# Core Questions
# in Philosophy

# Core Questions in Philosophy

## A Text with Readings

### Fifth Edition

## Elliott Sober

*University of Wisconsin–Madison*

Upper Saddle River, New Jersey 07458

**Library of Congress Cataloging-in-Publication Data**

Sober, Elliott.
  Core questions in philosophy : a text with readings / Elliott Sober.— 5th ed.
    p. cm.
  Includes bibliographical references and index.
  ISBN-13: 978-0-13-243778-3
  ISBN-10: 0-13-243778-3
  1.  Philosophy—Introductions.  I. Title.
  BD21.S615 2009
  100—dc22

                                                              2008005098


**Editor in Chief:** Sarah Touborg
**Senior Editor:** Dave Repetto
**Associate Editor:** Sarah Holle
**Editorial Assistant:** Carla Worner
**Director of Marketing:** Brandy Dawson
**Marketing Manager:** Lindsey Prudhomme
**Marketing Assistants:** Irene Fraga, Craig Deming
**Senior Managing Editor:** Mary Rottino
**Production Liaison:** Jean Lapidus
**Composition/Full-Service Project Management:** Pine Tree Composition
**Project Manager:** Jessica Balch
**Operations Specialist:** Cathleen Petersen
**Cover Design:** Margaret Kenselaar
**Cover Photo:** Getty Images, Inc.
**Printer/Binder:** R. R. Donnelley/Harrisonburg
**Cover Printer:** R. R. Donnelley/Harrisonburg

Pearson Education Ltd., London
Pearson Education Singapore, Pte. Ltd
Pearson Education Canada, Inc.
Pearson Education–Japan
Pearson Education Australia PTY, Limited

Pearson Education North Asia, Ltd., Hong Kong
Pearson Educación de Mexico, S.A. de C.V.
Pearson Education Malaysia, Pte. Ltd
Pearson Education, Upper Saddle River,
  New Jersey

10  9  8  7  6  5  4  3  2  1
ISBN-13 978-0-13-243778-3
ISBN-10    0-13-243778-3

*For Aaron*

# Contents

**Readings**

**Suggestions for Further Reading     145**


## PART III    Theory of Knowledge

**Chapters**

**Readings**

**Suggestions for Further Reading     254**


## PART IV    Philosophy of Mind

**Chapters**

## PART V  Ethics

### Chapters

### Readings

# Boxes

# Preface

The philosophical problems investigated in this book concern fundamental facts about our place in the universe. Many of us were brought up to believe that God exists, that there is a real difference between right and wrong, that we can freely choose what sort of lives to lead, and that it is possible for us to gain knowledge of the world we inhabit. A major goal of philosophy is to discover whether these opinions can be rationally defended or are just comfortable illusions.

*Core Questions in Philosophy* emphasizes the idea that philosophy is a subject devoted to *evaluating arguments* and *constructing theories*. This is not the same as describing the history of what various philosophers have thought. Although I discuss historical texts, I do so because they are rich sources of ideas pertinent to answering philosophical questions. The point is not to say solemn and respectful words about worthy figures now dead, but to engage them in dialogue—to grapple with the theories they have proposed, to criticize these theories, even to improve upon them.

Besides proposing answers to philosophical questions, I also try to make clear which questions I have *not* answered. I hope that the reader will approach what I say the way I have approached the philosophical texts I discuss. This is a book to argue with, to dissect. It isn't my goal to have the reader accept without question the conclusions I reach.

This work is a combination *textbook with readings*. In Parts II through V of the book, the chapters I wrote are followed by related readings (drawn from the writings of Plato, Aristotle, Aquinas, Anselm, Descartes, Locke, Hume, Kant, Mill, and others). The chapters are intended to flow together, so that the main areas covered—philosophy of religion, epistemology, philosophy of mind, and ethics—are connected to each other to make a coherent whole.

The chapters I wrote are intended to be *launching pads* from which readers can pursue issues on their own. I believe students are best able to think about philosophy if they first are provided with some basic tools and concepts. It is the purpose of the chapters to provide these *core ideas*.

The chapters often discuss the readings that follow, but the area of overlap is far from total. Many chapters contain material that isn't touched on in any reading; and the readings raise a wealth of issues that the chapters don't address. The chapters are intended to stand on their own as well as to provide points of entry into the readings.

Each chapter is followed by review questions and problems for further thought. These should help readers to consolidate their understanding of what I have said, and to think creatively about related problems. The chapters often contain material in boxes; these boxes provide, in a nutshell, a restatement of the main idea or a brief discussion of related matter that may interest the reader. A list of the boxes immediately follows the table of contents. Each main part of the book includes suggestions for further reading. There is also a glossary at the end of the book that provides simple definitions of the main concepts used.

Besides covering a number of traditional topics, this book also takes up some contemporary theories and problems, both from philosophy and from other disciplines. Creationism and evolutionary theory are hotly debated now. The issues they raise are continuous with a tradition of argument in philosophy of religion that goes back (at least) to Aquinas, Hume, and Paley. The relation of mind and body is a philosophical problem of long standing, but the ideas of Freud and Skinner get a hearing along with those of Descartes. In ethics there has long been a debate as to whether ethical truths are discovered or created. Plato and Sartre are separated by more than 2,000 years, but both speak to this issue. The problem of free will raises the question of whether every event is caused. Here, the contribution of modern physics must be brought into contact with a perennial problem of philosophy. Philosophy isn't the same as biology, psychology, or physics, but the problems of philosophy cannot be isolated from the sciences. One aim of this book is to connect philosophical problems with ideas derived from a wider culture.

In addition to rewriting each chapter for clarity (and in a few instances correcting what I think were mistakes in the previous edition), I have written a new chapter on Locke's arguments concerning the existence of objects outside one's own mind. I also have added new readings by Blaise Pascal, U.T. Place, Baron d'Holbach, and a new selection from Plato's *The Republic*.

The etymology of the word *philosopher* is *lover of wisdom*. This doesn't guarantee that all philosophers are wise, nor even that each individual philosopher is devoted to the attainment of wisdom. Philosophers *should* strive for wisdom; whether they do so, and whether they attain it, are separate questions.

Wisdom involves understanding—seeing how things fit together. When the pieces of a puzzle are fitted together, one attains a sense of wholeness. Current philosophy is embedded in a historical tradition of philosophical discourse. It also is connected to problems in the sciences, the other humanities, and the arts. This book aims to give the reader a sense of these multiple connections.

*Elliott Sober*
*University of Wisconsin–Madison*

# Acknowledgments

My debts to colleagues in philosophy at University of Wisconsin, Madison, are enormous. A fixed point in my work week has been discussions of the ideas and techniques that go into presenting central problems of philosophy to new students. My philosophical outlook, as well as the view I have of teaching, have been shaped by these conversations.

It is a pleasure to thank: Michael Byrd, Claudia Card, Fred Dretske, Ellery Eells, Berent Enç, Malcolm Forster, Martha Gibson, Paula Gottlieb, Daniel Hausman, Andy Levine, Steve Nadler, Terry Penner, Mark Singer, Dennis Stampe, Daniel Wikler, and Keith Yandell. They were generous enough to suffer my trespasses onto philosophical terrain that belonged more to them than to me. Some read parts of this book and gave me comments; others listened patiently while I tried out what I thought was a new angle.

The first four editions of *Core Questions in Philosophy* elicited a steady stream of correspondence and phone calls from teachers of philosophy and their students. These took a variety of forms; there was praise and blame, suggestions on how to do better, and even a few not-so-gentle suggestions that I should turn my attention to other projects. On the whole, though, I was happy with what I heard, though this didn't mean that I felt that I should leave the book unchanged. I thank everyone who took the trouble to let me know what they thought. Most (but not all), will find evidence that I listened to what they said in the way this edition differs from the ones before.

Deserving of special mention are: Richard Behling, Keith Butler, Paul Christopher, William R. Carter, Robert Cummins, Doug Frame, Phil Gasper, Ronald Glass, Richard Hanley, John Hines, Burton Hurdle, Charles Kielkopf, Gregory Mougin, Bradley Monton, Margaret Moore, William Russell Payne, Howard Prospersel, David Ring, Roy Sorensen, Whilhelm S. Wurzer, and Stephen Wykstra. The help they provided was extremely valuable. I also must thank the anonymous readers of previous editions of this textbook for their valuable suggestions. In addition, I'm grateful to Joel Velasco and John Koolage for their help in preparing this edition.

Writing an introduction to philosophy is a challenge. The challenge is to reconstruct what a problem or idea would sound like to someone who hasn't studied the subject before. The project requires that one return to the beginning—to the fundamentals of the subject. I hope what I found by beginning again will be useful to those who are beginning for the first time.

# PART I
# INTRODUCTION

## CHAPTER 1

## *What Is Philosophy?*

When asked "do you have a philosophy?" most people say "yes," but what do they mean? They usually have in mind a set of beliefs that they admit are difficult to prove are true, but that nonetheless are important to the way they think of themselves and the world they inhabit. Sometimes people describe their philosophies by saying what they think makes an action right or wrong. The statement "it's part of my philosophy that people should help each other" might be an example. A person's philosophy might include the fundamental ethical principles they believe. But people often have more than *ethics* in mind when they talk about their philosophies. A religious person might say that it is part of his or her philosophy that God exists; an atheist might say that it is part of his or her philosophy that there is no God and that there is no life after death. These propositions are important to the people who believe them. They describe what exists; philosophers would say that they are part of *metaphysics,* not ethics. Metaphysics is the part of philosophy that attempts to describe, in very general terms, what there is.

If everyday people think of their philosophies as the important beliefs they have that are difficult to prove, how does this idea of philosophy relate to how philosophers understand their own subject? Sometimes a term is used in ordinary talk in a way that differs dramatically from the way it is used by specialists. People sometimes say that tomatoes are vegetables, but a botanist will tell you that tomatoes are a fruit. Everyday people say they are concerned about "ecology," but biologists understand "ecology" in a very different way. Perhaps philosophers use the term "philosophy" in a way that departs fundamentally from what ordinary people mean when they say that they have a philosophy.

To gain a better purchase on what philosophy is, I'm going to discuss the question of what is distinctive about philosophy from two angles. First, I'll sketch some of the main philosophical problems that I'll examine in this book. That is, I'll describe some *examples* of philosophy. But giving examples doesn't really answer the question "What is philosophy?" If you asked "What is a mammal?" and I showed you a human being, a hippo, and a cat, these examples might give you a *hint* about what a mammal is. However, citing examples isn't the same as saying what it is to be a mammal. That is why there will be a second stage to my discussion of what philosophy is. After giving some examples of philosophical problems, I'll present some theories about what philosophy is. I believe these theories have merit, though, I admit, none is entirely adequate.

## EXAMPLES

The first philosophical problem we'll consider is whether God exists. Some philosophers have constructed arguments that attempt to establish that God exists; others have tried to show there is no God. I'll evaluate some of the more influential arguments and try to see whether they work.

The second problem we will consider concerns knowledge. It is pretty clear that belief and knowledge are different. Some people long ago thought that the earth is flat. They *believed* this, but they didn't know it, since it isn't true. Of course, they *thought* they knew it, but that's different. It also is pretty clear that true belief isn't the same as knowledge. If you believe something for no reason at all, but happen to be right by accident, you have true belief but not knowledge. For example, think of a gullible gambler at a racetrack who believes for no good reason that the first horse in every race will win. Occasionally this person will be right—he will have a true belief. But it isn't plausible to say that he knew, on those races about which he turned out to be right, that the first horse would win. So having knowledge involves something more than having a true belief.

The philosophical problem about knowledge will split into two parts. First, there are the questions: What is knowledge? What makes knowledge different from true belief? Second, there is the question: Do human beings ever know anything? One philosophical position we will consider answers this last question in the negative. Sure, we have beliefs. And granted, some of our beliefs are true. Knowledge, however, we never have. We don't even know those things we take to be most obvious. This position is called *philosophical skepticism*. We will consider arguments for skepticism and arguments that attempt to refute it.

The third philosophical subject that will be addressed in this book consists of a collection of topics from the philosophy of mind. The first of these is the so-called mind/body problem. You have a mind; you also have a brain. What is the relationship between these items? One possible answer is that they are identical. Although "mind" and "brain" are two words, they name the same thing, just like the names "Superman" and "Clark Kent." An alternative position in this area is called *dualism;* it says that the mind and the brain are different things. We will consider other theories that have been advanced about the mind/body problem as well.

Another topic from the philosophy of mind that we'll address concerns human freedom. Each of us has the personalities we have because we inherited a set of genes from our parents and then grew up in a sequence of environments. Genes plus environments make us the sorts of people we are. We didn't choose the genes we have, nor did we choose the environments we experienced in early life. These were thrust upon us from the outside. Each of us performs certain actions and abstains from performing others. This pattern of what we do and don't do results from the personalities we have. Can we be said to perform actions freely? Is it really in our control to perform some actions and abstain from others? Perhaps the fact that our actions are the results of factors outside our control (our genes and our early environment) shows that it is a mistake to say that we freely choose what we do. Of course, we talk in everyday life about people doing things "of their own free will." We also think of ourselves as facing real choices, as exercising control over what we do. However, the philosophical problem of freedom asks whether this common way of thinking is really defensible. Maybe freedom is just an illusion. Perhaps we tell ourselves a fairy tale about our own freedom because we can't face the fact that we aren't free. The philosophical problem will be to see whether we can be free if our personalities are the results of factors outside our control.

The last problem area I'll address is ethics. In everyday life, we frequently think that some actions are right and others are wrong. The philosophical problem about this familiar attitude divides into two parts. First, we'll consider whether there really are such things as ethical facts. Maybe talk about ethics, like talk about freedom, is just an elaborate illusion. Consider a parallel question about science. In every science, there are questions that are controversial. For example, physicists have different opinions about how the solar system began. But most of us think that there is something else to physics besides opinions. There are facts about what the world is really like.

Clashes of opinion occur in what I'll call the *subjective realm*. Here we find one human mind disagreeing with another. But facts about physics exist in the *objective realm*. Those facts exist independently of anybody's thinking about them. They are out there, and science aims to discover what they are. In science, there are both subjective opinions and objective facts—people have beliefs, but there also exists, independently of what anyone believes, a set of facts concerning the way the world really is. The question about ethics is whether both these realms (subjective and objective) exist in ethics, or if only one of them does. We know that people have different ethical opinions. The question is whether, in addition to those opinions, there are ethical facts. In other words, does ethics parallel the description I've just given of science, or is there a fundamental difference here? *Ethical subjectivism* is the philosophical thesis that there are no ethical facts, only ethical opinions. According to this position, the claim that "murder is always wrong" and the claim that "murder is sometimes permissible" are *both* misguided—there are no facts about the ethics of murder for us to have opinions about. We'll consider arguments supporting and criticizing this position.

|  | *Subjective Realm* | *Objective Realm* |
|---|---|---|
| *Science* | Scientific opinions | Scientific facts |
| *Ethics* | Ethical opinions | Ethical facts |

The second question that arises in ethics is this: If there are ethical facts, what are they? Here we assume a positive answer to the first question and then press on for more details. One theory we'll consider is *utilitarianism,* which says that the action you should perform in a given situation is the one that will produce the greatest happiness for the greatest number of individuals. This may sound like common sense, but in fact, I'll argue that there are some serious problems with this ethical theory.

## THREE THEORIES ABOUT WHAT PHILOSOPHY IS

I've just described a menu of four central philosophical problems: God, knowledge, mind, and ethics. What makes them all *philosophical* problems? Instead of giving examples, can we say something more general and complete about what distinguishes philosophy from other areas of inquiry? I'll offer three theories about what is characteristic of at least some philosophical problems.

Several of the problems just described involve *fundamental questions of justification.* There are many things that we believe without hesitation or reflection. These beliefs that are second nature to us are sometimes called "common sense." Common sense says that the senses (sight, hearing, touch, taste, and smell) provide each of us with knowledge of the world we inhabit. Common sense also says that people often act "of their own free will," and common sense holds that some actions are right while others are wrong. Philosophy examines the fundamental assumptions we make about ourselves and the world we inhabit and tries to determine whether those assumptions are rationally defensible.

Another characteristic of many philosophical questions is that they are very *general;* often they're more general than the questions investigated in specific sciences. Physicists have asked whether there are electrons; biologists have investigated whether genes exist; and geologists have sought to find out if the continents rest on movable plates. However, none of these sciences really bothers with the question of why we should think there are physical objects. The various sciences simply *assume* there are things outside the mind; they then focus on more specific questions about what those things are like. In contrast, it is a characteristically philosophical question to ask why you should believe that there is anything at all outside your mind. The idea that your mind is the only thing that exists is called *solipsism.* Philosophers have addressed the question of whether solipsism is true. This is a far more general question than the question of whether electrons, genes, or continental plates exist.

The third view of what philosophy is says that philosophy is the enterprise of *clarifying concepts.* Consider some characteristic philosophical questions: What is knowledge? What is freedom? What is justice? Each of these concepts applies to some things but not to others. What do the things falling under the concept have in common, and how do they differ from the things to which the concept does not apply?

We must be careful here, since many questions that aren't especially philosophical sound like the examples just given. Consider some characteristic scientific questions: What is photosynthesis? What is acidity? What is an electron? How does the first batch of questions differ from these? One difference between these questions concerns the ways in which *reason* and *observation* help answer them. You probably are aware that philosophy courses don't include laboratory sections. Philosophers usually don't perform experiments as part of their inquiries. Yet, in many sciences (though not in all), laboratory observation is central. This doesn't mean that observation plays no role in philosophy. Many of the philosophical arguments we will consider begin by making an observation. For example, in Chapter 5, I'll consider an argument for the existence of God that begins with the following assertion: Organisms are complicated things that are remarkably well adapted to the environments they inhabit. The thing to notice here is that this fact is something we know by observation. So philosophers, as well as scientists, do rely on observations.

Nonetheless, there is something distinctive about how observations figure in a philosophical inquiry. Usually the observations that are used in a philosophical theory are familiar and obvious to everyone. A philosopher will try to show by reasoning that those observations lead to some rather surprising conclusions. That is, although philosophy involves both observation and reasoning, it is the latter that in some sense does more of the work. As you will see in what follows, philosophical disputes often involve disagreements about reasoning; rarely are such disputes decidable by making an observation.

Each of these ways of understanding what philosophy is should be taken with a grain of salt (or perhaps with two). I think there is something to be said for each, even though each is somewhat simplified and distorting.

## THE NATURE OF PHILOSOPHY HAS CHANGED HISTORICALLY

One thing that makes it difficult to define "what philosophy is" is that the subject has been around at least since the ancient Greeks and has changed a great deal. There are many problems that are just as central to philosophy now as they were to the ancient Greeks, but there are other problems that have broken away from philosophy and now are thought of as purely scientific.

For example, ancient Greek philosophers discussed what the basic constituents of physical things are. Thales (who lived around 580 B.C.E) thought that everything is made of water; many other theories were discussed as well. Now such questions are thought to be part of physics, not philosophy. Similarly, until the end of the nineteenth century, universities put philosophy and psychology together in the same academic department. It is only recently that the two subjects have been thought of as separate. Scientists in the seventeenth century—for example, Isaac Newton—used the term "natural philosophy" to refer to what we now think of as science. The term "scientist" was invented in the nineteenth century by the British philosopher William Whewell. The idea that philosophy and science are separate subjects may seem clear now, but the separation we now find natural was not so obvious in the past. Many of the problems that we now regard as philosophical are problems that have not broken away from philosophy and found their way into the sciences. Perhaps there are problems now taken to be philosophical that future generations won't regard as such. The shifting historical nature of what counts as philosophy helps make it difficult to say anything very precise about what that subject is.

## PHILOSOPHICAL METHOD

Having tried to say something about what philosophy is, I now want to say something about what philosophy is *not* (at least not in this book). You may have the impression that doing philosophy involves lying under a tree staring up at the sky, making deep and mysterious pronouncements off the top of your head that sound very important but that are hard to make sense of when you try to think about them clearly. I'll call this the *mystical guru model* of philosophy. Your experience reading this book won't correspond to this impression.

There is, however, another experience you've probably had that comes closer. If you took a high school geometry course, you'll remember proving theorems from axioms. If your geometry course was like the one I had, the axioms were given to you with very little explanation of why you should believe them. Maybe they looked pretty obvious to you, and so you didn't wonder very much about their plausibility. Anyhow, the main task was to use the axioms to prove theorems. You started with the axioms as assumptions and then showed that if they are true, other statements must be true as well.

Philosophers tend to talk about "arguments" rather than "proofs." The goal is to try to reach answers to important philosophical questions by reasoning correctly from assumptions that are plausible. For example, in Chapter 4, I'll examine some attempts to prove that God exists. The idea here is to start with assumptions that practically anybody would grant are true and then show that these assumptions lead to the conclusion that there is a God. This resembles what you may have done in geometry: Starting with simple and supposedly obvious assumptions, you were able to establish something less obvious and more complex—for example, that the sum of the angles of a triangle equals two right angles (180 degrees).

Sometimes the philosophical questions we'll consider will strike you as difficult, deep, even mysterious. I won't shy away from such questions. I'll try, however, to address them with clarity and precision. The goal is to take hard questions and deal with them clearly, which, I emphasize, should never involve trying to pull the wool over someone's eyes by making deep-sounding pronouncements that mean who-knows-what.

## SUMMARY

I began this chapter by describing how everyday people use the term "philosophy." In fact, their usage is not so distant from what philosophers mean by the term. Philosophy *does* address the most fundamental beliefs we have about ourselves and the world we inhabit. Precisely because these assumptions are so central to the way we think and act, it is difficult to step back for a moment from these assumptions and examine them critically. The French have an expression, "the most difficult thing for a fish to see is water." Some assumptions are so natural and seemingly obvious that it is hard to see that we are making assumptions at all. Philosophy is the effort to help us identify these assumptions and evaluate them. Each of us *does* have a philosophy. What divides some people from others is their willingness to ask probing questions about what they believe and why. This is what philosophy as a discipline tries to add to the philosophies that each of us carries with us through our lives.

## Review Questions

1. What is the difference between objective and subjective?
2. If you want to say what philosophy is, why isn't it enough to list some examples of philosophical problems?

## A Problem for Further Thought

Which of the ideas presented here about what philosophy is also apply to mathematics? Which do not?

# CHAPTER 2

# *Deductive Arguments*

Philosophy involves constructing and evaluating arguments. In this respect, philosophy is no different from any other rational activity—mathematicians do this, as do economists, physicists, and people in everyday life. The distinctive thing about philosophy isn't that philosophers construct and evaluate arguments; what is distinctive is the kinds of questions those arguments aim to answer. In the previous chapter, I talked about what makes a question philosophical. The goal in this chapter is to develop some techniques that can be used to tell whether an argument is good or bad.

## ARGUMENTS

An argument divides into two parts: the premises and the conclusion. The premises and the conclusion are statements; each is expressed by a declarative sentence. Each is either true or false. When people argue that a given statement is true, they try to provide reasons for thinking this. The reasons are the premises of their argument; premises are assumptions. The statement to be established is the argument's conclusion.

In high school geometry, you talked about axioms and theorems. Axioms are assumptions (premises); the theorem (the conclusion) is what is supposed to follow from those assumptions. In geometry you may have spent little or no time asking whether the axioms are true. Not so for the philosophical arguments I discuss in this book. We'll want to see whether the premises are plausible. We'll also want to see whether the premises, if they were true, would provide a reason for thinking the conclusion is true as well. I'll pose these two questions again and again.

## GOOD ARGUMENTS

I now want to talk about different kinds of "good arguments." What does "good" mean? A good argument is *rationally persuasive;* it gives you a good reason to think the conclusion is true. Advertisers and politicians sometimes use arguments that trick people into believing what they say. These arguments sometimes persuade people, but they don't always provide *good* reasons.

A good argument should have true premises; if the premises are false, how could they provide you a good reason to believe the conclusion? But more is required than this. In the following argument, the premise is true, but it doesn't provide you a good reason to think that the conclusion is true:

Grass is green
_____

Roses are red

What is wrong here is that the premises are irrelevant to the conclusion. A good argument should contain true premises, but it also should cite premises that are related in the right way to the conclusion. The truth of the premises should give you a reason to think that the conclusion is true. The three types of "good argument" that I'll now describe differ in what relationship their premises and conclusions have to each other.

Good arguments can be divided into two categories, and one of those categories can be divided into two more:

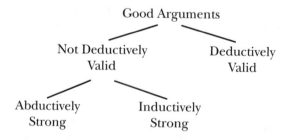

I'll treat the three categories (deductively valid, inductively strong, and abductively strong) as *mutually exclusive.* If an argument belongs to one category, it can't belong to any of the others. At the end of Chapter 3, I'll modify this classification slightly.

You may have heard some of this terminology before. Deduction is what you do in a mathematical proof. Induction involves sampling from a population to decide what its characteristics are. Abduction may be a less familiar term. It has nothing to do with kidnapping. The word was invented by the great nineteenth-century American philosopher Charles Sanders Peirce. Philosophers sometimes use the longer label "inference to the best explanation" to describe what Peirce meant by abduction.

I'll consider deduction in this chapter, induction and abduction in the next. The goal in each case is to describe some of the considerations that are relevant to deciding whether an argument is good or bad.

## DEDUCTIVE VALIDITY DEFINED

The first type of good argument consists of ones that are "deductively valid." Here are two examples of this type of argument:

| | |
|---|---|
| All fish swim. | All particles have mass. |
| All sharks are fish. | All electrons are particles. |
| ———————— | ———————— |
| All sharks swim. | All electrons have mass. |

In these arguments, the premises are the statements above the horizontal line; the conclusion is the statement below. These arguments say that the premises are true and that, therefore, the conclusion also is true.

Here is what deductive validity means:

> *A deductively valid argument* is an argument that has the following property: *IF* its premises were true, its conclusion would have to be true.

I've capitalized the word *IF.* I'd print it in bright colors if I could, because it is important not to forget this two-letter word. *A valid argument need not have true premises.* What is required is that the conclusion would have to be true, *IF* the premises were true. Take a minute to look at these two arguments. Convince yourself that they are deductively valid.

## "VALIDITY" IS A TECHNICAL TERM

What philosophers and logicians mean by "valid" doesn't have much in common with what we mean by "valid" in ordinary English. In everyday life, we say that a statement is "valid" if it is plausible or true. The technical use of the term that I just explained differs from ordinary usage in two ways. First, we never say that a *statement* or an *idea* is valid or invalid. Validity is a property of *arguments,* and of arguments only. Second, an argument can be valid even if the statements it contains are wildly implausible. A valid argument can have false premises and a false conclusion.

Here is an example:

All plants have minds.
All ladders are plants.
_____

All ladders have minds.

## LOGICAL FORM

What makes an argument deductively valid? The three example arguments described so far have different subject matters. The first is about fish, the second is about particles, and the third is about plants. Though they are about different things, they have the same structure. The structural property that they have in common is called their "logical form." Think of each argument as the result of substituting terms into the following skeleton:

All *B*s are *C*s
All *A*s are *B*s
_____

All *A*s are *C*s

This is the logical form of the three arguments given. You can think of *A*, *B*, and *C* as blanks into which terms may be substituted. Take a minute to see how the arguments just stated can be obtained from the above skeleton by substitution—by "filling in the blanks."

An argument is valid or invalid solely because of the logical form it has. The subject matter of the argument is irrelevant. Since the three example arguments have the same logical form, they are all valid or all invalid. They have the same logical form, so they are in the same boat. As already mentioned, they are valid. Indeed, each and every of the millions of arguments you can construct by substitution into the above skeleton is valid as well.

## INVALIDITY

The definition of validity tells you what a deductively *invalid* argument will be like. If there is even the smallest possibility that the conclusion could be false when the premises are true, then the argument is deductively invalid.

The ladder argument is valid, though all the statements it contains are false. Is the reverse situation possible? Can an argument be *invalid,* even though all the statements it contains are true? The answer is *yes.* Here's an example:

Emeralds are green.
_____

Lemons are yellow.

The premise is true and so is the conclusion. So why isn't the argument deductively valid? The definition of validity says that the premises in a valid argument must provide an *absolute guarantee* that the conclusion is true. But the fact that emeralds are green doesn't guarantee that lemons must be yellow. The color of lemons isn't entailed by the fact that emeralds are green. Validity concerns the *relationship* of premises to conclusion, not the question of whether the premises and the conclusion each happen to be true.

Sometimes it isn't so obvious that an argument is invalid. The above example is pretty blatant—the premise has nothing to do with the conclusion. But what do you think of the following argument? Is it valid or not?

> If Jones stands in the heavy rain without an umbrella, then Jones will get wet.
> Jones is wet.
> _____
>
> Jones was standing in the heavy rain without an umbrella.

Imagine that all three of the statements in this argument are true. Imagine that Jones is now standing before you soaking wet and that Jones just came in from the rain.

Even if all the statements in this argument are true, this argument is still invalid. It is just like the argument about emeralds and lemons. Though the premises and the conclusion happen to be true, the premises don't *guarantee* that the conclusion must be true.

How can we see this more clearly? I said before that all arguments that have the same logical form are in the same boat. This means that if the argument about Jones is invalid, so is each and every argument that has the same form. Let's begin by isolating the argument's logical form. Here it is:

> If $P$, then $Q$
> $Q$
> _____
>
> $P$

What do $P$ and $Q$ stand for in this argument skeleton? You can substitute any statement (declarative sentence) you please for these letters to obtain an argument with this logical form. Notice that the letters in this skeleton differ in their function from the letters in the previous skeleton. There, *A, B,* and *C* are blanks into which terms denoting kinds of things ("fish," "electrons," etc.) can be substituted.

Anyhow, we now have the logical form of the argument about Jones. If it is invalid, so are *all* arguments that have the same logical form. This means that if there is even one argument that has this logical form, in which the premises are true and the conclusion false, then the argument form is invalid. This will mean that the initial argument about Jones is invalid as well.

Here is an argument that has the same logical form as the argument about Jones that settles the question:

If Sam lives in Wisconsin, then Sam lives in the U.S.A.

Sam lives in the U.S.A.

---

Sam lives in Wisconsin.

The premises of this argument are true, but the conclusion, I assure you, is false. The Sam I'm talking about lives in California.

## TESTING FOR INVALIDITY

So here's a strategy to use if you want to know whether an argument is invalid: First, ignore the content and isolate the logical form (the "skeleton") of the argument. Get rid of the distracting subject matter since that is irrelevant; what you want to focus on is the logical form. Second, see if you can invent an argument that has this logical form in which the premises are true and the conclusion is false. If you can find even one rotten apple of this type, you are finished. If there is even one argument with this property, then *every* argument of that form is invalid.

When an argument has true premises and a false conclusion, it is quite obvious that the truth of the premises doesn't *guarantee* that the conclusion must be true. The premises can't be guaranteeing this, since the conclusion is false. But this tells you something general. It tells you that each and every argument of this form will be such that the premises don't guarantee the truth of the conclusion.

So far, I've presented some examples of arguments. I've explained that a valid argument needn't have true statements in it and that an argument composed solely of true statements needn't be valid. This should make you wonder whether there is any connection at all between the question of whether an argument is valid and the question of whether the premises and conclusion are true.

There *is* a connection. It is illustrated by the following table. If an argument is valid, it can exhibit three of the four following combinations in which the premises are either all true or not all true and the conclusion is either true or false:

|  |  | Premises | |
|---|---|---|---|
|  |  | All true | Not all true |
| Conclusion | True | Possible | Possible |
|  | False | Impossible | Possible |

This table indicates that a valid argument can't have true premises and a false conclusion. However, the fact that an argument is valid leaves open which of the other three cells the argument occupies.

What can be said of an *in*valid argument? If an argument is invalid, are any of the four combinations impossible? I leave this to you to figure out by consulting the definition of validity.

When you find an invalid argument, you may want to ask if the argument can be repaired. Is there anything that can be done to an invalid argument to make it valid? There is. By adding premises, you can turn a deductively invalid argument into a valid one. Consider the following argument:

> Smith lives in the U.S.A.
> ───────────
> Smith lives in Wisconsin.

This is invalid, but it can be made valid by adding a premise:

> Smith lives in the U.S.A.
> Everyone who lives in the U.S.A. lives in Wisconsin.
> ───────────
> Smith lives in Wisconsin.

Notice that the conclusion now follows from the premises. The trouble is the second premise is false.

In the preceding pair of arguments, fixing the defect of invalidity just substitutes one problem for another; instead of having to criticize an argument's invalidity, you have to criticize its premises for not being true. The following argument pair is different. Here one can repair the defect of invalidity and obtain a perfectly fine argument. Notice first that the following argument isn't deductively valid:

> Smith lives in Wisconsin.
> ───────────
> Smith lives in the U.S.A.

The argument can be repaired, however, by adding a premise:

> Smith lives in Wisconsin.
> Everyone who lives in Wisconsin lives in the U.S.A.
> ───────────
> Smith lives in the U.S.A.

This argument is valid and has true premises as well. You can see from these two pairs of arguments that invalidity is easy to fix. Just add premises. What is harder is to add premises that not only make the argument valid, but are true as well.

This idea will come up repeatedly when I discuss various philosophical arguments. I sometimes will claim an argument is invalid. When this happens, you should ask yourself whether the argument can be repaired. Often the price of making the argument valid (by adding a premise) is that you have to supply a new premise you think is false. In making this addition, you are trading one defect (invalidity) for another (false premises). If you can't repair the argument so that it is both valid and has all true premises, then you should consider the possibility that there is something fundamentally flawed about the whole line of argument. On the other hand, sometimes an invalid argument can be replaced by a valid one merely by supplying a true premise that maybe you neglected to mention because it is so obvious. In this case, the defect in the original argument isn't so fundamental.

So far I've emphasized two questions that we will want to ask about arguments:

(1) Is the argument deductively valid?

(2) Are all the premises true?

If the answer to both questions is *yes,* the conclusion of the argument must be true.

Arguments are tools. We use them to do things. When the goal is rational persuasion, a good argument will provide a good reason to think the conclusion is true. If an argument is deductively valid and has true premises, is that sufficient to make it good? To see why validity and true premises aren't enough, consider the following argument:

Lemons are yellow.
_____
Lemons are yellow.

---

### Conditionals

If/then statements are called conditionals. Conditional statements have other statements as components. For example, the statement "If pigs fly, then grass is green" is a statement of the form "If *P,* then *Q,*" where *P* and *Q* are themselves statements.

In the statement "If *P,* then *Q,*" *P* is called the *antecedent* and *Q* is called the *consequent.* A conditional doesn't say that its antecedent is true; the statement "If Joe drinks arsenic, then Joe will die" does not say that Joe drinks arsenic. A conditional doesn't say that its consequent is true; "If there is a nuclear war, then Washington will be attacked" doesn't say that Washington will be attacked.

Conditionals can be rewritten without changing what they say. Consider the statement "If you live in Wisconsin, then you live in the U.S.A." This is equivalent in meaning to saying that "If you don't live in the U.S.A., then you don't live in Wisconsin." The conditional "If *P,* then *Q*" is equivalent to "If not-*Q,* then not-*P,*" no matter what *P* and *Q* happen to be. Here's a piece of terminology: The statement "If not-*Q,* then not-*P*" is the *contrapositive* of the conditional "If *P,* then *Q.*" A conditional and its contrapositive are equivalent.

Consider the following two conditionals: "If *P,* then *Q*" and "If *Q,* then *P.*" Are they equivalent? That is, do they mean the same thing? The answer is *no.* "If you live in Wisconsin, then you live in the U.S.A." is true, but "If you live in the U.S.A., then you live in Wisconsin" is false. These two if/then statements can't mean the same thing, since what the one says is true while what the other says is false. "If *Q,* then *P*" is termed the *converse* of the conditional "If *P,* then *Q.*" A conditional and its converse are not equivalent.

Here the conclusion merely repeats what the premise asserts. This argument is valid and the premise is true. But there is something defective about this argument. What is it?

## CIRCULARITY, OR BEGGING THE QUESTION

The previous argument is *circular;* it *begs the question.* Suppose you didn't already have an opinion as to whether lemons are yellow. The above argument wouldn't help you resolve your uncertainty. The argument would be useless in this regard.

Good arguments are tools that help answer questions about whether their conclusions are true. A good argument should give you a reason to accept the conclusion if you don't already believe the conclusion is true. So besides checking to see if an argument is deductively valid and has true premises, you also should see if the argument begs the question.

## TRUTH

One other idea needs clearing up before I leave the topic of deductive validity. You'll notice that the definition of validity makes use of the concept of truth. What is truth?

There are deep philosophical questions here, most of which I'll skirt. My goal is to describe the concept of truth I use in this book. It is beyond the scope of this book to defend this choice or to fully develop its implications. To begin with, whether a statement is true is an entirely different question from whether you or anybody happens to believe it. Whether someone believes the statement "The Rocky Mountains are in North America" is a psychological question. If beings with minds had never populated the earth, no one would have thought about the location of this mountain range. But this doesn't affect the question of whether the statement

---

**Begging the Question**

To understand what makes an argument question-begging, it is useful to examine some examples.

Suppose you were trying to convince someone that God exists. The argument you give for thinking this is true is that the Bible says there is a God. Would this argument convince someone who didn't already believe that there is a God? Probably not. Anyone who doubts there is a God probably doesn't think that everything the Bible says is true.

Here's a second example. Someone is very suspicious about the reliability of consumer magazines. You try to convince him that *Consumer Reports* is reliable by pointing out that *Consumer Reports* ranks itself very highly in an article evaluating the reliability of consumer magazines. Probably your argument will fail to convince.

In these two examples, identify the premises and conclusion in each argument. Then describe what it is about the argument that makes it question-begging.

is true. There can be truths that no one believes. Symmetrically, there can be propositions that everyone thinks are true, but that aren't. There can be beliefs that aren't true.

When I say that a certain sentence has the property of being true, what am I saying? For example, when I say that the English sentence "The Rocky Mountains are in North America" is true, am I attributing some mysterious property to it? Not really. All I'm saying is that the world is the way the sentence says it is. When I say that the sentence is true, all I'm saying is that the Rocky Mountains are in North America. So in a way, the concept of truth is often "redundant." Sometimes when I use the concept of truth, I could say the same thing without using that concept.

In high school English, your teacher may have told you to avoid redundancy. If you hand in an essay containing the sentence "Oscar is an unmarried bachelor," the essay might come back with "unmarried" crossed out and the marginal comment "avoid redundancy." The word "unmarried" is redundant because "Oscar is an unmarried bachelor" means exactly the same thing as "Oscar is a bachelor." Adding the word "unmarried" is to spill useless ink. The Redundancy Theory of Truth claims that the word "true" is redundant in just this sense. "It is true that the Rockies are in North America" says exactly what the sentence "The Rockies are in North America" asserts. This helps show why truth isn't a mysterious property. If you believe a statement $P$, you also believe that $P$ is true. So, if you have any beliefs about the world at all, you should be quite comfortable applying the concept of truth to those beliefs.

## "TRUE FOR ME"

You'll see from these remarks that the expression "It is true for me" can be dangerously misleading. Sometimes saying that a statement is true "for you" just means that you believe it. If that is what you want to say, just use the word "belief" and leave truth out of it. However, there is a more radical idea that might be involved here. Sometimes people use the expression "true for me" to express the idea that each of us makes our own reality and that the beliefs we have constitute that reality. I'll assume this is a mistake. My concept of truth assumes a fundamental division between the way things really are and the way they may seem to be to this or that individual. This is what I meant in Chapter 1 by distinguishing the objective realm and the subjective realm.

## WISHFUL THINKING

Closely related to this distinction between objective and subjective is a piece of advice: *We should avoid wishful thinking.* Most of the things we believe aren't made true by our believing them. That the Rockies are in North America is a fact that is independent of our thought and language. We don't bring this geographic fact into being by thinking or talking in the way we do.

## SELF-FULFILLING PROPHESIES

In saying this, I'm not denying that the thoughts we have often affect the world out-side the mind. If I think to myself "I can't hit a baseball," this may have the effect that I do badly in the batter's box; here my believing something has the effect that the belief is made true. This is the idea of a "self-fulfilling prophesy." Notice how this causal chain works:

| *Thought* | *Action* | *Truth* |
|-----------|----------|---------|
| I believe that I won't hit the baseball. $\longrightarrow$ | I swing too high. $\longrightarrow$ | I don't hit the baseball. |

I have no problem with the idea that various statements may be caused to be true by individuals thinking thoughts to themselves. What I deny is that the mere act of think-ing, unconnected with action or some other causal pathway, can make statements true in the world outside the mind. I'm rejecting the idea that the world is arranged so that it spontaneously conforms to the ideas we happen to entertain.

Later in this book, I'll investigate whether there are any exceptions to this prin-ciple that says that we should avoid wishful thinking. Maybe there are some state-ments that become true just because we think they are. Here are some philosophical claims we'll consider:

> Mathematical statements and definitions are made true by our regarding them as such; for example, "2 + 3 = 5" is true just because we choose to define our terminology ("2," " + ," etc.) in the way we do (Chapter 4).

> Some statements about the contents of my own mind (for example, "I am in pain") are made true just by my believing they are true (Chapter 13).

> Ethical statements are true just because God, society, or some individual agent thinks they are (Chapter 31).

I'm mentioning these philosophical claims here without tipping my hand as to whether I think any of them is plausible. If any of them were correct, they would count as excep-tions to the pattern I've just described. For the moment, though, I'm merely noting that belief and truth are generally very separate questions.

---

## Review Questions

1. When is a statement or idea valid? (a trick question)
2. Define what it means to say that an argument is deductively valid.
3. Invent an example of a valid argument that has false premises and a true con-clusion. Invent an example of an invalid argument that has true premises and a true conclusion.

4. Can a statement be a premise in one argument and a conclusion in another? If you think so, give an example.
5. Which of the following argument forms is valid? Which is invalid? For each of the invalid ones, construct an example of an argument with that form in which the premises are true and the conclusion false:

|  |  |
|---|---|
| If *P,* then *Q* | If *P,* then *Q* |
| (a)  *P* | (b)  *Q* |
| ——————— | ——————— |
| *Q* | *P* |
| If *P,* then *Q* | If *P,* then *Q* |
| (c)  Not-*P* | (d)  Not-*Q* |
| ——————— | ——————— |
| Not-*Q* | Not-*P* |

For the argument forms you think are fallacious, invent names for these fallacies by using the vocabulary about conditionals presented in the box on page 14.
6. A sign on a store says "No shoes, no service." Does this mean that if you wear shoes, then you will be served?
7. What does it mean to say that an argument is "circular," that it "begs the question"? Construct an example of an argument of this type different from the ones presented in this chapter.
8. What does it mean to say that truth is objective, not subjective?

## Problems for Further Thought

1. The Redundancy Theory of Truth may seem plausible as an account of what the following sentence means:

   It is true that the Rockies are in North America.

   Does it work as well as an explanation of what the following sentence means?

   Some statements that are true have not been formulated yet.

2. Consider the following argument:

   I release an otherwise unsupported apple from my hand a few feet from the earth's surface.
   ———————
   The apple falls to earth.

   Is this argument deductively valid? What is the logical form of this argument?

3.  (Here is a problem that was drawn to my attention by Richard Behling.) In this chapter, I said that each argument has a *single* logical form. This is the skeleton into which terms can be substituted to obtain the argument. What I said is an oversimplification, however. A given argument can be obtained from *many* logical forms. For example, consider the following argument:

> Fred lives in California.
> If Fred lives in California, then Fred lives in the U.S.A.
> ─────────────────
> Fred lives in the U.S.A.

This argument can be obtained from *both* of the following skeletons by substitution:

$$\text{(a)} \quad \frac{\begin{array}{l} X \\ \textit{If X, then Y} \end{array}}{Y} \qquad\qquad\qquad \text{(b)} \quad \frac{\begin{array}{l} R \\ S \end{array}}{T}$$

Argument form (a) is valid, but (b) is *in*valid. The argument about Fred is valid.
   Here's the problem: Use the concept of logical form to define when an argument is valid, and when it is invalid, without falling into the trap of thinking that each argument has *exactly one* logical form.

4.  In this chapter, I claimed that there are "objective truths." Do you agree? Construct an argument in which you try to demonstrate that such things exist, or that they do not.

# CHAPTER 3

# *Inductive and Abductive Arguments*

In Chapter 2, I explained the idea of deductive validity. In a deductively valid argument the premises provide an *absolute guarantee* that the conclusion is true: If the premises are true, there is no way in the world that the conclusion can be false. If the premises are true, the conclusion can't be false.

## DEDUCTIVE VALIDITY IS A LIMITATION

This feature of deductive arguments may sound like a virtue. It is a good thing when an argument provides this sort of strong guarantee. This virtue, however, can also represent a kind of limitation. Granted, a deductively valid argument that has true premises can't have a false conclusion; but it also is a property of such arguments that the conclusion can't say anything that wasn't already contained in the premises.

To see what this means, consider what you could validly deduce from the result of some opinion survey. Suppose you were interested in finding out what percentage of registered voters in a county are Democrats. You don't feel like contacting each of them and asking, so you open the phone book and make, let's say, 1000 telephone calls.

Suppose the result of your survey is that 60 percent of the people called say they are Democrats. What you want to know is the percentage of Democrats in the whole county. Could you construct a deductively valid argument here? Can you deduce that (approximately) 60 percent of the voters are Democrats from a premise that describes the result of your survey? The answer is *no,* for two reasons. The fact that 60 percent of the people called *said* they are Democrats doesn't deductively guarantee that any of them are. And even if 60 percent of the people called are Democrats, you can't validly deduce from this that (approximately) 60 percent of the voters in the county are Democrats. That is, neither of the following arguments is deductively valid:

60% of the people called said they are Democrats.
_____

60% of the people called are Democrats.

60% of the people called are Democrats.
_____

Approximately 60% of the voters in the county are Democrats.

Why can't you deduce these things validly? The reason is that in a deductively valid argument, it is impossible for the conclusion to be false if the premises are true. But it *is* possible that everyone you called in your survey lied. In addition, it is possible that the percentage of Democrats in the whole county is only 25 percent, even if nobody lied in your phone survey. In saying this, I'm not saying that the people you called actually lied, and I'm not saying that the real percentage in the whole county is only 25 percent. I'm just saying that these are *possible,* given the result of your phone calls. The result of your telephone survey doesn't absolutely rule out these possibilities; this means you can't *deduce* the percentage of Democrats in the whole county from what the one-thousand people said on the phone.

So the absolute guarantee that a deductively valid argument provides has this limitation: Insisting that an argument be deductively valid prohibits you from reaching conclusions that go beyond the information given in the premises.

It would make sense to insist that an argument be deductively valid if you wanted to avoid even the smallest risk of having a false conclusion with true premises. However, we often are willing to gamble. For example, we might think that the result of the phone survey does provide information about the composition of the county. We might think that the survey provides a pretty good reason for concluding that about 60 percent of the county voters are Democrats. In saying this, though, the "good reason" isn't a deductively valid one.

## NONDEDUCTIVE INFERENCE—A WEAKER GUARANTEE

We have here a fundamental characteristic of nondeductive inference. Suppose we conclude that about 60 percent of the voters in the county are Democrats, based on the premise that 60 percent of the people called said they were Democrats. In this case the premise doesn't provide an absolute guarantee that the conclusion is true. However, there is a lesser kind of guarantee that this premise may provide. If the argument is a strong one, the premise makes the conclusion *probable;* it provides a *good reason* for thinking the conclusion is true; it makes the conclusion *plausible.* Instead of an absolute guarantee, we have here a weaker guarantee. You are running a risk of being wrong about your conclusion, even if your premise is true. But this risk might be a reasonable one to take. The conclusion might be a good bet, given that the premise is true.

## TWO GAMBLING STRATEGIES

The language in the previous paragraph suggests that you can think about the difference between deductive and nondeductive arguments in terms of ideas about gambling. Consider two sorts of gamblers. The first I'll call the *extreme conservative.* This individual refuses to wager unless winning is a sure thing. The second individual I'll call the *thoughtful risk taker.* This individual at times enters into risky gambles hoping to win. Each strategy has its virtue and its limitation. The virtue of the conservative strategy is that you'll never lose a gamble. Its limitation is that there are gambles you will decline to take that you could have won. The limitation of thoughtful risk taking is that you can lose money. Its virtue is that it can lead you to win wagers by taking risks.

Limiting yourself to deductive arguments is a conservative strategy. You avoid the risk of reaching false conclusions from true premises. The limitation is that you decline to say anything that goes beyond the evidence. Nondeductive arguments are riskier. The gain is that you can reach true conclusions that go beyond what the premises say; the risk is that you may reach a false conclusion from true premises.

## PREDICTIVE BELIEFS

In science as well as in everyday life, we make nondeductive inferences all the time. We often are prepared to take risks. Each of us has beliefs about the future. These, however, aren't deduced from the observations we made in the present and past.

## UNIVERSAL LAWS

Science is a risky business in another way. Scientists often try to reach conclusions about *universal laws*. An example is Isaac Newton's (1642–1727) universal law of gravitation, which you may have studied in high school. This law says that the gravitational attraction between two bodies is proportional to the products of their masses and is inversely proportional to the square of the distance between them. This law describes how much gravitational attraction there is between any two objects, no matter where those objects are located and no matter when those objects exist. Newton's law is *universal* in scope—it describes what is true at any time and place. This isn't an isolated example. In lots of sciences, there are universal statements that scientists think are well supported by evidence.

Could Newton have deduced his law from the observations he made and the experiments he conducted? *No.* His law is universal in scope. His observations, however, were conducted in a rather narrowly limited range of places and times. Newton didn't go backward in time to check if his law held true 3 million years ago. Nor did he send a spaceship to a distant galaxy to do the required measurements. When scientists conclude that a universal law is true or probably true, based on premises that describe the observations they have made, they aren't making deductively valid arguments.

Science is a very ambitious enterprise. Science ventures beyond what is strictly observed in the here and now, just as the conclusion in a nondeductive argument ventures beyond the information strictly contained in the premises.

## DETECTIVE WORK

I said before that nondeductive arguments are constantly used in both science and in everyday life. Newton was my scientific example. Let me describe the calculations of Sherlock Holmes as my everyday one.

Holmes was constantly telling Watson that he figures out detective problems by "deduction." Although Holmes was a very good detective, I doubt that he solved his puzzles by strictly deductive methods. Holmes didn't observe the crimes he was later called upon to investigate. What he observed were *clues.* For example, suppose Holmes is trying to solve a murder. He wonders whether Moriarty is the murderer. The clues Holmes gathers include a gun, a cigar butt, and a fresh footprint, all found at the scene of the crime. Suppose the gun has an "M" carved in the handle, the cigar is Moriarty's favorite brand, and the footprint is the size that would be produced by Moriarty's ample foot. Can Holmes deduce from these clues that Moriarty is the murderer? No. Although the information may make that conclusion plausible or probable, it doesn't absolutely rule out the possibility that someone else did the dirty deed.

I've been emphasizing that in a strong nondeductive inference, the premises make the conclusion plausible or probable; they don't absolutely guarantee that the conclusion must be true. I now want to talk about the difference between two sorts of nondeductive inference—inductive and abductive.

## INDUCTION

I'll begin with some properties of induction. Inductive inference involves taking a description of some sample and extending that description to items outside the sample. The voter survey discussed before provides an example:

> 60% of the county voters called are Democrats.
> ———————————
> Approximately 60% of the county voters are Democrats.

Notice that in this example the vocabulary present in the argument's conclusion is already used in the premise. Although the conclusion goes beyond what the premise asserts (which is what makes the argument nondeductive), no new concepts are introduced in the conclusion.

## TWO FACTORS INFLUENCE INDUCTIVE STRENGTH

In the case of deduction, I said that an inference is either deductively valid or it isn't. Validity is a yes/no affair. It is like pregnancy. Inductive strength, however, isn't a yes/no matter; arguments are either stronger or weaker. Inductive strength is a matter of degree.

Two factors affect how strong or weak an inductive argument is. The first is sample size. If you called 1,000 individuals in your phone survey, that would make the conclusion stronger than if you had called only 100. The second factor is the representativeness or unbiasedness of the sample. If you called 1,000 individuals drawn at random from a list of voters, that would make the resulting inference stronger than if you had called 1,000 members of labor unions. The percentage of Democrats in labor unions may be higher than that in the population as a whole. If so, you are biasing your sample by drawing it exclusively from a union membership list.

By making a telephone survey, you are failing to contact people who don't have phones. Is this a problem? That depends. If the percentage of Democrats with phones is approximately equal to the percentage of Democrats among registered voters, no bias is introduced. On the other hand, if people with phones are disproportionately Democrats or disproportionately Republicans, your phone survey will have introduced a bias.

How do you avoid having a biased sample? Sometimes this is done by "randomization." If you have a list of all the county voters, drawing names "at random" means that each name has the same chance of being selected. However, this process of selecting at random can fail to ensure an unbiased sample. For example, suppose you draw names at random, but all the people you contact happen to be women. If women are disproportionately Democrats or disproportionately Republicans, your sample is biased. I don't say that random draws from the voter list will *probably* result in this sort of bias. My point is just that randomizing doesn't absolutely guarantee that your sample is unbiased. I won't say more here about how you can avoid having a biased sample. This fine point aside, the basic idea is this: Inductive arguments are stronger or weaker according to (1) the sample size and (2) the unbiasedness of the sample.

## ABDUCTION

I now move to abduction—inference to the best explanation. I'll begin with an example of an abductive inference that was important in the history of science. After saying what is distinctive about this form of inference, I'll describe two principles that are relevant to deciding whether an abductive inference is strong or weak.

Gregor Mendel (1822–1884) was an experimental biologist who worked in a monastery in Moravia. He is credited with having discovered genes, the particles in living things that allow parents to transmit characteristics to offspring in reproduction.

## INFERRING WHAT ISN'T OBSERVED

The first thing to note about Mendel's discovery is that he never actually saw a gene (or an "element," as Mendel called them). Although more powerful microscopes made this possible later, Mendel never saw even one of them. Rather, Mendel reasoned that the observations he made could be explained if genes existed and had the characteristics he specified.

Mendel ran breeding experiments in the monastery's garden. He crossed tall pea plants with short ones and noted the proportion of tall and short plants among the offspring. Similarly, he crossed plants that had wrinkled peas with plants that had smooth peas, and he noted the mix of wrinkled and smooth plants among the progeny. He then crossed some of those offspring with each other, and he saw the proportion of various characteristics found in the next generation.

Mendel observed that when plants of certain sorts are crossed, their offspring exhibit characteristics in very definite proportions. Mendel asked himself a question that never figured in my discussion of induction. He asked *why* the crosses produced offspring with characteristics distributed into such proportions.

This why-question led Mendel to invent a story. He said, Suppose each plant contains particles (genes) that control the observed characteristics of tall and short, wrinkled and smooth, in certain specific ways. He conjectured that each parent contributes half its genes to the offspring and that this process occurs in accordance with definite rules. The whole invented story had this property: If the story were true, that would explain why the breeding experiments had the results that Mendel observed them to have.

It should be quite clear that Mendel's theory of the gene went beyond the observations then available to him. He never saw a gene, but his theory postulates the existence of such things. I noted before that it is a general feature of nondeductive inference, whether inductive or abductive, that the conclusion goes beyond the premises. We see here, however, a respect in which abduction differs from induction.

## ABDUCTION DIFFERS FROM INDUCTION

If Mendel had made an inductive inference, he simply would have claimed that the observed results of the experiments he ran in his garden would also occur anywhere the experiment was carried out. His experiment was made in Europe at the end of the nineteenth century. An inductive extension of the description of his experiment might conclude that the same results would occur in twentieth-century North America as well. Had Mendel limited himself to this suggestion, no one would remember him now as the father of genetics. His important inference was abductive, not inductive. He didn't simply claim the experiment could be replicated. Rather, he formulated a theoretical explanation of *why* the results occurred. Mendel's inference drew a conclusion concerning something he did *not* see (genes), based on premises that described what he *did* see (the results of the experimental crossings).

## CAN YOU DEDUCE THE EXPLANATION FROM THE OBSERVATIONS?

Let's attend to Mendel's inference more carefully. The following is *not* a deductively valid argument:

> Experimental crosses in the pea plants were observed to exhibit such-and-such results.
> _____
> There are genes, and they obey laws $L$.

Remember: You can't validly deduce a theory from a set of observations.

Why can't you do this? Basically, the last argument attempts to infer a theory about the cause from the observation of its effects. There are, however, lots of possible causes that might have been responsible for the observed effects. The argument is deductively invalid for the same reason the following argument is also invalid:

> A pistol with an "M" on the handle, an El Supremo cigar butt, and a size 12 footprint were found next to the murder victim's body.
> _____
> Moriarty is the murderer.

Though Moriarty may be the most plausible suspect, the clues, in themselves, don't absolutely guarantee that he must have done the deed. Mendel and Holmes were making an inference about what is *probably* true, given the observations. They weren't inferring what is *absolutely guaranteed* to be true by the observations.

## DEDUCING OBSERVATIONAL PREDICTIONS FROM A THEORY

If a set of observations doesn't deductively imply a theory, then perhaps the reverse is true: Maybe a theory deductively implies some observations. This corresponds more closely to what Mendel did. He saw that his theory of the gene implies that certain experimental results ought to occur. He then saw that those predictions came true. He concluded that the truth of the predictions was evidence that the theory is true.

## WHEN THE PREDICTION COMES TRUE

So a better representation of Mendel's inference might go like this. The theory entailed a prediction. The prediction came true. Hence, the theory is probably true. What we now need to see is that the following form of argument is not deductively valid:

> If there are genes and they obey laws *L,* then experimental crosses in the pea plants should exhibit such-and-such results.
> Experimental crosses in the pea plants were observed to exhibit such-and-such results.
> _____
> There are genes and they obey laws *L.*

This is deductively invalid for the same reason that the following argument is too:

> If Jones lives in Wisconsin, then Jones lives in the U.S.A.
> Jones lives in the U.S.A.
> _____
> Jones lives in Wisconsin.

Note that these two arguments have the same logical form.

Scientists often test their theories by seeing whether the predictions made by the theories come true. There is nothing wrong with doing this. The point, however, is that the truth of the theory doesn't follow deductively from the truth of the prediction. Scientists are reasoning *non*deductively when they decide that a theory is plausible because its predictions have come true. *Successful prediction isn't absolutely conclusive proof that the theory is true.*

## WHEN THE PREDICTION TURNS OUT TO BE FALSE

On the other hand, if the predictions entailed by Mendel's theory had come out false, that would have allowed him to deduce that the theory is mistaken. That is, the following argument *is* deductively valid:

If there are genes and they obey laws *L,* then experimental crosses in the pea plants should exhibit such-and-such results.

Experimental crosses in the pea plants didn't exhibit such-and-such results.

———————————

It is false that there are genes and they obey laws *L.*

In other words, *a failed prediction is conclusive proof that the theory implying the prediction is false.*

## HOW TRUE PREDICTIONS AND FALSE PREDICTIONS ARE INTERPRETED

Let's generalize these points. Let $T$ be a theory and $P$ a prediction the theory makes. If the prediction comes out true, we can't deduce that the theory is true. If, however, the prediction comes out false, we can deduce the theory is false:

| *Invalid* | *Valid* |
|---|---|
| If $T$, then $P$ | If $T$, then $P$ |
| $P$ | Not $P$ |
| ——————— | ——————— |
| $T$ | Not $T$ |

---

### Deducing That a Theory Is True

Recall from Chapter 2 that a deductively invalid argument can be turned into a valid one by adding premises. I now will exploit this fact to show how the truth of a theory can be deduced from the fact that it makes a successful prediction, *if you make certain further assumptions.*

Suppose we wish to design an experiment that tests two theories. Here the problem isn't one of evaluating a single theory, but of seeing which of two theories is more plausible. To test one theory ($T_1$) against another ($T_2$), we want to find a prediction over which they disagree. Suppose $T_1$ predicts that $P$ will be true, while $T_2$ predicts that $P$ will be false. If we assume that one or the other theory is true, we can find out whether $P$ comes true and then deduce which theory is true. For example, if $P$ turns out to be true, we can reason as follows:

$T_1$ or $T_2$
If $T_1$, then $P$.
If $T_2$, then not-$P$.
$P$

———————

$T_1$

Notice that this argument is deductively valid. Also note that if $P$ had turned out to be false, we could have deduced that $T_2$ is correct.

---

The difference between these two arguments—one deductively valid, the other not—suggests there is an important difference between the way scientists argue that theories are true and the way they argue that theories are false. It is possible to reject a theory just on the basis of the false predictions it makes, using a deductively valid argument; but it isn't possible to accept a theory just on the basis of the true predictions it makes, using a deductively valid argument. discuss this difference again in Chapter 8.

So far I've explained how a deductively valid argument can lead a scientist to reject a suggested explanation. But how do scientists ever interpret observations as providing strong evidence in favor of the explanations they consider? This must involve a nondeductive inference. But what are the rules that govern such inferences? I now present two ideas that are relevant to evaluating abductive arguments. These I call the *Surprise Principle* and the *Only Game in Town Fallacy*.

## THE SURPRISE PRINCIPLE: WHEN DOES SUCCESSFUL PREDICTION PROVIDE STRONG EVIDENCE?

I've argued that you can't validly deduce that a theory is true just from the fact that some prediction it makes comes true. But maybe only a small modification of this idea is needed. Perhaps all we need to say is that a theory is made highly probable or plausible when a prediction it makes comes true. I now want to explain why this reformulation also is mistaken.

An unconscious patient is brought into the emergency room of a hospital. What is wrong? What would explain the fact that the patient is unconscious? The doctor on duty considers the hypothesis that the patient is having a heart attack. How should the doctor test whether this hypothesis is true? Well, the hypothesis predicts that the patient will have a heart (after all, if someone is having a heart attack, he or she must have a heart). The doctor verifies that this prediction is correct—the patient, indeed, does have a heart. Has the doctor thereby obtained strong evidence that the patient is having a heart attack? Clearly not. This is an example in which you don't obtain serious support for a hypothesis just by showing that one of its predictions is correct.

You go to the gym, and someone tells you he is an Olympic weight lifter. You reason that if he is an Olympic weight lifter, he should be able to pick up the hat you are wearing. You offer him your hat; he lifts it without difficulty. Have you thereby obtained strong evidence that he is an Olympic weight lifter? Clearly not. Once again, the hypothesis under test isn't strongly supported by the fact that one of its predictions turns out to be correct.

What has gone wrong in these two cases? In the first example, the presence of a heart isn't strong evidence that the patient is having a heart attack. The reason is that you would expect the individual to have a heart even if he weren't having a heart attack. In the second example, the man's lifting the hat isn't strong evidence that he is an Olympic weight lifter. The reason is that you would expect him to be able to do this even if he weren't an Olympic lifter.

What should you look for if you want to test the hypothesis that the patient has had a heart attack? What you want to find is a symptom that you would expect to find if the patient were having a heart attack, *but would expect to not be present if the patient were not having a heart attack.* Suppose an erratic EKG (electrocardiogram) almost always occurs when there is a heart attack but rarely occurs when there is no heart attack. This means that the presence of an erratic EKG would be strong evidence that the patient is suffering a heart attack.

What sort of test should you use if you want to see if the man in the gym really is an Olympic weight lifter? Suppose Olympic weight lifters (of this man's weight) can almost always lift 400 pounds, but people who aren't Olympic lifters can rarely do this. This means that his managing to lift 400 pounds would be strong evidence that he is an Olympic weight lifter.

Think of the unconscious patient and the weight lifter as posing *discrimination problems.* The problem is to find evidence that strongly discriminates between two hypotheses. In the first example, the competing hypotheses are:

$H_1$: The patient is having a heart attack.
$H_2$: The patient isn't having a heart attack.

An erratic EKG strongly favors $H_1$ over $H_2$; the mere fact that the patient has a heart does not.

The same holds true for the second example. The problem is to find evidence that discriminates between the following two hypotheses:

$H_1$: This man is an Olympic weight lifter.
$H_2$: This man isn't an Olympic weight lifter.

The fact that the man can lift 400 pounds strongly favors $H_1$ over $H_2$; the fact that he can lift a hat does not.

The Surprise Principle describes what it takes for an observation to strongly favor one hypothesis over another:

> *The Surprise Principle:* An observation $O$ strongly supports $H_1$ over $H_2$ if both the following conditions are satisfied, but not otherwise: (1) if $H_1$ were true, $O$ is to be expected; and (2) if $H_2$ were true, $O$ would have been unexpected.

Let's apply this principle to the first example. Consider the observation that the patient has an erratic EKG. If the patient were having a heart attack ($H_1$), we would expect him to have an erratic EKG. And if the patient weren't having a heart attack ($H_2$), we would expect him not to have an erratic EKG. This explains why the erratic EKG is strong evidence of a heart attack—the EKG strongly favors $H_1$ over $H_2$. Now consider the observation that the patient has a heart. If the patient were having a heart attack, we would expect him to have a heart. But we would expect him to have a heart even if he weren't having a heart attack. This explains why the presence of a heart isn't strong evidence that the patient is having a heart attack—the observation

---

**No Surprise/Surprise**

The Surprise Principle involves two requirements. It would be more descriptive, though more verbose, to call the idea the No Surprise/Surprise Principle.

The Surprise Principle describes when an observation $O$ strongly favors one hypothesis ($H_1$) over another ($H_2$). There are two requirements:

(1) If $H_1$ were true, you would expect $O$ to be true.

(2) If $H_2$ were true, you would expect $O$ to be false.

That is, (1) if $H_1$ were true, $O$ would be unsurprising; (2) if $H_2$ were true, $O$ would be surprising.

The question to focus on is *not* whether the hypotheses ($H_1$ or $H_2$) would be surprising. The Surprise Principle has nothing to do with this. To apply the Surprise Principle, you must get clearly in mind what the hypotheses are and what the observation is.

---

doesn't strongly favor $H_1$ over $H_2$. We were looking for an explanation of why the erratic EKG provides telling evidence whereas the presence of a heart doesn't. The key is to be found in condition (2) of the Surprise Principle.

Take a few minutes to apply the Surprise Principle to the example of the weight lifter. Make sure you see how the principle explains why being able to lift a hat isn't strong evidence, whereas being able to lift 400 pounds is.

## EVIDENCE MAY DISCRIMINATE BETWEEN SOME HYPOTHESES WHILE FAILING TO DISCRIMINATE BETWEEN OTHERS

In the examples of the heart attack and the weight lifter, $H_2$ says only that $H_1$ is false. In other abductions, however, $H_2$ may say more than this. Suppose you see someone crossing campus carrying several philosophy books. You wonder whether the person is a philosophy major. Two hypotheses to consider are

$H_1$: The person is a philosophy major.
$H_2$: The person is an engineering major.

According to the Surprise Principle, the observation you have made favors $H_1$ over $H_2$. But now consider the following third hypothesis:

$H_3$: The person isn't a student, but is in the business of buying and selling philosophy books.

Although your observation discriminates between $H_1$ and $H_2$, it does not discriminate between $H_1$ and $H_3$.

This brings out an important fact about how the Surprise Principle applies to abductive inferences. *If you want to know whether an observation strongly supports a hypothesis, ask yourself what the alternative hypotheses are.* For an observation to strongly support a hypothesis is for it to strongly favor that hypothesis over the others with which it competes.

## TRUE PREDICTION ISN'T ENOUGH

The point of the examples about the unconscious patient and the weight lifter was to show why successful prediction doesn't automatically provide strong evidence. If someone is having a heart attack, that predicts that he will have a heart; but the presence of a heart isn't strong evidence the person is having a heart attack. If someone is an Olympic weight lifter, that predicts that he will be able to lift a hat; but lifting a hat isn't strong evidence the person is an Olympic weight lifter.

There is a scene in the Monty Python movie *The Life of Brian* that illustrates this idea. The setting is a marketplace. Around the perimeter of the market are assorted prophets and soothsayers. The camera pans from one to the other. We see that in each case, the prophet holds a crowd of people in rapt attention. The first prophet predicts that tomorrow a purple monster will rise out of the desert and devour three villages. The crowd is amazed at these predictions and no doubt will conclude that the prophet has special powers to foresee the future if the predictions come true. After showing us a few prophets of this sort, the camera comes to an individual who very calmly makes the following predictions: Tomorrow, many people will get up early. Others will sleep longer. Some people will decide to have breakfast, while others will postpone eating until later in the day. And so on. The joke is that the crowd in front of this guy is just as awestruck as the crowds were in front of the more outlandish prophets.

There is a lesson here. How would you test the hypothesis that someone has special powers to foresee the future? If he predicts events that people without special powers can easily predict, it isn't very impressive that his predictions come true. If, however, he predicts events that normal people aren't able to foresee, and then these predictions come true, we are more impressed. The Surprise Principle explains why the success of "safe" predictions provides less compelling evidence than the success of "daring" predictions.

Here's a related example of the Surprise Principle in action. Many people thought that the astrologer Jeanne Dixon had special powers to predict the future. After all, she predicted the assassination of President John F. Kennedy and several other events that no one could have guessed were going to happen. If Jeanne Dixon played it safe and only predicted events that everybody knew were going to happen, we wouldn't be impressed. But aren't we being sensible in reasoning that she probably does have special powers, since this and other daring predictions have come true?

Although this reasoning may seem to conform to the Surprise Principle, it doesn't. The thing people sometimes forget is that Jeanne Dixon made thousands of predictions and most of them turned out false. It isn't surprising at all that some handful of these should have come out true. Although Jeanne Dixon predicted the Kennedy assassination, which surprised (practically) everyone when it happened, it isn't at all surprising that someone with no special powers should be lucky a few times every thousand tries. The Surprise Principle, properly understood, tells us why we shouldn't take Jeanne Dixon's few successes as strong evidence that she had special powers.

## MODEST FAVORING

The Surprise Principle shows when an observation *strongly* favors one hypothesis over another. However, sometimes our observations are not so telling and unequivocal. Sometimes the observations ($O$) favor one hypothesis ($H_1$) over another ($H_2$), but only modestly. This will be true when $H_1$ confers on $O$ a higher probability than $H_2$ does, but the difference is modest. What the Surprise Principle and this idea about $O$'s modestly favoring $H_1$ over $H_2$ have in common is this: Both make use of the idea that an observation favors one hypothesis ($H_1$) over another ($H_2$). This will be true when the probability of $O$, according to $H_1$, exceeds the probability of $O$, according to $H_2$. We will examine the concept of probability in more detail in Chapter 18.

## THE SURPRISE PRINCIPLE SUMMARIZED

In summary, the Surprise Principle gives advice on what a hypothesis must do if it is to be strongly supported by the predictions it makes. First, the hypothesis shouldn't make false predictions. Second, among the true predictions the hypothesis makes, there should be predictions we would expect not to come true if the hypothesis were false.

When we ask whether an observation $O$ strongly supports some hypothesis $H_1$, the Surprise Principle requires that we specify what the alternative hypotheses are against which $H_1$ competes. It may turn out that $O$ strongly favors $H_1$ over $H_2$, but that $O$ doesn't strongly favor $H_1$ over $H_3$. The example of the person carrying philosophy books across campus illustrates this point.

## THE ONLY GAME IN TOWN FALLACY

I turn now to a second principle for evaluating abductive inferences. Suppose you and I are sitting in a cabin in the woods. We hear a strange rumbling sound in the attic. You ask, "I wonder what that could be?" I reply, "That is the sound of gremlins bowling in the attic." You, being a sensible person, reply, "I really don't think there are gremlins in the attic." I then challenge you to produce a more plausible explanation of the noises. You reply "Gosh, I really don't have any idea why those noises occurred.

---

### An Investment Swindle

Suppose you received a letter every month for a year from an investment firm. In each letter, a prediction is made as to whether "the stock of the month" will increase or decline in value during the next 30 days. You keep track of what happens to the stocks described each month. Each prediction comes true. Would you conclude from this that the investment firm has a method for reliably predicting stock market events?

Some years ago an "investment firm" sent out such letters, but the mailing was a swindle. The firm began with a list of 10,000 investors. In the first month, 5,000 investors received letters predicting that stock *A* would go up; the other 5,000 received letters saying that stock *A* would go down. The firm then waited to see which prediction came true. During the second month, the firm sent letters to the 5,000 people who had received a true prediction during the first month. In the second month, 2,500 investors received letters predicting that stock *B* would go up; the other 2,500 received letters saying that *B* would go down. The process was repeated, so that by the end of 10 months a small number of investors had received 10 letters, each containing a successful prediction.

The company then wrote to those people, asking each to invest a large sum of money. Most did so. The company then absconded with the funds. (This story is from Daniel Dennett's *Brainstorms: Philosophical Essays on Mind and Psychology,* Cambridge, Mass., MIT Press, 1978.)

The investors who were swindled thought they were making a reasonable abductive inference on the basis of the company's track record. Describe the premise, the conclusion, and the reasoning that led the investors to think the conclusion was highly plausible. Were the investors making a strong inference?

---

I just think your story is implausible." To this humble admission on your part, I make the following rejoinder: "Look, my story, if true, would explain why we just heard those strange noises. If you don't want to accept my explanation, you must produce a more plausible explanation of your own. If you can't, you have to accept my explanation of the noises."

What I just did was commit an abductive fallacy (mistake in reasoning), which I'll call the *Only Game in Town Fallacy*. The fact that you can't think of a more plausible explanation of the noises doesn't oblige you to accept the story I constructed. There is an alternative, which is simply to admit that the noises are something you don't know how to explain.

Abduction is sometimes described loosely as follows: If a theory explains some observation, and if no rival account is available that can do a better job of explaining it, then you should accept the theory. Although this description of abduction is roughly correct, it makes the mistake of sanctioning the Only Game in Town Fallacy. The fact that no rival account is better than the explanation I construct doesn't show my explanation is even minimally plausible. My gremlin theory is pretty silly, although maybe there is nothing now available that is clearly superior to it.

I won't at this point try to fine-tune the idea of abductive inference any further, even though there is lots more to be said about it. We now have before us the basic idea of inference to the best explanation. We've seen that it is an important part of the scientific method. And I've described two principles that help guide us in evaluating whether an abductive inference is strong or weak.

## Review Questions

1. What is the difference between deductive validity and inductive strength?
2. What is the difference between induction and abduction?
3. What factors affect how strong an inductive argument is?
4. Suppose a given observation discriminates between two hypotheses, but a second observation fails to do this. Construct an example, different from the ones presented in this chapter, illustrating the point. Show how the Surprise Principle applies to your example.
5. An observation can succeed in discriminating between hypotheses $H_1$ and $H_2$ but fail to discriminate between $H_1$ and $H_3$. Construct an example that illustrates this point that is different from the ones presented in this chapter. Show how the Surprise Principle applies to your example.
6. What is the Only Game in Town Fallacy? What does it mean to call it a "fallacy"?

## Problems for Further Thought

1. Suppose you wanted to find out what percentage of the adults in your county are vegetarians. You obtain a list of unmarried adults in the county and contact them to do a survey. Is this sample a biased one? Why or why not?
2. Although induction and abduction were described in this chapter as separate kinds of inference, they have a good deal in common. The Surprise Principle was introduced as applying to abduction, but it applies to induction as well. Suppose an urn is filled with 1,000 balls, each of them either red or green. You reach into the urn, sampling at random, and bring out 100 balls. Your sample contains 50 red balls and 50 green ones. Here are some hypotheses to consider:

   $H_1$: All the balls in the urn are green.
   $H_2$: 75% of the balls are green.
   $H_3$: 50% of the balls are green.
   $H_4$: 25% of the balls are green.

   Suppose you think that $H_1$ and $H_2$ are the only possibilities. Does the observation strongly support one over the other? Which? How does the Surprise Principle apply to this question? Suppose, instead, that you think that $H_2$ and $H_3$ are the only possibilities. Does the sample strongly support one over the other? If so, which? Suppose, finally, that you think that $H_2$ and $H_4$ are the only possibilites. Which is best supported? Why?

3. Why think that any of the beliefs you have about the world outside your own mind are true? For example, why are you now entitled to think there is a printed page in front of you? Presumably you believe this on the basis of sense experience (sight, touch, etc.). Construct an abductive argument whose conclusion is that there is a printed page in front of you. Make sure your inference obeys the Surprise Principle. Does this abductive argument prove there is a printed page in front of you? Explain.

4. At the beginning of Chapter 2, I presented deductive validity, inductive strength, and abductive strength as mutually exclusive categories. This means that if an argument belongs to one category, it doesn't belong to any of the others. This is generally correct, but not always. Here is an inductive argument that isn't deductively valid:

> I've observed 1,000 emeralds and all have been green.
> _____
> All emeralds are green.

However, by adding a premise, I can produce a deductively valid argument:

> I've observed 1,000 emeralds and all have been green.
> If there are over 500 emeralds in the universe, they will all have the same color.
> _____
> All emeralds are green.

Both of these arguments are inductive in the sense that both involve drawing a sample from a population and reaching a conclusion about that population. If so, some inductively strong arguments are also deductively valid.

The same point holds for abductively strong arguments. Usually they aren't deductively valid, but sometimes they are. Construct a strong abductive argument that obeys the Surprise Principle. Show how it can be made deductively valid by adding or modifying a premise.

5. There is a difference between *not expecting O* and *expecting not-O*. A person who never considers whether $O$ is true does not expect $O$, but it would be wrong to say that she expects not-$O$. Of course, if someone expects not-$O$, it will also be true that she does not expect $O$. Thus, "$S$ expects not-$O$" implies "$S$ does not expect $O$," but the reverse is not true. With this logical point in mind, explain why condition 2 of the Surprise Principle is formulated by saying "$H_2$ leads you to expect not-$O$," rather than saying that "$H_2$ does not lead you to expect $O$."

## Suggestions for Further Reading

### ON THE NATURE OF PHILOSOPHY
The essays in Charles Bontempo and S. Jack Odell (eds.), *The Owl of Minerva: Philosophers on Philosophy,* New York, McGraw-Hill, 1975.
Bertrand Russell, "The Value of Philosophy," in *The Problems of Philosophy,* Oxford, Oxford University Press, 1950.

### ON DIFFERENT FORMS OF ARGUMENT
Monroe Beardsley, *Thinking Straight,* Englewood Cliffs, New Jersey, Prentice Hall, 1975.
Irving Copi, *Informal Logic,* New York, Macmillan, 1986.
Robert Fogelin, *Understanding Arguments,* New York, Harcourt, Brace, Jovanovich, 1978.
Ronald Giere, *Understanding Scientific Reasoning,* New York, Holt, Rinehart, and Winston, 1984.
Merrilee Salmon, *Logic and Critical Thinking,* San Diego, Harcourt, Brace, Jovanovich, 1984.

# PART II
# PHILOSOPHY OF RELIGION

CHAPTER 4

## *Aquinas's First Four Ways*

Saint Thomas Aquinas (c. 1224–1274) was an enormously accomplished theologian and philosopher. In his masterwork, the *Summa Theologiae,* he presents five proofs that God exists (Aquinas called them "the five ways"). I'll discuss the first four now and the fifth in the next chapter.

Each of Aquinas's arguments begins with a simple observation that is supposed to be obvious to everyone. For example, the first argument begins with the observation that physical objects are in motion. Each argument then proceeds through various other premises to the conclusion that the explanation of the initial observation is that there is a God. Aquinas intends each of his proofs to be deductively valid.

In Chapter 3, I stressed that most of the hypotheses that scientists are interested in testing can't be deduced from observations. For example, Mendel couldn't deduce the existence and characteristics of genes from the observations he made on his pea plants. The same is true in Aquinas's arguments, as he fully realizes: You can't deduce the existence and characteristics of God just from the simple observations with which his arguments begin. The existence of motion doesn't, all by itself, deductively imply the existence of God. Aquinas's arguments always include additional principles. It is these further principles that are supposed to link the starting observation with the conclusion that God exists.

### THE CONCEPT OF GOD

Before describing Aquinas's arguments, I need to say something about what he means by "God" and how I'll use that term. Aquinas took God to be a person—one who is all-powerful (omnipotent), all-knowing (omniscient), and entirely good (omnibenevolent)—all-PKG, for short. This conception of God is a familiar one in the traditions of Judaism, Christianity, and Islam (though there is room to debate, in these traditions, whether God is properly described in this way and other religions have other views about what characteristics God has). I'll assume provisionally that God, if such a being exists, has the three characteristics just mentioned. If we don't start with some preliminary picture of what God is, we won't know what we are talking about when we ask whether God exists. However, it is important to bear in mind that this conception of God is not the only one that is possible. Indeed, in Chapter 11, I'll consider an argument that suggests that God, if there is such a being, can't be all-PKG. The definition of God as an all-PKG being is a useful place to begin discussion, but it is only a point of departure.

Another caveat I should mention is that my versions of Aquinas's arguments won't be accurate in all respects. It is often a subtle historical question what this or that philosopher had in mind in a given text. In this case and later in this book, when I discuss the ideas of other philosophers, I often will examine somewhat simplified versions of the arguments they constructed. You may well ask: Why is it worthwhile studying simplified versions of a great philosopher's arguments? Admittedly, there is a loss, but there also is a gain. The main point to be made here, at the beginning of an introductory text, is that it is useful to evaluate these simpler arguments before more subtle arguments are addressed. At any rate, there is ample philosophical material to think about in the arguments I'll describe, even if these arguments don't capture the thoughts of various great thinkers with total accuracy and completeness.

## THE FIRST TWO ARGUMENTS: MOTION AND CAUSALITY

Aquinas's first argument for the existence of God is the argument from motion. Here it is, formulated as a deductive argument:

(I)  (1)  In the natural world, there are objects that are in motion.

(2)  In the natural world, objects that are in motion are always caused to move by objects other than themselves.

(3)  In the natural world, causes must precede their effects.

(4)  In the natural world, there are no infinite cause/effect chains.

———————————

(5)  Hence there is an entity outside of the natural world (a *supe*rnatural being), which causes the motion of the first moving object that exists in the natural world.

———————————

(6)  Hence, God exists.

Aquinas's second argument generalizes the ideas found in the first. Whereas the first argument is about motion in particular, the second argument is about causality in general:

(II) (1) The natural world includes events that occur.

    (2) In the natural world, every event has a cause, and no event causes itself.

    (3) In the natural world, causes must precede their effects.

    (4) In the natural world, there are no infinite cause/effect chains.

_____

    (5) Hence there is an entity outside of nature (a supernatural being), which causes the first event that occurs in the natural world.

_____

    (6) Hence, God exists.

In both these arguments, I've drawn two horizontal lines to indicate that (5) is supposed to follow from premisses (1)–(4) and that (6) is supposed to follow from (5).

What do premises (2) and (3) mean in these two arguments? Let's begin with an object ($O_1$) that is in motion now. Since it is in motion, there must be an earlier object—call it $O_2$—that sent $O_1$ into motion. If $O_2$ was itself in motion, $O_2$ must trace back to a previous mover, $O_3$, and so on. In the second argument, the subject is causality, not motion, but the idea is basically the same.

Premise (4) says that there can't be a cause/effect chain that extends infinitely far back into the past. The idea is that cause/effect chains (or mover/movee chains) leading from the present back into the past have a finite number of links. The arrow in the following diagram represents the relationship of causality:

$$\text{Past} \qquad \text{Present} \qquad \text{Future}$$
$$O_f \longrightarrow \cdots \longrightarrow O_3 \longrightarrow O_2 \longrightarrow O_1 \longrightarrow \quad \cdots$$

Although Aquinas's argument focuses on chains that extend from present back into the past, his principle (4) also has implications about chains that extend from the present forward into the future. These also must have a finite number of links. Cause/effect chains must be finite in both directions.

I'll begin with a criticism aimed just at argument I; after that, I'll lump the two arguments together and formulate some objections that apply to both.

## AQUINAS ON THE CAUSE OF MOTION

Aquinas thinks (premises 1–2) that if an object is in motion, it must be caused to move by something outside itself. Aquinas got this idea from Aristotle's physics. Aristotle (384–322 B.C.) held that if an object continues to move, its motion must be sustained by a force that keeps it in motion. If you remove the force, the object stops moving.

This idea didn't survive into modern physics. You may remember from your high school physics course that Newton, in the seventeenth century, held that an object remains in constant uniform motion unless acted on by a force. Recall that one of Newton's laws of motion is $F = ma$. This means that if an object of mass $m$ is acted on by a force of value *F*, then it will accelerate to degree *a*. This Newtonian law says that an object that isn't acted on by a force won't accelerate, which means it will remain at rest *or in uniform motion*. Newton's laws say that an object can remain in motion forever without there being any force that sustains its motion.

Newton's laws do not exclude the following possibility: The universe contains exactly one physical object, which always moves in uniform motion without any forces ever acting on it. Of course, Newton's laws don't say that the universe we live in is like this. Our universe obviously contains more than one material object. My point, though, is that Newton's theory of motion was different from Aristotle's and so was different from Aquinas's. Aristotle and Aquinas thought that motion requires an outside force; Newton and more modern physical theories hold that it is acceleration, not simply change in position, that requires a force.

It is not difficult to rescue Aquinas's first argument from this Newtonian objection. Just replace his talk of motion with the concept of acceleration. If objects accelerate there must be a force that causes them to do so. Then we are led by the same line of reasoning to the conclusion that there must exist a supernatural entity that causes the first accelerating object in nature to accelerate.

## GOD IS A PERSON, NOT JUST A CAUSE THAT EXISTS OUTSIDE OF NATURE

I turn now to some problems that the two arguments share. First, it is important to see that proposition (S)—that there is an entity outside of nature that causes the first moving object in nature to move, or that causes the first event in nature to occur—does not guarantee the existence of God, where God is understood to mean a person with something like the three properties of omnipotence, omniscience, and omnibenevolence (an all-PKG being). As Aquinas himself realized, conclusion (6) does not follow from proposition (5), in either argument.

## THE BIRTHDAY FALLACY

Another problem arises when we ask whether the argument shows that there is *precisely one* first cause, or instead shows only that there is *at least one*. Suppose we grant that each causal chain in nature has a first member. According to Aquinas, each of these first members must be caused by some event outside of nature. However, it does not follow that there is exactly one such event outside of nature that set all causal chains in the natural world in motion. Here it is important to see the difference between the following two propositions; the first is different from and does not deductively imply the second:

> Every event in the natural world traces back to an event that occurs outside nature.

> There is a single event outside of the natural world to which each event in nature traces back.

The difference here parallels the logical difference between the following two propositions, the first of which is true and the second false:

> Every person has a birthday—a day on which he or she was born.
> There is a single day that is everybody's birthday.

I want to give a name to the mistaken idea that the second proposition follows from the first. I'll call it the *Birthday Fallacy*.

So one problem with arguments I and II is that they don't show there is exactly one first cause or unmoved mover; at best, they show that there is at least one. To think otherwise is to commit the Birthday Fallacy.

## WHY CAN'T NATURE BE INFINITELY OLD?

Another objection to Aquinas's first two arguments is his claim that cause/effect chains cannot extend infinitely far into the past. Why is this impossible? If the natural world were infinitely old, each event could be caused by an earlier event. Every event that occurs in nature could have a cause that also existed in nature, so there would be no reason to infer that something outside of nature must exist as the cause of what occurs inside.

Aquinas thinks he has an answer to this question. He doesn't simply *assume* that causal chains extending into the past must be finite in length; he has an *argument* that he thinks shows why this is so. Here is his argument, which I'll reconstruct in terms of an example of a present event—your reading this page now:

> You are reading this page now.
> A causal chain that extends from this present event infinitely into the past, by definition, lacks a first member.
> If a causal chain lacked a first member, then all subsequent events in the chain could not occur.
>
> ———————
>
> Hence, the causal chain leading up to your reading this page now must be finitely old.

The third premise is where this argument goes wrong. Even if we assume that no event in nature can happen without its having a cause, it does not follow that there has to be a first natural event.

Many traditional theists will agree that the world could have an infinite future—that it could go on forever. However, if an infinite future is possible, why is an infinite past ruled out? If there doesn't have to be a last event in the history of the natural world, why must there be a first? Why accept Aquinas's claim that causal chains can't extend infinitely into the past? Here Aquinas gets some help from modern physics, which views the universe as finitely old. Although it is conceivable that the universe is infinitely old, apparently there are scientific reasons to think that this isn't so.

## WHY MUST EVERY EVENT IN NATURE HAVE A CAUSE?

This brings me to my last objection to Aquinas's first two arguments for the existence of God. Even if the natural world is only finitely old, why must there be an explanation of the first event that occurs in nature? That is, why must *every* event that occurs in nature have a cause?

Do scientists assume that every event has a cause? Well, it is true that scientists often try to discover the causes of events that they observe. However, this activity of searching does not require that one actually *believe* that every event has a cause. Perhaps there are exceptions to this generalization. One tries to find causal explanations for the events one observes for this reason: If you don't look, you won't discover the cause if there is one. Better to look and fail to find than never to look at all.

## THE THIRD ARGUMENT: CONTINGENCY

Aquinas's third argument for the existence of God, like the first two, begins with an observation that everybody would agree is true. The observation is put in language that may be unfamiliar, but once explained, it seems clear enough. The observation is that contingent things exist. What does it mean to say that a thing is contingent? The opposite of contingency is necessity. What makes an object contingent or necessary?

## NECESSARY AND CONTINGENT BEINGS

You, I, the Washington Monument, the human race, the Earth, the solar system, and the Milky Way are all examples of contingent things. Although all of us exist, we needn't have existed. The world could have failed to include any of us. If the particular sperm and egg that produced you hadn't encountered each other, you wouldn't have come into existence. Your parents would have had other children or no children at all. Likewise for the human race; although the world obviously includes human beings, it needn't have. Contingent things depend for their existence on something or other happening. In contrast, a necessary being is something that must exist no matter what. It doesn't depend for its existence on anything.

## POSSIBLE WORLDS

I want to represent the concepts of necessity and contingency by introducing a new idea. Consider the totality of things that have existed, now exist, or will exist at any place in the universe. This totality comprises a giant object that I'll call "the actual world." Imagine a census of the objects in the actual world. We might display this census on a very long time line, in which the durations of various objects are represented:

```
/—w—/

    /—x—/          /—y—/          /—z—/
_____

Past                Now                Future
```

Notice that the life spans, or durations, of objects *w* and *x* overlap. Objects *w* and *x* existed in the past and now are no more. Object *y* came into existence in the past, exists now, and will continue to exist until some future date, when it will cease to be. Object *z* hasn't yet come into being, but it will. Of course, this is a dreadfully incomplete census of everything that was, is, or will be. Never mind. You get the idea: The actual world consists of everything that has existed, exists now, or will exist, anywhere in the universe.

We know the world needn't have had precisely the census it does. Some of the objects in this census might have failed to exist. Other objects, which don't actually exist, might have done so. Let's call each possible way the world might have been a "possible world." There are many of these.

We now may say that an object is contingent if it exists in some but not all possible worlds. And an object is necessary if it exists in all possible worlds. Suppose the following are the censuses found in several possible worlds. As before, the horizontal line represents time within a possible world:

| | | | |
|---|---|---|---|
| *wx* | *y* | *z* | Actual world |
| *ab* | *y* | *z* | Possible world 1 |
| *ac* | *d* | *z* | Possible world 2 |

Past     Present     Future

Notice that *w* exists in the actual world, but not in the two alternative possible worlds represented. On the other hand, *y* exists in the actual world and in the first possible world, but not in the second. Object *z* is different—it exists in all of the possible worlds depicted. Of course, there are more than three possible worlds, since there are more than two alternative ways the actual world might have been (the actual world, of course, is one of the possible worlds). Would *z* continue to appear if we listed not just a few possible worlds, but all of them? That is the question of whether *z* is a necessary being.

I cited some examples of contingent things—you, the Washington Monument, the Earth, and a few others. These examples might strike you as typical of everything that exists. That is, you might find plausible the following philosophical conjecture: Everything that exists is contingent. Familiar objects clearly have this property. But is *everything* contingent? Aquinas argues in his third proof of the existence of God that not everything is contingent. There is at least one necessary being—namely, God.

Here is how his proof goes:

III  (1)  Contingent things exist.

(2)  Each contingent thing has a time at which it fails to exist ("contingent things are not omnipresent").

---

(3)  So, if everything were contingent, there would be a time at which nothing exists (call this an "empty time").

(4)  That empty time would have been in the past.

(5)  If the world were empty at one time, it would be empty forever after (a conservation principle).

---

(6)  So, if everything were contingent, nothing would exist now.

(7)  But clearly, the world is not empty (see premise 1).

---

(8)  So there exists a being who is not contingent.

---

Hence, God exists.

Aquinas's argument has two stages. First, there is his defense of proposition (6), which is contained in premises (1)–(5). Second, there is his use of proposition (6) to establish the existence of God. Before considering why Aquinas thinks (6) is correct, I want to focus on his use of (6) and (7) to infer proposition (8).


## REDUCTIO AD ABSURDUM

Aquinas's proof of (8) from (6) and (7) has a distinctive logical form. His proof is a *reductio ad absurdum* argument (a "reductio," for short).

When I talked about deductive validity in Chapter 2, I emphasized that the word "valid" in logic and philosophy doesn't mean what it means in everyday life. The same holds for the idea of reducing something to absurdity. In ordinary speech this means something like "making a mockery of an idea." In logic, however, reductio arguments are perfectly good arguments—they are deductively valid.

Here's how a reductio argument works. You want to prove a proposition *P*. To do this, you argue that if *P* were false, some proposition *A* would have to be true. But you construct the argument so that *A* is an obvious falsehood (an "absurdity"). From this, you may validly conclude that *P* is true. Reductio arguments, in other words, have the following valid logical form:

If *P* is false, then *A* is true.

*A* is false.

——————————

*P* is true.

Aquinas tries to establish the existence of a necessary being by reductio. He argues that if only contingent beings existed, the world would now be empty. But it is obviously false that the world is now empty. Hence, not everything is contingent—there must exist at least one necessary being.

Let's now examine Aquinas's defense of proposition (6). Why should we think the world would now be empty if there were no necessary beings? Aquinas's reasons for thinking this are contained in premises (1)–(5).

## CONTINGENCY AND ETERNITY

I'll begin by registering an objection to premise (2). Contrary to Aquinas, I submit that a contingent thing can be eternal; the fact that an object is contingent doesn't mean that there must be a time at which it fails to exist. I'll grant that familiar contingent objects aren't eternal. You are an example. You might have failed to exist; in addition, there was a time before you were born and there will be a time after you die. But this is just an example. We want to know whether *all* contingent beings must fail to be eternal.

Notice first that the considerations affecting contingency differ from those affecting the question of eternity. How can you tell whether an object is contingent in a diagram like the one given before showing the actual world and two possible worlds? You look *down* the list of possible worlds, checking to see if the object in question is present in each one. In that diagram, we might say that contingency is represented "vertically." Eternality is different. To see whether an object present in a given possible world is eternal, you look *across* the representation of that possible world, checking to see if it exists at all times in that world. So eternality is represented "horizontally."

Could an object exist in only some possible worlds and still exist at all times in the actual world? That is, could an object be both contingent and eternal? Aquinas says no. Here is a consideration that suggests he may be wrong.

The idea that material objects are made of very small indivisible particles has had a long history, going back at least to the ancient Greeks. Of course, we no longer think of atoms as indivisible particles—we have long since learned to talk about subatomic particles. Suppose for the moment, however, that the word "atom" names such indivisible particles. These particles are the basic building blocks of all material things.

One idea that has been put forward in atomistic theories is that atoms (fundamental particles) can't be created or destroyed. Large objects made of atoms can be created and destroyed by assembling and disassembling collections of atoms. But the basic particles themselves can't be destroyed, because you can't break them into pieces. Again, I'm not saying that this is true of the objects we now regard as the smallest material particles. I mention it only to describe a possible view of atoms.

Atoms, on the view I'm describing, are eternal. If a given atom exists now, it has always existed and it always will exist. Let's call one of the atoms that populates the actual world by the name "Charlie." Charlie is eternal.

Does it follow that Charlie is a necessary being—that the world couldn't have failed to include him? I would say not. The world could have contained more atoms than it does, or fewer. Indeed, it doesn't seem impossible that the world might have been entirely empty of matter. So Charlie, like all the atoms that happen to actually exist, is a contingent being.

If this is right, then Aquinas's premise (2) is mistaken. Charlie, I've claimed, is a contingent being, but he is eternal. So contingent things needn't have a time at which they fail to exist.

The argument I've given against premise (2) depends on a particular theory about the nature of atoms. If atoms really are indestructible, I can claim to have refuted Aquinas's premise. But are they, in fact, indestructible? Again, remember I'm discussing the smallest units of matter here. This is how I'm using the word "atom."

## CONSERVATION LAWS IN PHYSICS

Current physics doesn't support the view that atoms are indestructible. Before Einstein, physics upheld a principle that said that the quantity of mass in the universe is constant. Einstein replaced this classical conservation law with another one. Mass isn't conserved; rather, a quantity that Einstein called "mass-energy" is conserved. This principle says that mass can be destroyed; it may be converted into energy. Modern physics, therefore, doesn't seem to allow me to tell my story about Charlie, the indestructible atom. So matter *can* be destroyed, according to current theory. But this doesn't mean that every contingently existing particle WILL be destroyed, sooner or later. It is the latter claim that Aquinas advances in premise (2). I don't know of any good reason to think this is so, although I'll leave the question open.

My conclusion thus far is that premise (2) is mistaken; a contingent thing doesn't have to have a time at which it fails to exist. Let's move on.

## THE BIRTHDAY FALLACY

The transition from premise (2) to statement (3) involves a fallacy. Even if we grant that every contingent entity has a time at which it fails to exist, we can't conclude that there is an empty time. The fallacy here is the same one discussed concerning Aquinas's first two arguments. Recall the point about birthdays; "Everybody has a birthday" does not deductively imply that there is a day that is everyone's birthday.

To make this point graphic, consider the following possible world, in which no object is eternal, and yet there is no empty time:

$$\longleftarrow\ /\!\!-\!1\!-\!/\quad /\!\!-\!3\!-\!/\quad\ \ /\!\!-\!5\!-\!/\quad\ \ \longrightarrow$$
$$\phantom{\longleftarrow}\quad /\!\!-\!2\!-\!/\quad\ /\!\!-\!4\!-\!/\quad\ \ /\!\!-\!6\!-\!/$$

| Past | Present | Future |
|------|---------|--------|

The arrows at the beginning and end indicate the pattern should be repeated indefinitely into the past and into the future. So the supposition that everything is contingent doesn't imply an empty time. But there is an additional unjustified step. Even if there does have to be an empty time, why must it have been in the past? I see no reason to assume this.

## NECESSARY BEINGS OTHER THAN GOD

I've noted some problems in Aquinas's attempted reductio proof that not everything is contingent. Suppose, however, that Aquinas could show that there is at least one necessary being. Could he conclude from this that God exists? I want to argue that this, too, doesn't follow. In discussing Aquinas's first two arguments, I claimed that the existence of God doesn't follow from the existence of a first cause. I now want to suggest that the existence of God doesn't follow from the existence of a necessary being.

To explain why this is so, I have to develop an idea from the philosophy of mathematics. Until now I've described necessity and contingency as properties of entities. You and I are contingent beings, for example. Now, however, I want to discuss the idea that contingency and necessity are properties of propositions. Propositions, or statements, are true or false. They also have the properties of necessity and contingency.

## NECESSARY AND CONTINGENT PROPOSITIONS

Necessity and contingency as properties of propositions are definable in a way that parallels the way this distinction applies to entities like you and me. A proposition is necessarily true if it is true in all possible worlds. A proposition is necessarily false if it is false in all possible worlds. Contingent propositions are true in some possible worlds and false in others. A true statement is contingent if it is true in the actual world, though false in some possible world.

It is easy to cite examples of contingent propositions. Consider the fact that the United States is in North America. This is true, though only contingently so. Consider the following contingent falsehood: The Rocky Mountains are no higher than 6,000 feet above sea level. This is false, but there are possible worlds in which it is true.

## MATHEMATICAL TRUTHS

Are there any necessary truths? Many philosophers have held that mathematical truths are necessarily true. Consider the fact that $7 + 3 = 10$. It isn't just that this happens to be true in the actual world. There is no possible world in which it is false. The sum of 7 and 3 could not fail to equal 10.

To see why this is at least a plausible view of mathematical propositions, you've got to be clear on what the proposition says. The proposition doesn't say that if you put seven rabbits together with three others, there will be ten bunnies forever after. Rabbits reproduce, but this doesn't contradict any fact of arithmetic. Take another example: If you pour 3 cups of sugar into 7 cups of water, you will not obtain 10 cups of liquid. But, again, this doesn't contradict the fact that $7 + 3 = 10$. Arithmetic is unaffected by this result; it just so happens that liquids and solids don't always combine additively.

## NAMES DIFFER FROM THE THINGS NAMED

Here is a somewhat more subtle point to notice. The proposition that $7 + 3 = 10$ doesn't say anything about the language we use in expressing that fact to ourselves. It is a contingent fact that human beings use the numeral "7" to refer to the number 7. We might have called that number by another name—we might have used the numeral "2" to denote the number 7. Similarly, it is a contingent fact that we use the symbol "=" to represent the relation of equality. So it is a contingent fact that the sentence "$7 + 3 = 10$" expresses what it does, and it is a contingent fact that that sentence expresses a true proposition rather than a false one. But this doesn't show that $7 + 3$ might not have equaled 10. The fact couldn't have been otherwise, even though we might have used our terminology differently.

The distinction I'm drawing here is very obvious in some contexts, though it is easy to lose sight of in others. Few things are more different than a thing and its name. You are a person, but your name isn't. Your name contains a certain number of letters, but you don't. Your name is a linguistic entity, but you aren't.

We mark this difference by using quotation marks. If we want to talk about a thing, we use its name. If we want to talk about the name of a thing, we put the name in quotation marks. So if I want to talk about a big mountain in western North America, I might say that the Rocky Mountains are tall. But if I want to talk about the mountain range's name, I'd say that the phrase "the Rocky Mountains" contains 17 letters.

## NUMBERS AREN'T NUMERALS

This is obvious when you think about it. When it comes to mathematics, however, we tend to confuse these ideas. Numerals are names of numbers. But the number and its name are different, just as the phrase "the Rocky Mountains" differs from the mountains themselves. I grant that it is a contingent matter that the sentence

"7 + 3 = 10" expresses a truth. I deny, however, that 7 + 3 might have failed to equal 10. The proposition is necessarily true, even though it is a contingent fact that the sentence expresses the proposition it does. Just as your name is part of a language, though you aren't, so the sentence "7 + 3 = 10" is part of a language, though the proposition it expresses isn't.

## SETS

So what does the proposition that 7 + 3 = 10 actually mean? It doesn't say anything about rabbit reproduction or about the way sugar and water combine when poured together. Nor does it say anything about the language we use. You can think of this statement as describing a basic property of mathematical objects called *sets*.

First, I need a bit of terminology. The *union* of two sets is the set that includes all the members of the first and all the members of the second, and no others. A set is any collection of objects. So the set {Groucho Marx, Napoleon, the Eiffel Tower} is a three-member set, and the set {Napoleon, the Rocky Mountains, the French Revolution} is also a three-member set. The items in a set needn't have anything special in common with each other. There are sets of similar things, but there also are sets of dissimilar things. The union of the two sets just mentioned is this set: {Groucho Marx, Napoleon, the Eiffel Tower, the Rocky Mountains, the French Revolution}.

The proposition that 7 + 3 = 10 can be understood to say the following: Consider any two sets where the first contains exactly seven objects and the second contains exactly three. If these sets have no common members, then the union of these two sets will have precisely ten members. Notice that the arithmetic proposition doesn't say that the Rocky Mountains exist, or that there are at least seven material things in the universe. The arithmetic fact doesn't rule out the possibility that the world contains no material objects at all. It simply describes a basic property of the operation of set-theoretic union.

## NECESSITY AND CERTAINTY ARE DIFFERENT

I need to add a final clarification of the thesis that mathematical truths are necessary. In saying that it is a necessary truth that 7 + 3 = 10, I'm not saying that I know that the proposition is true with absolute certainty. Nor am I saying that I'll never change my mind on the question of whether 7 + 3 equals 10.

This is a rather subtle point, because we sometimes express our lack of certainty about a proposition by saying that maybe the proposition isn't so. If I think there will be rain tomorrow, but entertain some small doubt that this will be so, I may express this by saying, "Possibly it won't rain tomorrow." But my certainty or uncertainty is a fact about *me*. It is a fact in the *subjective* realm. I want to distinguish this question from the question of whether a given proposition has the property of necessity or contingency. The latter question doesn't have anything special to do with me. Necessity and contingency are *objective*.

Here is a nonmathematical example that may make this clearer. Could there be perpetual motion machines? A machine of this sort wouldn't require any energy input to keep running, but it would provide a constant output of energy. Scientists for many hundreds of years tried to design such a machine. They always failed. Finally, in the nineteenth century, physicists working in the area called thermodynamics proved that perpetual motion machines are impossible.

Consider the proposition that there are or will be perpetual motion machines. This is, we now believe, a falsehood. Is it a necessary falsehood? I would say yes. It isn't just that no one will bother to build one; the point is that it is impossible to build one. This, at least, is what science tells us.

Now I'll ask an entirely separate question: Am I absolutely certain that no such machine will ever exist? I guess I'm not absolutely certain. After all, science has been wrong before, and so maybe it now is wrong when it says that such machines are impossible. Opinion has changed through history on the question of whether such machines could be built. Before the nineteenth century, many serious scientists thought such machines are possible. Later, opinion changed. Maybe it will change again.

So the certainty that a single scientist or a community of scientists may have about the issue may change. But there is something that doesn't change. Either it is possible for such things to exist or it isn't. This should convince you that *certainty* and *necessity* are different. People may change their degree of certainty about a proposition; they may even think at one time that the proposition is true, but later on think that it is false. However, the proposition itself doesn't change from true to false. Nor does a proposition cease to be necessary just because people stop believing it. So, to say that arithmetic truths are necessary isn't to say that people are certain about arithmetic. Nor is it to say that people have never changed their minds about arithmetic propositions. Again, these are questions about our attitudes toward the propositions. But whether a proposition is necessary or not has nothing to do with our attitudes. In this respect, necessity is like truth—both are objective issues, independent of what people happen to believe.

To sum up, I've described a prominent view in the philosophy of mathematics. It holds that arithmetic truths are necessary. I haven't provided that view with a complete defense, but I hope you can see what it asserts. I also hope it is at least somewhat plausible, even if it is not entirely convincing.

What has this material about mathematics to do with the conclusion of Aquinas's third proof? Recall that Aquinas reasons that if there is a necessary being, then God must exist. Part of my point in talking about mathematical necessity here is that I want to describe a necessary being that no one would think is God.

## NUMBERS ARE NECESSARY BEINGS

Consider the fact that arithmetic includes various existence statements. Besides asserting that $7 + 3 = 10$, arithmetic also asserts that there is a prime number immediately after 10. If, however, arithmetic truths are necessary, then it is a necessary truth that there exists a prime number immediately after 10. To put it bluntly, the philosophy of mathematics I've described holds that the number 11 is a necessary being. It exists in all possible worlds. This follows from the thesis that arithmetic truths are necessary and from the fact that arithmetic contains existence claims.

The conclusion that there is a God doesn't follow from the assertion that not everything is contingent. A philosopher of mathematics might claim that the number 11 is a necessary being, but this wouldn't entail that God exists. This is my last criticism of Aquinas's third argument.

## AQUINAS'S FOURTH ARGUMENT: PROPERTIES THAT COME IN DEGREES

I won't spend much time on Aquinas's fourth proof of the existence of God. It is rooted in an Aristotelian view of causality that seems radically implausible now. Here's the argument:

(1) Objects have properties to greater or lesser extents.

(2) If an object has a property to a lesser extent, then there exists some other object that has that property to the maximum possible degree (call this a maximum exemplar of the property).

(3) So, there is an entity that has all properties to the maximum possible degree.

———————————

Hence, God exists.

The argument begins with an observation that is obviously true: Some things are more powerful and some less; some are more intelligent and others less, and so on. The second premise, however, seems entirely implausible. The fact that Charlie Chaplin is less than maximally funny doesn't mean that there must exist a maximally funny comedian. And the fact that we are somewhat intelligent, though not perfectly so, doesn't seem to require that there exists a perfectly intelligent being.

The Aristotelian idea that Aquinas is using here is roughly as follows. Aristotle thought that fire is the maximally hot substance. When other objects are hot to some lesser degree, this is because fire is mixed in them to some extent. The property of heat can occur to a less than maximal degree in human beings, for example, only because there exists this substance, fire, which is hot to the maximum possible degree. Fire is the maximum exemplar of heat, from which lesser degrees of heat derive.

There are other problems with the argument. If each property has a maximum exemplar, it doesn't follow that there is an entity that is a maximum exemplar of all properties. Recall the Birthday Fallacy: The fact that everyone has a birthday doesn't imply that there is a single day on which everyone was born. So even if there is a maximum exemplar of intelligence, a maximum exemplar of power, and a maximum exemplar of moral goodness, it doesn't follow that there is a single entity who is all-knowing, all-powerful, and all-good.

Finally, there is the problem of contradiction. If intelligence has its maximum exemplar, then stupidity would have to have its maximum exemplar as well. By Aquinas's argument, this leads us to say that there is a single being who is both maximally intelligent and maximally stupid. But this is impossible. That concludes what I want to say about Aquinas's fourth way.

## CRITICIZING AN ARGUMENT VERSUS SHOWING THE ARGUMENT'S CONCLUSION IS FALSE

None of the four arguments I've discussed here is successful. Does this mean there is no God? It means no such thing. There may be other arguments for the existence of God that are convincing. That the four arguments discussed here don't work doesn't mean that no argument will work. Not one word has been said here that shows that atheism is true. All we have seen is that some arguments for theism are flawed. In the next chapter, I'll consider Aquinas's fifth argument for the existence of God. Maybe it will fare better.

---

### Review Questions

1. What objections are there to the first cause argument?
2. What is the Birthday Fallacy? How does it figure in the discussion of Aquinas's arguments?
3. Explain what it means for an object to be necessary or contingent. What is a "possible world"?
4. How are necessity and eternality related? How does this bear on Aquinas's third argument?
5. What is a reductio argument? Give an example.
6. What is the difference between necessity and certainty? What is meant by saying that necessity is "objective"?
7. What would it mean for something to be a first cause without being God? What would it mean for something to necessarily exist without being God?

---

### Problems for Further Thought

1. I formulated Aquinas's proofs by having him talk about objects that exist in "nature" (in "the natural world"). What does "nature" include? Does it include just the things we can see or hear or touch or taste or smell? After all, the selection from Aquinas in the Readings translates Aquinas as talking about the "sensible" world. How would interpreting his argument in this way affect its plausibility? What other interpretations of "nature" make sense in this context?

2.  In discussing Aquinas's third proof, I talked about Charlie the atom as an example of a thing that is both eternal and contingent. Could something exist that is both necessary and noneternal? It would exist at *some* time in each possible world, though it would not exist at *all* times in the actual world. Can you give an example of such a thing?

3.  I criticized Aquinas's third argument by discussing numbers, which I claimed exist necessarily. Can the argument be reformulated so that this objection no longer applies?

4.  I criticized Aquinas's fourth argument by discussing "maximum stupidity." Can Aquinas reply to this objection by claiming that stupidity is just the absence of intelligence?

## CHAPTER 5

# *The Design Argument*

There are three main traditional arguments for the existence of God—the cosmological argument, the design argument, and the ontological argument. Aquinas's first, second, and third ways, surveyed in the previous chapter, are instances of the first. The cosmological argument takes different forms, but all cite general features of the whole universe as evidence that there is a God. The second type of traditional argument—the design argument—is the one we'll consider in the present chapter; the ontological arugment will occupy our attention in Chapter 8.

Aquinas's fifth argument for the existence of God is an instance of what has come to be called the Argument from Design. The design argument has a variety of forms, some of which I'll describe. To start things off, here is a formulation that is close to the one Aquinas uses:

> (1) Among objects that act for an end, some have minds whereas others do not.
>
> (2) An object that acts for an end, but does not itself have a mind, must have been designed by a being that has a mind.
>
> (3) Hence, there exists a being with a mind who designed all mindless objects that act for an end.
>
> ————————————
>
> Hence, God exists.

Note as a preliminary point that the transition from (2) to (3) commits the Birthday Fallacy described in Chapter 4. If each mindless object that acts for an end has a designer, it doesn't follow that there is a *single* designer of all the mindless objects that act for an end.

## GOAL-DIRECTED SYSTEMS

What does Aquinas mean by "act for an end"? This phrase corresponds to the modern idea of a goal-directed system. Human beings act for an end because they have desires; these desires represent the ends or purposes or goals to which behavior is directed. Human beings are capable of goal-directed behavior because they have minds. Consider, however, a different example: a guided missile. It is a goal-directed system. Its goal or function is to reach and destroy its target. If the target veers off to the side, the missile can adjust its behavior so that it will achieve its purpose. Guided missiles are goal-directed systems, but they don't have minds. How is this possible? The answer is consistent with what Aquinas says in premise (2). Guided missiles are *artifacts*. They are devices built by creatures with minds—namely, human beings. This is how missiles obtained the machinery that allows them to engage in goal-directed behavior.

Are there other examples of goal-directed systems besides human beings and artifacts? Nonhuman organisms provide a third category. Even bacteria, which evidently don't have beliefs and desires, seek out nutrients and avoid poisonous chemicals. It seems plausible to describe them as having the goal of surviving and reproducing. They are able to modify their behavior to achieve these ends.

Does the list stop here—with human beings, artifacts, and nonhuman organisms? Aquinas followed Aristotle in thinking that even inanimate objects such as rocks and comets have goals. This idea pretty much went out of fashion with the Scientific Revolution in the seventeenth century. It now seems implausible to describe a rock as being hard "in order to resist destruction." It also seems strange to say that rocks fall toward the center of the Earth when they are released "in order to attain the location that it is in their nature to seek." But this is how Aristotle thought about rocks, and Aquinas followed him here. Both thought that everything, whether living or not, should be understood *teleologically*—that is, as a goal-directed system. (This will be discussed further in Chapter 34.) I won't take issue with this general teleological picture, except to note that it is far more encompassing than the one provided by modern science. However, this point does not affect the design argument as I have formulated it. What is required is just that *some* mindless objects are goal-directed.

## TWO KINDS OF DESIGN ARGUMENT

It will be useful to distinguish two kinds of design argument. Aquinas would have been willing to endorse them both. David Hume (1711–1776), who examined various design arguments in his *Dialogues Concerning Natural Religion* (1779), discusses both sorts. I'll call these two sorts of arguments *global* design arguments and *local* design arguments.

A global design argument cites some general feature of the whole universe and argues that this feature should be explained by the hypothesis that it is the product of intelligent design. An example would be the argument that proposes to explain why the laws of nature are simple. Newton himself argued that the simplicity of natural laws is evidence that there exists an intelligent and perfect God who was their author.

A local design argument focuses on a more specific feature that one or more object in the universe has and claims that the hypothesis that God exists is the best or the only plausible explanation of that fact. The example I'll consider here concerns features of the organisms we observe on Earth. They are goal-directed systems; they are complex systems equipped with the ability to modify their behavior so that they can survive and reproduce. In this Chapter, I'll begin with the local argument just mentioned, in which it is special features of living things (including ourselves) that are said to require explanation. In Chapter 7, I'll return to design arguments that are global.

## PALEY'S WATCH

In the eighteenth century and the early nineteenth century in Great Britain, design arguments were the rage. Numerous books were published arguing that the existence of God was required to explain this or that feature of the world we observe. One of the most influential works of this sort was produced by William Paley (1743–1805). Whereas Aquinas formulated his version of the design argument as a deductively valid argument, I'm going to interpret Paley's argument as an abductive argument, an inference to the best explanation.

Paley's striking formulation of the design argument goes like this: Suppose you were walking on a beach (actually, Paley talks about walking on a "heath") and found a watch lying on the sand. Opening it up, you see it is a complex and intricate piece of machinery. You also see that the parts of the watch work together to allow the hands to measure out equal intervals of time with considerable precision. What could explain the existence and characteristics of this object?

### $H_1$: **The Random Hypothesis**

One hypothesis to consider I will call the *Random Hypothesis*. By the random action of the waves on the sand, a watch was accidentally produced. Even if you think that this explanation is possible, I bet you agree that it isn't very plausible. The idea that waves beating on sand could produce a useful object of such intricacy doesn't make a lot of sense. It is about as plausible as suggesting that a monkey randomly pounding on a typewriter will write out the complete works of Shakespeare.

### $H_2$: **The Design Hypothesis**

A far more plausible explanation is the *Design Hypothesis*. The intricacy and usefulness of the watch suggest that it is the product of intelligence. This hypothesis says that the watch exists because there was a watchmaker who produced it.

Why do we think the Design Hypothesis is more plausible than the Random Hypothesis? If there were a designer at work, then it wouldn't be surprising that the watch is complex and well suited to the task of measuring temporal intervals. If, however, the only process at work were waves pounding on sand, then it would be enormously surprising that the watch has these characteristics. The observed features of the watch are possible, according to each hypothesis. But they are rather probable according to one and vastly improbable according to the other. In preferring the Design Hypothesis, we prefer the hypothesis that strains our credulity less.

I hope you see that Paley's argument uses the Surprise Principle described in Chapter 3. You've made some observations (call them $O$) and are considering whether $O$ strongly favors one hypothesis ($H_2$) over another ($H_1$). The Surprise Principle says that $O$ strongly favors $H_2$ over $H_1$ if $H_2$ says that $O$ is very probable while $H_1$ says that $O$ is quite improbable. $O$ would be unsurprising if $H_2$ were true, but $O$ would be very surprising if $H_1$ were true.

Not only do we infer the existence of a watchmaker from the watch we found; we also can infer something about the watchmaker's characteristics. We can say that the designer must have been fairly intelligent to produce an object of such intricacy. Chimps are somewhat intelligent, but it is dubious that a chimp could have made the watch. Rather, what we naturally infer is that the watchmaker must have had an intelligence at least on the order of human intelligence, given the features of the watch we observe.

## THE ANALOGY

So far in this argument, Paley is simply describing what common sense would say about the watch on the beach. Paley then suggests an analogy. Look around the living world. Notice that it is filled with organisms that are extremely intricate and well adapted to living in the environments they inhabit. In fact, organisms are far more complicated than watches. And as well suited as a watch is to the task of measuring time, organisms are even better suited to the tasks of surviving and reproducing.

How can we explain the fact that organisms are so amazingly intricate and well adapted? One possibility is the Random Hypothesis—that by a process akin to waves pounding on sand, orchids, crocodiles, and people came into existence. The other alternative is the Design Hypothesis—that an organism maker made the impressive pieces of machinery we call living things. Which explanation is more plausible? If the Random Hypothesis says that the existence of a watch is very improbable, then the Random Hypothesis also must say that the existence of these intricate and adapted organisms is very improbable. So if inferring the existence of a watchmaker is plausible in the first case, then inferring the existence of a designer of all life is plausible in the second.

Finally, we may ask how intelligent this maker of organisms must be, given the intricacy and fineness of adaptation that organisms exhibit. From what watches are like, we can infer that watchmakers must be pretty smart. By the same reasoning, we infer that the maker of organisms must be very, very intelligent—far more intelligent than human beings are. Paley's design argument concludes that the intricacy and adaptedness of organisms are best explained by postulating the existence of an *extremely* intelligent designer.

## ABDUCTIONS OFTEN POSTULATE UNOBSERVED ENTITIES

There is a point that pertains to all of Aquinas's arguments that should be emphasized here. The design argument claims there is something we observe—the complexity and adaptedness of living things—that is best explained by the hypothesis that there is a God. The conclusion of the argument concerns the existence of something we have not directly observed. Although there may be defects in this argument, the fact that it reaches a conclusion about a being we have not observed isn't one of them. Recall from Chapter 3 that abductive arguments frequently have this characteristic. It would cripple science to limit theorizing to a description of what scientists have actually observed. So my view of Paley's argument is that it is an abductive argument:

> Organisms are intricate and well suited to the tasks of survival and reproduction.
> ===========
> Hence, organisms were created by an intelligent designer.

I've drawn a double line here to indicate that the argument does not aim at being deductively valid.

To show this is a strong abductive argument, Paley argues that it is analogous to a second inference to the best explanation:

> The watch is intricate and well suited to the task of measuring time.
> ===========
> Hence, the watch was created by an intelligent designer.

Paley claims that if you grant that the second abductive argument is convincing, you should grant that the first one is convincing as well.

## HUME'S CRITICISMS OF THE DESIGN ARGUMENT

Hume's *Dialogues on Natural Religion* contain several criticisms of the design argument. Sometimes he is talking about global design arguments—ones that argue that the entire universe must be the product of intelligent design. At other times, Hume addresses local arguments—ones that focus on the adaptedness and intricacy of organisms.

I've claimed that design arguments are abductive. Hume paints a very different picture. He represents the arguments as being *inductive arguments* or *arguments from analogy*. This may not look like a very important difference, since all of these formulations involve a nondeductive inference. But you will see in what follows that two of Hume's criticisms of design arguments aren't very convincing if we think of the design argument as an inference to the best explanation.

## IS THE DESIGN ARGUMENT A WEAK ARGUMENT FROM ANALOGY?

In this section, I'll discuss a criticism of the argument from design that Hume develops in Part II of his *Dialogues* (see the paragraph beginning "What I chiefly scruple ... ").

To see what Hume has in mind when he talks about arguments from analogy, consider the following example of an analogy argument:

> Human beings circulate their blood.
> ===========================
> Dogs circulate their blood.

I've drawn a double line between the premise and the conclusion, again to indicate that the argument isn't deductively valid. In this argument, let's call human beings the *analogs* and dogs the *targets*. I say that dogs are the targets here because they are the items about which the argument aims to reach a conclusion. Hume suggests, with some plausibility, that such arguments are stronger or weaker depending on how similar the analogs are to the targets. To see what he means here, compare the above argument with the following one:

> Human beings circulate their blood.
> ===========================
> Plants circulate their blood.

This argument is quite weak, because human beings and plants aren't very similar.

We can formulate Hume's point by saying that an analogy argument has the following logical form:

> Object $A$ has property $P$.
> Object $A$ and object $T$ are similar to degree $n$.
> $n$[ ===========================
> $T$ has property $P$.

$A$ is the analog and $T$ is the target. The number $n$ measures the degree of similarity between $A$ and $T$. It goes from a minimum value of 0 (meaning that $A$ and $T$ aren't similar at all) to a maximum value of 1 (meaning that they share all their characteristics). This number also represents a probability—that is why "$n$" is next to the double line separating premises from conclusion. A high value of $n$ means that $A$ and $T$ are very similar and that the premises make the conclusion very probable. This expresses Hume's idea that the more similar $A$ and $T$ are, the more probable it is that the target object $T$ has the property found in the analog $A$.

Hume uses this idea about analogy arguments to criticize the design argument. He thinks the design argument has the following form:

> Watches are the products of intelligent design.
> $n$[ ===========================
> The universe is the product of intelligent design.

This is a very weak argument, Hume says, since the analog is really not very similar to the target. Watches resemble the universe as a whole in some ways, but fail to do so in a great many others. So *n* has a low value.

Here Hume is criticizing what I've called a global design argument—an argument that focuses on some large-scale feature of the entire universe. Hume's point, however, also applies to local design arguments—to arguments that focus on organisms and their characteristics:

$$n \left[ \frac{\text{Watches are the products of intelligent design.}}{\text{Organisms are the product of intelligent design.}} \right.$$

Hume's criticism is that organisms are really not very similar to watches. Watches are made of metal, but organisms aren't. Kangaroos hop around, but watches don't. Organisms reproduce and obtain nutrition from their environment, but watches don't. And so on. Since analog and target are so dissimilar, the analogy argument is a very weak one; *n* is low here as well.

Hume's idea is that the strength or weakness of an analogy argument depends on the *overall similarity* of target and analog. You look at all the known characteristics of target and analog and try to say how similar they are overall. I grant that if you did this, you would conclude that watches and kangaroos aren't very similar.

My view, however, is that this doesn't undermine the design argument at all when that argument is taken to be abductive. It is entirely irrelevant whether watches and kangaroos both have fur, or whether both hop around, or whether both reproduce. The design argument focuses on *a single pair of features* of each of these and asks how it should be explained. A watch's intricacy, as well as its being well suited to measuring time, require that we think of it as the product of intelligent design. Paley's claim is that an organism's intricacy, as well as its being well suited to the tasks of survival and reproduction, ought to be explained in the same way. It doesn't matter that the one is made of metal while the other isn't. *Overall* similarity is irrelevant.

The fundamental idea of Paley's argument is that the Surprise Principle tells us that the Design Hypothesis is better supported than the Random Hypothesis, given the observations we have made about living things. This argument stands on its own. To use the Surprise Principle in this case, it doesn't matter whether organisms are similar to watches or to anything else. I conclude that Hume is mistaken to criticize the design argument as a weak argument from analogy.

## IS THE DESIGN ARGUMENT A WEAK INDUCTION?

A second criticism that Hume levels at the design argument rests on thinking that the argument must be inductive if it is to make sense. (Here I have in mind the paragraph in Part II of the *Dialogues* that begins "And can you blame me … "; see especially the passage that begins "When two species of objects … ")

Recall from Chapter 2 that inductive arguments involve observing a sample and extrapolating from it to some claim about one or more objects not in the sample. For example, suppose I call a large number of voters registered in a county and find that most of them are Democrats. This seems to license the inference that the next voter I call will probably be a Democrat. Hume observes, again with some plausibility, that the strength of an inductive inference is influenced by sample size. In particular, if my sample had included only five individuals, I would be on rather shaky ground if I used this as my basis for predicting what the next voter called would be like. My inference would be on even shakier ground if I ventured a guess about the next telephone call having never sampled even a single voter. A sample size of zero is just plain silly; an inductive argument can't be weaker than that.

Hume claims that if we are to have a reason for thinking that the universe we inhabit is the product of intelligent design, we must base this conclusion on induction. What would this involve? We would have to examine a large number of other universes and see that most or all of them were the result of intelligent design. If our sample size were sufficiently large, that would justify a conclusion about the universe we inhabit. But how big *is* our sample size? How many universes have we observed being made by an intelligent designer? The answer is—zero. The only universe we have ever experienced is the one we inhabit. We have not seen our universe being made by an intelligent designer, nor have we seen an intelligent designer make the organisms that exist in our universe. So no inductive argument can be constructed here.

My view is that this is true, but irrelevant. Small sample size does weaken an inductive argument. However, the design argument isn't an inductive argument. Hume assumed that the only sorts of inferences worth taking seriously are inductive and deductive. I think this is a mistake. There is abduction as well. Mendel didn't have to observe that lots of different organisms have genes before he could conclude that his pea plants have genes. Mendel never saw a single gene, but this didn't prevent him from inferring their existence. His inference was abductive, not inductive.

I've reviewed two of Hume's criticisms of the design argument. They don't work. Of course, this doesn't mean that the argument has no flaws, only that we have yet to uncover one. The design argument that Paley formulated considers two competing hypotheses—the hypothesis of intelligent design and the hypothesis of random physical processes. In the mid-nineteenth century, a new hypothesis was formulated that we now need to consider as a third alternative—this is Darwin's theory of evolution by natural selection. In the next chapter, I'll describe what this hypothesis asserts and discuss how it compares with the hypothesis of intelligent design.

---

## Review Questions

1. What does it mean to say that the design argument is an abductive argument?
2. What is the difference between a global design argument and a local design argument?
3. How does Paley's argument about the watch use the Surprise Principle?

4. Hume formulated a principle that states how the strength of an analogy argument may be measured. What is it?
5. What two criticisms did Hume make of the design argument? Are these good criticisms if the argument is understood to be abductive in character?

---

### Problems for Further Thought

1. It might be suggested that one difference between Paley's argument about the watch and his argument about organisms is that we have seen watchmakers, but have never directly observed God. Does this point of difference undermine the force of Paley's design argument?
2. I mentioned in passing that modern science no longer takes seriously the idea that *all* things are goal-directed systems. Consider the following pair of propositions. Can you think of a reason that the first of them might be true, whereas the second might be rejected?

   The function of the heart is to pump blood.

   The function of rain is to provide farm crops with water.

   What does it mean to attribute a "function" to something?
3. In addition to the two criticisms that Hume makes of the design argument that are described in this chapter, Hume presents a third. He says that even if the design argument succeeds in showing that a designer made the universe (or the organisms in it), the argument does not succeed in establishing what characteristics that designer has. For this reason, the argument does not show that God exists. Is Hume's claim correct? How seriously does this undermine the design argument?

---

# CHAPTER 6

---

## *Evolution and Creationism*

Aquinas and Paley maintained that the intricacy and adaptedness of organisms can be explained only by viewing them as the product of intelligent design, but they were not able to consider an alternative theory that Charles Darwin (1809–1882) put on the table in 1859 when he published his book *The Origin of Species.* Modern-day creationists do consider what their predecessors could not; they reject Darwin's theory and maintain that the old design argument is still correct. My goal in this chapter is to give a sample of the kinds of arguments that one needs to consider in thinking about the evolution versus creation debate. As I promised at the end of Chapter 3, I'll here introduce a new principle that is important to abductive inference, which will supplement the Surprise Principle and the Only Game in Town Fallacy. Unfortunately, I won't have time to provide a full treatment of the philosophical issues, and there are lots of biological details that are important here that I won't be able to discuss.

## CREATIONISM

Creationists (sometimes calling themselves "scientific creationists" or "intelligent design theorists") are present-day defenders of the design argument. Although they agree among themselves that intelligent design is needed to explain some features of the living world, they disagree with each other about various points of detail. Some hold that the earth is young (around 10,000 years old), whereas others concede that it is ancient—about 4.5 billion years old, according to current geology. Some creationists maintain that each species (or basic "kind" of organism) was separately created by an intelligent designer, whereas others concede that biologists are right when they assert, as Darwin did, that all life on earth traces back to a common ancestor.

To clarify what creationism asserts, let's consider three possible relationships that might obtain among God ($G$), mindless evolutionary processes ($E$), and the complex adaptations that organisms are observed to have ($O$):

$$\text{(theistic evolutionism)} \qquad G \longrightarrow E \longrightarrow O$$
$$\text{(atheistic evolutionism)} \qquad E \longrightarrow O$$
$$\text{(creationism)} \qquad G \longrightarrow E \not\longrightarrow O$$

Theistic evolutionism says that God set mindless evolutionary processes in motion; these processes, once underway, suffice to explain the complex adaptations we observe organisms to have. Atheistic evolutionism denies that there is a God, but otherwise agrees with theistic evolutionism that mindless evolutionary processes are responsible for complex adaptations. Creationism disagrees with both theistic evolutionism and atheistic evolutionism. Creationism maintains that mindless evolutionary processes are incapable of giving rise to complex adaptations and that God directly intervenes in nature to bring these about. Creationism does not deny that evolution is responsible for some of the features we observe in nature; creationists concede that quantitative changes in a feature found in a species might be due to natural selection (an example of this sort of change will be described below). However, the emergence of genuinely novel, complex adaptive features is, for creationists, another story entirely.

You can see from these three options that belief in evolutionary theory is not the same as atheism. In my opinion, current evolutionary theory is neutral on the question of whether there is a God. Evolutionary theory can be supplemented with a claim, either *pro* or *con*, concerning whether God exists. Evolutionary theory also is consistent with agnosticism, which is the view that we don't know whether there is a God.

Evolutionary theory, however, is not consistent with creationism. Evolutionary theory holds that mindless evolutionary processes (including the process of natural selection) are responsible for the complex adaptations we observe; creationism denies this.

## SOME CREATIONIST ARGUMENTS

Some of the most frequently repeated creationist arguments contain mistakes and confusions. For example, some creationists have argued that evolutionary theory is on shaky ground because hypotheses about the distant past can't be proven with absolute certainty. They are right that evolutionary theory isn't absolutely certain, but then nothing in science is absolutely certain; recall the remarks in Chapter 3 about gambling. What one legitimately strives for in science is powerful evidence showing that one explanation is far more plausible than its competitors. Biologists now regard the hypotheses of evolution as about as certain as any hypothesis about the prehistoric past could be. Naturally, no scientist was on the scene some 3.8 billion years ago when life started to exist on Earth. However, it is nonetheless possible to have strong evidence about matters that one can't directly observe, as I hope my previous discussion of abduction has made clear.

Another example of an error that some creationists make is their discussion of the Second Law of Thermodynamics. They claim this law shows that it is impossible for order to arise from disorder by natural processes. Natural processes can lead an automobile to disintegrate into a junk heap, but creationists think the Second Law of Thermodynamics says that no natural process can cause a pile of junk to assemble itself into a functioning car. Here creationists are arguing that physics is inconsistent with the claim that life evolved from nonlife. What the Second Law actually says is that a *closed system* will (with high probability) move from states of greater order to states of lesser order. But if the system isn't closed, the law says nothing about what will happen. So if the Earth were a closed system, its overall level of disorder would have to increase. But, of course, the Earth is no such thing—energy from the sun is a constant input. If the universe as a whole as a closed system, then thermodynamics does entail that disorder will increase overall. But this overall trend doesn't prohibit "pockets" of order from arising and being maintained. The Second Law of Thermodynamics offers no basis for thinking that life couldn't have evolved from nonlife.

A full treatment of the evolution versus creationism debate would require me to describe the positive explanations that creationists have advanced. If you want to compare evolutionary theory and creationism, you can't just focus on whatever difficulties there may be in evolutionary ideas. You've also got to look carefully at what the alternative is. Doing this produces lots of difficulties for creationism. The reason is that creationists have either been woefully silent on the details of the explanation they want to defend, or they have produced detailed stories that can't withstand scientific scrutiny. For example, young earth creationists, as I mentioned, maintain that the earth is only a few thousand years old. This claim conflicts with a variety of very solid scientific findings, from geology and physics. It isn't just evolutionary theory that you have to reject if you buy into this version of creationism, but a good deal of the rest of science as well.

As I also indicated, there are many different versions of creationism. Creationism is not a single theory, but a cluster of similar theories. In the present chapter, I won't attempt to cover all these versions, but will focus on a few of the options. First let's look at the ABCs of Darwinism.

## DARWIN'S TWO-PART THEORY

Many of the main ideas that Darwin developed in *The Origin of Species* are still regarded by scientists as correct, but others have been refined or expanded. Still others have been junked entirely. Although evolutionary theory has developed a long way since Darwin's time, I'll take his basic ideas as a point of departure. Darwin's theory contains two main elements. First, there is the idea that all present-day life is related. The organisms we see didn't come into existence independently by separate creation. Rather, organisms are related to each other by a family tree. You and I are related. If we go back far enough in time, we'll find a human being who is an ancestor of both of us. The same is true of us and a chimp, though, of course, we must go back even further in time to reach a common ancestor. And so it is for any two present-day organisms. Life evolved from nonlife, and then descent with modification gave rise to the diversity we now observe.

Notice that this first hypothesis of Darwin's says nothing about *why* new characteristics arose in the course of evolution. If all life is related, why aren't all living things identical? The second part of Darwin's theory is the idea of natural selection. This hypothesis tries to explain why new characteristics appear and become common and why some old characteristics disappear. It is very important to keep these two elements in Darwin's theory separate. The idea that all present-day living things are related isn't at all controversial in modern science. The idea that natural selection is the principal cause of evolutionary change is *somewhat* controversial, although it is still by far the majority view among biologists. One reason it is important to keep these ideas separate is that some creationists have tried to score points by confusing them. Creationists sometimes suggest that the whole idea of evolution is something even biologists regard with great doubt and suspicion. However, the idea that all life is related isn't at all controversial. What is controversial, at least to some degree, are ideas about natural selection.

## NATURAL SELECTION

Here's a simple example of how natural selection works. Imagine a population of zebras that all have the same top speed. They can't run faster than 38 mph. Now imagine that a novelty appears in the population. A mutation occurs—a change in the genes found in some zebra—that allows that newfangled zebra to run faster at 42 mph, say. Suppose running faster is advantageous, because a fast zebra is less likely to be caught and eaten by a predator than a slow one is. Running fast enhances the organism's *fitness*—its ability to survive and reproduce. If running speed is passed on from parent to offspring, what will happen? What will occur (probably) is that the fast zebra will have more offspring than the average slow zebra. As a result, the percentage of fast zebras increases. In the next generation, fast zebras enjoy the same advantage, and so the characteristic of being fast will again increase in frequency. After a number of generations, we expect all the zebras to have this new characteristic. Initially, all the zebras ran at 38 mph. After the selection process runs its course, all run at 42 mph. So the process comes in two stages. First, a novel mutation occurs, creating the variation upon which natural selection operates. Then, natural selection goes to work changing the composition of the population:

| *Start* | ⟶ | *Then* | ⟶ *Finish* |
|---|---|---|---|
| 100% run at 38 mph. | | A novel mutant runs at 42 mph; the rest run at 38 mph. | 100% run at 42 mph. |

We may summarize how this process works by saying that natural selection occurs in a population of organisms when there is *inherited variation in fitness.* Let's analyze what this means. The organisms must *vary;* if all the organisms are the same, then there will be no variants to select among. What is more, the variations must be passed down from parents to offspring. This is the requirement of *inheritance.* Last, it must be true that the varying characteristics in a population affect an organism's *fitness*— its chance of surviving and reproducing. If these three conditions are met, the population will evolve. By this, I mean that the frequency of characteristics will change.

The idea of natural selection is really quite simple. What Darwin did was to show how this simple idea has many implications and applications. Merely stating this simple idea wouldn't have convinced anyone that natural selection is the right explanation of life's diversity. The power of the idea comes from the numerous detailed applications.

Notice that the introduction of novel characteristics into a population is a precondition for natural selection to occur. Darwin didn't have a very accurate picture of how novel traits arise. He theorized about this, but didn't come up with anything of lasting importance. Rather, it was later in the nineteenth century that Mendel started to fill in this detail. Genetic mutations, we now understand, are the source of the variation on which natural selection depends. One central idea that Darwin had about mutation, which twentieth-century genetics has vindicated, is that mutations do not occur because they would be useful to the organism; this is what biologists mean when they say that mutations occur "at random."

Creationists sometimes say that the process of evolution by natural selection is like a tornado blowing through a junkyard. The latter process cannot sweep together the scraps of metal laying around on the ground and assemble them into a functioning automobile. From this, creationists conclude that the former process is likewise incapable of creating novel adaptations. This analogy is fundamentally misleading. The tornado is a totally random process, like the spinning of a huge roulette wheel.

However, evolution by natural selection has two parts; mutations appear randomly, but then it is not a random matter which mutations increase in frequency and which decline. Selection is nonrandom. A better analogy than the tornado in the junk-yard is one that Darwin proposed in his 1873 book *The Variation of Animals and Plants Under Domestication:*

> Let an architect be compelled to build an edifice with uncut stones, fallen from a precipice. The shape of each fragment may be called accidental; yet the shape of each has been determined by the force of gravity, the nature of the rock, and the slope of the precipice,—events and circumstances all of which depend on natural laws; but there is no relation between these laws and the purpose for which each fragment is used by the builder. In the same manner the variations of each creature are determined by fixed and immutable laws; but these bear no relation to the living structure which is slowly built up through the power of natural selection, whether this be natural or artificial selection. (Darwin 1876, p. 236)

Notice that the little story I've told about zebra running speed describes a rather modest change that occurs *within* an existing species. Yet Darwin's 1859 book was called *The Origin of Species.* How does change within a species help explain the coming into existence of new species?

## SPECIATION

Darwin's hypothesis was that small changes in a population (like the one I just described) add up. Given enough little changes, the organisms will become very different. Modern evolutionists usually tell a story like the following one. Think of a single population of zebras. Imagine that a small number of zebras are separated from the rest of the population for some reason; maybe they wander off or a river changes course and splits the old population in two. If the resulting populations live in different environments, selection will lead them to become increasingly different. Characteristics that are advantageous in one population will not be advantageous in the other. After a long time, the populations will have diverged. They will have become so different from each other that individuals from the one can't breed with individuals from the other. Because of this, they will be two species, not two populations belonging to the same species.

Pretty much everybody in Darwin's day, including those who thought that God created each species separately, would have agreed that the little story about zebras evolving a greater speed could be true. The real resistance to Darwin's theory focused on his thesis that the mechanism responsible for small-scale changes *within* species also gives rise to large-scale changes, namely, to the origin of *new* species. This was a daring hypothesis, but it now is the mainstream view in evolutionary theory. Even so, biologists continue to debate the importance that natural selection has had in the evolutionary process. Modern evolutoinary theory describes other possible causes of evolutionary change. Which traits were due to natural selection and which were due to other evolutionary processes? There are a number of still unanswered questions in evolutionary biology about natural selection. Even biologists who hold that natural selection is the major cause of evolution are sometimes puzzled about how it applies in particular cases. For example, it is still rather unclear why sexual reproduction evolved. Some creatures reproduce sexually, others asexually. Why is this? Although there are open questions pertaining to natural selection, I want to emphasize that it isn't at all controversial that human beings share common ancestors with chimps. Don't confuse the idea of common ancestry with the idea of natural selection; these are separate elements in Darwin's theory.

## THE TREE OF LIFE

I turn now to this uncontroversial idea. Why do biologists think it is so clear that living things are related to each other—that there is a family tree of life on earth just like there is a family tree of your family? Two kinds of evidence have seemed persuasive. I won't give the details here; rather, I want to describe the *kinds* of arguments biologists deploy. As a philosopher, I'm more interested that you grasp the logic of the arguments; for the biological details, you should consult a biology book.

To illustrate how one line of argument works, consider this simple problem. Suppose I assign a philosophy class the job of writing an essay on the meaning of life. As I read through the papers, I notice that two students have handed in papers that are word-for-word identical. How should I explain this striking similarity? One possibility, of course, is that the students worked independently and by coincidence arrived at exactly the same result. The independent origin of the two papers isn't impossible. But I would regard this hypothesis as extremely implausible. Far more convincing is the idea that one student copied from the other or that each of them copied from a common source—a paper downloaded from the Internet, perhaps. This hypothesis is a more plausible explanation of the observed similarity of the two papers.

## THE PRINCIPLE OF THE COMMON CAUSE

The plagiarism example illustrates an idea that the philosopher Hans Reichenbach (in *The Direction of Time,* University of California Press, 1956) called the *Principle of the Common Cause.* Let's analyze the example more carefully to understand the rationale of the principle.

Why, in the case just described, is it more plausible that the students copied from a common source than that they wrote their papers independently? Consider how probable the matching of the two papers is, according to each of the two hypotheses. If the two students copied from a common source, then it is rather probable that the papers should closely resemble each other. If, however, the students worked independently, then it is enormously improbable that the two papers should be so similar. Here we have an application of the Surprise Principle described in Chapter 3: If one hypothesis says that the observations are very probable whereas the other hypothesis says that the observations are very improbable, then the observations strongly favor the first hypothesis over the second. The Principle of the Common Cause makes sense because it is a consequence of the Surprise Principle.

The example just described involves hypotheses that describe mental activity—when students plagiarize they use their minds, and the same is true when they write papers independently. However, it is important to see that the Principle of the Common Cause also makes excellent sense when the hypotheses considered do not describe mental processes. Here's an example: I have a barometer at my house. I notice that when it says "low," there usually is a storm the next day; and when it says "high," there usually is no storm the next day. The barometer reading on one day and the weather on the next are *correlated*. It may be that this correlation is just a coincidence; perhaps the two events are entirely independent. However, a far more plausible hypothesis is that the reading on one day and the weather on the next trace back to a common cause—namely, the weather at the time the reading is taken:

The common cause hypothesis is more plausible because it leads you to expect the correlation of the two observed effects. The separate cause hypothesis is less plausible because it says that the observed correlation is a very improbable coincidence. Notice that the hypotheses in this example do not describe the mental activities of agents.

## ARBITRARY SIMILARITIES AMONG ORGANISMS

I'll now apply this principle to the evolutionary idea of common ancestry. One reason biologists think all life is related is that all organisms (with some minor exceptions) use the same genetic code. To understand what this means, think of the genes in your body as a set of instructions for constructing more complex biological items—amino acids and then proteins. The total sequence of genes in your body and the sequence in a frog's are different. The striking fact, however, is that the gene that codes for a given amino acid in a frog codes for that very same amino acid in people. As far as we now know, there is no reason why the genes that code for a given amino acid had to code for that acid rather than some other. The code is arbitrary; there is no functional reason why it has to be the way it is. (Don't be misled by my talk of codes here. This word may suggest intelligent design, but this isn't what biologists mean. Genes *cause* amino acids to form; for present purposes, this is a perfectly satisfactory way to understand what it means for genes to "code for" this or that amino acid.)

How are we to explain the detailed similarity among the genetic codes that different species use? If the species arose independently of each other, we would expect them to use different genetic codes. But if those species all trace back to a common ancestor, it is to be expected that they will share the same genetic code. The Principle of the Common Cause underlies the belief that evolutionary biologists have that all living things on earth have common ancestors.

## USEFUL SIMILARITIES AMONG ORGANISMS

The reason a shared genetic code is evidence of common ancestry is that the code is arbitrary. There are lots of possible codes that would work. If there were only a single functional code, the fact that different species use this one code would not be evidence of common ancestry. Consider, for example the fact that sharks and dolphins both have a streamlined body shape. Both are shaped like torpedoes. Is this strong evidence that they have a common ancestor? I would say not. There is an obvious functional reason why large predators that spend their lives swimming through water should be shaped like this. If there is life in other galaxies that includes large aquatic predators, we would probably expect it to have this sort of shape. Even if life on earth and life on other galaxies are not descended from common ancestors, there are *some* similarities we still would expect to find. I conclude that the streamlined shape of dolphins and sharks isn't strong evidence that they evolved from a common ancestor. The Surprise Principle explains why some similarities, but not others, are evidence for the hypothesis that there is a tree of life uniting all organisms on earth.

The genetic code is one just one example of a similarity that can't be explained by its usefulness to the organism. There are lots of others. Consider the fact that human beings have tail bones, that we have appendices, and that human fetuses have gill slits. None of these features is useful. In fact, the appendix is worse than useless, since burst appendices kill many people. Biologists interpret these features as evidence that we share common ancestors with nonhuman organism. This and lots of other evidence points to the conclusion that we share common ancestors with monkeys, with other mammals, with fish, and with all other living things. In drawing this conclusion, biologists are using the Surprise Principle and the Principle of the Common Cause.

## IRREDUCIBLE COMPLEXITY

Although creationists have usually rejected the Darwinian hypothesis of common ancestry, not all have done so. What creationists universally reject is the thesis that natural selection is the correct explanation of the complex adaptations we observe in nature. Modern-day creationists are usually willing to grant that selection can explain small modifications in existing species, as in the earlier example about zebra running speed. But how can the gradual accumulation of modifications explain a feature like the vertebrate eye? This is the key objection that Michael Behe develops in

## Humans from Nonhumans, Life from Nonlife

When people hear about the idea of evolution, there are two parts of the theory that sometimes strike them as puzzling. First, there is the idea that human beings are descended from apelike ancestors. Second, there is the idea that life evolved from nonliving materials.

Scientists believe the first of these statements because there are so many striking similarities between apes and human beings. This isn't to deny that there are differences. However, the similarities (e.g., the fact that both have tail bones) would be expected if humans and apes have a common ancestor, but would be quite surprising if they came into existence independently..

There is a big difference between having evidence humans are descended from apelike ancestors and *having an explanation of precisely why this happened*. The evidence for a common ancestor is pretty overwhelming, but the details of why evolution proceeded in just the way it did are less certain. Students of human evolution continue to investigate why our species evolved as it did. In contrast, the claim that we did evolve isn't a matter of scientific debate.

What about the second idea—that life arose from nonlife? Why not maintain that God created the first living thing and then let evolution by natural selection produce the diversity we now observe? Notice that this is a very different idea from what creationists maintain. They hold that each species (or "basic kind" of organism) is the result of separate creation by God. They deny that present-day species are united by common descent from earlier life forms.

One main sort of evidence for thinking that life evolved from nonlife on Earth about 4 billion years ago comes from laboratory experiments. Scientists have created laboratory conditions that resemble the ones they believe were present shortly after the Earth came into existence about 4.5 billion years ago. They find that the nonliving ingredients present then can enter into chemical reactions, the products of which are simple organic materials. For example, it is possible to run electricity (lightning) through a "soup" of inorganic molecules and produce amino acids. Why is this significant? Amino acids are an essential stage in the process whereby genes construct an organism. Similar experiments have generated a variety of promising results. This subject in biology—*prebiotic evolution*—is very much open and incomplete. No one has yet been able to get inorganic materials to produce DNA, but the promising successes to date suggest that further work will further illuminate how life arose from nonlife.

Laboratory experiments don't aim to create a multicellular organism from inorganic materials. No one wants to make a chicken out of carbon, ammonia, and water. Evolution by natural selection proceeds by the accumulation of very small changes. So the transition from nonlife to life must involve the creation of a rather simple self-replicating molecule. Chickens came much later.

A self-replicating molecule is a molecule that makes copies of itself. A molecule of this sort is able to reproduce. With accurate replication, the offspring of a molecule will resemble its parent. Once a simple self-replicating molecule is in place, evolution by natural selection can begin. It may sound strange to describe a simple self-replicating molecule as being "alive." Such a molecule will do few of the things that a chicken does. But from the biological point of view, reproduction and heredity (that is, similarity between parents and offspring) are fundamental properties.

his 1966 book *Darwin's Black Box* when he introduces the concept of *irreducible complexity*. Behe defines an irreducibly complex system as one in which the whole system has a function, the system is made of many parts, and the system would not be able to perform its function if any of the parts were removed. Behe's idea is that the Darwinian process of natural selection involves adding one small part to another, with each modification improving the fitness of the organism. But what good is 1% of an eye? Creationists, Behe included, think that the answer is obvious—no good at all—and that this shows that evolutionary theory can't explain complex adaptations.

Biologists sometimes respond to this creationist claim by arguing that gradual modification *can* explain structures like the eye. A piece of light sensitive skin allows the organism to tell the difference between light and dark, and this is advantageous. Then, if this skin is shaped into a cup, the organism can not only tell whether it is light or dark, but can also tell from what direction the light is coming, and this provides a further advantage. Maybe it is not so obvious that the eye can't evolve one small step at the time. However, there is another, more fundamental, problem with Behe's argument. What we call "the parts" of a system may or may not correspond to the historical sequence of accumulating details. Consider the horse and its four legs. A horse with zero, one, or two legs cannot walk or run; suppose the same is true for a horse with three. In contrast, a horse with four legs can walk and run, and it thereby gains a fitness advantage. So far so good—the four-legged arrangement satisfies the definition of irreducible complexity. The mistake comes from thinking that horses (or their ancestors) had to evolve their four legs one leg at a time. In fact it's a mistake to think that a separate set of genes controls the development of each leg; rather, there is a single set that controls the development of appendages. A division of a system into parts that entails that the system is irreducibly complex may or may not correspond to the historical sequence of events through which the lineage passed. This point is obvious with respect to the horse's four legs, but needs to be borne in mind when other, less familiar, organic features are considered. What we call the "parts" of the eye may not correspond to the sequence of events that occurred in the eye's evolution.

## IS CREATIONISM TESTABLE?

So far I have outlined what Darwin's theory of evolution amounts to, the kind of evidence that biologists take seriously for the claim of common ancestry, and some objections that creationists make to this theory. The question I now want to consider concerns the theory that creationists themselves present. What is it? What predictions does it make? What evidence is there for the theory they present?

Here we need to consider some of the different versions that creationism might take. To get started, let's consider:

$H_1$: A superintelligent designer fashioned all the complex adaptations we observe organisms to have so that organisms would be perfectly adapted to their environment.

This hypothesis is disconfirmed by what we observe. Organisms often have highly imperfect adaptations. The eye that human beings use has a blindspot, though the eye of the octopus does not. And many spiders have eyes with built-in sunglasses, though human beings do not. Our eye is imperfect and so are lots of features that we and other organisms possess. Can we repair this defect in $H_1$? One way to do so is to make the hypothesis of intelligent design more modest in what it says:

> $H_2$: An intelligent designer fashioned all the complex adaptations we observe organisms to have.

The problem with $H_2$ is not that it makes false predictions, but that it makes none at all. $H_2$ is consistent with what we observe, no matter what our observations turn out to be. Features that are useful are consistent, as well as features that are neutral and features that are harmful. One of the features that scientists expect scientific theories to have is that they be testable, by which they mean that theories should make predictions that can be checked against observations. $H_2$, it appears, is not testable. This defect can also be remedied. Consider, for example, a third version of creationism:

> $H_3$: Organisms did not evolve. Rather, God created each species separately and endowed them with the very characteristics they would have had if they had evolved by natural selection.

$H_3$ is a wild card; it makes the same predictions that evolutionary theory makes. If so, what reason can there be to choose between these two theories?

## PREDICTIVE EQUIVALENCE

Evolutionary theory and $H_3$ are *predictively equivalent*. If evolutionary theory predicts that life will have a particular feature, so does $H_3$. Although imperfect adaptations disconfirm $H_1$, they are perfectly consistent with $H_3$. Does this mean that evolutionary theory is not well supported? I would say not. Consider the following pair of hypotheses:

> $J_1$: You are now looking at a printed page.
> $J_2$: You are now looking at a salami.

You have excellent evidence that $J_1$ is true and that $J_2$ is false. $J_1$ predicts that you are having particular sensory experiences; if $J_1$ is true, you should be having certain visual, tactile, and gustatory sensations (please take a bite of this page). $J_2$ makes different predictions about these matters. The sensory experiences you now are having strongly favor $J_1$ over $J_2$. Now, however, let's introduce a wild card. What evidence do you have that $J_1$ *as opposed to* $J_3$ is true:

> $J_3$: There is no printed page in front of you, but someone is now systematically misleading you into thinking that there is a printed page in front of you.

$J_1$ and $J_3$ are predictively equivalent. The experiences you now are having tell you that $J_1$ is more plausible than $J_2$, but they don't strongly favor $J_1$ over $J_3$. In the section of this book that focuses on Descartes's *Meditations* (Chapter 13), the problem of choosing between $J_1$ and $J_3$ will be examined in detail. For now, what I want you to see is this: When you ask whether some hypothesis is strongly supported by the evidence, you must ask yourself what the alternatives are against which the hypothesis is to be compared. If you compare $J_1$ with $J_2$, you'll conclude that $J_1$ is extremely well supported. However, the problem takes on a different character if you compare $J_1$ with $J_3$. The point applies to the competition between evolutionary theory and creationism. When you compare evolutionary theory with creatoinism, everything depends on which version of creationism you consider. Some versions make false predictions, some make no predictions, and some "piggy-back" on evolutionary theory, relying on that theory's ability to make predictions and then using those predictions.

## PREDICTION VERSUS ACCOMMODATION

Here a fourth version of creationism raises interesting questions. Suppose we examine the human eye in detail and observe that has a set of features that we'll call F. We then can construct the following version of creationism:

$H_4$: An intelligent designer made the human eye and gave it the set of features F.

Does $H_4$ make predictions? Well, it entails what we should observe. In fact, no theory can do a better job than $H_4$ does of fitting what we observe, since $H_4$ hits the nail precisely on the head. The problem is that $H_4$ merely accomodates the observations; it does not provide novel predictions. It is easy—too easy—to construct hypotheses such as $H_4$. Whenever you observe that O is true, you just construct the hypothesis that "an intelligent designer wanted O to be true and had the means to bring this about." If such hypotheses were satisfactory, there would be no need to do real science; we could shut down all of the costly research now underway and just invoke this tidy formula.

This suggests that we should supplement the two rules for abduction presented in Chapter 3. In addition to the Surprise Principle and the Only Game in Town Fallacy, we should require that a good theory make predictions that were not used in the construction of that theory. This is the requirement that theories shouldn't merely accommodate what we observe after the fact; in addition, they should make some predictions that are novel.

## DOES EVOLUTIONARY THEORY MAKE NOVEL PREDICTIONS?

What is sauce for the goose is sauce for the gander. If we demand that creationism make novel predictions, we should demand that evolutionary theory do the same. By prediction, I do not restrict myself to saying what will happen in the future. A prediction can involve observations that have not yet been made that reflect events that took place in the past. For example, the part of evolutionary theory that says that organisms possess common ancestors predicts that we should find intermediate fossil forms. Biology says that whales and cows have a common ancestor, so there should be fossils that have characteristics that are "in between." And if birds and dinosaurs have a common ancestor, there should be fossils that are intermediate here as well. Darwin worried about "the incompleteness of the fossil record," but there have been numerous fossil finds that fulfill the predictions of the hypothesis of common ancestry.

What about the other part of Darwin's theory, the hypothesis of natural selection? What does it predict? Here it is important to realize that there are many detailed theories in evolutionary theory that predict which traits will be favored by natural selection in which circumstances. For example, in human beings, slightly more boys than girls are born. In other species, there is extreme male bias, or a female bias, in the sex ratio at birth. Evolutionary theory provides theories that predict when a species should evolve one sex ratio and when it should evolve another. Another example concerns the nature of infectious disease. Suppose you are infected with a disease that is spread through the air; if you get sick, you will take to your bed and you will spread the disease less frequently. Compare this to a disease like diarrhea that is spread through feces. Even if you take to your bed, your feces will be taken from your room and sent into the environment, just as if you were well. Now think about these two patterns from the point of view of the organism that causes the disease. In the case of an airborne disease, selection favors infections that are mild over ones that are severe; in the case of a waterborne disease, selection favors just the opposite pattern. The *vector* of the disease—the details concerning how the disease is spread from infected to uninfected individuals—allows biologists to predict what traits the disease should evolve. These evolutionary ideas have recently been important in biological thinking about AIDS-HIV; see Paul Ewald's *The Evolution of Infectious Disease*, Oxford University Press, 1993, for discussion.

When I say that evolutionary theory makes predictions, I do not mean that it now is in a position to predict the whole detailed future of the planet's biosphere, nor that every detail of the past can be predicted either. There are many open questions in evolutionary, as in any science. However, the theory has made impressive strides since 1859. The same is not true of creationism. Paley compared the random hypothesis with the hypothesis of intelligent design and argued that the latter was better supported; Behe compares evolutionary theory to the hypothesis of intelligent design and draws the same conclusion. In the two hundred years between these two publications, no theory worthy of the name has been developed.

## CONCLUDING REMARKS

Creationism comes in many forms. Some of them make very definite predictions about what we observe. The version that says that God made organisms so that they are perfectly adapted to their environments makes predictions that do not accord with what we observe. Young earth creationism, which says that the earth is ten thousand years old, also makes predictions that conflict with what scientists observe. A third version of creationism says that God made organisms to look exactly as they would if they had evolved by the mindless process of natural selection; this makes the same predictions that evolutionary theory makes, and so our observations do not allow us to discriminate between evolutionary theory and this "mimicking" or "piggy-backing" version of creationism. Finally, the bare, minimalistic version of creationism that says that God had some (unspecified) impact on the traits of living things is, I suggest, untestable. We have not found a version of creationism that makes definite predictions about what we observe *and* that is better supported by the observations than evolutionary theory is. What is wanted here is not just a version of creationism that can accommodate the observations after we have made them, but one that tells us what we will observe before we make those observations. Is there a version of creationism that can do this?

## Review Questions

1. What are the two main elements of Darwin's theory?
2. Describe what the Principle of the Common Cause says. How is this principle related to the Surprise Principle? How is it used by biologists to decide whether different species have a common ancestor?
3. The geneticist François Jacob said (in "Evolution and Tinkering," *Science*, Vol. 196, 1977, pp. 1161–1166) that "natural selection does not work as an engineer works. It works like a tinkerer—a tinkerer who does not know exactly what he is going to produce but uses whatever he finds around him." What does Jacob mean here? How is this point relevant to evaluating whether the hypothesis of evolution or the hypothesis of intelligent design is a more plausible explanation of the characteristics of living things?
4. What does it mean to say that two theories are predictively equivalent? Can the design hypothesis be formulated so that the existence of imperfect adaptations isn't evidence against it?

## Problems for Further Thought

1. Louis Pasteur (1822–1895) developed scientific evidence against the hypothesis of "spontaneous generation." For example, he argued that maggots developing on rotten meat aren't the result of life springing spontaneously from nonliving materials; the maggots were hatched from eggs laid there by their parents. Does Pasteur's discovery mean life couldn't have evolved from nonliving materials?
2. Suppose you are a crew member on the starship *Enterprise*, bound for a new planet. You know there is intelligent life there; the question you want to answer

is whether these life forms have ever had any contact with Earth. Which sorts of observations would be relevant and which irrelevant to this question? Defend your interpretation. How does the Principle of the Common Cause apply to this problem?

**3.** Does Paley interpret the watch in a way that resembles what Behe means by irreducible complexity?

# CHAPTER 7

## *Can Science Explain Everything?*

In the previous chapter, we failed to identify a version of the design hypothesis that not only makes predictions, but also makes *novel* predictions, about the features we should observe in living things. It is a further question whether there are versions of creationism that do better than the versions I described. If there are not, then creationism should be discarded as an explanation of the characteristics that organisms possess. But this result would not show that the design hypothesis has no role to play at all. Perhaps there are other features of the universe, distinct from the ones discussed in biology, that we should explain by postulating the existence of an intelligent designer.

Here is another way to pose this problem: A *naturalistic* explanation seeks to explain features of the world by describing the processes in nature that produced them. A *super* naturalistic explanation, on the other hand, attempts to explain features of the world by describing the supernatural processes (the processes that occur outside of nature) that produced them. Is there reason to think that every feature of the world has a naturalistic explanation? If so, the hypothesis of a supernatural God isn't needed to explain anything.

The question I want to explore in this chapter is this: Should we expect that science will sooner or later explain everything that's true about the world we inhabit? That is, will science sooner or later be able to explain everything and do this without needing to postulate the existence of a supernatural God?

### SCIENTIFIC IGNORANCE

It is easy to find facts about the world that science can't explain now. Every scientific discipline has its open questions. These are the things that keep present-day scientists busy. Scientists don't spend their time repeating to each other things everybody already knows; rather, they devote their energies to trying to puzzle out answers to heretofore unanswered questions.

Because there are plenty of facts about the world that science can't now explain, it is easy to construct a particular kind of abductive argument for the existence of God.

### "But How Do You Explain God?"

Sometimes people object to the suggestion that the existence of God is the explanation of a fact by asking, "But how do you explain the existence of God?" The implications behind this question is that it isn't plausible to say that God explains something unless you are able to explain why God exists.

This criticism of abductive arguments for the existence of God isn't a good one. Mendel was right to think that the existence of genes explains something. However, Mendel had no idea how to explain the fact that genes exist. Here are two more examples that exhibit the same pattern. For hundreds of years before Newton's time, mariners had good evidence that the tides are correlated with the phases of the Moon, even though they had no very plausible explanation for why this should be so. As noted in the previous chapter, evolutionists have excellent evidence that human beings are descended from apelike ancestors, even though the explanation of this evolutionary event is still somewhat unclear. My conclusion is that if abductive arguments for the existence of God are defective, this isn't because no one knows how to explain why God exists.

I mentioned in the previous chapter that evolutionary theory is currently unable to explain why some species reproduce sexually while others don't. Consider the following theological explanation for this puzzling fact: There is a God, and God decided to make organisms reproduce in precisely the way they do. Whereas evolutionists can't (now) explain patterns of reproduction, a theologian can do this just by saying "it was God's will." I doubt that any scientist would argue that patterns of reproduction will *never* be explained scientifically. To be sure, evolutionists cannot *now* explain certain facts about sex. But science isn't over yet; it is reasonable to suspect that this example of scientific ignorance is only temporary.

## THE ONLY GAME IN TOWN FALLACY

What should we say *now?* Apparently, we now have two choices: We can accept the theological explanation sketched above, or we can admit that we have no explanation at all for why some species, but not others, reproduce sexually. I think it is clear that we aren't obliged to accept the theological explanation. To think we are required to accept the theological explanation just because it is the only one on the table is to commit the Only Game in Town Fallacy.

Recall the anecdote from Chapter 3. If you and I are sitting in a cabin and hear noises in the attic, it is easy to formulate an explanation of those noises. I suggest the noises are due to gremlins bowling. This hypothesis has the property that if it were true, it would explain why we heard the noises. But this fact about the gremlin hypothesis doesn't mean that the hypothesis is plausible.

Instead of accepting a theological explanation of why organisms reproduce as they do, we should consider the option of simply admitting that we at present don't understand why this is so. If my prediction about the future of evolutionary theory is correct, we eventually will have a satisfactory scientific explanation. We just have to be patient.

I now want to consider a very different kind of scientific ignorance. Suppose there are facts about the world that science *in principle* can't explain. It isn't a temporary gap, but a permanent one, that I now want to consider. If there are such facts, then the choice won't be between a theological explanation and a naturalistic explanation that science will eventually produce; the choice will be between a theological explanation and no explanation at all—not now nor in the future.

## THE TWO QUESTIONS

There are two questions I want to consider: (1) Are there any facts about the world that science is inherently incapable of explaining? (2) If there are, can we plausibly argue that the best explanation of why those facts are true is that God exists? To answer the first of these questions, I'll sketch a picture of how scientific explanation works. I then will argue that this view of scientific explanation implies that there are certain facts about the world that science can't ever explain. It isn't just that scientists haven't worked out the explanation *yet;* the point is that the nature of scientific explanation precludes their ever doing so.

## WHAT IS A SCIENTIFIC EXPLANATION?

There are two kinds of things science aims to explain. It aims to explain particular *events*, and it aims to explain *generalizations*. An example of the first type of problem would be the astronomer's question, "Why did the solar system come into existence?" An example of the second type would be the chemist's question, "Why does it take two atoms of hydrogen and one of oxygen for hydrogen and oxygen to combine to form a molecule of water?"

Don't confuse these two explanatory projects. Generalizations are true or false. Events aren't true or false; they happen or fail to happen. An event happens at a certain place and time. True generalizations, however, describe what is true of *all* places and times. I want to focus here on what scientists do when they explain *events*.

My thesis is that science explains an event by describing its causes. I'll assume further (although this isn't strictly necessary for what I want to conclude) that a cause has to precede its effects. So the causal explanation of an event $E_1$ that happens now is provided by citing one or more events in the past and showing how those events produced $E_1$. Suppose we show that $E_1$ was caused by $E_2$. We then might be interested in explaining why $E_2$ occurred. This might lead us to describe a still earlier event, $E_3$, and so on. This project leads us to describe causal chains that trace back into the past. You'll recall that Aquinas (Chapter 4) believed causal chains extending back into the past can have only a finite number of links. I make no assumption about this.

So far I've described two relationships that can obtain between events: (1) some events precede others in time, and (2) some events cause others. There is a third relationship. Some events are *parts* of other events. Consider the relationship between the storming of the Bastille and the French Revolution. The storming of the Bastille marked the beginning of the French Revolution. Both of these are events; the first is *part* of the second.

I want to focus on what science does when it tries to explain a spatiotemporal event. By "spatiotemporal," I simply mean that the event in question happened at some place and at some time. Of course, lots of events are "spread out." They don't occur in an instant, but take some length of time to occur. And they take place in a volume of space, not at a single spatial point. For example, the French Revolution lasted about 10 years, and it took place in France.

## A THESIS ABOUT EXPLANATION

My thesis is this: For science to be able to say why a spatiotemporal event $E$ occurred, there must be events in space and time that aren't included in $E$. I assume that no event explains itself. So if science is to explain $E$, there must be some event outside of $E$ (but still inside of space and time) that can be cited as the explanation.

It follows from this thesis that answerable questions about why this or that spatiotemporal event occurred must focus on events that are *part* of what happens in the history of the spatiotemporal universe. Such questions can't be answered if they ask why the *whole history* of the spatiotemporal universe was as it was. Consider an exhaustive description of the past, present, and future of what happens in space and time:

$$\cdots \longrightarrow E_3 \longrightarrow E_2 \longrightarrow E_1 \longrightarrow \cdots$$

$$\underline{\qquad\qquad\qquad\qquad\qquad\qquad\qquad\qquad\qquad\qquad}$$

Past                           Present      Future

$E_1$ is explicable, because there is something besides $E_1$ in the world that can be cited to do the explaining. If $E_1$ is part of some bigger event (the way the storming of the Bastille is part of the French Revolution), then that more inclusive event will be explicable only if there is something outside of it that we can cite by way of explanation. Such answerable questions about spatiotemporal events I'll call *local why-questions*. They focus on part of what has happened in the world's history. In contrast to them are *global why-questions*—questions that ask for an explanation of the totality of what has happened in the whole universe's history. I claim science can't answer global why-questions.

## WHY IS THERE SOMETHING RATHER THAN NOTHING?

Here's an example of a global why-question: *Why is there something rather than nothing?* This question doesn't ask why there is something *now*. That, of course, is a local question, which can be answered by saying that the universe was nonempty in the past, and then perhaps citing a conservation law (as Aquinas did—see Chapter 4) that says that if the world is nonempty at one time, it will be nonempty forever after. What I have in mind here is the question of why the universe *ever* contained anything. That is, why wasn't the universe entirely devoid of material objects throughout its history?

The spatiotemporal universe is the totality of everything that was, is, or will be, anywhere. There is nothing impossible about a universe that contains no material objects. Obviously the actual world isn't this way. The actual world (the one we inhabit) corresponds to one total history. An empty universe corresponds to a different total history. Both of these totalities are possible, but only one is actual. The question of why there is something rather than nothing asks why the first of these possible worlds, rather than the second, is actual. My claim is that science can't answer this question.

## CAN PHYSICS EXPLAIN THE ORIGIN OF THE UNIVERSE?

Don't be misled by the fact that physicists talk about explaining the "origin of the universe." This makes it sound like they are explaining why the universe is nonempty. My view is that they are doing no such thing. Rather they are addressing a different question. The Big Bang Theory doesn't show why the universe, in my sense of the word, came into existence. The universe, according to the way I am using the term, includes *everything* that there ever was, is, or will be. If the Big Bang produced what came after it, then the universe includes two stages: First, there was a Big Bang, and then there what happened next. The Big Bang doesn't explain why the whole universe exists; the Big Bang is *part* of the universe. The scientific question addressed by physicists is local, not global.

So the question "Why this totality, rather than that one?" isn't scientifically answerable, because it is global. Can a theological answer be provided? Let's imagine that God isn't a material object; he (or she or it) is outside the spatiotemporal totality I'm calling "the material universe." Can we explain why the material universe is nonempty by saying that God decided to make one totality actual rather than another?

## LEIBNIZ: GOD CHOOSES WHICH POSSIBLE WORLD TO ACTUALIZE

The seventeenth-century philosopher/scientist Gottfried Leibniz (1646–1716) thought this form of explanation is plausible. He said that God considered the set of all possible worlds and decided to make one of them actual. He did this by finding which world is best. This is why we live in the best of all possible worlds. If you think the world we inhabit is morally imperfect, you may doubt Leibniz's story. In Chapter 11, I'll consider this issue when I take up the problem of evil. However, the point of importance here is that Leibniz had another kind of perfection in mind, in addition to moral perfection. Leibniz thought this is the best of all possible worlds in the sense that this world has the maximum diversity of phenomena and the maximum simplicity of laws. Scientific laws are simple, but the kinds of events that happen in our world are enormously rich. This joint property of our world is what makes it perfect in this nonmoral sense.

I won't discuss the details of Leibniz's theory. My point is that he proposed a theological explanation for why there is something rather than nothing in the world of space and time. This fact about the world, being global, can't be scientifically explained. The question I want to pose is this: If a fact can be explained by the hypothesis that there is a God, but can't be explained scientifically, is this a good enough reason to conclude there is a God?

## CLARKE: GOD EXPLAINS WHY THE ACTUAL WORLD CONSISTS OF ONE TOTAL HISTORY RATHER THAN ANOTHER

Another anticipation of the argument for the existence of God we are considering is due to the British philosopher Samuel Clarke (1675–1729). Clarke thought he saw a way to improve an argument that Aquinas proposed. As noted in Chapter 4, Aquinas's second argument for the existence of God depends on the universe's being finitely old. Clarke's argument, presented in his 1705 book *A Demonstration of the Being and Attributes of God,* does not depend on that assumption. He asks us to consider the entire totality of events that occur in the world of space and time. Why did this history occur rather than some other? Clarke says that there are two possibilities: The entire history occurred for no reason at all, or it was brought into existence by a being who exists outside of space and time, namely, God. Clarke rejected the first suggestion as patently absurd; there *must* be a reason why the world is comprised of one total history rather than another. That reason is God. Clarke's argument is an instance of the cosmological argument.

If science is incapable of explaining why the world of space and time includes one total history rather than another, should we accept the claim that God exists because this hypothesis, if true, would explain this global fact? In similar fashion, should we accept the claim that God exists because it is able to explain why there is something rather than nothing (a fact that science is unable to explain)?

## THE ONLY GAME IN TOWN FALLACY, AGAIN

I think the answer to these questions is *no*. Once again, the Only Game in Town Fallacy needs to be considered. There is a second option besides accepting the only explanation available. This is to admit that there are things about the universe we don't understand *and never will.* Why there is something rather than nothing may be inherently inexplicable; the same may be true of the question of why the world contains one total set of events rather than another. I grant that *if* (1) there were an all-powerful God who exists outside of space and time and *if* (2) a God outside of the material world could nonetheless create a material world and *if* (3) God wanted to make the world nonempty, then this would explain why there is something rather than nothing in the spatiotemporal universe. These suppositions would explain the fact in question, but that doesn't show that this explanatory story is at all plausible.

## CAUSALITY

To see what is problematic about this suggested explanation, consider the causal relationship it says exists between God and the totality of the material universe. God is outside of space and time, but nonetheless manages to bring the whole material world into existence. This causal relationship is extremely hard to understand.

Think of the causal relationships we discuss in science and in everyday life. For example, we say that throwing the rock at the window caused the window to break. Here a causal relationship is said to obtain between two events, each of which occurred at a particular place and at a particular time. This is characteristic of well-understood claims about causality; in this case, *causation is a relationship that obtains between events that occur within space and time.* This is why it is so puzzling to say that a God outside of space and time causes the world of space and time to come into being.

I think it is misleading to use the statement "God did it" as a substitute for the statement "I really can't explain why this or that fact is true." The first statement advances an explanation, while the second admits to not having one. If the existence of God is to explain something, it must have more going for it than the fact that the observation under consideration is otherwise inexplicable.

I said before that evolutionary theory cannot now explain why some species reproduce sexually while others don't. This doesn't mean evolutionists can't make vague pronouncements such as "the pattern is due to natural selection." This vague remark is available to anyone who wants to make it. No scientist, however, would regard this single sentence as a satisfying explanation. The question—the main question—would be *how* natural selection managed to produce the results it did. What made sexual reproduction advantageous in some species and asexual reproduction advantageous in others? It is this more detailed question that, to date, has not been answered satisfactorily. There is an analogy here with the theological case. The theologian can say "God did it." The evolutionist can say "natural selection did it." A scientist would regard the latter explanation as unsatisfying, because it is too short on details. Why should the theological explanation be taken any more seriously? Part of what is missing in the theological story is any indication of *how* or *why* God did what he did. This may help explain why the theological explanation of patterns of reproduction should not be embraced. A theological explanation so short on details leaves too many questions unanswered to be convincing. In this circumstance, perhaps it is more plausible to admit we don't understand than to pretend that "God did it" gives us much by way of understanding.

A similar diagnosis can be offered of why the theological explanation of why there is something rather than nothing is so unsatisfying. To say "God did it" is to leave too much unexplained. How is it possible for something outside of space and time to cause the entire spatiotemporal universe to come into being? Why should God have preferred to actualize this possible world rather than any of the others? To the degree that we don't understand these matters, we should conclude that the theological explanation is really not much of an explanation at all.

My conclusion is that science may not be able to explain everything. There are facts now known to be true that science has not been able to account for. And even if science progresses, as I expect it to do, there will remain facts that are intrinsically resistant to scientific treatment. Not only has science not explained them yet, but also it never will, because it can't. Of course, we should be open to the possibility that explanations from outside of science may have some plausibility. My point here is that bringing in the existence of God is often to trade one mystery for another, with no net gain in our understanding.

## THE PRINCIPLE OF SUFFICIENT REASON

Clarke's argument makes use of an idea that has long been influential in philosophy. It is called *The Principle of Sufficient Reason*. This principle asserts that everything that happens in nature has an explanation; nothing happens for no reason at all. What can be said in favor of this principle? Scientists seem to assume it, or something like it, when they address a new problem. Consider some body of facts that science is currently not able to explain. For example, what is it about the organization of the human brain that allows us to have *conscious experience*? Neuroscientists assume that there is an answer to this question. This is why they set themselves the task of finding a scientific explanation of consciousness. But what assurance do they have that such an explanation exists?

Maybe it would make sense for scientists to assume that consciousness has an explanation even if they have no evidence at all that such an explanation exists. After all, if they look for explanation, they may find one (if such an explanation exists). But if they don't even look for an explanation, they will certainly fail to find it, even if there is one to be had. This is a strategic argument for its being sensible to look for an explanation of consciousness. It is not an argument that offers evidence that such an explanation exists. The fact that scientists search for explanations without a guarantee that they will succeed is not evidence that the Principle of Sufficient Reason is true.

## Review Questions

1. What is the difference between a global why-question and a local why-question?
2. Can science answer global why-questions? Why or why not?
3. Is it possible to have evidence that something exists without having an explanation for why the thing exists?
4. Consider the following argument: "If science can't explain some fact, but a theological story, if true, would explain that fact, then the fact is strong abductive evidence that the theological story is true." How is the Only Game in Town Fallacy relevant to assessing this argument?
5. What does it mean to say that causation is a relationship that obtains between events in space and time? If this were a correct claim about causation, what implications would it have for the idea that God explains the sorts of global facts discussed in this chapter?

## Problems for Further Thought

1.  Philosophers sometimes use the term *brute fact* to describe a fact that is so simple and obvious that it can't be justified or explained by appeal to any other fact. Consider the relationship between *x* and *y* described in the statement "*x* = *y*." This is the relationship of *identity*. This is a relationship that everything bears to itself; "the Eiffel Tower = the Eiffel Tower" is true, but "the Eiffel Tower = the Statue of Liberty" is false. What explains the fact that everything is self-identical? Is this true because of the way we use the identity sign "="? Is it a brute fact?

2.  In this chapter, I claimed that nothing explains itself. In everyday speech, however, we talk about something's being "self-explanatory." What does this mean? Is there a conflict between what I've said about explanation and the everyday idea? We also use the term "self-starter" to describe some people. Does this conflict with the idea that nothing causes itself?

3.  Blaise Pascal, a seventeenth-century philosopher whom I'll discuss in Chapter 10, once said, "The truth of religion lies in its very obscurity." What does this mean, and is it true?

## CHAPTER 8

# *The Ontological Argument*

The various arguments I've considered so far for the existence of God include premises we know to be true by experience. By using our senses (of sight, hearing, touch, etc.), we know that objects are in motion and that organisms are intricate and adapted to their environments. What is more, there is no other way to know these things; sensory experience is indispensable. Such propositions are called *a posteriori.* Notice the prefix *post*, meaning "after." An a posteriori truth is one that requires experience to be known (or justified). Accordingly, the arguments for the existence of God considered thus far are called *a posteriori* arguments.

## A POSTERIORI AND A PRIORI

Are all propositions a posteriori? Many philosophers have thought there are propositions that can be known to be true by reason alone. These propositions are termed *a priori.* Note the word "prior"; such propositions are knowable prior to, or independently of, experience. Standard examples are mathematical truths and definitions. We can know that $7 + 3 = 10$ and that bachelors are unmarried merely by thinking about the concepts involved. You don't have to do experiments or conduct surveys to find out whether such statements are true. Reason suffices.

Let's be clear on what it means to claim that a given proposition is a priori. To say that we know a priori that bachelors are unmarried doesn't mean we were born with the concepts of bachelorhood and marriage. For a proposition to be a priori, it isn't essential that the concepts contained in the proposition be *innate*. Maybe none of us is born with an understanding of the concept of a bachelor; maybe we must have various experiences to acquire that concept. Even if the concepts were acquired through experience, however, that wouldn't show the proposition fails to be a priori. To say that a proposition is a priori true means that *IF* you understand the concepts involved, then reason will suffice for you to decide that the proposition is true. Don't forget the *IF* in this idea. The idea that there is a priori knowledge doesn't require that there be innate concepts.

The Ontological Argument for the existence of God is an a priori argument. It aims to establish the truth of theism without reliance on any a posteriori premise. In particular, the idea is that we can prove that God must exist simply by examining the definition of the concept of God.

## DEFINITIONS AND EXISTENCE

This should strike you as a very surprising thing to try to do. Consider other definitions. For example, a bachelor is by definition an adult unmarried male. The thing to notice about this definition is that it doesn't imply there are any bachelors. If you think about it, this seems to be true of most definitions. You can define what it is to be a unicorn or a golden mountain, but the definitions won't settle whether there are such things.

When we consider concepts such as *bachelor, unicorn,* or *golden mountain,* the definitions specify what it would take to be an individual of the kind in question; the definitions don't say whether there are zero, one, or many things of that kind. The Ontological Argument claims the concept of God is different: From the definition of the concept of God, the existence of God is supposed to follow.

So the proposition that bachelors are unmarried is a priori, whereas the proposition that bachelors exist is a posteriori. The definition doesn't imply the existence claim. Are there any nontheistic examples of existence claims that can be known a priori? Perhaps existence claims in mathematics furnish examples. If mathematics is a priori, then mathematical existence claims are a priori. So it is an a priori truth that there exists a prime number between 12 and 14. It is philosophically debatable whether there are any a priori truths at all. I won't discuss that issue here, however, but will go along with the idea that mathematical truths are a priori. This means that since mathematics contains existence claims, there are (I'll assume) at least some existence statements that are a priori true. It follows that if there is a mistake in the Ontological Argument for the existence of God, it isn't to be found in the fact that the argument maintains that some existence claims are a priori true.

## ANSELM'S ARGUMENT

The Ontological Argument was formulated by Saint Anselm (1033–1109), who became archbishop of Canterbury. Aquinas, who lived in the thirteenth century, rejected this argument and recommended in its stead the five a posteriori arguments we examined in Chapters 4 and 5. Philosophers down to the present (including Descartes, whose *Meditations on First Philosophy* we'll discuss in Part II) have discussed the Ontological Argument and have constructed different versions of it. Here I'll consider a simplified formulation of the argument:

(O)  (1)  God is by definition the greatest being possible.

   (2)  A being who fails to exist in the actual world (while existing in other possible worlds) is less perfect than a being who exists in all possible worlds.

   ———————————

   Hence, God exists, necessarily.

I label the argument "O" for future reference.

### Premise (1): Conceivability and Possibility

Premise (1) is intended to capture what Anselm meant by saying that God is a being "than which none greater can be conceived." It isn't just that God is the most perfect being that happens to exist in the actual world. The actual world, after all, might contain only grossly imperfect beings, so that God's being the best of these wouldn't mean he is *all*-powerful, *all*-knowing, and *perfectly*-good. The idea is that God is a being who is the best possible being. There is no more perfect being in any possible world. (If you're a bit vague on the idea of a "possible world," go back to Chapter 4 and review.)

Although I gloss Anselm's first premise by saying that God is the best possible being, I want to note an important difference between possibility and conceivability. What is possible is an objective question; it doesn't depend on what people know or believe. Whether we can conceive of something, however, is a fact about us as knowing subjects. Hence, conceivability is a subjective notion. (This should remind you of the point made in Chapter 4 that necessity and certainty are different.)

What can be conceived of may vary from individual to individual. We can conceive of things that dogs can't conceive of; perhaps there are superintelligent beings elsewhere in the universe who can conceive of things that are beyond our grasp. In contrast, there is a sense of the term *possible*, which I'm using here, according to which what is possible doesn't vary from one thinker to another.

It is impossible, according to Einstein's special theory of relativity, for an object that has positive mass to go faster than the speed of light. This simply can't be done, no matter how powerful a rocket ship you build. Yet, I think this is something we can conceive of; we can describe what it would mean to go faster than the speed of light.

Newton thought that travel faster than the speed of light was possible. He not only could conceive of what this would be, he thought it was possible. We now view Newton as mistaken. It isn't possible to do this, and it never has been. For something to be possible, it isn't enough that you can conceive of its happening or that you can't see any reason why it couldn't happen.

If the human mind is limited in various ways, then maybe the most perfect being we can conceive of is still grossly imperfect in many ways. Maybe an ant can't conceive of a creature greater than an anteater, but that doesn't mean anteaters are the most perfect possible beings. Anselm, though he used the word "conceivable," really meant possible, I think. God isn't just the best being we frail human beings can conceptualize; God is supposed to be the best possible being.

## Premise (2): Necessary Existence Is a Perfection

If a being exists in all possible worlds, it is a necessary being, not a contingent one. Why does Anselm think God's perfection demands that God be a necessary being? A contingent thing depends for its existence on other things. You and I are contingent things; we exist only because certain other contingent beings acted as they did. But a truly perfect being, Anselm thinks, wouldn't depend for its existence on anything contingent. It would exist unconditionally. According to Anselm's second premise, a necessary being is more perfect than a contingent one. So if God has all the perfections, he must be a necessary being, not a contingent one.

The Ontological Argument *looks* like it is deductively valid: If God has all the perfections and if necessary existence is a perfection, then God exists necessarily. But from Anselm's time down to the present, there have been doubters. Many philosophers (both theists and atheists) have thought that the Ontological Argument must involve a mistake.

## GAUNILO'S CRITICISM

Anselm describes a criticism formulated by his contemporary, Gaunilo. Gaunilo says the argument must be defective, since if it were not, you could prove the existence of a perfect island by a similar a priori argument. What did Gaunilo have in mind?

Let's start with the concept of an island. The first point is that the concept of islandhood resembles the concept of bachelorhood. Its definition doesn't deductively imply that there are any objects of the kind defined. So any attempt to provide an a priori proof that islands exist must fail. Now let's define a new concept: Call it a *P*-island. A *P*-island is an island than which no greater island can be conceived. *P*-islands are just like ordinary islands, except they are, by definition, the best possible islands. Gaunilo thought there can be no a priori demonstration that there are *P*-islands. Perhaps no such thing exists, and if there happen to be *P*-islands, this isn't something that could be discovered by reason alone.

## A Priori/A Posteriori and Necessity/Contingency

In Chapter 4, the ideas of necessity and contingency were introduced. A possible world, roughly, is a way the world might be. A necessary truth is a proposition that is true in all possible worlds; a contingent truth is a proposition that is true in the actual world, but not in all possible worlds.

In this chapter, the ideas of *a priori* and *a posteriori* propositions were introduced. An a priori proposition can be known (or justified) independent of experience. How is the distinction between necessary and contingent propositions related to the distinction between a priori and a posteriori propositions?

This is a deep, controversial, and fundamental philosophical question. Some philosophers hold that the two distinctions divide up the propositions in exactly the same way. That is, they hold that all necessary propositions are a priori and that all contingent propositions are a posteriori. According to this theory, all the propositions that natural science discovers by observation are contingent.

Some of what I've said in previous chapters has assumed that this theory is false. I've suggested that empirical science (that is, science that relies on observation) is able to discover what is really possible. In Chapter 4, I mentioned some examples. I said that thermodynamics has discovered that perpetual motion machines are impossible (that is, it is a necessary truth that there are no perpetual motion machines); I also stated that Einstein's theories of relativity say that no particle (with positive rest mass) can go faster than the speed of light (that is, that objects with positive rest mass necessarily go slower than the speed of light). In other words, I've suggested that some a posteriori propositions are necessary, even though other a posteriori propositions are contingent.

What about a priori propositions? The examples discussed so far of a priori propositions (such as "bachelors are unmarried" and "2 + 3 = 5") are all cases of necessary truths. So the question remains: Are there any a priori propositions that are contingent? The examples I'll give provide a preview of material that will be discussed in Chapter 13. Consider the proposition each of us formulates when we say to ourselves "I exist." You know this proposition to be true without using sight, hearing, taste, touch, or smell. Thought alone allows you to see that it is true. So it is a priori. The same seems to be true for the proposition you formulate by saying to yourself "I am thinking." Yet, it isn't a necessary truth that you exist. You might have failed to do so. If this line of thinking is right, we may conclude that the proposition each of us considers when we say to ourselves "I exist" or "I am thinking" is a priori and contingent.

Fill in the following table with examples of the four types of propositions indicated:

|  | Necessary | Contingent |
|---|---|---|
| A priori |  |  |
| A posteriori |  |  |

Consider, however, the following argument, which mimics the structure of the Ontological Argument:

(I)  (1)  A *P*-island is by definition the greatest possible island.

   (2)  An island that fails to exist in the actual world (while existing in other possible worlds) is less perfect than an island that exists in all possible worlds.

———————

Hence, a *P*-island exists necessarily.

I label this argument "I" for future reference.

Gaunilo's conclusion wasn't that there are *P*-islands (as well as *P*-bagels, *P*-comedians, and so on). Rather, he thought this argument about islands must be defective. It seems crazy to think the existence of a perfect island could be established a priori. Gaunilo concluded that Anselm's argument must have a mistake in it as well. What sort of mistake did Gaunilo think these two arguments commit? He believed that the two premises of the Island Argument are true. But Gaunilo holds that these premises don't deductively imply the conclusion; the existence of a perfect island doesn't follow from these a priori premises. Gaunilo concludes that the Island Argument (I) is invalid. He takes this to show that the Ontological Argument (O) is also invalid.

## How Are the Ontological Argument and the Island Argument Related?

Notice that Gaunilo's argument was obtained from Anselm's by substituting "*P*-island" for "God," and "island" for "being." We saw in Chapter 2 that the validity of an argument depends on its form, not on its subject matter. Gaunilo was suggesting that since his Island Argument is invalid, so too is Anselm's argument about God, since they have the same logical form. Gaunilo thought the Island Conclusion doesn't follow from the Island Premises. By parity of reasoning, he claims Anselm's conclusion doesn't follow from Anselm's premises.

Gaunilo is making an argument about these two arguments. In particular, he attempts to show Anselm's argument is invalid by reductio (see Chapter 4 for this piece of terminology). Gaunilo argues as follows:

If the Ontological Argument is deductively valid, then the Island Argument is deductively valid.

The Island Argument is not deductively valid.

———————————

The Ontological Argument is not deductively valid.

## ANSELM'S REPLY

Anselm scornfully replies to this criticism. He says that his argument applies to God—the greatest possible being. It doesn't apply to a *P*-island—the greatest possible island. His idea is that islands are not the kind of thing that could have all the perfections. For example, islands can't have the perfection of intelligence. I think this criticism of Gaunilo misses the mark. Islands can have some perfections (shady places, beautiful beaches, nice drinking water, tropical fruit), even if they can't have all of them. A *P*-island is an island that is the most perfect possible island; this does not require that it be intelligent. As long as existence is one of the perfections that an island can have, Gaunilo's point seems correct.

Even so, Gaunilo's objection is, to my mind, incomplete. His reductio argument, if it works, shows that there has to be a mistake somewhere in Anselm's reasoning, but it doesn't show exactly where the mistake occurs. As noted before, Anselm's argument *looks* valid; if it isn't, we would like to see exactly where it goes wrong.

When Anselm dismisses Gaunilo's Island Argument, maybe he means that the Ontological Argument is deductively valid, while the Island Argument is not. However, this suggestion seems implausible, since deductive validity doesn't depend on an argument's subject matter, only on its form, and the two arguments seem to have the same logical form. Or maybe Anselm is claiming the premises of the Island Argument are implausible, though the premises of the Ontological Argument are quite plausible. If this were correct, the two arguments would be disanalogous. But the first premise of the Ontological Argument and the first premise of the Island Argument seem to be on a par. Anselm holds that his own definition of God is correct; it is hard to see how Gaunilo's definition of a *P*-island could be mistaken.

What about the second premises of the two arguments? If necessary existence is a perfection for beings in general, why isn't it a perfection for islands in particular? I feel a little shaky about my ability to make such judgments about "perfection," but I don't see why the second premise of the Ontological Argument should be accepted and the second premise of the Island Argument rejected. I conclude that the two arguments are fully parallel, contrary to what Anselm says in reply to Gaunilo. Gaunilo, I think, is on to something.

## DISPENSING WITH PERFECTION

Anselm's argument (O) makes use of the idea that God is perfect. Gaunilo's parody of Anselm—Gaunilo's Island Argument (I)—also makes use of that concept. Gaunilo and Anselm shared a worldview according to which everything in the universe occupies a particular position on the Great Chain of Being. At the top is God, next come the angels, then human beings, then animals, and then plants. Anselm and Gaunilo believed it was an entirely objective question how perfect a given thing is.

I want to suggest that we can see a defect in the Ontological Argument more clearly once we set aside the concept of perfection. Let's not worry about inferring a being's existence from its being perfect. Let's not worry about how perfect a particular thing is or about whether perfection is objective. Let's simply define a being as an existing thing and see what happens.

Unicorns don't exist. The concept of unicornhood isn't exemplified in the actual world. Consider, however, a new concept, which I call *E*-unicornhood. An *E*-unicorn is by definition something that is an existing unicorn. Does it follow from the definition of an *E*-unicorn that there are *E*-unicorns? Not at all. The concept includes the property of existence, but that doesn't imply that the concept is actually exemplified.

The definition simply describes what a thing must be like if it is to count as an *E*-unicorn. The definition tells us that if something is an *E*-unicorn, then that thing will have the property of existing. Now let's define the concept of an *E*-God. An *E*-God is a being who is all-powerful, all-knowing, and all-good and who actually exists. Does it follow from the definition of an *E*-God that there is an *E*-God? Not at all. The definition simply describes what a thing must be like if it is to count as an *E*-God. The definition tells us that if something is an *E*-God, then that thing will have the property of existing.

## CONCLUSION

When we define God, we are saying what properties a being must have to be God. Parallel remarks apply to defining unicorns or golden mountains. Anselm argued that our concept of God has built into it the idea that God necessarily exists. Just as God is by definition omnipotent, it also is true that God, by definition, necessarily exists. My criticism of the Ontological Argument comes to this: Let's grant that God is by definition the greatest possible being. And let us grant that necessary existence is a perfection. What follows from this is that necessary existence is part of the concept of God. Necessary existence is built into the concept of God, just as omnipotence is. But the fact that existence is built into a concept doesn't imply there are things to which the concept applies.

If we concede that God is defined as an omnipotent being, all this means is that if God exists, then that being must be omnipotent. Likewise, if we concede that God is defined as a necessarily existent being, we are merely saying that if there is a God, then that being necessarily exists. The definitions don't entail the existence of anything that is omnipotent nor of anything that necessarily exists. It is for this reason that the Ontological Argument is invalid.

---

## Review Questions

1. What is the difference between an a posteriori proposition and an a priori proposition? What is the difference between saying that a proposition is a priori and saying that it is innate? Give an example of an a posteriori existence claim and an example of an a priori existence claim.
2. What is the difference between saying that a proposition is possible and saying that it is conceivable?
3. How does Gaunilo's point about islands bear on Anselm's argument about God? What is a reductio argument? In what way is Gaunilo employing this form of argumentation?
4. Suppose God is, by definition, a being that exists in all possible worlds. Does it follow that God exists?

## Problems for Further Thought

1. Consult the original text of Anselm's argument and Gaunilo's reply. Give a formulation of the argument that is more true to the text than the one presented in this chapter.

2. I've argued that building the idea of existence into a concept doesn't ensure that anything actually exemplifies the concept. That is the point of considering *E*-unicorns. Now, however, consider the opposite problem. Is it possible to define a concept so that the definition ensures that *nothing* can exemplify it? Construct a definition that does this. How is it possible that definitions can have negative implications about existence, but not positive implications?

3. Do the following arguments have the same logical form? Explain your answer.

> God has every perfection.
> Existence is a perfection.
> ──────────────
> God exists.
> Sam has every novel by Dickens.
> *David Copperfield* is a novel by Dickens.
> ──────────────
> Sam has *David Copperfield*.

4. Suppose I define God as a necessarily existing being? Does it follow that God exists? If I assume that it is possible that God exists, would it then follow that God exists? If so, is this a convincing proof of God's existence?

5. In the selection from Hume's *Dialogues Concerning Natural Religion*, Philo, Demea, and Cleanthes discuss a priori and a posteriori arguments for the existence of God. What are their views on whether there can be an a priori proof that God exists?

## CHAPTER 9

# *Is the Existence of God Testable?*

Up to this point, I've taken the question of whether God exists to be perfectly meaningful. It may be difficult to answer, but I've assumed there *is* an answer. Theists, atheists, and agnostics agree on this. I've assumed the sentence "God exists" says something; the question is whether what it says is true, and whether we can know this.

## LOGICAL POSITIVISM

Some philosophers—advocates of the position called *logical positivism*—have an altogether different view of this problem. They hold that the sentence "God exists" is meaningless. It isn't true and it isn't false either. They hold that it is misguided to argue about whether God exists. Their idea is that we have been misled by a superficial grammatical similarity between the sentence "God exists" and the sentence "Genes exist." The latter expresses a scientific statement that can be justified or rejected by appeal to evidence. In contrast, the former sentence expresses no proposition at all. Positivism maintains that we shouldn't try to answer the question of whether God exists, but should reject it as meaningless. According to positivism, theists, atheists, and agnostics are all mistaken.

## THE TESTABILITY THEORY OF MEANING

Positivists advanced a theory that is supposed to justify this philosophical thesis. This is the *Testability Theory of Meaning*. It holds that for a sentence to be meaningful, it must be either a priori or a posteriori. The Testability Theory of Meaning also includes specific proposals for how these two categories should be understood.

As explained in Chapter 8, a truth is a priori if it can be justified without appeal to sense experience—it can be justified by reason alone. And a truth is a posteriori if it must rely on sense experience for its justification. This is what it means for a *truth* to be a priori or a posteriori. *Falsehoods* can fall into these categories as well. A mathematical truth like "$2 + 3 = 5$" can be justified by reason alone, but the mathematical falsehood "$2 + 4 = 7$" can be *disproved* by reason alone. Just as the statement "There is a book in front of you now" is an a posteriori truth, so the statement "There is no book in front of you now" is an a posteriori falsehood.

Some meaningful statements are true; others are false. In saying that each meaningful sentence is either a priori or a posteriori, positivists are saying that every meaningful sentence is *decidable in principle*. That is, they maintain that if $S$ is a meaningful sentence, then it is possible to figure out whether $S$ is true. If there is no way in principle to figure out whether $S$ is true, positivists conclude that $S$ is meaningless.

I now turn to the positivists' account of what makes a sentence a priori or a posteriori. Once each of these categories is clarified, they think the claim that God exists can be seen to fall into neither category. Positivists conclude the claim is meaningless.

## ANALYTICITY

Positivists (and some other philosophers besides) hold that all a priori statements are *analytic*. An analytic truth (as opposed to a *synthetic* one) is a definition or a deductive consequence of a definition. The truth of "All bachelors are unmarried" follows from the definitions of the terms that occur in it. "Either it is raining or it is not raining" likewise follows from the definitions of "or" and "not." Symmetrically, positivism maintains that all a posteriori statements are *synthetic*—if a sentence depends on sense experience for its justification, its truth doesn't follow from definitions alone.

Where does the sentence "God exists" fit into this classification? Positivists reject the whole strategy behind the Ontological Argument. They hold that "God exists" isn't decidable from definitions alone. So the sentence isn't a priori. This means that if "God exists" is meaningful, it must be a posteriori. We now must examine the account positivists give of what makes a sentence a posteriori.

## FALSIFIABILITY

Positivists say that the sentence "God exists" is *untestable.* There is no way to use observations to decide whether it is true. Defenders of the Testability Theory of Meaning have argued that sentences are tested by deducing predictions from them that can be checked by making observations. Mendel tested his genetic theory by deducing from it a prediction about the proportions of different characteristics that there should be in the pea plants he grew in his garden. He then was able to check these predictions observationally. Positivists argue that the sentence "God exists" makes no predictions whatever, so it is untestable.

Sometimes the idea of observational testability is developed with reference to the concept of *falsification.* If a theory makes a prediction that can be checked observationally, the theory runs the risk of being refuted by observations. This is what the influential philosopher of science Karl Popper (not a positivist himself) meant by saying that a scientific theory should be falsifiable. This doesn't mean a scientific theory should be false. *Falsifiable* doesn't mean *false.* What is crucial is that the theory rule out at least some possible observations. It must "stick its neck out."

In science, confirmation and disconfirmation are intimately connected. An experiment has different possible outcomes. If some outcomes would be evidence *in favor of* the hypothesis, then other outcomes would be evidence *against* it. If you propose an experiment for testing a hypothesis and you think that every possible result would indicate the hypothesis is true, there is no reason to run the experiment. The only way the experiment could offer you real evidence in favor of the hypothesis is if there were some possible results that would undermine the hypothesis. You then get evidence supporting the hypothesis if you run the experiment and find that those possible refuting outcomes don't come to pass. Getting evidence in favor of a hypothesis requires that the hypothesis rule out something. But what does the sentence "God exists" rule out? Is there anything we can imagine observing that would be evidence against theism? For example, if we observed that there is moral evil in the world, would that count against the hypothesis that there is a God? In Chapter 11, I'll discuss this question in some detail. For now, I'll merely note that theists have usually not taken the existence of evil to count against theism. They say that if the world had been morally perfect, that would be consistent with the existence of God; and if the world happens to contain moral evil, that too can be reconciled with theism. It seems that theists usually can reconcile their belief in God with just about anything they observe.

Consider the doomsday pronouncements that pop up from time to time in different religions. Every so often, some religious group gets the idea that God is about to bring the world to an end. Such predictions have yet to come true. What has been the result of these failed predictions? A few end-of-the-worlders have had their faith shaken. But, after some reflection, most theists have decided that the failed predictions of the end-of-the-worlders don't count against the hypothesis that there is a God. If the world had come to an end, theists would have taken this to support their belief that there is a God; but when the world fails to come to an end, these same people continue to believe that God exists.

I hope these remarks convey the flavor of what positivists are getting at when they claim that the hypothesis that God exists is untestable. I now want to be a little more precise about these ideas. I begin with two definitions:

> A hypothesis $H$ is *strongly falsifiable* if $H$ deductively implies at least one observation statement $O$.

> An *observation statement* is a statement whose truth or falsehood can be determined by direct observation.

Notice that strong falsifiability allows a hypothesis to be refuted by a valid deductive argument if the ob.servational prediction it makes turns out to be false:

> If $H$, then $O$.
> Not-$O$.
> _____
> Not-$H$

## AUXILIARY ASSUMPTIONS NEEDED

I agree that the hypothesis that God exists isn't strongly falsifiable. The same is true, however, of most of the hypotheses that science investigates. *Hypotheses rarely deductively imply predictions all by themselves.* Rather, the usual pattern is that you must conjoin auxiliary assumptions $A$ to a hypothesis $H$ to get $H$ to deductively imply an observational prediction $O$. It isn't $H$ that implies $O$, but $H\&A$ that does the trick.

I'll illustrate this idea with an example from outside science. Consider Sherlock Holmes again. Holmes wishes to test the hypothesis that Moriarty is the murderer. Does this hypothesis, all by itself, tell Holmes what he will observe at the scene of the crime? Not at all. Auxiliary assumptions are needed. If Holmes knows Moriarty wears a size 12 shoe, smokes El Supremo cigars, and fires a gun of type X, these auxiliary assumptions may lead him to expect to find certain clues. If he discovers a size 12 footprint, an El Supremo butt on the carpet next to the victim, and a bullet from a type X gun, his auxiliary assumptions may lead him to think that Moriarty is probably the murderer. On the other hand, if Holmes were to make *other* auxiliary assumptions, then the hypothesis that Moriarty is the murderer would lead Holmes to make quite different predictions. If Holmes thought that Moriarty didn't smoke, that he has a size 8 shoe, and that he prefers to use a knife, then the hypothesis that Moriarty is the murderer would *not* predict the clues Holmes found. The clues found at the scene of the crime don't say anything one way or the other about whether Moriarty is the murderer until auxiliary assumptions are added.

So most of the hypotheses we test don't, all by themselves, deductively imply observationally checkable statements. They do so only when supplemented with auxiliary assumptions. Where does this leave the thesis that the hypothesis that God exists isn't testable?

The sentence "God exists" is not strongly falsifiable, but that is uninteresting, since most scientific hypotheses aren't strongly falsifiable either. This brings us to the next question: Is the hypothesis that God exists testable when it is supplemented with auxiliary assumptions? The answer is *yes*. Consider the following candidates:

$A_1$: If there is a God, there will be living things in the world and they will be perfectly adapted to their environments.

$A_2$: If there is a God, there will be no living things.

$A_3$: If there is a God, there will be living things in the world, but they will not be perfectly adapted to their environments.

The hypothesis that there is a God, when conjoined with $A_1$, predicts something we can check by making observations. The same is true if we conjoin the theistic hypothesis with $A_2$ or with $A_3$. So there is a twofold parallel between the hypothesis that God exists and a scientific hypothesis (or a detective's hypothesis): The hypothesis isn't strongly falsifiable, but it is testable when conjoined with auxiliary assumptions. Does this mean that the hypothesis that God exists is no less testable than the hypotheses of science?

There does seem to be a difference between these cases, although it isn't to be characterized in terms of the idea of strong falsifiability. In the case of Holmes's testing whether Moriarty is the murderer, I noted that different sets of auxiliary assumptions entail different predictions about what Holmes will find at the scene of the crime. If $A_4$ is true, we get one set of predictions; if $A_5$ is true, we get a very different set.

$A_4$: Moriarty smokes El Supremo cigars, has a size 12 shoe, and uses a type X gun.

$A_5$: Moriarty does not smoke, has a size 8 shoe, and uses a knife as his preferred murder weapon.

If Holmes is to say whether the clues at the scene of the crime count for or against the hypothesis that Moriarty is the murderer, he must decide which of $A_4$ and $A_5$ is true.

### Neptune and Vulcan

Most hypotheses in science don't entail predictions all by themselves; they have to be conjoined to auxiliary assumptions to do so. This means that if the prediction turns out to be false, scientists face a choice. They can reject the hypothesis or they can reject the auxiliary assumptions.

Two episodes in nineteenth-century astronomy illustrate these two options. Working separately, John Adams and Urbain Leverrier used Newtonian physics plus assumptions about the planets then known to exist to predict where the orbit of Uranus should be. These assumptions included the idea that Uranus is the planet farthest from the sun. The prediction about Uranus' orbit obtained by conjoining Newton's theory with this assumption came out wrong. Adams and Leverrier therefore had to choose between rejecting Newtonian physics and rejecting one or more of the auxiliary assumptions. Because Newtonian theory was well supported by other observations, they were reluctant to reject it. They therefore suspected that the auxiliary assumptions were the culprit. They conjectured that Uranus isn't the last planet. Two years later, astronomers were able to confirm this conjecture; they observed the planet that we now call Neptune.

This same pattern of reasoning was subsequently applied to the planet Mercury. Newtonian physics plus auxiliary assumptions (including the assumption that there is no planet between Mercury and the sun) predict where Mercury's orbit should be. This prediction turned out to be false. Scientists therefore faced a choice. Either Newton's theory is wrong or at least one auxiliary assumption is mistaken. Following the pattern of reasoning that worked so well for the case of Uranus, some scientists conjectured that there is a planet lying between Mercury and the Sun. It was given the name "Vulcan."

As it turned out, this conjecture was mistaken. There is no such planet. It wasn't the auxiliary assumption (that there is no planet between Mercury and the Sun) that was responsible for the false prediction about Mercury's orbit; it was Newtonian physics itself that led to the error. Only when Newton's theories were replaced by Einstein's theories of relativity could the departure of Mercury's orbit from Newtonian values be explained.

In the reasoning about Uranus and the reasoning about Mercury, three sorts of statement play a role. There are theories *(T)*, auxiliary assumptions *(A)*, and predictions *(P)*. Describe the logical form of the arguments that the scientists formulated in the two cases.

## AUXILIARY ASSUMPTIONS MUST BE INDEPENDENTLY ESTABLISHED

In the scientific case, as well as in the case of detective work, there is an important fact about auxiliary assumptions that goes beyond what I've said so far. Not only are auxiliary assumptions needed if the hypothesis is to make observational predictions, in addition, *those auxiliary assumptions must be checkable independent of the hypothesis under test.* For example, Holmes can interpret the clues found at the scene of the crime once he decides whether $A_4$ or $A_5$ is true. Furthermore, he can find out whether $A_4$ or $A_5$ is true without his having to already know if Moriarty is the murderer.

Can the same be done for the auxiliary hypotheses about God's nature, like $A_1$, $A_2$, or $A_3$? This isn't so clear. It is easy enough to *invent* auxiliary hypotheses that reconcile what we observe with the hypothesis that God is responsible for what we observe. If we find that an organism is perfectly adapted to its environment, we can construct an auxiliary assumption that effects this reconciliation. If we find that the organism is imperfectly adapted, a different auxiliary assumption can be invented that does the same thing. The problem is, How do we figure out which of these auxiliary assumptions is true without assuming at the outset that God is responsible for what we observe? This is the problem we ran into in Chapter 5 when we considered different versions of creationism.

In the detective case, Holmes wouldn't endlessly revise his opinions about auxiliary assumptions just to preserve his faith that Moriarty must be the murderer. To do so would be to fall prey to an obsession, not to do good detective work. Holmes would find out which of $A_4$ and $A_5$ is true, and then use these independently confirmed auxiliary assumptions to test the hypothesis that Moriarty is the murderer. The result may be that Holmes is forced to conclude Moriarty is probably innocent of the crime. It is difficult to test the hypothesis that God exists because it is hard to determine which auxiliary assumptions to accept if you don't already believe that God exists.

How is what I'm saying different from what the Testability Theory of Meaning maintains? To begin with, I'm not using the idea of strong falsifiability to criticize the hypothesis that God exists. Nor am I claiming that no one will ever figure out how the hypothesis that God exists can be tested. Perhaps someday auxiliary assumptions will be independently discovered that can tell us what the hypothesis that God exists predicts about the observable world. My claim is just that this hasn't happened *yet*. In summary, positivists used the Testability Theory of Meaning to derive *timeless* verdict concerning the sentence "God exists." In contrast, I've used a different idea about testability (one that emphasizes the role of auxiliary assumptions) to argue for a verdict concerning how the issue of testability stands *now*.

## "GOD EXISTS" IS MEANINGFUL

I disagree with positivism on another count. I think the hypothesis that there is a God is meaningful. It is possible to discuss whether there is evidence for or against it. Also, the hypothesis obviously has various logical properties; I noted before that it, in conjunction with various auxiliary statements, deductively implies various predictions. This is enough to show that the sentence "God exists" isn't meaningless gibberish. A meaningful statement need not be decidable in principle.

## SUMMARY

I'll summarize my assessment of the Testability Theory of Meaning as follows. I think there are difficulties in testing the hypothesis that God exists. This, however, isn't because I endorse the criterion of falsifiability; I don't. The bare statement "God exists" does not entail observational predictions, but neither does the bare statement "electrons exist." The typical situation in science is that theoretical statements have observational consequences only when they are conjoined with auxiliary assumptions. It is easy to invent auxiliary assumptions that permit the hypothesis that God exists to make predictions. It also is easy to invent such assumptions so that the result is that the hypothesis makes *true* predictions. What is not so easy is to show that the auxiliary assumptions that permit the theistic hypothesis to make predictions are themselves well confirmed. Scientific testing requires that the auxiliary assumptions used be well supported by evidence; inventing them isn't enough.

## Review Questions

1. What does it mean to say that a hypothesis is strongly falsifiable? Does this mean it is false? Is the hypothesis that organisms contain genes strongly falsifiable?
2. What is an auxiliary assumption? How does testing the hypothesis that God exists depend on a choice of auxiliary assumptions?
3. What does it mean to say that Holmes could independently confirm the auxiliary assumptions he needs concerning Moriarty? Independent of what?
4. How does the Surprise Principle explain why the existence of miracles would be strong evidence for the existence of God? What problems need to be addressed if one wishes to argue for theism in this way?

## Problems for Further Thought

1. Consider the following passage from David Hume's "Essay on Miracles":

   > That no testimony is sufficient to establish a miracle unless the testimony be of such a kind, that its falsehood would be more miraculous than the fact which it endeavors to establish. . . . When any one tells me that he saw a dead man restored to life, I immediately consider with myself whether it be more probable that this person should either deceive or be deceived, or that the fact which he related should really have happened. I weigh the one miracle against the other, and according to the superiority which I discover, I pronounce my decision, and always reject the greater miracle. If the falsehood of his testimony would be more miraculous than the event which he relates, then, and only then, can he pretend to commend my belief or opinion.

   What general point about eyewitness testimony is Hume making here? Does Hume's argument show that miracles never happen?
2. Can positivists say that a sentence is meaningful even though we will never actually find out whether it is true? Can they say that a sentence is meaningful if it is impossible for us to discover whether it is true? Does this mean that sentences about the prehistoric past are meaningless?
3. The readings for this chapter include a selection from A. J. Ayer's *Language, Truth, and Logic* (1936). This was a very influential defense of logical positivism. In this selection, Ayer says that there is no conflict between science and religion.

He also says that positivism agrees with what many religious mystics maintain. Why does Ayer hold these views?

4. The concept of strong falsifiability was defined in this chapter. Define the parallel concept of strong verifiability. What problems are there with the claim that statements that are not a priori must be strongly verifiable?

5. Is the testability theory of meaning meaningful according to the standards it specifies? That is, is the theory either a consequence of definitions or testable via sense experience?

# CHAPTER 10

## *Pascal and Irrationality*

Blaise Pascal (1623–1662), a French physicist, philosopher, mathematician, and mystic, was interested in the question of whether it could be rational to believe in God even if you think it is enormously improbable that God exists. Suppose all the evidence is *against* God's existence—you regard the existence of God as a possibility, although you think it is extremely implausible. Can it still make sense to be a theist? Pascal was one of the founders of the modern mathematical theory of probability. His argument has come to be called *Pascal's Wager,* because Pascal argues that believing that God exists is a sensible wager, even if there is no evidence that God exists.

### PRUDENTIAL AND EVIDENTIAL REASONS FOR BELIEF

Before analyzing Pascal's argument, I want to describe two kinds of reasons someone might have for believing some proposition or for performing some action. Suppose one day we meet for lunch. I'm carrying a machine gun and a briefcase. I open the briefcase and show you that it contains $1,000,000. I show you that the gun is loaded. Then, I make you an offer I think you can't refuse. You probably do not believe the president of the United States is juggling candy bars at this very moment. You regard this proposition as very improbable, though you grant that it isn't entirely impossible. Here is my offer: If you can get yourself to believe that the president is juggling candy bars right now, I'll give you $1,000,000. If you don't believe this proposition, I'll shoot you with the machine gun. What is it reasonable for you to do, supposing that you think I'm entirely sincere in my threats and promises?

In one sense, it is rational to try to believe, even though you think the proposition in question is very improbable. It would be prudent (i.e., in your self-interest) to try to believe, supposing that you don't want to die and would like to have the million dollars. The kind of reason you have here I'll call a *prudential reason.*

In another sense, however, you don't have any reason to believe that the president of the United States is juggling candy bars right now. You have no evidence at all that the proposition is true. Let's describe this fact by saying that you don't have an *evidential reason* for believing the proposition in question.

Pascal's Wager is intended to provide you with a *prudential* reason for believing that God exists even if you think there is no *evidence* that there is a God. Even if you think all the evidence is against the existence of God, Pascal thinks he can give you a prudential reason for theism, so long as you grant that the existence of God is at least possible.

## WHEN DOES IT MAKE SENSE TO GAMBLE?

Before analyzing Pascal's argument, I need to mention one other detail, about gambling. Here is a fact about reasonable gambles: *It can make sense to bet on improbable outcomes if the payoff is big enough.* Suppose I offer you the following wager. If you pay

---

### The Expected Value of an Action

You have to decide between two actions: buying a lottery ticket and not buying one. If you buy the ticket, a card is drawn at random from a standard deck of cards. If the card is the ace of spades, you win $1,000,000. If not, you lose. The ticket costs $1. Should you buy the ticket, if your only goal is to maximize your cash resources?

The *expected value* (expected utility) of an action is the *average* payoff you would receive, if you performed the action again and again. If you buy the ticket, there is a 51/52 chance that the ace of spades will not appear; in this case, your resources will have dropped $1 (the cost of the ticket). On the other hand, if you buy the ticket, there is a 1/52 chance that you will win the million; in this case, your resources (taking account of the cost of the ticket) will have increased by *$999,999.* So the expected value of buying the ticket is

$$-(\$1)(51/52) + (\$999{,}999)(1/52) = \$19{,}230.$$

What is the expected value of the alternative action—of *not* buying the ticket? That depends on what you would do with the $1 in question. Suppose that you would simply put it in your pocket if you didn't buy into the lottery. In this case, you can be certain that your resources will neither increase nor decline. So the expected value of not buying a ticket is $0. Notice that buying the ticket has a higher expected value than not buying. So the rule in decision theory— to maximize expected utility (or value)—tells you to buy the ticket.

The expected value of buying the ticket is *not* the amount of money you can expect to get. If you enter the lottery, you'll either end up a dollar behind or $999,999 ahead. The expected value is what you would average if you bought into the lottery again and again. Most of the time, you'll lose; occasionally, you'll win. The average payoff per ticket over the long run is about $19,230.

The mathematical idea of an expectation applies to quantities other than value or utility. A probability theorist might say that the expected number of offspring for parents in the United States today is about 2.2. This doesn't mean that a couple can expect to have precisely this number of children. Rather, 2.2 is the expected number because it is the average. The same is true when life insurance companies describe the life expectancy of a person who now is 19 years old.

me $1, you will be allowed to draw a single card from a standard deck of cards. If the card drawn turns out to be the ace of spades, I'll give you $1,000,000. If it turns out to be some other card, you receive nothing, and so you are out the dollar you paid for the chance. Question: Does it make sense to buy into this gamble, assuming you can trust me to pay you if you win and that your goal is to maximize the amount of money you possess? The answer is yes. Although the probability of winning is only 1/52, the payoff if you win is so huge and the cost to you if you lose is so small that this is a great gamble to make. Bear this fact in mind as you consider Pascal's argument.

## PASCAL'S ARGUMENT

Pascal's Wager can be represented as a solution to a problem in decision theory. This is a modern theory that describes how an agent should choose among different available *actions* by seeing what the *utilities* are of the different *outcomes*. Be sure to get clear on how each of these italicized terms figures in Pascal's argument.

You have to decide whether or not to believe there is a God. These are the two possible actions—believing in God, or not believing. Separate from what you believe, there is the way the world is—either there is a God or there isn't. Hence, there are four possible outcomes—an outcome being composed of your performing an action when the world is a particular way. The four outcomes are represented in the following two-by-two table:

|  |  | Ways the World Might Be | |
|---|---|---|---|
|  |  | God Exists | God does not exist |
| Actions | Believe that God exists | $+^\circ$ | $-10$ |
|  | Do not believe that God exists | $-^\circ$ | $+10$ |

The upper-left entry represents the outcome in which you believe in God and there is a God. What is the result, if this should come to pass? Pascal says that the payoff to you is an infinite reward—you go to heaven. Suppose, on the other hand, that you occupy the lower-left cell. This is the outcome in which you don't believe there is a God, but God in fact exists. Here Pascal says you suffer an infinite punishment—you receive eternal damnation. What about the other two entries? If you believe in God, but there is no God, perhaps you will have wasted your time with religious rituals and observances you might have preferred to skip had you only known there is no God listening to your prayers. This isn't a horrible result, though it should be represented as a modest disutility—hence my entry of $-10$. On the other hand, if you don't believe in God and there is no God (the lower-right cell), you receive a modest benefit. Instead of engaging in religious practices that you may find boring at times, you can get involved in activities that are more rewarding. Pascal says that the entry in this cell represents a modest benefit; my chosen value for the utility here is $+10$.

To summarize the structure of the problem: you must decide which action to perform. The possible outcomes are the possible pairings of an available action with a different way the world might be. With each possible outcome, you associate a utility (a payoff), that represents how good or bad the outcome is for you.

How are the utilities of the different possible outcomes to be combined to reach a decision about which act is preferable? The *expected utility* of believing there is a God needs to take account of two possibilities: There is the utility you receive if you believe and there is a God, and the quite different utility you receive if you believe and there is no God. Likewise the expected utility of not believing must take account of both outcome possibilities (represented in the bottom row). Here is Pascal's solution. Even if you think the existence of God is very improbable (say, you assign it a probability of only $1/1,000,000$), the expected utility of believing is higher than the expected utility of not believing. The reason is that though the existence of God is very improbable, there is a huge benefit if you are a theist and God exists, but only a small cost if you are a theist and there is no God. It makes sense to bet on the existence of God, even if the existence of God is very improbable, for reasons that parallel the gamble I mentioned before. The gamble makes sense even though it is improbable that there is a God.

## FIRST CRITICISM OF PASCAL'S ARGUMENT

Two criticisms have been made of this wager, only one of which is decisive. First, some philosophers have objected to treating belief as an action. We can't decide to believe a proposition; belief isn't an action we control in this way. In my story about the president, you may recognize that it is in your interest to believe the president is now juggling candy bars. Believing this would be good for you, but that doesn't mean you can automatically make yourself believe the proposition. The objection to Pascal's argument is that it is a mistake to treat belief as a problem in decision theory, since decision theory is about choosing actions that you can perform if you want to.

Pascal recognized this difficulty. After stating his wager, he comments that people who are convinced his reasoning is sound may not be able to suddenly start being theists. He suggests to them that they go live among religious people. By doing this, habits of faith will gradually take hold. Pascal realized you can't simply decide to believe something. But he did see that you can choose to live your life in such a way that belief will come naturally after a while.

Pascal's comment means that the Wager can be reformulated so that the actions considered really are things under our control. Rather than treating belief and non-belief as things we can choose to do directly, let's recognize that sincere belief can only occur in the right setting, where the right habits have been developed. It also is worth mentioning that Pascal's Wager concerns what it is best for you to believe. The question of whether you can do what is best for you is a separate question.

## SECOND CRITICISM OF PASCAL'S ARGUMENT

The second objection to Pascal's argument is more telling. In Chapter 9, I discussed the difficulty of establishing what God would be like if such a being existed. This is the problem of independently confirming auxiliary hypotheses, as I called them, about God's nature.

Pascal's Wager makes very specific assumptions about what God would be like if there were such a being. The assumption is that God would send believers to heaven and nonbelievers to hell. But there are other conceptions to consider. For example, maybe God would reward those who lead a good life and would punish those who are bad, independently of what those individuals' theological opinions happen to be. Or consider another possibility: Perhaps God will send everyone to heaven except those who are convinced by Pascal's Wager.

The main problem with the Wager is that it makes assumptions about God's nature that are part of one religious tradition but not part of many others. How can one tell which assumptions are true? In the absence of a convincing argument, I see no reason to think Pascal's description of the payoffs is correct.

## THE ROLE OF REASON

Pascal argued that it can make sense to believe things that are totally unsupported by evidence. If you think evidence is the hallmark of rational belief, then you'll interpret Pascal as giving a justification of irrationality. Of course, he didn't abandon the standard of rationality altogether. He tried to provide a *rational argument* that we should believe in God even if there is no evidence that God exists. Pascal aimed to provide a prudential reason, not an evidential reason.

Pascal rejected the idea that evidential reasoning should determine whether or not we believe in God. Other religious thinkers have done the same thing, but for reasons that differ from Pascal's. For example, it has been suggested that God is so radically different from all the other beings that we know about that the methods of reasoning that are appropriate for discussing these other beings are no longer appropriate when the question is a theological one. God is said to be an infinite being, one who may stand outside of space and time and yet be able to influence what happens inside of space and time. God is also supposed to be all-powerful, all-knowing, and all-good. In all these respects, God is far different from the familiar objects about which we are accustomed to reasoning.

Let's grant that God is supposed to have these special features. Why do they show that reason isn't an appropriate tool to use in thinking about whether God exists? I noted in Chapter 2 and again in Chapter 9 that deductive validity depends on an argument's form, not on its subject matter. If this is right, then deductive reasoning should apply to the question of God's existence in the same way it applies to other questions.

Sometimes it is suggested that God is so shrouded in mystery that we can't hope to understand God by rational inquiry. Maybe this is right—maybe the issues are so mysterious that you'll never be able to see that God exists if you adhere to rational standards of argument. But why does this mean that those standards should be abandoned? Why not take this to mean that you shouldn't believe that God exists, precisely because no good argument can be produced for this conclusion?

I won't pursue these questions any further. Maybe it can be explained why usual standards of evidence and argument should be abandoned when the question is whether God exists. However, I know of no reason to think this.

## FREUD'S PSYCHOLOGICAL EXPLANATION OF THEISM

There is a curious fact here, one that really does require an explanation. If we were talking about virtually any topic from everyday or scientific life, no one would be very attracted by the advice that we should believe something on the basis of no evidence. Yet, when the question is whether God exists, people sometimes drop their critical standards. This isn't true of everyone, of course. It wasn't true of Anselm, Aquinas, Hume, or Paley, for example. Still, the idea of switching from reason to faith has been attractive to many.

There is a psychological question I want to pose here, even though I will not try to answer it. Why are people sometimes inclined to believe without evidence when the question is whether God exists, but are much less willing to take this attitude when the question is a different one?

In his essay, "The Future of an Illusion," Sigmund Freud (1856–1939), the founder of psychoanalysis, gave an answer that is worth pondering. Freud points out that the world is in many ways a frightening place. It is a relatively recent event in human history that people have come to exercise some mastery over nature, and even this recent mastery is enormously incomplete. Although we aren't threatened every day by wild animals, lightning, drought, famine, and flood, each of us has to face the inevitability of our own deaths. In this ultimate sense, we are as helpless as our ancient ancestors. With so much of nature out of our control, beyond our understanding, and threatening our survival, it isn't surprising that human beings should invent myths that provide a different and more appealing picture of our place in the cosmos. Instead of viewing the universe as indifferent to us, impersonal, incomprehensible, and dangerous, we construct a comprehensible picture of forces more powerful than ourselves who take an interest in our fate. Freud's hypothesis was that believing in God persists in human history because of the psychological benefits it provides to believers.

Pascal aimed to provide a prudential argument for believing that God exists. Freud was an atheist, but aimed to provide an explanation for why many people believe God exists. Pascal sought to justify theism; Freud didn't seek to justify it, but to explain it.

## A NEW PRUDENTIAL ARGUMENT

In spite of these differences, we can use some of Freud's observations to formulate a prudential argument for theism that is stronger than the one that Pascal provided. The stumbling block for Pascal was the assumptions he made about what God would be like if he existed. We can avoid these difficult questions about God's nature, however, and focus on something that is more familiar and closer to home—our own minds.

Suppose you are the sort of person who derives comfort and fulfillment from believing in God. Your belief in God provides your life with meaning. It gives you the courage to face adversity. Moreover, let's suppose that without believing in God, you would plunge into despair. You would become depressed, unable to live a productive life.

There are many people in the world who aren't like this. First, there are cheerful agnostics and atheists—people who manage to make a meaningful life for themselves without needing a theological framework. Second, there are people who remain tormented by despair even after they become theists. In both these cases, I'm talking about people whose general outlook is rather independent of the theological opinions they happen to have. Nevertheless, let's suppose there are some people for whom belief in God makes all the difference. Perhaps you are a person of this sort. If so, you can use these psychological facts to formulate a prudential argument for theism:

> If you believe in God, you will lead a happy and productive life.
> If you don't believe in God, you will fall into depression and despair.
> _____
> The way to maximize expected utility is for you to be a theist.

This argument resembles Pascal's in that it ignores whatever evidence there may be concerning whether God exists. But unlike Pascal's argument, this prudential argument doesn't make assumptions about what God would do to theists and atheists. This argument focuses on the psychological consequences of theism, not on speculations about heaven and hell. This argument is more difficult to refute than Pascal's. The major issue it raises is difficult and general. Should we allow prudential reasons to influence what we believe, or should we require that our beliefs be regulated by evidence alone?

## PRAGMATISM

*Pragmatism* is a general philosophical position that has implications about this question. This philosophical idea was developed in the nineteenth and twentieth centuries principally by Charles Sanders Peirce, William James, and John Dewey. In ordinary speech, "being pragmatic" means *being practical*. The philosophical position, however, isn't fully captured by the everyday meaning of the word. Pragmatists say that we should believe propositions that are useful to us. In everyday life, this usually means that we should be attentive to evidence. Suppose you are about to cross the street and want to know whether a bus is coming. The most useful thing to do here is to use your senses (sight, hearing, etc.). It would be silly to engage in wishful thinking—to refuse to consult any evidence and simply believe the proposition you'd like to have be true. In cases of this sort, the prudent thing to do is to attend to evidence. There are cases, however, in which prudential considerations can lead in one direction and evidential considerations in another. My story about the president juggling candy bars provides one example. A prudential argument for theism may provide another.

In *The Will to Believe* (1897), William James (1842–1910) says that a person is entitled to believe in God for purely prudential reasons (of the psychological sort described earlier) if the belief provides a "vital benefit" and if no decision about theism can be made on the basis of the evidence available. But why shouldn't a pragmatist be more liberal? Even if there were *substantial* evidence against there being a God, why shouldn't sufficiently large prudential benefits outweigh the evidential considerations? James's position doesn't provide a blanket justification of theism. As mentioned before, people who could lead happy productive lives without being theists can't claim they *need* to believe in God to avoid falling into despair. Yet, the spirit of pragmatism (if not the letter of James's formulation) seems to sanction believing in God if belief would be useful.

To do justice to the problems pragmatism raises, we would need to consider a variety of cases. If it is a matter of life and death, is it reasonable for someone to be a theist on purely prudential grounds? In less extreme cases, is the comfort provided by theism reason enough to believe in God? This raises complex questions about the attitudes we should take to our lives. Someone might reject pragmatic arguments for theism by saying that they prefer to look the universe square in the face without the benefit of comforting illusions. This person might prefer a life of honest uncertainty and doubt over a life made comfortable by beliefs that have no evidential basis.

The pragmatist says that we should believe what it is useful to believe. An opponent of pragmatism might insist that prudential considerations are always irrelevant; we should believe only those propositions that are well supported by evidence. This is the position that W. K. Clifford defended in his essay "The Ethics of Belief" (1877). He rejected James's position and maintained that "it is wrong always, everywhere, and for anyone, to believe anything upon insufficient evidence." Here is one of the arguments that Clifford gives:

> If I let myself believe anything on insufficient evidence, there may be no great harm done by the mere belief; it may be true after all, or I may never have occasion to exhibit it in outward acts. But I cannot help doing this great wrong towards Man, that I make myself credulous. The danger to society is not merely that it should believe wrong things, though that is great enough, but that it should become credulous and lose the habit of testing things and inquiring into them; for then it must sink back into savagery (p. 79).

Clifford's warning is exaggerated. It just isn't true that society will "sink back into savagery" if you believe a proposition without having any evidence for it. People in non-savage societies have been believing various propositions without having evidence for them for a long time. Clifford is here advancing a *consequentialist* argument; he is suggesting that the action in question is wrong because it has bad consequences. Another possible argument for Clifford's position would be that it is wrong *in itself* to believe upon insufficient evidence, regardless of whether this has good or bad consequences. This raises the question of why it is wrong in itself to so believe.

## Review Questions

1. What is the difference between a prudential reason and an evidential reason for believing something?
2. Can it ever make sense to bet on something that probably won't happen?
3. Given the payoffs Pascal assigns to outcomes, what is the expected value of believing in God? Of not believing?
4. Do people believe what they do because they "decide to believe"? If not, does it follow Pascal's argument is mistaken?
5. How does Pascal's argument depend on a set of auxiliary assumptions (in the sense of Chapter 9) about God's nature?
6. Describe a prudential argument for believing in God that avoids the problem that Pascal's argument confronts.
7. Why did Clifford reject James's pragmatic argument of theism? Evaluate the argument that Clifford presents for his position.

## Problems for Further Thought

1. In Chapter 7, I explained what the Principle of Sufficient Reason is and sketched an argument for why it might be useful to believe the principle even if there is no evidence that it is true. Work out the details of this decision-theoretic argument by constructing a 2-by-2 table for this problem that resembles the one used for Pascal's Wager. Is the argument successful?
2. In Chapter 7, I argued that there is a kind of question (a global question about why the whole history of the universe is as it is) that science cannot answer. Can science answer the question of whether we should accept James's or Clifford's position on the ethics of belief? If so, which scientific theory provides an answer to this question?
3. Ethicists often distinguish duties from superogatory acts. An action is a duty if it is something you must perform; an action is superogatory if it would be a good thing to do, but is not a duty. How does this distinction apply to Clifford's argument against James?

**4.** The Readings for this section of the book include an excerpt from Pascal's *Pensées* in which he states his wager. In fact, he states several wagers, steadily refining the wager he thinks is most relevant. What are these different wagers and how do they differ? Which are more convincing and which are less?

# CHAPTER 11

## *The Argument from Evil*

Most of the arguments considered so far concerning the existence of God have had theistic conclusions. I now turn to an issue many regard as providing an argument for atheism. It sometimes is thought that the fact that there is evil in the world (or that there is so much of it) proves there is no God. An argument to this effect is called an Argument from Evil. I'll consider three forms this argument might take. I think none of these successfully proves there is no God. Then I'll consider a fourth version of the argument from evil; here, instead of trying to prove that there is no God, the argument attempts to show something more modest—that the existence of evil is evidence against the hypothesis that God exists.

### FIRST VERSION OF THE ARGUMENT

The first form of the Argument from Evil is simple:

(1) If God were to exist, then that being would be all-powerful, all-knowing, and all-good (all-PKG, for short).

(2) If an all-PKG being existed, then there would be no evil.

(3) There is evil.

———————

Hence, there is no God.

The argument is deductively valid; convince yourself of this by identifying the argument's logical form.

Sometimes it is said that the first premise is a definition of what we mean by the concept of God. I'll say in a minute why I don't think (1) is a definition. Premise (2) is usually defended as follows. If God is all-good, he wants to prevent evil. If he is all-knowing, he knows the difference between right and wrong and knows how to prevent evil from coming into existence. And if he is all-powerful, he can prevent evil, should he wish to do so. So God, if he is all-PKG, has both the inclination and the ability to prevent evil from occurring.

## TWO KINDS OF EVIL

What does *evil* mean in premise (3)? Discussion of the Argument from Evil usually divides existing evils into two categories. There are the evils that are brought into existence by human actions, and there are the evils that exist because of natural events that aren't under human control. In the first category falls the suffering that human beings inflict on each other; the second category includes the suffering that human beings (and other creatures) experience because of natural disasters, such as earthquakes and plagues.

## POSSIBLE REACTIONS TO THE ARGUMENT

As mentioned before, the argument is valid. Hence, if you wish to reject the conclusion, you must reject one or more of the premises. What options are available?

One option is to deny the existence of evil (premise 3). For example, you could take the view that there really is no difference between right and wrong. This is the idea that the universe is morally neutral and that we human beings impose illusory moral categories upon it. This view about morality will be discussed in the fifth section of the book, especially in Chapters 29 and 30. For now I'll ignore this option. I'll assume that some of the murders, tortures, and other brutalities that have peppered human history really are morally bad. I also will assume that the world would have been a better place if some of the suffering caused by natural disasters hadn't occurred. This assumption—that premise (3) is correct—is shared by many, if not all, religious traditions.

Another option is to reject premise (1). You could interpret the existence of evil as showing merely that if there is a God, then God isn't all-PKG. This strategy grants premises (2) and (3), but then concludes that if God exists, he can't be exactly the way one religious tradition says he is.

The fact that this strategy is available shows, I think, that (1) isn't "true by definition." If the first premise really did define what the term "God" means, then the existence of evil couldn't be explained by rejecting this premise. But this does seem to be a real option. What we need to recognize is that premise (1) doesn't have the same status as the following sentence: "A bachelor is an unmarried man." Suppose we found that a man whom we thought is a bachelor in fact is married. Would this lead us to consider the possibility that maybe bachelors could be married? I think not. Premise (1) embodies one theory about what God's nature is. It is one theory among many possible theories, none of which deserves to be viewed as "true by definition." The ancient Greeks denied that the gods are all-PKG. Manicheanism and Zoroastrianism deny that God is all-powerful. So rejecting premise (1) is an option we need to consider as a way of explaining why evil exists.

## THEODICY AND DEFENSE

One other option remains: reject premise (2). This is the strategy pursued by theists who think premises (1) and (3) are true. If you think God is all-PKG and that evil is a reality, you need to show how God's being all-PKG doesn't imply that there should be no evil in the world.

There are two types of criticism that might be offered of premise (2). You could try to explain why it is false. This is the project known as "theodicy" in traditional Christian theology. Here you try to explain why an all-PKG God would allow evil to exist. Alternatively, there is the more modest criticism in which you try to show that we don't have a good reason to think that the premise is true. Contemporary philosophers of religion use the term "defense" to describe this second type of reply to the Argument from Evil. The distinction that separates theodicy from defense can be seen in the discussion of other arguments for the existence of God. For example, in Chapter 4, we considered an objection to the design argument that maintains that if God built organisms, they would be perfectly adapted to their environments. One way to criticize this argument is to suggest that there is no reason to think that God would have wanted each organism to be perfectly adapted. A more ambitious criticism would be the attempt to demonstrate what God's motives would be.

In any event, I think there is some plausibility in rejecting premise (2). Notice that premise (2) makes an extreme claim. It says that if an all-PKG God existed, there would exist not even a tiny amount of evil in the world.

## SOUL-BUILDING EVILS

Traditional theodicy has claimed that some evils have the property of being "soul-building." Soul-building evils are the ones that make us better people. Living through adversity strengthens our character; it makes us better people than we would have been if we had never suffered hardship.

I want to be careful about what I'm conceding here. I grant that *some* evils are soul-building. But I think it is a gross exaggeration to say this of *all* the evils that human beings have experienced. Sometimes suffering doesn't make the victim stronger; sometimes suffering destroys people. And even when people survive brutal tortures, do we really think that they are always better people for it? Sometimes they survive as mere shells. Even when torture victims in some sense are made stronger by their ordeals, do we still want to say that the experience has been worth it? If you think it was worthwhile for *them,* would *you* choose to undergo the torture yourself? There are some "strengths" that aren't worth having because they cost too much to acquire.

Sometimes it is suggested that when people are destroyed by the sufferings they endure, the souls of other people are strengthened by watching this happen. I think this is sometimes true, but it is often false. Sometimes the only effect on witnesses is that they are sickened by having to watch events they know full well are horrible. Sometimes people who witness the suffering of others react with callousness and indifference, and some suffering occurs in private. In these cases, there is no audience whose souls can be made stronger by watching the spectacle. Just as suffering often doesn't make the sufferer a better person, it also is true that one person's suffering often fails to improve the characters of witnesses. So in granting that *some* suffering is soul-building, I'm granting something about a rather small portion of the huge mountain of agony the human race has experienced.

Is the fact that some evils are soul-building enough to refute premise (2)? This isn't so clear. If it is desirable that we be strong of heart, why couldn't God have made us this way without us having to experience evil? The need for soul-building experiences is sometimes defended by an analogy concerning the way a benevolent parent treats a child. If you really care about your children, you won't shield them from all adversity. There are some experiences that involve pain and suffering that children need to have if they are to mature into morally sensitive and autonomous adults. If your child is being picked on by a bully at school, you may decide she has to tough it out for herself. Intervening would save her a few scrapes and bruises *now*, but you might decide as a parent that this wouldn't be in her long-term best interests.

You, as a parent, have the goal of seeing your children develop in a certain way. You choose not to prevent some bad things from happening to your child because you recognize that there is no other way for her to mature as you intend. Suppose, however, that you could have your child become a virtuous adult without her having to be kicked around by the bully. In this case, why would you allow the bully to continue to harass your child? A parent might allow soul-building evils to befall a child when there is no other way to have the child's soul grow strong, but the limitations that might justify a parent's choice aren't supposed to be present where God is concerned. If God is all-PKG, why couldn't he simply make us with strong souls? Defenders of the soul-building idea reply that God wants us to be able to be proud of our own achievements. If we suffer through adversity, we get credit for the strong souls that result. If, however, God simply gave us strong souls *gratis,* we would deserve no credit. We couldn't be proud of ourselves; at best, we would simply be grateful to a benevolent deity. To evaluate this suggestion, we must ask why it is so important that we be able to take credit for having strong characters. Why is it better to experience an evil and then get credit for having endured it? Why is this better than having a strong character because God made us that way from the start? I raise this question, but won't attempt to answer it. I'll concede for now that an all-PKG God would allow at least some evils to exist. Some soul-building evils are of this sort. In other words, I'll concede that premise (2) is false.

Does this mean there is no problem of evil—that the existence of evil poses no difficulty for the conception of God as an all-PKG being? I think not. The soul-building evils an all-PKG God would allow us to experience are a tiny portion of the evils we need to explain. What needs to be explained isn't why there is some evil *rather than none at all.* The deeper problem is to explain why there is so much evil, *rather than one ounce less.*

## SECOND VERSION OF THE ARGUMENT

So the second Argument from Evil is more difficult to refute. It takes the following form:

(1) If God were to exist, then that being would be all-PKG.
(4) If an all-PKG being existed, then the amount of evil would not exceed a soul-building minimum.

(5)  The amount of evil does exceed a soul-building minimum.

———————————

Hence, there is no God.

By "soul-building minimum," I mean the minimum amount of evil that would suffice to make us have strength of character. This argument is valid. Hence, if the conclusion is false, at least one of the premises must be false. The project of theodicy is to show that premise (4) is mistaken.


## FREE WILL

Is there a reason that an all-PKG being might have for permitting evils to exist that go beyond the soul-building minimum? It sometimes is suggested that this reason is to be found in the idea of *free will*. God made us free; this means it is up to us whether we do good or do evil. A consequence of this freedom is that there is more evil than would be strictly necessary for soul-building.

There is a question here that we will examine in detail in the section of this book on philosophy of mind. Why couldn't God have made us free agents who always freely choose to do what is right? Why assume that free people must sometimes perform evil actions? If a sinner can have free will, why can't a saint? After all, God is supposed to be a free being who never does evil things. This seems to show that being free and always doing what's right are not incompatible. Even if being free implies that you *could* do evil things, why does freedom imply that you *actually* choose to do so?

However, let's now set this point aside and assume, for the sake of argument, that human freedom requires that people sometimes produce evil and that this evil exceeds the minimum that would exist strictly from the point of view of soul-building. This means that premise (4) in the second argument is mistaken. But again, I want to emphasize that this doesn't fully solve the problem of evil. The problem is to account for the quantity of evil that exists. Let's grant that some evil must exist for soul-building and some more evil will be a consequence of human freedom. Does this explain the quantity of evil that the world contains?


## EXAMPLES, AND A THIRD VERSION OF THE ARGUMENT

Let's single out some horrendous evil that has befallen the human race. Think of all the suffering Hitler caused. How could an all-PKG God have allowed this to happen? Is the answer that God gave each of us free will? I think this appeal to the importance of human freedom doesn't begin to address the difficulty. Why didn't God intervene in human affairs on those rare occasions on which it would have made a dramatic difference? When the sperm and egg came together that produced Hitler, why didn't God prevent that fertilization event from happening? To do so would still have allowed human beings to be free; in addition, that brief intervention would allow there to be soul-building evils aplenty. Here I'm considering a minor foray into human affairs, not some major restructuring of human nature. Suppose that if Hitler had never existed, many of the terrible things he did would never have happened. The world would have been a much better place. Most theists would agree with this. So why didn't God influence the course of human history for the better? What you must see here is that appeals to soul-building and to freedom don't provide an answer. Causing Hitler to never be born would not have robbed his parents of free will.

Another way to make this point is to consider horrendous evils that come into existence for reasons having nothing to do with human action. Consider the bubonic plague. If God had prevented that disease from existing, much suffering and death would have been avoided. To intervene in the lives of the relevant microorganisms doesn't rob them of free will, since they don't have wills (minds) to begin with. Also, the amount of suffering that occurred because of the plague far exceeded what could be explained by the goal of soul-building. About one-third of the European population died agonizing deaths from bubonic plague. Would our souls have been less strong if some smaller percentage had perished?

These considerations lead to a third version of the Argument from Evil:

(1)  If God were to exist, then that being would be all-PKG.

(6)  If an all-PKG being existed, then there would be no more evil than the minimum required for soul-building and as a consequence of human freedom.

(7)  The quantity of evil found in human history exceeds the minimum required for soul-building and as a consequence of human freedom.

---

Hence, there is no God.

## A CRITICISM OF THE ARGUMENT

How might this third argument be criticized? If there is a God, and if premises (1) and (7) are true, what grounds can there be for rejecting premise (6)? The project of *theodicy* needs to produce a reason for thinking that (6) is false. The more modest project of *defense* merely has to show that we don't have a good reason to think that (6) is true. Whereas soul-building and free will were just presented in the context of a theodicy, I'll now shift gears and formulate a reply to this last argument that has the character of a defense.

Premise (6), like premises (2) and (4) in the preceding arguments, attempts to specify an upper bound on the amount of evil that an all-PKG God would allow to exist. But why think that we mere humans have the ability to figure this out? After all, God, if he exists, is vastly more intelligent than we are. It therefore is entirely possible that his plan for the world contains elements that we cannot understand or even imagine. Perhaps God allowed evils into the world beyond those required for soul-building and as a consequence of human freedom because these additional evils are required to obtain some greater good of which we are unaware. We need to be careful in how we formulate this criticism of the Argument from Evil. I am not asserting that premise (6) is false. I am giving a reason for thinking that we don't know that (6) is true. All of the versions of the Argument from Evil that I have surveyed attempt to circumscribe exactly how much evil there should be if an all-PKG being existed. To do this requires that we know a lot about what an all-PKG being would do. To the degree that we lack knowledge of what God's plan would be if he existed, we also lack the sort of knowledge that is needed for these arguments for atheism to succeed.

## TESTABILITY, AGAIN

In Chapters 6 and 9, I discussed whether the existence of God is testable. The reply I just formulated to the Argument from Evil raises the same issue. How much evil should we expect there to be if there were a God? Atheists who advance the Argument from Evil just described think they can answer this question. However, if we can't answer this question, we can't test the proposition that God exists by examining how much evil there is in the world.

## ANOTHER KIND OF ARGUMENT—THE EVIDENTIAL ARGUMENT FROM EVIIL

The arguments from evil formulated so far are deductively valid; the goal is to prove that an all-PKG God cannot exist, given this or that fact about the evils that exist. But there is reason to think that no such deductive argument can be made to work. Such an argument would have the following form:

> If an all-PKG God exists, then evils of kind X will not exist.
> Evils of kind X do exist.
> _____
> No all-PKG God exists.

This argument is deductively valid (what is its logical form?). The problem with this kind of argument is that it is hard to show that the first premise is true. The theist has the option of asserting that human beings are in no position to understand why an all-PKG God would allow evils of kind X to exist. However, the fact that we can't understand why these evils exist can hardly be said to entail that there is no such being.

There is a more modest formulation of the argument from evil that is worth considering. It is called the evidential argument from evil (see W. Rowe's article, "The Problem of Evil and Some Varieties of Atheism," *American Philosophical Quarterly* [1979] 16: 335–341). The goal here is merely to show that this or that kind of evil is evidence against the hypothesis that an all-PKG being exists; the argument does not claim that these evils prove that no such being exists. We can use the Surprise

Principle to formulate the argument. Let E be a proposition that describes in some detail the kinds and quantities of evil that exist:

> If an all-PKG God existed, you would expect E not to be true.
> If an all-PKG God did not exist, you would expect E to be true.
> The Surprise Principle.
> _____
>
> E is strong evidence against there being an all-PKG being.

The Surprise Principle describes what "strong" evidence means. It can be reformulated to define what evidence (strong or weak) means, and this allows us to construct an even more modest version of the evidential argument from evil:

> The truth of proposition E is more surprising if an all-PKG God exists than if there is no such being.
> The Modest Surprise Principle.
> _____
>
> E is evidence against there being an all-PKG being.

As an exercise, write down what the Modest Surprise Principle says.

    Is it true that the kinds and quantities of evil that exist are evidence against the existence of an all-PKG God? If not, what could count as evidence against this hypothesis?

---

## Review Questions

1. Consider the proposition that God is all-powerful, all-knowing, and all-good. Should we regard this proposition as a definition of what the word "God" means? If it isn't a definition, does this mean that the proposition is false?
2. It sometimes is suggested that imperfections must exist if human beings are to be able to form the idea of God (a perfect being). Is this a solution to the problem of evil?
3. Does the fact that some evils are soul-building while others are consequences of human freedom solve the problem of evil?
4. What is the difference between theodicy and defense as criticisms of the Argument from Evil? Illustrate this distinction by constructing an argument that has nothing to do with the existence of God.
5. A criticism was presented of the third Argument from Evil. The argument is valid. And the criticism did not claim that any of the premises are false. What, then, is the criticism?
6. What is the evidential argument from evil? Is it more successful than the arguments that attempt to prove that there is no God?

## Problems for Further Thought

1. The appeal to free will, which is part of the project of theodicy, includes the claim that (a) God is omnipotent (all-powerful) and the claim that (b) God cannot give us free will without there also being evil in the world. Are (a) and (b) compatible? How should the concept of "omnipotence" be understood?

2. Are there reasons beyond the goal of soul-building and the goal of giving us free will that an all-PKG God would have for allowing evil to exist? If so, would that solve the problem of evil?

3. Some people interpret the Bible as providing an adequate theodicy. According to their interpretation, Adam and Eve freely chose to sin in the Garden of Eden. When they did so, this effectively unleashed all of the rest of the evils that we find in the world. This theodicy apparently can explain *all* of the evil that there is, not just the evils that can be attributed to soul-building and to free will. Is this theodicy an adequate reply to the Argument from Evil?

4. Here's a question about the free will solution to the problem of evil. If God knows in advance what we'll do (which he must, if he is all-knowing), how can it be true that we have free will? This is question we'll address in Part IV.

# Readings

SAINT THOMAS AQUINAS

## Five Ways to Prove That God Exists

In this selection from **Summa Theologica** (Part 1, Question 2, Article 3), Saint Thomas Aquinas provides five proofs of the existence of God. In each, an obvious and uncontroversial observation is the starting premise.

The existence of God can be proved in five ways.

The first and more manifest way is the argument from motion. It is certain, and evident to our senses, that in the world some things are in motion. Now whatever is moved is moved by another, for nothing can be moved except it is in potentiality to that towards which it is moved; whereas a thing moves inasmuch as it is in act. For motion is nothing else than the reduction of something from potentiality to actuality. But nothing can be reduced from potentiality to actuality, except by something in a state of actuality. Thus that which is actually hot, as fire, makes wood, which is potentially hot, to be actually hot, and thereby moves and changes it. Now it is not possible that the same thing should be at once in actuality and potentiality in the same respect, but only in different respects. For what is actually hot cannot simultaneously be potentially hot; but it is simultaneously potentially cold. It is therefore impossible that in the same respect and in the same way a thing should be both mover and moved; *i.e.,* that it should move itself. Therefore, whatever is moved must be moved by another. If that by which it is moved be itself moved, then this also must needs be moved by another, and that by another again. But this cannot go on to infinity, because then there would be no first mover, and, consequently, no other mover, seeing that subsequent movers move only inasmuch as they are moved by the first mover; as the staff moves only because it is moved by the hand. Therefore it is necessary to arrive at a first mover, moved by no other; and this everyone understands to be God.

The second way is from the nature of efficient cause. In the world of sensible things we find there is an order of efficient causes. There is no case known (neither is it, indeed, possible) in which a thing is found to be the efficient cause of itself; for so it would be prior to itself, which is impossible. Now in efficient causes it is not possible to go on to infinity, because in all efficient causes following in order, the first is the cause of the intermediate cause, and the intermediate is the cause of the ultimate cause, whether the intermediate cause be several, or one only. Now to take away the cause is to take away the effect. Therefore, if there be no first cause among efficient causes, there will be no ultimate, nor any intermediate, cause. But if in efficient causes it is possible to go on to infinity, there will be no first efficient cause, neither will there be an ultimate effect, nor any intermediate efficient causes; all of which is plainly false. Therefore it is necessary to admit a first efficient cause, to which everyone gives the name of God.

The third way is taken from possibility and necessity, and runs thus. We find in nature things that are possible to be and not to be, since they are found to be generated, and to be corrupted, and consequently, it is possible for them to be and not to be. But it is impossible for these always to exist, for that which can not-be at some time is not. Therefore, if everything can not-be, then at one time there was nothing in existence. Now if this were true, even now there would be nothing in existence, because that which does not exist begins to exist only through something already existing. Therefore, if at one time nothing was in existence, it would have been impossible for anything to have begun to exist; and thus even now nothing would be in existence—which is absurd. Therefore, not all beings are merely possible, but there must exist something the existence of which is necessary. But every necessary thing either has its necessity caused by another, or not. Now it is impossible to go on to infinity in necessary things which have their necessity caused by another, as has been already proved in regard to efficient causes. Therefore we cannot but admit the existence of some being having of itself its own necessity, and not receiving it from another, but rather causing in others their necessity. This all men speak of as God.

The fourth way is taken from the gradation to be found in things. Among beings there are some more and some less good, true, noble, and the like. But *more* and *less* are predicated of different things according as they resemble in their different ways something which is the maximum, as a thing is said to be hotter according as it more nearly resembles that which is hottest; so that there is something which is truest, something best, something noblest, and, consequently, something which is most being, for those things that are greatest in truth are greatest in being, as it is written in *Metaphysics* II [a work of Aristotle]. Now the maximum in any genus is the cause of all in that genus, as fire, which is the maximum of heat, is the cause of all hot things, as is said in the same book. Therefore there must also be something which is to all beings the cause of their being, goodness, and every other perfection; and this we call God.

The fifth way is taken from the governance of the world. We see that things which lack knowledge, such as natural bodies, act for an end, and this is evident from their acting always, or nearly always, in the same way, so as to obtain the best result. Hence it is plain that they achieve their end, not fortuitously, but designedly. Now whatever lacks knowledge cannot move towards an end, unless it be directed by some being endowed with knowledge and intelligence; as the arrow is directed by the archer. Therefore some intelligent being exists by whom all natural things are directed to their end; and this being we call God.

## WILLIAM PALEY

# The Design Argument

In this selection from his ***Natural Theology*** (1836 edition), William Paley elaborates an argument for the existence of God that traces back at least to the last of Aquinas's five ways. His discussion of how one interprets a watch found on a heath is one of the most famous analogies proposed in the history of philosophy. The term "natural theology" means that the author attempts to establish the existence and nature of God by the same methods used in the natural sciences—observation and reasoning.

In crossing a heath, suppose I pitched my foot against a stone, and were asked how the stone came to be there: I might possibly answer, that for any thing I knew to the contrary, it had laid there for ever: nor would it perhaps be very easy to shew the absurdity of this answer. But suppose I had found a *watch* upon the ground, and it should be inquired how the watch happened to be in that place; I should hardly think of the answer which I had before given, that, for any thing I knew, the watch might have always been there. Yet why should not this answer serve for the watch as well as for the stone? why is it not as admissible in the second case, as in the first? For this reason, and for no other, viz, that, when we come to inspect the watch, we perceive (what we could not discover in the stone) that its several parts are framed and put together for a purpose, e.g. that they are so formed and adjusted as to produce motion, and that motion so regulated as to point out the hour of the day; that, if the different parts had been differently shaped from what they are, of a different size from what they are, or placed after any other manner, or in any other order, than that in which they are placed, either no motion at all would have been carried on in the machine, or none that would have answered the use that is now served by it. To reckon up a few of the plainest of these parts, and of their offices, all tending to one result:—We see a cylindrical box containing a coiled elastic spring, which, by its endeavor to relax itself, turns round the box. We next

William Paley, "The Design Argument," from *Natural Theology,* 1836.

observe a flexible chain (artificially wrought for the sake of flexure), communicating the action of the spring from the box to the fusee. We then find a series of wheels, the teeth of which catch in, and apply to each other, conducting the motion from the fusee to the balance, and from the balance to the pointer; and at the same time by the size and shape of those wheels so regulating that motion, as to terminate in causing an index, by an equable and measured progression, to pass over a given space in a given time. We take notice that the wheels are made of brass in order to keep them from rust; the springs of steel, no other metal being so elastic; that over the face of the watch there is placed a glass, a material employed in no other part of the work, but in the room of which, if there had been any other than a transparent substance, the hour could not be seen without opening the case. This mechanism being observed (it requires indeed an examination of the instrument, and perhaps some previous knowledge of the subject, to perceive and understand it; but being once, as we have said, observed and understood), the inference, we think, is inevitable, that the watch must have had a maker; that there must have existed, at some time, and at some place or other, an artificer or artificers, who formed it for the purpose which we find it actually to answer; who comprehended its construction and designed its use.

I. Nor would it, I apprehend, weaken the conclusion that we had never seen a watch made—that we had never known an artist capable of making one—that we were altogether incapable of executing such a piece of workmanship ourselves, or of understanding in what manner it was performed; all this being no more than what is true of some exquisite remains of ancient art, of some lost arts, and, to the generality of mankind, of the more curious productions of modern manufacture. Does one man in a million know how oval frames are turned? Ignorance of this kind exalts our opinion of the unseen and unknown artist's skill, if he be unseen and unknown, but raises no doubt in our minds of the existence and agency of such an artist, at some former time and in some place or other. Nor can I perceive that it varies at all the inference, whether the question arise concerning a human agent or concerning an agent of a different species, or an agent possessing in some respects a different nature.

II. Neither, secondly, would it invalidate our conclusion, that the watch sometimes went wrong, or that it seldom went exactly right. The purpose of the machinery, the design, and the designer might be evident, in whatever way we accounted for the irregularity of the movement, or whether we could account for it or not. It is not necessary that a machine be perfect, in order to show with what design it was made: still less necessary, where the only question is whether it were made with any design at all.

III. Nor, thirdly, would it bring any uncertainty into the argument, if there were a few parts of the watch concerning which we could not discover or had not yet discovered in what manner they conduced to the general effect; or even some parts, concerning which we could not ascertain whether they conduced to that effect in any manner whatever. For, as to the first branch of the case, if by the loss, or disorder, or decay of the parts in question, the movement of the watch were found in fact to be stopped, or disturbed, or retarded, no doubt would remain in our minds as to the utility or intention of these parts, although we should be unable to investigate the manner according to which, or the connection by which, the ultimate effect depended upon their action or assistance; and the more complex the machine, the more likely is this obscurity to arise. Then, as to the second thing supposed, namely, that there were parts which might be spared without prejudice to the movement of the watch, and that we had proved this by experiment, these superfluous parts, even if we were completely assured that they were such, would not vacate the reasoning which we had instituted concerning other parts. The indication of contrivance remained, with respect to them, nearly as it was before.

IV. Nor, fourthly, would any man in his senses think the existence of the watch with its various machinery accounted for, by being told that it was one out of possible combinations of material forms; that whatever he had found in the place where he found the watch, must have contained some internal configuration or other; and that this configuration might be the structure now exhibited; namely, of the works of a watch, as well as a different structure.

V. Nor, fifthly, would it yield his inquiry more satisfaction, to be answered that there existed in things a principle of order, which had disposed the parts of the watch into their present form and situation. He never knew a watch made by the principle of order; nor can he even form to himself an idea of what is meant by a principle of order, distinct from the intelligence of the watchmaker.

VI. Sixthly, he would be surprised to hear that the mechanism of the watch was no proof of contrivance, only a motive to induce the mind to think so.

VII. And not less surprised to be informed, that the watch in his hand was nothing more than the result of the laws of metallic nature. It is a perversion of language to assign any law as the efficient, operative cause of any thing. A law presupposes an agent; for it is only the mode according to which an agent proceeds: it implies a power; for it is the order according to which that power acts. Without this agent, without this power, which are both distinct from itself, the *law* does nothing, is nothing. The expression, "the law of metallic nature," may sound strange and harsh to a philosophic ear; but it seems quite as justifiable as some others which are more familiar to him, such as "the law of vegetable nature," "the law of animal nature," or, indeed, as "the law of nature" in general, when assigned as the cause of phenomena, in exclusion of agency and power, or when it is substituted into the place of these.

VIII. Neither, lastly, would our observer be driven out of his conclusion or from his confidence in its truth, by being told that he knew nothing at all about the matter. He knows enough for his argument; he knows the utility of the end; he knows the subserviency and adaptation of the means to the end. These points being known, his ignorance of other points, his doubts concerning other points, affect not the certainty of his reasoning. The consciousness of knowing little need not beget a distrust of that which he does know.

# DAVID HUME

# Critique of the Design Argument

In this selection from his ***Dialogues Concerning Natural Religion*** (1779), Hume describes a conversation between Cleanthes, Demea, and Philo. Hume did not publish this work during his lifetime, probably because he was apprehensive about what the public reaction would be.

Not to lose any time in circumlocutions, said Cleanthes, addressing himself to Demea, much less in replying to the pious declamations of Philo, I shall briefly explain how I conceive this matter. Look round the world: Contemplate the whole and every part of it: You will find it to be nothing but one great machine, subdivided into an infinite number of lesser machines, which again admit of subdivisions to a degree beyond what human senses and faculties can trace and explain. All these various machines, and even their most minute parts, are adjusted to each other with an accuracy which ravishes into admiration all men who have ever contemplated them. The curious adapting of means to ends, throughout all nature, resembles exactly, though it much exceeds, the productions of human contrivance—of human design, thought, wisdom, and intelligence. Since therefore the effects resemble each other, we are led to infer, by all the rules of analogy, that the causes also resemble, and that the Author of Nature is somewhat similar to the mind of man, though possessed of much larger faculties, proportioned to the grandeur of the work which he has executed. By this argument *a posteriori*, and by this argument alone, do we prove at once the existence of a Deity and his similarity to human mind and intelligence.

I shall be so free, Cleanthes, said Demea, as to tell you that from the beginning I could not approve of your conclusion concerning the similarity of the Deity to men, still less can I approve of the mediums by which you endeavor to establish it. What! No demonstration of the Being of God! No abstract arguments! No proofs *a priori*! Are these which have hitherto been so much insisted on by philosophers all fallacy, all sophism? Can we reach no farther in this subject than experience and probability? I will say not that this is betraying the cause of a Deity; but surely, by this affected candor, you give advantages to atheists which they never could obtain by the mere dint of argument and reasoning.

What I chiefly scruple in this subject, said Philo, is not so much that all religious arguments are by Cleanthes reduced to experience, as that they appear not to be even the most certain and irrefragable of that inferior kind. That a stone will fall, that fire will burn, that the earth has solidity, we have observed a thousand and a thousand times; and when any new instance of this nature is presented, we draw without hesitation the accustomed inference. The exact similarity of the cases gives us a perfect assurance of a similar event, and a stronger evidence is never desired nor sought after. But wherever you depart, in

David Hume, "Critique of the Design Argument," from *Dialogues Concerning Natural Religion*, edited by Norman Kemp Smith (Walton-on-Thames, England: Thomas Nelson and Sons Ltd., 1947).

the least, from the similarity of the cases, you diminish proportionably the evidence; and may at last bring it to a very weak *analogy,* which is confessedly liable to error and uncertainty. After having experienced the circulation of the blood in human creatures, we make no doubt that it takes place in Titius and Maevius; but from its circulation in frogs and fishes it is only a presumption, though a strong one, from analogy that it takes place in men and other animals. The analogical reasoning is much weaker when we infer the circulation of the sap in vegetables from our experience that the blood circulates in animals; and those who hastily followed that imperfect analogy are found, by more accurate experiments, to have been mistaken.

If we see a house, Cleanthes, we conclude, with the greatest certainty, that it had an architect or builder because this is precisely that species of effect which we have experienced to proceed from that species of cause. But surely you will not affirm that the universe bears such a resemblance to a house that we can with the same certainty infer a similar cause, or that the analogy is here entire and perfect. The dissimilitude is so striking that the utmost you can here pretend to is a guess, a conjecture, a presumption concerning a similar cause; and how that pretension will be received in the world, I leave you to consider.

It would surely be very ill received, replied Cleanthes; and I should be deservedly blamed and detested did I allow that the proofs of a Deity amounted to no more than a guess or conjecture. But is the whole adjustment of means to ends in a house and in the universe so slight a resemblance? the economy of final causes? the order, proportion, and arrangement of every part? Steps of a stair are plainly contrived that human legs may use them in mounting; and this inference is certain and infallible. Human legs are also contrived for walking and mounting; and this inference, I allow, is not altogether so certain because of the dissimilarity which you remark; but does it, therefore, deserve the name only of presumption or conjecture?

Good God! cried Demea, interrupting him, where are we? Zealous defenders of religion allow that the proofs of a Deity fall short of perfect evidence! And you, Philo, on whose assistance I depended in proving the adorable mysteriousness of the Divine Nature, do you assent to all these extravagant opinions of Cleanthes? For what other name can I give them? or, why spare my censure when such principles are advanced, supported by such an authority, before so young a man as Pamphilus?

You seem not to apprehend, replied Philo, that I argue with Cleanthes in his own way, and, by showing him the dangerous consequences of his tenets, hope at last to reduce him to our opinion. But what sticks most with you, I observe, is the representation which Cleanthes has made of the argument *a posteriori;* and, finding that that argument is likely to escape your hold and vanish into air, you think it so disguised that you can scarcely believe it to be set in its true light. Now, however much I may dissent, in other respects, from the dangerous principle of Cleanthes, I must allow that he has fairly represented that argument, and I shall endeavor so to state the matter to you that you will entertain no further scruples with regard to it.

Were a man to abstract from everything which he knows or has seen, he would be altogether incapable, merely from his own ideas, to determine what kind of scene the universe must be, or to give the preference to one state or situation of things above another. For as nothing which he clearly conceives could be esteemed impossible or implying a contradiction, every chimera of his fancy would be upon an equal footing; nor could he assign just reason why he adheres to one idea or system, and rejects the others which are equally possible.

Again, after he opens his eyes and contemplates the world as it really is, it would be impossible for him at first to assign the cause of any one event, much less the whole of things, or of the universe. He might set his fancy a rambling, and she might bring him in an infinite variety of reports and representations. These would all be possible; but, being all equally possible, he would never of himself give a satisfactory account for his preferring one of them to the rest. Experience alone can point out to him the true cause of any phenomenon.

Now, according to this method of reasoning, Demea, it follows (and is, indeed, tacitly allowed by Cleanthes himself) that order, arrangement, or the adjustment of final causes, is not of itself any proof of design, but only so far as it has been experienced to proceed from that principle. For aught we can know *a priori*, matter may contain the source or spring of order originally within itself, as well as mind does; and there is no more difficulty in conceiving that the several elements, from an internal unknown cause, may fall into the most exquisite arrangement, than to conceive that their ideas, in the great universal mind, from a like internal unknown cause, fall into that arrangement. The equal possibility of both these suppositions is allowed. But, by experience, we find (according to Cleanthes) that there is a difference between them. Throw several pieces of steel together, without shape or form they will never arrange themselves so as to compose a watch. Stone and mortar and wood, without an architect, never erect a house. But the ideas in a human mind, we see, by an unknown, inexplicable economy, arrange themselves so as to form the plan of a watch or house. Experience, therefore, proves that there is an original principle of order in mind, not in matter. From similar effects we infer similar causes. The adjustment of means to ends is alike in the universe, as in a machine of human contrivance. The causes, therefore, must be resembling.

I was from the beginning scandalized, I must own, with this resemblance which is asserted between the Deity and human creatures, and must conceive it to imply such a degradation of the Supreme Being as no sound theist could endure. With your assistance, therefore, Demea, I shall endeavor to defend what you justly call the adorable mysteriousness of the Divine nature, and shall refute this reasoning of Cleanthes, provided he allows that I have made a fair representation of it.

When Cleanthes had assented, Philo, after a short pause, proceeded in the following manner.

That all inferences, Cleanthes, concerning fact are founded on experience, and that all experimental reasonings are founded on the supposition that similar causes prove similar effects, and similar effects similar causes, I shall not at present much dispute with you. But observe, I entreat you, with what extreme caution all just reasoners proceed in the transferring of experiments to similar cases. Unless the cases be exactly similar, they repose no perfect confidence in applying their past observation to any particular phenomenon. Every alteration of circumstances occasions a doubt concerning the event; and it requires new experiments to prove certainly that the new circumstances are of no moment or importance. A change in bulk, situation, arrangement, age, disposition of the air, or surrounding bodies—any of these particulars may be attended with the most unexpected consequences. And unless the objects be quite familiar to us, it is the highest temerity to expect with assurance, after any of these changes, an event similar to that which before fell under our observation. The slow and deliberate steps of philosophers here, if anywhere, are distinguished from the precipitate march of the vulgar, who, hurried on by the smallest similitude, are incapable of all discernment or consideration.

But you can think, Cleanthes, that your usual phlegm and philosophy have been preserved in so wide a step as you have taken when you compared to the universe houses, ships, furniture, machines; and, from their similarity in some circumstances, inferred a similarity in their causes? Thought, design, intelligence, such as we discover in men and other animals, is no more than one of the springs and principles of the universe, as well as heat or cold, attraction or repulsion, and a hundred others which fall under daily observation. It is an active cause by which some particular parts of nature, we find, produce alterations on other parts. But can a conclusion, with any propriety, be transferred from parts to the whole? Does not the great disproportion bar all comparison and inference? From observing the growth of a hair, can we learn anything concerning the generation of a man? Would the manner of a leaf's blowing, even though perfectly known, afford us any instruction concerning the vegetation of a tree?

But allowing that we were to take the *operations* of one part of nature upon another for the foundation of our judgment concerning the *origin* of the whole (which never can be admitted), yet why select so minute, so weak, so bounded a principle as the reason and design of animals is found to be upon this planet? What peculiar privilege has this little agitation of the brain which we call *thought,* that we must thus make it the model of the whole universe? Our partiality in our own favor does indeed present it on all occasions, but sound philosophy ought carefully to guard against so natural an illusion.

So far from admitting, continued Philo, that the operations of a part can afford us any just conclusion concerning the origin of the whole, I will not allow any one part to form a rule for another part if the latter be very remote from the former. Is there any reasonable ground to conclude that the inhabitants of other planets possess thought, intelligence, reason, or anything similar to these faculties in men? When nature has so extremely diversified her manner of operation in this small globe, can we imagine that she incessantly copies herself throughout so immense a universe? And if thought, as we may well suppose, be confined merely to this narrow corner and has even there so limited a sphere of action, with what propriety can we assign it for the original cause of all things? The narrow views of a peasant who makes his domestic economy the rule for the government of kingdoms is in comparison a pardonable sophism.

But were we ever so much assured that a thought and reason resembling the human were to be found throughout the whole universe, and were its activity elsewhere vastly greater and more commanding than it appears in this globe; yet I cannot see why the operations of a world constituted, arranged, adjusted, can with any propriety be extended to a world which is in its embryo-state, and is advancing towards that constitution and arrangement. By observation we know somewhat of the economy, action, and nourishment of a finished animal; but we must transfer with great caution that observation to the growth of a foetus in the womb, and still more to the formation of an animalcule in the loins of its male parent. Nature, we find, even from our limited experience, possesses an infinite number of springs and principles which incessantly discover themselves on every change of her position and situation. And what new and unknown principles would actuate her in so new and unknown a situation as that of the formation of a universe, we cannot, without the utmost temerity, pretend to determine.

A very small part of this great system, during a very short time, is very imperfectly discovered to us; and do we thence pronounce decisively concerning the origin of the whole?

Admirable conclusion! Stone, wood, brick, iron, brass, have not, at this time, in this minute globe of earth, an order or arrangement without human art and contrivance; therefore, the universe could not originally attain its order and arrangement without something similar to human art. But is a part of nature a rule for another part very wide of the former? Is it a rule for the whole? Is a very small part a rule for the universe? Is nature in one situation a certain rule for nature in another situation vastly different from the former?

And can you blame me, Cleanthes, if I here imitate the prudent reserve of Simonides, who, according to the noted story, being asked by Hiero, *What God was?* desired a day to think of it, and then two days more; and after that manner continually prolonged the term, without ever bringing in his definition or description? Could you even blame me if I had answered, at first, *that I did not know,* and was sensible that this subject lay vastly beyond the reach of my faculties? You might cry out sceptic and railer, as much as you pleased; but, having found in so many other subjects much more familiar the imperfections and even contradictions of human reason, I never should expect any success from its feeble conjectures in a subject so sublime and so remote from the sphere of our observation. When two *species* of objects have always been observed to be conjoined together, I can *infer,* by custom, the existence of one wherever I *see* the existence of the other; and this I call an argument from experience. But how this argument can have place where the objects, as in the present case, are single, individual, without parallel or specific resemblance, may be difficult to explain. And will any man tell me with a serious countenance that an orderly universe must arise from some thought and art like the human because we have experience of it? To ascertain this reasoning it were requisite that we had experience of the origin of the worlds; and it is not sufficient, surely, that we have seen ships and cities arise from human art and contrivance....

Philo was proceeding in this vehement manner, somewhat between jest and earnest, as it appeared to me, when he observed some signs of impatience in Cleanthes, and then immediately stopped short. What I had to suggest, said Cleanthes, is only that you would not abuse terms, or make use of popular expressions to subvert philosophical reasonings. You know that the vulgar often distinguish reason from experience, even where the question relates only to matter of fact and existence, though it is found, where that *reason* is properly analyzed, that it is nothing but a species of experience. To prove by experience the origin of the universe from mind is not more contrary to common speech than to prove the motion of the earth from the same principle. And a caviller might raise all the same objections to the Copernican system which you have urged against my reasonings. Have you other earths, might he say, which you have seen to move?

Yes! cried Philo, interrupting him, we have other earths. Is not the moon another earth, which we see to turn round its center? Is not Venus another earth, where we observe the same phenomenon? Are not the revolutions of the sun also a confirmation, from analogy, of the same theory? All the planets, are they not earths which revolve about the sun? Are not the satellites moons which move round Jupiter and Saturn, and along with these primary planets round the sun? These analogies and resemblances, with others which I have not mentioned, are the sole proofs of the Copernican system; and to you it belongs to consider whether you have any analogies of the same kind to support your theory.

In reality, Cleanthes, continued he, the modern system of astronomy is now so much received by all inquirers, and has become so essential a part even of our earliest education, that we are not commonly very scrupulous in examining the reasons upon which it is founded. It is now become a matter of mere curiosity to study the first writers on that subject who had the full force of prejudice to encounter, and were obliged to turn their arguments on every side in order to render them popular and convincing. But if we peruse Galileo's famous *Dialogues* concerning the system of the world, we shall find that that great genius, one of the sublimest that ever existed, first bent all his endeavors to prove that there was no foundation for the distinction commonly made between elementary and celestial substances. The schools, proceeding from the illusions of sense, had carried this distinction very far; and had established the latter substances to be ingenerable, incorruptible, unalterable, impassible; and had assigned all the opposite qualities to the former. But Galileo, beginning with the moon, proved its similarity in every particular to the earth: its convex figure, its natural darkness when not illuminated, its density, its distinction into solid and liquid, the variations of its phases, the mutual illuminations of the earth and moon, their mutual eclipses, the inequalities of the lunar surface, etc. After many instances of this kind, with regard to all the planets, men plainly saw that these bodies became proper objects of experience, and that the similarity of their nature enabled us to extend the same arguments and phenomena from one to the other.

In this cautious proceeding of the astronomers you may read your own condemnation, Cleanthes; or rather may see that the subject in which you are engaged exceeds all human reason and inquiry. Can you pretend to show any such similarity between the fabric of a house and the generation of a universe? Have you ever seen nature in any such situation as resembles the first arrangement of the elements? Have worlds ever been formed under your eye, and have you had leisure to observe the whole progress of the phenomenon, from the first appearance of order to its final consummation? If you have, then cite your experience and deliver your theory.

# SAINT ANSELM AND GAUNILO

# The Ontological Argument

In this selection from the **Proslogion,** Saint Anselm attempts to provide an a priori proof of the existence of God. Gaunilo, a contemporary of Anselm's, presents two criticisms of the argument. In one of them, he claims that if Anselm's argument establishes the existence of God, then the existence of a perfect island would be provable a priori. Anselm replies to each of Gaunilo's criticisms.

## ANSELM

### Chapter II. That God Truly Is

O Lord, you who give understanding to faith, so far as you know it to be beneficial, give me to understand that you are just as we believe, and that you are what we believe.

We certainly believe that you are something than which nothing greater can be conceived.

But is there any such nature, since "the fool has said in his heart: God is not"?

However, when this very same fool hears what I say, when he hears of "something than which nothing greater can be conceived," he certainly understands what he hears.

What he understands stands in relation to his understanding (*esse in intellectu*), even if he does not understand that it exists. For it is one thing for a thing to stand in relation to our understanding; it is another thing for us to understand that it really exists. For instance, when a painter imagines what he is about to paint, he has it in relation to his understanding. However, he does not yet understand that it exists, because he has not yet made it. After he paints it, then he both has it in relation to his understanding and understands that it exists. Therefore, even the fool is convinced that "something than which nothing greater can be conceived" at least stands in relation to his understanding, because when he hears of it he understands it, and whatever he understands stands in relation to his understanding.

And certainly that than which a greater cannot be conceived cannot stand only in relation to the understanding. For if it stands at least in relation to the understanding, it can be conceived to be also in reality, and this is something greater. Therefore, if "that than which a greater cannot be conceived" only stood in relation to the understanding, then "that than which a greater cannot be conceived" would be something than which a greater can be conceived. But this is certainly impossible.

Therefore, something than which a greater cannot be conceived undoubtedly both stands in relation to the understanding and exists in reality.

### Chapter III. That It Is Impossible to Conceive That God Is Not

This so truly is that it is impossible to think of it as not existing.

It can be conceived to be something such that we cannot conceive of it as not existing.

This is greater than something which we can conceive of as not existing.

Therefore, if that than which a greater cannot be conceived could be conceived not to be, we would have an impossible contradiction: That than which a greater cannot be conceived would not be that than which a greater cannot be conceived.

Therefore, something than which a greater cannot be conceived so truly is, that it is impossible even to conceive of it as not existing.

This is you, O Lord our God. You so truly are that you cannot be thought not to be. And rightly so.

For if some mind could conceive of something better than you, the creature would rise above its Creator and would judge its Creator, which would be completely absurd.

Also, whatever else there is, except for you alone, can be conceived not to be.

Therefore, you alone, of all things exist in the truest and greatest way (*verissime et maxime esse*), for nothing else so truly exists and therefore everything else has less being.

Why, then, did the fool say in his heart: "God is not," since it is so obvious to the rational mind that you exist supremely above all things? Why, because he is stupid and foolish.

### Chapter IV. How the Fool Said in His Heart What Cannot Be Conceived

How was the fool able to "say in his heart" what he was unable to conceive? Or how was it that he could not conceive what he said in his heart? For to "say in one's heart" and to "conceive" are the same thing.

However, if—or rather because—he really did conceive of it (since he said it in his heart) and yet did not really say it in his heart (since he was unable to conceive of it), then there must be more than one way for something to be said in one's heart, or to be conceived.

Indeed, a thing is conceived of in one way when the word signifying it is thought; in another way when the very thing itself is understood.

Accordingly, God can be conceived not to be in the first way, but not at all in the second. Certainly no one who understands what God is can conceive that God is not. It is possible, however, for him to say this word in his heart, while giving it either no meaning at all or some alien meaning.

God is that than which a greater cannot be conceived. Whoever understands this correctly at least understands that he exists in such a way that even for thought he cannot not exist. Therefore, whoever understands that God is so cannot even conceive that he is not.

My thanksgiving to you, good Lord, my thanksgiving to you. For what I first believed through your giving I now so understand through your illumination that even if I did not want to believe that you are, I would be unable not to understand it.

## GAUNILO

Consider this example: Certain people say that somewhere in the ocean there is an island, which they call the "Lost Island" because of the difficulty or, rather, the impossibility of finding what does not exist. They say that it is more abundantly filled with inestimable riches and delights than the Isles of the Blessed, and that although it has no owner or inhabitant, it excels all the lands that men inhabit taken together in the unceasing abundance of its fertility.

When someone tells me that there is such an island, I easily understand what is being said, for there is nothing difficult here. Suppose, however, as a consequence of this, that he then goes on to say: You cannot doubt that this island, more excellent than all lands, actually exists somewhere in reality, because it undoubtedly stands in relation to your understanding. Since it is more excellent, not simply to stand in relation to the understanding, but to be in reality as well, therefore this island must necessarily be in reality. Otherwise, any other land that exists in reality would be more excellent than this island, and this island, which you understand to be the most excellent of all lands would then not be the most excellent.

If, I repeat, someone should wish by this argument to demonstrate to me that this island truly exists and is no longer to be doubted, I would think he were joking; or, if I accepted the argument, I do not know whom I would regard as the greater fool, me for accepting it or him for supposing that he had proved the existence of this island with any kind of certainty. He should first show that this excellent island exists as a genuine and undeniable real thing, and not leave it standing in relation to my understanding as a false or uncertain something.

## ANSELM

My reasoning, you claim, is as if something should say that there is an island in the ocean, which surpasses the whole earth in its fertility, but which is called a "Lost Island" because of the difficulty, or even impossibility, of finding something that does not exist; and as if he should then argue that no one can doubt that it actually does exist because the words describing it are easily understood.

I can confidently say that if anyone discovers for me something existing either in fact or at least in thought, other than "that than which a greater cannot be conceived," and is able to apply the logic of my argument to it, I shall find that "Lost Island" for him and shall give it to him as something which he will never lose again.

## GAUNILO

When it is asserted to the fool [in *Proslogion III*] that this "greater than all things" is such that even to thought it cannot not be, and yet when this is proved to him on no other ground than that otherwise this "greater than all things" would not be greater than all things, he can give the same answer and reply: When did *I* ever say that such a being, one that is "greater than all things," exists in reality, so that from this you could prove to me that it exists so fully in reality that it cannot be conceived not to be? First of all, it should be proved by some most certain argument that some superior reality, that is, a nature which is greater and better than everything that is, actually exists. From this we can then prove all the other qualities which must not be lacking from that which is greater and better than all things.

## ANSELM

That which cannot possibly not be is obviously something that can be conceived and understood. He who conceives of this conceives of something greater than he who conceives of that which has the possibility of not being. Therefore, while he is conceiving of "that than which a greater cannot be conceived," if he conceives that it has the possibility of not being, he is obviously not conceiving of "that than which a greater cannot be conceived." However, the same thing cannot be both conceived and not conceived at the same time. Therefore, he who conceives of "that than which a greater cannot be conceived" is not conceiving of what can, but of what cannot possibly, not be. For that reason, what he is conceiving must necessarily exist, because whatever is able not to exist is not that of which he is conceiving.

## ALFRED JULES AYER

# The Meaninglessness of Religious Discourse

In this selection from *Language, Truth and Logic* (1936), A. J. Ayer argues that the positivist theory of meaning shows that the claim that God exists is neither true nor false—it is meaningless.

It is now generally admitted, at any rate by philosophers, that the existence of a being having the attributes which define the god of any non-animistic religion cannot be demonstratively proved. To see that this is so, we have only to ask ourselves what are the premises from which the existence of such a god could be deduced. If the conclusion that a god exists is to be demonstratively certain, then these premises must be certain; for, as the conclusion of a deductive argument is already contained in the premises, any uncertainty there may be about the truth of the premises is necessarily shared by it. But we know that no empirical proposition can ever be anything more than probable. It is only *a priori* propositions that are logically certain. But we cannot deduce the existence of a god from an *a priori* proposition. For we know that the reason *a priori* propositions are certain is that they are tautologies. And from a

Alfred Jules Ayer, "Religious Discourse Is Meaningless," from *Language, Truth and Logic* (New York: Dover Books, 1936), pp. 114–120. Reprinted with permission.

set of tautologies nothing but a further tautology can be validly deduced. It follows that there is no possibility of demonstrating the existence of a god.

What is not so generally recognized is that there can be no way of proving that the existence of a god, such as the God of Christianity, is even probable. Yet this also is easily shown. For if the existence of such a god were probable, then the proposition that he existed would be an empirical hypothesis. And in that case it would be possible to deduce from it, and other empirical hypotheses, certain experiential propositions which were not deducible from those other hypotheses alone. But in fact this is not possible. It is sometimes claimed, indeed, that the existence of a certain sort of regularity in nature constitutes sufficient evidence for the existence of a god. But if the sentence "God exists" entails no more than that certain types of phenomena occur in certain sequences, then to assert the existence of a god will be simply equivalent to asserting that there is the requisite regularity in nature; and no religious man would admit that this was all he intended to assert in asserting the existence of a god. He would say that in talking about God, he was talking about a transcendent being who might be known through certain empirical manifestations, but certainly could not be defined in terms of those manifestations. But in that case the term "god" is a metaphysical term. And if "god" is a metaphysical term, then it cannot be even probable that a god exists. For to say that "God exists" is to make a metaphysical utterance which cannot be either true or false. And by the same criterion, no sentence which purports to describe the nature of a transcendent god can possess any literal significance.

It is important not to confuse this view of religious assertions with the view that is adopted by atheists, or agnostics.[1] For it is characteristic of an agnostic to hold that the existence of a god is a possibility in which there is no good reason either to believe or disbelieve; and it is characteristic of an atheist to hold that it is at least probable that no god exists. And our view that all utterances about the nature of God are nonsensical, so far from being identical with, or even lending any support to, either of these familiar contentions, is actually incompatible with them. For if the assertion that there is a god is nonsensical, then the atheist's assertion that there is no god is equally nonsensical, since it is only a significant proposition that can be significantly contradicted. As for the agnostic, although he refrains from saying either that there is or that there is not a god, he does not deny that the question whether a transcendent god exists is a genuine question. He does not deny that the two sentences "There is a transcendent god" and "There is no transcendent god" express propositions one of which is actually true and the other false. All he says is that we have no means of telling which of them is true, and therefore ought not to commit ourselves to either. But we have seen that the sentences in question do not express propositions at all. And this means that agnosticism also is ruled out.

Thus we offer the theist the same comfort as we gave to the moralist. His assertions cannot possibly be valid, but they cannot be invalid either. As he says nothing at all about the world, he cannot justly be accused of saying anything false, or anything for which he has insufficient grounds. It is only when the theist claims that in asserting

---

[1]This point was suggested to me by Professor H. H. Price.

the existence of a transcendent god he is expressing a genuine proposition that we are entitled to disagree with him.

It is not to be remarked that in cases where deities are identified with natural objects, assertions concerning them may be allowed to be significant. If, for example, a man tells me that the occurrence of thunder is alone both necessary and sufficient to establish the truth of the proposition that Jehovah is angry, I may conclude that, in his usage of words, the sentence "Jehovah is angry" is equivalent to "It is thundering." But in sophisticated religions, though they may be to some extent based on men's awe of natural process which they cannot sufficiently understand, the "person" who is supposed to control the empirical world is not himself located in it; he is held to be superior to the empirical world, and so outside it; and he is endowed with super-empirical attributes. But the notion of a person whose essential attributes are non-empirical is not an intelligible notion at all. We may have a word which is used as if it named this "person," but, unless the sentences in which it occurs express propositions which are empirically verifiable, it cannot be said to symbolize anything. And this is the case with regard to the word "god," in the usage in which it is intended to refer to a transcendent object. The mere existence of the noun is enough to foster the illusion that there is a real, or at any rate a possible entity corresponding to it. It is only when we enquire what God's attributes are that we discover that "God," in this usage, is not a genuine name.

It is common to find belief in a transcendent god conjoined with belief in an afterlife. But, in the form which it usually takes, the content of this belief is not a genuine hypothesis. To say that men do not ever die, or that the state of death is merely a state of prolonged insensibility, is indeed to express a significant proposition, though all the available evidence goes to show that it is false. But to say there is something imperceptible inside a man, which is his soul or his real self, and that it goes on living after he is dead, is to make a metaphysical assertion which has no more factual content than the assertion that there is a transcendent god.

It is worth mentioning that, according to the account which we have given of religious assertions, there is no logical ground for antagonism between religion and natural science. As far as the question of truth or falsehood is concerned, there is no opposition between the natural scientist and the theist who believes in a transcendent god. For since the religious utterances of the theist are not genuine propositions at all, they cannot stand in any logical relation to the propositions of science. Such antagonism as there is between religion and science appears to consist in the fact that science takes away one of the motives which make men religious. For it is acknowledged that one of the ultimate sources of religious feeling lies in the inability of men to determine their own destiny; and science tends to destroy the feeling of awe with which men regard an alien world, by making them believe that they can understand and anticipate the course of natural phenomena, and even to some extent control it. The fact that it has recently become fashionable for physicists themselves to be sympathetic towards religion is a point in favour of this hypothesis. For this sympathy towards religion marks the physicists' own lack of confidence in the validity of their hypotheses, which is a reaction on their part from the anti-religious dogmatism of nineteenth-century scientists, and a natural outcome of the crisis through which physics has just passed.

It is not within the scope of this enquiry to enter more deeply into the causes of religious feeling, or to discuss the probability of the continuance of religious belief. We are concerned only to answer those questions which arise out of our discussion of the possibility of religious knowledge. The point which we wish to establish is that there cannot be any transcendent truths of religion. For the sentences which the theist uses to express such "truths" are not literally significant.

An interesting feature of this conclusion is that it accords with what many theists are accustomed to say themselves. For we are often told that the nature of God is a mystery which transcends the human understanding. But to say that something transcends the human understanding is to say that it is unintelligible. And what is unintelligible cannot significantly be described. Again, we are told that God is not an object of reason but an object of faith. This may be nothing more than an admission that the existence of God must be taken on trust, since it cannot be proved. But it may also be an assertion that God is the object of a purely mystical intuition, and cannot therefore be defined in terms which are intelligible to the reason. And I think there are many theists who would assert this. But if one allows that it is impossible to define God in intelligible terms, then one is allowing that it is impossible for a sentence both to be significant and to be about God. If a mystic admits that the object of his vision is something which cannot be described, then he must also admit that he is bound to talk nonsense when he describes it.

For his part, the mystic may protest that his intuition does reveal truths to him, even though he cannot explain to others what these truths are; and that we who do not possess this faculty of intuition can have no ground for denying that it is a cognitive faculty. For we can hardly maintain *a priori* that there are no ways of discovering true propositions except those which we ourselves employ. The answer is that we set no limit to the number of ways in which one may come to formulate a true proposition. We do not in any way deny that a synthetic truth may be discovered by purely intuitive methods as well as by the rational method of induction. But we do say that every synthetic proposition, however it may have been arrived at, must be subject to the test of actual experience. We do not deny *a priori* that the mystic is able to discover truths by his own special methods. We wait to hear what are the propositions which embody his discoveries, in order to see whether they are verified or confuted by our empirical observations. But the mystic, so far from producing propositions which are empirically verified, is unable to produce any intelligible propositions at all. And therefore we say that his intuition has not revealed to him any facts. It is no use his saying that he has apprehended facts but is unable to express them. For we know that if he really had acquired any information, he would be able to express it. He would be able to indicate in some way or other how the genuineness of his discovery might be empirically determined. The fact that he cannot reveal what he "knows," or even himself devise an empirical test to validate his "knowledge," shows that his state of mystical intuition is not a genuinely cognitive state. So that in describing his vision the mystic does not give us any information about the external world; he merely gives us indirect information about the condition of his own mind.

These considerations dispose of the argument from religious experience, which many philosophers still regard as a valid argument in favour of the existence of a god. They say that it is logically possible for men to be immediately acquainted with God, as they are immediately acquainted with a sense-content, and that there is no reason why one should be prepared to believe a man when he says that he is seeing a yellow patch, and refuse to believe him when he says that he is seeing God. The answer to this is that if the man who asserts that he is seeing God is merely asserting that he is experiencing a peculiar kind of sense-content, then we do not for a moment deny that his assertion may be true. But, ordinarily, the man who says that he is see-ing God is saying not merely that he is experiencing a religious emotion, but also that there exists a transcendent being who is the object of this emotion; just as the man who says that he sees a yellow patch is ordinarily saying not merely that his visual sense-field contains a yellow sense-content, but also that there exists a yellow object to which the sense-content belongs. And it is not irrational to be prepared to believe a man when he asserts the existence of a yellow object, and to refuse to believe him when he asserts the existence of a transcendent god. For whereas the sentence "There exists here a yellow-coloured material thing" expresses a genuine synthetic proposi-tion which could be empirically verified, the sentence "There exists a transcendent god" has, as we have seen, no literal significance.

We conclude, therefore, that the argument from religious experience is altogether fallacious. The fact that people have religious experiences is interesting from the psy-chological point of view, but it does not in any way imply that there is such a thing as religious knowledge, any more than our having moral experiences implies that there is such a thing as moral knowledge. The theist, like the moralist, may believe that his experiences are cognitive experiences, but, unless he can formulate his "knowledge" in propositions that are empirically verifiable, we may be sure that he is deceiving him-self. It follows that those philosophers who fill their books with assertions that they intuitively "know" this or that moral or religious "truth" are merely providing material for the psychoanalyst. For no act of intuition can be said to reveal a truth about any mat-ter of fact unless it issues in verifiable propositions. And all such propositions are to be incorporated in the system of empirical propositions which constitutes science.

## BLAISE PASCAL

# Belief in God — What Do You Have to Lose?

Blaise Pascal (1623–1662) was a follower of Jansenism, a branch of Catholicism that was active in France in the sixteenth to eighteenth centuries. Jansenism was based on the writings of the sixteenth-century Dutch theologian Cornelius Jansen and was inspired by the writings of St. Augustine; it was condemned by the Church as heretical. In a letter he had sewn inside his cloak, Pascal describes having a mystical experience that changed his life; it made him realize that "the God of Abraham, Isaac, and Jacob is not the God of the philosophers." Pascal was con-vinced that God is far too different from us for us to have any evidence concerning whether he exists. Pascal nonetheless argued that it is rational to believe in God. In the following passage

From Blaise Pascal, *Pensées*, Section 3, "Of the Necessity of the Wager" (number 233), translated by W. F. Trotter. URL: http://www.leaderu.com/cyber/books/pensees/pensees.html.

from his *Pensées,* a book that was posthumously assembled from his notes, Pascal sets forth his now-famous wager. In fact, he gives the wager different formulations. Try to discern what these different arguments of Pascal's are and how they differ.

If there is a God, He is infinitely incomprehensible, since, having neither parts nor limits, He has no affinity to us. We are then incapable of knowing either what He is or if He is. This being so, who will dare to undertake the decision of the question? Not we, who have no affinity to Him.

Who then will blame Christians for not being able to give a reason for their belief, since they profess a religion for which they cannot give a reason? They declare, in expounding it to the world, that it is a foolishness, *stultitiam;* and then you complain that they do not prove it! If they proved it, they would not keep their word; it is in lacking proofs that they are not lacking in sense. "Yes, but although this excuses those who offer it as such and takes away from them the blame of putting it forward without reason, it does not excuse those who receive it." Let us then examine this point, and say, "God is, or He is not." But to which side shall we incline? Reason can decide nothing here. There is an infinite chaos which separated us. A game is being played at the extremity of this infinite distance where heads or tails will turn up. What will you wager? According to reason, you can do neither the one thing nor the other; according to reason, you can defend neither of the propositions.

Do not, then, reprove for error those who have made a choice; for you know nothing about it. "No, but I blame them for having made, not this choice, but a choice; for again both he who chooses heads and he who chooses tails are equally at fault, they are both in the wrong. The true course is not to wager at all."

Yes; but you must wager. It is not optional. You are embarked. Which will you choose then? Let us see. Since you must choose, let us see which interests you least. You have two things to lose, the true and the good; and two things to stake, your reason and your will, your knowledge and your happiness; and your nature has two things to shun, error and misery. Your reason is no more shocked in choosing one rather than the other, since you must of necessity choose. This is one point settled. But your happiness? Let us weigh the gain and the loss in wagering that God is. Let us estimate these two chances. If you gain, you gain all; if you lose, you lose nothing. Wager, then, without hesitation that He is. "That is very fine. Yes, I must wager; but I may perhaps wager too much." Let us see. Since there is an equal risk of gain and of loss, if you had only to gain two lives, instead of one, you might still wager. But if there were three lives to gain, you would have to play (since you are under the necessity of playing), and you would be imprudent, when you are forced to play, not to chance your life to gain three at a game where there is an equal risk of loss and gain. But there is an eternity of life and happiness. And this being so, if there were an infinity of chances, of which one only would be for you, you would still be right in wagering one to win two, and you would act stupidly, being obliged to play, by refusing to stake one life against three at a game in which out of an infinity of chances there is one for you, if there were an infinity of an infinitely happy life to gain. But there is here an infinity of an infinitely happy life to gain, a chance of gain against a finite number of chances of loss, and what you stake is finite. It is all divided; where-ever the infinite is and there is not an infinity of chances of loss against that of gain, there is no time to hesitate, you must give all. And thus, when one is forced to play, he must renounce reason to preserve his life, rather than risk it for infinite gain, as likely to happen as the loss of nothingness.

For it is no use to say it is uncertain if we will gain, and it is certain that we risk, and that the infinite distance between the certainly of what is staked and the uncertainty of what will be gained, equals the finite good which is certainly staked against the uncertain infinite. It is not so, as every player stakes a certainty to gain an uncertainty, and yet he stakes a finite certainty to gain a finite uncertainty, without transgressing against reason. There is not an infinite distance between the certainty staked and the uncertainty of the gain; that is untrue. In truth, there is an infinity between the certainty of gain and the certainty of loss. But the uncertainty of the gain is proportioned to the certainty of the stake according to the proportion of the chances of gain and loss. Hence it comes that, if there are as many risks on one side as on the other, the course is to play even; and then the certainty of the stake is equal to the uncertainty of the gain, so far is it from fact that there is an infinite distance between them. And so our proposition is of infinite force, when there is the finite to stake in a game where there are equal risks of gain and of loss, and the infinite to gain. This is demonstrable; and if men are capable of any truths, this is one.

"I confess it, I admit it. But, still, is there no means of seeing the faces of the cards?" Yes, Scripture and the rest, etc. "Yes, but I have my hands tied and my mouth closed; I am forced to wager, and am not free. I am not released, and am so made that I cannot believe. What, then, would you have me do?"

True. But at least learn your inability to believe, since reason brings you to this, and yet you cannot believe. Endeavour, then, to convince yourself, not by increase of proofs of God, but by the abatement of your passions. You would like to attain faith and do not know the way; you would like to cure yourself of unbelief and ask the remedy for it. Learn of those who have been bound like you, and who now stake all their possessions. These are people who know the way which you would follow, and who are cured of an ill of which you would be cured. Follow the way by which they began; by acting as if they believed, taking the holy water, having masses said, etc. Even this will naturally make you believe, and deaden your acuteness. "But this is what I am afraid of." And why? What have you to lose?

# WILLIAM JAMES

## The Will to Believe

William James (1842–1910) was an influential psychologist and philosopher who helped found the American school of philosophy known as pragmatism. In the present essay, James argues that we sometimes face decisions about what to believe that can and should be made on

William James, "The Will to Believe," from *The Will to Believe and Other Essays in Popular Philosophy* (New York: Longmans Green & Co., 1897).

some basis other than the evidence at hand. His argument is an updated version of Pascal's Wager (Chapter 10).

1. ... Let us give the name of *hypothesis* to anything that may be proposed to our belief; and just as the electricians speak of live and dead wires, let us speak of any hypothesis as either *live* or *dead.* A live hypothesis is one which appeals as a real possibility to him to whom it is proposed. If I ask you to believe in the Mahdi, the notion makes no electric connection with your nature—it refuses to scintillate with any credibility at all. As an hypothesis it is completely dead. To an Arab, however (even if he be not one of the Mahdi's followers), the hypothesis is among the mind's possibilities: it is alive. This shows that deadness and liveness in an hypothesis are not intrinsic properties, but relations to the individual thinker. They are measured by his willingness to act irrevocably. Practically, that means belief; but there is some believing tendency wherever there is willingness to act at all.

Next, let us call the decision between two hypotheses an *option.* Options may be of several kinds. They may be—first, *living* or *dead;* secondly, *forced* or *avoidable;* thirdly, *momentous* or *trivial;* and for our purposes we may call an option a *genuine* option when it is of the forced, living, and momentous kind.

(1) A living option is one in which both hypotheses are live ones. If I say to you: "Be a theosophist or be a Mohammedan," it is probably a dead option, because for you neither hypothesis is likely to be alive. But if I say: "Be an agnostic or be a Christian," it is otherwise: trained as you are, each hypothesis makes some appeal, however small, to your belief.

(2) Next, if I say to you: "Choose between going out with your umbrella or without it," I do not offer you a genuine option, for it is not forced. You can easily avoid it by not going out at all. Similarly, if I say, "Either love me or hate me," "Either call my theory true or call it false," your option is avoidable. You may remain indifferent to me, neither loving nor hating, and you may decline to offer any judgment as to my theory. But if I say, "Either accept this truth or go without it," I put on you a forced option, but there is no standing place outside of the alternative. Every dilemma based on a complete logical disjunction, with no possibility of not choosing, is an option of this forced kind.

(3) Finally, if I were Dr. Nansen and proposed to you to join my North Pole expedition, your option would be momentous; for this would probably be your only similar opportunity, and your choice now would either exclude you from the North Pole sort of immortality altogether or put at least the chance of it into your hands. He who refuses to embrace a unique opportunity loses the prize as surely as if he tried and failed. *Per contra,* the option is trivial when the opportunity is not unique, when the stake is insignificant, or when the decision is reversible if it later prove unwise. Such trivial options abound in the scientific life. A chemist finds an hypothesis live enough to spend a year in its verification: he believes in it to that extent. But if his experiments prove inconclusive either way, he is quit for his loss of time, no vital harm being done. It will facilitate our discussion if we keep all these distinctions in mind. ...

2. ... The thesis I defend is ... this: *Our passional nature not only lawfully may, but must, decide an option between propositions, whenever it is a genuine option that cannot by its*

*nature be decided on intellectual grounds; for to say, under such circumstances, "Do not decide, but leave the question open," is itself a passional decision—just like deciding yes or no—and is attended with the same risk of losing the truth. . . .*

3. . . . Wherever the option between losing truth and gaining it is not momentous, we can throw the chance of *gaining truth* away, and at any rate save ourselves from any chance of *believing falsehood,* by not making up our minds at all till objective evidence has come. In scientific questions, this is almost always the case; and even in human affairs in general, the need of acting is seldom so urgent that a false belief to act on is better than no belief at all. Law courts, indeed, have to decide on the best evidence attainable for the moment, because a judge's duty is to make law as well as to ascertain it, and (as a learned judge once said to me) few cases are worth spending much time over: the great thing is to have them decided on *any* acceptable principle, and got out of the way. But in our dealings with objective nature we obviously are recorders, not makers, of the truth; and decisions for the mere sake of deciding promptly and getting on to the next business would be wholly out of place. Throughout the breadth of physical nature facts are what they are quite independently of us, and seldom is there any such hurry about them that the risks of being duped by believing a premature theory need be faced. The questions here are always trivial options, the hypotheses are hardly living (at any rate not living for us spectators), the choice between believing truth or falsehood is seldom forced. The attitude of special balance is therefore the absolutely wise one if we would escape mistakes. What difference, indeed, does it make to most of us whether we have or have not a theory of the Röntgen rays, whether we believe or not in mind-stuff, or have a conviction about the causality of conscious states? It makes no difference. Such options are not forced on us. On every account it is better not to make them, but still keep weighing reasons *pro et contra* with an indifferent hand.

I speak, of course, here of the purely judging mind. For purposes of discovery such indifference is to be less highly recommended, and science would be far less advanced than she is if the passionate desires of individuals to get their own faiths confirmed had been kept out of the game. . . . If you want an absolute duffer in an investigation, you must, after all, take the man who has no interest whatever in its results: he is the warranted incapable, the positive fool. The most useful investigator, because the most sensitive observer, is always he whose eager interest in one side of the question is balanced by an equally keen nervousness lest he become deceived. Science has organized this nervousness into a regular *technique,* her so-called method of verification; and she has fallen so deeply in love with the method that one may even say she has ceased to care for truth by itself at all. It is only truth as technically verified that interests her. The truth of truths might come in merely affirmative form, and she would decline to touch it. Such truth as that, she might repeat with Clifford, would be stolen in defiance of her duty to mankind. Human passions, however, are stronger than technical rules. "*Le œur a ses raisons,*" as Pascal says, "*que la raison ne connaît pas*"[1]; and however indifferent to all but the bare rules the game the umpire,

---

[1]The heart has its reasons, that reason does not know.

the abstract intellect, may be, the concrete players who furnish him the materials to judge of are usually, each one of them, in love with some pet "live hypothesis" of his own. Let us agree, however, that wherever there is no forced option, the dispassionately judicial intellect with no pet hypothesis, saving us, as it does, from dupery at any rate, ought to be our ideal.

The question next arises: Are there not somewhere forced options in our speculative questions, and can we (as men who may be interested at least as much in positively gaining truth as in merely escaping dupery) always wait with impunity till the coercive evidence shall have arrived? It seems *a priori* improbable that the truth should be so nicely adjusted to our needs and powers as that. In the great boarding-house of nature, the cakes and the butter and the syrup seldom come out so even and leave the plates so clean. Indeed, we should view them with scientific suspicion if they did.

4 *Moral questions* immediately present themselves as questions whose solution cannot wait for sensible proof. A moral question is a question not of what sensibly exists, but of what is good, or would be good if it did exist. Science can tell us what exists; but to compare the *worths*, both of what exists and of what does not exist, we must consult not science, but what Pascal calls our heart. Science herself consults her heart when she lays it down that the infinite ascertainment of fact and correction of false belief are the supreme goods for man. Challenge the statement, and science can only repeat it oracularly, or else prove it by showing that such ascertainment and correction bring men all sorts of other goods which man's heart in turn declares. The question of having moral beliefs at all or not having them is decidedly by our will. Are our moral preferences true or false, or are they only odd biological phenomena, making things good or bad for *us*, but in themselves indifferent? How can your pure intellect decide? If your heart does not *want* a world of moral reality, your head will assuredly never make you believe in one. Mephistophelian scepticism, indeed, will satisfy the head's play-instincts much better than any rigorous idealism can. Some men (even at the student age) are so naturally cool-hearted that the moralistic hypothesis never has for them any pungent life, and in their supercilious presence the hot young moralist always feels strangely ill at ease. The appearance of knowingness is on their side, of *naivete* and gullibility on his. Yet, in the articulate heart of him, he clings to it that he is not a dupe, and that there is a realm in which (as Emerson says) all their wit and intellectual superiority is no better than the cunning of a fox. Moral scepticism can no more be refuted or proved by logic than intellectual scepticism can. When we stick to it that there *is* truth (be it of either kind), we do so with our whole nature, and resolve to stand or fall by the results. The sceptic with his whole nature adopts the doubting attitude; but which of us is the wiser, Omniscience only knows.

Turn now from these wider questions of good to a certain class of questions of fact, questions concerning personal relations, states of mind between one man and another. *Do you like me or not?*—for example. Whether you do or not depends, in countless instances, on whether I meet you half-way, am willing to assume that you must like me, and show you trust and expectation. The previous faith on my part in your liking's existence is in such cases what makes your liking come. But if I stand aloof, and refuse to budge an inch until I have objective evidence ... ten to one your liking never comes. How many women's hearts are vanquished by the mere sanguine insistence of some man that they *must* love him! He will not consent to the hypothesis that they cannot. The desire for a certain kind of truth here brings about that special truth's existence; and so it is in innumerable cases of other sorts. Who gains promotions, boons, appointments, but the man in whose life they are seen to play the part of live hypotheses, who discounts them, sacrifices other things for their sake before they have come, and takes risks for them in advance? His faith acts on the powers above him as a claim, and creates its own verification.

A social organism of any sort whatever, large or small, is what it is because each member proceeds to his own duty with a trust that the other members will simultaneously do theirs. Wherever a desired result is achieved by the co-operation of many independent persons, its existence as a fact is a pure consequence of the precursive faith in one another of those immediately concerned. A government, an army, a commercial system, a ship, a college, an athletic team, all exist on this condition, without which not only is nothing achieved, but nothing is even attempted. A whole train of passengers (individually brave enough) will be looted by a few highwaymen, simply because the latter can count on one another, while each passenger fears that if he makes a movement of resistance, he will be shot before anyone else backs him up. If we believed that the whole carfull would rise at once with us, we should each severally rise, and trainrobbing would never be attempted. There are, then, cases where a fact cannot come at all unless a preliminary faith exists in its coming. *And where faith in a fact can help create the fact,* that would be an insane logic which should say that faith running ahead of scientific evidence is the "lowest kind of immorality" into which a thinking being can fall. Yet such is the logic by which our scientific absolutists pretend to regulate our lives!

5. In truths dependent on our personal action, then, faith based on desire is certainly a lawful and possibly an indispensable thing.

But now, it will be said, these are all childish human cases, and have nothing to do with great cosmical matters, like the question of religious faith. Let us then pass on to that. Religions differ so much in their accidents that in discussing the religious question we must make it very generic and broad. What then do we now mean by the religious hypothesis? Science says things are; morality says some things are better than other things; and religion says essentially two things.

First, she says that the best things are the more eternal things, the overlapping things, the things in the universe that throw the last stone, so to speak, and say the final word. "Perfection is eternal"—this phrase of Charles Secretan seems a good way of putting this first affirmation of religion, an affirmation which obviously cannot yet be verified scientifically at all.

The second affirmation of religion is that we are better off even now if we believe her first affirmation to be true.

Now, let us consider what the logical elements of this situation are *in case the religious hypothesis in both its branches be really true.* (Of course, we must admit that possibility at the outset. If we are to discuss the question at all, it must involve a living option. If for any of you religion be a hypothesis that cannot, by any living possibility, be true, then you need go no farther. I speak to the "saving remnant" alone.) So proceeding, we see, first, that religion offers itself as a *momentous* option. We are supposed to gain, even now, by our belief, and to lose by our non-belief, a certain vital good. Secondly, religion is a *forced* option, so far as that good goes. We cannot escape the issue by remaining sceptical and waiting for more light, because, although we do avoid error in that way *if religion be untrue,* we lose the good, *if it be true,* just as certainly as if we positively chose to disbelieve. It is as if a man should hesitate indefinitely to ask a certain woman to marry him because he was not perfectly sure that she would prove an angel after he brought her home. Would he not cut himself off from that particular angel-possibility as decisively as if he went and married someone else? Scepticism, then, is not avoidance of option; it is option of a certain particular kind of risk. *Better risk loss of truth than chance of error*—that is your faith-vetoer's exact position. He is actively playing his stake as much as the believer is; he is backing the field against the religious hypothesis, just as the believer is backing the religious hypothesis against the field. To preach scepticism to us as a duty until "sufficient evidence" for religion be found, is tantamount therefore to telling us, when in the presence of a religious hypothesis, that to yield to our fear of its being error is wiser and better than to yield to our hope that it may be true. It is not intellect against all passions, then; it is only intellect with one passion laying down its law. And by what, forsooth, is the supreme wisdom of this passion warranted? Dupery for dupery, what proof is there that dupery through hope is so much worse than dupery through fear? I, for one, can see no proof; and I simply refuse obedience to the scientist's command to imitate his kind of option, in a case where my own stake is important enough to give me the right to choose my own form of risk. If religion be true and the evidence for it be still insufficient, I do not wish, by putting your extinguisher upon my nature (which feels to me as if it had after all some business in this matter), to forfeit my sole chance in life of getting upon the winning side—that chance depending, of course, on my willingness to run the risk of acting as if my passional need of taking the world religiously might be prophetic and right.

All this is on the supposition that it really may be prophetic and right, and that, even to us who are discussing the matter, religion is a live hypothesis which may be true. Now, to most of us religion comes in a still further way that makes a veto on our active faith even more illogical. The more perfect and more eternal aspect of the universe is represented in our religions as having personal form. The universe is no longer a mere It to us, but a *Thou,* if we are religious; and any relation that may be possible from person to person might be possible here. For instance, although in one sense we are passive portions of the universe, in another we show a curious autonomy, as if we were small active centres on our own account. We feel, too, as if the appeal of religion to us were made to our own active good-will, as if evidence might be forever withheld from us unless we met the hypothesis half-way. To take a trivial illustration: just as a man who is in a company of gentlemen made no advances, asked a warrant for every concession, and believed no one's word without proof, would cut himself off by such churlishness from all the social rewards that a more trusting spirit would earn—so here, one who should shut himself up in snarling logicality and try to make the gods extort his recognition willy-nilly, or not get it at all, might cut himself off forever from his only opportunity of making the gods' acquaintance. This feeling, forced on us we know not whence, that by obstinately believing that there are gods (although not to do so would be so easy both for our logic and our life) we are doing the universe the deepest service we can, seems part of the living essence of the religious hypothesis. If the hypothesis were true in all its parts, including this one, then pure intellectualism, with its veto on our making willing advances, would be an absurdity; and some participation of our sympathetic nature would be logically required. I, therefore, for one, cannot see my way to accepting the agnostic rules for truth-seeking, or willfully agree to keep my willing nature out of the game. I cannot do so for this plain reason, that *a rule of thinking which would absolutely prevent me from acknowledging certain kinds of truth if those kinds of truth were really there, would be an irrational rule.* That for me is the long and short of the formal logic of the situation, no matter what the kinds of truth might materially be.

I confess I do not see how this logic can be escaped. But sad experience makes me fear that some of you may still shrink from radically saying with me, *in abstracto,* that we have the right to believe at our own risk any hypothesis that is live enough to tempt our will. I suspect, however, that if this is so, it is because you have got away from the abstract logical point of view altogether, and are thinking (perhaps without realizing it) of some particular religious hypothesis which for you is dead. The freedom to "believe what we will" you apply to the case of some patent superstition; and the faith you think of is the faith defined by the schoolboy when he said, "Faith is when you believe something that you know ain't true." I can only repeat that this is misapprehension. *In concreto,* the freedom to believe can only cover living options which the intellect of the individual cannot by itself resolve; and living options never seem absurdities to him who has them to consider. When I look at the religious question as it really puts itself to concrete men, and when I think of all the possibilities which both practically and theoretically it involves, then this command that we shall put a stopper on our heart, instincts, and courage, and *wait*—acting of course meanwhile more or less as if religion were *not* true—till doomsday, or till such time as our intellect and senses working together may have raked in evidence enough—this command, I say, seems to me the queerest idol ever manufactured in the philosophic cave. Were we scholastic absolutists, there might be more excuse. If we had an infallible intellect with its objective certitudes, we might feel ourselves disloyal to such a perfect organ of knowledge in not trusting to it exclusively, in not waiting for its releasing word. But if we are empiricists, if we believe that no bell in us tolls to let us know for certain when truth is in our grasp, then it seems a piece of idle fantasticality to preach so solemnly our duty of waiting for the bell. Indeed we *may* wait if we will—I hope you do not think that I am denying that—but if we do so, we do so at our peril as much as if we believed. In either case we *act*, taking our life in our hands. No one of us ought to issue vetoes to the other, nor should we bandy words of abuse. We ought, on the contrary, delicately and profoundly to respect one another's mental freedom: then only shall we bring about the intellectual republic; then only shall we have that spirit of inner tolerance without which all our outer tolerance is soulless, and which is empiricism's glory; then only shall we live and let live, in speculative as well as in practical things. . . .

## Suggestions for Further Reading

### ON THE DEBATE BETWEEN CREATIONISM AND EVOLUTIONARY THEORY

Douglas Futuyama, *Science on Trial: The Case for Evolution,* New York, Pantheon, 1982.

Dwayne Gish, *Evolution? The Fossils Say No!* San Diego, Creation-Life Publishers, 1979.

Phillip Johnson, *Defeating Darwinism by Opening Minds,* Downers Grove, IL, Intervarsity Press, 1997.

Philip Kitcher, *Abusing Science: The Case Against Creationism,* Cambridge, Massachusetts, MIT Press, 1982.

Henry Morris, *Scientific Creationism,* San Diego, Creation-Life Publishers, 1974.

Michael Behe, *Darwin's Black Box,* New York, Free Press, 1996.

Robert Pennock, *Tower of Babel—The Evidence against the New Creationism,* Cambridge, Massachusetts, MIT Press, 1998.

### ON THE TESTABILITY OF RELIGIOUS CLAIMS

Essays by Antony Flew, R. M. Hare, and Basil Mitchell, "Theology and Falsification," in Antony Flew and Alisdair MacIntyre (eds.), *New Essays in Philosophical Theology,* New York, Macmillan, 1966.

Carl Hempel, "Empiricist Criteria of Cognitive Significance: Problems and Changes," in *Aspects of Scientific Explanation,* New York, Free Press, 1965.

Elliott Sober, "Testability," Proceedings and Addresses of the American Philosophical Association, 1999. Available at the Web site http://philosophy.wisc.edu/sober.

### ON THE ONTOLOGICAL ARGUMENT

John Hick and Arthur McGill (eds.), *The Many-Faced Argument: Recent Studies on the Ontological Argument for the Existence of God.* London, Macmillan, 1968.

Alvin Plantinga, *The Nature of Necessity.* Oxford, Oxford University Press, 1974.

### ON PASCAL'S WAGER

James Cargile, "Pascal's Wager," *Philosophy,* vol. 41, pp. 229–236, 1966.

William Lycan and George Schlesinger, "You Bet Your Life: Pascal's Wager Defended," in J. Feinberg and R. Schafer-Landau (eds.), *Reason and Responsibility,* Belmont, California, Wadsworth, 1999.

Gregory Mougin and Elliott Sober, "Betting against Pascal's Wager," *Nous,* vol. 28, pp. 382–395, 1994.

Blaise Pascal, *Penseé,* Everyman's Library, London, J. M. Dent & Sons, 1958.

## ON THE ARGUMENT FROM EVIL

Robert M. Adams, "Must God Create the Best?" *Philosophical Review,* vol. 81, pp. 317–332, 1972.

Richard Swinburne, "The Problem of Evil," in Stuart Brown (ed.), *Reason and Religion,* Ithaca, Cornell University Press, 1977.

Peter Van Inwagen, "The Magnitude, Duration, and Distribution of Evil—A Theodicy," *Philosophical Topics,* vol. 16, 1988.

## ON RECENT WORK IN PHILOSOPHY OF RELIGION

William Mann, *The Blackwell Guide to Philosophy of Religion,* New York: Blackwell Publishers, 2004.

# PART III
# THEORY
# OF KNOWLEDGE

## CHAPTER 12

### *What Is Knowledge?*

#### EPISTEMOLOGY

In everyday life, in science, and in philosophy as well, we talk of "knowing" things. We also say that some beliefs are "strongly supported by evidence"; we say that they are "justified" or "well confirmed." We not only describe *ourselves* with such terms; we also apply them to *others*.

*Epistemology* is the part of philosophy that tries to understand such concepts. Epistemologists try to evaluate the commonsense idea that we (often, if not always) have knowledge and that we are (often, if not always) rationally justified in the beliefs we have. Some philosophers have tried to defend these commonsense ideas with philosophical argumentation. Others have developed a philosophical position that involves denying these commonsense ideas. A philosopher who claims that we don't have knowledge, or that our beliefs aren't rationally justified, is defending some version of *philosophical skepticism*.

In this chapter, I'll begin with some remarks about the problem of knowledge. In the next chapter, I'll examine the views of the seventeenth-century French philosopher René Descartes. Descartes tried to show that we really do possess knowledge of the world; he tried to refute the skeptic. After evaluating Descartes' views about knowledge, I'll turn to an alternative way of thinking about knowledge, *the Reliability* Theory of Knowledge (Chapter 14).

After this discussion of the problem of knowledge, I'll examine the idea of rational justification. The eighteenth-century Scottish philosopher David Hume, whose views on the Argument from Design we considered in Chapter 5, argued that the beliefs we have that are based on induction aren't rationally justified. Hume was a skeptic about induction. We'll consider his argument for this philosophical position and also the attempts some philosophers have made to show that Hume's startling thesis is mistaken. The last chapter in this part of the book discusses a central problem in epistemology—how do we know that things exist that are outside our own minds?

So let's get started with the problem of knowledge. Before we can ask whether we know anything, we have to get clear on what knowledge is. To focus ideas, I want to distinguish three different ways we talk about knowledge. Only one of these will be our concern in what follows.

## THREE KINDS OF KNOWLEDGE

Consider the differences that separate the following three statements, each concerning an individual, whom I'll call *S* (the subject):

(1)  *S* knows how to ride a bicycle.

(2)  *S* knows the president of the United States.

(3)  *S* knows that the Rocky Mountains are in North America.

Right now I'm not interested in saying which of these statements is true. The point is that they involve different kinds of knowledge.

The kind of knowledge described in (3) I'll call *propositional knowledge.* Notice that the object of the verb in (3) is a proposition—something that is either true or false. There is a proposition—that the Rockies are in North America—and (3) asserts that *S* knows that that proposition is true. Statements (1) and (2) don't have this structure. For example, the object of the verb in (2) isn't a proposition, but a person. A similar kind of knowledge would be involved if I said that *S* knows Chicago. Statement (2) says that *S* is related to an object—a person, place, or thing—so I'll say that (2) describes an instance of *object knowledge.* Is there a connection between object knowledge and propositional knowledge? Maybe to know the president of the United States, you must know some propositions that are about him. But which propositions? To know the president, do you have to know what state he comes from? This doesn't seem essential. The same holds true for each other fact about the man: There doesn't seem to be any particular proposition you've got to know for you to know him.

There is another aspect of the idea of object knowledge, one that is rather curious. Suppose I've read lots of books about the president. I know as many propositions about him as you might wish. Still, it won't be true that I know him, because I've never met him. Knowing people seems to require some sort of direct acquaintance. But it is hard to say exactly what is needed here. If I once was introduced to the president at some large party, that wouldn't be enough for me to say that I "know" him. It isn't just direct acquaintance, but something more. I won't try to describe this further. I'll merely conclude that propositional knowledge, no matter how voluminous, isn't sufficient for object knowledge. Object knowledge requires some sort of direct acquaintance with the object. In contrast propositional knowledge does not require that you have direct acquaintance with the objects that the proposition is about; *S* can know that the Rockies are in North America though she has never seen them.

I turn next to the kind of knowledge described in statement (1). I'll call this *know-how* knowledge. What does it mean to know how to do something? I think this idea has little connection with propositional knowledge. My son Aaron knew how to ride a bike when he was five years old. This means he had certain abilities—he knew how to keep his balance, how to pedal, and so on. If you asked a physicist to describe what Aaron was doing that allowed him to ride the bike, the physicist could write out a set of propositions. There would be facts about gravity, forward momentum, and balancing of forces. But Aaron wasn't a physicist at age five. He didn't know the propositions that the physicist specifies. Aaron *obeyed* the physical principles that the physicist describes—his behavior conformed to what they say—but he didn't do this by learning the propositions in question. Aaron had know-how knowledge, but little in the way of propositional knowledge.

---

### Necessary and Sufficient Conditions

Consider the following suggested definition of what a bachelor is:

For any *S, S* is a bachelor if and only if

(1)  *S* is an adult.

(2)  *S* is male.

(3)  *S* is unmarried.

I'm not claiming that this definition precisely captures what "bachelor" means in ordinary English. Rather, I want to use it as an example of a proposed definition.

The definition is a generalization. It concerns any individual you care to consider. The definition makes two claims: The first is that *IF* the individual has characteristics (1), (2), and (3), then the individual is a bachelor. In other words, (1), (2), and (3) are together *sufficient* for being a bachelor. The second claim is that *IF* the individual is a bachelor, then the individual has all three characteristics. In other words, (1), (2), and (3) are each *necessary* for being a bachelor.

We can define what a necessary condition is and what a sufficient condition is as follows:

"*X* is a necessary condition for *Y*" means that if *Y* is true, then *X* is true.

"*X* is a sufficient condition for *Y*" means that if *X* is true, then *Y* is true.

What does the expression "if and only if" mean in this proposed definition of bachelorhood? It means that the conditions listed are both necessary and sufficient. A good definition will specify necessary and sufficient conditions for the concept one wishes to define.

This means that there can be two sorts of defect in a proposed definition. A definition can fail to provide conditions that are sufficient. It also can provide conditions that aren't necessary. And, of course, it can fall down on both counts. Which sorts of defects are present in the following suggested definitions?

*S* is a bachelor if and only if *S* is male.

*S* is a bachelor if and only if *S* is an unmarried human adult male who is tall and lives in Ohio.

The first definition is said to be "too broad"; it admits too much. The second is "too narrow"; it admits too little.

Conversely, it is possible for a physicist to have detailed knowledge of the physical principles that describe successful bike riding and yet not know how to ride a bike. The physicist may lack the ability to perform the behaviors, but not because there is some proposition he or she fails to grasp. I conclude that propositional knowledge is neither necessary nor sufficient for knowing how to perform some task. The two concepts of knowledge are quite separate.

The subject of this and the following two chapters is *propositional knowledge,* not *object knowledge* or *know-how knowledge.* The goal is to understand what propositional knowledge is. We want to answer the following question: What are the necessary and sufficient conditions for it to be true that *S* knows that *p,* where *p* is some proposition—for example, the proposition that the Rockies are in North America?

## TWO REQUIREMENTS FOR KNOWLEDGE: BELIEF AND TRUTH

Two ideas that form part of the concept of knowledge should be noted at the outset. First, if *S* knows that *p,* then *S* must believe that *p.* Second, if *S* knows that *p,* then *p* must be true. Knowledge requires both *belief* and *truth.*

I won't try to argue for the first of these requirements, but will just assume it is correct. The second does require some explanation, however. People sometimes say they know things that, in fact, turn out to be false. But this isn't a case of knowing things that are untrue, but of people *thinking* they know things that happen to be untrue.

Knowledge has an objective and a subjective side. You should remember this pair of concepts from Chapter 1. A fact is objective if its truth doesn't depend on the way anyone's mind is. It is an objective fact that the Rocky Mountains are more than 10,000 feet above sea level. A fact is subjective, on the other hand, if it isn't objective. The most obvious example of a subjective fact is a description of what's going on in someone's mind.

Whether someone believes the Rockies are more than 10,000 feet above sea level is a subjective matter, but whether the mountains really are that high is an objective matter. Knowledge requires both an objective and a subjective element. For *S* to know that *p, p* must be true and the subject, *S,* must believe that *p* is true.

I've just cited two necessary conditions for knowledge: Knowledge requires belief, and knowledge requires truth. Is that it? That is, are these two conditions not just separately necessary but also jointly sufficient? Is true belief enough for knowledge?

## PLATO: TRUE BELIEF ISN'T SUFFICIENT FOR KNOWLEDGE

In the dialogue called *The Theaetetus,* the Greek philosopher Plato (c. 430–345 B.C.), who was Aristotle's teacher, argues the answer is *no.* Orators and lawyers sometimes trick people into believing things; sometimes those things happen to be true. According to Plato, people who have been duped in this way have true beliefs, but they don't have knowledge.

Of course, the fact that orators and lawyers intend to deceive isn't crucial for Plato's point. Think of an individual, Clyde, who believes the story about Groundhog

Day. Clyde thinks that if the groundhog sees its shadow, then spring will come late. Clyde puts this silly principle to work this year. He receives the news about the behavior of the Official Designated Groundhog, and so he believes that spring will come late. Suppose Clyde turns out to be right about the late spring. If there is no real connection between the groundhog seeing its shadow and the coming of a late spring, then Clyde will have a true belief (that spring will come late), but he won't have knowledge.

So what else is needed, besides true belief, for someone to have knowledge? A natural suggestion is that knowledge requires justification. The problem with Clyde is that he didn't satisfy this further requirement (though perhaps he thought he did). Justification, notice, can't just mean that the subject *thinks* he has a reason; otherwise we'd have to conclude that Clyde knows how long winter will last just because he believes that he has a reason for thinking this.

## JUSTIFICATION

What does it mean to say that an individual is "justified" in believing a proposition? Sometimes we start believing that a proposition is true because we consider an argument that describes the evidence available. Mendel believed that genes exist because of the data he collected from his pea plants. Sherlock Holmes believed that Moriarty was the murderer because of the evidence he found at the crime scene. Should we conclude that people are justified in believing a proposition only when their belief in the proposition was caused by their considering an argument? This isn't always plausible. When I believe that I have a headache, I don't construct an argument in which the evidence is laid out in a set of propositions that constitute my premises. Still, it would seem that I am justified in believing that I have a headache. This suggests that there is such a thing as *noninferential justification*. Some of the propositions we believe are apprehended more or less "directly"; they are not inferred from other propositions that we believe.

What, then, does "justification" mean when it is used in accounts of what knowledge is? When we talk about someone's action being *morally* justified, we mean that the action does not violate any *moral* duties that the person has. Perhaps "justified belief" should be understood in a similar way. We should think of individuals as having certain duties concerning how their beliefs should be formed. A belief is justified if the process by which it was formed does not violate any duties that the person has. To make sense of this suggestion, we'd have to say what duties we have that govern how we are supposed to form our beliefs. Are we obliged to base our beliefs on the evidence that is available, and only on the evidence? This, I take it, is what I do when I believe that I have a headache. However, this suggestion requires further exploration; some of the issues were touched on in Chapter 10, on Pascal's Wager.

Even though the concept of "justification" requires further attention, it is plausible to think that this is one of the necessary ingredients that defines what knowledge is. Knowing that a proposition is true requires more than just having a true belief. The third requirement is that your belief be "justified."

## THE JTB THEORY

Suppose knowledge requires these three conditions. Is that it? That is, are these conditions not just separately necessary, but jointly sufficient? I'll call the theory of knowledge that asserts this the *JTB Theory*. It says that knowledge is one and the same thing as justified true belief:

> (JTB)   For any individual *S* and any proposition *p*, *S* knows
> that *p* if and only if
>
> (1)  *S* believes that *p*.
>
> (2)  *p* is true.
>
> (3)  *S* is justified in believing that *p*.

The JTB Theory states a generalization. It says what knowledge is for *any* person *S* and *any* proposition *p*. For example, let *S* be you and let *p* = "the moon is made of green cheese." The JTB Theory says this: If you know that the moon is made of green cheese, then statements (1) to (3) must be true as well. And if you don't know the moon is made of green cheese, then at least one of statements (1) to (3) must be false. As in the definition of bachelorhood discussed in the preceding box, the expression "if and only if" says that we are being given necessary and sufficient conditions for the defined concept.

## THREE COUNTEREXAMPLES TO THE JTB THEORY

In 1963 the U.S. philosopher Edmund Gettier published a pair of counterexamples to the JTB Theory ("Is Justified True Belief Knowledge?" *Analysis,* 1963, Vol. 23, pp. 121–123). What is a *counterexample?* It is an example that goes counter to what some general theory says. A counterexample to a generalization shows that the generalization is false. The JTB Theory says that *all* cases of justified true belief are cases of knowledge. Gettier thought his two examples show that an individual can have justified true belief without having knowledge. If Gettier is right, then the three conditions given by the JTB Theory aren't sufficient, even if they are necessary.

Here is one of Gettier's examples: Smith works in an office. He knows that someone will soon be promoted. The boss, who is very reliable, tells Smith that Jones is going to get the promotion. Smith has just counted the coins in Jones's pocket, finding there to be 10 coins there. Smith therefore has excellent evidence for the following proposition:

> (a)  Jones will get the promotion and Jones has 10 coins in his pocket.

Smith then deduces from this statement the following:

> (b)  The man who will get the promotion has 10 coins in his pocket.

Now suppose that, unknown to Smith, Jones will *not* get the promotion. Rather it is Smith himself who will be promoted. And suppose Smith also happens to have 10 coins in his pocket. Smith believes (b); and (b) is true. Gettier also claims that Smith is justified in believing (b), since Smith deduced it from (a). Although (a) is false, Smith had excellent reason to think that it is true. Gettier concludes that Smith has a justified true belief in (b), but Smith doesn't know that (b) is true.

Gettier's other example exhibits the same pattern. The subject validly deduces a true proposition from a proposition that is very well supported by evidence even though it is, unbeknownst to the subject, false. I now want to describe a kind of counterexample to the JTB Theory in which the subject reasons *non*deductively.

The British philosopher, logician, and social critic Bertrand Russell (1872–1970) described a very reliable clock that stands in a town square. This morning you walk by it and glance up to find out what the time is. As a result, you come to believe that the time is 9:55. You are justified in believing this, based on your correct assumption that the clock has been very reliable in the past, but suppose that, unbeknownst to you, the clock stopped exactly 24 hours ago. You now have a justified true belief that it is 9:55, but you don't know that this is the correct time.

Let me add a third example to Gettier's Smith/Jones story and to Russell's clock. You buy a ticket in a fair lottery. "Fair" means that one ticket will win and every ticket has the same chance. There are one thousand tickets and you get ticket number 452. You look at this ticket, think for a moment, and then believe the following proposition: Ticket number 452 will not win. Suppose that when the drawing occurs a week later, you are right. Your belief was true. In addition, it was extremely well justified; after all, its probability was extremely close to unity— there was only one chance in a thousand you would be mistaken. Yet, I think we want to say in this case that you didn't *know* that the ticket would fail to win. Here is a third case of justified true belief that isn't knowledge. Note that the reasoning here is nondeductive.

## WHAT THE COUNTEREXAMPLES HAVE IN COMMON

In all three of these cases, the subject has *highly reliable,* but not *infallible,* evidence for the proposition believed. The boss *usually* is right about who will be promoted; the clock *usually* is right as to what the time is; and it *usually* is true that a ticket drawn at random in a fair lottery doesn't win. Of course, *usually* doesn't mean *always.* The sources of information that the subjects exploit in these examples are *highly* reliable, but not *perfectly* reliable. All the sources of information are prone to error to at least some degree.

Do these examples really refute the JTB theory? That depends on how we understand the idea of justification. If highly reliable evidence is enough to justify a belief, then the counterexamples do refute the JTB theory. But if justification requires perfectly infallible evidence, then these examples don't undermine the JTB theory.

My view is that justifying evidence needn't be infallible. I think we can have rational and well-supported beliefs even when we aren't entitled to be absolutely certain that what we believe is true. This is the point of strong inductive and abductive arguments (Chapter 3) From this, I conclude that justified true belief is not sufficient for knowledge.

## AN ARGUMENT FOR SKEPTICISM

What more is required? The lottery example suggests the following idea. In this case, you *probably* won't be mistaken when you believe that ticket number 452 will lose, but high probability isn't enough. To know that the ticket will lose, it must be *impossible* for you to be mistaken. You don't have knowledge in this example, because there is a chance (small though it may be) that you will be wrong.

There is some plausibility to this suggestion about what knowledge requires. The problem is that this idea seems to lead immediately to skepticism—to the conclusion that we don't know anything. For it seems that virtually all the beliefs we have are based on evidence that isn't infallible. Consider, just briefly, the beliefs we have that depend on the testimony of our senses. We use vision, hearing, touch, and so forth, to gather evidence about the way the world is. Do the resulting beliefs count as knowledge? The problem is that the senses are sometimes misleading.

Right now, you believe you are looking at a printed page. You believe this because of the visual experiences you now are having. Do you *know* that there is a printed page in front of you? According to the present suggestion, for this to be true, it must be the case that you couldn't possibly be mistaken in believing what you do. But the fact of the matter seems to be that you *could* be mistaken. You might be hallucinating, or dreaming, or your senses might be malfunctioning in some other way.

So here's where we are. The JTB Theory is mistaken. JTB doesn't suffice for knowledge. As an alternative to the JTB theory, we have this suggestion: Knowledge requires the impossibility of error. This suggestion, plausible though it may be as a diagnosis of why you don't have knowledge in the lottery example, allows us to formulate the following argument for skepticism:

> If *S* knows that *p*, then it isn't possible that *S* is mistaken in believing that *p*.
> It is possible that *S* is mistaken in believing that *p*.
> _____
> *S* doesn't know that *p*.

This form of argument can be used to argue that *a posteriori* knowledge does not exist. Recall from Chapter 8 that a proposition is *a posteriori* if it can be known only through the testimony of sense experience. The skeptic claims that beliefs based on sense experience aren't totally immune from the possibility of error. People make perceptual mistakes—for example, in cases of illusion, hallucination, and dreaming. Since we can't absolutely rule out the possibility of error, the skeptic concludes that we must admit that the senses don't provide us with knowledge.

---

### Is Skepticism Self-Refuting?

Skeptics claim that people don't know anything. Can skeptics claim to know that what they say is true? If not, does that show that their philosophical thesis is false?

It is a contradiction to say that you know that no one (including yourself) knows anything. But a skeptic can *assert* that people lack knowledge without claiming to *know* that this is so. In addition, a skeptic can claim to provide a *good argument* for skepticism. This isn't contradictory.

The thesis that no one knows anything, if true, can't be known to be true. But that doesn't show that the position is false. If you think that all truths are knowable, you will say that this skeptical thesis can't be true. But why think that all truths are knowable? Why not think, instead, that the universe may contain truths that we are incapable of knowing?

Another way for skeptics to avoid contradicting themselves is to be modest. Instead of claiming that no one knows *anything,* they could limit themselves to the claim that no one ever knows anything *through the testimony of the senses.* If this more limited kind of skepticism could be supported by an *a priori* argument, the position wouldn't be self-refuting.

---

This argument for skepticism is deductively valid. (Identify its logical form.) The first premise seems to describe a plausible requirement for knowing the proposition in question. The second premise also seems plausible; it just says that the beliefs we have aren't absolutely immune from the possibility of error. If you want to reject skepticism, you must refute one or both of these premises.

Although the above argument has fairly plausible premises, its conclusion is pretty outrageous. I think I know lots of things, and I believe this is true of you as well. It is hard to accept the idea that I don't know that I have a hand. If you think that you now know there is a printed page in front of you, you should too balk at this argument for skepticism. The skeptical argument contradicts a fundamental part of our commonsense picture of the way we are related to the world around us. Common sense says that people sometimes have knowledge of the world they inhabit; the skeptical argument says that common sense is mistaken in this respect. If there is a mistake in the argument, where is it?

---

## Review Questions

1. Explain how object knowledge, know-how knowledge, and propositional knowledge differ.

2. What do the following pieces of terminology mean? (i) *X* is a necessary condition for *Y;* (ii) *X* is a sufficient condition for *Y;* (iii) *X* is true if and only if *Y* is true; (iv) *o* is a counterexample to the statement "All emeralds are green."

3. Why think that true belief isn't sufficient for knowledge? What is the JTB theory? What is the difference between highly reliable evidence and absolutely infallible evidence?

4. Describe the three counterexamples to the JTB Theory (Gettier's, Russell's, and the lottery example). Do these counterexamples show that JTB isn't necessary or that it isn't sufficient for knowledge?
5. What is skepticism? What is the argument for skepticism given at the end of this chapter? Is the argument deductively valid?

## Problems for Further Thought

1. People sometimes say, concerning a proposition that is difficult to take to heart, "I know it is true, but I don't believe it." Does this refute the claim that if *S* knows that *p,* then *S* believes that *p?*
2. I suggested that we lack knowledge in the lottery example because knowledge requires the impossibility of error. Can you think of a different explanation for why we lack knowledge in this or in the other two examples that were used against the JTB Theory?

## CHAPTER 13

# *Descartes' Foundationalism*

René Descartes (1596–1650) is sometimes described as the father of modern philosophy. The kind of epistemology he tried to develop is called *foundationalism.* Before launching into the details of Descartes' philosophy, I want to describe what kind of approach to the problem of knowledge foundationalism provides.

## FOUNDATIONALISM

The word *foundationalism* should make you think of a building. What keeps a building from falling over? The answer has two parts. First, there is a solid foundation. Second, the rest of the building, which I'll call the superstructure, is attached securely to that solid foundation. Descartes wanted to show that (many if not all of) the beliefs we have about the world are cases of genuine knowledge. To show this, he wanted to divide our beliefs into two categories. There are the foundational beliefs, which are perfectly solid. Then, there are the superstructural beliefs, which count as knowledge because they rest securely on that solid foundation.

Besides this metaphor from architecture, there is another that should help you understand what Descartes' project is. You probably had a geometry course in high school. Here you studied Euclid's development of the subject. Recall that Euclid, who lived about 2,200 years ago, divided the propositions of geometry into two categories. First, there are the axioms of geometry. These are supposed to be simple and totally obvious truths. Second, there are the theorems, which at first glance are somewhat less obvious. Euclid shows that the theorems are true by showing how they can be deduced from the axioms.

A foundationalist theory of knowledge could also be called a Euclidean theory of knowledge. To show that a given body of beliefs counts as knowledge, we use the following strategy: First, we identify the beliefs that will provide the foundations of knowledge (the axioms). These must be shown to have some special property, like being totally beyond doubt. In a moment, I'll clarify what Descartes had in mind by this "special property." Second, we show that the rest of our beliefs count as knowledge because they bear some special relationship to the foundational items. In Euclid's geometry, the special relationship was deductive implication.

Euclid, of course, was interested only in the beliefs we have about geometry. Descartes had a more comprehensive ambition. He was interested in the totality of what we believe. But whether the problem is to describe the foundations of geometry or the foundations of knowledge as a whole, there are two ideas that must be clarified. We need to identify what the foundational items are, and we need to describe the relationship that must obtain between foundational and superstructural items that qualifies the latter as knowledge. In doing so, we need to remember that the building metaphor is only a metaphor. What makes the foundation of a house solid is that the walls are thick and hard and are set deeply into solid ground. But foundational beliefs aren't foundational because they are thick and hard and planted deeply in dirt. What, then, does it mean, for a belief to be foundational?

## EUCLID'S PARALLEL POSTULATE

If your high school geometry was like mine, you spent most of your time seeing what theorems could be proved from the axioms. You spent little or no time seeing why the axioms should be regarded as true. You were told that they are "obvious," or that they should just be accepted on faith. Maybe your teacher said that geometry is just a game and the axioms are the rules. In fact, the question about the axioms is a serious one. One of Euclid's starting assumptions—his so-called fifth postulate—bothered geometers for about two thousand years. This postulate says the following: Through a point that is not on a given straight line, there is exactly one line that is parallel to the given line. In other words, the parallel postulate says that if you extend all the lines passing through this point to infinity, exactly one of them will fail to intersect the initial line.

A number of subsequent geometers felt that this assumption of Euclid's was less obvious than the others assumptions he used. As a result, they tried to show that it could be proved from the other axioms. Geometers repeatedly failed to do this, and eventually established that the parallel postulate couldn't be proved from Euclid's other assumptions. That is, they showed the parallel postulate is *independent* of the other assumptions. This means that the denial of the parallel postulate is consistent with Euclid's other assumptions. It then transpired that non-Euclidean geometries could be developed, ones that retain Euclid's other assumptions but reject his parallel postulate.

The details of this story don't matter here. The history of geometry does show, however, that it sometimes isn't so clear whether a given statement is "obviously true." Perhaps Euclid thought that the parallel postulate was obvious. If so, that would have been his justification for treating it as something that doesn't have to be proved; it would stand on its own as an axiom/postulate. This doesn't mean, however, that subsequent geometers had to regard Euclid's judgment as beyond question. What strikes one person as obvious may not be so obvious to someone else.

## DESCARTES' METHOD OF DOUBT

Now let's consider Descartes' approach to the problem of knowledge. Descartes' goal is to refute skepticism. He wants to show that we really do have knowledge of the world we inhabit. His strategy for achieving this goal is foundationalist in character. This means the first item on his agenda must be to identify the beliefs that are foundational.

At the beginning of his *Meditations on First Philosophy* (1641), Descartes proposes a method for determining which of the beliefs he has are foundational. He called this the *method of doubt*. You see whether it is possible to doubt a proposition. If it is possible to do this, you set the belief aside—it isn't foundational. If it isn't possible to do so (that is, if the belief is *indubitable*), then the belief is a foundational item. Notice that failing the method of doubt test doesn't mean that the belief is *false*. It just means the belief isn't *absolutely certain*.

Descartes doesn't try to apply this method to beliefs one at a time. Think of all the beliefs you have—there are millions (at least). You believe that 1 is a number. You believe that 2 is a number. And so on. It would be time consuming and also boring to try to consider each belief separately. Rather, what Descartes does is consider *kinds* of beliefs; he considers whether all the beliefs in this or that category pass or fail the method of doubt test.

---

### Indubitability

Very few propositions are made true just by your believing them. You can believe that there are unicorns, but that doesn't make such creatures pop into existence.

Consider the proposition "I am thinking." If you believe that this is true, then it must be true. Believing is a kind of thinking. Descartes thinks that the same is true for propositions of the form "I seem to see that $p$." He also thinks that this is true for propositions that say that you believe that $p$ or want it to be true that $q$ (where $p$ and $q$ are propositions). If you believe them, they must be true.

If a proposition is made true by your believing it, then it has this property: You can't describe a situation in which you believe the proposition but the proposition is false. Descartes determines whether a proposition is dubitable by seeing whether he can describe a situation of this kind. This means that a proposition is indubitable if the proposition is made true by the act of believing it.

Are there indubitable propositions that aren't made true by your believing them? Some philosophers have held that simple logical truths, like "It is raining or it is not raining," are beyond doubt. Is it plausible to maintain that these are made true by your believing them?

## THE METHOD APPLIED TO A POSTERIORI BELIEFS

The first category Descartes considers is the set of beliefs that depend for their justification on sense experience. Many of our beliefs are based on sight, hearing, touch, taste, and smell. These propositions are a posteriori (Chapter 8). Is it possible to doubt these beliefs? Descartes says that the answer is *yes*. Your present belief that there is a printed page in front of you is based on vision. Vision, however, can be misleading. Psychologists tell us about hallucinations and illusions. Maybe you've had such experiences yourself. If not, remember Macbeth, who was certain a dagger was hovering in front of him. Besides hallucinations, there is the fact of dreaming. In a dream you may find yourself believing there is a printed page in front of you. You may find yourself having visual experiences just like the ones you are having now. But in the dream, your belief is mistaken. Descartes takes this to show that the belief you have right now might be mistaken.

So beliefs that rest on the testimony of the senses fail the method of doubt test. Let's be clear on why Descartes thinks they do so. Descartes shows such beliefs are dubitable by constructing a story of a particular kind. You now believe that there is a printed page in front of you on the basis of a set of visual experiences. Let's call the proposition you believe *B* and the experiences you now are having *E*. Your belief that *B* is true rests on your having experiences *E*. Descartes holds that *B* can be doubted because he can describe a situation in which you have *E* and believe *B* even though *B* is false. Dreams and hallucinations show how this can happen. Descartes shows that a class of beliefs is dubitable by constructing a story of this sort.

## DUBITABILITY IS A LOGICAL, NOT A PSYCHOLOGICAL, PROPERTY

In saying that a belief is dubitable, Descartes isn't saying that we are able to take seriously the idea that it might be false. The proposition that there is a page in front of you is dubitable in Descartes' sense; this doesn't mean you are now about to take seriously the possibility that no page is present. A proposition is dubitable when a certain sort of story can be constructed; dubitability is thus a logical property that a proposition has. It has nothing to do with whether we can get ourselves to believe that the proposition might be false.

## THE METHOD APPLIED TO BELIEFS BASED ON RATIONAL CALCULATION

Descartes next turns his attention to propositions of mathematics. I believe that $2 + 3 = 5$. I believe that squares have four sides. Descartes remarks that these are true "whether I'm awake or asleep." These propositions are *a priori* (recall this piece of vocabulary from Chapter 8). They don't depend for their justification on sensory experience. Do propositions justified by reason, independent of sense experience, pass the method of doubt test? Descartes thinks they fail. How could this be true? Descartes asks us to imagine that our minds are deceived by an "evil demon."

Imagine that an evil demon causes our faculty of reasoning to find propositions totally obvious that in fact are false. If this were so, we might believe that $2 + 3 = 5$ even though the proposition isn't true.

These conclusions—all reached in the first of the *Meditations*—are entirely negative. *A posteriori* beliefs about the character of the world outside the mind are dubitable. We see this by considering dreams and hallucinations. *A priori* propositions also are dubitable. We see this by considering the evil demon. If no belief in these two categories passes the method of doubt test, which beliefs could be the foundations of knowledge? What category of belief could possibly satisfy this very stringent requirement?

## I AM THINKING, THEREFORE I EXIST

In an earlier work, the *Discourse on the Method* (1637), Descartes identifies a pair of propositions that pass the test:

> I noticed that while I was trying to think everything false, it must be that I, who was thinking this, was something. And observing that this truth, *I am thinking, therefore I exist* [ *Je pense, donc je suis; Cogito ergo sum* in Latin], was so solid and secure that the most extravagant suppositions of the skeptics could not overthrow it, I judged that I need not scruple to accept it as the first principle of the philosophy I was seeking.

In the *Second Meditation,* Descartes focuses on the belief "I am, I exist" as the first proposition that can be judged beyond doubt.

To understand what Descartes is driving at, you must think about yourself, formulating your thoughts in the first person. When Descartes considers the proposition "I am thinking," you aren't supposed to consider the proposition "Descartes is thinking." Rather, you should say to yourself precisely what Descartes says to himself.

Consider my belief that I am thinking. I can't doubt this. I can't construct a story in which I believe this proposition, though it is false. For if I *believe* the proposition, then I am thinking, and so the proposition is true. So the attempt to doubt the proposition fails; the attempt to doubt it proves that it must be true. The proposition "I am thinking" passes the method of doubt test.

There are two important characteristics of the proposition "I am thinking" that you should note. First, it is important that the proposition is in the first person. When Descartes considers "I am thinking," he concludes that this proposition passes the method of doubt test. However, if he had considered "Descartes is thinking," the result would have been different. It *is* possible for Descartes to doubt that there is someone named "Descartes." He can invent a story in which there is no such person as Descartes; the fact that such a story can be constructed shows that the proposition is dubitable. The second feature of the proposition "I am thinking" is that it involves a psychological property. I can't doubt that I am thinking, but I can doubt that I am now in North America. Both beliefs are first person, but only the former is psychological.

As noted, Descartes maintains that the proposition "I exist" also passes the method of doubt test. Take a few minutes to formulate an argument, similar to the one just described for "I am thinking," that shows that this is so.

So far, we have two propositions that Descartes thinks can serve as foundations for the rest of what we know. I can't doubt that I am thinking; nor can I doubt that I exist. This is a meager foundation. Just as it would be hard to erect a big building on a foundation made of two bricks, so it would be difficult to ground the whole of what we know about the world on this paltry foundation of two beliefs.

There is more, however. Consider propositions solely about the contents of your own present sensory experiences. Such propositions describe the way things *seem* to be, not the way they in fact *are*. You now seem to see a page in front of you. Descartes thinks that all such first-person descriptions of the way things seem are indubitable. To understand Descartes' point, it is essential to recognize the difference between the following two propositions:

> There is a page in front of me.
>
> I seem to see a page in front of me.

It is pretty clear, as noted earlier, that the first of these can be doubted. That's the point about dreams and illusions. Descartes maintains that the second proposition is different. He holds that it has this peculiar property: If you believe that the proposition is true, then you can't be mistaken. If you *believe* that you seem to see a page in front of you, then you *do* seem to see a page in front of you. You can't be mistaken in your beliefs about the way things seem to be.

So the foundation of knowledge has just been augmented. "I am thinking" and "I exist" are indubitable, and so are the many first-person beliefs about the way things seem.

## THESIS OF THE INCORRIGIBILITY OF THE MENTAL

Descartes went even further. He thought that people have infallible access to what they believe and desire. Introspection ("looking inward") is a method that the mind can use to accurately grasp its own contents. This is sometimes expressed by saying that Descartes believed in *the thesis of the incorrigibility of the mental*. Although "There is a page in front of me" isn't indubitable, Descartes thought "I believe that there is a page in front of me" is indubitable. If you believe that you have that belief, then it must be true that you have that belief. Ditto for desires. If you believe that you want some ice cream, then it must be true that you want some ice cream.

A great deal of work in psychology in the last hundred years shows that this incorrigibility thesis isn't plausible. Sigmund Freud, whose views on religion came up in Chapter 10, argued that we often misunderstand what we really believe and what we really want. At times our beliefs and desires would be very upsetting to us if we were conscious of them. So, as a defense mechanism, our minds repress them. The result is that we often have mistaken beliefs about what we really think and want. An example of this is Freud's theory of the Oedipus complex. Freud held that little boys want to kill their fathers and marry their mothers. If you asked a little boy whether he wanted to do this, however, he probably would sincerely answer *no*. You might well ask: What evidence can there be for this theory? If little boys deny having these desires, why think they have them? Freud's answer is that this theory is a plausible explanation of what little boys *do*. It is their behavior that we must consider, not just what they say they believe and desire. Verbal reports about what we think and want are evidence as to what our beliefs and desires really are. Sincere reports, however, don't settle the matter, since behavior may provide *other* evidence that is relevant.

Although this idea—that we often have a false picture of our own beliefs and desires—is very important in Freud's theories, it isn't unique to them. A great deal of other work in psychology also denies Descartes' thesis of incorrigibility. See, for example, the article by R. Nesbett and T. Wilson called "Telling More Than We Can Know" (*Psychological Review* 84: 231–259). Descartes wants to include *all* first-person reports of his own beliefs and desires as foundations. Each, he thought, passes the method of doubt test. Freud and many other psychologists would disagree. I'm on their side.

Where does this leave Descartes' project of identifying the foundations of knowledge? The foundations include *I am thinking* and *I exist* and all first-person reports about the way the world seems to be. Another example of an indubitable belief might be "I am in pain." Descartes' view was that if you believe that you are in pain, then you are in pain.

In Chapter 2, I pointed out that for a very large class of our beliefs, there is a huge difference between believing a proposition and that proposition's actually being true. To believe that the Rockies are over ten thousand feet is one thing; for the mountains to actually be that high is another. It is misguided wishful thinking to hold that believing the proposition guarantees that it is true. This sensible separation of belief and truth, which seems right for a wide class of propositions, is called into question by the special examples that Descartes thought pass the method of doubt test. According to Descartes, "I am in pain" must be true if I think it is. The same holds for "I am thinking" and "I seem to see a page in front of me." These are cases in which wishful thinking seems to work.

## DO FIRST-PERSON PSYCHOLOGICAL BELIEFS PROVIDE A SUFFICIENT FOUNDATION?

These propositions, Descartes thought, are foundational. We can't be mistaken in believing them. Some philosophers have disagreed with Descartes' claim. They have maintained that it is possible to be mistaken in holding some of these beliefs. I'm not going to address that matter here. Instead, I want to consider another problem. Recall the architectural metaphor discussed at the beginning of this chapter. An adequate foundation for a building must have two properties. It must be (1) secure and (2) sufficient to support the house. The foundations of knowledge are subject to the same requirements. According to Descartes, they must be indubitable. In addition, it must be possible to rest everything else we know on them. Don't forget that the method of doubt is intended to identify the foundations; the entire superstructure is supposed to rest on that basis.

Descartes, as I mentioned before, wasn't a skeptic. He thought that we know lots of things about the world outside our own minds. For example, you know that there is a page in front of you now. This belief about the external world isn't indubitable; it didn't pass the method of doubt test. Nevertheless, It Is (Descartes would agree) something you know. How can Descartes show that this is true? Recall the Euclidean analogy. We've just identified some axioms of the system of knowledge. Do these suffice to prove some theorems? We must show how you know there is a page in front of you by showing how this proposition is connected with foundational ones. In Euclidean geometry, we justify theorems by deducing them from axioms. How can a superstructural belief be shown to be knowledge? We must show that it is connected with foundational pieces of knowledge in the right way. But what is this special connection supposed to be?

Can deduction do the trick? Euclid deduced theorems from axioms. Can Descartes deduce propositions about the world outside the mind from beliefs that are first-person psychological reports? To show that you know that there is a page in front of you, maybe we should try to deduce that proposition in the following way:

I seem to see a page in front of me.

There is a page in front of me.

The premise of this argument is foundational. The problem is that it does not deductively imply the conclusion. The existence of a page in front of me doesn't deductively follow from the way things seem to me now. That's the point noted before about dreams and hallucinations.

The premise given isn't enough. Even if I augmented it with other reports about my present psychological state (for example, "I seem to feel a page," "I seem to taste a page," etc.) that still wouldn't be enough. Such premises might be ones about which I'm perfectly certain, but they don't provide a sufficient foundation for the beliefs I have about the world outside the mind. Such arguments are not deductively valid.

## AN ADDITIONAL FOUNDATIONAL BELIEF: GOD EXISTS AND IS NO DECEIVER

Descartes saw quite clearly that the argument just represented needs an additional premise, one that will bridge the gap between first-person psychological premises and a conclusion that describes the world outside the mind. Descartes thought the proposition that *God exists and is no deceiver* provides the additional premise that he needs.

How would this additional premise solve Descartes' problem? Descartes had the following picture in mind: God created your mind and situated you in the world. What sort of mind did God give you? Obviously, he didn't give you a mind that reaches true conclusions about the world on each and every occasion. Your mind isn't infallible. On the other hand, God would not have furnished you with a mind that leads you to false beliefs about the world no matter how carefully you reason and no matter how much evidence you consult. If God had done this, he would have been a deceiver. Descartes thinks that God created us with minds that have the capacity to attain true beliefs about the world. We are neither infallible nor are we hopelessly trapped by falsehood. Rather, we are somewhere in the middle: We can reach true beliefs if we are careful about how we use the minds that God bestowed upon us. This is the kind of mind that an all-PKG god would have given us. But why think that such a being exists?

## HOW TO PROVE THAT GOD EXISTS

I've just explained what role the proposition that God exists and is no deceiver is supposed to play in Descartes' theory of knowledge. However, if this proposition is to be a part of the foundations, it must be indubitable. It must pass the method of doubt test. Descartes has to show that the proposition that God exists and is no deceiver is not just true, but that it is indubitable. Here Descartes seems to be trying to do the impossible. Isn't it obvious that it is possible to doubt that God exists and is no deceiver? After all, atheists or agnostics don't believe that God exists. Isn't this enough to show that it is *possible* to doubt that God exists and is no deceiver?

Descartes thinks that atheists and agnostics have not considered the matter carefully enough. They *think* they can doubt the proposition, but they have not really grasped what this would really involve. (Recall Anselm's comment about the "fool" "said in his heart what cannot be conceived.") Descartes believes that he has a proof of the existence of God whose premises are *indubitable*. In addition, the proof is so simple that once you attend carefully to it, you can't doubt that there is a god. This is the proof that Descartes lays out in the *Third Meditation*. Here it is, in outline:

(1) My idea of God is an idea of a perfect being.

(2) There must be at least as much perfection in the cause as there is in the effect.

_____

Hence, the cause of my idea is a perfect being—namely, God himself.

Once you inspect this proof, the proposition that God exists is like the proposition *I am thinking*—it is impossible to doubt that it is true.

Descartes thinks he knows premise (1) of this argument by introspection. By looking inward at the contents of his own mind, he can discern this fact about himself. Premise (1), Descartes believes, is indubitable. As to premise (2), Descartes thinks that it is an indubitable principle about causality. It can be broken into two components. First, there is the idea that every event has a cause. Second, there is the idea that the cause must be at least as perfect as the effect. It isn't clear why we should accept these principles about causality. For example, why couldn't some events occur for no reason at all? This is a question we explored in Chapters 4 and 7. Descartes needs to show not only that it is *true* that every event has a cause, but that this proposition is *indubitably* true. This is something that he does not succeed in doing.

Premise (2) needs to be clarified. Descartes distinguishes two kinds of perfection (or "reality") that an idea or representation might possess. To find out how *objectively* perfect a representation is, you must find out how perfect the thing is that the representation represents. Two photographs of a saint must have the same degree of objective perfection; two photographs of a trash can will have the same degree of objective perfection as well. And if saints are more perfect than trash cans, the first pair will have more objective perfection than the second.

This characterization of objective perfection requires a little fine-tuning. A picture of a unicorn has a certain degree of objective perfection, even though there are no unicorns. So, to determine how objectively perfect the picture is, you must ask yourself this question: If the picture represented something that actually existed, how perfect would that thing be?

I hope you can see from the definition of objective perfection why Descartes thinks that his concept of God has the maximum amount of objective perfection. This is something that Descartes can say just by examining his concept of God. Indeed, it is something that an atheist might agree to as well. If there were a God, then that being would have all the perfections; this means that the atheist's concept of God is objectively perfect.

The concept of objective perfection allows some representations to be ranked higher than others. My idea of God is at the top. Somewhere below that is my idea of a saint. And still further down the list is my idea of a trash can. The second kind of perfection that Descartes discusses is different. This is what Descartes calls an idea's *formal perfection*. All mental contents have the same degree of formal perfection, because they all are made of the same stuff. To see what Descartes has in mind here, consider paintings. These may differ in their degree of objective perfection, but all are made of canvas and paint. In this sense, they have the same degree of formal perfection. Descartes thinks the same holds for all the ideas I may have.

In the argument for the existence of God that I just sketched, Descartes is talking about the *objective* perfection of his idea of God. Let's reformulate the argument to make this explicit:

(1) My idea of God is objectively perfect.

(2) If an idea is objectively perfect, then the cause of that idea must be a perfect being.

———————

Hence, God exists.

Premise (2) strikes me as implausible. Here is a way to see that it is false. I claim that people could form their concept of God (a perfect being) in the following way. They could look at *imperfect* things in the world and thereby form the idea of *limited* intelligence, *limited* goodness, and *limited* power. Then, by applying the concept of negation (the concept we express by the word "not") to these ideas, they would obtain the idea of a being who has *unlimited* intelligence, goodness, and power. This seems to be an entirely possible causal explanation for why we have the idea of a perfect being. If it is possible, then (2) is false.

In the *Third Meditation,* Descartes explicitly considers this suggestion. He rejects the idea that we might have acquired the concept of perfection by seeing imperfect things and then applying the concept of negation. You should consider Descartes' argument and decide whether you think it works. Descartes thinks the only possible explanation for the fact that we have an idea of a perfect being is that a perfect being actually exists and caused us to have this idea. Leaving this exercise to you, I'll conclude that Descartes' causal argument for the existence of God is defective. Descartes wanted to show that "God exists" isn't just true, but indubitably true. This proposition was to be a foundational element in the structure of our knowledge. The argument he gave falls short of this ambitious goal.

## THE CLARITY AND DISTINCTNESS CRITERION

If God is no deceiver, how can we tell whether the beliefs we have are true? Descartes thought that if we inspect them carefully, and make sure that they are clear and distinct, we can be certain that they are correct. Descartes maintained that *clear and distinct* beliefs must be true. If you reason carefully and use your mental faculties in the way that God intended them to be used, you can obtain knowledge of the world you inhabit. Descartes thinks you have an indubitable grasp of the contents of your own mind; he also thinks that you can know indubitably that God exists and is no deceiver. This foundation, he believes, provides a sufficient and secure basis for you to gain knowledge of the world you inhabit.

## THE CARTESIAN CIRCLE

Scholars argue over whether Descartes' argument for the existence of God has a defect that goes beyond the fact that some of his premises are dubious. They have suggested that the argument is circular, given its place in Descartes' larger philosophical program. Recall that Descartes wants to prove that God exists and is no deceiver in order to be able to conclude that clear and distinct ideas must be true.

Descartes' argument for the existence of God, like all arguments, involves the use of reason. For us to recognize that the argument establishes the existence of God, we must use the faculty of reasoning we possess. Descartes' argument begins by examining his concept of God and determining that this is the idea of a perfect being. Descartes therefore seems to be using the clarity and distinctness criterion in arguing that God exists. Descartes vehemently denied that he was guilty of circular reasoning. This problem has come to be known as the Problem of the Cartesian Circle.

Here's how I see this issue: Descartes is using the method of doubt test to assemble foundations for knowledge. His goal is to assemble enough premises by this procedure so that he can show that we have knowledge of the world outside our minds. The existence of a God who is no deceiver is supposed to be one of these premises. Descartes thought his causal argument for the existence of God is beyond doubt; he thought that as you reason your way through the argument, you must find it irresistible.

Why should we agree that the proposition "Every event has a cause" is beyond doubt? Descartes' view seems to be that when we consider the proposition carefully, using the full resources of clarification and logic that we possess, we will be driven to conclude that the proposition must be true. This seems to mean that we are applying the clarity and distinctness criterion. If so, Descartes is reasoning in a circle.

## CONCLUSION

Where does this leave the project of refuting skepticism? Descartes thought that first-person psychological beliefs are indubitable. He recognized that this, by itself, isn't enough to show that the beliefs we have provide us with genuine knowledge of the world outside the mind. Additional premises are needed. The following example argument shows how Descartes wanted to bridge the gap between the indubitable knowledge we have of our own minds and the beliefs we have about the world outside our minds:

(1)  I now believe that the object in front of me is a page.

(2)  My present belief is clear and distinct.

(3)  Clear and distinct ideas are true.

There is a page in front of me.

The argument is valid. If the premises are true, the conclusion also must be true. Descartes' foundationalism can be understood as a pair of claims about this argument. First, he claims that the premises of this argument are *indubitable*. Second, he thinks that the conclusion of the argument is a proposition we *know* because it follows from these indubitable premises. I've already discussed premise (1); Descartes thought that it was indubitable. But what of the next two premises? There is a tension between these two claims.

Suppose we grant Descartes that premise (3) is right—that a clear and distinct idea can't fail to be true. If we grant this, then it isn't so obvious that my present belief about what is in front of me really is clear and distinct. I may *think* that it is, but this appearance may be deceiving. So if (3) is right, (2) can't be beyond doubt. Alternatively, suppose we are able to tell, by introspection, whether a belief is clear and distinct. That will be enough to underwrite the truth of (2). In that case, there is no longer any absolute assurance that (3) is right. The problem here concerns whether we should see "clarity and distinctness" as a purely subjective characteristic of a belief. If I can tell just by examining the contents of my own beliefs whether they are "clear and distinct," I see no reason to say that a clear and distinct belief must be true. On the other hand, if we treat "clarity and distinctness" as a characteristic that is necessarily connected with truth, I don't see how I can tell whether a belief is "clear and distinct" just by introspection.

Descartes tried to refute the following skeptical argument, which I described at the end of the previous chapter:

Knowledge requires the impossibility of error.

It now is possible that I am mistaken in believing that there is a page in front of me.

---

Hence, I don't know that there is a page in front of me.

Descartes accepted the first premise but denied the second. Descartes concedes that we often make mistakes. The senses sometimes play tricks on us, and so does our faculty of reasoning. But the fact that this *sometimes* happens doesn't show that it is happening *now*. If I am now reasoning in a careful and logically rigorous way, then I can't now be mistaken in what I believe, or so Descartes maintained. So Descartes' reply to the skeptic's argument can be put like this:

If God exists and is no deceiver and I now have a clear and distinct belief that there is a page in front of me, then I can't be mistaken in thinking that there is a page in front of me.

God exists and is no deceiver and I now have a clear and distinct belief that there is a page in front of me.

---

I can't be mistaken in thinking that there is a page in front of me.

The problem is that Descartes' argument for the second premise of this last argument wasn't successful. He wasn't able to prove that we are embedded in the world in the special way described by the hypothesis that God exists and is no deceiver. In consequence, he wasn't able to refute the skeptic's argument.

## Review Questions

1. What is foundationalism in epistemology? What does it have to do with Euclidean geometry? With building a house?
2. What is the method of doubt test? What does Descartes use this method to do? What fails the test? What passes?

3. What does it mean to say that there is a "gap" between our first-person psychological beliefs and the beliefs we have about the world outside the mind?
4. Descartes thought that proving that God exists would help show why we are able to have knowledge of the world around us. Why did he think this? Is the proposition that "God exists and is no deceiver" foundational, according to Descartes?
5. Analyze Descartes' causal argument for the existence of God. Suppose that one of Aquinas's arguments for the existence of God is valid and has true premises. Could Descartes have used it, instead of his causal argument, to prove that God exists?
6. What is the Problem of the Cartesian Circle?
7. In the previous chapter, an argument for skepticism was presented. How would Descartes evaluate this argument?

## Problems for Further Thought

1. Which of the following propositions pass the method of doubt test? How are they different from each other?

> I saw Joe run.
>
> I seem to remember seeing Joe run.
>
> I remember seeming to see Joe run.

2. Can someone mistakenly believe that he or she seems to see a coffee cup? Can someone mistakenly believe he or she is in pain?
3. I suggested that our idea of a perfect being might be obtained by observing imperfect things and then using the concept of negation. Descartes considers this suggestion in the *Third Meditation* and rejects it (consult the paragraph that begins "Nor should I imagine that I do not perceive..."). What reason does Descartes give for rejecting this explanation? Are his reasons plausible?
4. In his book *The Principles of Philosophy* (1644), Descartes defines clarity and distinctness as follows:

> I term that "clear" which is present and apparent to an attentive mind, in the same way that we see objects clearly when, being present to the regarding eye, they operate upon it with sufficient strength. But the "distinct" is that which is so precise and different from all other objects that it contains within itself nothing but what is clear.... Perceptions may be clear without being distinct, but cannot be distinct without also being clear.

Given this definition, can a clear and distinct idea be false?

## CHAPTER 14

# *The Reliability Theory of Knowledge*

### DESCARTES: KNOWLEDGE IS INTERNALLY CERTIFIABLE

According to Descartes, *knowledge is internally certifiable.* What does this mean? It means that if I know some proposition *p*, then there exists an argument that shows that *p* must be true, *whose premises are either* a priori *true or knowable by introspection.* Recall how Descartes would explain why I now know that there is a page in front of me:

I believe that there is a page in front of me.

My belief that there is a page in front of me is clear and distinct.

Clear and distinct ideas are true.

There is a page in front of me.

The first two premises I know by *introspection*—by gazing within my own mind and examining its contents. How do I know that the third premise is true? I know by introspection that I have an idea of a perfect God; I (supposedly) know *a priori* that an idea of a perfect being must be caused by a perfect being. Putting these two thoughts together, I deduce that God—a perfect being—must exist. The third premise is supposed to follow from this.

Notice that the word "knowledge" does not appear in the displayed argument. So what does this argument have to do with the issue of whether I *know* that there is a page in front of me? For Descartes, I know that the concluding proposition is true because I know the premises are true. And how do I know the premises? I know these by introspection and *a priori* reasoning.

I want to name the elements in this argument. There is a *subjective premise,* an *objective conclusion,* and a *linking premise.* The subjective premise describes what is going on in the subject's mind ("I believe that there is a page in front of me"). The objective conclusion makes a claim about the world outside the subject's mind ("There is a page in front of me"). The linking premise (or premises) shows how the subjective premise necessitates the objective conclusion ("If I have a particular belief and it is clear and distinct, then it is true").

This vocabulary can be used to say what is characteristic of Descartes's approach to the problem of knowledge. His idea—that knowledge is internally certifiable—comes to this: *If the subject knows that the objective conclusion is true, then the subject must know that the linking premise is true and must know this independently of sense experience.* By introspection and *a priori* reasoning, I can establish the required connection between what is inside the mind and what is outside it.

The theory of knowledge I'll discuss in this chapter involves a very different approach from that taken by Descartes. It agrees with Descartes that knowledge requires the existence of a connection between what is going on inside the mind and what is going on outside it. Knowledge requires that a particular linking premise be true. But according to the *Reliability Theory of Knowledge*, the linking premise doesn't have to be knowable by introspection and *a priori* reasoning. In fact, this theory maintains that the subject doesn't have to know that the linking premise is true at all. It just has to *be* true. This approach to the problem of knowledge was first proposed by Fred Dretske (in "Conclusive Reasons," *Australasian Journal of Philosophy,* Vol. 49, 1971) and by David Armstrong (in *Belief, Truth, and Knowledge,* Cambridge University Press, 1973).

## WHAT MAKES A THERMOMETER RELIABLE?

The Reliability Theory of Knowledge claims there is an important analogy between knowledge and a reliable measuring device. If you know that there is a page in front of you now, then your belief is related to the world outside your mind in the same way that the reading of a reliable thermometer is related to the temperature.

Thermometers are devices that form representations of temperature. The height of the mercury column is the representation; the ambient temperature is the thing represented. Thermometer readings represent temperature, just as your beliefs represent the world outside your mind. Thermometer readings can be accurate or inaccurate, just as beliefs can be true or false. What makes a thermometer reliable? Does this just mean that its readings are accurate? To see why this isn't enough, consider a thermometer that is used just once. Suppose, on that one occasion, the thermometer said "98 degrees Fahrenheit" and the temperature happened to be 98 degrees Fahrenheit. The reading was accurate, but that doesn't mean that the thermometer was reliable. For all I've said, the thermometer may have been stuck. If so, it wasn't reliable, even though its one and only reading was accurate. A reliable thermometer is one for which there is a *necessary connection* between readings and temperatures. If the thermometer reads *n* degrees Fahrenheit, then the temperature *must be n* degrees Fahrenheit. If a thermometer is reliable, then its reading *must be* correct; it can't be mistaken in what it says. A stuck thermometer isn't reliable, even when its readings happen to be correct. It is unreliable because its readings are correct only *by accident.*

Do reliable thermometers exist? I think so. The mercury thermometers we use to check whether we have fevers are examples. In saying this, I'm not denying two obvious facts. First, a thermometer can be reliable in one set of circumstances but not in another. A mercury thermometer wouldn't be very useful for measuring temperature if it were wrapped in insulation before being placed in your mouth. The second point is that in saying that a thermometer is reliable, I'm not denying that it would be unreliable if it were broken. Hitting a reliable thermometer with a hammer will usually be enough to make it unreliable. So there are two things that help make a thermometer reliable. First, it has to be used in the right environment (for example, don't wrap it in insulation if you want to take somebody's temperature). Second, the internal makeup of the device has to be right (for example, the glass tube that holds the mercury can't be broken).

Notice that reliability is an objective feature of the relationship between the thermometer and its environment. The question is whether the thermometer and its environment make the following claim true: *If the thermometer says that the temperature is n degrees Fahrenheit, then the temperature must be n degrees Fahrenheit.* It is an entirely separate question whether anybody realizes that this thermometer/environment relationship obtains. Whether we notice this fact is a subjective question, but whether the relationship obtains is an objective matter.

Let's imagine that you take a thermometer out of a child's mouth, see that it reads 99 degrees Fahrenheit, and then announce: "The thermometer is reliable, and so the baby's temperature is 99 degrees Fahrenheit." Suppose a contentious philosopher (like me) comes along and tries to refute your claim. I say:

> Your thermometer isn't reliable. It is unreliable because I can conceive of a circumstance in which its reading would be false. For example, I can conceive of a situation in which the thermometer is wrapped in insulation. In that case, the thermometer reading wouldn't be correct. I also can conceive of the thermometer's being broken. In that case as well, the thermometer reading wouldn't be correct. It follows from the fact that I can conceive of these things that your thermometer isn't reliable.

Should you be convinced by my argument? I think not. Whether the thermometer is reliable *here and now* has nothing to do with what I can imagine. Granted, if the situations I described *actually* obtained, then the thermometer wouldn't be reliable, but from this it doesn't follow that the thermometer is unreliable in the actual circumstances in which it is used.

## RELEVANCE TO THE PROBLEM OF KNOWLEDGE

How does this discussion of reliable thermometers bear on the problem of knowledge? The Reliability Theory of Knowledge says that an individual knows a proposition if the individual is related to the proposition the way a reliable thermometer is related to the temperature it measures. A reliable thermometer wouldn't say *n* degrees Fahrenheit unless the temperature were *n* degrees Fahrenheit. An individual knows that there is a page in front of her precisely when she wouldn't have believed that there is a page in front of her unless there were one there. Another way to express this idea is by using the concept of *causality*. A thermometer is reliable in a given circumstance if the only thing that could cause the thermometer to read *n* degrees Fahrenheit is that the temperature really is *n* degrees Fahrenheit. Similarly, *S* knows that there is a page in front of her in a given circumstance if the only thing that could cause *S* to believe this is that there really is a page in front of her.

I hope the connection between thermometers and knowledge is starting to become clear. Suppose *S* believes that there is a page in front of her. We want to know whether this belief is an instance of knowledge. The answer should depend on the *actual* relationship that obtains between *S* and her environment. Suppose *S*'s sensory system is functioning normally; she isn't hallucinating, for example. In addition, suppose that there are no evil demons around who might choose to provide *S* with misleading evidence. If so, it may be true that *S* is a reliable indicator of the presence of a page. If you want to answer the question of whether *S* knows that there is a page present, it will be entirely irrelevant to point out that if *S* had taken a hallucinatory drug or if *S* were plagued by an evil demon, then *S*'s belief would be (or might be) false. These *hypothetical* considerations do nothing to undermine the claim that *S*'s sensory state is a reliable indicator of what is going on in her environment.

Here's how the Reliability Theory of Knowledge characterizes what knowledge is:

(RTK)  *S* knows that *p* if and only if

    (1)  *S* believes that *p*.

    (2)  *p* is true.

    (3)  in the circumstances that *S* occupies, if *S* believes that *p*, then *p* must be true.

The third condition can also be formulated in either of the following two ways:

In the circumstances that *S* occupies, *S* wouldn't believe that *p* unless *p* were true.

In the circumstances that *S* occupies, it is impossible that *S* believe *p* and *p* be false.

Notice that the Reliability Theory of Knowledge makes use of the concepts of *necessity* and *impossibility*. To understand this theory of knowledge, we need to look more carefully at what these concepts mean.

## THREE CONCEPTS OF IMPOSSIBILITY

I want to discuss three kinds of impossibility. Consider the following three statements:

    (1)  Joe can't be a married bachelor.

    (2)  Joe can't go faster than the speed of light.

    (3)  Joe can't tie his shoes now.

The word "can't" in each of these indicates that something is *impossible*, but different kinds of impossibility are involved.

The first statement is logically necessary. It has to be true, just by virtue of logic and the definitions of the terms involved. If definitions and their deductive consequences are *a priori* true (Chapter 8), then (1) expresses a necessary truth that is *a priori*.

In contrast, statement (2) isn't *a priori*. We know that it is true because Einstein's theory of relativity—an *a posteriori* theory—says that it is so. Statement (2) is said to be *nomologically necessary* (from *nomos*, meaning "law"). It is necessary because of a law of nature, in this case an *a posteriori* law of physics.

Statement (3) differs from the first two examples. Its truth doesn't follow from logic or definitions. Nor does its truth follow from any law of nature—physical or biological or whatever. Rather, to see that (3) is true, you have to take into account particular facts about Joe. Joe can't tie his shoes now because he is carrying several bags of groceries. I'll call this third sort of necessity *circumstantial necessity*. By this I mean that the statement is necessarily true only because of facts about the circumstances described. There is an additional fact about type (3) necessity that I should note. Whether we judge (3) true or false depends on how we interpret it. That is, (3) is ambiguous. If we interpret it to mean that Joe can't tie his shoes because he is otherwise occupied, (3) may be true. Suppose, however, we take (3) to mean that even if Joe put down the bags, he still couldn't tie his shoes. If that is how we interpret (3), we may judge it false. This is an important feature of statements that are circumstantially necessary—they are *ambiguous*.

When I say that a thermometer is reliable, I mean that it and its environment are related in a special way. I'm saying that its circumstances are such that its readings *must* be correct. In saying this, I'm using the concept of *circumstantial necessity*. Similarly, when I say that *S* knows that there is a page in front of her, I'm saying that she is related to her environment in a special way. I'm saying that she can't be mistaken in believing what she does. Here again, I'm using the concept of circumstantial necessity.

Suppose that a real printed page is the only thing that could get *S* to believe that a printed page is before her. Her senses are functioning normally. There are no evil demons lurking about who provide misleading evidence. If this is so, and if *S* subsequently believes the proposition in question, then *S* will *know* that there is a printed page in front of her. This is what the reliability theory says. In this circumstance, her belief will be related to the world the way the reading of a reliable thermometer is related to the temperature.

## TO HAVE KNOWLEDGE, YOU DON'T HAVE TO BE ABLE TO CONSTRUCT A PHILOSOPHICAL ARGUMENT REFUTING THE SKEPTIC

It is important to notice that the claims that *S* knows some proposition *p* isn't refuted by the fact that *S* may not be able to defend her knowledge claim against clever philosophical interrogation. If I asked *S* how she knows that her impressions aren't caused by an evil demon, she may draw a blank. If I ask her how she knows that she isn't dreaming, she may admit that she can't construct an argument proving that she isn't dreaming. Such philosophical puzzles may even lead *S* to say "I guess I don't know that there is a printed page in front of me." But her comment doesn't show that she lacks knowledge. Rather, it shows only that *S* doesn't believe that she knows there is a printed page in front of her.

If *S* is like a reliable thermometer, she has knowledge. Being like a reliable thermometer, however, doesn't require that *S* has the ability to construct fancy philosophical arguments that show she is like a thermometer. Thermometers can't construct philosophical arguments, yet they are sometimes reliable. *S* may be similar. She may be unable to refute the skeptic, but that doesn't show she lacks knowledge. *S* may even be a skeptic herself. She may believe that she lacks knowledge, but that doesn't entail that she really lacks it. Just as it is possible to mistakenly believe that a thermometer is unreliable, so it is possible to mistakenly believe that an individual lacks knowledge. In fact, it is possible to have false beliefs about one's own situations: *S* can believe that she lacks knowledge and yet be wrong.

---

### The KK-Principle

According to the Reliability Theory of Knowledge, knowing a proposition doesn't imply that you know that you know it. That is, the reliability theory rejects what is called the *KK-principle*. The following several paragraphs about this principle will be somewhat tough to grasp—so take a deep breath, read them slowly, and then read them again.

The *KK-principle* says that if *S* knows that *p*, then *S* knows that she knows that *p*. But I've just argued that the following is possible: *S* knows that *p*, but *S* doesn't believe that she knows that *p*. It follows that *S* might know that *p* even though she doesn't know that she knows that *p*. So if I'm right, the KK-principle is false.

If the KK-principle were true, *S* could prove that she lacked knowledge just by becoming a philosophical skeptic. This would be very *convenient*—wouldn't it be nice to be able to prove some thesis just by believing it?

Suppose *S* believed, maybe for no reason at all, that she lacked knowledge. If so, the KK-principle would imply that, indeed, she did lack knowledge. To see why, consider the following argument:

(1) If you do not believe that you have knowledge, then you don't know that you have knowledge.

(2) If you don't know that you have knowledge, then you don't have knowledge.

---

If you do not believe that you have knowledge, then you don't have knowledge.

This argument is deductively valid (what is its logical form?). Notice that premise (1) is correct; it follows from the fact that knowing a proposition requires that you believe the proposition. Premise (2) would be true if the KK-principle were correct. So if the KK-principle were true, believing that skepticism is true would be enough to ensure that skepticism is true, but if knowing is like being a reliable thermometer, this has got to be wrong.

The Reliability Theory of Knowledge holds that whether an agent knows something is settled by the objective relationship that obtains between the agent's belief and the environment. Whether the agent believes that this relationship obtains is irrelevant. The reliability theory rejects the KK-principle.

In summary, the Reliability Theory of Knowledge explains why *S* knows that there is a page in front of her by describing the following argument:

> *S* believes that there is a page in front of her.
>
> In the circumstances *S* occupies, she wouldn't believe that there is a page in front of her unless there were a page in front of her.
> ───────────────
> There is a page in front of *S*.

This argument doesn't use the word "know." So what does it have to do with knowledge? According to the reliability theory, *S* knows that the concluding proposition is true because the premises are true. But *S* doesn't have to *know* that the premises are true. Nor does *S* have to produce an argument independent of sense experience for the premises. This shows why the reliability theory rejects Descartes' claim that knowledge is internally certifiable.

One virtue of the reliability theory is that it explains what is wrong with a standard skeptical argument. The skeptic claims that *S* doesn't know that there is a printed page in front of her on the grounds that it is possible to imagine that *S* is deluded in some way. You can imagine a situation in which *S* believes what she does, but is mistaken. The reliability theory shows why this act of imagination is irrelevant to the question of whether *S* has knowledge *in the real world situation that she occupies.*

## A CONSEQUENCE OF THE RELIABILITY THEORY

To conclude this discussion, I want to consider an implication that the reliability theory has. It involves a fact about circumstantial necessity that I mentioned before. This is the fact that claims of circumstantial necessity often are ambiguous. I'll restate the point and then show how it is relevant to the reliability theory.

Consider the statement "Joe can't tie his shoes now." Suppose I make this comment to you while we are looking at Joe, who is carrying two heavy bags of groceries. Is the quoted remark true? Here are two ways of interpreting it:

(1) If Joe tries to tie his shoes while holding the bags of groceries, he will fail.

(2) If Joe tries to tie his shoes after first putting down the groceries, he will fail.

If we interpreted "Joe can't tie his shoes now" to mean (1), it will be true; if we interpreted it to mean (2), it will be false. Which reading you choose affects whether you will say that the quoted claim is true.

To see how this idea applies to the Reliability Theory of Knowledge, let's switch examples—from knowing that there is a printed page in front of you to knowing that there is a barn in the field next to the road on which you are driving. Suppose one day you go for a drive in Dane County, which is where Madison, Wisconsin, is located. On your drive, you look at a field and say, "There is a barn in that field." Suppose that the proposition you've asserted is true. Is this belief of yours a case of knowledge? The reliability theory says that we must ask whether, in the circumstances you occupy, there is anything besides a real barn that could have caused you to believe a barn is present. The problem I want to focus on is that it isn't clear how to decide what is included and what is excluded by the expression "in the circumstances you occupy."

First I need to define the idea of a *fool's barn*. Fool's gold looks like gold, but isn't gold at all. A fool's barn is something that looks like a barn but isn't one. Suppose there are no fool's barns in Dane County. The only things that look like barns are real barns. This means that if I describe the circumstances you occupy by saying that you are in Dane County, then it will be true that the only thing that could have made you think a barn is present is a real barn. Hence, your belief counts as a case of knowledge.

Now let's broaden our vision. In Hollywood, there are fool's barns. These are the facades used in movie sets. When viewed from one angle, they look like barns, but they aren't buildings at all. So if you were driving around Hollywood and came to believe that a barn was present, your belief would not count as knowledge (even if your belief happened to be true). The reason is that, around Hollywood, there are things besides real barns that can make you believe a barn is present.

So if your circumstances are restricted to Dane County, you might know that a barn is present; if your circumstances are restricted to Hollywood, you wouldn't. But now consider a puzzle. I initially suggested that the circumstances you occupy are limited to the objects in Dane County. Given this array of objects, I argued that a real barn is the only thing (in the circumstances you occupy) that could cause you to think that a barn is present. But why describe your circumstances so narrowly? Why not describe your circumstances as including all the objects in the United States? If I describe your situation in this way, it will be false that the only thing that could cause you to believe a barn is present is a real barn.

Here is the point: When we assert or deny that the only thing *in the circumstances* that could cause you to believe that a barn is present is a real barn, we are making reference to the environment you occupy. The environment may be thought of as composed of a set of objects. If we describe that set narrowly, it may be true that the only thing in the set that could cause your belief is a real barn. If we describe the set more broadly, this may no longer be true. So whether you know, on your drive through Dane County, that there is a barn on the hill next to the road depends on how we choose to describe the "circumstances you occupy." There are many true descriptions we might select. Narrow ones will entail that you have knowledge; broader ones will entail that you do not.

## THESIS OF THE RELATIVITY OF KNOWLEDGE

The claim I just made about knowledge may be put this way: *Knowledge is relative.* Whether $S$ knows that $p$ depends on (is relative to) a choice. "$S$ is in Dane County" and "$S$ is in the United States" are equally correct descriptions of the circumstances that $S$ occupies. Which one we consider depends on our interests.

Let's be clear what this relativity thesis asserts. When you say that something is relative, you should always be prepared to say *what* it is relative to. The thesis that knowledge is relative is the thesis that whether an agent knows a proposition depends on (is relative to) a specification of his or her circumstances. These circumstances can be specified in different equally correct ways, and so there is no unique answer to the question of whether the agent has knowledge.

Let's consider a down-to-earth example of relativity that does not concern knowledge. Mary and Alice are walking down the street, side by side. Is Mary walking to the left of Alice? Well, that depends on the point of view. If you look at them from the front, you get one answer. If you look at them from the back, you get the other. The key thing to notice is that $x$'s being to the left of $y$ isn't a relation between $x$ and $y$ alone. It involves some third item, $z$.

Does $S$ know that $p$? The suggestion now being considered is that the question is incomplete, that is, whether $S$ knows that $p$ depends on a third item besides the agent $S$ and the proposition $p$. It depends on a specification of $S$'s environment. There are different true ways to describe $S$'s environment. $S$ is in Dane County. But it also is true that $S$ is in the United States. Relative to one specification of the environment—call it $E_1$—$S$ knows that $p$. But relative to another equally true specification of the environment—call it $E_2$—$S$ doesn't know that $p$.

## WHAT DOES THE RELATIVITY THESIS SAY ABOUT SKEPTICISM?

The thesis that knowledge is relative has interesting implications about skepticism. Skepticism, recall, is the position that people don't have knowledge. Its opposite is the more commonsense idea that people often (if not always) know the propositions they believe. If the relativity thesis is true, then each of these theses is true in one sense but false in another. If the agent's environment is given a very broad specification, then skepticism is true. If the environment is given a narrower specification, then the opposite position will be correct. Notice, however, that there is no conflict between the following two claims:

(1)   $S$ knows that $p$, relative to $E_1$.

(2)   $S$ doesn't know that $p$, relative to $E_2$.

These statements don't conflict with each other, any more than the next pair conflicts with each other.

---

**What's Relative about Einstein's Theory of Relativity?**

Sometimes people say that Einstein proved that "Everything is relative." This isn't true. Neither is the more modest claim that Einstein proved that everything in physics is relative.

To say that a statement is relative isn't to say that it is subjective or arbitrary. Rather, it is to say that the statement is incomplete in a particular way. Whether Sue is walking to the left of Mary is a relative matter. That means that there exists some third item, beyond the two people mentioned, that must be referred to if the statement is to be true or false. To say just that Sue is to the left of Mary is to fail to express a complete thought.

It takes no enormous insight or creativity to see that whether one person is walking to the left of another is a relative, not an absolute, matter. In contrast, Einstein's idea that simultaneity is relative is anything but obvious. It was a brilliant theoretical conjecture, something that isn't at all suggested by our commonsense talk about space and time. Consider two events that occur at different places. Common sense suggests that either the events are simultaneous with each other or they aren't. Einstein's theory says that this isn't true. Whether two events are simultaneous depends on the choice of some third item—something called a *rest frame*. Relative to one rest frame, the events are simultaneous, but relative to another equally "correct" rest frame, they aren't. Simultaneity is relative, not absolute.

Einstein didn't say that everything in physics is relative. For example, in the special theory of relativity he defines a quantity called *the space–time interval*. This quantity measures the amount of separation that there is between events; it takes account of both spatial and temporal distances. The space–time interval between two events isn't relative to the choice of a rest frame. Space–time interval is absolute, not relative.

---

(3) Mary is walking to the left of Sue, when they are viewed from the front.

(4) Mary is not walking to the left of Sue, when they are viewed from the back.

So the dispute between skepticism and common sense seems to end in a stalemate, not in a victory for either side, if the relativity thesis is correct. Each position is correct in one sense but incorrect in another. This consequence follows from the Reliability Theory of Knowledge once we acknowledge that claims about circumstantial necessity are ambiguous.

---

## Review Questions

1. At the beginning of this chapter, I said that Descartes held that knowledge is "internally certifiable." What does this mean? Does the Reliability Theory of Knowledge agree?

2. What is the difference between logical necessity, nomological necessity, and circumstantial necessity?

3. What does it mean to say that claims about circumstantial necessity are "ambiguous"?

4. What does it mean to say that a thermometer is "reliable"? What analogy does the Reliability Theory of Knowledge see between reliable thermometers and knowledge?

5. How does the Reliability Theory of Knowledge assess the following skeptical argument: "I can imagine that my senses are now malfunctioning. Hence, I don't now know that there is a printed page in front of me."

6. What does it mean to say that knowledge is "relative"? Relative to what?

7. Does the relativity thesis entail that skepticism is correct?

---

## Problems for Further Thought

1. For any proposition *p*, we can construct the sentence "*S* knows that *p*." Since "*S* knows that lemons are yellow" is a sentence, we can construct the sentence "*S* knows that *S* knows that lemons are yellow." We can repeat this operation as many times as we please. The KK-principle says that if *S* knows that *p*, then *S* knows that *S* knows that *p*. Formulate similar principles for truth (the TT-principle), belief (the BB-principle), and surprise (the SS-principle). Are any of these principles plausible? Defend your answers.

2. Whether a ring is made of gold depends on the materials that the jeweler chooses when the ring is made. Does this mean that whether a ring is made of gold is a relative matter? How is this example different from the two claims about relativity discussed in this chapter?

3. Do you think that nonhuman organisms have knowledge? For example, do dogs? What is required for dogs to have knowledge, according to the reliability theory? How do these requirements differ from what would be demanded by the view that knowledge is internally certifiable? If dogs have knowledge, does this count as a point in favor of one conception of knowledge?

---

## CHAPTER 15

---

# *Justified Belief and Hume's Problem of Induction*

In this chapter, I will present a new problem in epistemology. So far, I've discussed the concept of *knowledge*, examining Descartes' foundationalism (Chapter 13) and the Reliability Theory of Knowledge (Chapter 14). The problem to be considered here concerns the idea of justified belief.

## KNOWLEDGE VERSUS JUSTIFIED BELIEF

Before starting, let's be clear on how this problem differs from the previous one. What is the difference between knowledge and justified belief? Two differences should be clear. First, if *S* knows that *p*, then *p* must be true; whereas *S*'s having a justified belief that *p* doesn't require that *p* be true. Knowledge requires truth, but justified belief doesn't. The second difference is that knowledge requires the impossibility of error; justified belief does not. Recall the lottery example discussed in Chapter 12. Suppose you believe, before the drawing, that ticket number 346 will not win in a fair lottery containing one thousand tickets. Suppose your belief turns out (after the drawing) to have been true. I claim you didn't *know* that the ticket wouldn't win. Nevertheless, I claim that you had strong evidence for thinking the ticket would lose. Your belief was reasonable, or justified. (I'll use these two terms interchangeably.)

These comparisons of knowledge and justified belief are summarized in the following table:

|  | Is truth required? | Is the impossibility of error required? |
|---|---|---|
| Knowledge | Yes | Yes |
| Justified belief | No | No |

As the lottery example illustrates, the evidence we have for many of the beliefs we hold falls short of providing absolute certainty. We sometimes use the concept of *probability* to describe such cases. We say that ticket number 346 *probably* won't win, to indicate that we aren't absolutely sure that it won't. Similarly, we might also say that our present experiences make the beliefs we have about the world outside the mind highly probable. Your present experiences don't make it absolutely certain that there is a printed page in front of you, but it does seem plausible to say that your experiences make it very probable that there is a printed page before you.

## SKEPTICISM ABOUT JUSTIFIED BELIEF

Until now I've talked about skepticism as if it were a single thesis. Now I want to distinguish skepticism about knowledge from a second kind of skepticism, which concerns the idea of justified belief.

Although skepticism about knowledge sounds like a shocking thesis at first hearing, once one grasps what it says, it doesn't fundamentally undermine our picture of ourselves and the world we inhabit. If knowledge requires the *impossibility* of error, perhaps we should concede that we don't know many things. Of course, we often talk about the knowledge we have, but perhaps this is just sloppy talk. This concession to skepticism isn't terribly threatening, because it allows us to hold onto the idea that our beliefs about the world aren't groundless and arbitrary. We can still say that they are "reasonable" and "well justified," even if they aren't entitled to be labeled "knowledge." Skepticism about knowledge doesn't entail skepticism about rational belief. This is why it is possible to abandon the claim that we have knowledge without thereby giving up the idea that our beliefs are rational.

There is a second form of skepticism that is far more disturbing. This form of skepticism rejects our claim to rationality. According to this more radical form of skepticism, we aren't rationally justified in believing what we do. It is this type of skepticism that is involved in Hume's views on induction. Hume claimed that the beliefs we have about the future and the beliefs we have concerning generalizations can't be rationally justified. It isn't just that we can't be *certain* that the sun will rise tomorrow. And it's not just that we don't *know* that the sun will rise tomorrow. According to Hume, we have no rational justification at all for this or for any other expectation we have about the future.

## HUME'S SKEPTICAL THESIS ABOUT INDUCTION

We constantly form expectations about what the future will be like or about which generalizations (statements of the form "All *As* are *B*") are true, based on evidence that isn't deductively conclusive. Our beliefs about the future are based on perception and memory, but you can't deduce what the future will be like from premises that describe just the present and the past. Let's focus on an example in order to get clear on this simple point. Suppose I have observed many emeralds and have found each of them to be green. I then formulate the prediction "The next emerald I observe will be green"; or maybe I formulate the generalization "All emeralds are green." (Just so this can be an example of the kind I want, suppose that emeralds aren't green *by definition*.)

Common sense says that we are rational in believing the predictions and generalizations we do if those beliefs are based on lots of evidence. Looking at lots of emeralds and finding that each is green seems to justify my expectation that the next emerald I examine will be green. Now it is obvious that we can't *deduce* generalizations or predictions from our past observations. Yet, the following appear to be perfectly sensible *nondeductive* arguments:

I've observed numerous emeralds, and each has been green.

(GEN)    ========================

Hence, all emeralds are green.


I've observed numerous emeralds, and each has been green.

(PRED)   ========================

Hence, the next emerald I observe will be green.

I've drawn a double line between premises and conclusions to indicate that these arguments aren't deductively valid. In both the generalization argument (GEN) and the prediction argument (PRED), we think that the conclusion reached is rationally justified by the premises. We think that it isn't a mere prejudice to hold, in each case, that the premise provides good evidence for the truth of the conclusion. Hume's thesis is that this conviction can't be rationally defended.

It is important to see that Hume's thesis goes far beyond the undisturbing claim that the GEN and PRED arguments just given aren't deductively valid. That much is obvious. Rather, Hume is saying that the premises in those arguments don't rationally justify their conclusions. Hume's view is that there is absolutely no rational justification for the beliefs we have that are predictions or generalizations. His view is that it is merely a habit we have that we regard such premises as providing good reason to believe such conclusions. This is a habit we can't abandon; it is part of human nature to expect the future to resemble the past. But it is a habit that we can't rationally defend. When challenged by the skeptic to rationally justify this pattern in our thinking, we can only say that this is the way human beings in fact operate. We can't produce a good argument to rationally justify this habit of mind.

## HUME'S ARGUMENT THAT INDUCTION CAN'T BE RATIONALLY JUSTIFIED

Why did Hume reach this startling conclusion about induction? (Here I'll reconstruct the argument that Hume gives in Part II of the section from *An Enquiry Concerning Human Understanding* called "Skeptical Doubts Concerning the Operations of the Understanding.") Hume thought that the arguments GEN and PRED require an additional premise. As they stand, the premise doesn't support the conclusion. If the observation is to support the generalization or the prediction, then we must assume that the future will resemble the past. This assumption Hume calls the *Principle of the Uniformity of Nature* (PUN).

Hume thought that this principle plays an indispensable role in each and every inductive argument we make. The example concerns the color of emeralds. Consider, however, the belief that the sun will rise tomorrow. This predictive belief is based on the premise that the sun has risen on each of the days that we have bothered to make an observation. Why should these *past* observations support the prediction I make about *tomorrow*? Hume thought that I must be assuming that nature is uniform—that the future will resemble the past. Hume says that without this assumption, the past would be no guide to the future.

So each and every inductive argument presupposes PUN: We must assume PUN if the observational premise is to support the prediction or generalization stated in the argument's conclusion. This means that if the conclusion we reach is rationally defensible, then a good argument must be available for thinking that PUN is true. If PUN can't be defended, then anything we believe that depends on assuming that PUN is true must likewise be indefensible.

We now can state Hume's skeptical argument:

(1) Every inductive argument requires PUN as a premise.

(2) If the conclusion of an inductive argument is rationally justified by the premises, then those premises must themselves be rationally justifiable.

(3) So, if the conclusion of an inductive argument is justified, there must be a rational justification for PUN.

(4) If PUN is rationally justifiable, then there must be a good inductive argument or a good deductive argument for PUN.

(5) There is no good inductive argument for PUN, since any inductive argument for PUN will be circular.

(6) There cannot be a good deductive argument for PUN, since PUN is not *a priori* true, nor does PUN deductively follow from the observations we have made to date.

(7) So, PUN is not rationally justifiable.

---

Hence, there is no rational justification for the beliefs we have that take the form of predictions or generalizations.

In a nutshell, Hume's claim is that the beliefs we have about emerald color and tomorrow's sunrise (and lots of other beliefs as well) aren't rationally justifiable. This is because they rest on an assumption that can't be rationally justified.

## WHY CAN'T PUN BE JUSTIFIED?

Let's look more carefully at steps (4) to (6) in the argument. Consider what PUN asserts; it says that the future will resemble the past—that past uniformities will continue to obtain in the future. Is this something that we could know to be true on the basis of induction? If it were, the inductive argument would look like this:

Nature has been uniform in my past observations.

---

Nature in general is uniform.

Recall that Hume claims that *all* inductive arguments require that PUN be assumed as a premise, but the above argument is inductive. Notice that if we insert PUN as a premise, as Hume requires, the argument becomes circular—it assumes as a premise the very proposition it tries to establish as a conclusion.

What about the other sort of justification? Can we give a deductive justification of PUN? Here again, Hume holds that the answer is *no*. The argument isn't deductively valid; the general uniformity principle can't be deduced from the observations I've made in the past.

Hume considers, and rejects, a second possible sort of deductive argument. Could PUN be a definitional truth, deducible from the definitions of the terms it uses? If PUN were a definitional truth, it would have the same sort of *a priori* justification that "All bachelors are unmarried" possesses. Hume rejects this idea by saying that there is "no contradiction" in supposing that the universe should suddenly cease to be uniform. It isn't a definitional truth that past regularities will continue into the future, Hume says.

## SUMMARY OF HUME'S ARGUMENT

It now should be clear how Hume's skeptical argument proceeds. First, there is a claim: Every inductive argument requires the premise that nature is uniform. Second, Hume argues that no rational justification can be given for that premise. He defends this assertion by considering three options: (1) an inductive argument in favor of PUN, (2) a deduction of PUN from past observations, and (3) a deduction of PUN from definitions. He asserts that none of these ways of defending PUN is going to work. This means that PUN can't be justified. Hume concludes that the inductive inferences we make aren't rationally justifiable.

## Review Questions

1. What is the difference between knowledge and justified belief? Does skepticism about knowledge entail skepticism about rational justification? What do each of these skeptical theses assert?
2. Hume says that we can't deduce what the future will be like from our present observations and memories. Does Hume's skeptical thesis say anything more than this?
3. What is the Principle of the Uniformity of Nature?
4. What is Hume's skeptical argument about induction?

## Problems for Further Thought

1. Is the claim that nature is uniform falsifiable (Chapter 9)? That is, can you describe a possible observation that would count against this claim?
2. Is it possible that *all* of our beliefs could be rationally justified? Would this be possible if we had a finite number of beliefs? In answering, explain what you think it means to say that a belief is rationally justified?

## CHAPTER 16

# *Can Hume's Skepticism Be Refuted?*

In the previous chapter, I described Hume's skeptical argument about induction as focusing on the Principle of the Uniformity of Nature (PUN). This principle, recall, says that the future will resemble the past. In this chapter, I'll criticize this version of Hume's argument. Then I'll formulate Hume's argument in another way. After that, I'll examine two criticisms that have been made of Hume's startling argument. Again, you want to be clear on what Hume's conclusion is. He didn't merely say that our predictions are uncertain; he said that they have *no rational justification whatever.* They are the product of a rationally indefensible habit that is deeply entrenched in human nature.

### WHAT DOES THE PRINCIPLE OF THE UNIFORMITY OF NATURE SAY?

PUN says that the future will resemble the past. Recall that Hume held that every time we make an induction—inferring that the sun will rise tomorrow or that the next emerald we observe will be green—we are assuming that nature is uniform. So PUN is supposed to be an assumption that is required by each and every inductive argument. But what, exactly, does PUN mean? Does it mean that nature is uniform *in each and every respect?* If so, it is pretty clear that we don't think that PUN is true. Summer leaves are green, but we don't expect autumn to resemble summer in this respect. So if we understand PUN in this way, the principle is not, contrary to Hume, something we are always assuming.

Let's try a second interpretation. Maybe PUN means that the future will resemble the past *in some respect.* This does seem to be something we believe. This is such a modest principle, however, that it is hard to see how it will help very much in the task of inferring what the future will be like. If I want to know whether future emeralds will be green or blue based on my observation that so far they all have been green, this version of PUN is pretty useless. It doesn't tell me whether it makes sense to expect emeralds to remain green or to expect a change.

These two attempts to clarify what PUN says illustrate a general problem. No one yet has been able to clarify the principle so that it has both of the following properties:

(1)  PUN is plausible.

(2)  PUN gives definite advice about what we should infer from the observations we have made.

There is a third characteristic that Hume's argument about induction attributes to PUN. This is the idea that PUN plays an indispensable role in the way we think about the world:

(3)  If we want to make inductive inferences about the world, PUN is something we must believe, no matter what else we believe.

This last condition expresses the idea that PUN is an assumption—a presupposition—that underlies the whole project of inductive inference.

If it is hard to formulate PUN so that it satisfies (1) and (2), it will be even harder to clarify the principle so that it satisfies (1), (2), and (3). I haven't proved that it is impossible to do this. But no one has done so yet. For this reason, I suggest we drop the formulation of Hume's argument that involves PUN. Instead, I'll consider a different version of Hume's argument that induction can't be rationally justified.

## A NEW CONCEPT: DEGREES OF RELIABILITY

This new version of Hume's argument involves the idea that a method of inference possesses *some degree of reliability*. Induction is a method of inference. Like other methods of inference, it makes predictions and says what generalizations are true based on a set of observations. We can say of a method of inference *how often* the predictions or generalizations it endorses have been true. A method that usually leads to truth is highly reliable; one that rarely does so is very unreliable.

This use of the concept of reliability departs somewhat from the one employed by the Reliability Theory of Knowledge (Chapter 14). There I discussed reliability as an on/off concept; a thermometer is either reliable or it isn't. Moreover, a reliable thermometer, in the sense employed there, *must* make true claims about the temperature.

Notice that the concept of *degrees of reliability* isn't an on/off concept. In addition, a highly reliable method of inference can sometimes lead to falsehood. The point is that it does so *rarely*. A method of inference is highly reliable if the predictions it makes are *usually* true.

Induction is a rule that scientists use to evaluate hypotheses in the light of evidence. A scientist makes a number of observations—call them *O*. The goal is to say which hypothesis among a set of competing hypotheses is most plausible in the light of those observations. For example, suppose you've examined numerous emeralds and all have been green (call this *O*). The problem is to say which of the following hypotheses is better supported in the light of those observations:

$(H_1)$ All emeralds are green.
$(H_2)$ All emeralds are green until the year 2050; thereafter, they are blue.

Common sense suggests that $H_1$ is more plausible than $H_2$ in the light of the observations *O*. The philosophical question is to explain why this is so. Hume denied that this evaluation of the competing hypotheses can be rationally defended.

## WHAT IS A RULE OF INFERENCE?

Rules of inference provide *licenses*. A fishing license permits you to fish. A rule of inference permits you to draw conclusions. In the previous example, induction permits you to conclude that  is probably true, given *O*. That is, induction is a rule of inference that connects premise to conclusion in the following argument:

> I've examined lots of emeralds and all have been green.
>
> I[ ================
>
> All emeralds are green.

I've drawn a double line to indicate that the argument is not deductively valid. I've written an "I" beside the double line to indicate that the rule of inference being used is induction. The problem of induction is to explain why we are entitled to use this inference rule.

## DOES THE PAST RELIABILITY OF INDUCTION PROVIDE AN ANSWER?

Common sense may suggest that we are entitled to use induction now, because induction has been reliable in the past. Induction has often been used to make predictions, and the predictions endorsed by inductive arguments usually, if not always, turned out to be correct. This is why we rightly take seriously what induction tells us. Hume rejected this attempt to justify induction. Let's examine it more carefully. Here is the argument we need to consider:

> Induction has been highly reliable in the past.
>
> ================
>
> Induction will be highly reliable now and in the future.

The premise of this argument is something we know by having observed the past track record of the inductive method. The conclusion makes a claim about what will be true now and in the future.

Every argument must use a rule of inference to license the transition from its premises to its conclusion. What rule of inference is used here? Can the conclusion be validly deduced from the premise? *No.* That is why I've drawn a double line. This is an *inductive* argument; induction (I) is the rule of inference that is being used.

Hume's point about this argument is that it is *circular* or *question-begging*. The philosophical question is whether induction can be rationally justified. This argument simply assumes that induction is legitimate. You can't justify using induction now by appeal to the fact that induction has been successful in the past.

## HUME'S ARGUMENT REFORMULATED

So Hume's skeptical argument about induction can be formulated as follows:

(1) To rationally justify induction, you must show that induction will be reliable.

(2) To show that induction will be reliable, you must construct an inductive argument or a deductively valid argument.

(3)  You can't show that induction will be reliable by an inductive argument; that would be question-begging.

(4)  You can't validly deduce that induction will be reliable from premises describing the past reliability of induction (or from definitions).

---

Hence, induction cannot be rationally justified.

This argument doesn't say anything about the Principle of the Uniformity of Nature (PUN). Can it be refuted?

## STRAWSON: IT IS ANALYTIC THAT INDUCTION IS RATIONAL

Hume claimed that a rational justification for using induction must show that the method will probably be reliable. The British philosopher Peter Strawson (in *Introduction to Logical Theory,* Methuen, 1952) challenged this. Strawson rejects premise (1) of Hume's argument. Strawson's idea is a simple one. He thinks that the statement "Induction is rational" is like the statement "Bachelors are unmarried." Both are *a priori* truths. Both are deductive consequences of the definitions of the terms that occur in them. According to Strawson, induction is, by definition, a rational activity.

Strawson doesn't claim "Induction will be reliable" is an *a priori* truth. He agrees with Hume that this isn't true by definition. But he thinks that you don't have to establish that an inference rule will be reliable if you want to show that using the rule is rational. Hume thought that rationality requires reliability. Strawson denies this. According to Strawson, it is entirely rational to use inductive methods to formulate our beliefs about the future, even though we can offer no good reason for expecting that the method will probably lead to true beliefs. If it turns out later that we were entirely mistaken about what we thought the world would be like, no one can accuse us of having been irrational. We would have behaved perfectly reasonably even though we ended up with false beliefs.

I find Strawson's argument unconvincing. Methods of inference are methods for doing things. Consider an analogy—*recipes.* Suppose I told you that I have a great recipe for making a cake. To determine whether this is true, you would want to see if the method is reliable. The point of the recipe is to produce nice cakes. You evaluate the recipe by seeing if it is a reliable instrument. It would puzzle you if I said that a particular recipe is excellent even though I granted that there is no reason whatever to think that using the recipe will probably result in a nice cake. This, however, is just what Strawson is saying about induction. The point of induction is to reach true beliefs about the world. That is the goal of inference. Whether it is reasonable to use induction or some other method depends on whether the method is a reliable instrument for attaining the specified goal. If it can't be shown that the instrument will attain the goal, it is hard to see how using the instrument is rationally justified. Strawson's mistake, I think, is to hold that the rationality of a method has nothing to do with its reliability.

## BLACK: INDUCTION CAN BE INDUCTIVELY JUSTIFIED

I turn now to an attempt at providing an inductive justification of induction. The American philosopher Max Black (in "Inductive Support of Inductive Rules," *Problems of Analysis,* Cornell University Press, 1954) argued that once you look carefully at what *circularity* means, you'll see that the inductive justification of induction isn't circular at all. That is, Black holds that the following argument provides a perfectly good reason for accepting the conclusion:

> Induction has been highly reliable until now.
> I[ ═══════════════
> Probably, induction will be highly reliable if we use it now and in the future.

Once again, I use the letter "I" to indicate that the rule of inference that licenses passing from the premise to the conclusion is the principle of induction.

What does Black think it means for an argument to be circular? His suggestion is roughly as follows: If an argument is circular, then the conclusion occurs as one of the premises. This isn't Black's exact formulation, but it captures the spirit of what he says. For Black, circularity involves a relationship between the conclusion and the premises. It has nothing to do with what rule of inference is used to get from premise to conclusion. I hope it is clear why, if you accept Black's definition of circularity, that the above inductive justification of induction isn't circular. The point I want to make, however, is that Black's definition is too narrow. I think there is a broader definition of circularity that shows that the above argument is circular. It is this: An argument is circular if it couldn't possibly convince someone that the conclusion is true if they didn't believe the conclusion already. A circular argument can't change anybody's mind. If you have doubts about induction, the above argument isn't going to lay them to rest.

Besides this, there is another problem confronting Black's suggestion. Consider a bizarre rule of inference that is the mirror image of induction. It is called *counterinduction.* Induction tells you to expect past regularities to continue into the future. Counterinduction tells you to expect past regularities *not* to continue. For example, counterinduction licenses the following inference:

> I've examined lots of emeralds and all have been green.
> I[ ═══════════════
> Future emeralds will not all be green.

Of course, induction would lead to a quite different conclusion. The problem of induction is, in part, to explain why we should use induction rather than counterinduction to formulate our predictions about the future.

What has this to do with Black's proposal? Black claims that the inductive justification of induction isn't circular. If he is right, then neither is the following argument:

Counterinduction has been highly unreliable until now.

I[ ═══════════

Probably, counterinduction will be highly reliable if we use it now and in the future.

Here we have a counterinductive justification of counterinduction.

Counterinduction has had a poor track record in the past. How should we expect it to do in the future? That depends on what rule of inference we use. If we use induction, we will expect counterinduction's dismal past track record to continue into the future. If, however, we use counterinduction, we expect the pattern to reverse. Since the method has been unreliable in the past, we expect that counterinduction will be *reliable* in the future. So we have two arguments to compare: the inductive justification of induction and the counterinductive justification of counterinduction. Which method of inference—induction or counterinduction—should we now use? The problem with Black's inductive justification of induction is that it gives us no reason to reject the counterinductive justification of counterinduction. This means that Black's favored inductive justification of induction, even if it is noncircular in Black's sense of the term, doesn't show why we should use induction rather than counterinduction. Hume's problem has not been solved.

Is it possible to refute Hume's argument? We have examined two attempts to do so. I think both fail. This does not mean that there is no way to prove Hume wrong. In the next chapter, I'll consider this problem from a different angle.

---

## Review Questions

1. When we try to clarify exactly what the Principle of the Uniformity of Nature says, we run into a problem. What is the problem?
2. How can Hume's skeptical argument about induction be formulated without mentioning PUN?
3. What is Strawson's justification of induction? What objection to it was presented in this chapter?
4. What is Black's inductive justification of induction? What two objections to it were presented in this chapter?
5. What does it mean to say that a rule of inference is a "license"? What is the difference between the license provided by induction and the license provided by counterinduction?

## Problems for Further Thought

1. The problem of induction involves explaining why the observation of many emeralds, all of them green, supports $H_1$ better than $H_2$:

    $H_1$: All emeralds are green.

    $H_2$: All emeralds are green until 2050; thereafter, they are blue.

    Can the Surprise Principle (Chapter 3) be used to show that the observations strongly favor $H_1$ over $H_2$? Explain your answer.
2. Hume considers, and rejects, two kinds of arguments that might justify induction—deductive arguments and inductive arguments. Would considering abductive arguments change the sort of conclusion that Hume reaches about induction?
3. Consider the rules of inference that are used in arguments we think are deductively valid. How can these rules be justified? Formulate a skeptical problem about deduction that is similar to Hume's problem about induction. Can this problem be solved?
4. Maybe Hume's Principle of the Uniformity of Nature should be formulated as the claim that the laws of nature are the same at all times and places. Is this claim true? Does it give definite advice about what we should infer from a given body of observations? Is it an assumption of all inductive reasoning?

## CHAPTER 17

# *Beyond Foundationalism*

In the previous chapter, I briefly considered two attempts to refute Hume's skeptical argument about induction. I argued that neither is successful. However, the failures of these two criticisms don't show that induction can't be justified. So the question remains: Can Hume's skepticism be refuted?

### HUME'S PROBLEM AND DESCARTES' PROBLEM

In this chapter, I'm going to argue that if we understand the idea of rational justification in the way Hume did, then he was right that induction can't be rationally justified. Notice that the thesis I'll be arguing for has an *IF* in it. I won't claim that Hume's skepticism is correct. My conclusion will be more modest: Skepticism is correct, *IF* the task of rational justification is understood in the way Hume understood it.

To defend this thesis, I want to describe a similarity between a problem that Descartes confronted and the one that Hume addressed. Descartes asked, how does my present mental state justify the beliefs I have about the world outside my mind? Hume asked, how do the observations I have made of my physical environment justify the beliefs I have about the future? The parallelism between these two problems is illustrated in the following diagram:

| | *Level* | *Kind of Belief* | *Examples* |
|---|---|---|---|
| Hume's problem | 3 | Predictions and generalizations | "The sun will rise tomorrow." |
| | 2 | Present and past observations | "The sun is now rising." "The sun has risen each day that I have made an observation." |
| Descartes' problem | 1 | Indubitable beliefs | "I now seem to see a sunrise." "I now seem to remember that the sun has risen each day that I have made an observation." |

In this diagram, I've divided beliefs into three categories. Hume was asking how beliefs at level 3 can be justified. Descartes was asking how beliefs in level 2 can be justified.

Both Descartes and Hume were foundationalists in the way they approached questions about knowledge and justification. By this, I mean that each held that *IF* a belief is rationally justified or known, then it is justified or known solely on the basis of its relationship to beliefs at lower levels. Foundationalism holds that justification flows from bottom to top, not in the other direction. Beliefs are justified because of their relationship to other beliefs that are more certain.

Hume thought that *IF* beliefs in category 3 were justified, they would have to be justified solely on the basis of items in category 2. Descartes thought that *IF* beliefs in category 2 were justified, they would have to be justified solely on the basis of items in category 1. Notice that both of these points are *IF*-statements. They don't assert that the beliefs in question actually are justified; the point is that Descartes and Hume agreed about what would have to be true *IF* the items in question were justified. This is something on which a skeptic and a nonskeptic might agree.

In spite of this similarity between the way Descartes and Hume formulated their respective problems about justification, they ended up defending very different solutions. Remember that Hume was a skeptic, whereas Descartes was not. Hume claimed that level 3 beliefs cannot be justified, whereas Descartes argued that level 2 beliefs can be justified.

I now want to advance a thesis about Descartes' problem and then extend that thesis so that it applies to Hume's problem as well. Let's grant Descartes that each of us is absolutely certain about his or her own present psychological state. My point is that these level 1 beliefs aren't enough to justify the beliefs I have about the physical environment I inhabit (level 2). I need an additional assumption concerning the *relationship* between levels 1 and 2. This connecting principle might take the form of claiming that God exists and is no deceiver, or it might take some other form. But the contents of my own experience are simply not enough, taken all by themselves.

The parallel thesis about Hume's problem is as follows: If my beliefs about my present and past environment (items at level 2) are to justify the predictions and generalizations I believe (items at level 3), then I have to assume something about the *relationship* between levels 2 and 3. The principle of the uniformity of nature ("the future will resemble the past") is an example of this type of bridge principle. Or some other bridge principle might be proposed. The point is that my present perceptions and memories are simply not enough, taken all by themselves.

Be clear on what I'm suggesting. First, let's note an obvious point: Level 1 statements don't deductively imply level 2 statements, and level 2 statements don't deductively imply level 3 statements. This should be obvious from the examples of level 1, 2, and 3 beliefs given in the diagram.

My point isn't this obvious fact about deductive relationships. I want to make a more ambitious claim. Not only do lower level statements fail to deductively imply higher level statements; I also claim that lower level statements, all by themselves, are not enough to provide a justification for higher level statements. Lower level statements, taken by themselves, don't even provide good evidence for higher level statements.

## WHETHER *X* IS EVIDENCE FOR *Y* DEPENDS ON BACKGROUND ASSUMPTIONS *Z*

This is a pretty radical thesis, I admit. Do your present experiences provide evidence about the physical environment you occupy? For example, does statement (a) below provide a rational justification for believing statement (b)?

(a) You seem to see a printed page in front of you now.
(b) There is a printed page in front of you now.

I claim that the answer depends on what you assume about the *relationship* between your present experiences and the world outside your mind. Given one set of assumptions, statement (a) might be excellent evidence that statement (b) is true. But given a different set of assumptions, statement (a) would be good evidence that statement (b) is false. The point is that the assumptions you make, one way or the other, go beyond what is contained in level 1. Assumptions about the relationship of levels 1 and 2 aren't, properly speaking, contained in level 1. I hope my discussion of Descartes makes plausible what I'm saying about the relationship of (a) and (b). If you assume that the environment is "normal" and that your senses are functioning properly, then (a) is evidence favoring (b). If you assume that your senses are misleading you, however, then (a) would be evidence against (b).

What would the parallel claim be about the relationship of statements at levels 2 and 3? For example, does statement (c) provide strong evidence for statement (d)?

(a)  I've examined lots of emeralds and all have been green.

(b)  All emeralds are green.

We naturally take (c) to be evidence favoring (d). How could this be otherwise? Well, suppose you believed the following statement (the example is due to I. J. Good, "The White Shoe Is a Red Herring," *British Journal for the Philosophy of Science*, Vol. 17, 1967, p. 322):

> Either there are lots of emeralds, of which 99 percent are green, or there are very few emeralds, and all of them are green.

If you believed this, then (c) would be evidence *against* (d). On the other hand, if you believed the following statement, then (c) would provide evidence in favor of (d):

> If you examine lots of emeralds and all have been found to be green, then probably all emeralds are green.

Notice that the two possible assumptions just listed aren't strictly at level 2.

Whether (c) is evidence for or against (d) depends on what assumptions you make. If you make no assumptions about the relationship of level 2 and level 3, then the evidence described in (c) can't be interpreted as either favorable or unfavorable to (d). In a way, the present idea is something that has already come up in this book. I've already pointed out that hypotheses are testable only when background assumptions are added to them (Chapter 9). Here's an elaboration of that idea: When you test a hypothesis *H* and obtain some observations *O*, it will usually be true that *O* is evidence for or against *H* only because of the background assumptions (*A*) you made.

## ANOTHER RELATIVITY THESIS

We have here another example of a relativity thesis in philosophy. The idea of relativity, recall, came up in Chapter 14 in connection with the problem of knowledge. There it was argued that the Reliability Theory of Knowledge leads to the conclusion that whether *S* knows some proposition *p* depends on how one chooses to describe the environment that *S* inhabits. Different equally true descriptions of *S*'s circumstances lead to opposite conclusions about whether *S* has knowledge. The present point concerns the concept of evidence, not the concept of knowledge. Is statement (c) evidence for statement (d)? No answer can be given until a third term is specified. Relative to one set of assumptions, the answer is *no,* but relative to another the answer is *yes.* We shouldn't ask whether one statement is evidence for another, but whether one statement is evidence for another relative to a set of background assumptions.

## FOUNDATIONALISM LEADS TO SKEPTICISM

I'm claiming that the evidence relationship involves three things, not just two. Whether *O* is evidence for *H* depends on background assumptions (*A*). What impact does this point have on the problems that Hume and Descartes pursued about the concept of rational justification? My suggestion is that the problems they posed lead right to skepticism. If the challenge is to see if level 3 beliefs can be justified *solely by level 2 beliefs*, we must conclude that this can't be done. Likewise, if the problem is to see if level 2 beliefs can be justified *solely by level 1 beliefs*, we are forced to reach a negative conclusion in this case as well. Descartes wasn't a skeptic about the rational justifiability of level 2 beliefs. Hume was a skeptic about the rational justifiability of level 3 beliefs. My claim is that if we adopt a foundationalist understanding of what rational justification involves, then Descartes was wrong and Hume was right. In both Descartes' problem and Hume's problem, foundationalism leads to skepticism.

## A NONFOUNDATIONALIST APPROACH TO JUSTIFICATION

However, I don't think this shows that our beliefs are totally lacking in rational justification. Rather, I believe that the foundationalist misunderstands what it takes to rationally justify a belief. We *can* justify a level 3 belief. We do this by appealing to the other beliefs we have, some of which will themselves be at level 3. The same holds for the beliefs we have at level 2.

Think of how the task of justification works in everyday life and in science. If a scientist makes a prediction, or if we do this in our everyday lives, how are these predictions to be defended? If we say that the sun will rise tomorrow, we can support this prediction by appealing to other beliefs we have about the way the solar system has worked *and will continue to work*. In everyday life and science, we allow people to justify their beliefs at level 3 by appealing to other beliefs that also are at level 3. Often, predictions are justified by citing generalizations. In doing this, we aren't following the rules that foundationalism lays down. We aren't justifying a belief at one level strictly in terms of beliefs that are at lower levels.

What does this imply about whether our beliefs about the world are rationally justified? My point is to focus on what it means to ask for a rational justification. If we understand that idea in a foundationalist way, we will be led straight to skepticism—to the conclusion that the beliefs we have aren't rationally justifiable. On the other hand, if we recognize that the idea of rational justification needn't be understood in a foundationalist way, skepticism doesn't threaten. In everyday life and in science, we frequently say that our beliefs are justified. When we do this, we aren't using a foundationalist understanding of the idea of rational justification. I'm suggesting that we are often perfectly correct when we say that this or that belief is well justified. Such claims are correct, in part, because rational justification is usually not understood in the way the foundationalist demands.

## STANDARDS OF JUSTIFICATION OFTEN DEPEND ON THE AUDIENCE

Our standards of rational justification often depend on the audience we have in mind. Suppose you believe some proposition that some other person doesn't. Your goal is to rationally persuade the other individual that you are right. In doing this, you will feel free to use as a premise in your argument any belief that the two of you share. If you agree about lots of things, there will be many propositions that you can use as premises. If, however, your disagreement is more pervasive, you will be much more limited in the premises you can use, and if you somehow disagreed about *everything*, it would be impossible to construct a rational argument that shows this person that the proposition in question is correct.

In everyday life, it is a familiar occurrence that one person rationally justifies some proposition to another. The same is true in science and in courts of law. This can happen because the two parties agree about enough; what they share is sufficient to allow an argument to be constructed that shows whether the proposition under dispute is correct. Matters change, however, when we ask someone to justify a proposition *to a skeptic*. A skeptic won't agree with you about many of the things you take for granted. If skeptics differ with you on sufficiently many beliefs, perhaps it will be impossible to rationally convince them that the proposition is true.

Foundationalists say that when you try to provide a rational justification of some proposition *p*, you must construct an argument that would be compelling *to a skeptic who doubts all the propositions that are at the same level as p*. This is one sort of activity, but there are others. A more familiar problem of rational justification is to construct an argument that would convince someone who doesn't already believe *p*, but who has lots of other beliefs at the same level as *p*. Even if the foundationalist's problem is insoluble, this doesn't mean that more familiar problems of rational justification are too.

## TWO METAPHORS—BUILDING A BUILDING AND REPAIRING A RAFT

In Chapter 13, we examined the foundationalist idea that justifying our beliefs resembles building a building on solid foundations. The foundations must be perfectly solid; otherwise, the entire superstructure will be insecure. This is a good metaphor for foundationalism. Antifoundationalists think that it is fundamentally misleading. When we take up philosophical problems about rational justification, we already have many beliefs. Our job is not to strip them down to an indubitable core and then build them back up. Rather, what we need to do is to ask if we should change any of the beliefs we already have. Otto Neurath (1882–1945) expressed this view of philosophy in the following analogy: "We are like sailors who must rebuild their ship on the open sea, without being able to dismantle the ship in dry dock or being able to reconstruct it from the best components." Solid foundations are impossible, but that doesn't mean that our beliefs are completely unjustified.

## Review Questions

1. What is meant by saying that we have beliefs at level 1, level 2, and level 3? How does a foundationalist understand what it means for a belief at a level to be rationally justified? Are there any beliefs that are located at none of these three levels?
2. A relativity thesis is advanced in this chapter concerning the idea of evidence. What is that thesis? How does it go beyond the "obvious" fact that level 2 beliefs don't deductively imply beliefs at level 3?
3. How could the observation of lots of green emeralds be evidence against the claim that all emeralds are green?
4. Foundationalists understand the problem of rational justification in one way, but people in ordinary life usually think of the problem in another. What is the difference?

## Problems for Further Thought

In Chapter 7, I argued that scientific explanation is possible only for local why-questions. In the present chapter, I argued that you can rationally justify a proposition to someone only if you agree with that person about something. What similarities are there between these two theses?

## CHAPTER 18

# *Locke on the Existence of External Objects*

The last problem I want to discuss in this chapter on epistemology concerns the beliefs we have about the physical objects in our environment. Consider your present belief that there is a book in front of you. There are several epistemological questions we could ask about this belief. Does this belief count as knowledge? Are you justified in believing the proposition that there is a book before you? What evidence do you have that this proposition is true? It is the last of these that I want to discuss. I'll do so by examining some ideas that the English philosopher John Locke (1632–1704) presents in his *Essay Concerning Human Understanding*.

Philosophers call the book in front of you an "external" object, meaning that it is not in your mind. Your mind can be thought of as "an internal world." It is populated by beliefs, desires, and feelings. Books and tables are physical objects in the external world. The experiences you now are having—for example, your present visual and tactile sensations—seem to provide you with evidence that there is a book in front of you. But how can what transpires in the internal world of your mind provide evidence concerning what is going on in the external world of physical objects? Maybe there is no book in front of you. Maybe you are just hallucinating.

This is a question we examined in Chapters 13 and 17 in connection with Descartes' foundationalism. We discussed Descartes' theistic answer, that God is no deceiver, which means that if I am careful in my reasoning, I will not err in trusting the testimony of my senses. Locke read and learned from Descartes, but he provides a different kind of answer to this question. In Book 4, Chapter 11, of the *Essay*, Locke tries to show that there are features that we can discern *in* our experience that show that those experiences provide evidence for the existence of external objects.

Before we get started on the details of Locke's argument, it is worth considering the kind of argument that Locke is attempting to construct. Suppose you are walking through an art gallery and are looking at several paintings that were all painted by a single artist. You wonder whether these paintings are pictures of real-world scenes or are fantasies produced by the artist's imagination. It seems that you can't answer this question just by looking at the paintings. If the paintings are similar to each other, that doesn't seem to help, since an artist can produce similar paintings by looking at a single part of the external world, or by merely imagining a series of similar scenes. But suppose the paintings all contain unicorns and mermaids. Isn't this evidence that the paintings are fantasies, not paintings of a real-world scene? Maybe so, but here you are relying on information you have—that there are no unicorns and mermaids. This information isn't something you learned by looking at the paintings. If this is the right thing to say about the paintings in the gallery, how can Locke succeed in showing that the content of our experience provides evidence that there are external, physical objects?

Locke points out that "nobody can, in earnest, be so skeptical as to be uncertain of the existence of those things which he sees and feels." This is a correct psychological point. None of us is capable of seriously doubting that there are physical objects in our environment. One might say that it is part of *human nature* to think that an external world exists. However, this *psychological* point does not address the question of *epistemology*. Why *should* you think that the content of your experience provides evidence for the existence of external things? Locke gives the following answer: "This is certain: the confidence that our faculties do not herein deceive us is the greatest assurance we are capable of concerning the existence of material beings." This isn't much of an argument. Locke is talking about the following two propositions

- Your sense organs do not deceive you.
- There are external objects.

He is saying that you are entitled to be confident that the first is true, and that this assures you that the second proposition is true as well. The problem is that the two propositions aren't separable in the way Locke suggests. Given the experiences you now are having, the first entails the second, and given the experiences you now are having, the second entails the first. The two propositions stand or fall together; it is a mistake to think that knowing that the first is true provides a reason for believing the second. Someone who questions the second proposition will also want to question the first; the argument that Locke presents *begs the question* (Chapter 2).

Locke then provides four more "concurrent reasons" for thinking that our experience provides evidence for the existence of external objects. Let's see if he does a better job of solving this problem.

## LOCKE'S FIRST ARGUMENT—"THOSE THAT WANT THE ORGANS OF ANY SENSE"

Locke's first reason has to do with people who are blind or lack some other (functioning) sense organ:

> Those that want the organs of any sense, never can have the ideas belonging to that sense produced in their minds. This is too evident to be doubted: and therefore we cannot but be assured that they come in by the organs of that sense, and no other way. The organs themselves, it is plain, do not produce them: for then the eyes of a man in the dark would produce colours, and his nose smell roses in the winter: but we see nobody gets the relish of a pineapple, till he goes to the Indies, where it is, and tastes it.

Locke is arguing as follows:

> People who are blind do not have visual sensations.
> The visual experiences of sighted people are not caused by their eyes.
> ─────────────
> The visual experiences of sighted people are caused by external things.

Is the argument valid? If not, maybe a double line should be drawn between premises and conclusion to indicate that the premises are supposed to show that the conclusion of plausible or probable, not that it must be true. Also, are the premises true?

## LOCKE'S SECOND ARGUMENT—"IDEAS WHICH FORCE THEMSELVES UPON ME"

Locke notes that sensation and memory are experienced differently:

> When my eyes are shut, or windows fast, I can at pleasure recall to my mind the ideas of light, or the sun, which former sensations had lodged in my memory; so I can at pleasure lay by that idea, and take into my view that of the smell of a rose, or taste of sugar. But, if I turn my eyes at noon towards the sun, I cannot avoid the ideas which the light or sun then produces in me. So that there is a manifest difference between the ideas laid up in my memory, (over which, if they were there only, I should have constantly the same power to dispose of them, and lay them by at pleasure,) and those which force themselves upon

me, and I cannot avoid having. And therefore it must needs be some exterior cause, and the brisk acting of some objects without me, whose efficacy I cannot resist, that produces those ideas in my mind, whether I will or no.

Locke's argument might be put like this:

> I cannot mentally control whether I have the visual experiences I have.
> Those visual experiences have causes.
> _____
> The causes of those visual experiences are external to my mind.

Again, assess this argument: Do the premises provide a good reason to believe the conclusion? Are the premises true?


## LOCKE'S THIRD ARGUMENT—"PLEASURE OR PAIN"

Locke's next argument also focuses on a difference between sensation and memory—in this case, the memory of a sensation:

> Pleasure or pain, which accompanies actual sensation, accompanies not the returning of those ideas without the external objects. Add to this, that many of those ideas are produced in us with pain, which afterwards we remember without the least offence. Thus, the pain of heat or cold, when the idea of it is revived in our minds, gives us no disturbance; which, when felt, was very troublesome; and is again, when actually repeated: which is occasioned by the disorder the external object causes in our bodies when applied to them: and we remember the pains of hunger, thirst, or the headache, without any pain at all; which would either never disturb us, or else constantly do it, as often as we thought of it, were there nothing more but ideas floating in our minds, and appearances entertaining our fancies, without the real existence of things affecting us from abroad.

Locke then adds that "the same may be said of pleasure." Here is how I see Locke's argument:

> When I have a headache, I feel pain.
> When I remember the headache, I don't feel pain.
> This difference must have a cause.
> _____
> The difference is that an external object causes the headache, but not the memory of the headache.

Yes, same old drill—evaluate Locke's argument.

## LOCKE'S FOURTH ARGUMENT—"OUR SENSES ASSIST ONE ANOTHER'S TESTIMONY"

This is my favorite:

> Our senses assist one another's testimony of the existence of outward things, and enable us to predict. Our senses in many cases bear witness to the truth of each other's report, concerning the existence of sensible things without us. He that sees a fire, may, if he doubt whether it be anything more than a bare fancy, feel it too; and be convinced, by putting his hand in it.

In Chapter 6, on evolution and creationism, I discussed the principle of the common cause. Locke is using this principle here. When two students submit word-for-word identical essays, it is possible that they wrote them independently. However, it is far more plausible to think that they copied their essays from a common source—say, from a Web site on the Internet. Another example discussed in that chapter is the striking resemblance between the words in French, Spanish, and Italian for the numbers. This similarity might be a coincidence, but it is far more plausible to think that the similarities exist because these different languages are descendants of a common ancestor—Latin.

In Locke's example, the visual experience of fire tends to be accompanied by a tactile sensation of warmth. Why are these correlated? True, it might be a coincidence. However, it is far more plausible to think that the correlation is due to a common cause—an external object that causes both the visual impression *and* the feeling of warmth. The same kind of argument can be developed concerning the different memories you have that are in agreement. Your visual impression right now resembles the experience you had a second ago, and also resembles the experience you had the second before that. You know that this resemblance exists by accessing your memories. The resemblance is plausibly explained by postulating the existing of an external object that persists through time—the book before you—which is the common cause of various experiences and subsequent memory traces.

These considerations don't *prove* that there are external objects, but the argument that makes use of the Principle of the Common Cause does seem to establish something more modest—that the content of your experience is *evidence* for the existence of things that are outside of your experience—an external world.

---

## Review Questions

1. How is Locke's approach to the question of how we have knowledge of (or evidence for) the existence of physical objects external to the mind different from that of Descartes?
2. Describe Locke's four arguments and evaluate them. Are they deductive arguments, inductive, or abductive?

**3.** In Chapter 6, the principle of the common cause was presented and it was said to be a consequence of the Surprise Principle, introduced in Chapter 3. How does the Surprise Principle apply to the fourth of Locke's arguments?

## Problem for Further Thought

In discussing Locke's fourth argument, I describe two possible hypotheses. What are they? Are there other possibilities? If so, does considering them affect the conclusion of the argument?

# Readings

## RENÉ DESCARTES

## Meditations on First Philosophy

In this work, René Descartes (1596–1650) tries to discover to what extent he has genuine knowledge of the world he inhabits. He pursues a foundationalist strategy. First, he attempts to discover which of his beliefs are beyond doubt. These will be the foundations for the rest of what he knows. Second, the task is to show how these foundational items support the rest of his knowledge.

Besides addressing the problem of knowledge, Descartes also considers the relationship that obtains between his mind and his body. In the **Sixth Meditation** he argues that these are distinct objects. This position—**dualism**—is discussed in the next section of the text on philosophy of mind.

### SYNOPSIS OF THE SIX FOLLOWING MEDITATIONS

In the First Meditation I set forth the reasons for which we may, generally speaking, doubt about all things and especially about material things, at least as long as we have no other foundations for the sciences than those which we have hitherto possessed. But although the utility of a Doubt which is so general does not at first appear, it is at the same time very great, inasmuch as it delivers us from every kind of prejudice, and sets out for us a very simple way by which the mind may detach itself from

René Descartes, *Meditations on First Philosophy*, edited and translated by Elizabeth Haldane and G. R. T. Ross, in *The Philosophical Works of Descartes*, vol. 1 (Cambridge University Press, 1969), pp. 140–199. Reprinted by permission of Cambridge University Press.

the senses; and finally it makes it impossible for us ever to doubt those things which we have once discovered to be true.

In the Second Meditation, mind, which making use of the liberty which pertains to it, takes for granted that all those things of whose existence it has the least doubt, are non-existent, recognises that it is however absolutely impossible that it does not itself exist. This point is likewise of the greatest moment, inasmuch as by this means a distinction is easily drawn between the things which pertain to mind—that is to say to the intellectual nature—and those which pertain to body.

But because it may be that some expect from me in this place a statement of the reasons establishing the immortality of the soul, I feel that I should here make known to them that having aimed at writing nothing in all this Treatise of which I do not possess very exact demonstrations, I am obliged to follow a similar order to that made use of by the geometers, which is to begin by putting forward as premises all those things upon which the proposition that we seek depends, before coming to any conclusion regarding it. Now the first and principal matter which is requisite for thoroughly understanding the immortality of the soul is to form the clearest possible conception of it, and one which will be entirely distinct from all the conceptions which we may have of body; and in this Meditation this has been done. In addition to this it is requisite that we may be assured that all the things which we conceive clearly and distinctly are true in the very way in which we think them; and this could not be proved previously to the Fourth Meditation. Further we must have a distinct conception of corporeal nature, which is given partly in this Second, and partly in the Fifth and Sixth Meditations. And finally we should conclude from all this, that those things which we conceive clearly and distinctly as being diverse substances, as we regard mind and body to be, are really substances essentially distinct one from the other; and this is the conclusion of the Sixth Meditation. This is further confirmed in this same Meditation by the fact that we cannot conceive of body excepting in so far as it is divisible, while the mind cannot be conceived of excepting as indivisible. For we are not able to conceive of the half of a mind as we can do of the smallest of all bodies; so that we see that not only are their natures different but even in some respects contrary to one another. I have not however dealt further with this matter in this treatise, both because what I have said is sufficient to show clearly enough that the extinction of the mind does not follow from the corruption of the body, and also to give men the hope of another life after death, as also because the premises from which the immortality of the soul may be deduced depend on an elucidation of a complete system of Physics. This would mean to establish in the first place that all substances generally—that is to say all things which cannot exist without being created by God—are in their nature incorruptible, and that they can never cease to exist unless God, in denying to them his concurrence, reduce them to nought; and secondly that body, regarded generally, is a substance, which is the reason why it also cannot perish, but that the human body, inasmuch as it differs from other bodies, is composed only of a certain configuration of members and of other similar accidents, while the human mind is not similarly composed of any accidents, but is a pure substance. For although all the accidents of mind be changed, although, for instance, it think certain things, will others, perceive others, etc., despite all this it does not emerge from these changes another mind: the human body on the other hand becomes a different thing from the sole fact that the figure or form of any of its portions is found to be changed. From this it follows that the human body may indeed easily enough perish, but the mind [or soul of man (I make no distinction between them)] is owing to its nature immortal.

In the third Meditation it seems to me that I have explained at sufficient length the principal argument of which I make use in order to prove the existence of God. But none the less, because I did not wish in that place to make use of any comparisons derived from corporeal things, so as to withdraw as much as I could the minds of readers from the senses, there may perhaps have remained many obscurities which, however, will, I hope, be entirely removed by the Replies which I have made to the Objections which have been set before me. Amongst others there is, for example, this one, "How the idea in us of a being supremely perfect possesses so much objective reality [that is to say participates by representation in so many degrees of being and perfection] that it necessarily proceeds from a cause which is absolutely perfect." This is illustrated in these Replies by the comparison of a very perfect machine, the idea of which is found in the mind of some workman. For as the objective contrivance of this idea must have some cause, i.e. either the science of the workman or that of some other from whom he has received the idea, it is similarly impossible that the idea of God which is in us should not have God himself as its cause.

In the fourth Meditation it is shown that all these things which we very clearly and distinctly perceive are true, and at the same time it is explained in what the nature of error or falsity consists. This must of necessity be known both for the confirmation of the preceding truths and for the better comprehension of those that follow. (But it must meanwhile be remarked that I do not in any way there treat of sin—that is to say of the error which is committed in the pursuit of good and evil, but only of that which arises in the deciding between the true and the false. And I do not intend to speak of matters pertaining to the Faith or the conduct of life, but only of those which concern speculative truths, and which may be known by the sole aid of the light of nature.)

In the fifth Meditation corporeal nature generally is explained, and in addition to this the existence of God is demonstrated by a new proof in which there may possibly be certain difficulties also, but the solution of these will be seen in the Replies to the Objections. And further I show in what sense it is true to say that the certainty of geometrical demonstrations is itself dependent on the knowledge of God.

Finally in the Sixth I distinguish the action of the understanding from that of the imagination; the marks by which this distinction is made are described. I here show that the mind of man is really distinct from the body, and at the same time that the two are so closely joined together that they form, so to speak, a single thing. All the errors which proceed from the senses are then surveyed, while the means of avoiding them are demonstrated, and finally all the reasons from which we may deduce the existence of material things are set forth. Not that I judge them to be very useful in establishing that which they prove, to wit, that there is in truth a world, that men possess bodies, and other such things which never have been doubted by anyone of sense; but because in considering these closely we come to see that they are neither so strong nor so evident as those arguments which lead us to the knowledge of our mind and of God; so that these last must be the most certain and most evident facts which can fall within the cognizance of the human mind. And this is the whole matter that I have tried to prove in these Meditations, for which reason I here omit to speak of many other questions with which I dealt incidentally in this discussion.

## MEDITATIONS ON THE FIRST PHILOSOPHY IN WHICH THE EXISTENCE OF GOD AND THE DISTINCTION BETWEEN MIND AND BODY ARE DEMONSTRATED

### Meditation I: Of the Things Which May Be Brought Within the Sphere of the Doubtful

It is now some years since I detected how many were the false beliefs that I had from my earliest youth admitted as true, and how doubtful was everything I had since constructed on this basis; and from that time I was convinced that I must once for all seriously undertake to rid myself of all the opinions which I had formerly accepted, and commence to build anew from the foundation, if I wanted to establish any firm and permanent structure in the sciences. But as this enterprise appeared to be a very great one, I waited until I had attained an age so mature that I could not hope that at any later date I should be better fitted to execute my design. This reason caused me to delay so long that I should feel that I was doing wrong were I to occupy in deliberation the time that yet remains to me for action. To-day, then, since very opportunely for the plan I have in view I have delivered my mind from every care [and am happily agitated by no passions] and since I have procured for myself an assured leisure in a peaceable retirement, I shall at last seriously and freely address myself to the general upheaval of all my former opinions.

Now for this object it is not necessary that I should show that all of these are false—I shall perhaps never arrive at this end. But inasmuch as reason already persuades me that I ought no less carefully to withhold my assent from matters which are not entirely certain and indubitable than from those which appear to me manifestly to be false, if I am able to find in each one some reason to doubt, this will suffice to justify my rejecting the whole. And for that end it will not be requisite that I should examine each in particular, which would be an endless undertaking; for owing to the fact that the destruction of the foundations of necessity brings with it the downfall of the rest of the edifice, I shall only in the first place attack those principles upon which all my former opinions rested.

All that up to the present time I have accepted as most true and certain I have learned either from the senses or through the senses; but it is sometimes proved to me that these senses are deceptive, and it is wiser not to trust entirely to anything by which we have once been deceived.

But it may be that although the senses sometimes deceive us concerning things which are hardly perceptible, or very far away, there are yet many others to be met with as to which we cannot reasonably have any doubt, although we recognise them by their means. For example, there is that fact that I am here, seated by the fire, attired in a dressing gown, having this paper in my hands and other similar matters. And how could I deny that these hands and this body are mine, were it not perhaps that I compare myself to certain persons, devoid of sense, whose cerebella are so troubled and clouded by the violent vapours of black bile, that they constantly assure us that they think they are kings when they are really quite poor, or that they are clothed in purple when they are really without covering, or who imagine that they have an earthenware head or are nothing but pumpkins or are made of glass. But they are mad, and I should not be any the less insane were I to follow examples so extravagant.

At the same time I must remember that I am a man, and that consequently I am in the habit of sleeping, and in my dreams representing to myself the same things or sometimes even less probable things, than do those who are insane in their waking moments. How often has it happened to me that in the night I dreamt that I found myself in this particular place, that I was dressed and seated near the fire, whilst in reality I was lying undressed in bed! At this moment it does indeed seem to me that it is with eyes awake that I am looking at this paper; that this head which I move is not asleep, that it is deliberately and of set purpose that I extend my hand and perceive it; what happens in sleep does not appear so clear nor so distinct as does all this. But in thinking over this I remind myself that on many occasions I have in sleep been deceived by similar illusions, and in dwelling carefully on this reflection I see so manifestly that there are no certain indications by which we may clearly distinguish wakefulness from sleep that I am lost in astonishment. And my astonishment is such that it is almost capable of persuading me that I now dream.

Now let us assume that we are asleep and that all these particulars, e.g. that we open our eyes, shake our head, extend our hands, and so on, are but false delusions; and let us reflect that possibly neither our hands nor our whole body are such as they appear to us to be. At the same time we must at least confess that the things which are represented to us in sleep are like painted representations which can only have been formed as the counterparts of something real and true, and that in this way those general things at least, i.e. eyes, a head, hands, and a whole body, are not imaginary things, but things really existent. For, as a matter of fact, painters, even when they study with the greatest skill to represent sirens and satyrs by forms the most strange and extraordinary, cannot give them natures which are entirely new, but merely make a certain medley of the members of different animals; or if their imagination is extravagant enough to invent something so novel that nothing similar has ever before been seen, and that then their work represents a thing purely fictitious and absolutely false, it is certain all the same that the colours of which is compared are necessarily real. And for the same reason, although these general things, to wit, [a body], eyes, a head, hands, and such like, may be imaginary, we are bound at the same time to confess that there are at least some other objects yet more simple and more universal, which are real and true; and of these just in the same way as with certain real colours, all these images of things which dwell in our thoughts, whether true and real or false and fantastic, are formed.

To such a class of things pertains corporeal nature in general, and its extension, the figure of extended things, their quantity or magnitude and number, as also the place in which they are, the time which measures their duration, and so on.

That is possibly why our reasoning is not unjust when we conclude from this that Physics, Astronomy, Medicine and all other sciences which have as their end the consideration of composite things, are very dubious and uncertain; but that Arithmetic, Geometry and other sciences of that kind which only treat of things that are very simple and very general, without taking great trouble to ascertain whether they are actually existent or not, contain some measure of certainty and an element of the indubitable. For whether I am awake or asleep, two and three together always form five, and the square can never have more than four sides, and it does not seem possible that truths so clear and apparent can be suspected of any falsity [or uncertainty].

Nevertheless I have long had fixed in my mind the belief that an all-powerful God existed by whom I have been created such as I am. But how do I know that He has not brought it to pass that there is no earth, no heaven, no extended body, no magnitude, no place, and that nevertheless [I possess the perceptions of all these things and that] they seem to me to exist just exactly as I now see them? And, besides, as I sometimes imagine that others deceive themselves in the things which they think they know best, how do I know that I am not deceived every time that I add two and three, or count the sides of a square, or judge of things yet simpler, if anything simpler can be imagined? But possibly God has not desired that I should be thus deceived, for He is said to be supremely good. If, however, it is contrary to His goodness to have made me such that I constantly deceive myself, it would also appear to be contrary to His goodness to permit me to be sometimes deceived, and nevertheless I cannot doubt that He does permit this.

There may indeed be those who would prefer to deny the existence of a God so powerful, rather than believe that all other things are uncertain. But let us not oppose them for the present, and grant that all that is here said of a God is a fable; nevertheless in whatever way they suppose that I have arrived at the state of being that I have reached—whether they attribute it to fate or to accident, or make out that it is by a continual succession of antecedents, or by some other method—since to err and deceive oneself is a defect, it is clear that the greater will be the probability of my being so imperfect as to deceive myself ever, as is the Author to whom they assign my origin the less powerful. To these reasons I have certainly nothing to reply, but at the end I feel constrained to confess that there is nothing in all that I formerly believed to be true, of which I cannot in some measure doubt, and that not merely through want of thought or through levity, but for reasons which are very powerful and maturely considered; so that henceforth I ought not the less carefully to refrain from giving credence to these opinions than to that which is manifestly false, if I desire to arrive at any certainty [in the sciences].

But it is not sufficient to have made these remarks, we must also be careful to keep them in mind. For these ancient and commonly held opinions still revert frequently to my mind, long and familiar custom having given them the right to occupy my mind against my inclination and rendered them almost masters of my belief; nor will I ever lose the habit of deferring to them or of placing my confidence in them, so long as I consider them as they really are, i.e. opinions in some measure doubtful, as I have just shown, and at the same time highly probable, so that there is much more reason to believe in than to deny them. That is why I consider that I shall not be acting amiss, if, taking of set purpose a contrary belief, I allow myself to be deceived, and for a certain time pretend that all these opinions are entirely false and imaginary, until at last, having thus balanced my former prejudices with my latter [so that they cannot divert my opinions more to one side than to the other], my judgment will no longer be dominated by bad usage or turned away from the right knowledge of the truth. For I am assured that there can be neither peril nor error in this course, and that I cannot at present yield too much to distrust, since I am not considering the question of action, but only of knowledge.

I shall then suppose, not that God who is supremely good and the fountain of truth, but some evil genius not less powerful than deceitful, has employed his whole energies in deceiving me; I shall consider that the heavens, the earth, colours, figures, sound, and all other external things are nought but the illusions and dreams of which this genius has availed himself in order to lay traps for my credulity; I shall consider myself as having no hands, no eyes, no flesh, no blood, nor any senses, yet falsely believing myself to possess all these things; I shall remain obstinately attached to this idea, and if by this means it is not in my power to arrive at the knowledge of any truth, I may at least do what is in my power [i.e. suspend my judgment], and with firm purpose avoid giving credence to any false thing, or being imposed upon by this arch deceiver, however powerful and deceptive he may be. But this task is a laborious one, and insensibly a certain lassitude leads me into the course of my ordinary life. And just as a captive who in sleep enjoys an imaginary liberty, when he begins to suspect that his liberty is but a dream, fears to awaken, and conspires with these agreeable illusions that the deception may be prolonged, so insensibly of my own accord I fall back into my former opinions, and I dread awakening from this slumber, lest the laborious wakefulness which would follow the tranquillity of this repose should have to be spent not in daylight, but in the excessive darkness of the difficulties which have just been discussed.

### Meditation II: Of the Nature of the Human Mind; and That It Is More Easily Known Than the Body

The Meditation of yesterday filled my mind with so many doubts that it is no longer in my power to forget them. And yet I do not see in what manner I can resolve them; and, just as if I had all of a sudden fallen into very deep water, I am so disconcerted that I can neither make certain of setting my feet on the bottom, nor can I swim and so support myself on the surface. I shall nevertheless make an effort and follow anew the same path as that on which I yesterday entered, i.e. I shall proceed by setting aside all that in which the least doubt could be supposed to exist, just as if I had discovered that it was absolutely false; and I shall ever follow in this road until I have met with something which is certain, or at least, if I can do nothing else, until I have learned for certain that there is nothing in the world that is certain. Archimedes, in order that he might draw the terrestrial globe out of its place, and transport it elsewhere, demanded only that one point should be fixed and immoveable; in the same way I shall have the right to conceive high hopes if I am happy enough to discover one thing only which is certain and indubitable.

I suppose, then, that all the things that I see are false; I persuade myself that nothing has ever existed of all that my fallacious memory represents to me. I consider that I possess no senses; I imagine that body, fatigue, extension, movement and place are but the fictions of my mind. What, then, can be esteemed as true? Perhaps nothing at all, unless that there is nothing in the world that is certain.

But how can I know there is not something different from those things that I have just considered, of which one cannot have the slightest doubt? Is there not some God, or some other being by whatever name we call it, who puts these reflections into my mind? That is not necessary, for is it not possible that I am capable of producing them myself? I myself, am I not at least something? But I have already denied that I had senses and body. Yet I hesitate, for what follows from that? Am I so dependent on body and senses that I cannot exist without these? But I was persuaded that there was nothing in all the world, that there was no heaven, no earth, that there were no minds, nor any bodies: was I not then likewise persuaded that I did not exist? Not at all; of a surety I myself did exist since I persuaded myself of something [or merely because I thought of something]. But there is some deceiver or other, very powerful and very cunning, who ever employs his ingenuity in deceiving me. Then without doubt I exist also if he deceives me, and let him deceive me as much as he will, he can never cause me to be nothing so long as I think that I am something. So that after having reflected well and carefully examined all things, we must come to the definite conclusion that this proposition: I am, I exist, is necessarily true each time that I pronounce it, or that I mentally conceive it.

But I do not yet know clearly enough what I am, I who am certain that I am; and hence I must be careful to see that I do not imprudently take some other object in place of myself, and thus that I do not go astray in respect of this knowledge that I hold to be the most certain and most evident of all that I have formerly learned. That is why I shall now consider anew what I believed myself to be before I embarked upon these last reflections; and of my former opinions I shall withdraw all that might even in a small degree be invalidated by the reasons which I have just brought forward, in order that there may be nothing at all left beyond what is absolutely certain and indubitable.

What then did I formerly believe myself to be? Undoubtedly I believed myself to be a man. But what is a man? Shall I say a reasonable animal? Certainly not; for then I should have to inquire what an animal is, and what is reasonable; and thus from a single question I should insensibly fall into an infinitude of others more difficult; and I should not wish to waste the little time and leisure remaining to me in trying to unravel subtleties like these. But I shall rather stop here to consider the thoughts which of themselves spring up in my mind, and which were not inspired by anything beyond my own nature alone when I applied myself to the consideration of my being. In the first place, then, I considered myself as having a face, hands, arms, and all that system of members composed of bones and flesh as seen in a corpse which I designated by the name of body. In addition to this I considered that I was nourished, that I walked, that I felt, and that I thought, and I referred all these actions to the soul: but I did not stop to consider what the soul was, or if I did stop, I imagined that it was something extremely rare and subtle like a wind, a flame, or an ether, which was spread throughout my grosser parts. As to body I had no manner of doubt about its nature, but thought I had a very clear knowledge of it; and if I had desired to explain it according to the notions that I had then formed of it, I should have described it thus: By the body I understand all that which can be defined by a certain figure: something which can be confined in a certain place, and which can fill a given space in such a way that every other body will be excluded from it; which can be perceived either by touch, or by sight, or by hearing, or by taste, or by smell: which can be moved in many ways not, in truth, by itself, but by something which is foreign to it, by which it is touched [and from which it receives impressions]: for to have the power of self-movement, as also of feeling or of thinking, I did not consider to appertain to the nature of body: on the contrary, I was rather astonished to find that faculties similar to them existed in some bodies.

But what am I, now that I suppose that there is a certain genius which is extremely powerful, and, if I may say so, malicious, who employs all his powers in deceiving me? Can I affirm that I possess the least of all those things which I have just said pertain to the nature of body? I pause to consider, I revolve all these things in my mind, and I find none of which I can say that it pertains to me. It would be tedious to stop to enumerate them. Let us pass to the attributes of soul and see if there is any one which is in me? What of nutrition or walking [the first mentioned]? But if it is so that I have no body it is also true that I can neither walk nor take nourishment. Another attribute is sensation. But one cannot feel without body, and besides I have thought I perceived many things during sleep that I recognised in my waking moments as not having been experienced at all. What of thinking? I find here that thought is an attribute that belongs to me; it alone cannot be separated from me. I am, I exist, that is certain. But how often? Just when I think; for it might possibly be the case if I ceased entirely to think, that I should otherwise cease altogether to exist. I do not now admit anything which is not necessarily true: to speak accurately I am not more than a thing which thinks, that is to say a mind or a soul, or an understanding, or a reason, which are terms whose significance was formerly unknown to me. I am, however, a real thing and really exist; but what thing? I have answered: a thing which thinks.

And what more? I shall exercise my imagination [in order to see if I am not something more]. I am not a collection of members which we call the human body: I am not a subtle air distributed through these members, I am not a wind, a fire, a vapour, a breath, nor anything at all which I can imagine or conceive; because I have assumed that all these were nothing. Without changing that supposition I find that I only leave myself certain of the fact that I am somewhat. But perhaps it is true that these same things which I supposed were non-existent because they are unknown to me, are really not different from the self which I know. I am not sure about this, I shall not dispute about it now; I can only give judgment on things that are known to me. I know that I exist, and I inquire what I am, I whom I know to exist. But it is very certain that the knowledge of my existence taken in its precise significance does not depend on things whose existence is not yet known to me; consequently it does not depend on those which I can feign in imagination. And indeed the very term *feign* in imagination proves to me my error, for I really do this if I image myself a something, since to imagine is nothing else than to contemplate the figure or image of a corporeal thing. But I already know for certain that I am, and that it may be that all these images, and, speaking generally, all things that relate to the nature of body are nothing but dreams [and chimeras]. For this reason I see clearly that I have as little reason to say, "I shall stimulate my imagination in order to know more distinctly what

I am," than if I were to say, "I am now awake, and I perceive somewhat that is real and true: but because I do not yet perceive it distinctly enough, I go to sleep of express purpose, so that my dreams may represent the perception with greatest truth and evidence." And, thus, I know for certain that nothing of all that I can understand by means of my imagination belongs to this knowledge which I have of myself, and that it is necessary to recall the mind from this mode of thought with the utmost diligence in order that it may be able to know its own nature with perfect distinctness.

But what then am I? A thing which thinks. What is a thing which thinks? It is a thing which doubts, understands, [conceives], affirms, denies, wills, refuses, which also imagines and feels.

Certainly it is no small matter if all these things pertain to my nature. But why should they not so pertain? Am I not that being who now doubts nearly everything, who nevertheless understands certain things, who affirms that one only is true, who denies all the others, who desires to know more, is averse from being deceived, who imagines many things, sometimes indeed despite his will, and who perceives many likewise, as by the intervention of the bodily organs? Is there nothing in all this which is as true as it is certain that I exist, even though I should always sleep and though he who has given me being employed all his ingenuity in deceiving me? Is there likewise any one of these attributes which can be distinguished from my thought, or which might be said to be separated from myself? For it is so evident of itself that it is I who doubts, who understands, and who desires, that there is no reason here to add anything to explain it. And I have certainly the power of imagining likewise; for although it may happen (as I formerly supposed) that none of the things which I imagine are true, nevertheless this power of imagining does not cease to be really in use, and it forms part of my thought. Finally, I am the same who feels, that is to say, who perceives certain things, as by the organs of sense, since in truth I see light, I hear noise, I feel heat. But it will be said that these phenomena are false and that I am dreaming. Let it be so; still it is at least quite certain that it seems to me that I see light, that I hear noise and that I feel heat. That cannot be false; properly speaking it is what is in me called feeling; and used in this precise sense that is no other thing than thinking.

From this time I begin to know what I am with a little more clearness and distinction than before; but nevertheless it still seems to me, and I cannot prevent myself from thinking, that corporeal things, whose images are framed by thought, which are tested by the senses, are much more distinctly known than that obscure part of me which does not come under the imagination. Although really it is very strange to say that I know and understand more distinctly these things whose existence seems to me dubious, which are unknown to me, and which do not belong to me, than others of the truth of which I am convinced, which are known to me and which pertain to my real nature, in a word, than myself. But I see clearly how the case stands: my mind loves to wander, and cannot yet suffer itself to be retained within the just limits of truth. Very good, let us once more give it the freest rein, so that, when afterwards we seize the proper occasion for pulling up, it may the more easily be regulated and controlled.

Let us begin by considering the commonest matters, those which we believe to be the most distinctly comprehended, to wit, the bodies which we touch and see; not indeed bodies in general, for these general ideas are usually a little more confused, but let us consider one body in particular. Let us take, for example, this piece of wax: it has been taken quite freshly from the hive, and it has not yet lost the sweetness of the honey which it contains; it still retains somewhat of the odour of the flowers from which it has been culled; its colour, its figure, its size are apparent; it is hard, cold, easily handled, and if you strike it with the finger, it will emit a sound. Finally all the things which are requisite to cause us distinctly to recognise a body, are met within it. But notice that while I speak and approach the fire what remained of the taste is exhaled, the smell evaporates, the colour alters, the figure is destroyed, the size increases, it becomes liquid, it heats, scarcely can one handle it, and when one strikes it, no sound is emitted. Does the same wax remain after this change? We must confess that it remains; none would judge otherwise. What then did I know so distinctly in this piece of wax? It could certainly be nothing of all that the senses brought to my notice, since all these things which fall under taste, smell, sight, touch, and hearing, are found to be changed, and yet the same wax remains.

Perhaps it was what I now think, viz. that this wax was not that sweetness of honey, nor that agreeable scent of flowers, nor that particular whiteness, nor that figure, nor that sound, but simply a body which a little while before appeared to me as perceptible under these forms, and which is now perceptible under others. But what, precisely, is it that I imagine when I form such conceptions? Let us attentively consider this, and, abstracting from all that does not belong to the wax, let us see what remains. Certainly nothing remains excepting a certain extended thing which is flexible and movable. But what is the meaning of flexible and movable? Is it not that I imagine that this piece of wax being round is capable of becoming square and of passing from a square to a triangular figure? No, certainly it is not that, since I imagine it admits of an infinitude of similar changes, and I nevertheless do not know how to compass the infinitude by my imagination, and consequently this conception which I have of the wax is not brought about by the faculty of imagination. What now is this extension? Is it not also unknown? For it becomes greater when the wax is melted, greater when it is boiled, and greater still when the heat increases; and I should not conceive [clearly] according to truth what wax is, if I did not think that even this piece that we are considering is capable of receiving more variations in extension than I have ever imagined. We must then grant that I could not even understand through the imagination what this piece of wax is, and that it is my mind alone which perceives it. I say this piece of wax in particular, for as to wax in general it is yet clearer. But what is this piece of wax which cannot be understood excepting by the [understanding or] mind? It is certainly the same that I see, touch, imagine, and finally it is the same which I have always believed it to be from the beginning. But what must particularly be observed is that its perception is neither an act of vision, nor of touch, nor of imagination, and has never been such although it may have appeared formerly to be so, but only an intuition of the mind, which may be imperfect and confused as it was formerly, or clear and distinct as it is at present, according as my attention is more or less directed to the elements which are found in it, and of which it is composed.

Yet in the meantime I am greatly astonished when I consider [the great feebleness of mind] and its proneness to fall [insensibly] into error; for although without giving expression to my thoughts I consider all this in my own mind, words often impede me and I am almost deceived by the terms of ordinary language. For we say that we see the same wax, if it is present, and not that we simply judge that it is the same from its having the same colour and figure. From this I should conclude that I knew the wax by means of vision and not simply by the intuition of the mind; unless by chance I remember that, when looking from a window and saying I see men who pass in the street, I really do not see them, but infer that what I see is men, just as I say that I see wax. And yet what do I see from the window but hats and coats which may cover automatic machines? Yet I judge these to be men. And similarly solely by the faculty of judgment which rests in my mind, I comprehend that which I believed I saw with my eyes.

A man who makes it his aim to raise his knowledge above the common should be ashamed to derive the occasion for doubting from the forms of speech invented by the vulgar; I prefer to pass on and consider whether I had a more evident and perfect conception of what the wax was when I first perceived it, and when I believed I knew it by means of the external senses or at least by the common sense as it is called, that is to say by the imaginative faculty, or whether my present conception is clearer now that I have most carefully examined what it is, and in what way it can be known. It would certainly be absurd to doubt as to this. For what was there in this first perception which was distinct? What was there which might not as well have been perceived by any of the animals? But when I distinguish the wax from its external forms, and when, just as if I had taken from it its vestments, I consider it quite naked, it is certain that although some error may still be found in my judgment, I can nevertheless not perceive it thus without a human mind.

But finally what shall I say of this mind, that is, of myself, for up to this point I do not admit in myself anything but mind? What then, I who seem to perceive this piece of wax so distinctly, do I not know myself, not only with much more truth and certainty, but also with much more distinctness and clearness? For if I judge that the wax is or exists from the fact that I see it, it certainly follows much more clearly that I am or that I exist myself from the fact that I see it. For it may be that what I see is not really wax, it may also be that I do not possess eyes with which to see anything; but it cannot be that when I see, or (for I no longer take account of the distinction) when I think I see, that I myself who think am nought. So if I judge that the wax exists from the fact that I touch it, the same thing will follow, to wit, that I am; and if I judge that my imagination, or some other cause, whatever it is, persuades me that the wax exists, I shall still conclude the same. And what I have here remarked of wax may be applied to all other things which are external to me [and which are met with outside of me]. And further, if the [notion or] perception of wax has seemed to me clearer and more distinct, not only after the sight or the touch, but also after many other causes have rendered it quite manifest to me, with how much more [evidence] and distinctness must it be said that I now know myself, since all the reasons which contribute to the knowledge of wax, or any other body whatever, are yet better proofs of the nature of my mind! And there are so many other things in the mind itself which may contribute to the elucidation of its nature, that those which depend on body such as these just mentioned, hardly merit being taken into account.

But finally here I am, having insensibly reverted to the point I desired, for, since it is now manifest to me that even bodies are not properly speaking known by the senses or by the faculty of imagination, but by the understanding only, and since they are not known from the fact that they are seen or touched, but only because they are understood, I see clearly that there is nothing which is easier for me to know than my mind. But because it is difficult to rid oneself so promptly of an opinion to which one was accustomed for so long, it will be well that I should halt a little at this point, so that by the length of my meditation I may more deeply imprint on my memory this new knowledge.

## Meditation III: Of God, That He Exists

I shall now close my eyes, I shall stop my ears, I shall call away all my senses, I shall efface even from my thoughts all the images of corporeal things, or at least (for that is hardly possible) I shall esteem them as vain and false; and thus holding converse only with myself and considering my own nature, I shall try little by little to reach a better knowledge of and a more familiar acquaintanceship with myself. I am a thing that thinks, that is to say, that doubts, affirms, denies, that knows a few things, that is ignorant of many [that loves, that hates], that wills, that desires, that also imagines and perceives; for as I remarked before, although the things which I perceive and imagine are perhaps nothing at all apart from me and in themselves, I am nevertheless assured that these modes of thought that I call perceptions and imaginations, inasmuch only as they are modes of thought, certainly reside [and are met with] in me.

And in the little that I have just said, I think I have summed up all that I really know, or at least all that hitherto I was aware that I knew. In order to try to extend my knowledge further, I shall now look around more carefully and see whether I cannot still discover in myself some other things which I have not hitherto perceived. I am certain that I am a thing which thinks; but do I not then likewise know what is requisite to render me certain of a truth? Certainly in this first knowledge there is nothing that assures me of its truth, excepting the clear and distinct perception of that which I state, which would not indeed suffice to assure me that what I say is true, if it could ever happen that a thing which I conceived so clearly and distinctly could be false; and accordingly it seems to me that already I can establish as a general rule that all things which I perceive very clearly and very distinctly are true.

At the same time I have before received and admitted many things to be very certain and manifest, which yet I afterwards recognised as being dubious. What then were these things? They were the earth, sky, stars and all other objects which I apprehended by means of the senses. But what did I clearly [and distinctly] perceive in them? Nothing more than that the ideas or thoughts of these things were presented to my mind. And not even now do I deny that these ideas are met with in me. But there was yet another thing which I affirmed, and which, owing to the habit which I had formed of believing it, I thought I perceived very clearly, although in truth I did not perceive it at all, to wit, that there were objects outside of me from which these ideas proceeded, and to which they were entirely similar. And it was in this that I erred, or, if perchance my judgment was correct, this was not due to any knowledge arising from my perception.

But when I took anything very simple and easy in the sphere of arithmetic or geometry into consideration, e.g. that two and three together made five, and other things of the sort, were not these present to my mind so clearly as to enable me to affirm that they were true? Certainly if I judged that since such matters could be doubted, this would not have been so for any other reason than that it came into my mind that perhaps a God might have endowed me with such a nature that I may have been deceived even concerning things which seemed to me most manifest. But every time that this preconceived opinion of the sovereign power of a God presents itself to my thought, I am constrained to confess that it is easy to Him, if He wishes it, to cause me to err, even in matters in which I believe myself to have the best evidence. And, on the other hand, always when I direct my attention to things which I believe myself to perceive very clearly, I am so persuaded of their truth that I let myself break out into words such as these: Let who will deceive me, He can never cause me to be nothing while I think that I am, or some day cause it to be true to say that I have never been, it being true now to say that I am, or that two and three make more or less than five, or any such thing in which I see a manifest contradiction. And, certainly, since I have no reason to believe that there is a God who is a deceiver, and as I have not yet satisfied myself that there is a God at all, the reason for doubt which depends on this opinion alone is very slight, and so to speak metaphysical. But in order to be able altogether to remove it, I must inquire whether there is a God as soon as the occasion presents itself; and if I find that there is a God, I must also inquire whether He may be a deceiver; for without a knowledge of these two truths I do not see that I can ever be certain of anything.

And in order that I may have an opportunity of inquiring into this in an orderly way [without interrupting the order of meditation which I have proposed to myself, and which is little by little to pass from the notions which I find first of all in my mind to those which I shall later on discover in it] it is requisite that I should here divide my thoughts into certain kinds, and that I should consider in which of these kinds there is, properly speaking, truth or error to be found. Of my thoughts some are, so to speak, images of the things, and to these alone is the title "idea" properly applied; examples are my thought of a man or of a chimera, of heaven, of an angel, or [even] of God. But other thoughts possess other forms as well. For example in willing, fearing, approving, denying, though I always perceive something as the subject of the action of my mind, yet by this action I always add something else to the idea which I have of that thing; and of the thoughts of this kind some are called volitions or affections, and others judgments.

Now as to what concerns ideas, if we consider them only in themselves and do not relate them to anything else beyond themselves, they cannot properly speaking be false; for whether I imagine a goat or a chimera, it is not less true that I imagine the one than the other. We must not fear likewise that falsity can enter into will and into affections, for although I may desire evil things, or even things that never existed, it is not the less true that I desire them. Thus there remains no more than the judgments which we make, in which I must take the greatest care not to deceive myself.

But the principal error and the commonest which we may meet with in them, consists in my judging that the ideas which are in me are similar or conformable to the things which are outside me; for without doubt if I considered the ideas only as certain modes of my thoughts, without trying to relate them to anything beyond, they could scarcely give me material for error.

But among these ideas, some appear to me to be innate, some adventitious, and others to be formed [or invented] by myself; for, as I have the power of understanding what is called a thing, or a truth, or a thought, it appears to me that I hold this power from no other source than my own nature. But if I now hear some sound, if I see the sun, or feel heat, I have hitherto judged that these sensations proceeded from certain things that exist outside of me; and finally it appears to me that sirens, hippogryphs, and the like, are formed out of my own mind. But again I may possibly persuade myself that all these ideas are of the nature of those which I term adventitious, or else that they are all innate, or all fictitious: for I have not yet clearly discovered their true origin.

And my principal task in this place is to consider, in respect to those ideas which appear to me to proceed from certain objects that are outside me, what are the reasons which cause me to think them similar to these objects. It seems indeed that I am taught this lesson by nature; and, secondly, I experience in myself that these ideas do not depend on my will nor therefore on myself—for they often present themselves to my mind in spite of my will. Just now, for instance, whether I will or whether I do not will, I feel heat, and thus I persuade myself that this feeling, or at least this idea of heat, is produced in me by something which is different from me, i.e. by the heat of the fire near which I sit. And nothing seems to me more obvious than to judge that this object imprints its likeness rather than anything else upon me.

Now I must discover whether these proofs are sufficiently strong and convincing. When I say that I am so instructed by nature, I merely mean a certain spontaneous inclination which impels me to believe in this connection, and not a natural light which makes me recognise that it is true. But these two things are very different; for I cannot doubt that which the natural light causes me to believe to be true, as, for example, it has shown me that I am from the fact that I doubt, or other facts of the same kind. And I possess no other faculty whereby to distinguish truth from falsehood, which can teach me that what this light shows me to be true is not really true, and no other faculty that is equally trustworthy. But as far as [apparently] natural impulses are concerned, I have frequently remarked, when I had to make active choice between virtue and vice, that they often enough led me to the part that was worse, and this is why I do not see any reason for following them in what regards truth and error.

And as to the other reason, which is that these ideas must proceed from objects outside me, since they do not depend on my will, I do not find it any the more convincing. For just as these impulses of which I have spoken are found in me, notwithstanding that they do not always concur with my will, so perhaps there is in me some faculty fitted to produce these ideas without the assistance of any external things, even though it is not yet known by me; just as, apparently, they have hitherto always been found in me during sleep without the aid of any external objects.

And finally, though they did proceed from objects different from myself, it is not a necessary consequence that they should resemble these. On the contrary, I have noticed that in many cases there was a great difference between the object and its idea. I find, for example, two completely diverse ideas of the sun in my mind; the one derives its origin from the senses, and should be placed in the category of adventitious ideas; according to this idea the sun seems to be extremely small; but the other is derived from astronomical reasonings, i.e. is elicited from certain notions that are innate in me, or else it is formed by me in some other manner; in accordance with it the sun appears to be several times greater than the earth. These two ideas cannot, indeed, both resemble the same sun, and reason makes me believe that the one which seems to have originated directly from the sun itself, is the one which is most dissimilar to it.

All this causes me to believe that until the present time it has not been by a judgment that was certain [or premeditated], but only by a sort of blind impulse that I believed that things existed outside of, and different from me, which, by the organs of my senses, or by some other method whatever it might be, conveyed these ideas or images to me [and imprinted on me their similitudes].

But there is yet another method of inquiring whether any of the objects of which I have ideas within me exist outside of me. If ideas are only taken as certain modes of thought, I recognise amongst them no difference or inequality, and all appear to proceed from me in the same manner; but when we consider them as images, one representing one thing and the other another, it is clear that they are very different one from the other. There is no doubt that those which represent to me substances are something more, and contain so to speak more objective reality within them [that is to say, by representation participate in a higher degree of being or perfection] than those that simply represent modes or accidents; and that idea again by which I understand a supreme God, eternal, infinite, [immutable], omniscient, omnipotent, and Creator of all things which are outside of Himself, has certainly more objective reality in itself than those ideas by which finite substances are represented.

Now it is manifest by the natural light that there must at least be as much reality in the efficient and total cause as in its effect. For pray, whence can the effect derive its reality, if not from its cause? And in what way can this cause communicate this reality to it, unless it possessed it in itself? And from this it follows, not only that something cannot proceed from nothing, but likewise that what is more perfect—that is to say, which has more reality within itself—cannot proceed from the less perfect. And this is not only evidently true of those effects which possess actual or formal reality, but also of the ideas in which we consider merely what is termed objective reality. To take an example, the stone which has not yet existed not only cannot now commence to be unless it has been produced by something which possesses within itself, either formally or eminently, all that enters into the composition of the stone [i.e. it must possess the same things or other more excellent things than those which exist in the stone] and heat can only be produced in a subject in which it did not previously exist by a cause that is of an order [degree or kind], at least as perfect as heat, and so in all other cases. But further, the idea of heat, or of a stone, cannot exist in me unless it has been placed within me by some cause which possesses within it at least as much reality as that which I conceive to exist in the heat or the stone. For although this cause does not transmit anything of its actual or formal reality to my idea, we must not for that reason imagine that it is necessarily a less real cause; we must remember that [since every idea is a work of the mind] its nature is such that it demands of itself no other formal reality than that which it borrows from my thought, of which it is only a mode [i.e. a manner or way of thinking]. But in order that an idea should contain some one certain objective reality rather than another, it must without doubt derive it from some cause in which there is at least as much formal reality as this idea contains of objective reality. For if we imagine that something is found in an idea which is not found in the cause, it must then have been derived from nought; but however imperfect may be this mode of being by which a thing is objectively [or by representation] in the understanding of its idea, we cannot certainly say that this mode of being is nothing, nor, consequently, that the idea derives its origin from nothing.

Nor must I imagine that, since the reality that I consider in these idea is only objective, it is not essential that this reality should be formally in the causes of my ideas, but that it is sufficient that it should be found objectively. For just as this mode of objective existence pertains to ideas by their proper nature, so does the mode of formal existence pertain to the causes of those ideas (this is at least true of the first and principal) by the nature peculiar to them. And although it may be the case that one idea gives birth to another idea, that cannot continue to be so indefinitely; for in the end we must reach an idea whose cause shall be so to speak an archetype, in which the whole reality [or perfection] which is so to speak objectively [or by representation] in these ideas is contained formally [and really]. Thus the light of nature causes me to know clearly that the ideas in me are like [pictures or] images which can, in truth, easily fall short of the perfection of the objects from which they have been derived, but which can never contain anything greater or more perfect.

And the longer and the more carefully that I investigate these matters, the more clearly and distinctly do I recognise their truth. But what am I to conclude from it all in the end? It is this, that if the objective reality of any one of my ideas is of such a nature as clearly to make me recognise that it is not in me either formally or eminently, and that consequently I cannot myself be the cause of it, it follows of necessity that I am not alone in the world, but that there is another being which exists, or which is the cause of this idea. On the other hand, had no such an idea existed in me, I should have had no sufficient argument to convince me of the existence of any being beyond myself; for I have made very careful investigation everywhere and up to the present time have been able to find no other ground.

But of my ideas, beyond that which represents me to myself, as to which there can be no difficulty, there is another which represents a God, and there are others representing corporeal and inanimate things, others angels, others animals, and others again which represent to me men similar to myself.

As regards the ideas which represent to me other men or animals, or angels, I can however easily conceive that they might be formed by an admixture of the other ideas which I have of myself, of corporeal things, and of God, even although there were apart from me neither men nor animals, nor angels, in all the world.

And in regard to the ideas of corporeal objects, I do not recognise in them anything so great or so excellent that they might not have possibly proceeded from myself; for if I consider them more closely, and examine them individually, as I yesterday examined the idea of wax, I find that there is very little in them which I perceive clearly and distinctly. Magnitude or extension in length, breadth, or depth, I do so perceive; also figure which results from a termination of this extension, the situation which bodies of different figure preserve in relation to one another, and movement or change of situation; to which we may also add substance, duration and number. As to other things such as light, colours, sounds, scents, tastes, heat, cold and the other tactile qualities, they are thought by me with so much obscurity and confusion that I do not even know if they are true or false, i.e. whether the ideas which I form of these qualities are actually the ideas of real objects or not [or whether they only represent chimeras which cannot exist in fact]. For although I have before remarked that it is only in judgments that falsity, properly speaking, or formal falsity, can be met with, a certain material falsity may nevertheless be found in ideas, i.e. when these ideas represent what is nothing as though it were something. For example, the ideas which I have of cold and heat are so far from clear and distinct that by their means I cannot tell whether cold is merely a privation of heat, or heat a privation of cold, or whether both are real qualities, or are not such. And inasmuch as [since ideas resemble images] there cannot be any ideas which do not appear to represent some things, if it is correct to say that cold is merely a privation of heat, the idea which represents it to me as something real and positive will not be improperly termed false, and the same holds good of other similar ideas.

To these it is certainly not necessary that I should attribute any author other than myself. For if they are false, i.e. if they represent things which do not exist, the light of nature shows me that they issue from nought, that is to say, that they are only in me in so far as something is lacking to the perfection of my nature. But if they are true, nevertheless because they exhibit so little reality to me that I cannot even clearly distinguish the thing represented from non-being, I do not see any reason why they should not be produced by myself.

As to the clear and distinct idea which I have of corporeal things, some of them seem as though I might have derived them from the idea which I possess of myself, as those which I have of substance, duration, number, and such like. For [even] when I think that a stone is a substance, or at least a thing capable of existing of itself, and that I am a substance also, although I conceive that I am a thing that thinks and not one that is extended, and that the stone on the other hand is an extended thing which does not think, and thus there is a notable difference between the two conceptions—they seem, nevertheless, to agree in this, that both represent substances. In the same way, when I perceive that I now exist and further recollect that I have in former times existed, and when I remember that I have various thoughts of which I can recognise the number, I acquire ideas of duration and number which I can afterwards transfer to any object that I please. But as to all other qualities of which the ideas of corporeal things are composed, to wit, extension, figure, situation and motion, it is true that they are not formally in me, since I am only a thing that thinks; but because they are merely certain modes of substance [and so to speak the vestments under which corporeal substance appears to us] and because I myself am also a substance, it would seem that they might be contained in me eminently.

Hence there remains only the idea of God, concerning which we must consider whether it is something which cannot have proceeded from me myself. By the name God I understand a substance that is infinite [eternal, immutable], independent, all-knowing, all-powerful, and by which I myself and everything else, if anything else does exist, have been created. Now all these characteristics are such that the more diligently I attend to them, the less do they appear capable of proceeding from me alone; hence, from what has been already said, we must conclude that God necessarily exists.

For although the idea of substance is within me owing to the fact that I am substance, nevertheless I should not have the idea of an infinite substance—since I am finite—if it had not proceeded from some substance which was veritably infinite.

Nor should I imagine that I do not perceive the infinite by a true idea, but only by the negation of the finite, just as I perceive repose and darkness by the negation of movement and light; for, on the contrary, I see that there is manifestly more reality in infinite substance than in finite, and therefore that in some way I have in me the notion of the infinite earlier than the finite—to wit, the notion of God before that of myself. For how would it be possible that I should know that I doubt and desire, that is to say, that something is lacking to me, and that I am not quite perfect, unless I had within me some idea of a Being more perfect than myself, in comparison with which I should recognise the deficiencies of my nature?

And we cannot say that this idea of God is perhaps materially false and that consequently I can derive it from nought [i.e. that possibly it exists in me because I am imperfect], as I have just said is the case with ideas of heat, cold and other such things; for, on the contrary, as this idea is very clear and distinct and contains within it more objective reality than any other, there can be none which is of itself more true, nor any in which there can be less suspicion of falsehood. The idea, I say, of this Being who is absolutely perfect and infinite, is entirely true; for although, perhaps we can imagine that such a Being does not exist, we cannot never-the less imagine that His idea represents nothing real to me, as I have said of the idea of cold. This idea is also very clear and distinct; since all that I conceive clearly and distinctly of the real and the true, and of what conveys some perfection, is in its entirety contained in this idea. And this does not cease to be true although I do not comprehend the infinite, or though in God there is an infinitude of things which I cannot comprehend, nor possibly even reach in any way by thought; for it is of the nature of the infinite that my nature, which is finite and limited, should not comprehend it; and it is sufficient that I should understand this, and that I should judge that all things which I clearly perceive and in which I know that there is some perfection, and possibly likewise an infinitude of properties of which I am ignorant, are in God formally or eminently, so that the idea which I have of Him may become the most true, most clear, and most distinct of all the ideas that are in my mind.

But possibly I am something more than I suppose myself to be, and perhaps all those perfections which I attribute to God are in some way potentially in me, although they do not yet disclose themselves, or issue in action. As a matter of fact I am already sensible that my knowledge increases [and perfects itself] little by little, and I see nothing which can prevent it from increasing more and more into infinitude; nor do I see, after it has thus been increased [or perfected], anything to prevent my being able to acquire by its means all the other perfections of the Divine nature; nor finally why the power I have of acquiring these perfections, if it really exists in me, shall not suffice to produce the ideas of them.

At the same time I recognise that this cannot be. For, in the first place, although it were true that every day my knowledge acquired new degrees of perfection, and that there were in my nature many things potentially which are not yet there actually, nevertheless these excellences do not pertain to [or make the smallest approach to] the idea which I have of God in whom there is nothing merely potential [but in whom all is present really and actually]; for it is an infallible token of imperfection in my knowledge that it increases little by little. And further, although my knowledge grows more and more, nevertheless I do not for that reason believe that it can ever be actually infinite, since it can never reach a point so high that it will be unable to attain to any greater increase. But I understand God to be actually infinite, so that He can add nothing to His supreme perfection. And finally I perceive that the objective being of an idea cannot be produced by a being that exists potentially only, which properly speaking is nothing, but only by a being which is formal or actual.

To speak the truth, I see nothing in all that I have just said which by the light of nature is not manifest to anyone who desires to think attentively on the subject; but when I slightly relax my attention, my mind, finding its vision somewhat obscured and so to speak blinded by the images of sensible objects, I do not easily recollect the reason why the idea that I possess of a being more perfect than I, must necessarily have been placed in me by a being which is really more perfect; and this is why I wish here to go on to inquire whether I, who have this idea, can exist if no such being exists.

And I ask, from whom do I then derive my existence? Perhaps from myself or from my parents, or from some other source less perfect than God; for we can imagine nothing more perfect than God, or even as perfect as He is.

But [were I independent of every other and] were I myself the author of my being, I should doubt nothing and I should desire nothing, and finally no perfection would be lacking to me; for I should have bestowed on myself every perfection of which I possessed any idea and should thus be God. And it must not be imagined that those things that are lacking to me are perhaps more difficult of attainment than those which I already possess; for, on the contrary, it is quite evident that it was a matter of much greater difficulty to bring to pass that I, that is to say, a thing or a substance that thinks, should emerge out of nothing, than it would be to attain to the knowledge of many things of which I am ignorant, and which are only the accidents of this thinking substance. But it is clear that if I had of myself possessed this greater perfection of which I have just spoken [that is to say, if I had been the author of my own existence], I should not at least have denied myself the things which are the more easy to acquire [to wit, many branches of knowledge of which my nature is destitute]; nor should I have deprived myself of any of the things contained in the idea which I form of God, because there are none of them which seem to me specially difficult to acquire: and if there were any that were more difficult to acquire, they would certainly appear to me to be such (supposing I myself were the origin of the other things which I possess) since I should discover in them that my powers were limited.

But though I assume that perhaps I have always existed just as I am at present, neither can I escape the force of this reasoning, and imagine that the conclusion to be drawn from this is, that I need not seek for any author of my existence. For all the course of my life may be divided into an infinite number of parts, none of which is in any way dependent on the other; and thus from the fact that I was in existence a short time ago it does not follow that I must be in existence now, unless some cause at this instant, so to speak, produces me anew, that is to say, conserves me. It is as a matter of fact perfectly clear and evident to all those who consider with attention the nature of time, that, in order to be conserved in each moment in which it endures, a substance has need of the same power and action as would be necessary to produce and create it anew, supposing it did not yet exist, so that the light of nature shows us clearly that the distinction between creation and conservation is solely a distinction of the reason.

All that I thus require here is that I should interrogate myself, if I wish to know whether I possess a power which is capable of bringing it to pass that I who now am shall still be in the future; for since I am nothing but a thinking thing, or at least since thus far it is only this portion of myself which is precisely in question at present, if such a power did reside in me, I should certainly be conscious of it. But I am conscious of nothing of the kind, and by this I know clearly that I depend on some being different from myself.

Possibly, however, this being on which I depend is not that which I call God, and I am created either by my parents or by some other cause less perfect than God. This cannot be, because, as I have just said, it is perfectly evident that there must be at least as much reality in the cause as in the effect; and thus since I am a thinking thing, and possess an idea of God within me, whatever in the end be the cause assigned to my existence, it must be allowed that it is likewise a thinking thing and that it possesses in itself the idea of all the perfections which I attribute to God. We may again inquire whether this cause derives its origin from itself or from some other thing. For if from itself, it follows by the reasons before brought forward, that this cause must itself be God; for since it possesses the virtue of self-existence, it must also without doubt have the power of actually possessing all the perfections of which it has the idea, that is, all those which I conceive as existing in God. But if it derives its existence from some other cause than itself, we shall again ask, for the same reason, whether this second cause exists by itself or through another, until from one step to another, we finally arrive at an ultimate cause, which will be God.

And it is perfectly manifest that in this there can be no regression into infinity, since what is in question is not so much the cause which formerly created me, as that which conserves me at the present time.

Nor can we suppose that several causes may have concurred in my production, and that from one I have received the idea of one of the perfections which I attribute to God, and from another the idea of some other, so that all these perfections indeed exist somewhere in the universe, but not as complete in one unity which is God. On the contrary, the unity, the simplicity or the inseparability of all things which are in God is one of the principal perfections which I conceive to be in Him. And certainly the idea of this unity of all Divine perfections cannot have been placed in me by any cause from which I have not likewise received the ideas of all the other perfections; for this cause could not make me able to comprehend them as joined together in an inseparable unity without having at the same time caused me in some measure to know what they are [and in some way to recognise each one of them].

Finally, so far as my parents [from whom it appears I have sprung] are concerned, although all that I have ever been able to believe of them were true, that does not make it follow that it is they who conserve me, nor are they even the authors of my being in any sense, in so far as I am a thinking being; since what they did was merely to implant certain dispositions in that matter in which the self—i.e. the mind, which alone I at present identify with myself—is by me deemed to exist. And thus there can be no difficulty in their regard, but we must of necessity conclude from the fact alone that I exist, or that the idea of a Being supremely perfect—that is of God—is in me, that the proof of God's existence is grounded on the highest evidence.

It only remains to me to examine into the manner in which I have acquired this idea from God; for I have not received it through the senses, and it is never presented to me unexpectedly, as is usual with the ideas of sensible things when these things present themselves, or seem to present themselves, to the external organs of my senses; nor is it likewise a fiction of my mind, for it is not in my power to take from or to add anything to it; and consequently the only alternative is that it is innate in me, just as the idea of myself is innate in me.

And one certainly ought not to find it strange that God, in creating me, placed this idea within me to be like the mark of the workman imprinted on his work; and it is likewise not essential that the mark shall be something different from the work itself. For from the sole fact that God created me it is most probable that in some way he has placed his image and similitude upon me, and that I perceive this similitude (in which the idea of God is contained) by means of the same faculty by which I perceive myself—that is to say, when I reflect on myself I not only know that I am something [imperfect], incomplete and dependent on another, which incessantly aspires after something which is better and greater than myself, but I also know that He on whom I depend possesses in Himself all the great things towards which I aspire [and the ideas of which I find within myself], and that not indefinitely or potentially alone, but really, actually and infinitely; and that thus He is God. And the whole strength of the argument which I have here made use of to prove the existence of God consists in this, that I recognise that it is not possible that my nature should be what it is, and indeed that I should have in myself the idea of a God, if God did not veritably exist— a God, I say, whose idea is in me, i.e. who possesses all those supreme perfections of which our mind may indeed have some idea but without understanding them all, who is liable to no errors or defect [and who has none of all those marks which denote imperfection]. From this it is manifest that He cannot be a deceiver, since the light of nature teaches us that fraud and deception necessarily proceed from some defect.

But before I examine this matter with more care, and pass on to the consideration of other truths which may be derived from it, it seems to me right to pause for a while in order to contemplate God Himself, to ponder at leisure His marvellous attributes, to consider, and admire, and adore, the beauty of this light so resplendent, at least as far as the strength of my mind, which is in some measure dazzled by the sight, will allow me to do so. For just as faith teaches us that the supreme felicity of the other life consists only in this contemplation of the Divine Majesty, so we continue to learn by experience that a similar meditation, though incomparably less perfect, causes us to enjoy the greatest satisfaction of which we are capable in this life.

## Meditation IV: Of the True and the False

I have been well accustomed these past days to detach my mind from my senses, and I have accurately observed that there are very few things that one knows with certainty respecting corporeal objects, that there are many more which are known to us respecting the human mind, and yet more still regarding God Himself; so that I shall now without any difficulty abstract my thoughts from the consideration of [sensible or] imaginable objects, and carry them to those which, being withdrawn from all contact with matter, are purely intelligible. And certainly the idea which I possess of the human mind inasmuch as it is a thinking thing, and not extended in length, width and depth, nor participating in anything pertaining to body, is incomparably more distinct than is the idea of any corporeal thing. And when I consider that I doubt, that is to say, that I am an incomplete and dependent being, the idea of a being that is complete and independent, that is of God, presents itself to my mind with so much distinctness and clearness—and from the fact alone that this idea is found in me, or that I who possess this idea exist, I conclude so certainly that God exists, and that my existence depends entirely on Him in every moment of my life—that I do not think that the human mind is capable of knowing anything with more evidence and certitude. And it seems to me that I now have before me a road which will lead us from the contemplation of the true God (in whom all the treasures of science and wisdom are contained) to the knowledge of the other objects of the universe.

For, first of all, I recognise it to be impossible that He should ever deceive me; for in all fraud and deception some imperfection is to be found, and although it may appear that the power of deception is a mark of subtilty or power, yet the desire to deceive without doubt testifies to malice or feebleness, and accordingly cannot be found in God.

In the next place I experienced in myself a certain capacity for judging which I have doubtless received from God, like all the other things that I possess; and as He could not desire to deceive me, it is clear that He has not given me a faculty that will lead me to err if I use it aright.

And no doubt respecting this matter could remain, if it were not that the consequence would seem to follow that I can thus never be deceived; for if I hold all that I possess from God, and if He has not placed in me the capacity for error, it seems as though I could never fall into error. And it is true that when I think only of God [and direct my mind wholly to Him], I discover [in myself] no cause of error, or falsity; yet directly afterwards, when recurring to myself, experience shows me that I am nevertheless subject to an infinitude of errors, as to which, when we come to investigate them more closely, I notice that not only is there a real and positive idea of God or of a Being of supreme perfection present to my mind, but also, so to speak, a certain negative idea of nothing, that is, of that which is infinitely removed from any kind of perfection; and that I am in a sense something intermediate between God and nought, i.e. placed in such a manner between the supreme Being and nonbeing, that there is in truth nothing in me that can lead to error in so far as a sovereign Being has formed me; but that, as I in some degree participate likewise in nought or in non-being, i.e. in so far as I am not myself the supreme Being, and as I find myself subject to an infinitude of imperfections, I ought not to be astonished if I should fall into error. Thus do I recognise that error, in so far as it is such, is not a real thing depending on God, but simply a defect; and therefore, in order to fall into it, that I have no need to possess a special faculty given me by God for this very purpose, but that I fall into error from the fact that the power given me by God for the purpose of distinguishing truth from error is not infinite.

Nevertheless this does not quite satisfy me; for error is not a pure negation [i.e. is not the simple defect or want of some perfection which ought not to be mine], but it is a lack of some knowledge which it seems that I ought to possess. And on considering the nature of God it does not appear to me possible that He should have given me a faculty which is not perfect of its kind, that is, which is wanting in some perfection due to it. For if it is true that the more skillful the artisan, the more perfect is the work of his hands, what can have been produced by this supreme Creator of all things that is not in all its parts perfect? And certainly there is no doubt that God could have created me so that I could never have been subject to error; it is also certain that He ever wills what is best; is it then better that I should be subject to err than that I should not?

In considering this more attentively, it occurs to me in the first place that I should not be astonished if my intelligence is not capable of comprehending why God acts as He does; and that there is thus no reason to doubt of His existence from the fact that I may perhaps find many other things besides this as to which I am able to understand neither for what reason nor how God has produced them. For, in the first place, knowing that my nature is extremely feeble and limited, and that the nature of God is on the contrary immense, incomprehensible, and infinite, I have no further difficulty in recognising that there is an infinitude of matters in His power, the causes of which transcend my knowledge; and this reason suffices to convince me that the species of cause termed final, finds no useful employment in physical [or natural] things; for it does not appear to me that I can without temerity seek to investigate the [inscrutable] ends of God.

It further occurs to me that we should not consider one single creature separately, when we inquire as to whether the works of God are perfect, but should regard all his creations together. For the same thing which might possibly seem very imperfect with some semblance of reason if regarded by itself, is found to be very perfect if regarded as part of the whole universe; and although, since I resolved to doubt all things, I as yet have only known certainly my own existence and that of God, nevertheless since I have recognised the infinite power of God, I cannot deny that He may have produced many other things, or at least that He has the power of producing them, so that I may obtain a place as a part of a great universe.

Whereupon, regarding myself more closely, and considering what are my errors (for they alone testify to there being any imperfection in me), I answer that they depend on a combination of two causes, to wit, on the faculty of knowledge that rests in me, and on the power of choice or of free will—that is to say, of the understanding and at the same time of the will. For by the understanding alone I [neither assert nor deny anything, but] apprehend the ideas of things as to which I can form a judgment. But no error is properly speaking found in it, provided the word error is taken in its proper signification; and though there is possibly an infinitude of things in the world of which I have no idea in my understanding, we cannot for all that say that it is deprived of these ideas [as we might say of something which is required by its nature], but simply it does not possess these; because in truth there is no reason to prove that God should have given me a greater faculty of knowledge than He has given me; and however skilful a workman I represent Him to be, I should not for all that consider that He was bound to have placed in each of His works all the perfections which He may have been able to place in some. I likewise cannot complain that God has not given me a free choice or a will which is sufficient, ample and perfect, since as a matter of fact I am conscious of a will so extended as to be subject to no limits. And what seems to me very remarkable in this regard is that of all the qualities which I possess there is no one so perfect and so comprehensive that I do not very clearly recognise that it might be yet greater and more perfect. For, to take an example, if I consider the faculty of comprehension which I possess, I find that it is of very small extent and extremely limited, and at the same time I find the idea of another faculty much more ample and even infinite, and seeing that I can form the idea of it, I recognise from this very fact that it pertains to the nature of God. If in the same way I examine the memory, the imagination, or some other faculty, I do not find any which is not small and circumscribed, while in God it is immense [or infinite]. It is free-will alone or liberty of choice which I find to be so great in me that I can conceive no other idea to be more great; it is indeed the case that it is for the most part this will that causes me to know that in some manner I bear the image and similitude of God. For although the power of will is incomparably greater in God than in me, both by reason of the knowledge and the power which, conjoined with it, render it stronger and more efficacious, and by reason of its object, inasmuch as in God it extends to a great many things; it nevertheless does not seem to me greater if I consider it formally and precisely in itself: for the faculty of will consists alone in our having the power of choosing to do a thing or choosing not to do it (that is, to affirm or deny, to pursue or to shun it), or rather it consists alone in the fact that in order to affirm or deny, pursue or shun those things placed before us by the understanding, we act so that we are unconscious that any outside force constrains us in doing so. For in order that I should be free it is not necessary that I should be indifferent as to the choice of one or the other of two contraries; but contrariwise the more I lean to the one—whether I recognise clearly that the reasons of the good and true are to be found in it, or whether God so disposes my inward thought—the more freely do I choose and embrace it. And undoubtedly both divine grace and natural knowledge, far from diminishing my liberty, rather increase it and strengthen it. Hence this indifference which I feel, when I am not swayed to one side rather than to the other by lack of reason, is the lowest grade of liberty, and rather evinces a lack or negation in knowledge than a perfection of will: for if I always recognised clearly what was true and good, I should never have trouble in deliberating as to what judgment or choice I should make, and then I should be entirely free without ever being indifferent.

From all this I recognise that the power of will which I have received from God is not of itself the source of my errors—for it is very ample and very perfect of its kind—any more than is the power of understanding; for since I understand nothing but by the power which God has given me for understanding, there is no doubt that all that I understand, I understand as I ought, and it is not possible that I err in this. Whence then come my errors? They come from the sole fact that since the will is much wider in its range and compass than the understanding, I do not restrain it within the same bounds, but extend it also to things which I do not understand: and as the will is of itself indifferent to these, it easily falls into error and sin, and chooses the evil for the good, or the false for the true.

For example, when I lately examined whether anything existed in the world, and found that from the very fact that I considered this question it followed very clearly that I myself existed, I could not prevent myself from believing that a thing I so clearly conceived was true: not that I found myself compelled to do so by some external cause, but simply because from great clearness in my mind there followed a great inclination of my will; and I believed this with so much the greater freedom or spontaneity as I possessed the less indifference towards it. Now, on the contrary, I not only know that I exist, inasmuch as I am a thinking thing, but a certain representation of corporeal nature is also presented to my mind; and it comes to pass that I doubt whether this thinking nature which is in me, or rather by which I am what I am, differs from this corporeal nature, or whether both are not simply the same thing; and I here suppose that I do not yet know any reason to persuade me to adopt the one belief rather than the other. From this it follows that I am entirely indifferent as to which of the two I affirm or deny, or even whether I abstain from forming any judgment in the matter.

And this indifference does not only extend to matters as to which the understanding has no knowledge, but also in general to all those which are not apprehended with perfect clearness at the moment when the will is deliberating upon them: for, however probable are the conjectures which render me disposed to form a judgment respecting anything, the simple knowledge that I have that those are conjectures alone and not certain and indubitable reasons, suffices to occasion me to judge the contrary. Of this I have had great experience of late when I set aside as false all that I had formerly held to be absolutely true, for the sole reason that I remarked that it might in some measure be doubted.

But if I abstain from giving my judgment on any thing when I do not perceive it with sufficient clearness and distinctness, it is plain that I act rightly and am not deceived. But if I determine to deny or affirm, I no longer make use as I should of my free will, and if I affirm what is not true, it is evident that I deceive myself; even though I judge according to truth, this comes about only by chance, and I do not escape the blame of missing my freedom; for the light of nature teaches us that the knowledge of the understanding should always precede the determination of the will. And it is in the misuse of the free will that the privation which constitutes the characteristic nature of error is met with. Privation, I say, is found in the act, in so far as it proceeds from me, but it is not found in the faculty which I have received from God, nor even in the act in so far as it depends on Him.

For I have certainly no cause to complain that God has not given me an intelligence which is more powerful, or a natural light which is stronger than that which I have received from Him, since it is proper to the finite understanding not to comprehend a multitude of things, and it is proper to a created understanding to be finite; on the contrary, I have every reason to render thanks to God who owes me nothing and who has given me all the perfections I possess, and I should be far from charging Him with injustice, and with having deprived me of, or wrongfully withheld from me, these perfections which He has not bestowed upon me.

I have further no reason to complain that He has given me a will more ample than my understanding, for since the will consists only of one single element, and is so to speak indivisible, it appears that its nature is such that nothing can be abstracted from it [without destroying it]; and certainly the more comprehensive it is found to be, the more reason I have to render gratitude to the giver.

And, finally, I must also not complain that God concurs with me in forming the acts of the will, that is the judgment in which I go astray, because these acts are entirely true and good, inasmuch as they depend on God; and in a certain sense more perfection accrues to my nature from the fact that I can form them, than if I could not do so. As to the privation in which alone the formal reason of error or sin consists, it has no need of any concurrence from God, since it is not a thing [or an existence], and since it is not related to God as to a cause, but should be termed merely a negation [according to the significance given to these words in the Schools]. For in fact it is not an imperfection in God that He has given me the liberty to give or withhold my assent from certain things as to which He has not placed a clear and distinct knowledge in my understanding; but it is without doubt an imperfection in me not to make a good use of my freedom, and to give my judgment readily on matters which I only understand obscurely. I nevertheless perceive that God could easily have created me so that I never should err, although I still remained free, and endowed with a limited knowledge, viz. by giving to my understanding a clear and distinct intelligence of all things as to which I should ever have to deliberate; or simply by His engraving deeply in my memory the resolution never to form a judgment on anything without having a clear and distinct understanding of it, so that I could never forget it. And it is easy for me to understand that, in so far as I consider myself alone, and as if there were only myself in the world, I should have been much more perfect than I am, if God had created me so that I could never err. Nevertheless I cannot deny that in some sense it is a greater perfection in the whole universe that certain parts should not be exempt from error as others are than that all parts should be exactly similar. And I have no right to complain if God, having placed me in the world, has not called upon me to play a part that excels all others in distinction and perfection.

And further I have reason to be glad on the ground that if He has not given me the power of never going astray by the first means pointed out above, which depends on a clear and evident knowledge of all the things regarding which I can deliberate, He has at least left within my power the other means, which is firmly to adhere to the resolution never to give judgment on matters whose truth is not clearly known to me; for although I notice a certain weakness in my nature in that I cannot continually concentrate my mind on one single thought, I can yet, by attentive and frequently repeated meditation, impress it so forcibly on my memory that I shall never fail to recollect it whenever I have need of it, and thus acquire the habit of never going astray.

And inasmuch as it is in this that the greatest and principal perfection of man consists, it seems to me that I have not gained little by this day's Meditation, since I have discovered the source of falsity and error. And certainly there can be no other source than that which I have explained; for as often as I so restrain my will within the limits of my knowledge that it forms no judgment except on matters which are clearly and distinctly represented to it by the understanding, I can never be deceived; for every clear and distinct conception is without doubt something, and hence cannot derive its origin from what is nought, but must of necessity have God as its author—God, I say, who being supremely perfect, cannot be the cause of any error; and consequently we must conclude that such a conception [or such a judgment] is true. Nor have I only learned to-day what I should avoid in order that I may not err, but also how I should act in order to arrive at a knowledge of the truth; for without doubt I shall arrive at this end if I devote my attention sufficiently to those things which I perfectly understand; and if I separate from these that which I only understand confusedly and with obscurity. To these I shall henceforth diligently give heed.

## Meditation V: Of the Essence of Material Things, and Again, of God, That He Exists

Many other matters respecting the attributes of God and my own nature or mind remain for consideration; but I shall possibly on another occasion resume the investigation of these. Now (after first noting what must be done or avoided, in order to arrive at a knowledge of the truth) my principal task is to endeavour to emerge from the state of doubt into which I have these last days fallen, and to see whether nothing certain can be known regarding material things.

But before examining whether any such objects as I conceive exist outside of me, I must consider the ideas of them in so far as they are in my thought, and see which of them are distinct and which confused.

In the first place, I am able distinctly to imagine that quantity which philosophers commonly call continuous, or the extension in length, breadth, or depth, that is in this quantity, or rather in the object to which it is attributed. Further, I can number in it many different parts, and attribute to each of its parts many sorts of size, figure, situation and local movement, and, finally, I can assign to each of these movements all degrees of duration.

And not only do I know these things with distinctness when I consider them in general, but, likewise [however little I apply my attention to the matter], I discover an infinitude of particulars respecting numbers, figures, movements, and other such things, whose truth is so manifest, and so well accords with my nature, that when I begin to discover them, it seems to me that I learn nothing new, or recollect what I formerly knew—that is to say, that I for the first time perceive things which were already present to my mind, although I had not as yet applied my mind to them.

And what I here find to be most important is that I discover in myself an infinitude of ideas of certain things which cannot be esteemed as pure negations, although they may possibly have no existence outside of my thought, and which are not framed by me, although it is within my power either to think or not to think them, but which possess natures which are true and immutable. For example, when I imagine a triangle, although there may nowhere in the world be such a figure outside my thought, or ever have been, there is nevertheless in this figure a certain determinate nature, form, or essence, which is immutable and eternal, which I have not invented, and which in no wise depends on my mind, as appears from the fact that diverse properties of that triangle can be demonstrated, viz. that its three angles are equal to two right angles, that the greatest side is subtended by the greatest angle, and the like, which now, whether I wish it or do not wish it, I recognise very clearly as pertaining to it, although I never thought of the matter at all when I imagined a triangle for the first time, and which therefore cannot be said to have been invented by me.

Nor does the objection hold good that possibly this idea of a triangle has reached my mind through the medium of my senses, since I have sometimes seen bodies triangular in shape; because I can form in my mind an infinitude of other figures regarding which we cannot have the least conception of their ever having been objects of sense, and I can nevertheless demonstrate various properties pertaining to their nature as well as to that of the triangle, and these must certainly all be true since I conceive them clearly. Hence they are something, and not pure negation; for it is perfectly clear that all that is true is something, and I have already fully demonstrated that all that I know clearly is true. And even although I had not demonstrated this, the nature of my mind is such that I could not prevent myself from holding them to be true so long as I conceive them clearly; and I recollect that even when I was still strongly attached to the objects of sense, I counted as the most certain those truths which I conceived clearly as regards figures, numbers, and the other matters which pertain to arithmetic and geometry, and, in general, to pure and abstract mathematics.

But now, if just because I can draw the idea of something from my thought, it follows that all which I know clearly and distinctly as pertaining to this object does really belong to it, may I not derive from this an argument demonstrating the existence of God? It is certain that I no less find the idea of God, that is to say, the idea of a supremely perfect Being, in me, than that of any figure or number whatever it is; and I do not know any less clearly and distinctly that an [actual and] eternal existence pertains to this nature than I know that all that which I am able to demonstrate of some figure or number truly pertains to the nature of this figure or number, and therefore, although all that I concluded in the preceding Meditations were found to be false, the existence of God would pass with me as at least as certain as I have ever held the truths of mathematics (which concern only numbers and figures) to be.

This indeed is not at first manifest, since it would seem to present some appearance of being a sophism. For being accustomed in all other things to make a distinction between existence and essence, I easily persuade myself that the existence can be separated from the essence of God, and that we can thus conceive God as not actually existing. But, nevertheless, when I think of it with more attention, I clearly see that existence can no more be separated from the essence of God than can its having its three angles equal to two right angles be separated from the essence of a [rectilinear] triangle, or the idea of a mountain from the idea of a valley; and so there is not any less repugnance to our conceiving a God (that is, a Being supremely perfect) to whom existence is lacking (that is to say, to whom a certain perfection is lacking), than to conceive of a mountain which has no valley.

But although I cannot really conceive of a God without existence any more than a mountain without a valley, still from the fact that I conceive of a mountain with a valley, it does not follow that there is such a mountain in the world; similarly although I conceive of God as possessing existence, it would seem that it does not follow that there is a God which exists; for my thought does not impose any necessity upon things, and just as I may imagine a winged horse, although no horse with wings exists, so I could perhaps attribute existence to God, although no God existed.

But a sophism is concealed in this objection; for from the fact that I cannot conceive a mountain without a valley, it does not follow that there is any mountain or any valley in existence, but only that the mountain and the valley, whether they exist or do not exist, cannot in any way be separated one from the other. While from the fact that I cannot conceive God without existence, it follows that existence is inseparable from Him, and hence that He really exists; not that my thought can bring this to pass, or impose any necessity on things, but, on the contrary, because the necessity which lies in the thing itself, i.e. the necessity of the existence of God determines me to think in this way. For it is not within my power to think of God without existence (that is of a supremely perfect Being devoid of a supreme perfection) though it is in my power to imagine a horse either with wings or without wings.

And we must not here object that it is in truth necessary for me to assert that God exists after having presupposed that He possesses every sort of perfection, since existence is one of these, but that as a matter of fact my original supposition was not necessary, just as it is not necessary to consider that all quadrilateral figures can be inscribed in the circle; for supposing I thought this, I should be constrained to admit that the rhombus might be inscribed in the circle since it is a quadrilateral figure, which, however, is manifestly false. [We must not, I say, make any such allegations because] although it is not necessary that I should at any time entertain the notion of God, nevertheless whenever it happens that I think of a first and a sovereign Being, and, so to speak, derive the idea of Him from the storehouse of my mind, it is necessary that I should attribute to Him every sort of perfection, although I do not get so far as to enumerate them all, or to apply my mind to each one in particular. And this necessity suffices to make me conclude (after having recognised that existence is a perfection) that this first and sovereign Being really exists; just as though it is not necessary for me ever to imagine any triangle, yet, whenever I wish to consider a rectilinear figure composed only of three angles, it is absolutely essential that I should attribute to it all those properties which serve to bring about the conclusion that its three angles are not greater than two right angles, even although I may not then be considering this point in particular. But when I consider which figures are capable of being inscribed in the circle, it is in no wise necessary that I should think that all quadrilateral figures are of this number; on the contrary, I cannot even pretend that this is the case, so long as I do not desire to accept anything which I cannot conceive clearly and distinctly. And in consequence there is a great difference between the false suppositions such as this, and the true ideas born within me, the first and principal of which is that of God. For really I discern in many ways that this idea is not something factitious, and depending solely on my thought, but that it is the image of a true and immutable nature; first of all, because I cannot conceive anything but God himself to whose essence existence [necessarily] pertains; in the second because it is not possible for me to conceive two or more Gods in this same position; and, granted that there is one such God who now exists, I see clearly that it is necessary that He should have existed from all eternity, and that He must exist eternally; and finally, because I know an infinitude of other properties in God, none of which I can either diminish or change.

For the rest, whatever proof or argument I avail myself of, we must always return to the point that it is only those things which we conceive clearly and distinctly that have the power of persuading me entirely. And although amongst the matters which I conceive of in this way, some indeed are manifestly obvious to all, while others only manifest themselves to those who consider them closely and examine them attentively; still, after they have once been discovered, the latter are not esteemed as any less certain than the former. For example, in the case of every right-angled triangle, although it does not so manifestly appear that the square of the base is equal to the squares of the two other sides as that this base is opposite to the greatest angle; still, when this has once been apprehended, we are just as certain of its truth as of the truth of the other. And as regards God, if my mind were not pre-occupied with prejudices, and if my thought did not find itself on all hands diverted by the continual pressure of sensible things, there would be nothing which I could know more immediately and more easily than Him. For is there anything more manifest than that there is a God, that is to say, a Supreme Being, to whose essence alone existence pertains?

And although for a firm grasp of this truth I have need of a strenuous application of mind, at present I not only feel myself to be as assured of it as of all that I hold as most certain, but I also remark that the certainty of all other things depends on it so absolutely, that without this knowledge it is impossible ever to know anything perfectly.

For although I am of such a nature that as long as I understand anything very clearly and distinctly, I am naturally impelled to believe it to be true, yet because I am also of such a nature that I cannot have my mind constantly fixed on the same object in order to perceive it clearly, and as I often recollect having formed a past judgment without at the same time properly recollecting the reasons that led me to make it, it may happen meanwhile that other reasons present themselves to me, which would easily cause me to change my opinion, if I were ignorant of the facts of the existence of God, and thus I should have no true and certain knowledge, but only vague and vacillating opinions. Thus, for example, when I consider the nature of a [rectilinear] triangle, I who have some little knowledge of the principles of geometry recognise quite clearly that the three angles are equal to two right angles, and it is not possible for me not to believe this so long as I apply my mind to its demonstration; but so soon as I abstain from attending to the proof, although I still recollect having clearly comprehended it, it may easily occur that I come to doubt its truth, if I am ignorant of there being a God. For I can persuade myself of having been so constituted by nature that I can easily deceive myself even in those matters which I believe myself to apprehend with the greatest evidence and certainty, especially when I recollect that I have frequently judged matters to be true and certain which other reasons have afterwards impelled me to judge to be altogether false.

But after I have recognised that there is a God—because at the same time I have also recognised that all things depend upon Him, and that He is not a deceiver, and from that have inferred that what I perceive clearly and distinctly cannot fail to be true—although I no longer pay attention to the reasons for which I have judged this to be true, provided that I recollect having clearly and distinctly perceived it no contrary reason can be brought forward which could ever cause me to doubt of its truth; and thus I have a true and certain knowledge of it. And this same knowledge extends likewise to all other things which I recollect having formerly demonstrated, such as the truths of geometry and the like; for what can be alleged against them to cause me to place them in doubt? Will it be said that my nature is such as to cause me to be frequently deceived? But I already know that I cannot be deceived in the judgment whose grounds I know clearly. Will it be said that I formerly held many things to be true and certain which I have afterwards recognised to be false? But I had not had any clear and distinct knowledge of these things, and not as yet knowing the rule whereby I assure myself of the truth, I had been impelled to give my assent from reasons which I have since recognised to be less strong than I had at the time imagined them to be. What further objection can then be raised? That possibly I am dreaming (an objection I myself made a little while ago), or that all the thoughts which I now have are no more true than the phantasies of my dreams? But even though I slept the case would be the same, for all that is clearly present to my mind is absolutely true.

And so I very clearly recognise that the certainty and truth of all knowledge depends alone on the knowledge of the true God, in so much that, before I knew Him, I could not have a perfect knowledge of any other thing. And now that I know Him I have the means of acquiring a perfect knowledge of an infinitude of things, not only of those which relate to God Himself and other intellectual matters, but also of those which pertain to corporeal nature in so far as it is the object of pure mathematics [which have no concern with whether it exists or not].

### Meditation VI: Of the Existence of Material Things, and of the Real Distinction Between the Soul and Body of Man

Nothing further now remains but to inquire whether material things exist. And certainly I at least know that these may exist in so far as they are considered as the objects of pure mathematics, since in this aspect I perceive them clearly and distinctly. For there is no doubt that God possesses the power to produce everything that I am capable of perceiving with distinctness, and I have never deemed that anything was impossible for

Him, unless I found a contradiction in attempting to conceive it clearly. Further, the faculty of imagination which I possess, and of which, experience tells me, I make use when I apply myself to the consideration of material things, is capable of persuading me of their existence; for when I attentively consider what imagination is, I find that it is nothing but a certain application of the faculty of knowledge to the body which is immediately present to it, and which therefore exists.

And to render this quite clear, I remark in the first place the difference that exists between the imagination and pure intellection [or conception]. For example, when I imagine a triangle, I do not conceive it only as a figure comprehended by three lines, but I also apprehend these three lines as present by the power and inward vision of my mind, and this is what I call imagining. But if I desire to think of a chiliagon, I certainly conceive truly that it is a figure composed of a thousand sides, just as easily as I conceive of a triangle that it is a figure of three sides only; but I cannot in any way imagine the thousand sides of a chiliagon [as I do the three sides of a triangle], nor do I, so to speak, regard them as present [with the eyes of my mind]. And although in accordance with the habit I have formed of always employing the aid of my imagination when I think of corporeal things, it may happen that in imagining a chiliagon I confusedly represent to myself some figure, yet it is very evident that this figure is not a chiliagon, since it in no way differs from that which I represent to myself when I think of a myriagon or any other many-sided figure; nor does it serve my purpose in discovering the properties which go to form the distinction between a chiliagon and other polygons. But if the question turns upon a pentagon, it is quite true that I can conceive its figure as well as that of a chiliagon without the help of my imagination; but I can also imagine it by applying the attention of my mind to each of its five sides, and at the same time to the space which they enclose. And thus I clearly recognise that I have need of a particular effort of mind in order to effect the act of imagination, such as I do not require in order to understand, and this particular effort of mind clearly manifests the difference which exists between imagination and pure intellection.

I remark besides that this power of imagination which is in one, inasmuch as it differs from the power of understanding, is in no wise a necessary element in my nature, or in [my essence, that is to say, in] the essence of my mind; for although I did not possess it I should doubtless ever remain the same as I now am, from which it appears that we might conclude that it depends on something which differs from me. And I easily conceive that if some body exists with which my mind is conjoined and united in such a way that it can apply itself to consider it when it pleases, it may be that by this means it can imagine corporeal objects; so that this mode of thinking differs from pure intellection only inasmuch as mind in its intellectual activity in some manner turns on itself, and considers some of the ideas which it possesses in itself; while in imagining it turns towards the body, and there beholds in it something conformable to the idea which it has either conceived of itself or perceived by the senses. I easily understand, I say, that the imagination could be thus constituted if it is true that body exists; and because I can discover no other convenient mode of explaining it, I conjecture with probability that body does exist; but this is only with probability, and although I examine all things with care, I nevertheless do not find that from this distinct idea of corporeal nature, which I have in my imagination, I can derive any argument from which there will necessarily be deduced the existence of body.

But I am in the habit of imagining many other things besides this corporeal nature which is the object of pure mathematics, to wit, the colours, sounds, scents, pain, and other such things, although less distinctly. And inasmuch as I perceive these things much better through the senses, by the medium of which, and by the memory, they seem to have reached my imagination, I believe that, in order to examine them more conveniently, it is right that I should at the same time investigate the nature of sense perception, and that I should see if from the ideas which I apprehend by this mode of thought, which I call feeling, I cannot derive some certain proof of the existence of corporeal objects.

And first of all I shall recall to my memory those matters which I hitherto held to be true, as having perceived them through the senses, and the foundations on which my belief has rested; in the next place I shall examine the reasons which have since obliged me to place them in doubt; in the last place I shall consider which of them I must now believe.

First of all, then, I perceived that I had a head, hands, feet, and all other members of which this body—which I considered as a part, or possibly even as the whole, of myself—is composed. Further I was sensible that this body was placed amidst many others, from which it was capable of being affected in many different ways, beneficial and hurtful, and I remarked that a certain feeling of pleasure accompanied those that were beneficial, and pain those which were harmful. And in addition to this pleasure and pain, I also experienced hunger, thirst, and other similar appetites, as also certain corporeal inclinations towards joy, sadness, anger, and other similar passions. And outside myself, in addition to extension, figure, and motions of bodies, I remarked in them hardness, heat, and all other tactile qualities, and, further, light and colour, and scents and sounds, the variety of which gave me the means of distinguishing the sky, the earth, the sea, and generally all the other bodies, one from the other. And certainly, considering the ideas of all these qualities which presented themselves to my mind, and which alone I perceived properly or immediately, it was not without reason that I believed myself to perceive objects quite different from my thought, to wit, bodies from which those ideas proceeded; for I found by experience that these ideas presented themselves to me without my consent being requisite, so that I could not perceive any object, however desirous I might be, unless it were present to the organs of sense; and it was not in my power not to perceive it, when it was present. And because the ideas which I received through the senses were much more lively, more clear, and even, in their own way, more distinct than any of those which I could of myself frame in meditation, or than those I found impressed on my memory, it appeared as though they could not have proceeded from my mind, so that they must necessarily have been produced in me by some other things. And having no knowledge of those objects excepting the knowledge which the ideas themselves gave me, nothing was more likely to occur to my mind than that the objects were similar to the ideas which were caused. And because I likewise remembered that I had formerly made use of my senses rather than my reason, and recognised that the ideas which I formed of myself were not so distinct as those which I perceived through the senses, and that they were most frequently even composed of portions of these last, I persuaded myself easily that I had no idea in my mind which had not formerly come to me through the senses. Nor was it without some reason that I believed that this body (which by a certain special right I call my own) belonged to me more properly and more strictly than any other; for in fact I could never be separated from it as from other bodies; I experienced in it and on account of it all my appetites and affections, and finally I was touched by the feeling of pain and the titillation of pleasure in its parts, and not in the parts of other bodies which were separated from it. But when I inquired, why, from some, I know not what, painful sensation, there follows sadness of mind, and from the pleasurable sensation there arises joy, or why this mysterious pinching of the stomach which I call hunger causes me to desire to eat, and dryness of throat causes a desire to drink, and so on, I could give no reason excepting that nature taught me so; for there is certainly no affinity (that I at least can understand) between the craving of the stomach and the desire to eat, any more than between the perception of whatever causes pain and the thought of sadness which arises from this perception. And in the same way it appeared to me that I had learned from nature all the other judgments which I formed regarding the objects of my senses, since I remarked that these judgments were formed in me before I had the leisure to weigh and consider any reasons which might oblige me to make them.

But afterwards many experiences little by little destroyed all the faith which I had rested in my senses; for I from time to time observed that those towers which from afar appeared to me to be round, more closely observed seemed square, and that colossal statues raised on the summit of these towers, appeared as quite tiny statues when viewed from the bottom; and so in an infinitude of other cases I found error in judgments founded on the external senses. And not only in those founded on the external senses, but even in those founded on the internal as well; for is there anything more intimate or more internal than pain? And yet I have learned from some persons whose arms or legs have been cut off, that they sometimes seemed to feel pain in the part which had been amputated, which made me think that I could not be quite certain that it was a certain member which pained me, even although I felt pain in it. And to those grounds of doubt I have lately added others, which are very general; the first is that I never have believed myself to feel anything in waking moments which I cannot also sometimes believe myself to feel when I sleep, and as I do not think that these things which I seem to feel in sleep, proceed from objects outside of me, I do not see any reason why I should have this belief regarding objects which I seem to perceive while awake. The other was that being still ignorant, or rather supposing myself to be ignorant, of the author of my being, I saw nothing to prevent me from having been so constituted by nature that I might be deceived even in matters which seemed to me to be most certain. And as to the grounds on which I was formerly persuaded of the truth of sensible objects, I had not much trouble in replying to them. For since nature seemed to cause me to lean towards many things from which reason repelled me, I did not believe that I should trust much to the teachings of nature. And although the ideas which I receive by the senses do not depend on my will, I did not think that one should for that reason conclude that they proceeded from things different from myself, since possibly some faculty might be discovered in me—though hitherto unknown to me—which produced them.

But now that I begin to know myself better, and to discover more clearly the author of my being, I do not in truth think that I should rashly admit all the matters which the senses seem to teach us, but, on the other hand, I do not think that I should doubt them all universally.

And first of all, because I know that all things which I apprehend clearly and distinctly can be created by God as I apprehend them, it suffices that I am able to apprehend one thing apart from another clearly and distinctly in order to be certain that the one is different from the other, since they may be made to exist in separation at least by the omnipotence of God; and it does not signify by what power this separation is made in order to compel me to judge them to be different: and, therefore, just because I know certainly that I exist, and that meanwhile I do not remark that any other thing necessarily pertains to my nature or essence, excepting that I am a thinking thing, I rightly conclude that my essence consists solely in the fact that I am a thinking thing [or a substance whose whole essence or nature is to think]. And although possibly (or rather certainly, as I shall say in a moment) I possess a body with which I am very intimately conjoined, yet because, on the one side, I have a clear and distinct idea of myself inasmuch as I am only a thinking and unextended thing, and as, on the other, I possess a distinct idea of body, inasmuch as it is only an extended and unthinking thing, it is certain that this [that is to say, my soul by which I am what I am], is entirely and absolutely distinct from my body, and can exist without it.

I further find in myself faculties employing modes of thinking peculiar to themselves, to wit, the faculties of imagination and feeling, without which I can easily conceive myself clearly and distinctly as a complete being; while, on the other hand, they cannot be so conceived apart from me, that is without an intelligent substance in which they reside, for [in the notion we have of these faculties, or, to use the language of the Schools] in their formal concept, some kind of intellection is comprised, from which I infer that they are distinct from me as its modes are from a thing. I observe also in me some other faculties such as that of change of position, the assumption of different figures and such like, which cannot be conceived, any more than can the preceding, apart from some substance to which they are attached, and consequently cannot exist without it; but it is very clear that these faculties, if it be true that they exist, must be attached to some corporeal or extended substance, and not to an intelligent substance, since in the clear and distinct conception of these there is some sort of extension found to be present, but no intellection at all. There is certainly further in me a certain passive faculty of perception, that is, of receiving and recognising the ideas of sensible things, but this would be useless to me [and I could in no way avail myself of it], if there were not either in me or in some other thing another active faculty capable of forming and producing these ideas. But this active faculty cannot exist in me [inasmuch as I am a thing that thinks] seeing that it does not presuppose thought, and also that those ideas are often produced in me without my contributing in any way to the same, and often even against my will; it is thus necessarily the case that the faculty resides in some substance different from me in which all the reality which is objectively in the ideas that are produced by this faculty is formally or eminently contained, as I remarked before. And this substance is either a body, that is, a corporeal nature in which there is contained formally [and really] all that which is objectively [and by representation] in those ideas, or it is God Himself, or some other creature more noble than body in which that same is contained eminently. But, since God is no deceiver, it is very manifest that He does not communicate to me these ideas immediately and by Himself, nor yet by the intervention of some creature in which their reality is not formally, but only eminently, contained. For since He has given me no faculty to recognise that this is the case, but, on the other hand, a very great inclination to believe [that they are sent to me or] that they are conveyed to me by corporeal objects, I do not see how He could be defended from the accusation of deceit if these ideas were produced by causes other than corporeal objects. Hence we must allow that corporeal things exist. However, they are perhaps not exactly what we perceive by the senses, since this comprehension by the senses is in many instances very obscure and confused; but we must at least admit that all things which I conceive in them clearly and distinctly, that is to say, all things which, speaking generally, are comprehended in the object of pure mathematics, are truly to be recognised as external objects.

As to other things, however, which are either particular only, as, for example, that the sun is of such and such a figure, etc., or which are less clearly and distinctly conceived, such as light, sound, pain and the like, it is certain that although they are very dubious and uncertain, yet on the sole ground that God is not a deceiver, and that consequently He has not permitted any falsity to exist in my opinion which He has not likewise given me the faculty of correcting, I may assuredly hope to conclude that I have within me the means of arriving at the truth even here. And first of all there is no doubt that in all things which nature teaches me there is some truth contained; for by nature, considered in general, I now understand no other thing than either God Himself or else the order and disposition which God has established in created things; and by my nature in particular I understand no other thing than the complexus of all the things which God has given me.

But there is nothing which this nature teaches me more expressly [nor more sensibly] than that I have a body which is adversely affected when I feel pain, which has need of food or drink when I experience the feelings of hunger and thirst, and so on; nor can I doubt there being some truth in all this.

Nature also teaches me by these sensations of pain, hunger, thirst, etc., that I am not only lodged in my body as a pilot in a vessel, but that I am very closely united to it, and so to speak so intermingled with it that I seem to compose with it one whole. For if that were not the case, when my body is hurt, I, who am merely a thinking thing, should not feel pain, for I should perceive this wound by the understanding only, just as the sailor perceives by sight when something is damaged in his vessel; and when my body has need of drink or food, I should clearly understand the fact without being warned of it by confused feelings of hunger and thirst. For all these sensations of hunger, thirst, pain, etc. are in truth none other than certain confused modes of thought which are produced by the union and apparent intermingling of mind and body.

Moreover, nature teaches me that many other bodies exist around mine, of which some are to be avoided, and others sought after. And certainly from the fact that I am sensible of different sorts of colours, sounds, scents, tastes, heat, hardness, etc., I very easily conclude that there are in the bodies from which all these diverse sense-perceptions proceed certain variations which answer to them, although possibly these are not really at all similar to them. And also from the fact that amongst these different sense-perceptions some are very agreeable to me and others disagreeable, it is quite certain that my body (or rather myself in my entirety, inasmuch as I am formed of body and soul) may receive different impressions agreeable and disagreeable from the other bodies which surround it.

But there are many other things which nature seems to have taught me, but which at the same time I have never really received from her, but which have been brought about in my mind by a certain habit which I have of forming inconsiderate judgments on things; and thus it may easily happen that these judgments contain some error. Take, for example, the opinion which I hold that all space in which there is nothing that affects [or makes an impression on] my senses is void; that in a body which is warm there is something entirely similar to the idea of heat which is in me; that in a white or green body there is the same whiteness or greenness that I perceive; that in a bitter or sweet body there is the same taste, and so on in other instances; that the stars, the towers, and all other distant bodies are of the same figure and size as they appear from far off to our eyes, etc. But in order that in this there should be nothing which I do not conceive distinctly, I should define exactly what I really understand when I say that I am taught somewhat by nature. For here I take nature in a more limited signification than when I term it the sum of all the things given me by God, since in this sum many things are comprehended which only pertain to mind (and to these I do not refer in speaking of nature) such as the notion which I have of the fact that what has once been done cannot ever be undone and an infinitude of such things which I know by the light of nature [without the help of the body]; and seeing that it comprehends many other matters besides which only pertain to body, and are no longer here contained under the nature of nature, such as the quality of weight which it possesses and the like, with which I also do not deal; for in talking of nature I only treat of those things given by God to me as a being composed of mind and body. But the nature here described truly teaches me to flee from things which cause the sensation of pain, and seek after the things which communicate to me the sentiment of pleasure and so forth; but I do not see that beyond this it teaches me that from those diverse sense-perceptions we should ever form any conclusion regarding things outside of us, without having [carefully and maturely] mentally examined them beforehand. For it seems to me that it is mind alone, and not mind and body in conjunction, that is requisite to a knowledge of the truth in regard to such things. Thus, although a star makes no larger an impression on my eye than the flame of a little candle there is yet in me no real or positive propensity impelling me to believe that it is not greater than that flame; but I have judged it to be so from my earliest years, without any rational foundation. And although in approaching fire I feel heat, and in approaching it a little too near I even feel pain, there is at the same time no reason in this which could persuade me that there is in the fire something resembling this heat any more than there is in it something resembling the pain; all that I have any reason to believe from this is, that there is something in it, whatever it may be, which excites in me these sensations of heat or of pain. So also, although there are spaces in which I find nothing which excites my senses, I must not from that conclude that these spaces contain no body; for I see in this, as in other similar things, that I have been in the habit of perverting the order of nature, because these perceptions of sense having been placed within me by nature merely for the purpose of signifying to my mind what things are beneficial or hurtful to the composite whole of which it forms a part, and being up to that point sufficiently clear and distinct, I yet avail myself of them as though they were absolute rules by which I might immediately determine the essence of the bodies which are outside me, as to which, in fact, they can teach me nothing but what is most obscure and confused.

But I have already sufficiently considered how, notwithstanding the supreme goodness of God, falsity enters into the judgments I make. Only here a new difficulty is presented—one respecting those things the pursuit or avoidance of which is taught me by nature, and also respecting the internal sensations which I possess, and in which I seem to have sometimes detected error [and thus to be directly deceived by my own nature]. To take an example, the agreeable taste of some food in which poison has been intermingled may induce me to partake of the poison, and thus deceive me. It is true, at the same time, that in this case nature may be excused, for it only induces me to desire food in which I find a pleasant taste, and not to desire the poison which is unknown to it; and thus I can infer nothing from this fact, except that my nature is not omniscient, at which there is certainly no reason to be astonished, since man, being finite in nature, can only have knowledge the perfectness of which is limited.

But we not infrequently deceive ourselves even in those things to which we are directly impelled by nature, as happens with those who when they are sick desire to drink or eat things hurtful to them. It will perhaps be said here that the cause of their deceptiveness is that their nature is corrupt, but that does not remove the difficulty, because a sick man is none the less truly God's creature than he who is in health; and it is therefore as repugnant to God's goodness for the one to have a deceitful nature as it is for the other. And as a clock composed of wheels and counter-weights no less exactly observes the laws of nature when it is badly made, and does not show the time properly, than when it entirely satisfies the wishes of its maker, and as, if I consider the body of a man as being a sort of machine so built up and composed of nerves, muscles, veins, blood and skin, that although there were no mind in it at all, it would not cease to have the same motions as at present, exception being made of those movements which are due to the direction of the will, and in consequence depend upon the mind [as opposed to those which operate by the disposition of its organs], I easily recognise that it would be as natural to this body, supposing it to be, for example, dropsical, to suffer the parchedness of the throat which usually signifies to the mind the feeling of thirst, and to be disposed by this parched feeling to move the nerves and other parts in the way requisite for drinking, and thus to augment its malady and do harm to itself, as it is natural to it, when it has no indisposition, to be impelled to drink for its good by a similar cause. And although, considering the use to which the clock has been destined by its maker, I may say that it deflects from the order of its nature when it does not indicate the hours correctly;

and as, in the same way, considering the machine of the human body as having been formed by God in order to have in itself all the movements usually manifested there, I have reason for thinking that it does not follow the order of nature when, if the throat is dry, drinking does harm to the conservation of health, nevertheless I recognise at the same time that this last mode of explaining nature is very different from the other. For this is but a purely verbal characterisation depending entirely on my thought, which compares a sick man and a badly constructed clock with the idea which I have of a healthy man and a well made clock, and it is hence extrinsic to the things to which it is applied; but according to the other interpretation of the term nature I understand something which is truly found in things and which is therefore not without some truth.

But certainly although in regard to the dropsical body it is only so to speak to supply an extrinsic term when we say that its nature is corrupted, inasmuch as apart from the need to drink, the throat is parched; yet in regard to the composite whole, that is to say, to the mind or soul united to this body, it is not a purely verbal predicate, but a real error of nature, for it to have thirst when drinking would be hurtful to it. And thus it still remains to inquire how the goodness of God does not prevent the nature of man so regarded from being fallacious.

In order to begin this examination, then, I here say, in the first place, that there is a great difference between mind and body, inasmuch as body is by nature always divisible, and the mind is entirely indivisible. For, as a matter of fact, when I consider the mind, that is to say, myself inasmuch as I am only a thinking thing, I cannot distinguish in myself any parts, but apprehend myself to be clearly one and entire; and although the whole mind seems to be united to the whole body, yet if a foot, or an arm, or some other part, is separated from my body, I am aware that nothing has been taken away from my mind. And the faculties of willing, feeling, conceiving, etc. cannot be properly speaking said to be its parts, for it is one and the same mind which employs itself in willing and in feeling and understanding. But it is quite otherwise with corporeal or extended objects, for there is not one of these imaginable by me which my mind cannot easily divide into parts, and which consequently I do not recognise as being divisible; this would be sufficient to teach me that the mind or soul of man is entirely different from the body, if I had not already learned it from other sources.

I further notice that the mind does not receive the impressions from all parts of the body immediately, but only from the brain, or perhaps even from one of its smallest parts, to wit, from that in which the common sense is said to reside, which, whenever it is disposed in the same particular way, conveys the same thing to the mind, although meanwhile the other portions of the body may be differently disposed, as is testified by innumerable experiments which it is unnecessary here to recount.

I notice, also, that the nature of body is such that none of its parts can be moved by another part a little way off which cannot also be moved in the same way by each one of the parts which are between the two, although this more remote part does not act at all. As, for example, in the cord *ABCD* [which is in tension] if we pull the last part *D*, the first part *A* will not be moved in any way differently from what would be the case if one of the intervening parts *B* or *C* were pulled, and the last part *D* were to remain unmoved. And in the same way, when I feel pain in my foot, my knowledge of physics teaches me that this sensation is communicated by means of nerves dispersed through the foot, which, being extended like cords from there to the brain, when they are contracted in the foot, at the same time contract the inmost portions of the brain which is their extremity and place of origin, and then excite a certain movement which nature has established in order to cause the mind to be affected by a sensation of pain represented as existing in the foot. But because these nerves must pass through the tibia, the thigh, the loins, the back and the neck, in order to reach from the leg to the brain, it may happen that although their extremities which are in the foot are not affected, but only certain ones of their intervening parts [which pass by the loins or the neck], this action will excite the same movement in the brain that might have been excited there by a hurt received in the foot, in consequence of which the mind will necessarily feel in the foot the same pain as if it had received a hurt. And the same holds good of all the other perceptions of our senses.

I notice finally that since each of the movements which are in the portion of the brain by which the mind is immediately affected brings about one particular sensation only, we cannot under the circumstances imagine anything more likely than that this movement, amongst all the sensations which it is capable of impressing on it, causes mind to be affected by that one which is best fitted and most generally useful for the conservation of the human body when it is in health. But experience makes us aware that all the feelings with which nature inspires us are such as I have just spoken of; and there is therefore nothing in them which does not give testimony to the power and goodness of the God [who has produced them]. Thus, for example, when the nerves which are in the feet are violently or more than usually moved, their movement, passing through the medulla of the spine to the inmost parts of the brain, gives a sign to the mind which makes it feel somewhat, to wit, pain, as though in the foot, by which the mind is excited to do its utmost to remove the cause of the evil as dangerous and hurtful to the foot. It is true that God could have constituted the nature of man in such a way that this same movement in the brain would have conveyed something quite different to the mind; for example, it might have produced consciousness of itself either in so far as it is in the brain, or as it is in the foot, or as it is in some other place between the foot and the brain, or it might finally have produced consciousness of anything else whatsoever; but none of all this would have contributed so well to the conservation of the body. Similarly, when we desire to drink, a certain dryness of the throat is produced which moves its nerves, and by their means the internal portions of the brain; and this movement causes in the mind the sensation of thirst, because in this case there is nothing more useful to us than to become aware that we have need to drink for the conservation of our health; and the same holds good in other instances.

From this it is quite clear that, notwithstanding the supreme goodness of God, the nature of man, inasmuch as it is composed of mind and body, cannot be otherwise than sometimes a source of deception. For if there is any cause which excites, not in the foot but in some part of the nerves which are extended between the foot and the brain, or even in the brain itself, the same movement which usually is produced when the foot is detrimentally affected, pain will be experienced as though it were in the foot, and the sense will thus naturally be deceived; for since the same movement in the brain is capable of causing but one sensation in the mind, and this sensation is much more frequently excited by a cause which hurts the foot than by another existing in some other quarter, it is reasonable that it should convey to the mind pain in the foot rather than in any other part of the body. And although the parchedness of the throat does not always proceed, as it usually does, from the fact that drinking is necessary for the health of the body, but sometimes comes from quite a different cause, as is the case with dropsical patients, it is yet much better that it should mislead on this occasion than if, on the other hand, it were always to deceive us when the body is in good health; and so on in similar cases.

And certainly this consideration is of great service to me, not only in enabling me to recognise all the errors to which my nature is subject, but also in enabling me to avoid them or to correct them more easily. For knowing that all my senses more frequently indicate to me truth than falsehood respecting the things which concern that which is beneficial to the body, and being able almost always to avail myself of many of them in order to examine one particular thing, and, besides that, being able to make use of my memory in order to connect the present with the past, and of my understanding which already has discovered all the causes of my errors, I ought no longer to fear that falsity may be found in matters every day presented to me by my senses. And I ought to set aside all the doubts of these past days as hyperbolical and ridiculous, particularly that very common uncertainty respecting sleep, which I could not distinguish from the waking state; for at present I find a very notable difference between the two, inasmuch as our memory can never connect our dreams one with the other, or with the whole course of our lives, as it unites events which happen to us while we are awake. And, as a matter of fact, if someone, while I was awake, quite suddenly appeared to me and disappeared as fast as do the images which I see in sleep, so that I could not know from whence the form came nor whither it went, it would not be without reason that I should deem it a spectre or a phantom formed by my brain [and similar to those which I form in sleep], rather than a real man. But when I perceive things as to which I know distinctly both the place from which they proceed, and that in which they are, and the time at which they appeared to me; and when, without any interruption, I can connect the perceptions which I have of them with the whole course of my life, I am perfectly assured that these perceptions occur while I am waking and not during sleep. And I ought in no wise to doubt the truth of such matters, if, after having called up all my senses, my memory, and my understanding, to examine them, nothing is brought to evidence by any one of them which is repugnant to what is set forth by the others. For because God is in no wise a deceiver, it follows that I am not deceived in this. But because the exigencies of action often oblige us to make up our minds before having leisure to examine matters carefully, we must confess that the life of man is very frequently subject to error in respect to individual objects, and we must in the end acknowledge the infirmity of our nature.

## DAVID HUME

# Induction Cannot Be Rationally Justified

In this excerpt from his ***An Enquiry Concerning Human Understanding,*** Hume (1711–1776) argues that there can be no rational justification of the inductions that people perform. The reason is that all such inductions depend on the Principle of the Uniformity of Nature, and this principle cannot be given a rational justification.

## SKEPTICAL DOUBTS CONCERNING THE OPERATIONS OF THE UNDERSTANDING

### Part I

All the objects of human reason or inquiry may naturally be divided into two kinds, to wit, "Relations of Ideas," and "Matters of Fact." Of the first kind are the sciences of Geometry, Algebra, and Arithmetic, and, in short, every affirmation which is either intuitively or demonstratively certain. *That the square of the hypotenuse is equal to the square of the two sides* is a proposition which expresses a relation between these figures. *That three times five is equal to the half of thirty* expresses a relation between these numbers. Propositions of this kind are discoverable by the mere operation of thought, without dependence on what is anywhere existent in the universe. Though there never were a circle or triangle in nature, the truths demonstrated by Euclid would forever retain their certainty and evidence.

Matters of fact, which are the second objects of human reason, are not ascertained in the same manner, nor is our evidence of their truth, however great, of a like nature with the foregoing. The contrary of every matter of fact is still possible, because it can never imply a contradiction and is conceived by the mind with the same facility and distinctness as if ever so conformable to reality. *That the sun will not rise tomorrow* is no less intelligible a proposition and implies no more contradiction than the affirmation *that it will rise.* We should in vain, therefore, attempt to demonstrate its falsehood. Were it demonstratively false, it would imply a contradiction and could never be distinctly conceived by the mind.

It may, therefore, be a subject worthy of curiosity to inquire what is the nature of that evidence which assures us of any real existence and matter of fact beyond the present testimony of our senses or the records of our memory. This part of philosophy, it is observable, had been little cultivated either by the ancients or moderns; and, therefore, our doubts and errors in the prosecution of so important an inquiry may be the more excusable while we march through such difficult paths without any guide or direction. They may even prove useful by exciting curiosity and destroying that implicit faith and security which is the bane of all reasoning and free inquiry. The discovery of defects in the common philosophy, if any such there be, will not,

David Hume, "Induction Cannot Be Rationally Justified," from *An Enquiry Concerning Human Understanding,* edited by Charles W. Hendel (New York: Macmillan, 1957), pp. 40–53.

I presume, be a discouragement, but rather an incitement, as is usual, to attempt something more full and satisfactory than has yet been proposed to the public.

All reasoning concerning matters of fact seem to be founded on the relation of *cause* and *effect*. By means of that relation alone we can go beyond the evidence of our memory and senses. If you were to ask a man why he believes any matter of fact which is absent, for instance, that his friend is in the country or in France, he would give you a reason, and this reason would be some other fact: as a letter received from him or the knowledge of his former resolutions and promises. A man finding a watch or any other machine in a desert island would conclude that there had once been men in that island. All our reasonings concerning fact are of the same nature. And here it is constantly supposed that there is a connection between the present fact and that which is inferred from it. Were there nothing to bind them together, the inference would be entirely precarious. The hearing of an articulate voice and rational discourse in the dark assures us of the presence of some person. Why? Because these are the effects of the human make and fabric, and closely connected with it. If we anatomize all the other reasonings of this nature, we shall find that they are founded on the relation of cause and effect, and that this relation is either near or remote, direct or collateral. Heat and light are collateral effects of fire, and the one effect may justly be inferred from the other.

If we would satisfy ourselves, therefore, concerning the nature of that evidence which assures us of matters of fact, we must inquire how we arrive at the knowledge of cause and effect.

I shall venture to affirm, as a general proposition which admits of no exception, that the knowledge of this relation is not, in any instance, attained by reasonings *a priori*, but arises entirely from experience, when we find that any particular objects are constantly conjoined with each other. Let an object be presented to a man of ever so strong natural reason and abilities—if that object be entirely new to him, he will not be able, by the most accurate examination of its sensible qualities, to discover any of its causes or effects. Adam, though his rational faculties may be supposed, at the very first, entirely perfect, could not have inferred from the fluidity and transparency of water that it would suffocate him, or from the light and warmth of fire that it would consume him. No object ever discovers, by the qualities which appear to the senses, either the causes which produced it or the effects which will arise from it; nor can our reason, unassisted by experience, ever draw any inference concerning real existence and matter of fact.

This proposition, *that causes and effects are discoverable, not by reason, but by experience,* will readily be admitted with regard to such objects as we remember to have once been altogether unknown to us, since we must be conscious of the utter inability which we then lay under of foretelling what would arise from them. Present two smooth pieces of marble to a man who has no tincture of natural philosophy; he will never discover that they will adhere together in such a manner as to require great force to separate them in a direct line, while they make so small a resistance to a lateral pressure. Such events as bear little analogy to the common course of nature are also readily confessed to be known only by experience, nor does any man imagine that the explosion of gunpowder or the attraction of a loadstone could ever be discovered by arguments *a priori*. In like manner, when an effect is supposed to depend upon an intricate machinery or secret structure of parts, we make no difficulty in attributing all our knowledge of it to experience. Who will assert that he can give the ultimate reason why milk or bread is proper nourishment for a man, not for a lion or tiger?

But the same truth may not appear at first sight to have the same evidence with regard to events which have become familiar to us from our first appearance in the world, which bear a close analogy to the whole course of nature, and which are supposed to depend on the simple qualities of objects without any secret structure of parts. We are apt to imagine that we could discover these effects by the mere operation of our reason without experience. We fancy that, were we brought on a sudden into this world, we could at first have inferred that one billiard ball would communicate motion to another upon impulse, and that we needed not have waited for the event in order to pronounce with certainty concerning it. Such is the influence of custom that where it is strongest it not only covers our natural ignorance but even conceals itself, and seems not to take place, merely because it is found in the highest degree.

But to convince us that all the laws of nature and all the operations of bodies without exception are known only by experience, the following reflections may perhaps suffice. Were any object presented to us, and were we required to pronounce concerning the effect which will result from it without consulting past observation, after what manner, I beseech you, must the mind proceed in this operation? It must invent or imagine some event which it ascribes to the object as its effect; and it is plain that this invention must be entirely arbitrary. The mind can never possibly find the effect in the supposed cause by the more accurate scrutiny and examination. For the effect is totally different from the cause, and consequently can never be discovered in it. Motion in the second billiard ball is a quite distinct event from motion in the first, nor is there anything in the one to suggest the smallest hint of the other. A stone or piece of metal raised into the air and left without any support immediately falls. But to consider the matter *a priori*, is there anything we discover in this situation which can beget the idea of a downward rather than an upward or any other motion in the stone or metal?

And as the first imagination or invention of a particular effect in all natural operations is arbitrary where we consult not experience, so must we also esteem the supposed tie or connection between the cause and effect which binds them together and renders it impossible that any other effect could result from the operation of that cause. When I see, for instance, a billiard ball moving in a straight line toward another, even suppose motion in the second ball should by accident be suggested to me as the result of their contact or impulse, may I not conceive that a hundred different events might as well follow from that cause? May not both these balls remain at absolute rest? May not the first ball return in a straight line or leap off from the second in any line or direction? All these suppositions are consistent and conceivable. Why, then, should we give the preference to one which is no more consistent or conceivable than the rest? All our reasonings *a priori* will never be able to show us any foundation for this preference.

In a word, then, every effect is a distinct event from its cause. It could not, therefore, be discovered in the cause, and the first invention or conception of it, *a priori*, must be entirely arbitrary. And even after it is suggested, the conjunction of it with the cause must appear equally arbitrary, since there are always many other effects which, to reason, must seem fully as consistent and natural. In vain, therefore, should we pretend to determine any single event or infer any cause or effect without the assistance of observation and experience.

Hence we may discover the reason why no philosopher who is rational and modest has ever pretended to assign the ultimate cause of any natural operation, or to show distinctly the action of that power which produces any single effect in the universe. It is confessed that the utmost effort of human reason is to reduce the principles productive of natural phenomena to a greater simplicity, and to resolve the many particular effects into a few general causes, by means of reasonings from analogy, experience, and observation. But as to the causes of these general causes, we should in vain attempt their discovery, nor shall we ever be able to satisfy ourselves by any particular explication of them. These ultimate springs and principles are totally shut up from human curiosity and inquiry. Elasticity, gravity, cohesion of parts, communication of motion by impulse—these are probably the ultimate causes and principles which we shall ever discover in nature; and we may esteem ourselves sufficiently happy if, by accurate inquiry and reasoning, we can trace up the particular phenomena to, or near to, these general principles. The most perfect philosophy of the natural kind only staves off our ignorance a little longer, as perhaps the most perfect philosophy of the moral or metaphysical kind serves only to discover larger portions of it. Thus the observation of human blindness and weakness is the result of all philosophy, and meets us, at every turn, in spite of our endeavors to elude or avoid it.

Nor is geometry, when taken into the assistance of natural philosophy, ever able to remedy this defect or lead us into the knowledge of ultimate causes by all that accuracy of reasoning for which it is so justly celebrated. Every part of mixed mathematics proceeds upon the supposition that certain laws are established by nature in her operations, and abstract reasonings are employed either to assist experience in the discovery of these laws or to determine their influence in particular instances where it depends upon any precise degree of distance and quantity. Thus it is a law of motion, discovered by experience, that the moment or force of any body in motion is in the compound ratio or proportion of its solid contents and its velocity, and, consequently, that a small force may remove the greatest obstacle or raise the greatest weight if by any contrivance or machinery we can increase the velocity of that force so as to make it an overmatch for its antagonist. Geometry assists us in the application of this law by giving us the just dimensions of all the parts and figures which can enter into any species of machine, but still the discovery of the law itself is owing merely to experience; and all the abstract reasonings in the world could never lead us one step toward the knowledge of it. When we reason *a priori* and consider merely any object or cause as it appears to the mind, independent of all observation, it never could suggest to us the notion of any distinct object, such as its effect, much less show us the inseparable and inviolable connection between them. A man must be very sagacious who could discover by reasoning that crystal is the effect of heat, and ice of cold, without being previously acquainted with the operation of these qualities.

## Part II

But we have not yet attained any tolerable satisfaction with regard to the question first proposed. Each solution still gives rise to a new question as difficult as the foregoing and leads us on to further inquiries. When it is asked, *What is the nature of all our reasonings concerning matter of fact?* the proper answer seems to be, That they are founded on the relation of cause and effect. When again it is asked, *What is the foundation of all our reasonings and conclusions concerning that relation?* it may be replied in one word, *experience.* But if we still carry on our sifting humor and ask, *What is the foundation of all conclusions from experience?* this implies a new question which may be of more difficult solution and explication. Philosophers that give themselves airs of superior wisdom and sufficiency have a hard task when they encounter persons of inquisitive dispositions, who push them from every corner to which they retreat, and who are sure at least to bring them to some dangerous dilemma. The best expedient to prevent this confusion is to be modest in our pretensions and even to discover the difficulty ourselves before it is objected to us. By this means we may make a kind of merit of our very ignorance.

I shall content myself in this section with an easy task and shall pretend only to give a negative answer to the question here proposed. I say, then, that even after we have experience of the operations of cause and effect, our conclusions from that experience are *not* founded on reasoning or any process of the understanding. This answer we must endeavor both to explain and to defend.

It must certainly be allowed that nature has kept us at a great distance from all her secrets and has afforded us only the knowledge of a few superficial qualities of objects, while she conceals from us those powers and principles on which the influence of these objects entirely depends. Our senses inform us of the color, weight, and consistency of bread, but neither sense nor reason can ever inform us of those qualities which fit it for the nourishment and support of the human body. Sight or feeling conveys an idea of the actual motion of bodies, but as to that wonderful force or power which would carry on a moving body forever in a continued change of place, and which bodies never lose but by communicating it to others, of this we cannot form the most distant conception. But notwithstanding this ignorance of natural powers and principles, we always presume when we see like sensible qualities that they have like secret powers, and expect that effects similar to those which we have experienced will follow from them. If a body of like color and consistency with that bread which we have formerly eaten be presented to us, we make no scruple of repeating the experiment and foresee with certainty like nourishment and support. Now this is a process of the mind or thought of which I would willingly know the foundation. It is allowed on all hands that there is no known connection between the sensible qualities and the secret powers, and, consequently, that the mind is not led to form such a conclusion concerning their constant and regular conjunction by anything which it knows of their nature. As to past *experience,* it can be allowed to give *direct* and *certain* information of those precise objects only, and that precise period of time which fell under its cognizance: But why this experience should be extended to future times and to other objects which, for aught we know, may be only in appearance similar, this is the main question on which I would insist. The bread which I formerly ate nourished me; that is, a body of such sensible qualities was, at that time, endued with such secret powers. But does it follow that other bread must also nourish me at another time, and that like sensible qualities must always be attended with like secret powers? The consequence seems nowise necessary. At least, it must be acknowledged that there is here a consequence drawn by the mind that there is a certain step taken, a process of thought, and an inference which wants to be explained. These two propositions are far from being the same: *I have found that such an object has always been attended with such an effect,* and *I foresee that other objects which are in appearance similar will be attended with similar effects.* I shall allow, if you please, that the one proposition may justly be inferred from the other: I know, in fact, that it always is inferred. But if you insist that the inference is made by a chain of reasoning, I desire you to produce that reasoning. The connection between these propositions is not intuitive. There is required a medium which may enable the mind to draw such an inference, if indeed it be drawn by reasoning and argument. What that medium is I must confess passes my comprehension; and it is incumbent on those to produce it who assert that it really exists and is the original of all our conclusions concerning matter of fact.

This negative argument must certainly, in process of time, become altogether convincing if many penetrating and able philosophers shall turn their inquiries this way, and no one be ever able to discover any connecting proposition or intermediate step which supports the understanding in this conclusion. But as the question is yet new, every reader may not trust so far to his own penetration as to conclude, because an argument escapes his inquiry, that therefore it does not really exist. For this reason it may be requisite to venture upon a more difficult task, and, enumerating all the branches of human knowledge, endeavor to show that none of them can afford such an argument.

All reasonings may be divided into two kinds, namely, demonstrative reasoning, or that concerning relations of ideas, and moral reasoning, or that concerning matter of fact and existence. That there are no demonstrative arguments in the case seems evident, since it implies no contradiction that the course of nature may change and that an object, seemingly like those which we have experienced, may be attended with different or contrary effects. May I not clearly and distinctly conceive that a body, falling from the clouds and which in all other respects resembles snow, has yet the taste of salt or feeling of fire? Is there any more intelligible proposition than to affirm that all the trees will flourish in December and January, and will decay in May and June? Now, whatever is intelligible and can be distinctly conceived implies no contradiction and can never be proved false by any demonstrative argument or abstract reasoning *a priori.*

If we be, therefore, engaged by arguments to put trust in past experience and make it the standard of our future judgment, these arguments must be probable only, or such as regard matter of fact and real existence, according to the division above mentioned. But that there is no argument of this kind must appear if our explication of that species of reasoning be admitted as solid and satisfactory. We have said that all arguments concerning existence are founded on the relation of cause and effect, that our knowledge of that relation is derived entirely from experience, and that all our experimental conclusions proceed upon the supposition that the future will be conformable to the past. To endeavor, therefore, the proof of this last supposition by probable arguments, or arguments regarding existence, must be evidently going in a circle and taking that for granted which is the very point in question.

In reality, all arguments from experience are founded on the similarity which we discover among natural objects, and by which we are induced to expect effects similar to those which we have found to follow from such objects. And though none but a fool or madman will ever pretend to dispute the authority of experience or to reject that great guide of human life, it may surely be allowed a philosopher to have so much curiosity at least as to examine the principle of human nature which gives this might authority to experience and makes us draw advantage from that similarity which nature has placed among different objects. From causes which appear similar, we expect similar effects. This is the sum of all our experimental conclusions. Now it seems evident that, if this conclusion were formed by reason, it would be as perfect at first, and upon one instance, as after ever so long a course of experience; but the case is far otherwise. Nothing is so like as eggs, yet no one, on account of this appearing similarity, expects the same taste and relish in all of them. It is only after a long course of uniform experiments in any kind that we attain a firm reliance and security with regard to a particular event. Now, where is that process of reasoning which, from one instance, draws a conclusion so different from that which it infers from a hundred instances that are nowise different from that single one? This question I propose as much for the sake of information as with an intention of raising difficulties. I cannot find, I cannot imagine any such reasoning. But I keep my mind still open to instruction if anyone will vouchsafe to bestow it on me.

Should it be said that, from a number of uniform experiments, we *infer* a connection between the sensible qualities and the secret powers, this, I must confess, seems the same difficulty, couched in different terms. The question still occurs, On what process of argument is this *inference* founded? Where is the medium, the interposing ideas which join propositions so very wide of each other? It is confessed that the color, consistency, and other sensible qualities of bread appear not of themselves to have any connection with the secret powers of nourishment and support; for otherwise we could infer these secret powers from the first appearance of these sensible qualities without the aid of experience, contrary to the sentiment of all philosophers, and contrary to plain matter of fact. Here, then, is our natural state of ignorance with regard to the powers and influence of all objects. How is this remedied by experience? It only shows us a number of uniform effects resulting from certain objects, and teaches us that those particular objects, at that particular time, were endowed with such powers and forces. When a new object endowed with similar sensible qualities is produced, we expect similar powers and forces, and look for a like effect. From a body of like color and consistency with bread, we expect like nourishment and support. But this surely is a step or progress of the mind which wants to be explained. When a man says, *I have found, in all past instances, such sensible qualities, conjoined with such secret powers,* and when he says, *similar sensible qualities will always be conjoined with similar secret powers,* he is not guilty of tautology, nor are these propositions in any respect the same. You say that the one proposition is an inference from the other; but you must confess that the inference is not intuitive, neither is it demonstrative. Of what nature is it then? To say it is experimental is begging the question. For all inferences from experience suppose, as their foundation, that the future will resemble the past and that similar powers will be conjoined with similar sensible qualities. If there be any suspicion that the course of nature may change, and that the past may be no rule for the future, all experience becomes useless and can give rise to no inference or conclusion. It is impossible, therefore, that any arguments from experience can prove this resemblance of the past to the future, since all these arguments are founded on the supposition of that resemblance. Let the course of things be allowed hitherto ever so regular, that alone, without some new argument or inference, proves not that for the future it will continue so. In vain do you pretend to have learned the nature of bodies from your past experience. Their secret nature, and consequently all their effects and influence, may change without any change in their sensible qualities. This happens sometimes, and with regard to some objects. Why may it not happen always, and with regard to all objects? What logic, what process of argument secures you against this supposition? My practice, you say, refutes my doubts. But you mistake the purport of my question. As an agent, I am quite satisfied in the point; but as a philosopher who has some share of curiosity, I will not say skepticism, I want to learn the foundation of this inference. No reading, no inquiry has yet been able to remove my difficulty or give me satisfaction in a matter of such importance. Can I do better than propose the difficulty to the public, even though, perhaps, I have small hopes of obtaining a solution? We shall at least, by this means, be sensible of our ignorance, if we do not augment our knowledge.

I must confess that a man is guilty of unpardonable arrogance who concludes, because an argument has escaped his own investigation, that therefore it does not really exist. I must also confess that, though all the learned, for several ages, should have employed themselves in fruitless search upon any subject, it may still, perhaps, be rash to conclude positively that the subject must therefore pass all human comprehension. Even though we examine all the sources of our knowledge and conclude them unfit for such a subject, there may still remain a suspicion that the enumeration is not complete or the examination not accurate. But with regard to the present subject, there are some considerations which seem to remove all this accusation of arrogance or suspicion of mistake.

It is certain that the most ignorant and stupid peasants, nay infants, nay even brute beasts, improve by experience and learn the qualities of natural objects by observing the effects which result from them. When a child has felt the sensation of pain from touching the flame of a candle, he will be careful not to put his hand near any candle, but will expect a similar effect from a cause which is similar in its sensible qualities and appearance. If you assert, therefore, that the understanding of the child is led into this conclusion by any process of argument or ratiocination, I may justly require you to produce that argument, nor have you any pretense to refuse so equitable a demand. You cannot say that the argument is abstruse and may possibly escape your inquiry, since you confess that it is obvious to the capacity of a mere infant. If you hesitate, therefore, a moment or if, after reflection, you produce an intricate or profound argument, you, in a manner, give up the question and confess that it is not reasoning which engages us to suppose the past resembling the future, and to expect similar effects from causes which are to appearance similar. This is the proposition which I intended to enforce in the present section. If I be right, I pretend not to have made any mighty discovery. And if I be wrong, I must acknowledge myself to be indeed a very backward scholar, since I cannot now discover an argument which, it seems, was perfectly familiar to me long before I was out of my cradle.

## Suggestions for Further Reading

### ON DESCARTES
Bernard Williams, *Descartes: The Project of Pure Inquiry*, London, Harvester Press, 1978.
Margaret Wilson, *Descartes*, London, Routledge and Kegan Paul, 1978.

### ON THE RELIABILITY THEORY OF KNOWLEDGE
David Armstrong, *Belief, Knowledge, and Truth*, London, Cambridge University Press, 1973.
Fred Dretske, *Knowledge and the Flow of Information*, Cambridge, Massachusetts, MIT Press, 1981.
Alvin Goldman, "A Causal Theory of Knowing," *Journal of Philosophy,* vol. 64, pp. 357–372, 1967.
Robert Nozick, *Philosophical Explanations*, Cambridge, Massachusetts, Harvard University Press, 1981.

### ON HUME
Barry Stroud, *Hume*, London, Routledge and Kegan Paul, 1977.

### ON INDUCTION
Nelson Goodman, *Fact, Fiction, and Forecast*, Indianapolis, Bobbs Merrill, 1965.
Ian Hacking, *An Introduction to Probability and Inductive Logic*, London, Cambridge University Press, 2001.
Wesley Salmon, *Foundations of Scientific Inference*, Pittsburgh, Pennsylvania, University of Pittsburgh Press, 1968.
Brian Skyrms, *Choice and Chance*, Belmont, California, Wadsworth, 1986.
Elliott Sober, *Reconstructing the Past—Parsimony, Evolution, and Inference*, Cambridge, Massachusetts, MIT Press, chapter 2.

# PART IV
# PHILOSOPHY OF MIND

## CHAPTER 19

### *Dualism and the Mind/Body Problem*

This section of the book is on philosophy of mind. I discuss three problems. The first is the mind/body problem (Chapters 19–23), the second is the problem of free will (Chapters 24–26), and the last is the problem of psychological egoism (Chapter 27). The mind/body problem and the problem of free will both address the broad issue of how the mind is related to the physical world of cause and effect. Is the mind a different thing from the body, or is the mind part of the physical world? If your beliefs and desires are caused by physical events outside of yourself, how can it be true that you act the way you do of your own free will? The last problem—the problem of psychological egoism—concerns the motives that drive us to act. Are people genuinely moved by the welfare of others, or is all behavior, in reality, selfish?

These three problems concern different stages in the causal chain that leads from genes and environment, to the mind, to action:

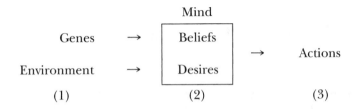

The mind/body problem concerns the nature of the objects and events that exist at stage 2 in this diagram. What is a mind? What are beliefs and desires? The problem of free will concerns the relation of stage 1 to stage 2. If our beliefs and desires are caused by the genes we possess and the environments we have inhabited, how can we possess free will? The problem of psychological egoism concerns the relationship of stages 2 and 3. If the actions we perform are caused by the desires we have, won't it be true that all action is fundamentally selfish—aimed at satisfying the actor's own desires, not at satisfying the needs of others? These are only preliminary statements of the philosophical problems. Each needs to be refined.

## WHAT IS THE MIND/BODY PROBLEM?

The question posed by the mind/body problem is simple: What is the relationship between the mental and the physical? I have a mind, which contains various beliefs, desires, sensations, and emotions. I also have a brain; this physical thing is a structured piece of tissue containing an intricate web of neurons. Are the mind and the brain one and the same thing? Are my beliefs, desires, emotions, and sensations identical with physical things found in my brain? Or are the mind and the brain different objects? Perhaps the mind isn't a physical thing at all.

## DESCARTES' DUALISM

In the previous section, the discussion of Descartes focused on his epistemology. Descartes also advanced a solution to the mind/body problem. It is this view, now called Cartesian Dualism, that I'll discuss in this chapter. Dualism is the idea that there are two kinds of things in the world. There are physical objects on the one hand, and, on the other, there are mental objects (like minds, pains, beliefs, etc.). According to dualism, brains and the bodies in which they are found are physical things; the mind, which is a nonphysical object, is distinct from both the whole body and is also distinct from all of the body's physical parts. Descartes didn't deny that there is a causal interaction between the mental and the physical: taking aspirin can cure headaches, and the sound of trumpets can lift your spirits. In the other direction, it seems undeniable that beliefs and desires can cause the parts of your body to move in various ways (speaking, walking, etc.). But granting this two-way interaction did not lead Descartes to abandon dualism.

## THE MIND/BRAIN IDENTITY THEORY

One alternative to dualism is provided by the Mind/Brain Identity Theory. This theory makes a claim about objects and also about the properties those objects possess. First, it says that your mind and your brain are one and the same object. Second, it claims that the mental properties you have (for example, believing that fire is hot, or wanting some ice cream, or being in pain) are physical properties; to be in pain is to have some physical event occur in your central nervous system.

   The identity theory asserts that mental terminology and physical terminology describe the same items in the world. The following analogy may be instructive. People for a long time used the term "water" to denote various items in the world. This term was used in everyday life. At a certain point in the history of science, it was discovered that water is made of $H_2O$ molecules. The discovery was that water and $H_2O$ are one and the same thing. There certainly is a difference between the two pieces of terminology "water" and "$H_2O$." The first word has been used by ordinary people for a very long time. The second term was introduced much more recently, as part of a scientific theory. Yet it does not follow from this that the terms denote different things. Water is identical with $H_2O$, as chemistry has discovered.

Philosophers who defend the Mind/Brain Identity Theory say that the same point applies to the relationship of mental terms and neurophysiological terms. Common sense has for a very long time deployed such terms as "belief," "desire," "pain," and "mind." The identity theory suggests that what happened to water will happen to the mind. Eventually neurophysiology will discover the nature of the mind, just as chemistry discovered the nature of water. Once various scientific theories have been developed, we will be able to say what it is to believe that snow is white, what it is to want some coffee, what it is to feel pain, what it is to have a mind. In each case, the answer will be given in the vocabulary provided by brain science. We now have only a very partial picture of what these neurophysiological theories will be like. However, the identity theory predicts that science is headed in the direction of a purely materialistic account of the mind. The mind is a physical thing, even though we now have only an incomplete picture of what its physical nature is.

In addition to dualism and the Mind/Brain Identity Theory, there are other solutions to the mind/body problem that I'll discuss. These are logical behaviorism (Chapter 20) and functionalism (Chapter 23). Rather than describing them right now, I'll turn to the task of analyzing Cartesian Dualism.

## IMMORTALITY OF THE SOUL

Before I present Descartes' arguments for dualism, I should note a connection between the mind/body problem and an issue in the philosophy of religion. If you believe the doctrine of the immortality of the soul but also hold that the body disintegrates at death, you may be attracted by dualism. The issue of whether the soul is immortal, of course, isn't the same as the question of whether there is a God. After all, there are many religions that deny the immortality of the soul. Conceivably someone might hold that the soul survives the death of the body and yet deny that there is a God. But historically it is worth remembering that what we might call "traditional" Christianity (this includes the Christianity of Descartes' time) espouses the doctrine of immortality. Dualism makes room for this possibility.

If the soul is part of the mind (even if it isn't the entirety of the mind) and if the soul lives forever and the body does not, we have an argument for dualism. However, this isn't Descartes' argument for dualism. Why not? Perhaps the reason is that anyone who doubts dualism will also probably doubt that any part of the mind survives the death of the body. So you aren't going to convince anyone that dualism is true by beginning with the premise that the soul is immortal.

## LEIBNIZ'S LAW

Note a structural feature of the argument for dualism that I just described. The argument defends dualism by trying to find a property that the mind has but the brain lacks; the property in question is immortality. Quite apart from whether this argument works, we should note a perfectly sensible principle that it uses. The idea is that if *m* and *b* are identical, then they must have all the same properties. This principle is called Leibniz's Law, after the seventeenth-century philosopher/mathematician (who, incidentally, co-invented the calculus with Newton. In Chapter 7, I briefly discussed Leibniz's belief that we live in the best of all possible worlds). Leibniz's Law is sometimes called the principle of the *indiscernibility of identicals*. It states that if you can find even one property that *m* has and *b* lacks, then you will have shown that *m* and *b* are distinct entities. You'll see this principle at work in both of the arguments that Descartes presents for dualism. The following form of argument is deductively valid:

> *m* has property *P*.
>
> *b* does not have property *P*.
>
> If *m* has a property that *b* lacks, then $m \neq b$.
> _____
>
> $m \neq b$.

Be sure you see how the argument concerning immortality has this logical form. The argument is valid. This means that if you reject the conclusion, you must reject at least one of the premises. I suggest that the third premise (Leibniz's Law) is true. Therefore, if you reject the conclusion, you must reject one of the first two premises.

## DESCARTES' FIRST ARGUMENT FOR DUALISM—THE INDUBITABLE EXISTENCE ARGUMENT

Now let's look at Descartes' first argument for dualism. In Chapter 13, I discussed how Descartes uses the method of doubt in his epistemology. He also uses the idea of doubt in his discussion of the mind/body problem.

In the *Second Meditation,* Descartes claims you can't doubt that you have a mind. If you try to doubt that you have a mind, you will find yourself entertaining a thought, and so you must grant that you have a mind after all. Descartes thought that the existence of the body has a quite different status. He thought that it *is* possible for you to doubt that you have a body. After all, you *can* entertain the thought that you are a disembodied spirit. Descartes concludes that your mind has a property that your body lacks. You can doubt the existence of the one, but not the existence of the other. Dualism follows, by Leibniz's Law.

Perhaps you are suspicious of what Descartes says about your body. Is it really possible for you to doubt that you have a body? Can you conceive of yourself being a disembodied spirit? You also should consider Descartes' other premise. Is Descartes right that you can't doubt that you have a mind?

I'm not going to pursue these questions here. I'll grant Descartes that he *can't* doubt that he has a mind and that he *can* doubt that he has a body. I want to consider whether dualism validly follows from these premises. To see whether this follows, we must be very explicit about what the property is that the mind is said to have and the body is said to lack. Descartes claims that his mind has the property of *indubitable existence,* and that his body lacks that property. Let's look more closely at this property. For an object $X$ to have this property means that the "owner" of $X$ can't doubt that $X$ exists. I say "owner" since *my* mind does not have indubitable existence *for you.* I take it that *you* have no trouble entertaining the thought that *I* don't have a mind. It is the first-person case that matters here—a person can't doubt the existence of his or her own mind.

## AN ANALOGY

There is a subtle mistake in Descartes' argument. I'm going to argue that psychological concepts such as "doubts," "wants," and so on, can be deceptive. They appear to be genuine properties, and so Leibniz's Law seems to apply to them. But this appearance is deceptive. Indubitable existence is not a genuine property at all.

I'll illustrate this idea by an example. Lois Lane wants to marry Superman. She doesn't realize that Superman and Clark Kent are one and the same person. Clark Kent, you'll recall, is the most incompetent reporter at the *Daily Planet.* If you ask Lois whether she wants to marry Clark Kent, she will say "No!" Does it follow from this (via Leibniz's Law) that Superman and Clark Kent are two different people? Of course not. The following argument is not valid:

> Lois Lane wants to marry Superman.
> Lois Lane does not want to marry Clark Kent.
> _____
> Superman is not identical with Clark Kent.

On the surface, it looks as if this argument is valid, given Leibniz's Law. It describes a property that Superman has and Clark Kent lacks, and concludes that they are non-identical. What you must see is that the argument does not describe any such property. Leibniz's Law, properly understood, does not license the conclusion of nonidentity. The two premises are true, but the conclusion does not follow from them; it is false.

Superman and Clark Kent have exactly the same properties. This isn't contradicted by the fact that Lois Lane wants one of the following *propositions* to be true and the other to be false:

> Lois Lane marries Superman.
> Lois Lane marries Clark Kent.

The fact that Lois desires one of these propositions to be true and the other to be false does not show that Superman and Clark Kent have different properties. The propositions are different; the people are identical.

Likewise, Descartes says that I am able to doubt one, but not the other, of the following two *propositions:*

I have a brain.
I have a mind.

But from this it does not follow that my brain has a different property from my mind. The propositions are different; the objects may, for all that, be identical.

## PROPOSITIONAL ATTITUDES AND ABOUTNESS

The crucial distinction we have to note here is this: Doubting and desiring are attitudes we have to *propositions;* doubting, desiring, and believing are examples of *propositional attitudes.* Perhaps there are some propositions whose truth cannot be doubted, whereas there are other propositions that we are able to doubt. Surely we desire that some propositions, but not others, should be true. But separate from this issue concerning propositions there is the issue of what *objects* those propositions are about. Here is the lesson I draw from the example about Lois Lane: *Even if one proposition is desired whereas another is not, it does not follow that what the first proposition is about differs from what the second proposition is about.* The same point holds when we consider other propositional attitudes, like doubting. What follows from these two statements?

Lois Lane wants it to be true that Lois Lane marries Superman.
Lois Lane does not want it to be true that Lois Lane marries Clark Kent.

What follows is that the proposition *Lois Lane marries Superman* is a different proposition from the proposition *Lois Lane marries Clark Kent.* What does *not* follow is that the person the first proposition is about (Superman) differs from the person the second proposition is about (Clark Kent). (Note to the reader: if you think that Superman and Clark Kent are different individuals, please invent an example in which a single person has two names and show how this example illustrates the relevant point about propositional attitudes and aboutness.)

What follows from these two statements?

I can't doubt that I have a mind.
I can doubt that I have a body.

What follows is that the proposition *I have a mind* is a different proposition from the proposition *I have a body.* What does *not* follow is that the object the first proposition is about (my mind) differs from the object the second proposition is about (my body).

With this diagnosis in hand, let's go back to Descartes' argument for dualism. He says that his mind has the property of indubitable existence, whereas his body does not have that property. It *sounds* as if Descartes is describing a property that the one thing has but the other thing lacks. But this, I claim, is deceptive. Indubitable existence is not a property of an object; rather, doubting is something we do or fail to do to propositions. To say that my mind indubitably exists is just to say that I cannot doubt a particular proposition. To say that my body does not indubitably exist is just to say that I can doubt a particular proposition. From this difference between propositions, however, nothing follows concerning whether those propositions are about the same or different things. This argument for dualism is invalid.

## Sense and Reference

The philosopher/logician Gottlob Frege (1848–1925) wanted to explain a difference that separates the following two statements:

> The Evening Star is the Evening Star.
> The Evening Star is the Morning Star.

The first of these is obviously true; it is a logical truth of the form "$a = a$." It is *a priori*; anyone who understands the meanings of the terms will be able to see that it is true, there being no need for astronomical observation. The second statement is different. It describes a discovery that astronomers made; it is *a posteriori*. The phrase "*the Evening Star*" is used to refer to the first star to appear in the evening. "*The Morning Star*" is an expression that is used to refer to the last star to disappear in the morning. It was discovered that these are one and the same object—namely, the planet Venus.

Notice that the terms occurring in the two statements refer to exactly the same thing. How, then, can the statements express different thoughts? Frege said that the explanation of this fact is that terms have sense (meaning) as well as reference. Although "*the Morning Star*" and "*the Evening Star*" are terms that refer to the same thing (the planet Venus), the two expressions aren't synonymous; they have different meanings. Frege thought that synonymous terms must refer to the same thing, but that terms that refer to the same thing need not be synonymous. The meaning of a term determines its reference, but not conversely. He also believed that the "truth value" of a statement (that is, whether the statement is true or false) is settled just by the reference of the terms it contains.

Consider the statement "The inventor of bifocals is dead." This statement is true. If Frege were right to say that the truth value of a statement is determined by the reference of the terms it contains, then we should be able to remove any term we choose, replace it with a coreferring term, and have the resulting statement still be true. We can do this; "the inventor of bifocals" and "the first U.S. ambassador to France" are coreferential. Substituting one for the other, we obtain the following sentence: "The first U.S. ambassador to France is dead." This statement is true. In this case, a true statement remains true if one of its terms is replaced by another that is coreferring.

Statements describing propositional attitudes posed a problem for Frege. Even though "*Superman*" and "*Clark Kent*" refer to the same person, the first, but not the second, of the following statements is true:

> Lois Lane wanted to marry Superman.
> Lois Lane wanted to marry Clark Kent.

To account for this fact, Frege suggested that terms in such sentences don't refer to the objects that they normally refer to. Normally, "Superman" and "Clark Kent" refer to a person. But in the above pair of sentences, Frege claimed that a shift occurs; the first refers to the meaning of the term "Superman," while the second refers to the meaning of the term "Clark Kent."

*Continued*

Since these terms have different meanings, it won't be true that the terms in the first sentence refer to precisely the same things that the terms in the second sentence refer to. This makes it possible for the first sentence to be true and the second false. In this way, Frege was able to retain his principle that the truth value of a sentence is determined by the reference of its constituent terms.

When you say, "Lois Lane shook hands with Superman," you are referring to Superman. When you say "Lois Lane wanted to marry Superman," you aren't referring to Superman, according to this proposal of Frege's. If you believe that you are referring to Superman in both statements, then you will reject Frege's account of how statements about propositional attitudes should be understood.

## DESCARTES' SECOND ARGUMENT FOR DUALISM—THE DIVISIBILITY ARGUMENT

I turn now to Descartes' second argument for dualism. It is far simpler than the one just analyzed. In the *Sixth Meditation*, Descartes claims that physical things have spatial parts. For example, a surgeon could divide my brain into pieces. My mind, however, does not have spatial parts. If so, dualism follows, by Leibniz's Law. Descartes also says that the body, but not the mind, has *extension*. By this he means that the body, but not the mind, takes up physical space; it has spatial location. This also leads to dualism by Leibniz's Law.

I'll treat these two arguments together: If the body has the properties of divisibility and extension, but the mind does not, dualism follows. I think that Descartes' argument here is valid. The question is whether his premises are true. I'll grant Descartes that it sounds odd to say that my mind has spatial parts and that it is located between my ears. It also sounds strange to say that my mind weighs about five pounds and has blood vessels running through it. How are we to explain the fact that such claims sound funny to us? One explanation is that they can't be true. If this were right, dualism would follow, since we then would have cited properties that my brain has but my mind does not. However, there is another possible explanation for why it sounds odd to say that my mind has spatial parts, or weighs five pounds, or has blood vessels running through it. The explanation is that these ideas are unfamiliar. The assertions sound jarring because they radically depart from what we happen to believe.

Consider the claim that water is $H_2O$. Before the advent of the atomic theory, the claim that a liquid is made of numerous tiny particles may have sounded pretty strange to people. But this, of course, does not mean that water could not be made of molecules of $H_2O$. For this reason, I claim that Descartes' second argument for dualism is inconclusive. If the mind and the brain really are identical, then many surprising facts may follow.

I conclude that Descartes' arguments for dualism do not work. The first argument (involving the idea of indubitable existence) is invalid. The second argument (involving the ideas of divisibility and extension) is valid, but it begs the question. There seems to be no reason to accept the premises (that the mind is indivisible and lacks extension) unless you already believe that the conclusion (dualism) is true. These negative verdicts don't show that dualism is false. All I've claimed so far is that these two arguments don't work. I now turn to a criticism that has been made of dualism.

## CAUSALITY BETWEEN THE PHYSICAL AND THE NONPHYSICAL

One of the main stumbling blocks for dualism has been the idea, endorsed by Cartesian Dualism, that there can be causal interactions between physical and nonphysical things. Descartes thought that physical events in your body can cause sensations in your mind. These sensations, like all mental events, allegedly lack spatial location. But how can events that are located in space bring about events that lack spatial location? And how are causal relations in the opposite direction possible? In *The Passions of the Soul*, Descartes claimed that the pineal gland in the brain is the jumping off point for this interaction. Nerve impulses reach the pineal gland and then manage to affect the mind, even though the mind is not located anywhere at all. Conversely, your mind (which is no place at all) influences your body by making an impact on the pineal gland. This is pretty mysterious, and dualists since Descartes have not managed to make this process any more comprehensible.

Causality is something we understand best when we consider two physical events that are linked by a physical signal. When we say that throwing the switch on the wall caused the ceiling light to go on, we are talking about two physical events that occur at different times and at different places. These two events are connected by the flow of electricity. We not only know *that* throwing the switch caused the light to go on; we also know *how* throwing the switch managed to bring this about. If we were unable to detect a physical signal passing from the switch to the light, we would be puzzled about how the first event was able to cause the second. Similarly, if I said that throwing the switch caused an event that isn't located anywhere at all, you would be puzzled how electricity or any other physical signal could reach an event that has no spatial location.

In light of the difficulty of understanding how causality can "cross over" from the mental to the physical and back again, wouldn't it be simpler to account for the causal interaction of the mind and the body by adopting the identity theory? If the mind and the brain are identical, it isn't terribly puzzling how your beliefs and desires can cause you to behave in various ways. This doesn't prove that the Mind/Brain Identity Theory is correct; the point is just that what is a hard question for dualism to answer isn't especially hard for the identity theory.

---

## Review Questions

1. What does dualism assert? What is the Mind/Brain Identity Theory?
2. What is Leibniz's Law? How is it used in arguments supporting dualism?
3. "I can't doubt that I have a mind, but I can doubt that I have a body. Hence, my mind isn't identical with my body." Is this argument valid?
4. "My brain is divisible into spatial parts, is located between my ears, weighs about five pounds, and has blood vessels running through it. My mind has none of these properties. Hence, my brain and my mind are nonidentical." Is this argument valid? If it is valid, must dualism be true?
5. Dualism has been thought to make mysterious how the mind and the body can causally interact. What problem is involved here?

## Problems for Further Thought

1. Descartes says that he can conceive of himself being a disembodied spirit (that is, having a mind but no body). What does conceiving of something mean? Does Descartes' claim entail that it is possible for him to be a disembodied spirit? (See discussion of conceivability and possibility in Chapter 8.)

2. Is a statue identical with the stone it is made of? Is an organism identical with the collection of cells in its body? Can Leibniz's Law be used to show that either of these claims of identity is false?

3. In the *Sixth Meditation*, Descartes argues that he is *essentially* a thinking thing. An essential property of a thing is a property that the thing must have if it is to exist. Could Descartes be deprived of thought and still be Descartes? Could Descartes have been born without the capacity of thought and still be Descartes? If Descartes can't doubt that he thinks, is that enough to show that Descartes is essentially a thinking thing?

4. It was suggested in this chapter that we understand causality best when there is a physical signal that passes from cause to effect (the electricity example). However, the fact that "absences" are sometimes causes suggests that causality need *not* involve a physical signal. For example, suppose a patient dies because his doctor fails to give him medicine. There is no "physical signal" between doctor and patient in this case, but there is causation. Does this point solve the objection to dualism that concerns the nature of causality?

5. Frank Jackson (in "What Mary Didn't Know," *Journal of Philosophy*, 1986: 83: 291–295) gives the following argument against physicalism (which he describes as the claim that all facts are physical facts):

> Mary is confined to a black-and-white room, is educated through black-and-white books and through lectures relayed on black-and-white television. In this way she learns everything there is to know about the physical nature of the world. She knows all the physical facts about us and our enviroment, in a wide sense of "physical" which includes everything in *completed* physics, chemistry, and neurophysiology, and all there is to know about the causal and relational facts consequent upon all this, including of course functional roles. If physicalism is true, she knows all there is to know. For to suppose otherwise is to suppose that there is more to know than every physical fact, and that is what physicalism denies.

> Physicalism is not the noncontroversial thesis that the actual world is largely physical, but the challenging thesis that it is entirely physical. This is why physicalists must hold that complete physical knowledge is complete knowledge simpliciter.... The claim here is not that, if physicalism is true, only what is expressed in explicitly physical language is an item of knowledge. It is that, if physicalism is true, then if you know everything expressed or expressible in explicitly physical language, you know everything.

It seems, however, that Mary does not know all there is to know. For when she is let out of the black-and-white room or given a color television, she will learn what it is like to see something red, say. This is rightly described as *learning*—she will not say "ho, hum." Hence, physicalism is false.

Assess Jackson's argument using the ideas concerning aboutness and propositional attitudes presented in this chapter.

# CHAPTER 20

## *Logical Behaviorism*

In 1949 Gilbert Ryle, a philosopher at Oxford University, published an influential book called *The Concept of Mind.* In it he presented a solution to the mind/body problem that has come to be called logical behaviorism. His views have something in common with those expressed by Ludwig Wittgenstein in his posthumously published *Philosophical Investigations* (1953). Later, an American philosopher deeply influenced by Wittgenstein, Norman Malcolm, elaborated this philosophical position in his book *Dreaming* (1959).

Logical behaviorism is a thesis about the meaning of the mentalistic terms we use in ordinary speech. Logical behaviorism tries to describe what we mean when we talk of an individual's thoughts, beliefs, intentions, dreams, and sensations. This thesis about meaning is quite different from a doctrine called methodological behaviorism, which I'll discuss in the next chapter. Methodological behaviorism is a thesis about science. It doesn't offer a linguistic analysis of ordinary speech; rather, it gives advice about how a productive science of psychology should be developed. Logical behaviorism advances both negative and positive claims. The negative part presents criticisms of other views of the mind. The positive part is an account of what mentalistic terminology means.

### THE ATTACK ON "THE GHOST IN THE MACHINE"

Ryle thought that the commonsense view of the mind is deeply confused. According to Ryle, common sense is committed to the idea that mental states are inner causes of behavior. To see what he means, suppose we ask why Joe lifted the cup to his lips. A commonsense answer might be that he did this because he *wanted* a drink of water and *believed* that there was water in the cup. This commonsense explanation says that mental states are inner states that Joe occupies, ones which cause his outward behavior. According to common sense, we see the behavior (the drinking), but we don't see the beliefs and desires that cause it. The beliefs and desires are "inside"; they can't be directly observed, though their effects—behavior—can be. I'll use the term "mentalism" to name this commonsense idea that mental states are inner causes of behavior. Ryle thought that this natural picture is deeply confused—mentalism is one-half of what he called the myth of "the Ghost in the Machine."

Ryle also held that common sense embraces *dualism*. This is the other half of what Ryle calls the myth of the Ghost in the Machine. Although Ryle lumped mentalism and dualism together, we need to keep them separate. Mentalism and dualism are different. Someone who thinks that the mind and the brain are identical—that mental states are states of the central nervous system—would reject dualism but would agree that mental states are inner causes of behavior. So mentalism does not imply dualism.

Why did Ryle reject mentalism—that minds exist and are quite different from the behaviors they cause? I'll discuss one of his main reasons. Ryle thought that the view of minds as inner causes leads to what I'll call *third-person skepticism*.

## LOGICAL BEHAVIORISM SAYS MENTALISM IS FALSE BECAUSE IT LEADS TO SKEPTICISM

Ryle's argument goes as follows. If mental states were inner, then the mental states of others would be hidden from us. Each of us would be able to observe the behaviors of others, but not the beliefs and desires that others have. Because of this, we wouldn't be able to know what others think or want. At best, the only facts we would know about the mind would come to us via *first-person introspection*. I can tell by examining my own mind what I think, want, and feel. However, if mental states were inner, I would have no way of knowing anything about what mental states you occupy. Ryle thought we clearly do have knowledge of the mental characteristics of others. He concluded that mental states can't be inner causes of behavior.

The deductively valid argument that Ryle advances goes like this:

(1) If mental states were inner causes of behavior, we would not have knowledge of the mental states of others.

(2) We do have knowledge of the mental states of others.

———————————

Hence, mental states are not inner causes of behavior.

Since the argument is valid, if you want to reject the conclusion, you must reject one or both of the premises. My view is that premise (2) is true. I also think that the conclusion is false. This means that I must reject premise (1). To do this, I must explain how we can have knowledge of the inner mental states of others.

## DO WE KNOW ABOUT THE MENTAL STATES OF OTHERS BY ANALOGY WITH OUR OWN CASE?

A traditional argument for how we could have knowledge of the mental states of others is via an *argument by analogy*. In 1948 Bertrand Russell advanced this argument in his book *Human Knowledge: Its Scope and Limits,* but the argument has been put forward by many philosophers. It is offered as a solution to the so-called "problem of other minds." I know by introspection that I have a mind. I also see by observing my own body that I behave in certain ways. I note that some of my behaviors tend to be associated with some of my mental states. For example, when I hurt my finger by stabbing it with a pin, I tend to say "Ouch!" I then look at others and notice that they produce certain behaviors. They say "Ouch!" on some occasions. I reason, by analogy, that others probably have minds and occupy the mental states that I do when I produce the same behaviors.

So the analogy argument goes like this:

> In my own case, I notice that when I produce behavior *B*, I usually am in mental state *M*.
>
> I observe that another individual (*O*) is now producing behavior *B*.
>
> ═══════════════
>
> So, *O* is now in mental state *M*.

The double line indicates that the argument isn't supposed to be deductively valid. Rather, the analogy argument says that the conclusion is probable if the premises are true. This analogy argument aims to show how we can have knowledge of the inner mental states of others. If the argument works, it refutes Ryle's claim that mentalism leads to third-person skepticism. But is the analogy argument persuasive?

The usual criticism of this argument is that it is very weak because the evidence is limited to my own case. It is like arguing that since *I* own a green chair, probably *everyone* has one. I agree with this criticism: An induction from one's own case to a conclusion about *all* human beings bases too ambitious a conclusion on too slender an evidential basis. The sample size is too small. Although the analogy argument does not refute premise (1) in Ryle's argument, I still think this premise is mistaken. We can see why by thinking about abduction, not induction.

## ABDUCTION

Let's view the beliefs and desires we attribute to others as theoretical postulates. We don't directly observe what other individuals think and want; we observe their behavior. We then invent a "theory" whose adequacy is judged by its ability to explain and predict behavior. My suggestion is that there are many cases in which the ascription of mental states to others is well confirmed by the behaviors we observe. (Of course, there also are cases in which our claims about what people think and want are undermined by what we subsequently observe them do, but that isn't in dispute.)

What's the difference between this solution to the problem of other minds and the analogy argument? In the analogy argument, I begin with an observation of myself and then seek to extend that description to other individuals. In the abductive argument, I make no mention of introspection. Mendel never observed a gene, but that is no objection to his theory. The fact that genes are inner causes of how tall a pea plant grows, or of whether its peas will be wrinkled or smooth, does not mean that we can't know about genes (see Chapter 3). Likewise, the view that mental states are inner causes of behavior does not lead to third-person skepticism. Ryle's criticism of mentalism is mistaken.

There is a simple but important distinction that needs to be drawn here. The following two questions are different; they need not have the same answers:

(1)  Is proposition *P* about observable things and only observable things?

(2)  Is proposition *P* testable by observation?

The Mendelian case and the case of claims about the mental states of others provide examples in which the answers are (1) *no* and (2) *yes*.

This discussion of the problem of other minds should remind you of material covered in Chapter 5 concerning the role of analogy and induction in the Argument from Design for the existence of God. Hume criticized the Argument from Design for being a weak analogy argument and for being a weak induction. How is my reply to Hume similar to the reply I've just made to Ryle?

## LOGICAL BEHAVIORISM'S POSITIVE THESIS—ITS ANALYSIS OF MENTALISTIC VOCABULARY

In addition to criticizing mentalism, Ryle also advances a positive thesis about how talk of beliefs and desires should be understood. Logical behaviorists maintain not just that belief is *not* an inner state; they also make a positive claim about what it *is* for an agent to believe something.

Logical behaviorism says that the meanings of mentalistic terms can be specified purely in terms of behavior. For example, what does it mean to say that someone wants a drink of water? The following proposal, though false, at least is consistent with the requirements that logical behaviorism imposes on the problem:

$$S \text{ wants to drink water} =_{df} S \text{ drinks.}$$

The subscript "df" means that the two statements are said to be equivalent by definition. This proposal is false; people who want a drink of water don't always get to drink. Notice, however, that the proposal obeys the rules that logical behaviorism lays down. The proposal analyzes the meaning of a mentalistic term ("wants to drink water") in purely behavioral language ("drinks"). Behaviorists usually admit that proposals like this one are too crude. They suggest, instead, that the meaning of mentalistic terminology cannot be given in terms of *actual* behavior, but can be given in terms of *dispositions* to behave. A more satisfactory suggestion, logical behaviorists maintain, is the following:

$$S \text{ wants to drink some water} =_{df} S \text{ is disposed to drink water.}$$

I have two criticisms of this proposal. First, it is incomplete. When the proposal is fleshed out, it turns out not to be consistent with the requirements of logical behaviorism. Second, I'll claim that even if the proposal were true, it would not establish what logical behaviorists hold—namely, that mentalistic terminology does not describe inner causes of outward behavior.

## THE DISPOSITIONAL ANALYSIS OF DESIRE IS INCOMPLETE

I begin with the charge of incompleteness. Wanting to drink water is supposed to be a disposition to drink water. Suppose Joe wants to drink some water and we place a cup of water before him, but he does not drink. Why not? The answer might be that he does not *believe* the cup contains water. However, this means that the behaviorist's proposed definition must be corrected as follows:

> *S* wants to drink water =$_{df}$ *S* is disposed to drink those things that *S* believes are water.

Notice that the proposal now is not consistent with behaviorist requirements. The present proposal analyzes a desire in terms of a disposition to behave *and* a belief. So we have not analyzed the mentalistic concept in *purely* behavioral terms.

I doubt that behaviorists can overcome this problem. Our commonsense mentalistic concepts seem to have the following property: Attributing a *single* mentalistic property to an agent does not, by itself, have implications concerning how the agent will behave. What has such implications are *batches* of mentalistic properties. If an agent wants, above all else, to drink water *and* believes that the cup before him contains water, perhaps this implies that he will reach for the cup and drink its contents (but what if he is paralyzed?). However, the desire *by itself* has no such implication and neither does the belief.

## A DISPOSITIONAL ANALYSIS DOES NOT REFUTE MENTALISM

My second objection to logical behaviorism's proposal for how mentalistic terms are to be analyzed is this: Even if mentalistic concepts could be analyzed purely in terms of behavioral dispositions, that would not disprove the idea that mental states are inner causes of outward behavior. To see why, I want to describe an analogy that David Armstrong (whose views on the Reliability Theory of Knowledge were discussed in Chapter 14) noticed between the supposed dispositional property of wanting a drink and other nonmental properties that clearly are dispositional in character. Dispositional properties are often named in English with "ible" or "able" suffixes. For example, to say that a lump of sugar is *soluble* is to say that it is disposed to dissolve. Solubility is a dispositional property. It is not hard to give a "behavioral analysis" of solubility. To say that something is soluble is to say that it is disposed to behave in a certain way when placed in a certain situation:

> *X* is soluble (in water) =$_{df}$ If *X* were immersed (in water), then *X* would dissolve.

Dissolving is a behavior; to immerse something is to place it in a particular sort of environment. This definition of solubility conforms to behavioristic requirements, since it makes no mention of the inner state that soluble substances might occupy. I have no objection to this behaviorist definition of solubility. My point is that the adequacy of this definition does not imply that there is no inner state of lumps of sugar that makes them dissolve when immersed. In fact, chemistry provides a scientific description of the inner features of sugar that make sugar dissolve when immersed in water. Solubility is a dispositional property, but this is consistent with the fact that soluble substances have internal, structural properties that make them behave as they do.

How is this relevant to the logical behaviorist's attempt to analyze mental states? Even if wanting to drink water were a behavioral disposition—one that could be described without mentioning any inner state of the organism—this would not show that wants aren't inner states. On the contrary, there is every reason to think that when something has a dispositional property, there is a physical basis of that disposition. When an organism is disposed to drink water, it is entirely appropriate to ask what it is about the organism's internal makeup that disposes it to act in this way. This completes my criticism of logical behaviorism's positive thesis. I claim that the meanings of mentalistic terms (like "wants," "believes") cannot be analyzed in purely behavioral language. In addition, I have argued that even if such an analysis could be provided (by describing mental states as "dispositions to behave"), it would not follow that mental states aren't inner causes of behavior.

---

### Pain without Pain Behavior?

Curare, the poison that some South American Indians have used on their darts, paralyzes its subject. In the 1930s and 1940s, scientists purified curare and studied its effects on the central nervous system. At first, some doctors thought that curare was a painkiller; they noticed that if you give curare to your patient before surgery, the patient will not move under the knife. After surgery, the patients complained that they experienced great pain, but for a time, the physicians didn't believe them (many of the patients were children). Eventually a physician volunteered to undergo surgery with curare; he reported that the pain was vivid and excruciating. After that, doctors realized that curare isn't a painkiller; it simply immobilizes.

Daniel Dennett (in "Why You Can't Make a Computer That Feels Pain," *Brainstorms*, MIT Press, 1978) suggests the following puzzle. An amnesiac is a drug that makes you forget. Suppose that you gave someone curare and an amnesiac before surgery. Would the individual feel pain? The patient would not say "ouch" or writhe during surgery. And after surgery, the patient would not say "that was horribly painful." Let's use the term "pain behavior" to name any behavior that usually accompanies pain. In Dennett's puzzle, there is no pain behavior, either during surgery or after. The question is, can there be pain without pain behavior? Dennett's example suggests that the answer is *yes*. Would you be prepared to undergo surgery with curare and an amnesiac as the only drugs you get? If not, the reason is probably that you think that you would still feel pain.

What does this example show about the claim that mentalistic terms do not describe the inner causes of behavior, but describe only the behavior itself?

## Review Questions

1. What is the "problem of other minds"? Does the analogy argument from one's own case solve this problem? Ryle thought that the mental states of others would be unknowable if mental states were inner causes of behavior. Why did Ryle think this?
2. What is logical behaviorism? Can a logical behaviorist analysis be given of the statement "Jones believes that there is rat poison in the gravy"?
3. Suppose that a mentalistic concept (like wanting to drink water) could be analyzed as a disposition to behave. Would that show that wants aren't inner causes of behavior?

## Problems for Further Thought

1. I've suggested that an abductive argument can solve the problem of other minds. Construct such an argument, making clear how the Surprise Principle (Chapter 3) applies.
2. What does it mean to say that *X* is "nothing but" *Y*? It can't mean just that *X* wouldn't exist if *Y* didn't. We wouldn't exist without oxygen. It doesn't follow that we are "nothing but" oxygen.
3. Russell attempted to solve the problem of other minds by introducing a postulate that he says "is not required in physics." What is this postulate? How does it apply to the problem of other minds? Is the postulate also applicable to examples concerning physical objects that have nothing to do with the mind? Are there exceptions to this principle? Are there many such exceptions?

# CHAPTER 21

## *Methodological Behaviorism*

Logical behaviorism was the subject of the last chapter; methodological behaviorism is the subject of the present one. Although the names sound similar, the doctrines themselves are very different. Logical behaviorism says that the meanings of commonsense mentalistic concepts can be analyzed in purely behavioral terms. Methodological behaviorism is not a thesis about what such commonsense terms mean; rather, it is a recommendation for how the science of psychology ought to be pursued.

In a curious way, methodological and logical behaviorism take opposite views on the nature of commonsense mentalistic language. As noted earlier, logical behaviorism *rejects* the idea that beliefs and desires are inner states that cause behavior.

Methodological behaviorism, by contrast, *accepts* the idea that our commonsense mentalistic vocabulary refers to inner states. Methodological behaviorism then argues that a scientific psychology should avoid talking about beliefs and desires precisely because they are inner states.

In this chapter, I'll divide methodological behaviorism into a negative and a positive thesis. (This is similar to my division of logical behaviorism into a negative and a positive thesis in the previous chapter.) First, I'll analyze the negative thesis; this is the claim that psychology should *not* attempt to explain behavior in terms of people's beliefs and desires. Then, I'll consider methodological behaviorism's positive thesis; this is the idea that people's behavior *can* be explained solely in terms of their history of conditioning.

## THE NEGATIVE THESIS: PSYCHOLOGY SHOULD AVOID BELIEF/DESIRE EXPLANATIONS

Why should psychology avoid explaining the behavior of agents by attributing beliefs and desires to them? B. F. Skinner, who was a leading proponent of behaviorism, provided several answers to this question in his books *Science and Human Behavior* (New York, Free Press, 1953), *Beyond Freedom and Dignity* (New York, Knopf, 1971), and *About Behaviorism* (New York, Random House, 1974). Skinner's first objection to mentalistic explanation is that beliefs and desires aren't observable. They are hidden. All we can directly observe is the behaviors of others, not what goes on in their minds. By now, my view of this kind of argument should be clear. Science legitimately talks about things that aren't or can't be observed. The fact that beliefs and desires can't be observed directly doesn't mean that claims about an individual's beliefs and desires can't be tested by observing behavior. For example, suppose I claim that Jane wants a drink of water and believes that there is water in the cup before her. Suppose I further claim that she has no other desires that would override her desire for the water. These claims about the agent's mind predict that she will reach for the water and drink it. If that prediction fails, I've gained evidence against the description just formulated about Jane's mind. As in the Mendelian case, claims about what is not observed can be tested by examining what they imply about what can be observed.

Another reason that Skinner gives for rejecting mentalistic theories is that they are "too easy." In the example, I attributed to Jane a combination of beliefs and desires that predict something about her behavior. Suppose she doesn't reach for the water. What will I do? I'll modify my claim about what she thinks and wants. I won't abandon my assumption that Jane has beliefs and desires and that these cause her behavior. So, apparently, the assumption of mentalism—that behavior is caused by beliefs and desires of some sort—isn't tested by observing behavior. Indeed, it appears that no matter what Jane does, I can always formulate a belief/desire story that is consistent with what I observe.

I want to clarify this point of Skinner's by distinguishing *specific belief/desire hypotheses* from what I'll call *the mentalistic thesis*, which is the claim that an individual's behaviors are caused by the beliefs and desires he or she possesses. The specific attributions are testable against the data of behavior; however, the mentalistic thesis does not seem to be. Skinner believes that the claims of science must be testable by observation; hence, he concludes, the mentalistic thesis does not deserve to be part of a scientific psychology. Notice that even if the mentalistic thesis is untestable, this would not imply that *specific belief/desire attributions* are untestable. The requirement that scientists should only put forward theories that are testable has the curious consequence that they are allowed to advance specific belief/desire explanations but are not allowed to say that mentalism is true. But mentalism is *logically entailed* by each specific belief/desire explanation. Can't we assert what our confirmed theories entail?

In Chapter 9, I discussed the idea that scientific claims should be testable. I argued that the thesis of strong falsifiability is implausible. I now want to make a related point: *There are many perfectly respectable scientific statements that cannot be refuted by the result of a single experiment.* In the present case, we have an example of this kind of statement. Statements that describe the basic tenets of a *research program* are not strongly falsifiable. Mentalism is such a thesis; it says that theories explaining behavior can be developed by extending and refining the ordinary concepts of belief and desire. Time will tell whether this is a good idea for psychology or a dead end. The fact that a single theory within this framework fails does not show that the whole framework is bankrupt. One rotten apple need not show that the barrel is spoiled.

Curiously enough, precisely the same point applies to Skinner's own research program. Skinner rejects mentalism and espouses behaviorism. This is the thesis that behaviors can be explained by describing the stimuli people have received from their environments. Skinner says we don't need to describe the inner states—mental or physical—of individuals in order to explain their behavior. This behaviorist thesis states the framework of the Skinnerian research program. Suppose I follow its dictates and construct a detailed behaviorist explanation of why you are now reading this page. Suppose further that this explanation turns out to be mistaken. Does that refute behaviorism as a general research program? I would say not (and Skinner would probably agree).

It is appropriate to demand that *specific explanations* be testable against the data of observations. It is not appropriate to demand that *theses about the framework of a research program* should be strongly falsifiable. Mentalism can't be faulted on the ground that it isn't testable. Specific mentalistic hypotheses can be tested. Time will tell whether the general thesis of mentalism will turn out to be correct. In this sense, the framework of mentalism, like the framework of behaviorism, *is* testable—it is testable "in the long run."

## METHODOLOGICAL BEHAVIORISM'S POSITIVE THESIS

I'll now consider methodological behaviorism's positive claim—that behavior can be explained without describing the inner states of the organism. I believe that there is a simple fact about people that shows that behaviorism can't be successful—that the kind of explanations it demands do not exist. Recall that methodological behaviorism does not deny that we have inner mental states. It claims, rather, that psychology does not need to discuss them in its attempt to explain behavior. So behaviorism grants that the causal chain linking environmental stimuli to behavior has the following structure:

$$\text{Environment} \longrightarrow \text{Inner state of organism} \longrightarrow \text{Behavior}$$

Methodological behaviorism maintains that my present behavior can be explained in terms of (1) the past environments I've occupied and the behaviors I produced in them, and (2) my present environment.

Skinner's theory of stimulus conditioning shows how such explanations can be constructed. In his research, Skinner manipulated the behavior of chickens and other organisms by placing them into a totally controlled environment—a *Skinner box*. For example, a chicken can be conditioned to peck at a key in its cage when the light is on. This is how. When the chicken is first placed in the box, it will peck occasionally. The box is so arranged that if the chicken pecks when the light is on, it receives a pellet of food. After some time, the chicken's pecking starts to happen pretty much only when the light goes on. In this stimulus/response experiment, the chicken is conditioned to peck when the light is on. The conditioning works by rewarding the chicken in some circumstances but not in others.

Suppose that this conditioning process has taken place. You then look into the cage and see that the chicken is pecking. How might you explain this behavior? A mentalistic explanation might say that the chicken is now pecking because it wants food and believes, based on its past experience, that pecking produces pellets of food. This is a mentalistic explanation—it is stated in terms of beliefs and desires. Skinner believes that this mentalistic story is entirely unnecessary. You can give a behaviorist explanation of the present behavior as follows: (1) in the past, the chicken was conditioned to peck when the light was on; (2) right now, the light is on. Notice that Skinner's explanation makes no mention of beliefs and desires. We can formulate the behaviorist explanation as a deductive argument:

> If the light is on, then the chicken pecks.
> The light is on now.
> ═══════════════════════
> Hence, the chicken now pecks.

You explain the present behavior by deducing it from the two facts listed as premises.

Skinner thinks that what is true of the chicken's pecking in the experiment is true of all the chicken's behaviors, both those produced in the box and those that occur in less controlled environments (like the barnyard). In addition, Skinner believes that human beings are like the chicken in relevant respects. Each of our behaviors can be explained by describing our history of stimulus conditioning. This is the thesis on which the behaviorist research program rests. We don't need to talk about what human beings think and want if we are to explain what human beings do.

## FIRST OBJECTION TO BEHAVIORISM'S POSITIVE THESIS: NOVEL BEHAVIORS

Are we like the chicken in a Skinner box? Critics of behaviorism, like the linguist Noam Chomsky, have claimed that *novel behaviors* cannot be explained in the way the behaviorist demands. Let's look with some care at an example of Skinner's to see what this criticism means.

Suppose you are walking down the street one day and a robber jumps out of the shadows, sticks a gun in your face, and says "your money or your life." You fumble nervously and then hand over your wallet. How should your behavior be explained? What makes the behavior novel is that you have never been robbed before. The only time anyone ever waved a gun in your face was when you were a child and the gun was a water gun. In that case, you didn't hand over your wallet; rather, you giggled and ran away. So why didn't you do the same thing this time?

The behaviorist needs to show that the present stimulus situation is similar to past ones in which you behaved similarly. Skinner explains the chicken's present pecking by saying that the *present* situation is like *past* situations in which the chicken pecked. The similarity is that the light is on in the Skinner box. The problem is that the present robbery is similar to many past situations you have been in. It is similar to your childhood playing with water guns. It is also similar to the time your mother threatened to spank you if you didn't clean up your room. After all, the robbery involved a gun *and* a threat. Which of these past experiences is the right one to appeal to in explaining your present behavior?

Remember that you have never been robbed before. The only time anyone waved a gun in your face it was a water gun and you giggled and ran away. And when your mom threatened to spank you, you apologized and cleaned up your room; you did not hand her your wallet. What past episodes can a behaviorist say are similar to, and also explain, your current behavior? An obvious answer is that you learned in the past that you should accommodate those who threaten you. Perhaps you were rewarded in the past for doing this and so the behavioral pattern became fixed. Although this sounds like the right sort of explanation to develop, it isn't true to the demands of behaviorism.

In the chicken case, there was a *physical property* of the earlier stimulus situations that recurs in the present. In the past, *the light was on*. In the present case, *the light is on*. It is perfectly permissible for a behaviorist to describe the history of conditioning in terms of such physical properties. What the behaviorist can't say, however, is that you are the sort of individual who behaves in ways you *believe* are accommodating when you *believe* that you are being threatened. This description of your stimulus history refers to inner mental states. These are just the items that the behaviorist says should *not* be included in the explanation.

I doubt that there is a physical similarity between past threats and the present one. In the past, your mom may have said, "If you don't clean up your room, I'll give you a spanking." Your behavioral response was not to hand your wallet over, but to apologize and tidy things up. The only way to describe how this past event is similar to the present robbery is to describe your beliefs and desires.

If our behaviors always obeyed patterns that were describable in terms of *physical similarities* between past and present stimulus conditions, behaviorism might work. But this often seems to be radically untrue. In lots of cases, what makes the past similar to the present is that we conceptualize past and present in similar ways. Take this mentalistic similarity away and behaviorism delivers radically mistaken predictions. In terms of purely physical similarities, I suppose that your participation in a water gun battle may be more similar to the present robbery than your being scolded by your mother. If you were to behave now in ways that are similar to the ways you behaved in previous *physically similar* past events, the prediction would be that you would giggle and run away.

It is an important fact about us that small physical differences in a stimulus often make enormous differences in the response, and huge physical differences in the stimulus often make no difference in the response. If a robber walks into a bank and hands the teller a note that says "You give me the cash," the teller produces one response. If the note had said "Me give you the cash," the response might be very be different. The notes aren't *that* different physically, so why was the response so different? Likewise, receiving a paper with a few marks on it can produce the same result as hearing a verbal command. But the marks on paper ("You give me the cash") and a verbal message ("Empty the cash drawers into this sack") are physically very different.

---

**Minimal Explanation versus Deep Explanation**

The behavior of a conditioned chicken in a Skinner box can be explained without describing the chicken's internal state. Why is the chicken now pecking the key? Skinner's answer is that the chicken pecks whenever the light is on, and the light is now on.

Since we have explained the behavior without mentioning the chicken's internal state, Skinner concludes that describing the internal state would be of no explanatory relevance. You don't need to describe what is going on inside, so why bother?

I grant that the purely behavioral account is an adequate explanation. However, I think that there can be a deeper explanation of the chicken's behavior.

Consider an analogy. Why did this white cube just dissolve? A behaviorist might answer by noting that (1) the cube was made of sugar, (2) it was just immersed in water, and (3) all sugar dissolves when immersed in water. Granted, this is an explanation. But it is possible to do better.

What is it about sugar that makes it dissolve when immersed? Here we request information about the internal structure of the sugar lump. Since sugar is water soluble but wood is not, we expect that the one has an internal state that the other lacks. Once described, this internal state of the lump of sugar is relevant to explaining why it just dissolved.

The chicken pecks when the light is on. Surely we can ask what it is about this chicken that makes it peck when the light is on. A conditioned chicken has a disposition to behave that an unconditioned chicken does not have. It is legitimate to expect that the one has an internal state that the other lacks. Once described, this internal state of the conditioned chicken is relevant to explaining why it now is pecking.

Perhaps it is possible to explain the chicken's behavior in the way the methodological behaviorist demands. However, this does not mean that other explanations that violate behaviorist principles are irrelevant to understanding why the chicken pecks.

Behaviorism sounds plausible for two reasons. First, it is true that claims about the mental states of individuals should be tested against behavioral data. Second, an individual's behavior is importantly influenced by the environments he or she has experienced. Neither of these truisms, however, shows what methodological behaviorism maintains—that it is possible to explain (and predict) behavior without mentioning mental states.

## SECOND OBJECTION TO BEHAVIORISM'S POSITIVE THESIS: IT ASSUMES THAT ENVIRONMENTAL DETERMINISM IS TRUE

One final shortcoming of methodological behaviorism should be noted. Behaviorism is a radically environmentalist doctrine. That is, when it comes to the nature/nurture problem—the problem of saying how much a behavior is explained by genes and how much by environment—the behaviorist is entirely on the side of the environment. By saying that *inner states* need not be described in explaining behavior, the behaviorist is excluding genes as well as environmentally acquired mental states. My point is that environmentalism may be true in some cases, but not in others.

Returning to the example of the chicken, it is interesting to note that there are some behaviors that you can't condition a chicken to perform. Speaking English is something that human beings learn to do when they are in the right kind of environment. A chicken in the same environment will not acquire this skill. Why not? Since the environments are the same, the answer can't be environmental. Presumably, there is a genetic difference between chickens and human beings that explains this behavioral difference.

What is true between species may also be true, in some cases, within a species. There may be genetic differences between human beings that are relevant to explaining differences in their behaviors. This is now a controversial area of investigation. My point is that methodological behaviorism assumes in advance of any detailed scientific analysis that environmental variables suffice to explain behavior. This should not be assumed as a matter of doctrine, but should be empirically investigated on a case-by-case basis.

Scientists are now considering the possibility that there may be a significant genetic component in diseases such as depression and schizophrenia. That is, in addition to the environmental causes of these conditions, there also may be genetic causes. In contrast, no one now believes that there is a genetic component in explaining why some people speak one language while others speak another. In this case, variation in the behavior has an entirely environmental explanation.

Environmental determinism is the view that genetic differences do not help explain any behavioral differences. Genetic determinism is the view that environmental differences do not help explain any behavioral differences. Both these views are too sweeping and extreme to be plausible. First, we must consider different behaviors separately. The kind of explanation we offer for schizophrenia may differ from the kind we want to give for speaking English. Second, we must recognize that there are "mixed" proposals that deserve a hearing; we want to consider the idea that some behaviors have both environmental and genetic causes.

## THE TWO OBJECTIONS SUMMARIZED

In conclusion, there are two kinds of questions, that methodological behaviorism can't address. The first is the kind of question typified by the robbery example. When I ask how your present behavior of handing over the money is explained by your previous experiences, it seems essential to describe your beliefs and desires. There is no purely physical similarity between the present holdup and your previous environments that provides an explanation. Rather, the similarity exists only because you conceptualize the present situation in a way that resembles the way you conceptualized previous (physically different) situations. Second, there is the idea of genetic (nonenvironmental) causes of behavior. If these exist, then methodological behaviorism will be unable to explain in some cases why some organisms behave differently from others. Methodological behaviorism began by rejecting mentalism; it claimed that mental states are irrelevant to explaining behavior. But, in fact, its thesis excludes brain science and genetics as well. The real thrust of behaviorism is to claim that the explanation of behavior need not describe the *inner state* of the organism. Mentalism describes what goes on inside, but so do brain science and genetics.

By focusing on what happens in tightly controlled environments, behaviorism may seem to have established a general pattern for explaining all behavior. It is true that the pecking of the chicken in the Skinner box can be handled in the way Skinner demands. However, it is a mistake to think that successful explanation in this case can be generalized to all other behaviors. Take the chicken out of the Skinner box and perhaps it will produce novel behaviors, just as you did when the robber said "your money or your life." And apart from the issue of novel behaviors, there is the nature/nurture issue, which methodological behaviorism settles in advance of looking at the relevant data.

---

### Review Questions

1. What is the difference between methodological behaviorism and logical behaviorism?
2. What is mentalism? Is mentalism testable? How does the distinction between specific explanations and framework assumptions about a research program bear on this question?
3. Why do so-called "novel" behaviors pose a problem for methodological behaviorism? What does *novel* mean? Isn't every behavior novel in some respect or other?
4. What does methodological behaviorism say about the relevance of genetics and brain science to the explanation of behavior? Why would innate differences in behavior be a problem for behaviorism?

## Problems for Further Thought

1. Some psychotherapists call themselves "behaviorists." They treat patients with phobias (extreme fears) by helping them modify fear behavior (like increased heart rate, perspiration, anxiety) rather than by helping them understand why they have the array of beliefs and desires that produce the reaction. Consider people who are enormously afraid of being in closed areas (claustrophobia). Instead of trying to get a claustrophobic individual to understand why he or she has this fear, a behavioral therapist might concentrate on "desensitizing" the individual. The goal would be to modify the individual's behavior. Treatment might begin with very brief exposures to closed areas; gradually, as the patient gains confidence, longer exposures would be attempted. Here's the question: Do the criticisms I've made of methodological behaviorism imply that behavioral therapy will not be effective? Defend your answer.

2. *Saying that lemons are yellow* is a kind of event. Can it be defined by its physical characteristics? Is *saying the English sentence "lemons are yellow"* definable by its physical characteristics? What is the difference between these two kinds of events?

3. If I strike your knee with a hammer, it will jerk. Is this due to the beliefs and desires you have? If not, why is your going to a movie tonight any different?

## CHAPTER 22

# *The Mind/Brain Identity Theory*

So far I've examined two theories about the nature of the mind and its relationship to the body. These were Cartesian Dualism (Chapter 19) and logical behaviorism (Chapter 20). Methodological behaviorism (Chapter 21), recall, isn't a thesis about the nature of the mind; since methodological behaviorism recommends that scientific explanations of behavior ignore the mind, it doesn't say much about what the mind is.

## THE IDENTITY THEORY IS AN *A POSTERIORI* CLAIM

Cartesian Dualism and logical behaviorism are very different positions. Yet the arguments that each presents have something in common: Neither appeals to any scientific finding as evidence for what it maintains. Cartesian Dualism says that we can recognize by introspection and philosophical reasoning that the mind has a property that the body lacks. Logical behaviorism says that we can see that mental states are not inner causes of behavior just by analyzing the meanings of commonsense mentalistic terms. Both theories are defended by arguments that are intended to be *a priori*.

The Mind/Brain Identity Theory isn't just a different theory from those surveyed so far; it also is a different *kind* of theory. The identity theory argues for its solution to the mind/body problem by describing the progress that science has made so far and by predicting the progress that science will make in the future. The relationship of the mind and the body, says the identity theory, is something that science discovers by observation and experiment. It isn't something that armchair philosophy—introspection and linguistic analysis—can hope to resolve. The identity theory is offered as an *a posteriori* proposition about the relationship of mind and body.

## MATERIALISM

The identity theory asserts that the history of science has been marked by success after success for a doctrine called *materialism* or *physicalism*. This is the view that every object is a material (physical) object. But what does that mean—that every object has at least one physical property? There must be more to materialism than this. After all, Descartes and other dualists agree that your thoughts have temporal location. For example, yesterday, you wanted an ice cream cone; this is a physical property that your desire had. What distinguishes materialism from dualism is this: Materialists hold that if two objects are different in any way at all, they must exhibit physical differences. If you love jazz and I do not, then there must be a physical difference between us. If we were physically exactly the same, either we'd both love jazz or neither of us would. The materialist's slogan is *no difference without a physical difference*. Dualists disagree with this principle. They think it is possible that two physically identical lumps of matter might be such that one of them has a mind while the other does not. A jazz lover and a jazz hater might be molecule-for-molecule identical; they would be physically identical but psychologically distinct. Dualists think this is possible because they think that the mind is a not a material object at all.

## PROGRESS IN SCIENCE

If we consider earlier centuries of human knowledge, we find phenomena that weren't well understood scientifically. For example, lightning was once profoundly perplexing. The ancient Greeks thought that lightning was Zeus's thunderbolt. But in the eighteenth and nineteenth centuries, the science of electricity established that lightning is an electrical discharge. Science was able to take a phenomenon that earlier had seemed to defy physical description and show that it can be understood within the framework of the laws of physics. Consider a statement that describes this scientific discovery:

Lightning is one and the same thing as a kind of electrical discharge.

This statement wasn't established by analyzing the meaning of the word *lightning*. The statement isn't an *a priori* truth, knowable by linguistic analysis; rather, it is an *a posteriori* truth that the science of electricity discovered. It could be established only by observation and experiment.

In the past century, there was a similar perplexity about the nature of life. What is the difference between living things and things that are not alive? A doctrine called *vitalism* held that living things contain a nonphysical substance that animates them with life—an *élan vita* (a vital fluid). In this century, vitalism has been undermined by the discoveries of molecular biology. We now know that life is a physicochemical phenomenon. Organisms are made of the same basic elements (carbon, oxygen, etc.) as nonliving things. Life differs from nonlife because of how these basic physical constituents are arranged. There is no extra nonphysical ingredient that magically makes organisms "alive."

Biology in the last one hundred years has discredited vitalism. The discovery of the molecular basis of life has been a triumph for materialism. By this I don't mean that each and every detail of the physical basis of life is well understood; if this were true, there would no longer be a need for research in molecular biology and biochemistry. Rather, what I mean is that the details are sufficiently well understood that there is no longer any real doubt that metabolism, reproduction, digestion, respiration, and so on are all physical processes.

## DUALISM RESEMBLES VITALISM

Cartesian Dualism and vitalism are similar. Dualism says that an individual's mind is a nonmaterial substance. Thinking beings therefore are said to contain a nonphysical ingredient not found in beings that don't have minds. Vitalism says that living things contain a nonphysical substance—an *élan vital*—that is unique to them. Just as dualism opposes a materialistic solution to the mind/body problem, so vitalism opposes a materialistic answer to the question of how biological and physical processes are related to each other.

The Mind/Brain Identity Theory says that what has happened to the problem of life is in the process of happening to the problem of mind. We now have some knowledge of the physical basis—the neurophysiological basis—of the mind. If science progresses the way it has in other areas, this materialistic understanding will broaden and deepen. The identity theory predicts that science will fully vindicate the thesis that an individual's mind and brain are one and the same entity. Each mental characteristic (for example, believing that snow is white, wanting a drink, feeling pain) is identical with some physical characteristic. The identity theory is a version of materialism: Mental objects are physical objects and mental characteristics are physical characteristics.

During the 1950s and 1960s, identity theorists—for example, U. T. Place, in "Is Consciousness a Brain Process?" and J. J. C. Smart, in "Sensations and Brain Processes" (both reprinted in V. Chappell [ed.], *The Philosophy of Mind,* Prentice-Hall, 1962)— gave the following as an example of what they meant. Brain scientists at that time suggested that feeling pain is one and the same event as having the c-fibers in one's brain fire. This neurophysiological hypothesis about the physical basis of pain later turned out to be untrue. This didn't deter identity theorists, however, who are quite happy to leave it to science to work out the details of the general hypotheses they formulate. The identity theorist claims that feeling pain is identical with being in *some physical state or other;* it is for science to tell us precisely what this physical state is.

## A CORRELATION EXPERIMENT

Consider this example in more detail. How might a scientist investigate the connection of pain and c-fiber firing? The scientist would want to find out if people experience pain whenever their c-fibers fire and if people have their c-fibers fire whenever they experience pain. Here's a simple experiment that would help determine if these mental and physical events co-occur. A probe inserted into the subject's brain would indicate when the c-fibers fire. Perhaps the subject's own testimony, based on introspection, would indicate when he or she experiences pain. The experimenter occasionally hits the subject's thumb with a hammer. Ignoring complications, suppose that different human subjects, when placed in the same (morally questionable) experiment, generate the same data. Suppose that the data show a perfect correlation between experiences of pain and c-fiber firings—the one kind of event occurs if and only if the other does.

Does this, by itself, show that the identity theory is true? No. Recall that dualism is consistent with there being a perfect correlation of mental events and physical events. Dualism claims that feeling pain and having your c-fibers fire are *two* distinct kinds of event. The identity theory, on the other hand, says that feeling a pain and having one's c-fibers fire are perfectly correlated because they are one and the same kind of event.

How are we to choose between dualism and the identity theory? One consideration, mentioned in Chapter 19, is that dualism makes it difficult to understand how mind and body can causally interact. The identity theory, on the other hand, has no difficulty accommodating this fact. However, the fourth Problem for Further Thought at the end of Chapter 19 suggests that this objection to dualism rests on a questionable assumption about what causality involves. Is there some other basis on which to choose between dualism and the identity theory?

## THE PRINCIPLE OF PARSIMONY

Identity theorists offer a second reason for rejecting dualism. They claim that the identity theory is more parsimonious (simpler) than dualism. Their idea is that the scientific method says we should prefer simpler theories over more complex ones, when both are consistent with the observations. It isn't just that more parsimonious ideas are easier to think about or are aesthetically more pleasing. Rather, their idea is that more parsimonious theories are more likely to be *true.*

The identity theory is more parsimonious because it claims (if the experiment just described were to yield a perfect correlation) that feeling pain and having one's c-fibers fire are one and the same event. A dualist, on the other hand, says that these are two different events. The Principle of Parsimony, sometimes called "Ockham's Razor" after the medieval philosopher William of Ockham, is an abductive principle. It says that we should prefer explanations that minimize the number of entities, processes, and events they postulate. The usual slogan is "don't multiply entities beyond necessity," though this isn't in Ockham's writings. Since one is a smaller number than two, the mind/brain identity theory is more parsimonious than dualism. Identity theorists count this as a reason for thinking that the identity theory is true and dualism is false, given that both are consistent with the observed correlation of mental and physical states.

In the vitalism controversy, no biologist took seriously the idea that an *élan vital* exists once the physical bases of life processes became reasonably clear. Rather, the conclusion was that an organism's being alive is nothing above and beyond its having certain physical processes going on in its body. To say otherwise would be to admit a further entity—an *élan vital*—without necessity. This would contradict the Principle of Parsimony. Biologists took this principle to heart once they obtained physical explanations of life processes. They realized that there was no reason to postulate the existence of an *élan vital*. For this reason, vitalism was rejected and materialism accepted. If a perfect correlation could be found between mental characteristics and physical ones, what reason could there be to postulate the existence of an immaterial mind—one that just happens to exhibit psychological characteristics that are correlated with the physical characteristics of the brain? This seems entirely gratuitous—a violation of the Principle of Parsimony. For this reason, the identity theory suggests that dualism should be rejected and materialism accepted, if science discovers perfect correlations between mental and physical characteristics.

Let's be clear on what the Principle of Parsimony recommends. In the problem of life, the principle leads one to *deny* the existence of an immaterial vital substance. It doesn't say that one should *suspend judgment* as to whether such a substance exists. Likewise, mind/brain identity theorists argue that parsimony offers a reason to think that immaterial minds do not exist. Their recommendation is not to suspend judgment about dualism, but to conclude that dualism is false. In both cases, Ockham's Razor leads one to conclude that *X* does not exist, not to conclude that one should suspend judgment as to whether *X* exists.

There is an interesting and difficult philosophical problem here, which I won't attempt to solve: Why should the greater simplicity or parsimony of a theory be a reason to think that the theory is true? Does using the Principle of Parsimony in this way require that we assume that nature is simple? This seems to be the rationale that Isaac Newton offers for using the principle in scientific reasoning (see the accompanying box). If using the principle requires that we assume that nature is simple, what evidence do we have that nature really is simple? This question should remind you of the question we asked in connection with Hume's views on induction in Chapters 15–17 concerning the principle of the uniformity of nature.

There is an alternative argument for using the principle of parsimony that does not rest on the assumption that nature is simple. The history of science shows that using the principle of parsimony has repeatedly led to important scientific advances. In Aristotle's physics (which we considered briefly in Chapter 4), the motions of celestial bodies and the motions of objects here on earth are said to follow different rules. One of the great achievements of Newton's physics is that it provided a single

**Newton on Parsimony**

The Principle of Parsimony has been used in many scientific debates. In his *Principles of Natural Philosophy* (1690), Newton presents four "Rules of Reasoning in Philosophy." The first two concern abduction, the second two induction:

1. *We are to admit no more causes of natural things than such as are both true and sufficient to explain their appearances.* To this purpose the philosophers say that Nature does nothing in vain, and more is in vain when less will serve; for Nature is pleased with simplicity and affects not the pomp of superfluous causes.

2. *Therefore to the same natural effects we must, as far as possible, assign the same causes.* As to respiration in a man and in a beast, the descent of stones in Europe and in America, the light of our culinary fire and of the sun, the reflection of light in the earth and in the planets.

3. *The qualities of bodies, which admit neither intensification nor remission of degrees, and which are found to belong to all bodies within the reach of our experiments, are to be esteemed the universal qualities of all bodies whatsoever.* For since the qualities of bodies are only known to us by experiments, we are to hold for universal all such as universally agree with experiments, and such as are not liable to diminution can never be quite taken away. We are certainly not to relinquish evidence of experiments for the sake of dreams and vain fictions of our own devising; nor are we to recede from the analogy of Nature, which is wont to be simple and always consonant to itself....

4. *In experimental philosophy we are to look upon propositions inferred by general induction from phenomena as accurately or very nearly true, notwithstanding any contrary hypotheses that may be imagined, till such time as other phenomena occur by which they may either be made more accurate or liable to exceptions.* This rule we must follow, that the argument of induction not be evaded by hypotheses.

Rule 1 is relevant to the debate between the identity theory and dualism. Rule 2 is similar to the Principle of the Common Cause discussed in connection with the Argument from Design (Chapter 6). Rule 3 bears on the relevance of Descartes' method of doubt (Chapter 13) to the progress of science.

set of laws that covered both. Newton's theory is in this respect simpler than Aristotle's. The rejection of vitalism in the nineteenth and twentieth centuries provides another such example. These achievement are important scientific milestones. However, we must be careful not to attend only to episodes in which more parsimonious theories turned out to be better than their less parsimonious rivals. There also have been episodes in which the opposite turned out to be true.

## Review Questions

1. What is materialism? Is it the view that money is the most important thing?
2. What is vitalism? Is vitalism shown to be true by the fact that living things contain DNA while nonliving things do not?

3. In what way is vitalism (as a solution to the problem of life) similar to dualism (as a solution to the problem of mind)? What is meant by "the problem of life" and "the problem of mind"?
4. What is the Principle of Parsimony? Why is dualism said to be less parsimonious than the identity theory?
5. Does the Principle of Parsimony agree with the following claim: "Since dualism and the identity theory both predict that mental events will be correlated with physical events, there is no way to choose between the two theories"?

---

## Problems for Further Thought

1. Suppose we observe a perfect correlation between some mental property (like feeling pain) and some physical property (like having one's c-fibers fire). Apply the Surprise Principle (Chapter 3) to see whether this observation strongly favors the identity theory over dualism.
2. In the passage from *Principles of Natural Philosophy* quoted in this chapter, Newton defends the Principle of Parsimony by saying that "Nature does nothing in vain." Is this idea consistent with what we now know about natural selection (Chapter 6)?
3. In the readings for this section of the text, there is a selection by Bertrand Russell on the problem of other minds. He proposes to solve this problem by introducing a postulate. What does this postulate say? How is it related to the Principle of Parsimony? Does this postulate solve the problem?
4. The principle of parsimony is often thought to be relevant to the question of whether God exists. Formulate and evaluate an argument for atheism that makes use of this principle.
5. In a reading at the end of this chapter, the psychologist U. T. Place defends the identity theory, but does not mention the principle of parsimony. He does so by describing a situation in which the correlation between two events justifies the conclusion that the two are identical. Evaluate Place's argument.

---

## CHAPTER 23

---

# *Functionalism*

In the previous chapter, I described the Mind/Brain Identity Theory as applying to the mind/body problem the general thesis that *everything is material*. Minds aren't made of an immaterial substance; rather, people have minds and mental characteristics by virtue of the fact that they have brains that possess various sorts of physical structure.

In the 1960s and 1970s, several philosophers—preeminently, Hilary Putnam (in "The Nature of Mental States" in H. Putnam, *Mind, Language, and Reality,* Cambridge University Press, 1975) and Jerry Fodor (in *Psychological Explanation,* Random House, 1968)—developed a criticism of the identity theory. They espoused a point of view that came to be called "functionalism." Although functionalism does not reject materialism, it does reject one important part of the identity theory. Functionalism has two parts—one negative, the other positive. The negative part describes what psychological states are *not.* This is the functionalist critique of the identity theory. The positive part advances a proposal about what psychological states *are.* I'll take these two ideas in order.

## FUNCTIONALISM'S NEGATIVE THESIS: WHAT'S WRONG WITH THE IDENTITY THEORY?

To begin with, I need to draw a commonsense distinction. Suppose someone says to you, looking at your clothing, "We own the same shirt." What might this mean? There are two choices. One is that you and this person own the same *kind* of shirt. The other is that the very shirt on your back is jointly owned by the two of you.

## THE TYPE/TOKEN DISTINCTION

Let's introduce some terminology to mark this distinction. Unique physical objects are called *tokens.* Kinds (or properties) are called *types.* The unique physical object that you are now wearing is a token of many types. It is a token of the type *shirt;* it also is a token of the type *blue,* and a token of the type *clothing.* To say that a single token is a token of many types is merely to say that a single object has many properties.

Conversely, a given type may have zero, one, or many tokens that fall under it. *Unicorn* is a type of animal that has no instances; there are no tokens of that type. *Golden mountain* is a type of geological object, one that happens to have no exemplars. You can see just from this pair of examples that two types (properties) may apply to exactly the same tokens and still be distinct types. Being a unicorn isn't the same property as being a golden mountain, even though the set of unicorns has precisely the same members as the set of golden mountains.

How does the type/token distinction apply to the mind/body problem? The identity theory has two parts. It makes a claim about psychological tokens and also a claim about psychological types. The former category—of psychological tokens—includes the following: Descartes' mind, the pain I felt in my foot last Thursday, Jones's thinking to herself today that lemons are yellow. Each of these is a token, and the identity theory says that each is identical with some physical token.

In addition, there are psychological types (properties); the identity theory makes a claim about these as well. For example, there is the property of having a mind, the property of feeling pain, the property of believing that lemons are yellow, and so on. Note that these types each have numerous tokens falling under them. Each type, therefore, describes something that various tokens have in common. The identity theory says that each of these psychological types (properties) is identical with some physical property or other.

## MULTIPLE REALIZABILITY

Functionalism rejects what the identity theory says about psychological types. Functionalists hold that psychological properties are not identical with physical properties. Instead, functionalists argue that psychological types are *multiply realizable*. I explain this idea with an example.

Consider a type that isn't psychological—the property of *being a mousetrap*. Each token mousetrap is a physical object. But think of all the different ways there are to build a mousetrap. Some are made of wood and wire and are loaded with cheese. Others are made of plastic and catch mice by injecting them with curare. Still others are made of a team of philosophers, who stalk around armed with inverted wastepaper baskets. There are many, perhaps endlessly many, ways to build a mousetrap.

Is there a single physical characteristic that all mousetraps have in common, and which non-mousetraps lack? This seems highly dubious. Each token mousetrap is a physical thing, but the property of being a mousetrap (the type) doesn't seem to be a physical property at all.

How does this analogy bear on the plausibility of the Mind/Brain Identity Theory? There is more than one (physical) way to build a mousetrap. The analogy is that there may be many physical ways to build a creature that has a mind, and more than one way for a being with a mind to have this or that psychological property.

---

### The Birthday Fallacy, Again

The Birthday Fallacy, introduced in Chapter 4, is the mistake you make if you confuse the following two statements:

> Everyone has a birthday.
> There is a single day on which everyone was born.

The first is true; the second false. You'd be making the same mistake if you confused the following two statements:

> Each mousetrap has physical properties that allow it to catch mice.
> There is a single set of physical properties that all mousetraps have in common that allows them to catch mice.

The first is true; the second false. How can the Birthday Fallacy be used to describe functionalism's criticism of the identity theory?

## COULD A COMPUTER HAVE PSYCHOLOGICAL CHARACTERISTICS?

Consider computers. It isn't very plausible to regard very simple computers as having beliefs and desires. My desk calculator no more "knows" facts about simple arithmetic than my stove "knows" recipes for making soup. Rather, human beings use these devices to do arithmetic or to make soup. A desk calculator, in this respect, is like paper and pencil. It facilitates *our* calculations, but doesn't itself engage in mental activity.

Don't be misled by the fact that we sometimes use mentalistic terms to describe simple computers. For example, we talk about computer "memory." However, I don't think my home computer literally remembers anything. This is just a metaphor. If I write some thoughts on a piece of paper and those scribbles are not erased, it is true that the piece of paper has "retained" the inscriptions I placed there. But the piece of paper does not remember anything. In this respect, I think a simple computer is just like a piece of paper.

So I don't think that very simple machines have minds or mental states. But let's now use our imaginations and think about what the future may bring. Could there be computers that have mental states? Could computers be built that perceive—see and hear, for example? Could computers be built that remember? Could a computer reason? Could a computer be built that has wants and needs and preferences?

Functionalists have generally regarded these as very real possibilities. Perhaps current computers can't do these things, and perhaps computer scientists at times exaggerate how close they are to making computers with these abilities. But take seriously for a moment the possibility that computers eventually will be built that have one or more of these mental abilities.

This possibility has serious implications for the identity theory. These computers, let's suppose, won't be made of protein. Perhaps they will be made of silicon chips. There seems to be no reason to expect that these thinking machines must be physically very much like the brains we have. Just as there are many physical ways to build a mousetrap, so there seem to be many physical ways to have a mind and to have particular mental states.

## MULTIPLE REALIZABILITY WITHIN THE CLASS OF LIVING THINGS

We don't need to consider the future of computer science to see the point of the idea of multiple realizability. Organisms other than human beings have psychological states. Some can perceive and remember and feel pain, even if they aren't capable of all the complex thoughts and feelings that human beings can experience. Is it reasonable to suppose that these psychological states in other species must be based on precisely the same physical structures that are present in human beings?

Even within the human species, there may be variation in the physical structures used to encode this or that mental state. Indeed, even within a single human being there may be many ways that the brain can encode a single piece of information. When you believe that lemons are yellow at two different times, maybe the brain structure that encodes your belief at the one time differs from the brain structure that encodes it at the other time.

This is functionalism's criticism of the identity theory. A given mental type—believing that lemons are yellow, wanting a drink of water, feeling pain—is not identical with any single physical type. The reason the identity theory is false is that psychological types have multiple physical realizations. This point might be formulated slightly sarcastically by saying that functionalism accuses the identity theory of being a "chauvinist" doctrine. (This quip is due to Ned Block, "Troubles with Functionalism," in W. Savage [ed.], *Perception and Cognition,* University of Minnesota Press, 1978.) Identity theorists say that a computer or another species must be like us physically if it is to have a mind and mental characteristics. Functionalism regards this as implausibly restrictive. This, then, is the negative thesis that functionalism advances. Mental properties are *not* identical with physical properties. Notice that this rejection of type-identity is consistent with accepting token-identity. Perhaps being a mousetrap isn't a physical property, but each mousetrap is a physical thing. Perhaps believing that lemons are yellow isn't a physical property, but my present state of believing that lemons are yellow might still be identical with a physical state that my brain occupies. Functionalism rejects the identity theory's thesis of *type*-identity, not its thesis of *token*-identity.

The identity theory is a version of materialism. So is functionalism. The identity theory denies that minds are made of an immaterial substance; it denies that disembodied spirits exist. Functionalism agrees. The following table shows how these two theories are related to each other, and also to dualism:

|  | *Dualism* | *Functionalism* | *Identity theory* |
|---|---|---|---|
| Are mental types identical with physical types? | No | No | Yes |
| Are mental tokens identical with physical tokens? | No | Yes | Yes |

In a sense, functionalism is an intermediate position; it is conceptually "in between" dualism and the identity theory.

## FUNCTIONALISM'S POSITIVE THESIS

So much for the negative thesis. What positive account does functionalism provide of what the mind and its properties are like? The name *functionalism* suggests what this positive account is. Let's return to the property of being a mousetrap. This property, I've argued, is not identical with any single physical property. What, then, makes something a mousetrap? What do the mousetraps have in common that makes them different from the non-mousetraps? A vague, though suggestive, answer is that being a mousetrap is a functional property; a mousetrap is any device that functions to turn a free mouse into a caught one. Mousetraps are things that play a particular causal role. Any device that produces certain effects in certain circumstances counts as a mousetrap, regardless of what physical materials it is made of or how it is physically constructed.

What does it mean, then, to claim that psychological properties are "functional" properties? Let's consider a psychological state *X* that has the following characteristics:

> When an individual believes that there is water in a cup in front of him and the individual is in state *X*, the individual drinks from the cup.

> When an individual believes that a well contains water and the individual is in state *X*, then the individual will draw water from the well and drink it.

Each of these two statements is a *conditional;* it describes what an agent will do *if* the agent has a particular belief and is in state *X.* Can you guess from these two conditionals what state *X* is? A reasonable conjecture is that *X* is the desire to drink water. Of course, there is more to this desire than what these two conditionals describe. Functionalism maintains that these conditionals, and others like them, describe what it is to have a particular desire. Any state that plays the right causal role will be the desire to drink water. The physical composition of the state does not matter. Psychological states are to be understood in terms of their causal relations to behavior and to other mental states.

This example concerning state *X* suggests the following functionalist proposal for understanding what it is for an agent to have a desire:

*S* wants proposition *P* to be true if and only if, if *S*'s beliefs are true, then *S* will cause *P* to become true. Notice that this proposal describes desire as a state that plays a particular causal role: When added to beliefs, desires produce actions of certain sorts. As plausible as this suggestion might be at first glance, there are problems. First, people don't always get what they want when their beliefs are true. A pitcher may want to strike out a batter and may have true beliefs about how to achieve this, but still the pitcher fails. The second objection is that people sometimes cause propositions to come true that they don't want to come true. When I drink from the cup, I cause my moustache to get damp, but this isn't something I want. So there is a defect in the functionalist proposal just stated for understanding what desire is. Perhaps it can be repaired. Maybe there is something right about the idea that mental states are to be understood in terms of their causal connections with behavior and with other mental states.

## SENSATIONS

The kind of difficulty we have been considering is especially prominent when we shift our attention from beliefs and desires to sensations. Consider what a functionalist says about the nature of pain, for example. When people are in pain, they are inclined to say "Ouch!" They are inclined to withdraw their bodies from the stimulus they think is causing the pain. And being in pain diminishes a person's attention span and has other psychological effects as well.

Suppose I exhaustively described the causes and the effects of being in pain. These would involve the relationship of being in pain to external stimuli, to behavior, and to other psychological states. Some of these I just mentioned. It is sometimes suggested that this functionalist account of pain leaves out the most important fact about pain—the fact that pain *hurts*. A state may play the functional role of pain and still not be a pain state, or so this objection asserts. If this is right, then functionalism will fail as an account of the nature of pain.

I won't try to answer this question of whether functionalism is adequate. Perhaps there are some psychological phenomena that functionalism cannot adequately characterize. Maybe sensations (like pain) are counterexamples. Even if this is true, however, there may be other psychological states for which functionalism is adequate; perhaps belief and desire can be understood along functionalist lines. This is now a controversial issue in philosophy.

## SUMMARY

I have argued that dualism, logical behaviorism, and the Mind/Brain Identity Theory are each inadequate. I think there is nothing wrong with mentalism—the view that beliefs and desires are inner causes of outward behavior. Behavior *provides evidence* about what an agent's mental states are, but behavior does not

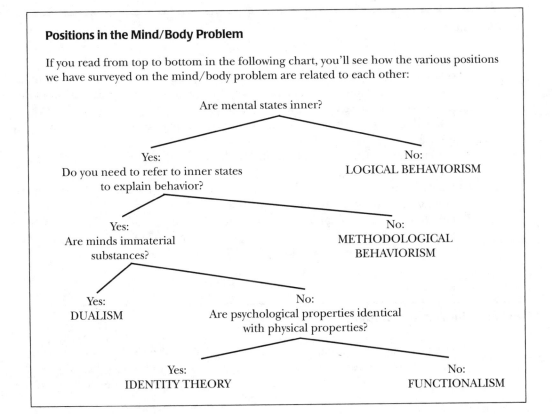

**Positions in the Mind/Body Problem**

If you read from top to bottom in the following chart, you'll see how the various positions we have surveyed on the mind/body problem are related to each other:

Are mental states inner?

Yes:
Do you need to refer to inner states to explain behavior?

No:
LOGICAL BEHAVIORISM

Yes:
Are minds immaterial substances?

No:
METHODOLOGICAL BEHAVIORISM

Yes:
DUALISM

No:
Are psychological properties identical with physical properties?

Yes:
IDENTITY THEORY

No:
FUNCTIONALISM

*define* what it is to be in a given mental state. To make sense of mentalism, we need not think that an agent's mind is made of some strange immaterial substance (as dualism maintains). Individuals have minds in virtue of the physical organization of their bodies. This, however, does not require that all the individuals who possess some psychological characteristic (like feeling pain, or believing that lemons are yellow) have some single physical characteristic in common. My conclusion is that functionalism's negative thesis is correct; it is plausible to hold that psychological states are multiply realizable. As for the positive thesis that functionalism advances, it remains to be seen whether an adequate functionalist account of different mental states can be developed.

In the rest of this section of the book, I'll explore two other philosophical problems about the mind. If human beings act as they do because of what they think and want, and if what they think and want is caused by things outside of themselves, how can human beings have free will? This problem is addressed in Chapters 24 to 26. After that, I'll consider the problem of psychological egoism. If human beings act on the basis of what they think and want, doesn't it follow that people always act selfishly—that they try to satisfy their own wants and never care, ultimately, about the welfare of others?

## Review Questions

1. I return home from a furniture store and report to my family, "They're selling our sofa." I look at the plate of food in front of my son and say, "That is what I ate for lunch." How does the type/token distinction help identify an ambiguity that is present in each of these two remarks?

2. What does it mean to say that a psychological property (a type) is multiply realizable?

3. Functionalists criticize the Mind/Brain Identity Theory for being "chauvinistic." What does this mean?

4. How is it possible to reject the identity theory without thinking that there are immaterial minds (disembodied spirits)?

5. Functionalists try to characterize what it is to have a psychological property (like feeling pain, or believing that Washington is the capital of the United States) by describing that property's "causal role." What does that mean?

## Problems for Further Thought

1. The fact that two types apply to exactly the same tokens isn't enough to ensure that they are identical. For example, *being a unicorn* and *being a golden mountain* are different types (properties), even though they apply to exactly the same

objects (namely, to no objects at all). Can the same point be made with respect to types that are exemplified? Can two types be different, even though they apply to the same (nonempty) set of objects? Describe an example of this sort.

2. In Chapter 6, I discussed the concept of fitness that is used in evolutionary theory. What would it mean to say that fitness is *multiply realizable?* Is it plausible to claim that fitness has this characteristic?

3. Here is *the inverted spectrum problem:* You have a particular characteristic sensation when you look at red things and a quite different sensation when you look at green things. Is it possible that someone has precisely the reverse arrangement? This individual would have a red sensation when he looks at green things and a green sensation when he looks at red things. His behavior, including his use of language, would be precisely the same as yours. For example, he would apply the term "red" to fire engines and the term "green" to grasshoppers. If spectrum inversion is possible, what consequences does this have for functionalism's positive thesis about the nature of mental states?

# CHAPTER 24

## *Freedom, Determinism, and Causality*

In the previous chapters about the mind/body problem, there was a simple idea that no theory contested. Dualists, identity theorists, and functionalists all grant that the mind and the physical world causally interact. Your beliefs and desires cause your body to move in various ways. In addition, mental states themselves have causal antecedents in the physical world. What you now believe and the preferences you now have—indeed, your personality as a whole—can be traced back to experiences you have had. These experiences were themselves caused by items in your physical environment. In addition, modern science recognizes that some features of your mind may be influenced by the genetic endowment you received from your parents.

So just as the human mind has effects on the physical environment, so too does the physical world—both inside and outside our own bodies—affect our mental states. The following diagram represents these causal relationships:

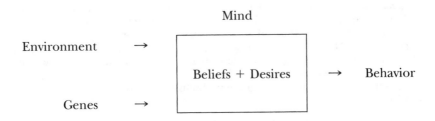

## THE PROBLEM OF FREEDOM

The puzzle about the existence of human freedom can now be given a preliminary formulation. Your beliefs and desires, and hence your behavior, are caused by things outside your control. You didn't freely choose the genes you have or the sequence of environments in which you grew up. If you didn't freely choose them, how can it be said that any of your behaviors is the result of free choices on your part? How can you be responsible for actions that were caused by events (long ago) over which you exercised no control? It looks like you are no more free than a computer; a computer behaves as it does because it was programmed to do so, and so, apparently, do you.

Another way to see the problem is to attend to a different feature of the above causal picture. Suppose your behavior is the result of your beliefs and desires just as a computer's behavior is the result of its programming. There is a feature of the computer's situation that seems also to characterize your own. Given the computer's program, it can't act differently from the way it does. Suppose a computer is programmed to compute the sum of two numbers. This means that if you input 7 and 5, then the computer can't fail to output 12. The computer can't act other than the way it does.

Are we like computers in this respect? Given the beliefs and desires we presently have, isn't it inevitable that we do precisely what we do? Our beliefs and desires leave open what we will do no more than a computer's program leaves open what it will do. This fact about the computer, and about ourselves if we are like the computer, seems to entail that we are not free agents. The reason is that if an action is performed freely, then it must have been possible for the agent to have done otherwise. If I freely lift a cup of coffee to my lips, then it must have been possible for me to refrain from lifting the cup to my lips. But given the beliefs and desires I had,

---

### Transitivity

Some objects stand in relation to others. Alice *is taller than* Ben. David *loves* Edward. The italicized terms denote relationships. The names flanking the italicized term refer to objects that are said to be related to each other.

Some relations are transitive; others are not. If Alice is taller than Ben and Ben is taller than Cathy, then Alice is taller than Cathy. A relation $R$ is said to be transitive precisely when it has this property:

For any three objects $a$, $b$, and $c$, if $a$ bears $R$ to $b$, and $b$ bears $R$ to $c$, then $a$ must bear $R$ to $c$.

*Being taller than* is a transitive relation. *Loving* is not a transitive relationship. The fact that David loves Edward and Edward loves Flo does not guarantee that David loves Flo.

*Causality* is a relation that obtains between events. Holmes's pulling the trigger caused Moriarty to die. Moriarty's death caused alarm to spread in the London underworld. Does it follow that Holmes's pulling the trigger caused alarm to spread in the London underworld? That is, is causality a transitive relation?

Does the Distant Causation Argument, discussed in this chapter, assume that causality is transitive?

I couldn't have done anything other than lift the cup to my lips. Our actions are the inevitable consequences of the minds we have, just as a computer's output is the inevitable consequence of its program.

I've just pointed out two features of the causal relationships depicted in the preceding diagram. Each suggests its own argument for the thesis that no human action is free. I'll call the first argument the *Distant Causation Argument;* it focuses on the idea that our behaviors are caused by factors (our genes and early childhood environment) that were beyond our control. I'll call the second argument the *Could-Not-Have-Done-Otherwise Argument;* it focuses on the claim that we can't act other than the way our beliefs and desires cause us to act. Both these arguments will be discussed later. Before reading further, write out each of these arguments, with premises and conclusions stated carefully, and make sure that what you come up with is an argument that is deductively valid. Once you do this, it should be clear that if we sometimes act freely, at least one premise in each argument must be false. Notice also that both these arguments reach a conclusion of total generality; each concludes that *not one* of our actions is performed freely. This goes beyond the more modest idea that *some* of our actions aren't performed freely.

## EXAMPLES OF UNFREE ACTS

It is controversial whether the Distant Causation Argument or the Could-Not-Have-Done-Otherwise Argument are right in their claim that human beings never act freely. However, it is not especially controversial that some human actions are not performed freely. Here I want to give two examples. The first is a behavior produced by *brainwashing.* Consider the case of Patty Hearst. Heiress to the newspaper fortune, Hearst was kidnaped and abused mentally and physically by her captors for several months in 1974. She then participated with them in a bank robbery. Later, she was caught and brought to trial. There was never any doubt that Hearst helped rob the bank. The question was whether she did so of her own free will. The defense attorneys tried to establish that Hearst didn't have free will at the time; they argued that her captors had so distorted her mental faculties that she was a mere pawn in their hands. Her actions were an expression of *their* wants, not of *hers,* or so they argued. The prosecution tried to show that Hearst was a free agent; they argued that even though she had been abused, she was a willing participant in the bank robbery. The prosecution won the case, and Patty Hearst went to jail. Quite apart from whether this was the right outcome, I want to draw your attention to an idea on which both the defense and the prosecution agreed: People who do what they do because of brainwashing aren't acting of their own free will. Here, then, is one kind of behavior that I think we can safely regard as unfree.

The second category of unfree behavior was described by Freud. Freud describes a man who obsessively washes his hands. He is caught in the grip of a compulsion. Even after normal people would recognize that their hands are clean, the compulsive handwasher keeps scrubbing away. Sometimes the compulsion is so extreme that the person's flesh is eaten away, exposing the bone. "They can't help themselves," we may want to say. Another example of this sort is kleptomania. A kleptomaniac is someone driven by the compulsion to steal. Even when they recognize that stealing is ruining their lives, kleptomaniacs find themselves powerless to change their behavior. Perhaps some people steal of their own free will; this does not seem to be true of kleptomaniacs.

Even philosophers who think that we sometimes act freely usually concede that brainwashing and compulsions rob us of our freedom. The question is whether there are *other* categories of behavior that are genuinely free. The Distant Causation Argument and the Could-Not-Have-Done-Otherwise Argument answer this question in the negative.

## ARE ALL BEHAVIORS LIKE THOSE PRODUCED BY BRAINWASHING AND COMPULSIONS?

To decide whether we ever act freely, you need to decide whether some of our behaviors differ significantly from the unfree behaviors just described. If brainwashing robs us of freedom, what should we say about the way a normal upbringing shapes us into the kinds of people we are? If indoctrination robs people of their freedom, what effect does education have on the possibility of free action? If a victim of brainwashing isn't responsible for what he or she does, how can we say that "normal" individuals are responsible for what they do?

Shifting now to the examples of compulsive behavior, we can ask—if compulsive behavior is unfree, what should we say about normal cases of rational deliberation in which people act on the basis of the wants they have? Perhaps the only difference between someone said to have a compulsion and a "normal" person is that they have different wants. It is unusual to want to wash your hands two hundred times a day, but not so unusual to want to wash them once after they get covered with dirt. If this is the only thing that distinguishes compulsive behavior from normal behavior, why say that the one is any less free than the other? To understand what freedom is, we need to answer questions such as these.

## A CLASH OF PLAUSIBLE CONCEPTIONS

The problem of freedom involves an apparent clash between two very fundamental ways we have of conceiving of ourselves. First, there is the idea that we are part of the causal network. Our actions don't spring from nothing; rather, they trace back to the beliefs, desires, and other mental features we possess. These mental characteristics didn't spring out of nothing; they too have their causal antecedents in our genes and environment. Second, there is the idea that (at least sometimes) we perform actions of our own free will. Is there a clash between these two ideas, or can they be reconciled?

The arguments considered above concerned two different stages of the causal process represented in the figure. The Distant Causation Argument concerns the relationship of your actions to your genes and environment. The Could-Not-Have-Done-Otherwise

Argument concerns the relationship of your actions to your beliefs and desires. In spite of this difference, the two arguments have something in common. Both assert that your actions are caused, and both assert that some fact about how your actions are caused shows those actions are not free. As noted before, if you think that some actions are performed freely, you must reject one or the other of these two premises.

## WHAT IS CAUSALITY?

For the rest of this chapter, I want to focus on the second of these key concepts. What does it mean to say that some events "cause" others? Understanding causality has been a very deep philosophical problem at least since David Hume's work in the eighteenth century. I won't attempt to get to the bottom of this cluster of problems. I will, however, try to clarify what causality is—enough so that we can better understand the problem of seeing the relationship between causality and freedom.

What does it mean to say that striking a match caused the match to ignite? This doesn't mean that the striking was, all by itself, enough to get the match to light. After all, besides being struck, the match had to be dry and there had to be oxygen in the air. So the first fact about causality is this: *A cause need not be a sufficient condition for its effect.* The second fact about causality is that there usually are many ways to get a particular effect to occur. Striking the match caused it to light, but that doesn't mean that striking the match was the only way to get the match to catch fire. Using a magnifying glass to focus sunlight on the match head would have done the trick. And putting the match into a heated frying pan also would have worked. So the second fact is this: *Causes often are not necessary for their effects to occur.* (See Chapter 12 to review the definitions of necessary and sufficient conditions.)

I now want to note a difference between *a* cause of an event and what we may term *the whole cause* of that event. Striking the match is *a* cause of its lighting. It is, however, only part of the whole set of causally relevant facts. Suppose I somehow were able to list all the causally relevant facts about the match at a given time. At that time, the match is struck in a certain way, there is oxygen present, the match is dry, and so on. Given all this information, what can we conclude about what will happen next?

## DETERMINISM

Can we say that the match *may* light? Yes. Can we say something more—namely, that the match *must* light, given this complete specification of all the earlier causal facts? The idea that a complete description of the causal facts guarantees what will happen next is the thesis of *determinism*. This thesis says that if you list all the causally relevant facts pertaining to the match and its environment at a given time, these facts uniquely determine what will happen next. The match's future is not left open by its present state. Given the match's present state, there is only one option as to what will happen next.

Sometimes we describe the causally relevant facts about an object so that the description does leave open what will happen next. For example, suppose we say that a pair of dice is fair. If this is all we know, we should conclude that the probability that the dice will land double-six on the next roll is 1/36. The fact that the dice are fair and that you're now rolling them does not allow you to say what *must* happen. All you can say is that the dice *may* land double-six, but it also is true that they *may* fail to do so. This does not mean that the pair of dice violates the thesis of determinism. That thesis says only that a *complete* description of the system determines what will happen next. Perhaps causal determinism is true and my description of the dice is incomplete. This has some plausibility. For example, I didn't describe exactly how the dice would be rolled, what the surface is like on which they land, or what the wind conditions are that affect them as they leave your hand. Causal determinism says only that if *all* the causally relevant facts are set out, these will leave open only one possible future for the pair of dice.

## INDETERMINISM

Is determinism true? Before I answer this question, let's be clear on what it would be for determinism to be false. If determinism is false, then the world is indeterministic. This means that a complete description of the causal facts at one time leaves open what will happen next. In such a universe, all you can say is that the present state of a system makes some futures more probable than others; the point is that even a complete description of the present will leave open more than one possible future.

Until the twentieth century, determinism was a plausible and widely accepted thesis about the world. Newton's laws of motion, for example, are deterministic in character. You may recall from high school physics that those laws do not make use of the concept of probability. For example, "$F = ma$" says that if a billiard ball of mass $m$ is acted on by a force of magnitude $F$, the ball will have an acceleration equal to $F/m$. The law does not say that this will "probably" happen, as if there are other possibilities that could happen instead. Rather, the law says what must happen if the object is acted on in a certain way. This Newtonian picture about how physical objects move provides a suggestive model for how *all* events in nature ultimately will be described. Living things are more complicated than billiard balls; creatures with minds are more complicated than many living things. The idea I want to consider, however, says that all things that are made of matter are ultimately governed by the laws of physics. So, since Newtonian theory is deterministic, the idea is that the behaviors of living things and of things with minds also must be deterministic in character. The thought behind this generalized Newtonian thesis is that "determinism percolates up." If elementary particles are deterministic, so is everything that is made of elementary particles. If a person's mind is a material object, then his or her beliefs, desires, and subsequent behaviors are governed by deterministic laws. I'm not saying that Newton was right about elementary particles, and I'm not saying that the mind is a physical thing made of elementary particles. Rather, I want you to consider is a certain idea: *If* all matter is deterministic and *if* a person's mind is a material thing, then human behavior is physically determined.

One of the if's in what I've just described—the idea that matter is deterministic—wasn't much questioned until the twentieth century. It was then that Niels Bohr, Werner Heisenberg, and Erwin Schrödinger developed the Quantum Theory. This theory is now interpreted in different ways by physicists, but what might be called the standard interpretation (called "the Copenhagen interpretation," for Bohr's hometown) is that the Quantum Theory says that the behavior of particles is not deterministic. According to this interpretation of the theory, even a complete description of a physical system leaves open what its future will be like. Some futures will be more probable than others, but the number of possibilities is always greater than one. In short, the present does not determine the future—chance is part of the way the world is.

It is by no means settled that the Copenhagen interpretation is the best interpretation of the Quantum Theory. Nor is it inconceivable that this very well confirmed scientific theory will one day be replaced by another, which assures us that the universe is deterministic. But what seems clear now is that one can't simply *assume* that determinism must be right. Perhaps the universe is deterministic, and then again, perhaps it is not. This is a scientific question to be settled by scientific investigation. One can't decide *a priori* whether determinism is true.

Suppose we are made of matter. Suppose that our psychological characteristics aren't due to the presence of some immaterial substance (as Cartesian Dualism asserts), but are consequences of how the matter we are made of is structured. If this is right, then I suggest that our behavior must be like the behaviors of physical particles. If chance influences the behavior of particles, then chance also influences the behavior of people. That is, I'm advancing the thesis that *in*determinism percolates up. If physical things don't obey deterministic laws, then our beliefs and desires don't determine what our actions will be. Rather those beliefs and desires make some actions vastly more probable than others. Similarly our genes plus the environments we inhabit do not determine what our thoughts and wants will be. Again the relationship is probabilistic, not deterministic.

Most philosophers who have written about the issue of human freedom have not worried about the implications of the Quantum Theory. Usually they have assumed that

---

### Two Uses of Probability

We often use the concept of probability to describe our *lack of knowledge*. When we say that a coin has an equal chance of landing heads or tails on the next toss, we often mean that the coin is evenly balanced (fair) and that we don't know exactly how it will be tossed or what the wind conditions will be.

If determinism is true, then the only reason we need to talk about probabilities is that we lack a complete description of the coin's initial state. Recall that determinism says that a complete description of a system at one time uniquely determines what will happen next; the present can't leave open different future possibilities that each has some chance of coming true. That is, if determinism is true, then we need the concept probability only to describe something subjective—namely, the fact that we sometimes (or always) lack complete information.

On the other hand, if determinism is false, then probability describes an objective fact about the world. Chance is a feature of the way things happen. In this case, probability talk isn't simply a way to represent our ignorance.

In short, whether determinism is true affects how we can use the concept of probability.

matter is deterministic and then have considered what this implies about the question of whether we are free. This is entirely understandable for people such as David Hume, who wrote about the issue of freedom long before the Quantum Theory came on the scene; Hume was writing in the heyday of the Newtonian world picture.

## DOES INDETERMINISM MAKE US FREE?

If the world is indeterministic, how does that fact affect the issue of whether we are free? My suspicion is that the shift from determinism to indeterminism does not make much of a difference. The reason I say this is that if you suspect that determinism rules out freedom, you'll probably be inclined to think that we wouldn't be free if indeterminism were true instead.

Suppose you think we can't have free will on the grounds that our thoughts and wants are causally determined by factors outside our control. We don't freely choose the genes we have, or the environments we inhabit in early childhood. These are thrust upon us. They shape the kinds of people we are as well as the specific beliefs and desires we have. Given all this, how can our actions be regarded as free? This is the thought expressed in the Distant Causation Argument. Maybe you find the Distant Causation Argument somewhat plausible. The question I want to ask is whether you would change your mind about freedom if chance were introduced into the above story. That is, suppose that your beliefs and desires were due to genes, environments, *and chance*. I suggest that if determinism robs you of freedom, chance seems to rob you of freedom as well.

The same point applies to the Could-Not-Have-Done-Otherwise Argument. Suppose you agree with this argument's thesis—that our actions can't be free, since they are inevitable, given the beliefs and desires we have. Would introducing chance into this story make more room for freedom? I think not. If the fact that your beliefs and desires determine your action makes you unfree, I think you'd still be unfree if your actions were caused by your beliefs, desires, *and chance*. To make this point graphic, consider a kind of brain surgery. Suppose you now are a deterministic system: Your beliefs and desires determine what you will do. I now offer you a brain implant, whereby a tiny roulette wheel is introduced into your deliberation processes. If you think you are unfree as a deterministic system, would the operation make you free? This seems implausible. Before the operation, you were a slave to your beliefs and desires. After the surgery, you are a slave to your beliefs, desires, and to the implanted roulette wheel. The shift from being a deterministic system to being an indeterministic system has not made a difference as far as the question of freedom is concerned.

## CAUSALITY IS THE ISSUE, NOT DETERMINISM

My suggestion is that determinism *and* indeterminism *both* pose a problem for human freedom. The reason is that causality can exist in an indeterministic universe just as much as it can in a deterministic one. If your mental states are caused by factors outside your control, how you can be a free agent.? Whether these causal factors *determine* your behavior is not essential.

It isn't hard to visualize how some events can cause others in a deterministic universe. If striking the match causes the match to light, determinism tells us that the striking completed a set of causal conditions that determines that the match must light. But how can some events cause others if determinism is false? The following example (due to Fred Dretske and Aaron Snyder, "Causal Irregularity," *Philosophy of Science,* Vol. 39, 1972, pp. 69–71) shows, I think, that this is possible. Suppose a roulette wheel is connected to a gun, which is pointed at a cat. If I spin the roulette wheel and the ball lands on 00, this will cause the gun to fire, which then will kill the cat. Suppose that the roulette wheel is an indeterministic system—spinning the wheel does not determine where the ball will drop. Now suppose I spin the wheel and the ball happens to fall on 00, thereby killing the cat. It seems to me that my spinning the wheel caused the cat to die, even though the process is not deterministic. The death of the cat *traces back* to my spinning the wheel. For this to be true, it is not required that my spinning the wheel *made it inevitable* that the cat would die. This is why it is possible to have causation without determinism.

Thus, my hunch is that the real problem is not to see whether determinism and freedom can be reconciled, but to see whether causality and freedom can be reconciled. However, since the traditional positions about freedom all focus on deterministic causation, I'll do the same.

## WHAT DOES DETERMINISM SAY ABOUT THE CAUSATION OF BEHAVIOR?

To fix ideas, let's be clear on how the thesis of determinism would apply to the diagram given earlier. This diagram represents the idea that your genes and environment cause your present mental state, and that this, in turn, causes your behavior. What do these causal relations mean, if causality is understood deterministically? Let's suppose for a moment that this diagram is *complete*. That is, suppose it represents *all* the factors that influence your mental state and your subsequent behavior. What does the thesis of determinism say about this chain? It asserts the following: Given your genes and environment, you couldn't have had a set of beliefs and desires different from the set you in fact possess, and given your beliefs and desires, you couldn't have performed an action different from the action you in fact produced. Determinism, recall, is the thesis that the facts at one time uniquely determine what comes next.

## DETERMINISM DIFFERS FROM FATALISM

Determinism is an entirely different doctrine from the idea termed *fatalism.* It is easy to understand what fatalism says by seeing how it figures in the Greek myth about Oedipus. Oedipus was a victim of fate. The Fates decreed that he would kill his father and marry his mother. In the story, Oedipus does these things in spite of himself. The Fates somehow ensured that Oedipus would find himself in this sorry state of affairs no matter what choices he made and no matter what he did.

Determinism says that the present determines the future; it does *not* say that the future is cast in stone, unaffected by what is true of the present. Determinism is entirely consistent with the idea that what is true at a later time *depends* on what is true earlier. Determinism does not rule out the idea that if the past had been different, the present would be different. Determinism does not rule out the idea that I can affect what the future will be like by now acting one way rather than another. Fatalism denies this; it says that the future is *independent* of what you do in the present.

Newton said that billiard balls are deterministic systems. If you hit the ball in a certain way (call it $W_1$), then the ball will move to a certain position (call it $P_1$) on the table. But Newtonian physics also says that if you hit the ball in some *other* way ($W_2$), the ball will move to a *different* position ($P_2$). Notice that in this theory, the present *makes a difference* to the future. The future is under the control of the present.

What would it be for Oedipus to be a deterministic system? This does not require us to think that there are such things as the Fates. Oedipus would be a deterministic system if his actions were deterministically controlled by his beliefs and desires. If Oedipus has one set of beliefs and desires (call it $S_1$), then Oedipus produces one action (call it $A_1$). But if he had had a different set of beliefs and desires ($S_2$), his action would have been entirely different ($A_2$).

Here is a picture of Oedipus according to which he is a deterministic system, but fatalism is false: Oedipus's beliefs and desires, plus the environment he was in, ensured that he would kill his father and marry his mother. But if he had had a different set of beliefs and desires, he would not have done this.

It is easy to confuse determinism and fatalism, even though they are very different ideas. In fact, they are almost opposite in what they say. Fatalism says that our beliefs and desires make no difference as far as what actions we perform and as far as what happens to us. In a sense, fatalism says that our beliefs and desires are impotent; they don't have the power to make a difference. But determinism, if we model it on the Newtonian idea, says that our beliefs and desires are not impotent; they causally control what we do and thereby powerfully influence what happens to us.

According to fatalism, there is no point in *trying* to do something. If it is fated that you will get an *A* in a course, you will get an *A* whether you try to get one or not; and if it is fated that you will get a *D*, you will, whether you try to avoid this fate or not. On the other hand, to think that your efforts influence what happens to you—to think that trying makes a difference to the grade you receive—is to reject fatalism.

Greek mythology talked about the Fates. I'll assume that there are no such things. I'll assume that fatalism is false. This leaves open the separate question of whether determinism is true. Most previous writers on the free will problem have assumed that causality requires determinism. I hope you see why I reject this connection; I think that causality is a fact about the world we inhabit, whether or not determinism turns out to be true.

## Review Questions

1. What is the Distant Causation Argument? What is the Could-Not-Have-Done-Otherwise Argument? What do these arguments have in common? How do they differ?
2. Two examples were given of unfree actions. What were they?
3. What does the thesis of determinism assert? What is indeterminism? How do these theses employ the concept of a "sufficient condition" and the concept of a "complete description"?
4. An unusual sort of brain surgery was described in this chapter. What was it and what relevance does it have to the problem of free will?
5. What is fatalism? Is it accurately described by the saying, "que sera, sera" ("whatever will be, will be")? How does fatalism differ from determinism?

## A Problem for Further Thought

Suppose the Fates decided to get Oedipus to kill his father and marry his mother by controlling what Oedipus thinks and wants. If this were so, how would determinism differ from fatalism?

## CHAPTER 25

# *A Menu of Positions on Free Will*

In this chapter, I'll present a menu of standard philosophical positions about the relationship of freedom and determinism. I then will make some critical remarks about some of the positions. This will set the stage for the positive proposal I'll make in the next chapter about how the idea of freedom of the will should be understood.

### "COMPATIBILITY" DEFINED

Before proceeding, I need to define a piece of terminology from logic. To say that two propositions are *compatible* is to say that the truth of one wouldn't rule out the truth of the other. Incompatibility means conflict; if one proposition were true, the other would have to be false. Two propositions can be compatible even though neither is, in fact, true. And two propositions can be incompatible even though both are false. Consider the following three statements:

(1) My shirt is green all over.

(2) My shirt is red all over.

(3) My shirt is torn.

Propositions (1) and (2) are incompatible. (1) and (3) are compatible. Do these two pieces of information tell you what color my shirt is? Do they tell you whether the shirt is torn? The answer to both questions is *no*.

## INCOMPATIBILISM AND COMPATIBILISM

*Incompatibilism* is a thesis about the problem of free will. It doesn't claim that determinism is true. It also doesn't claim that we are unfree. It merely asserts an if/then statement: *If determinism is true, then we aren't free.*

If two propositions (*D* and *F*) are incompatible, there are three possibilities: *D* is true and *F* is false; *D* is false and *F* is true; or *D* and *F* are both false. What is excluded by the claim of incompatibility is that both propositions are true. Of the three possible positions an incompatibilist can take, two have been prominent in philosophical discussion. The first holds that determinism is true and that we aren't free. This position has come to be called *hard determinism.* The second says that we are free and that our actions are not causally determined. This position is called *libertarianism.* These two positions agree that you freedom and determinism can't both be true, but they disagree about which proposition is true and which is false.

Opposed to incompatibilism is the idea that determinism does not rule out the possibility that we are free. This view, not surprisingly, is called *compatibilism.* In principle, there are four possible subvarieties of compatibilism. If propositions *D* and *F* are compatible, then the options are (1) *D* and *F* are both true; (2) *D* and *F* are both false; (3) *D* is true and *F* is false; or (4) *D* is false and *F* is true. Of these four possible positions, only one has been discussed much in the philosophical literature. This viewpoint is called *soft determinism;* it holds that our actions are both free and causally determined. The basic idea here is that freedom does not require the absence of determinism, but rather requires that our actions be caused in a particular way.

So the basic menu of standard positions is as follows:

I. Incompatibilism (if determinism is true, then we lack freedom).
   A. Hard Determinism: Incompatibilism and determinism are true, so we lack freedom.
   B. Libertarianism: Incompatibilism is true and we are free, so determinism is false.
   C.

II. Compatibilism (if determinism were true, that wouldn't rule out the possibility that we are free).

    A.  Soft Determinism: Compatibilism and determinism are true, and we are free.

    B, C, D.

Note that this outline leaves some possible positions unlabeled. Be sure you understand what the unlabeled options are. My own view falls in II.B; I'm a compatibilist. As explained in the previous chapter, I don't think one can assume that determinism is true. I do, however, think that some of our actions are performed freely. The kind of compatibilist position I endorse will be described in the next chapter.

The three labeled positions display three patterns of similarity and difference. Soft determinism and libertarianism agree that we are free, hard and soft determinism agree that determinism is true, and hard determinism and libertarianism agree that incompatibilism is correct. To understand how these three positions are related, we can schematize each as endorsing an argument. Let $F$ be the proposition that some of our actions are free and $D$ the proposition that determinism is true. Here is each position's characteristic argument:

| | |
|---|---|
| *Hard determinism:* | If $D$, then not-$F$ |
| | $D$ |
| | ——————— |
| | Not $F$ |
| *Libertarianism:* | If $D$, then not-$F$ |
| | $F$ |
| | ——————— |
| | Not $D$ |
| *Soft determinism:* | $F$ |
| | $D$ |
| | ——————— |
| | $F$ and $D$ are compatible |

Note that each of these arguments is deductively valid. Our task is to figure out which of the premises are plausible.


## LIBERTARIANISM

I'll begin by considering libertarianism. The philosopher C. A. Campbell (1897–1974) is the libertarian on whom I'll focus. Before I describe how Campbell defends libertarianism, let me note that "libertarianism" in the problem of free will is an entirely different doctrine from the idea that goes by that name in political philosophy. Libertarians in political philosophy argue that the state should not interfere in buying

---

### The Normative Problem of Freedom

Libertarianism, soft determinism, and hard determinism take different stances on the question of whether we, in fact, are free. They don't advance claims as to whether it is a good thing or a bad thing to be free. In other words, these theories concern *descriptive*, not *normative*, issues.

There is a separate issue about freedom that arises in political philosophy. It involves the question of which freedoms people have a right to. Do people have rights to particular liberties, which may not be violated by other individuals or by the state? This is a normative question about what people should and shouldn't do. It isn't the same as the question of whether people have free will.

Freedoms, in this normative sense, can come into conflict. Some defenders of capitalism hold that people should be free to engage in buying and selling without regulation by the state. However, this can result in "boom and bust" cycles that produce widespread suffering. If freedom from want is an entitlement that people have, then certain economic freedoms may have to be regulated or curtailed. This and other normative questions about the freedoms that people are entitled to will be discussed in the section of the text on ethics.

---

and selling or in other spheres of life. This is a *normative* view—a claim about the way things ought to be. On the other hand, libertarianism in the problem of free will is a *descriptive* claim, not a normative one. It asserts that we are free agents and that determinism is false. Libertarianism as a view about free will does not say whether it is good news or bad that we have free will.

Libertarians usually think they can tell by introspection that at least some of their actions aren't determined by the beliefs, desires, and other psychological characteristics they have. For example, Campbell, in his book *Selfhood and Godhood* (Allen and Unwin, 1957), focuses on the fact that we sometimes perform actions that are "out of character." When we do this, he says, it isn't true that our actions are determined by the characters we have.

I have two objections to this line of thinking. First, as noted in Chapter 13, there is no reason to place such complete trust in introspection. The beliefs we form about ourselves by "gazing within" can be both incomplete and inaccurate. They can be incomplete, because there may be facts about ourselves of which we aren't conscious—facts that introspection fails to detect. In addition, introspection can be inaccurate, because there are psychological mechanisms that systematically distort the way we appear to ourselves. Freud stressed both these ideas. In the latter category, he argued that some of the beliefs and desires we have would cause us great pain if we realized that we had them. As a "defense mechanism," introspection provides us with a false picture of what we really think and want. Although this view about introspection is characteristically Freudian, it is important to realize that many other approaches in psychology also endorse it. There is broad consensus that we shouldn't take the testimony of introspection at face value.

There is an additional difficulty with Campbell's view. He says that when we act out of character, our actions aren't determined by what our minds are like. I disagree. Consider a person who is usually cowardly but manages to act courageously on a given occasion. Is it plausible to think that the courageous act can't be explained by what the person's mind was like? I find this highly dubious. I suspect that there are aspects of the person's mind that came into play. Perhaps a combination of unusual circumstances led the person to muster his or her courage in a way that earlier had not been possible. So I really don't see that the actions we call "acting out of character" pose a problem for determinism. Campbell assumes that the phrase "acting out of character" means that the action isn't caused by the agent's character. But this is to misunderstand what the phrase means. When people who usually have been cowardly manage to act courageously, we might say "Evidently, they had it in them." This testifies to the fact that "acting out of character" isn't something we think of as uncaused.

Campbell accepts incompatibilism, thinks that introspection shows that we sometimes produce free acts, and so concludes that determinism must be false. I've suggested that this introspective argument against determinism is very weak. If you think that free will and determinism are incompatible, I don't see how the introspective impression we have that we are free can be decisive. The behaviorist psychologist B. F. Skinner, whose views I discussed in Chapter 21, wrote a book called *Beyond Freedom and Dignity* (Knopf, 1971). Skinner is an incompatibilist; in fact, he is a hard determinist. His view is that the introspective picture we have of ourselves as free agents is an illusion. It is a comforting idea—a fairy tale we tell ourselves. I don't agree with Skinner's hard determinism. My present point, however, is that I think Skinner is right not to take introspection at face value. Baron d'Holbach, another hard determinist, took the same view of introspection in the eighteenth century; an excerpt from his book, *The System of Nature*, is reprinted at the end of this section of the book.

If I thought that incompatibilism were true, I'd try to find out if human actions are determined. I would do this by seeing what science has to say about determinism and what psychology has to say about the causation of behavior. Campbell accepts incompatibilism, but argues in the opposite direction. He decides via introspection that some of our actions are free, and he concludes that our actions can't be causally determined. This, I think, is the wrong order in which to address the questions. Notice that Campbell's position, as I've presented it here, doesn't *argue* that incompatibilism is true. Rather, Campbell *assumes* that incompatibilism is true. He uses this as one of his premises to argue for the conclusion that our actions aren't causally determined.

## TWO SOFT DETERMINIST THEORIES

I turn now to the standard form that compatibilist theorizing takes—soft determinism. Soft determinist theories try to construct a plausible theory of what freedom is, one that shows why freedom is not ruled out by the alleged fact that our actions are determined. I think the two compatibilist theories I'll now consider are defective. However, they provide lessons concerning how a more successful compatibilist theory might be constructed.

The goal of a compatibilist theory is to show that an act is performed freely if it is caused in a particular sort of way; freedom doesn't require the absence of causality, but the right sort of causality. The goal is to make room for freedom in a world of causes.

## HUME

I'll begin with the compatibilist account of freedom advanced by David Hume. His idea was that an action is performed freely when the agent could have done otherwise, had the agent wanted to. Suppose you accept an employer's offer of a summer job. Hume says you act freely if you could have declined the offer had you wanted to. By the same token, when you hand the robber your wallet after the robber says, "Your money or your life," you do so of your own free will, if the following were true: Had you wanted to die rather than stay alive, you could have refused to hand over your wallet. So Hume's theory is that free actions are ones that are under the causal control of the agent's beliefs and desires. When an action is under the agent's control in this way, it will be true that if the agent had had a different set of wants, the agent would have selected and performed a different action. Hume's is a compatibilist theory because it says that an action is free if it is causally related to the agent's beliefs and desires in a particular way.

What would an *unfree* action be like, according to Hume's theory? Suppose you want to leave the room but you can't because you are handcuffed to the floor. In this case, you don't remain in the room freely. You stay in the room *whether you want to or not*. What you do is not under the control of your beliefs and desires.

Here is another example of unfreedom. Suppose I perform a brain operation on you. I disconnect your beliefs and desires from the nerves that send impulses to the rest of your body. I then implant a radio transmitter so that your body receives instructions from me. Now it is *my* beliefs and desires that dictate what *you* say and do. Your actions are no longer under the causal control of your own beliefs and desires. In this bizarre arrangement, your body would become a robot—a slave to my will. It would do what *I* want because I want it. We might observe you drinking water, depositing money into my bank account, and so on. But you wouldn't be doing these things of your own free will. Hume's theory explains why your actions are unfree in this case.

## FIRST OBJECTION TO HUME'S THEORY: COMPULSIVE BEHAVIOR

I think the main objection to Hume's theory is to be found in cases of *compulsive behavior.* Think of the kleptomaniac discussed in the previous chapter. A kleptomaniac is a thief whose desire to steal is overpoweringly strong. Kleptomaniacs want to steal though they may be completely convinced that they will be caught and punished. Even with full knowledge that stealing will hurt them rather than help, they continue to steal. Kleptomaniacs are caught in the grip of an obsession. They are slaves to a desire that isn't diminished by the realization that acting on the desire does them more harm than good. There are thieves who aren't kleptomaniacs, of course. When they decide whether to steal, their decision is affected by information about the chances of being caught and punished. None of this information makes any difference to a kleptomaniac. The kleptomaniac is *stuck;* his desire isn't sensitive in the familiar way to considerations about self-interest.

I claim that when kleptomaniacs steal, they are not doing so freely. Kleptomaniacs lack freedom of will with respect to the issue of whether they steal. Yet, kleptomaniacs satisfy Hume's requirements for what it takes to be free. Kleptomaniacs want, above all, to steal things. When a kleptomaniac steals, he does so because of the desires he has. If he hadn't wanted to steal, he wouldn't have done so. The kleptomaniac's actions are under the control of his beliefs and desires. The problem is that there is something about the desires themselves and the way they work that make the kleptomaniac unfree.

The causal diagram from the previous chapter can be used to illustrate why Hume's account of freedom looks for freedom in the wrong place:

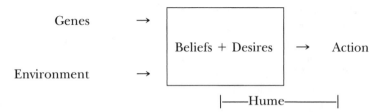

Hume's theory defines freedom in terms of a relation that obtains between beliefs and desires on the one hand and action on the other. For Hume, free actions are ones that are controlled by the agent's desires. The case of compulsive behavior provides an objection to Hume's account. It is the nature of the kleptomaniac's desires that makes him unfree. This suggests that a compatibilist theory shouldn't ignore the earlier links in the above causal chain.

## SECOND OBJECTION TO HUME'S THEORY: LOCKE'S LOCKED ROOM

There is a second, more subtle, problem with Hume's account. In his *Essay Concerning Human Understanding* (1690), John Locke (1632–1704) describes a man who decides to remain in a room in order to talk with a friend. Unbeknown to the man, the door of the room has been locked. The man remains in the room voluntarily, although it is false that he could have done otherwise had he chosen to do so. Locke's point is that an action can be voluntary even though the agent was not free to do otherwise. I want to add a comment about this example that Locke does not endorse. I think the man in the room stays there *of his own free will.* He freely chooses to stay in the room even though he is not free to exit it. If this is correct, Hume's theory is mistaken. For you to have performed some action of your own free will, it is not essential that you could have performed some other action if you had wanted to do so.

Here's another example that illustrates the same point. Take any action that an agent performed of his or her own free will. For example, suppose that Joe attended a concert last night of his own free will. Now imagine that if he hadn't decided to go to the concert, he would have been kidnapped and taken there against his will. Joe didn't know about this plot when he was deciding whether he would attend. The point is that Joe attended the concert of his own free will, even though he couldn't have done otherwise.

There is an important difference between the man locked in the room (though he doesn't know he is) and the kleptomaniac. The kleptomaniac's thought processes have malfunctioned; it is because of this malfunction that he does not steal of his own free will. But there is nothing wrong with the mind of the man in Locke's example. His will is free, although he isn't free to act in certain ways.

## DOES COERCION ROB US OF FREE WILL?

This contrast is important to bear in mind when you think about another important issue for the free will problem—coercion. Consider a robber who coerces you into handing over your cash by saying (convincingly), "Your money or your life." The robber has robbed you of your money. But has he also robbed you of your free will?

The robber presents you with an option—you can keep your money and die, or hand over your wallet and live. One option he has taken away from you is for you to keep your money *and* stay alive as well. You aren't free to do that. But has the robber robbed you of your free will?

This is a hard problem, but let me tentatively venture this answer: In many cases (if not in all), coerced actions don't rob their victims of free will. Of course, they can rob their victims of many things that are precious. And, of course, it often is wrong to place people in situations in which they have the choices (and only the choices) that the robber offers them. My point, however, is that the robbery victim's calculation—that he is better off surrendering the wallet—is very different from the kleptomaniac's "decision" to steal. The robbery victim's mind is functioning well; it is the circumstances in which the victim finds himself that are objectionable. In contrast, something has gone wrong with the kleptomaniac's mind, and it is this mental incapacity that makes him unfree.

## A SECOND COMPATIBILIST PROPOSAL: THE RELEVANCE OF SECOND-ORDER DESIRES

I now want to consider a second compatibilist theory, one that is intended to meet the problem posed by compulsive behavior. This theory has been defended by Gerald Dworkin (in "Acting Freely," *Nous,* Vol. 4, 1970, pp. 367–383) and by Harry Frankfurt (in "Freedom of the Will and the Concept of a Person," *Journal of Philosophy,* Vol. 68, 1971, pp. 5–20). The idea is that people in the grip of a compulsion are unfree because they act on the basis of desires they would rather not have. Suppose you asked a kleptomaniac whether he would prefer to not have an overpowering desire to steal. The kleptomaniac might sadly reply that he would be glad to have this monkey off his back.

The proposal we are considering requires us to distinguish first-order from second-order desires. A second-order desire is a desire about what one's desires should be like. "I'd like to be less selfish" is a second-order remark. It says that I would like to care more about the welfare of others. "I'd like to have an ice cream" or "I'd like Jones to get a raise" are first-order desires. They express desires about what should be true in the world outside one's own mind. So the proposal is that people act freely when their second-order desires are related in a specific way to their first-order desires. To do an action *A* of one's own free will is to do *A* because one has desires *D,* where one doesn't mind having *D.* This last clause means that one doesn't have the second-order desire that *D* be dropped from one's list of first-order desires.

Although this proposal implies that many people who are in the grip of compulsions are unfree, it still is defective. Imagine a kleptomaniac who is so warped by his compulsion that he can't even recognize that it is harming him. Imagine a compulsive handwasher who has been brainwashed into thinking that handwashing is the greatest thing in the world. Such individuals may not mind having the desires they have. That, however, doesn't show they have free will; it shows only that they don't mind being unfree. This theory of freedom, like Hume's, fails to explain why some forms of compulsive behavior are unfree. This doesn't mean that no compatibilist theory will work, just that the two I've just examined aren't satisfactory. In the next chapter, I outline a third compatibilist account.

---

## Review Questions

1. What does it mean to say that *X* and *Y* are compatible? What does incompatibility mean? What do *X* and *Y* stand for?
2. Define compatibilism, incompatibilism, hard determinism, libertarianism, and soft determinism.
3. What argument have libertarians given for thinking some actions are free? Assess this argument.
4. In the *Fourth Meditation,* Descartes argues that the will is infinite (that is, unlimited, and so absolutely free) as follows:

   > I know from experience that it [my will or freedom of choice] is not restricted in any way. . . . This is because the will simply consists in our ability to do or not do something (that is, to affirm or deny, to pursue or avoid); or rather, it consists simply in the fact that when the intellect puts something forward for affirmation or denial or for pursuit or avoidance, our inclinations are such that we do not feel we are determined by any external force.

   What is Descartes' argument? Evaluate its plausibility.
5. Explain Hume's theory of freedom. What makes it a compatibilist theory? Why does compulsive behavior provide a counterexample to this theory? Why does Locke's example of the man locked in the room provide a counterexample to

Hume's theory? Hume suggests necessary and sufficient conditions for freedom. Which of these objections shows the conditions aren't necessary? Which shows they are not sufficient?

6. Are the following propositions equivalent in meaning? (I) *S* did *A* of her own free will; (II) *S* was free to not do *A*.

7. In Chapter 12, I explained that a definition can be defective because it fails to provide necessary conditions, or because it fails to provide sufficient conditions. What sort of defect in Hume's definition of freedom is involved in (1) the example of compulsive behavior; (2) the example of the locked room?

## Problems for Further Thought

1. In the selection from Campbell's *Selfhood and Godhood* reprinted at the end of this section of the book, Campbell argues that some actions occur neither by chance nor by necessity. These are examples of *creative activity*, "in which [ ... ] nothing determines the act save the agent's doing it." According to Campbell, these are the acts that are free. Define what "chance" and "necessity" mean, taking into account the definitions of determinism and indeterminism provided in the previous chapter. Do your definitions allow that some actions may fall into neither category?

2. Political philosophers have often been interested in describing how much freedom of action a society allows its members. Would it be reasonable to measure this by determining how many of a person's desires are satisfiable in the society? There is an objection to this proposal similar to the objection I've formulated to the Dworkin/Frankfurt theory of freedom. What is it?

3. How does the idea of circumstantial necessity introduced in Chapter 14 apply to the present chapter?

## CHAPTER 26

# *Compatibilism*

In the previous chapter, I presented and criticized two compatibilist theories of freedom. Each sought to show that freedom doesn't require the absence of causality; both say that an action is free when it arises by a certain sort of causal process. In this chapter, I present a third compatibilist theory, one inspired by an idea suggested by my colleagues Dennis Stampe and Martha Gibson (in their "Of One's Own Free Will," *Philosophy and Phenomenological Research*, Vol. 52, 1992, pp. 529–556). After presenting a simplified version of this theory, I'll describe an objection to it.

I won't propose a way of meeting this objection, but will leave the problem of freedom unsolved. However, I do hope to convince you that compatibilism is a plausible view, even though I don't claim that a completely plausible compatibilist theory has yet been articulated.

## THE WEATHER VANE ANALOGY

I'll begin with an analogy. Consider a weather vane. This is a device that farmers put on top of their barns to tell them in which direction the wind is blowing. We talk about weather vanes being "stuck." We also talk about weather vanes being "free." What does this mean?

A free weather vane is one that responds to certain causal influences. If the wind is blowing north, a free weather vane will point north. The behavior of a free weather vane isn't uncaused. A stuck weather vane, on the other hand, doesn't respond to the wind's direction. When a weather vane is stuck pointing due north, there is a causal explanation for why it is pointing in that direction. The explanation, however, has nothing to do with the direction of the wind. So the difference between a free weather vane and a stuck one isn't that the position of the former is uncaused, whereas the position of the latter has a causal explanation. Both are caused to point in a certain direction by something or other. The difference isn't in *whether* the behavior is caused, but in *what* causes it.

I've just described the ordinary meaning of "free" when it is applied to weather vanes. Notice that our commonsense understanding of this idea involves a compatibilist theory of what it is for a weather vane to be free. The idea is to use this as an analogy for constructing a compatibilist theory of what it is for the will to be free. Of course, weather vanes don't have minds, whereas the issue of freedom of the will has to do with a feature of the mind. Let's press on, however, and see if the analogy can be developed.

## FUNCTION AND MALFUNCTION

Why do we say that the vane is free when it is causally responsive to the wind's direction? Why don't we describe a weather vane whose swivel is rusted solid as free, since in that case the direction it points isn't influenced by the wind? A stuck weather vane, after all, is free from the wind's influences. I suggest that the answer is to be found in the fact that the weather vane has a *function*. When it performs its function, its behavior is caused by the wind's direction. When it is stuck, it can't perform its function.

How can this idea about function be applied to the human mind? If we think of different parts of the mind as having functions, then freedom of the will exists if the mind is functioning properly. A malfunction, on the other hand, may result in a "stuck" will—one that is unfree.

Consider the following diagram, which shows how beliefs and desires are formed and then lead, via deliberation, to intentions and thence to action:

The box labeled "BGD" is the belief-generating device. It is the part of the mind that produces beliefs. Beliefs are its output. The belief-generating device takes account of evidence (other beliefs and experiences); these are its inputs. The BGD malfunctions when it isn't sensitive to evidence—when it outputs beliefs in a way that ignores the evidence at hand. Perhaps paranoia—the irrational and unshakable conviction that the whole world is conspiring against you—can be described as a malfunction of the BGD. In this situation, the person's beliefs are "stuck." The BGD has malfunctioned because it isn't responsive to evidence.

The DGD is the desire-generating device. It produces desires. Its inputs are the things that cause us to have the desires we do. I've put a question mark where the inputs to the DGD go; the inputs to this device are the things the device is sensitive to when it is functioning properly. Later, I'll discuss what function the DGD might have.

The BGD and the DGD output beliefs and desires, which are fed into a device that carries out deliberations. This device takes into account the agent's beliefs and desires and decides on the basis of them what the agent should do. This device completes its work when the agent forms the intention to perform some action.

By analogy with the weather vane, a person has free will when the various components involved in the process described in the diagram are functioning properly. Proper functioning is to be understood to mean that the BGD and the DGD are sensitive to certain sorts of causal influences.

## WHAT DOES IT MEAN TO ASCRIBE A FUNCTION TO SOMETHING?

Before we can develop this idea much further, we must have some idea of what the word "function" means. In the case of the weather vane, we know what the function of the object is, because it was created by human beings for a certain purpose. If farmers put such objects on their barns for purely ornamental reasons, we might not regard them as malfunctioning when their swivels rust solid. But farmers want weather vanes to respond to the wind's direction; this is their intended function.

If the human mind were created by an Intelligent Designer, and if we could find out why that Designer gave people the kinds of minds they have, we could say what functions the mind and its components subserve. However, if we want a naturalistic, not a theological, account of what it is for parts of the mind to have functions, we must set this idea about an Intelligent Designer (God) to one side.

Consider an analogous problem. We say that the function of the heart is to pump blood. What makes this true? After all, the heart does lots of things. It takes up space in your chest cavity. It also makes noise. But we don't say that the function of the heart is to take up space or to make noise. The problem is that the heart has many effects, but only some of these effects are what the heart is *for*—what it has as its function. If the heart were created by an Intelligent Designer, that would solve our problem. The Designer's intentions would settle what the function of the heart is. But I'll assume that we want a naturalistic, not a theological, account of heart function. We want to make sense of the idea of function without having to rely on the existence of an Intelligent Designer.

My proposal is that we understand the biological function of the heart in terms of the historical explanation of why people and other organisms have hearts. The reason hearts evolved is that they provided a benefit to the organisms possessing them. The benefit was that hearts pumped blood. As a side effect of the evolution of such blood pumps, it turned out that organisms had noise makers in their chests. But the heart didn't evolve because it made noise. Making noise provided no advantage for survival and reproduction.

Here, then, is a naturalistic account of what it is for an object (or characteristic) to have a function. We don't have to imagine that the object is present because of Intelligent Design. Natural selection (discussed in Chapter 6) is a perfectly satisfactory mechanism. My proposal is that "the function of $o$ is to do $F$" means that $o$ is present because $o$'s do $F$. The function of the heart is to pump blood (rather than make noise), since individuals have hearts because hearts pump blood (not because they make noise). (For elaboration of this way of understanding the concept of function, see Larry Wright, "Functions," *Philosophical Review*, Vol. 85, 1973, pp. 70–86.)

## THE FUNCTION OF THE DESIRE-GENERATING DEVICE

Why do individuals have desires? More specifically, why do individuals have devices (DGDs) that construct desires? What use could this faculty have had in our evolutionary past? The suggestion I want to consider is that the DGD has the function of representing what is good for the organism. Consider the case of thirst. When an organism gets dehydrated, it would be good for the organism to get some water. Organisms with minds seek out water when they are dehydrated because their DGD produces a desire for water. Like any device, the DGD might malfunction; if it fails to produce a desire for water when the organism is dehydrated, this could handicap the organism in its struggle to survive.

Bear in mind that there are other ways besides forming desires to get organisms to perform actions that satisfy their biological needs. Bacteria are capable of behaviors that satisfy their needs, but they don't have minds (or desires) to help them do this. The suggestion, then, is that the DGD has the function of representing what would be good for the organism; it isn't part of this suggestion that a DGD is the only way to get an organism to act so as to satisfy its needs.

Recall what this claim about the function of the DGD actually means. It means that we possess DGDs because, historically, such devices represented what was good for the organisms that possessed them; organisms with such devices did better at surviving and reproducing than ones that lacked them (or had DGDs that were constructed differently). If this is right, we can understand why individuals who are in the grip of a compulsion aren't free. Their DGD is stuck; it is malfunctioning because it no longer can represent what would be good for the agent. Kleptomaniacs want to steal even though stealing isn't good for them; indeed, kleptomaniacs sometimes want to steal even when they *know* that it isn't good for them to have this want. Likewise, a compulsive handwasher has an overpowering desire to keep washing his hands even though there is ample evidence available that this is a harm, not a help.

A similar explanation can be given for why brainwashing is able to rob people of their freedom. When people are brainwashed, they are given beliefs and desires on which they subsequently act. These beliefs and desires are "implanted" by short-circuiting the normal function of the belief- and desire-generating devices. The process of brainwashing causes the BGD and the DGD to malfunction. This is why individuals who are brainwashed to perform some action don't perform that action of their own free will.

So my proposal about freedom is this: An agent freely performs an action if the agent's mind is functioning properly. This includes the idea that the agent's DGD is able to perform the function of representing what is good for the agent. In addition, the idea of well-functioning includes the idea that the agent can rationally deliberate, given the beliefs and desires he or she has.

Although the present proposal and Hume's idea are both compatibilist theories, they are different. Hume thought the crucial consideration was whether the agent's desires control the agent's behavior. The idea I've just described says that it is the entire psychological process—from belief and desire formation through the formation of an intention to act—that settles whether the agent's action is free.

I now want to consider what the present theory of freedom would say in reply to the arguments described in Chapter 24. Each of these arguments, recall, aimed to show that we can't be free, because of some fact about how our beliefs, desires, and actions are caused.

## REPLY TO THE DISTANT CAUSATION ARGUMENT

I turn first to the Distant Causation Argument, which I represent as follows:

(1) If an agent freely performs an action, then the agent is responsible for the action.

(2) Agents are not responsible for actions that are caused by factors outside their control.

(3) Every action an agent performs is caused by factors (genes and early childhood environments) over which the agent had no control.

———————

No action is performed freely.

The compatibilist theory of freedom advanced in this chapter (the "Weather Vane Theory") must reject this argument. But how? The argument is deductively valid.

(Identify its logical form.) Therefore, if the conclusion is false, one or more of the premises must be false.

## WHAT DOES RESPONSIBILITY MEAN?

To reply to this argument, I need to examine the concept of *responsibility*. Consider what it means to say that a storm was responsible for some crop damage. Here "responsible for" simply means "causes."

If we use this understanding of the concept of responsibility to clarify premise (2) of the Distant Causation Argument, we can see that premise (2) is false. A storm can cause crop damage even though there were causes of the crop damage that the storm didn't control. Consider the following causal chain:

$$X \longrightarrow \text{Storm} \longrightarrow \text{Crop damage}$$

The storm was caused by earlier events $X$, which existed before the storm occurred. If causation is transitive (see the box on transitivity in Chapter 24), $X$ caused the crop damage. The storm didn't exercise any influence over $X$, since $X$ happened before the storm even existed. But this does not entail that the storm didn't cause the crop damage.

So the fact that the crop damage had "distant causes" doesn't mean that the storm wasn't responsible for the crop damage. By the same token, I conclude that premise (2) in the Distant Causation Argument is false.

## MORAL RESPONSIBILITY

It might be replied, in defense of the Distant Causation Argument, that "responsibility" isn't the simple causal concept I've just described. After all, if Patty Hearst was brainwashed by her kidnappers, we might say that she wasn't responsible for robbing the bank. This doesn't mean, however, that she played no causal role in the robbery.

If the storm wasn't responsible for the crop damage, this means that the storm didn't cause the damage. But if Patty Hearst wasn't responsible for what she did, this doesn't mean that she didn't do what she did. What, then, is the difference? We sometimes say that we don't "hold" people responsible for some of the things they do. In contrast, it sounds funny to say that we don't hold the storm responsible for what it did. Holding $X$ responsible, and deciding not to hold $X$ responsible, implies that we regard $X$ as a moral agent.

When we say that we don't hold Patty Hearst responsible for what she did, I think we mean that we don't *blame* her for her action. We don't think she deserves moral criticism for the robbery if she did it while brainwashed. If an agent is *morally responsible* for an event (a bank robbery, say), this means (1) that the agent caused the event; and (2) that the occurrence of the event reflects on the agent's moral character. Moral responsibility differs from the simpler idea of causal responsibility; it is this latter concept that we apply to storms, there being no implication of moral praise and blame in such cases.

Suppose we interpret the Distant Causation Argument to be talking about moral responsibility in the sense just described. Understood in this way, premise (2) is still false. We are morally responsible for many (if not all) of the actions we perform, though the beliefs and desires that cause those actions are themselves results of factors outside our control. The reason is that much of what we do shows what sort of moral character we have.

To say that someone is morally responsible for doing something wrong doesn't automatically mean that he or she should be punished. Unfortunately, the law often seems to connect these two issues. If members of the jury think that Patty Hearst shouldn't be punished for robbing the bank, they must find that she wasn't responsible for what she did. There is a question here that needs to be faced head on, however, one that shouldn't be allowed to slip by. Suppose someone does something wrong, and we take this to indicate a defect in the person's moral character. Maybe the rather minor lies that people tell have this feature. But surely we don't want to pass laws that say that anyone who lies will go to jail or pay a fine. The reason might be that this legalistic apparatus would intrude into private life so much that society would be worse rather than better as a result. We hold people responsible when they do such things, but this doesn't mean we think they should be punished.

The Distant Causation Argument tries to make it look like agents have nothing to do with the actions they perform—as if it is people's genes and environments that cause their actions, *rather than the agents themselves*. But this is absurd—*we* cause things to happen and these actions reflect on our characters, even though there are causal explanations for why we are the way we are.

## REPLY TO THE COULD-NOT-HAVE-DONE-OTHERWISE ARGUMENT

A second argument was presented in Chapter 24 that attempts to show that we lack free will. This is the Could-Not-Have-Done-Otherwise Argument, which can be represented as follows:

(1) If an agent freely performs some action $A$, then the agent could have done otherwise (that is, could have performed some action other than $A$).

(2) People can't perform actions other than the ones they do, in fact, perform.

———————————

Agents never act freely.

Since I believe that the conclusion of this argument is false, I must reject one or both of the premises.

Actually I think that both are defective. Premise (1) is mistaken for reasons that Locke brought out in his discussion of the man who decides of his own free will to remain in a room to talk to a friend; unbeknownst to him, the door was locked. This was discussed in the previous chapter. Premise (2) also should be examined carefully. In Chapter 14, I formulated an idea that I called the thesis of the ambiguity of necessity. Statements about necessity and possibility often are ambiguous. The example I discussed there was the statement "Joe can't tie his shoes." Interpreted one way, the statement is true (Joe is holding two bags of groceries). Interpreted in another way, the statement is false (if he put down the groceries, he could do it).

I think premise (2) in the above argument is ambiguous. It could mean either of the following:

(2a)  Given the very beliefs and desires the agent had, and given that the agent rationally deliberated, he could not have performed a different action from the one he did.

(2b)  Even if the agent had had a different set of beliefs and desires, the agent still could not have produced an action different from the one he did.

Proposition (2a) basically says that rational deliberation is a deterministic process—beliefs and desires determine a unique choice of action, if those beliefs and desires are rationally evaluated. Since I don't think that determinism is true, I doubt that (2a) is correct. Even if it were correct, however, I don't see why that would show that we are never free. Even if weather vanes were deterministic systems, that wouldn't show that they are never free. I believe the same holds true of the human mind.

Proposition (2b) denies that the agent's beliefs and desires make a difference; (2b) says that the agent would have done the same thing even if the agent had had different beliefs and desires. I think that this statement is false—it is basically the doctrine of fatalism, which I discussed and set aside in Chapter 24.

In summary, proposition (2) is ambiguous. If it is clarified to mean proposition (2a), then it fails to show that we are unfree. If it is clarified to mean proposition (2b), then it is false. I conclude that the Could-Not-Have-Done-Otherwise Argument fails to show that freedom is an illusion.

## ARE COERCED ACTIONS UNFREE?

The Distant Causation Argument and the Could-Not-Have-Done-Otherwise Argument don't refute compatibilism in general or the Weather Vane Theory in particular. I now want to consider an objection that is aimed specifically at the Weather Vane Theory. It criticizes the theory for what the theory says about coerced action.

It seems natural to say that coerced acts aren't performed freely. However, when the robber coerces you into surrendering your wallet, it doesn't seem to be true that your mind has malfunctioned. You correctly realize it is in your best interest to hand over your wallet, and so that is what you do. Action under coercion is often no different from other, less dramatic, actions produced by rational deliberation, at least as far as the inner workings of the mind are concerned. So if coerced actions are always unfree, the Weather Vane Theory is in trouble, since the theory says that we act freely when our minds are functioning properly.

My reply is to claim that coercion doesn't rob an individual of free will. I think that when you hand your wallet to the robber because you want to stay alive, your will is functioning perfectly well. Your situation here is different from that of a kleptomaniac or compulsive handwasher, whose DGDs have malfunctioned.

Maybe there are *some* cases of coercion that rob people of their free will. Suppose that the robber's threat frightens you so much that you totally lose your capacity to think clearly. You are so overcome by fear that you hand over your wallet, but not for any good reason. In this case, perhaps the coerced action is unfree. However, I think that many (perhaps most) cases of coercion aren't like this. People in such situations rarely "lose their heads"; often they show a considerable degree of care and self-control (you gingerly hand over your wallet, all the while assuring the robber that you

---

### What Is Coercion?

The robber says, "Your money or your life." You would prefer to stay alive without forfeiting your money, but that option isn't available. The choice is clear, and so you hand over the money.

You are in a grocery store and want a loaf of bread. The grocer will let you have the loaf only if you pay $3. You would prefer to have the loaf without handing over the money, but that option isn't available. The choice is clear, and so you hand over the money.

The robber has coerced you; the grocer has not. What is the difference?

There is a moral difference: What the robber did was wrong, but the grocer did nothing wrong. However, this doesn't seem to define what coercion is. You can coerce people for morally impeccable reasons. Suppose you are using a life preserver for a pillow and I need to throw the preserver to someone who is drowning. If you refuse to hand it over willingly, I may have to coerce you. But in coercing you, I've done nothing wrong.

There is a difference in magnitude: In the robbery example, you want to stay alive far more than you want to hold onto your wallet. In the grocer case, you would rather get the loaf than keep the $3, but the difference between these outcomes is far less momentous. Does this mean that coercion means putting people in situations in which it makes a great deal of difference to them what they do? Suppose I offer you $1,000 if you smile. Have I coerced you into smiling? You would much rather have the money and smile than forego the money and not smile. That doesn't make my offer coercive, however.

Some years ago, there was a program of testing new drugs in prisons. Prisoners would receive time off their sentences if they agreed to run the risk of being guinea pigs. The program was discontinued, partly because the offer was thought to be coercive. Do you agree that this offer would be coercive?

Let's return to the original question: What distinguishes the grocer from the robber? What, in short, is coercion?

have no intention of resisting). I conclude that a coerced action doesn't have to involve the will's being unfree.

## AN OBJECTION TO THE WEATHER VANE THEORY: FREE, RATIONAL SELF-SACRIFICE

Although the three objections I've just discussed don't undermine the Weather Vane Theory of Freedom, the one I'll discuss now poses a serious challenge. According to the Weather Vane Theory, the function of the desire-generating device (DGD) is to produce desires that represent what is good for the agent. I want to argue that this thesis is either too vague or is mistaken, if we consider the case of *rational self-sacrifice.*

Consider people who calmly and rationally decide to sacrifice their own interests to help others (perhaps their family or friends or nation). A soldier, for example, decides to throw himself on a grenade in order to save the lives of his comrades. Is it possible for a soldier to do this of his own free will?

I would say *yes*, but what does the Weather Vane Theory say? We have to ask whether the DGD is functioning properly here. Does the desire that it produces—the desire to sacrifice the agent's life to save the lives of his comrades—really represent what is good for the agent? Interpreted in one way, the answer seems to be *no*. The self-sacrifice would be good for others, not good for the soldier himself. If the DGD has the function of representing what is good for the agent, then it seems to have malfunctioned in this instance.

The other alternative is to interpret the account given of the function of the DGD so that the soldier's DGD isn't malfunctioning in this case. We might say that the soldier's DGD *is* representing what is good for him to do, since he believes a moral principle that says that this sort of self-sacrifice is morally required. But now "representing what is good for the agent" is being interpreted to mean "representing what the agent *thinks* is good." The problem with this way of understanding the function of the DGD is that the kleptomaniac who thinks that stealing is the best thing in the world also will be said to have a well-functioning DGD.

This suggests, I think, that the description I've been using of the DGD needs to be modified. I don't think rational self-sacrifice indicates that the individual's will is unfree. According to the Weather Vane Theory, this requires that the individual's DGD not have malfunctioned. To be able to say this, however, we need to revise the description of what the function of the DGD is.

This is all I'll say about the problem of freedom of the will. I hope you now understand what a compatibilist theory of freedom would be like. Even though the Weather Vane Theory isn't satisfactory as it stands, this theory, I think, suggests that there may be some merit in the compatibilist position. There does seem to be a difference between people engaged in normal rational deliberation and people who are caught in the grip of a compulsion. The Weather Vane Theory seeks to characterize what this difference is. It remains an open question in philosophy how the concept of freedom of the will should be understood.

## Review Questions

1. In this chapter, I sketched a commonsense picture of what it means to say that a weather vane is "free." What is this commonsense idea? Why say that it is compatibilist in character?
2. A weather vane has a function because it was designed by people to do something. What could it mean to say that the heart functions to pump blood, if the heart isn't the product of Intelligent Design?
3. What is the difference between saying that *X* is causally responsible for *Y* (as in "The storm was responsible for the crop damage") and saying that *X* is morally responsible for *Y*?
4. What is mistaken in the Distant Causation Argument and in the Could-Not-Have-Done-Otherwise Argument?
5. Are coerced actions performed freely? What consequence does the answer to this question have for the Weather Vane Theory?
6. What problem does the existence of rational self-sacrifice pose for the Weather Vane Theory?

## Problems for Further Thought

1. In Chapter 5 on the Argument from Design, I said that Aristotle's teleological conception of the universe has been rejected by modern science. People, tools, and nonhuman organisms are goal-directed systems, but it seems implausible to think of a mountain or the solar system in this way. In the present chapter, I presented an account of what it means to ascribe a function to something. How does this account help explain why it is mistaken, for example, to say that the function of rain is to provide farm crops with water?
2. Can the Weather Vane Theory of Freedom be revised so that it avoids the counterexample presented here of free, rational self-sacrifice? How might this be done?

## CHAPTER 27

# *Psychological Egoism*

In earlier chapters, I've used a standard and commonsense model of what rational deliberation is. This model was employed in the discussion of Pascal's Wager (Chapter 10) and in the three chapters (24–26) on the free will problem. The idea is that rational deliberators decide what to do by taking account of their beliefs and desires. This commonsense idea has been made precise by the science called decision theory; rational agents are said to "maximize expected utility." This idea seems to lead to the conclusion that people are fundamentally selfish: They act so as to achieve the goals they have—they act to get what they want. Not only is this true of a person we would ordinarily call selfish—for example, a business executive whose only goal is to make as much money as possible. The idea seems to apply to everybody. Even Mother Teresa, who devoted her life to helping the needy in India, would count as selfish, according to this idea. It is true that Mother Teresa didn't strive for wealth or material comfort. Her values placed fundamental importance on reducing the amount of suffering in the world. However, in devoting her life to this, she aimed at satisfying her own goals. Mother Teresa gained satisfaction from her work, just as business executives gain satisfaction from theirs. If Mother Teresa had done something else with her life, she would have felt guilty. Mother Teresa's payoff came from reducing the suffering of others; she gained a feeling of satisfaction and avoided the guilt feelings she would have experienced if she had done something else. Business executives also gain satisfaction; theirs comes in the currency of dollars and cents. The idea is that both act on the basis of their own wants; both do what they do in order to gain a feeling of satisfaction (and to avoid negative feelings like guilt).

The previous paragraph expresses in an imprecise way the idea I'll call psychological egoism (PE, for short). In this chapter, I clarify what PE says and argue that in some important ways it is false. I won't reject the model of decision making used so far—that rational agents act on the basis of the beliefs and desires they have. However, I'll argue that PE does not follow from this model. Even though Mother Teresa tried to get what she wanted, just as the ruthless business executive does, there yet may be important differences between them. I'll try to clarify what these are.

## TWO TRUISMS

I want to formulate what PE says more precisely. Let's begin by identifying two propositions that are not in dispute. The debate over whether PE is true is *not* settled by the following facts:

(1) Rational agents decide which action to perform by consulting their beliefs and desires.

(2) At times, rational agents are guided by desires that are other-directed.

Proposition (1) describes the model of rational deliberation I've been assuming. It says nothing about what the *content* is of people's desires; it doesn't say *what* people want. Statement (1) says that whatever it is that a rational agent wants, that agent's behavior will be aimed at achieving those goals. The debate over PE isn't settled by (1); (1) is a "truism" to which defenders and critics of PE can agree. Proposition (2) also is a truism. It says that people often have desires that concern the situations of others. A benevolent person may want others to suffer less. A sadist may want others to suffer more. Both of these individuals have what I'll call *other-directed preferences*. It makes a difference to them what the situations of other people are like.

I'll use the term "other-directed preference" to refer to preferences that people have about the situations of others, preferences that don't mention their own situation. If I prefer that *others suffer less rather than more,* this is an other-directed preference that I have; note that the italicized words, which specify the content of the preference, refer to others, but not to me. Similarly, a *self-directed preference* is any preference I have that refers to my own well-being, but does not say anything about the situation of others. If I prefer that *I have more money rather than less,* this is a self-directed preference that I have. Some preferences are neither purely self-directed nor purely other-directed. They are *mixed.* If I want to be the best chess player in the world, this is a preference whose content refers both to me and to others.

Proposition (2) does not refute PE. I might genuinely desire that your back gets scratched, but I would be an egoist if my only reason for wanting this is that I see it as a way to have my back get scratched as well. PE does not deny the existence of other-directed preferences. Rather, PE asserts that when we want others to do well (or ill), we don't care about others for their own sakes; the only reason we care about what happens to them is that we think that their welfare will affect our own welfare. PE maintains that concern for others is *purely instrumental, never ultimate.*

## GOALS AND SIDE EFFECTS OF AN ACT

The philosopher/psychologist William James (1842–1910), whose ideas about "the will to believe" we examined in Chapter 10 on Pascal's Wager, discusses PE in his influential book *The Principles of Psychology* (London, Henry Holt, 1890). He notes a fact about PE that we should consider. James points out (as did Aristotle) that an action may bring a feeling of satisfaction to an agent without the action's having been done in order to obtain the feeling. James thought that many altruistic acts are of this sort. We help people because we genuinely care about their situations. It happens that our helping others is accompanied by our receiving a glow of satisfaction. But, according to James, obtaining the glow is not the goal; it is an unintended side effect. James thinks that the glow of satisfaction we get when we see others benefit from our help is no more the goal of our action than is burning coal the goal of sailing steamships across the Atlantic.

If James were right, PE would be false. A defender of PE, however, would deny part of what James is saying. A defender of PE might say that James has the story precisely backward. It is true that an action can produce an effect that isn't the real goal of the action. But a psychological egoist might say that when we help others, what we really are after is the glow of satisfaction; the fact that others receive a benefit is merely a side effect of our trying to make ourselves feel good. There is a point of agreement between James and this defender of PE. Although they disagree over which effect of the helping behavior is the goal and which is the mere side effect, they agree that there is a difference between the two. So let's identify a third proposition on which the two sides concur:

> (3) That an action has a particular effect does not necessarily mean that it was performed in order to produce that effect.

It is easy to see why (3) is correct, quite apart from the issue of whether PE is true.


## A SIMPLE EXAMPLE

In order to clarify what PE asserts, I want to focus on a simple example. You see an advertisement in a magazine. It asks you to send a check for $10 to help starving children. You are fairly well-off. You could find enjoyable things to do with the $10, but the picture in the ad is pathetic. You believe that a $10 contribution will make a real difference for the people involved (it won't solve the whole problem, of course). You think for a moment and then put a $10 check in the mail to the charity.

In this case, were you an altruist or an egoist? On the surface, it may appear that you were altruistically motivated. After all, it seems that you wrote the check because you felt a genuine concern for the starving children. An advocate of PE, however, would maintain that your real motives, of which you perhaps aren't fully conscious, were purely selfish. You derived a glow of satisfaction—a nice feeling about yourself—from the donation. You also avoided feeling guilty. These psychological benefits were the *real* motives for your behavior, or so PE asserts.

To decide what your motivation was in this situation, I want to describe four kinds of people. Three of them have altruistic motives; one of them has only egoistic motives. After I've explained these four possibilities, I'll consider how we might go about deciding which of the four categories you occupy.


## FOUR PREFERENCE STRUCTURES

The first type of individual I'll call the Pure Egoist. This individual cares nothing for the welfare of others; the only thing that matters to a Pure Egoist is his or her own situation.

The following two-by-two table illustrates the preferences of the Pure Egoist. The table answers two questions about this individual. What preference does he have as to whether he will receive a benefit? What preference does he have as to whether the children do better rather than worse? The first question has to do with his self-directed preferences; the second concerns his other-directed preferences.

The Pure Egoist

Other-directed

|  |  | + | − |
|---|---|---|---|
|  | + | 4 | 4 |
| Self-directed |  |  |  |
|  | − | 1 | 1 |

The Pure Egoist cares only that he himself receive more (+) rather than less (−) of whatever the benefit is that is at issue. It is a matter of indifference to this person whether the children do better (+) or worse (−). This individual isn't benevolent; he also isn't malevolent. He simply does not care one way or the other about others.

The numbers in this table represent the order of the agent's preferences. The absolute values have no meaning; I could as easily have used "9" and "5" instead of "4" and "1."

If you were a Pure Egoist, would you give $10 to charity? Donating the money would have two effects. You would receive a glow of satisfaction; and the children would be made better off. On the other hand, not donating the money also would have two effects. You would feel guilty about yourself; and the children would be worse off. (For simplicity, I'm ignoring how you feel about retaining $10 or giving it away.) In this situation, there are two possible actions, whose consequences are represented in the table by the upper-left entry (+ to self and + to other) and the entry in the lower-right (− to self and − to other). In this situation, the Pure Egoist will choose the first action; he will donate the $10 to charity. He therefore will choose an action that benefits others. This benefit to others, however, is not the goal of his action, but rather is a mere side effect. If you were a Pure Egoist, you would help the starving children, but your real motive would be to make yourself feel good.

The second personality type is the mirror image of the Pure Egoist. It is the Pure Altruist:

The Pure Altruist

Other-directed

|  |  | + | − |
|---|---|---|---|
|  | + | 4 | 1 |
| Self-directed |  |  |  |
|  | − | 4 | 1 |

This individual cares nothing about his own situation, but only wants the other person to be better off. What would a Pure Altruist do if he had to choose between the actions represented by the entries in the upper-left and lower-right cells of the table? He either must benefit both self and other, or benefit neither. Notice that the Pure Altruist will choose the action that benefits both himself and the other person. If you were a Pure Altruist, you would donate the money to charity. A consequence of doing this would be that you would feel good about yourself. However, in this case, the benefit to self would be a side effect of the act, not the act's real motive.

In a choice between the upper-left and lower-right cells, the Pure Altruist will do the same thing that the Pure Egoist will do. Their actions will be the same, but their motives will differ. The Pure Egoist acts solely in order to benefit himself; benefits to others are just side effects. The Pure Altruist acts solely to benefit others; benefits to self are just side effects.

## PEOPLE ARE RARELY PURE ALTRUISTS OR PURE EGOISTS

Which of these preference structures describes real people? I think that in the vast majority of cases, the answer is *neither.* In most choice situations, most of us care about both self *and* others. We don't like to feel guilty; we also enjoy the glow of satisfaction that comes from thinking well of ourselves. Most of us have preferences about having other goods (like money) as well. But besides these self-directed preferences, we also have other-directed preferences. We often are either benevolent or malevolent in what we want concerning the situation of others.

Both the Pure Egoist and the Pure Altruist have only one kind of preference. Real people usually have both. So we must complicate our representation.

I now introduce a third character—the S-over-O Pluralist.

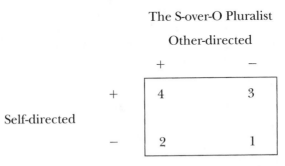

The S-over-O Pluralist

Other-directed

This individual prefers that he be better off rather than worse off (since $4 > 2$ and $3 > 1$). He also prefers that other people be better off rather than worse off (since $4 > 3$ and $2 > 1$). So this individual has both self-directed and other-directed preferences. This is why I call him a Pluralist. I've called this person an S-over-O Pluralist because of what he does when self-interest *conflicts* with the interests of others. Suppose the choice is between two actions. The first action provides him with a benefit while the other individual goes without; this is the outcome in the upper-right box. The second action provides the other with a benefit while he himself goes without; this is the lower-left outcome. When self-interest and the welfare of others conflict, the S-over-O Pluralist gives priority to himself (3 > 2). His self-directed preference is *stronger* than his other-directed preference.

What's the difference between the S-over-O Pluralist and the Pure Egoist? The Pure Egoist doesn't care at *all* about the situation of others. The S-over-O Pluralist *does* prefer that others be better off rather than worse. Both, however, say "me first" when self-interest conflicts with the welfare of others.

The last character I want to describe is the O-over-S Pluralist:

The O-over-S Pluralist

Other-directed

|  | + | − |
|---|---|---|
| + | 4 | 2 |
| − | 3 | 1 |

Self-directed

The O-over-S Pluralist cares about others and about himself as well; this is why he is a pluralist. I call him an O-over-S Pluralist to describe what he does when self-interest and the interests of others conflict. If an O-over-S Pluralist has to choose between the upper-right and lower-left cells, he will choose the lower left (3 > 2). He will sacrifice his own well-being so that the interests of the other person will be satisfied.

Notice that, of the four motivational structures I have described, only one of them completely lacks an altruistic motive. Psychological egoism says that people are Pure Egoists; it denies that people are ever motivational pluralists.

It should not be assumed that all of a person's motives, throughout his or her life, correspond to just one of these four motivational structures. For example, a person might be a Pure Egoist in one situation and an S-over-O Pluralist in another. These motivational structures are not intended to describe stable traits of people, but the traits that a person might have in a given situation in which there is a choice between actions that have consequences both for self and for someone else.

I noted before that when a Pure Altruist or a Pure Egoist face a choice between the upper-left and lower-right cells, they behave in the same way—both choose the action that benefits both self and other. The same is true of the S-over-O Pluralist and the O-over-S Pluralist. The four characters behave identically when self-interest *coincides* with the welfare of others. This means that how people behave in such situations is completely uninformative; the behavior does not help you figure out which of the four motivational structures they have. This is precisely what is going on in the example in which you donate $10 to charity. You would have donated the money no matter which of these four preference structures you possessed. How, then, are we to tell whether you are an altruist or an egoist?

The difference between Pure Egoists and S-over-O Pluralists, on the one hand, and O-over-S Pluralists and Pure Altruists, on the other, shows up when there is a *conflict* between helping one's self and having others be better off. In a situation of this sort, the agent must choose between being in the upper-right box (+ to self, − to other) and the lower-left box (− to self, + to other). People who choose to help others at cost to themselves in such conflict situations can't be Pure Egoists. However, people who help themselves and ignore the needs of others may be Pure Egoists, or they may be S-over-O Pluralists. To help figure out what your motives were when you gave $10 to the charity, let's put you in this sort of conflict situation.

When you contemplated sending $10 to the charity, there was no conflict between self-interest and the welfare of the starving children; the action that made you feel good also made the starving children better off. Because self-interest and the welfare of others *coincided,* it was impossible to tell what your motivation for helping was. To gain insight into your motives, we must ask what you would have done if there had been a conflict between self-interest and the welfare of the starving children.

## AN EXPERIMENTAL TEST

To visualize what such a conflict situation would be like, suppose I had made you the following promise as you sat at your desk deliberating about whether to write a check to the charity that would feed the starving children:

> Once you decide whether to write the check, I'll give you a pill that will cause you to *misremember* what you did. Thus, if you write the check, the pill will cause you to believe that you didn't, and so you will end up feeling guilty. And if you decide not to write the check, the pill will cause you to believe that you did do so, in which case you will end up feeling good about yourself.

Suppose you trust me to do what I say I'll do. Will you write the check or not? if you are in this hypothetical situation, self-interest and the welfare of others conflict. You can *either* feel good about yourself *or* help the starving children. You can't do both. What you choose shows what matters more to you.

My prediction is that you might well choose to write the check. If so, you have altruistic motives. It is false that the only thing you care about is feeling good about yourself. If, on the other hand, you decide not to write the check, how should this behavior be interpreted? I suggest that it is ambiguous. It is consistent with your being a Pure Egoist, but the behavior also is consistent with your being an S-over-O Pluralist.

When people send checks to charity in the real world, it may not be entirely clear why they do so. We can determine what their preference structures are if we consider what they would have done if self-interest and the interest of others had conflicted.

The experiment described here is a way to think about that kind of situation. My guess is that many people who give money to charity have altruistic motives in the sense defined here.

If so, psychological egoism is false as a generality. At least sometimes, people care about others, not just out of self-interest, but because the welfare of others is one of their ultimate concerns. This doesn't mean they don't care about themselves. It also doesn't mean that people don't value the glow of satisfaction and the freedom from guilt feelings they receive from helping others. Altruistically motivated people don't have to be Pure Altruists.

---

**Apportioning Causal Responsibility**

Events usually have more than one cause. A fatal car crash may be due to a slippery road surface, to the driver's carelessness, to the condition of the car's tires, to the position of a concrete wall, and so on. It is a mistake to think that precisely one of these was the "real" cause; each factor played a causal role.

Once we recognize that an event has many causes, we may wish to say which was "more important." The following situation provides an example of how the issue of apportioning causal responsibility may be addressed.

Suppose that you are a farmer who grows two fields of corn. The corn in the first field is shorter than the corn in the second. Upon investigation, you find that the corn in the first field has received less water and less fertilizer than the corn in the second. You suspect that the extra fertilizer going to the second field may have helped the corn there to grow taller; you also think that the additional water going to the second field may have been a help as well. Your question is, did these factors really make a difference? And if so, which was more important, the extra fertilizer or the extra water?

This problem can be represented by a two-by-two table. The corn in the first field received one unit of fertilizer and one unit of water; the corn in the second field received two units of each. The entries in the table represent the average height of the corn in each field:

|  |  | Water | |
|---|---|---|---|
|  |  | W1 | W2 |
| Fertilizer | F1 | 1 |  |
|  | F2 |  | 4 |

What experiment would you perform to find out whether an increase in fertilizer makes a difference? How would you find out whether an increase in water makes a difference? What would it mean to say that each makes a difference, but that one makes more of a difference than the other?

How is this problem related to the issue of egoism and altruism discussed in this chapter?

## A SECOND EXPERIMENTAL TEST

Here's a second experiment that may help clarify whether you had any altruistic motives when you sent the $10 check to the charity. As you are thinking about whether to do so, I tell you the following:

> As soon as you write the check or decide not to do so, I will give you a drug that will erase your memory of what you did, but will leave the rest of your mind intact. It isn't up to you whether you take this drug; my assistants will administer it to you regardless of whether you want it, and regardless of whether you decide to write the check to the charity

This drug is an amnesiac. If you were a pure egoist, would you write the check to the charity? If the only thing you care about is feeling good about yourself (and avoiding feeling guilty), the drug I'll give you will block that effect. If so, whether you write the check to the charity should be a matter of indifference if you are a pure egoist. If you write the check anyway, this is evidence that you are not a pure egoist. And if other people would write the check anyway, that would show that they are not pure egoists.

## CONCLUSION

My thesis is not that people *always* have altruistic ultimate motives. Nor am I claiming that people have *only* altruistic motives. Rather, my claim is that some people some of the time have altruistic motives, even if they also have self-directed motives as well. This is enough to show that PE is false as a general theory of human motivation.

## Review Questions

1. Give an example of an action that has two consequences, one of which was the goal of the action, the other of which was an unintended consequence.
2. What are self-directed and other-directed preferences? Give examples of each. Are there preferences that fall into neither category?
3. Represent each of the following preference structures by drawing a two-by-two table: (I) a *radical egalitarian* (someone who cares only that self and other receive the same degree of benefit); (II) a *utilitarian* (someone whose one concern is that more people benefit rather than fewer); (III) someone who is purely *malevolent* (who doesn't care about himself, but wants only that others be worse off rather than better).

4.  What is the difference between the Pure Egoist and the Pure Altruist? There is a kind of choice situation in which these two individuals will behave in the same way. Describe a case of this kind.

5.  What is the difference between the O-over-S Pluralist and the Pure Altruist? What is the difference between the S-over-O Pluralist and the Pure Egoist?

6.  There is a kind of choice situation in which people who have altruistic motives will behave differently from people who do not. Describe a case of this kind.

7.  When you help someone and this makes you feel good, how can you tell whether your motivation was altruistic or egoistic (or both)?

## Problems for Further Thought

1.  In both the experiments I described, there is a *time lag* between my describing the pill to you and your deciding what you will do. Suppose you decide to send the check to charity. I claimed this behavior shows you have an altruistic motive. Could a defender of PE reply that you felt good about yourself in the time between my describing the pill to you and your deciding whether to write the check, and that your behavior was therefore selfishly motivated?

2.  Suppose people with altruistic preference structures have them because their parents rewarded them with love and approval for helping others. Would this show that people are really egoists—that what really motivates them is parental approval?

3.  In this chapter, I tried to clarify what it means to ask *whether* someone is altruistically motivated. Two quantitative issues remain. How would you measure *how* altruistic someone is? And what would it mean to say that one person is *more altruistic* than another?

4.  (Suggested by Roy Sorensen) In the experiments described in this chapter, I assumed that the only egoistic motive that you might have is your wanting to feel good about yourself. This assumption allowed me to claim that if you donate to charity in the experiment, your motives are not exclusively egoistic. However, perhaps psychological egoism can be saved as a theory if we expand the list of what pure egoists care about. Why can't egoism maintain that people who donate to charity have the ultimate goal of being generous people. This goal is self-directed—the claim is that people want to have a certain type of personality. Evaluate this suggestion.

5.  It is sometimes suggested that people donate money to charity only because this leads others to admire and respect them. The pill-taking experiment described in this chapter provides a way of testing this. Can you think of another way to test this hypothesis, one that is less science-fictiony?

6.  The excerpt from Plato's *Republic* in the Readings describes an argument that Glaucon makes for psychological egoism. He claims that people never seek justice for its own sake, but do so only because it is a means to some selfish end. Use the material in this chapter to analyze Glaucon's argument.

# Readings

BERTRAND RUSSELL

## Other Minds Are Known by Analogy
## from One's Own Case

In this excerpt from **Human Knowledge: Its Scope and Limits** (1948), Russell argues that each of us knows about the mental characteristics of other people by analogy with our own case. You know by introspection which of your various mental states occurs when you behave in specific ways. Hence, the observation that others behave in similar ways makes it probable that they occupy similar mental states.

In Chapter 20, I described Ryle's objection to this argument. It resembles an objection (discussed in Chapter 5) that Hume made to the Argument from Design.

The problem with which we are concerned is the following. We observe in ourselves such occurrences as remembering, reasoning, feeling pleasure, and feeling pain. We think that sticks and stones do not have these experiences, but that other people do. Most of us have no doubt that the higher animals feel pleasure and pain, though I was once assured by a fisherman that "Fish have no sense nor feeling." I failed to find out how he had acquired this knowledge. Most people would disagree with him, but would be doubtful about oysters and starfish. However this may be, common sense admits an increasing doubtfulness as we descend in the animal kingdom, but as regards human beings it admits no doubt.

Bertrand Russell, "Other Minds Are Known by Analogy from One's Own Case," from *Human Knowledge: Its Scope and Limits* (London: Unwin Hyman Ltd., 1948), pp. 482–486. Reproduced with permission of Taylor & Francis Books Ltd., with acknowledgment to the Bertrand Russell Peace Foundation.

It is clear that belief in the minds of others requires some postulate that is not required in physics, since physics can be content with a knowledge of structure. My present purpose is to suggest what this further postulate may be.

It is clear that we must appeal to something that may be vaguely called "analogy." The behavior of other people is in many ways analogous to our own, and we suppose that it must have analogous causes. What people say is what we should say if we had certain thoughts, and so we infer that they probably have these thoughts. They give us information which we can sometimes subsequently verify. They behave in ways in which we behave when we are pleased (or displeased) in circumstances in which we should be pleased (or displeased). We may talk over with a friend some incident which we have both experienced, and find that his reminiscences dovetail with our own; this is particularly convincing when he remembers something that we have forgotten but that he recalls to our thoughts. Or again: you set your boy a problem in arithmetic, and with luck he gets the right answer; this persuades you that he is capable of arithmetical reasoning. There are, in short, very many ways in which my responses to stimuli differ from those of "dead" matter, and in all these ways other people resemble me. As it is clear to me that the causal laws governing my behavior have to do with "thoughts," it is natural to infer that the same is true of the analogous behavior of my friends.

The inference with which we are at present concerned is not merely that which takes us beyond solipsism, by maintaining that sensations have causes about which *something* can be known. This kind of inference ... suffices for physics.... We are concerned now with a much more specific kind of inference, the kind that is involved in our knowledge of the thoughts and feelings of others—assuming that we have such knowledge. It is of course obvious that such knowledge is more or less doubtful. There is not only the general argument that we may be dreaming; there is also the possibility of ingenious automata. There are calculating machines that do sums much better than our schoolboy sons; there are gramophone records that remember impeccably what So-and-so said on such-and-such an occasion; there are people in the cinema who, though copies of real people, are not themselves alive. There is no theoretical limit to what ingenuity could achieve in the ways of producing the illusion of life where in fact life is absent.

But, you will say, in all such cases it was the thoughts of human beings that produced the ingenious mechanism. Yes, but how do you know this? And how do you know that the gramophone does *not* "think"?

There is, in the first place, a difference in the causal laws of observable behavior. If I say to a student, "Write me a paper on Descartes's reasons for believing in the existence of matter," I shall, if he is industrious, cause a certain response. A gramophone record might be so constructed as to respond to this stimulus, perhaps better than the student, but if so it would be incapable of telling me anything about any other philosopher, even if I threatened to refuse to give it a degree. One of the most notable peculiarities of human behavior is change of response to a given stimulus. An ingenious person could construct an automaton which would always laugh at his jokes, however often it heard them; but a human being, after laughing a few times, will yawn, and end by saying, "How I laughed the first time I heard that joke."

But the differences in observable behavior between living and dead matter do not suffice to prove that there are "thoughts" connected with living bodies other than my own. It is probably possible theoretically to account for the behavior of living bodies by purely physical causal laws, and it is probably impossible to refute materialism by external observation alone. If we are to believe that there are thoughts and feelings other than our own, that must be in virtue of some inference in which our own thoughts and feelings are relevant, and such an inference must go beyond what is needed in physics.

I am, of course, not discussing the history of how we come to believe in other minds. We find ourselves believing in them when we first begin to reflect; the thought that Mother may be angry or pleased is one which arises in early infancy. What I am discussing is the possibility of a postulate which shall establish a rational connection between this belief and data, e.g., between the belief "Mother is angry" and the hearing of a loud voice.

The abstract schema seems to be as follows. We know, from observation of ourselves, a causal law of the form "A causes B," where A is a "thought" and B a physical occurrence. We sometimes observe a B when we cannot observe any A; we then infer an unobserved A. For example: I know when I say, "I'm thirsty," I say so, usually, because I am thirsty, and therefore, when I hear the sentence "I'm thirsty" at a time when I am not thirsty, I assume that someone else is thirsty. I assume this more readily if I see before me a hot, drooping body which goes on to say, "I have walked twenty desert miles in this heat with never a drop to drink." It is evident that my confidence in the "inference" is increased by increased complexity in the datum and also by increased certainty of the causal law derived from subjective observation, provided the causal law is such as to account for the complexities of the datum.

It is clear that insofar as plurality of causes is to be suspected, the kind of inference we have been considering is not valid. We are supposed to know "A causes B," and also to know that B has occurred; if this is to justify us in inferring A, we must know that *only* A causes B. Or, if we are content to infer that A is probable, it will suffice if we can know that in most cases it is A that causes B. If you hear thunder without having seen lightning, you confidently infer that there was lightning, because you are convinced that the sort of noise you heard is seldom caused by anything except lightning. As this example shows, our principle is not only employed to establish the existence of other minds but is habitually assumed, though in a less concrete form, in physics. I say "a less concrete form" because unseen lightning is only abstractly similar to seen lightning, whereas we suppose the similarity of other minds to our own to be by no means purely abstract.

Complexity in the observed behavior of another person, when this can all be accounted for by a simple cause such as thirst, increases the probability of the inference by diminishing the probability of some other cause. I think that in ideally favorable circumstances the argument would be formally as follows:

From subjective observation I know that A, which is a thought or feeling, causes B, which is a bodily act, e.g., a statement. I know also that, whenever B is an act of my own body, A is its cause. I now observe an act of the kind B in a body not my own, and I am having no thought or feeling of the kind A. But I still believe, on the basis of self-observation, that only A can cause B; I therefore infer that there was an A which caused B, though it was not an A that I could observe. On this ground I infer that other people's bodies are associated with minds, which resemble mine in proportion as their bodily behavior resembles my own.

In practice, the exactness and certainty of the above statement must be softened. We cannot be sure that, in our subjective experience, A is the only cause of B. And even if A is the only cause of B in our experience, how can we know that this holds outside our experience? It is not necessary that we should know this with any certainty; it is enough if it is highly probable. It is the assumption of probability in such cases that is our postulate. The postulate may therefore be stated as follows:

> If, whenever we can observe whether A and B are present or absent, we find that every case of B has an A as a causal antecedent, then it is probable that most B's have A as causal antecedents, even in cases where observation does not enable us to know whether A is present or not.

This postulate, if accepted, justifies the inference to other minds, as well as many other inferences that are made unreflectingly by common sense.

## U. T. PLACE

# Is Consciousness a Brain Process?

U. T. Place (1924–2000) was a British psychologist and philosopher who studied with Gilbert Ryle at Oxford University. Though Place was much influenced by Ryle's behaviorism, he helped develop a very different approach to the mind/body problem, arguing that mental states are identical with neurophysiological states. The following essay is partly behavioristic and partly antibehavioristic. Is Place's position consistent?

*Abstract*: The thesis that consciousness is a process in the brain is put forward as a reasonable scientific hypothesis, not to be dismissed on logical grounds alone. The conditions under which two sets of observations are treated as observations of the same process, rather than as observations of two independent correlated processes, are discussed. It is suggested that we can identify consciousness with a given pattern of brain activity, if we can explain the subject's introspective observations by reference to the brain processes with which they are correlated. It is argued that the problem of providing a physiological explanation of introspective observations is made to seem more difficult than it really is by the "phenomenological fallacy," the mistaken idea that descriptions of the appearances of things are descriptions of the actual state of affairs in a mysterious internal environment.

From U. T. Place, "In Consciousness a Brain Process?" *British Journal for Psychology* 47: 44–50.

# I. INTRODUCTION

The view that there exists a separate class of events, mental events, which cannot be described in terms of the concepts employed by the physical sciences no longer commands the universal and unquestioning acceptance among philosophers and psychologists which it once did. Modern physicalism, however, unlike the materialism of the seventeenth and eighteenth centuries, is behavioristic. Consciousness on this view is either a special type of behavior, "sampling" or "running-back-and-forth" behavior as Tolman has it,[1] or a disposition to behave in a certain way, an itch, for example, being a temporary propensity to scratch. In the case of cognitive concepts like "knowing," "believing," "understanding," "remembering," and volitional concepts like "wanting" and "intending," there can be little doubt, I think, that an analysis in terms of dispositions to behave is fundamentally sound.[2] On the other hand, there would seem to be an intractable residue of concepts clustering around the notions of consciousness, experience, sensations, and mental imagery, where some sort of inner process story is unavoidable.[3] It is possible, of course, that a satisfactory behavioristic account of this conceptual residuum will ultimately be found. For our present purposes, however, I shall assume that this cannot be done and that statements about pains and twinges, ab out how things look, sound, and feel, about things dreamed of or pictured in the mind's eye, are statements referring to events and processes which are in some sense private or internal to the individual of whom they are predicated. The question I wish to raise is whether in making this assumption we are inevitably committed to a dualist position in which sensations and mental images form a separate category of processes over and above the physical and physiological processes with which they are known to be correlated. I shall argue that an acceptance of inner processes does not entail dualism and that they thesis that consciousness is a process in the brain cannot be dismissed on logical grounds.

# II. THE "IS" OF DEFINITION AND THE "IS" OF COMPOSITION

I want to stress from the outset that in defending the thesis that consciousness is a process in the brain, I am not trying to argue that when we describe our dreams, fantasies, and sensations we are talking about processes in our brains. That is, I am not claiming that statements about sensations and mental images are reducible to or analyzable into statements about brain processes, in the way in which "cognition statements" are analyzable into statements about behavior. To say that statements about consciousness are statements about brain processes is manifestly false. This is shown (a) by the fact that you can describe your sensations and mental imagery without

---

[1]E. C. Tolman, *Purposive Behavior in Animals and Men* (Berkeley 1932).

[2]L. Wittgenstein, *Philosophical Investigations* (Oxford 1953); G. Ryle, *The Concept of Mind* (University of Chicago Press 1949).

[3]U. T. Place, "The Concept of Heed," *British Journal of Psychology*, 1955, 45: 243–255.

knowing anything about your brain processes or even that such things exist, (b) by the fact that statements about one's consciousness and statements about one's brain processes are verified in entirely different ways, (c) by the fact that there is nothing self-contradictory about the statement "X has a pain but there is nothing going on in his brain." What I do want to assert, however, is that the statement "Consciousness is a process in the brain," although not necessarily true, is not necessarily false. "Consciousness is a process in the brain" in my view is neither self-contradictory nor self-evident; it is a reasonable scientific hypothesis, in the way that the statement "Lightning is a motion of electric charges" is a reasonable scientific hypothesis.

The all but universally accepted view that an assertion of identify between consciousness and brain processes can be ruled out on logical grounds alone derives, I suspect, from a failure to distinguish what we may call the "is" of definition and the "is" of composition. The distinction I have in mind here is the difference between the function of the word "is" in statements like "A square is an equilateral rectangle," "Red is a color," "To understand an instruction is to be able to act appropriately under the appropriate circumstances," and its function in statements like "His table is an old packing case," "Her hat is a bundle of straw tied together with string," "A cloud is a mass of water droplets or other particles in suspension." These two types of "is" statements have one thing in common. In both cases it makes sense to add the qualification "and nothing else." In this they differ from those statements in which the "is" is an "is" of predication; the statements "Toby is eighty years old and nothing else," "Her hat is red and nothing else," or "Giraffes are tall and nothing else," for example, are nonsense. This logical feature may be described by saying that in both cases both the grammatical subject and the grammatical predicate are expressions which provide an adequate characterization of the state of affairs to which they both refer.

In another respect, however, the two groups of statements are strikingly different. Statements like "A square is an equilateral rectangle" are necessary statements which are true by definition. Statements like "His table is an old packing-case," on the other hand, are contingent statements which have to be verified by observation. In the case of statements like "A square is an equilateral rectangle" or "Red is a color," there is a relationship between the meaning of the expression forming the grammatical predicate and the meaning of the expression forming the grammatical subject, such that whenever the subject expression is applicable the predicate must also be applicable. If you can describe something as red then you must also be able to describe it is colored. In the case of statements like "His table is an old packing-case," on the other hand, there is no such relationship between the meanings of the expressions "his table" and "old packing-case"; it merely so happens that in this case both expressions are applicable to and at the same time provide an adequate characterization of the same object. Those who contend that the statement "Consciousness is a brain process" is logically untenable, base their claim, I suspect, on the mistaken assumption that if the meanings of two statements or expressions are quite unconnected, they cannot both provide an adequate characterization of the same object or state of affairs: if something is a state of consciousness, it cannot be a brain process, since there is nothing self-contradictory in supposing that someone feels a pain when there is nothing happen inside his skull. By the same token we might be led to conclude that a table cannot be an old packing-case, since there is nothing self-contradictory in supposing that someone has a table, but is not in possession of an old packing-case.

## III. THE LOGICAL INDEPENDENCE OF EXPRESSIONS AND THE ONTOLOGICAL INDEPENDENCE OF ENTITIES

There is, of course, an important difference between the table/packing-case and the consciousness/brain process case in that the statement "His table is an old packing-case" is a particular proposition which refers only to one particular case, whereas the statement "Consciousness is a process in the brain" is a general or universal proposition applying to all states of consciousness whatever. It is fairly clear, I think, that if we lived in a world in which all tables without exception were packing-cases, the concepts of "table" and "packing-case" in our language would not have their present logically independent status. In such a world a table would be a species of packing-case in much the same way that red is a species of color. It seems to be a rule of language that whenever a given variety of object or state of affairs has two characteristics or sets of characteristics, one of which is unique to the variety of object or state of affairs in question, the expression used to refer to the characteristic or set of characteristics which defines the variety of object or state of affairs in question will always entail the expression used to refer to the other characteristic or set of characteristics. If this rule admitted of no exception it would follow that any expression which is logically independent of another expression which uniquely characterizes a given variety of object or state of affairs must refer to a characteristic or set of characteristics which is not normally or necessarily associated with the object or state of affairs in question. It is because this rule applies almost universally, I suggest, that we are normally justified in arguing from the logical independence of two expressions to the ontological independence of the states of affairs to which they refer. This would explain both the undoubted force of the argument that consciousness and brain processes must be independent entities because the expressions used to refer to them are logically independent and, in general, the curious phenomenon whereby questions about the furniture of the universe are often fought and decided merely on a point of logic.

The argument from the logical independence of two expressions to the ontological independence of the entities to which they refer breaks down in the case of brain processes and consciousness, I believe, because this is one of a relatively small number of cases where the rule stated above does not apply. These exceptions are to be found, I suggest, in those case where the operations which have to be performed in order to verify the presence of the two sets of characteristics inhering in the object or state of affairs in question can seldom if ever be performed simultaneously. A good example here is the case of the cloud and the mass of droplets or other particles in suspension. A cloud is a large semi-transparent mass with a fleecy texture suspended in the atmosphere whose shape is subject to continual and kaleidoscopic change. When observed at close quarters, however, it is found to consist of a mass of tiny particles, usually water droplets, in continuous motion. On the basis of this second observation we conclude that a cloud is a mass of tiny particles and nothing else. But there is no logical connection in our language between a cloud and a mass of tiny particles; there is nothing self-contradictory in talking about a cloud which is not composed of tiny particles in suspension. There is no contradiction involved in supposing that clouds consist of a dense mass of fibrous tissue; indeed, such a consistency seems to be implied by many of the functions performed by clouds in fairy stories and mythology. It is clear from this that the terms "cloud" and "mass of tiny particles in suspension" mean quite different things. Yet we do not conclude from this that there must be two things, the mass of particles in suspensions and the cloud. The reason for this, I suggest, is that although the characteristics of being a cloud and being a mass of tiny particles in suspension are invariably associated, we never make the observations necessary to verify the statement "That is a cloud" and those necessary to verify the statement "This is a mass of tiny particles in suspension" at one and the same time. We can observe the micro-structure of a cloud only when we are enveloped by it, a condition which effectively prevents us from observing those characteristics which from a distance lead us to describe it as a cloud. Indeed, so disparate are those two experiences that we use different words to describe them. That which is a cloud when we observe it from a distance becomes a fog or mist when we are enveloped by it.

## IV. WHEN ARE TWO SETS OF OBSERVATIONS OBSERVATIONS OF THE SAME EVENT?

The example of the cloud and the mass of tiny particles in suspension was chosen because it is one of the few cases of a general proposition involving what I have called the "is" of composition which does not involve us in scientific technicalities. It is useful because it brings out the connection between the ordinary everyday case of the "is" of composition like the table/packing-case example and the more technical cases like "Lightning is a motion of electric charges" where the analogy with the consciousness/brain process case is most marked. The limitation of the cloud/tiny particles in suspension case is that it does not bring out sufficiently clearly the crucial problems of how the identity of the states of affairs referred to by the two expressions is established. In the cloud case the fact that something is a cloud and the fact that something is a mass of tiny particles in suspension are both verified by the normal processes of visual observation. It is arguable, moreover, that he identity of the entities referred to by the two expression is established by the continuity between the two sets of observations as the observer moves towards or way from the cloud. In the case of brain processes and consciousness there is no such continuity between the two sets of observations involved. A closer introspective scrutiny will never reveal the passage of nerve impulses over a thousand synapses in the way that a closer scrutiny of a cloud will reveal a mass of tiny particles in suspension. The operations required to verify statements about consciousness and statements about brain processes are fundamentally different.

To find a parallel for this feature we must examine other case where an identity is asserted between something whose occurrence is verified by the ordinary processes of observation and something whose occurrence is established by special procedures. For this purpose I have chosen the case where we say that lightning is a motion of electric charges. As in the case of consciousness, however closely we scrutinize the lightning we shall never be able to observe the electric charges, and just as the operations for determining the nature of one's state of consciousness are radically different from those involved in determining those involved in determining he nature of one's brain processes, so the operations for determining the occurrence of lightning are radically different form those involved in determining the occurrence of a motion of electric charges. What is it, therefore, that leads us to say that the two sets of observations are observations of the same event? It cannot be merely the fact that the two sets of observations are systematically correlated such that whenever there is lightning there is always a motion of electric charges. There are innumerable cases of such correlations where we have no temptation to say that the two sets of observations are observations of the same event. There is a systematic correlation, for example, between the movement of the tides and the stages of the moon, but this does not lead us to say that records of tidal levels are records of the moon's stages or vice versa. We speak rather of a causal connection between two independent events or processes.

The answer here seems to be that we treat the two sets of observations as observations of the same event in those cases where the technical scientific observations set in the context of the appropriate body of scientific theory provide an immediate explanation of the observations made by the man in the street. Thus we conclude that lightning is nothing more than a motion of electric charges, because we know that a motion of electric charges through the atmosphere, such as occurs when lightning is reported, gives rise to the type of visual stimulation which would lead an observer to report a flash of lightning. In the moon/tide case, on the other hand, there is no such direct causal connection between the stages of the moon and the observations made by the man who measures the height of the tide. The causal connection is between the moon and the tides, not between the moon and the measurement of the tides.

## V. THE PHYSIOLOGICAL EXPLANATION OF INTROSPECTION AND THE PHENOMENOLOGICAL FALLACY

If this account is correct, it should follow that in order to establish the identity of consciousness and certain processes in the brain, it would be necessary to show that the introspective observations reported by the subject can be accounted for in terms of processes which are known to have occurred in his brain. In the light of this suggestion it is extremely interesting to find that when a physiologist, as distinct from a philosopher, finds it difficult to see how consciousness could be a process in the brain, what worries him is not any supposed self-contradiction involved in such an assumption, but the apparent impossibility of accounting for the reports given by the subject of his consciousness processes in terms of the known properties of the central nervous system. Sir Charles Sherrington has posed the problem as follows:

> The chain of events stretching from the sun's radiation entering the eyes to, on the one hand, the contraction of the papillary muscles, and on the other, to the electrical disturbances in the brain-cortex are all straightforward steps in a sequence of physical "causation," such as, thanks to science, are intelligible. But in the second serial chain there follows on, or attend, the stage of brain-cortex

reaction an event or set of events quite inexplicable to us, which both as to themselves and as to the causal tie between them and what preceded them science does
not help us; a set of events seemingly incommensurable with any of the events
leading up to it. The self "sees" the sun; it senses a two-dimensional disc of brightness, located in the "sky," this last a field of lesser brightness, and overhead shaped
as a rather flattened dome, coping the self and a hundred other visual things as
well. Of hint that this is within the head there is none. Vision is saturated with this
strange property called "projection," the unargued inference that what it sees is
at a "distance" from the seeing "self," Enough has been said to stress that in the
sequence of events a step is reached where a physical situation in the brain leads
to a psychical, which however contains no hint of he brain of any other bodily
part. . . . The supposition has to be, it would see, two continuous series of events,
one physico-chemical, the other psychical, and at times interaction between them.[4]

Just as the physiologist is not likely to be impressed by the philosopher's con-
tention that there is some self-contradiction involved in supposing consciousness to
be a brain process, so the philosopher is unlikely to be impressed by the considerations which lead Sherrington to conclude that there are two sets of events, one
physico-chemical, the other psychical. Sherrington's argument, for all its emotional
appeal, depends on a fairly simple logical mistake, which is unfortunately all too frequently made by psychologists and physiologists and not infrequently in the past by
the philosophers themselves. This logical mistake, which I shall refer to as the "phenomenological fallacy," is the mistake of supposing that when the subject describes
his experience, when he describes how things look sound, smell, taste, or feel to him,
he is describing the literal properties of objects and events on a peculiar sort of internal cinema or television screen, usually referred to in the modern psychological literature as the "phenomenal field." If we assume, for example, that when a subject
reports a green after-image he is asserting the occurrence inside himself of an object
which is literally green, it is clear that we have on our hands an entity for which there
is no place in the world of physics. In the case of the green after-image there is no
green object in the subject's environment corresponding to the description that he
gives. Nor is there anything green in his brain; certainly there is nothing which could
have emerged when he reported the appearance of the green after-image. Brain
processes are not the sort of things to which color concepts can be properly applied.
   The phenomenological fallacy on which this argument is based depends on the
mistaken assumption that because our ability to describe things in our environment
depends on our consciousness of them, our description of things that are primarily
descriptions of our conscious experience and only secondarily, indirectly and infer-
entially descriptions of the objects and events in our environments. It is assumed
that because we recognize things in our environment by their look, sound, smell,
taste, and feel, we begin by describing their phenomenal properties, i.e. the properties
of the looks, sounds, smells, tastes, and feels which they produced in us, and infer

---

[4]Sir Charles Sherrington, *The Integrative Action of the Nervous System* (Cambridge 1947), pp. xx–xxi.

their real properties from their phenomenal properties. In fact, the reverse is the case. We begin by learning to recognize the real properties of things in our environment. We learn to recognize them, of course, by their look, sound, smell, taste, and feel; but this does not mean that we have to learn to describe the look, sound, smell, taste, and feel of things before we can describe the things themselves. Indeed, it is only after we have learned to describe the things in our environment that we learn to describe our consciousness of them. We describe our conscious experience not in terms of of the mythological "phenomenal properties" which are supposed to inhere in the mythological "phenomenal field," but by reference to the actual physical properties of he concrete physical objects, events, and processes which normally, though not perhaps in the present instance, give rise to the sort of conscious experience which we are trying to describe. In other words, when we describe the after-image as green, we are not saying that there is something, the after-image, which is green; we are saying that we are having the sort of experience which we normally have when, and which we have learned to describe as, looking at a green patch of light.

Once we rid ourselves of the phenomenological fallacy we realize that the problem of explaining introspective observations in terms of brain processes is far from insuperable. We realize that here is nothing that the introspecting subject says about his conscious experiences which is inconsistent with anything the physiologist might want to say about the brain processes which cause him to describe the environment and his consciousness of that environment in the way he does. When the subject describes his experience by saying that a light which is in fact stationary appears to move, all the physiologist or physiological psychologist has to do in order to explain the subject's introspective observations is to show that the brain process which is causing the subject to describe his experience in this way is the sort of process which normally occurs when he is observing an actual moving object and which therefore normally causes him to report the movement of an object in his environment. Once the mechanism whereby the individual describes what is going on in his environment has been worked out, all that is required to explain the individual's capacity to make introspective observations is an explanation of his ability to discriminate between those case where his normal habits of verbal descriptions are appropriate to the stimulus situation and those case where they are not, and an explanation of how and why, in those case where the appropriateness of his normal descriptive habits is in doubt, he learns to issue his ordinary descriptive protocols preceded by a qualifactory phrases like "it appears," "looks," "feels," etc.[5]

---

[5]I am greatly indebted to my fellow-participants in a series of informal discussion on this topic which took place in the Department of Philosophy, University of Adelaide, in particular to Mr. C. B. Martin for his persistent and searching criticism of my earlier attempts to defend the thesis that consciousness is a brain process, to Professor D. A. T. Gasking, of the University of Melbourne, for clarifying many of the logical issues involved, and to Professor J. J. C. Smart for moral support and encouragement in what often seemed a lost cause.

## BARON D'HOLBACH

# Determinism Shows That Free Will Is an Illusion

Paul-Henri Thiry, Baron d'Holbach (1723–1789), was an important philosopher in the French Enlightenment. He was a materialist and one of the first self-described atheists writing in Europe. In these excerpts from Chapter 11 of his book, ***The System of Nature***, d'Holbach argues that human beings are thoroughly enmeshed in the deterministic processes that govern nature and that, in consequence, free will is an illusion. D'Holbach published this book under a pseudonym; it was called "the atheist's Bible."

In whatever manner he is considered, he is connected to universal nature, and submitted to the necessary and immutable laws that she imposes on all the beings she contains, according to their peculiar essences or to the respective properties with which, without consulting them, she endows each particular species. Man's life is a line that nature commands him to describe upon the surface of the earth, without his ever being able to swerve from it, even for an instant. He is born without his own consent; his organization does in nowise depend upon himself; his ideas come to him involuntarily; his habits are in the power of those who cause him to contract them; he is unceasingly modified by causes, whether visible or concealed, over which he has no control, which necessarily regulate his mode of existence, give the hue to his way of thinking, and determine his manner of acting. He is good or bad, happy or miserable, wise or foolish, reasonable or irrational, without his will being for any thing in these various states. Nevertheless, in despite of the shackles by which he is bound, it is pretended he is a free agent, or that independent of the causes by which he is moved, he determines his own will, and regulates his own condition....

The will, as we have elsewhere said, is a modification of the brain, by which it is disposed to action, or prepared to give play to the organs. This will is necessarily determined by the qualities, good or bad, agreeable or painful, of the object or the motive that acts upon his senses, or of which the idea remains with him, and is resuscitated by his memory. In consequence, he acts necessarily, his action is the result of the impulse he receives either from the motive, from the object, or from the idea which has modified his brain, or disposed his will. When he does not act according to this impulse, it is because there comes some new cause, some new motive, some new idea, which modifies his brain in a different manner, gives him a new impulse, determines his will in another way, by which the action of the former impulse is suspended: thus, the sight of an agreeable object, or its idea, determines his will to set him in action to procure it; but if a new object or a new idea more powerfully attracts him, it gives a new direction to his will, annihilates the effect of the former, and prevents the action by which it was to be procured. This is the mode in which reflection, experience, reason, necessarily arrests or suspends the action of man's will: without

These portions from Chapter 11 of d'Holbach's *The System of Nature* (1770) were translated by H. D. Robinson in 1860.

this he would of necessity have followed the anterior impulse which carried him towards a then desirable object. In all this he always acts according to necessary laws, from which he has no means of emancipating himself. If when tormented with violent thirst, he figures to himself in idea, or really perceives a fountain, whose limpid streams might cool his feverish want, is he sufficient master of himself to desire or not to desire the object competent to satisfy so lively a want? It will no doubt be conceded, that it is impossible he should not be desirous to satisfy it; but it will be said—if at this moment it is announced to him that the water he so ardently desires is poisoned, he will, notwithstanding his vehement thirst, abstain from drinking it: and it has, therefore, been falsely concluded that he is a free agent. The fact, however, is, that the motive in either case is exactly the same: his own conservation. The same necessity that determined him to drink before he knew the water was deleterious, upon this new discovery equally determines him not to drink; the desire of conserving himself either annihilates or suspends the former impulse; the second motive becomes stronger than the preceding, that is, the fear of death, or the desire of preserving himself, necessarily prevails over the painful sensation caused by his eagerness to drink: but, it will be said, if the thirst is very parching, an inconsiderate man without regarding the danger will risk swallowing the water. Nothing is gained by this remark: in this case, the anterior impulse only regains the ascendency; he is persuaded that life may possibly be longer preserved, or that he shall derive a greater good by drinking the poisoned water than by enduring the torment, which, to his mind, threatens instant dissolution: thus the first becomes the strongest and necessarily urges him on to action. Nevertheless, in either case, whether he partakes of the water, or whether he does not, the two actions will be equally necessary; they will be the effect of that motive which finds itself most puissant; which consequently acts in the most coercive manner upon his will. This example will serve to explain the whole phenomena of the human will. This will, or rather the brain, finds itself in the same situation as a bowl, which, although it has received an impulse that drives it forward in a straight line, is deranged in its course whenever a force superior to the first obliges it to change its direction. The man who drinks the poisoned water appears a madman; but the actions of fools are as necessary as those of the most prudent individuals. The motives that determine the voluptuary and the debauchee to risk their health, are as powerful, and their actions are as necessary, as those which decide the wise man to manage his. But, it will be insisted, the debauchee may be prevailed on to change his conduct: this does not imply that he is a free agent; but that motives may be found sufficiently powerful to annihilate the effect of those that previously acted upon him; then these new motives determine his will to the new mode of conduct he may adopt as necessarily as the former did to the old mode. . . .

The errors of philosophers on the free agency of man, have arisen from their regarding his will as the *primum mobile,* the original motive of his actions; for want of recurring back, they have not perceived the multiplied, the complicated causes which, independently of him, give motion to the will itself; or which dispose and modify his brain, whilst he himself is purely passive in the motion he receives. Is he the master of desiring or not desiring an object that appears desirable to him? Without doubt it will be answered, no: but he is the master of resisting his desire, if he reflects on the consequences. But, I ask, is he capable of reflecting on these consequences, when his soul is hurried along by a very lively passion, which entirely depends upon his natural organization, and the causes by which he is modified? Is it in his power to add to these consequences all the weight necessary to counterbalance his desire? Is he the master of preventing the qualities which render an object desirable from residing in it? I shall be told: he ought to have learned to resist his passions; to contract a habit of putting a curb on his desires. I agree to it without any difficulty. But in reply, I again ask, is his nature susceptible of this modification? Does his boiling blood, his unruly imagination, the igneous fluid that circulates in his veins, permit him to make, enable him to apply true experience in the moment when it is wanted? And even when his temperament has capacitated him, has his education, the examples set before him, the ideas with which he has been inspired in early life, been suitable to make him contract this habit of repressing his desires? Have not all these things rather contributed to induce him to seek with avidity, to make him actually desire those objects which you say he ought to resist. . . .

In short, the actions of man are never free; they are always the necessary consequence of his temperament, of the received ideas, and of the notions, either true or false, which he has formed to himself of happiness; of his opinions, strengthened by example, by education, and by daily experience. So many crimes are witnessed on the earth only because every thing conspires to render man vicious and criminal; the religion he has adopted, his government, his education, the examples set before him, irresistibly drive him on to evil: under these circumstances, morality preaches virtue to him in rain. In those societies where vice is esteemed, where crime is crowned, where venality is constantly recompensed, where the most dreadful disorders are punished only in those who are too weak to enjoy the privilege of committing them with impunity, the practice of virtue is considered nothing more than a painful sacrifice of happiness. Such societies chastise, in the lower orders, those excesses which they respect in the higher ranks; and frequently have the injustice to condemn those in the penalty of death, whom public prejudices, maintained by constant example, have rendered criminal. Man, then, is not a free agent in any one instant of his life; he is necessarily guided in each step by those advantages, whether real or fictitious, that he attaches to the objects by which his passions are roused: these passions themselves are necessary in a being who unceasingly tends towards his own happiness; their energy is necessary, since that depends on his temperament; his temperament is necessary, because it depends on the physical elements which enter into his composition; the modification of this temperament is necessary, as it is the infallible and inevitable consequence of the impulse he receives from the incessant action of moral and physical beings.

In despite of these proofs of the want of free agency in man, so clear to unprejudiced minds, it will, perhaps, be insisted upon with no small feeling of triumph, that if it be proposed to any one, to move or not to move his hand, an action in the number of those called *indifferent,* he evidently appears to be the master of choosing; from which it is concluded that evidence has been offered of his free agency. The reply is, this example is perfectly simple; man in performing some action which he is resolved on doing, does not by any means prove his free agency: the very desire of displaying this quality, excited by the dispute, becomes a necessary motive, which decides his will either for the one or the other of these actions: what deludes him in this instance, or that which persuades him he is a free agent at this moment, is, that he does not discern the true motive which sets him in action, namely, the desire of convincing his opponent: if in the heat of the dispute he insists and asks, "Am I not the master of throwing myself out of the window?" I shall answer him, no; that whilst he preserves his reason there is no probability that the desire of proving his free agency, will become a motive sufficiently powerful to make him sacrifice his life to the attempt: if, notwithstanding this, to prove he is a free agent, he should actually precipitate himself from the window, it would not be a sufficient warranty to conclude he acted freely, but rather that it was the violence of his temperament which spurred him on to this folly. Madness is a state, that depends upon the heat of the blood, not upon the will. A fanatic or a hero, braves death as necessarily as a more phlegmatic man or a coward flies from it.

It *is* said that free agency is the absence of those obstacles competent to oppose themselves to the actions of *man,* or to the exercise of his faculties: at is pretended that he is a free agent whenever, making use of these faculties, he produces the effect he has proposed to himself. In reply to this reasoning, it is sufficient to consider that it in nowise depends upon himself to place or remove the obstacles that either determine or resist him; the motive that causes his action is no more in his own power than the obstacle that impedes him, whether this obstacle or motive be within his own machine or exterior of his person: he is not master of the thought presented to his mind, which determines his will; this thought is excited by some cause independent of himself. To be undeceived on the system of his free agency, man has simply to recur to the motive by which his will is determined; he will always find this motive is out of his own control. It is said: that in consequence of an idea to which the mind gives birth, man acts freely if he encounters no obstacle. But the question is, what gives birth to this idea in his brain? was he the master either to prevent it from presenting itself, or from renewing itself in his brain? Does not this idea depend either upon objects that strike him exteriorly and in despite of himself, or upon causes, that without his knowledge, act within himself and modify his brain? Can he prevent his eyes, east without design upon any object whatever, from giving him an idea of this object, and from moving his brain? He is not more master of the obstacles; they are the necessary effects of either interior or exterior causes, which always act according to their given properties. A man insults a coward, this necessarily irritates him against his insulter, but his will cannot vanquish the obstacle that cowardice places to the object of his desire, because his natural conformation, which does not depend upon himself, prevents his having courage. In this case, the coward is insulted in despite of himself; and against his will is obliged patiently to brook the insult he has received. . . .

It is the great complication of motion in man, it is the variety of his action, it is the multiplicity of causes that move him, whether simultaneously or in continual succession, that persuades him he is a free agent: if all his motions were simple, if the causes that move him did not confound themselves with each other, if they were distinct, if his machine were less complicated, he would perceive that all his actions were necessary, because he would be enabled to recur instantly to the cause that made him act. A man who should be always obliged to go towards the west, would always go on that side; but he would feel that, in so going, he was not a free agent: if he had another sense, as his actions or his motion, augmented by a sixth, would be still more varied and much more complicated, he would believe himself still more a free agent than he does with his five senses. It is, then, for want of recurring to the causes that move him; for want of being able to analyze, from not being competent to decompose the complicated motion of his machine, that man believes himself a free agent: it is only upon his own ignorance that he founds the profound yet deceitful notion he has of his free agency; that he builds those opinions which he brings forward as a striking proof of his pretended freedom of action. If, for a short time, each man was willing to examine his own peculiar actions, search out their true motives to discover their concatenation, he would remain convinced that the sentiment he has of his natural free agency, is a chimera that must speedily be destroyed by experience. Nevertheless it must be acknowledged that the multiplicity and diversity of the causes which continually act upon man, frequently without even his knowledge, render it impossible, or at least extremely difficult for him to recur to the true principles of his own peculiar actions, much less the actions of others: they frequently depend upon causes so fugitive, so remote from their effects, and which, superficially examined, appear to have so little analogy, so slender a relation with them, that it requires singular sagacity to bring them into light. This is what renders the study of the moral man a task of such difficulty; this is the reason why his heart is an abyss, of which it is frequently impossible for him to fathom the depth....

If he understood the play of his organs, if he was able to recall to himself all the impulsions they have received, all the modifications they have undergone, all the effects they have produced, he would perceive that all his actions are submitted to that *fatality*, which regulates his own particular system, as it does the entire system of the universe: no one effect in him, any more than in nature, produces itself by *chance*; this, as has been before proved, is a word void of sense. All that passes in him; all that is done by him; as well as all that happens in nature, or that is attributed to her, is derived from necessary causes, which act according to necessary laws, and which produce necessary effects from whence necessarily flow others. *Fatality*, is the eternal, the immutable, the necessary order, established in nature; or the indispensable connection of causes that act, with the effects they operate. Conforming to this order, heavy bodies fall; light bodies rise; that which is analogous in matter reciprocally attracts; that which is heterogeneous mutually repels; man congregates himself in society, modifies each his fellow; becomes either virtuous or wicked; either contributes to his mutual happiness, or reciprocates his misery; either loves his neighbor, or hates his companion necessarily, according to the manner in which the one acts upon the other. From whence it may be seen, that the same necessity which regulates the physical, also regulates the moral world, in which every thing is in consequence submitted to fatality. Man, in running over, frequently without his own knowledge, often in despite of himself, the route which nature has marked out for him, resembles a swimmer who is obliged to follow the current that carries him along: he believes himself a free agent, because he sometimes consents, sometimes does not consent, to glide with the stream, which, notwithstanding, always hurries him forward; he believes himself the master of his condition, because he is obliged to use his arms under the fear of sinking.

# DAVID HUME

# Of Liberty and Necessity

In this passage from ***An Enquiry Concerning Human Understanding*** (1748), Hume defends what has come to be called a "soft determinist" solution to the problem of free will. He maintains that actions are both free and causally determined. A free action, for Hume, is one in which the agent could have done otherwise had the agent wished to do so.

It might reasonably be expected in questions which have been canvassed and disputed with great eagerness, since the first origin of science and philosophy, that the meaning of all the terms, at least, should have been agreed upon among the disputants; and our enquiries, in the course of two thousand years, been able to pass from words to the true and real subject of the controversy. For how easy may it seem to give exact definitions of the terms employed in reasoning, and make these definitions, not the mere sound of words, the object of future scrutiny and examination? But if we consider the matter more narrowly, we shall be apt to draw a quite opposite conclusion. From this circumstance alone, that a controversy has been long kept on foot, and remains still undecided, we may presume that there is some ambiguity in the expression, and that the disputants affix different ideas to the terms employed in the controversy. For as the faculties of the mind are supposed to be naturally alike in every individual; otherwise nothing could be more fruitless than to reason or dispute together; it were impossible, if men affix the same ideas to their terms, that they could so long form different opinions of the same subject; especially when they communicate their views, and each party turn themselves on all sides, in search of arguments which may give them the victory over their antagonists. It is true, if men attempt the discussion of questions which lie entirely beyond the reach of human capacity, such as those concerning the origin of worlds, or the economy of the intellectual system or region of spirits, they may long beat the air in their fruitless contests, and never arrive at any determinate conclusion. But if the question regard any subject of common life and experience, nothing, one would think, could preserve the dispute so long undecided but some ambiguous expressions, which keep the antagonists still at a distance, and hinder them from grappling with each other.

This has been the case in the long disputed question concerning liberty and necessity; and to so remarkable a degree that, if I be not much mistaken, we shall find, that all mankind, both learned and ignorant, have always been of the same opinion with regard to this subject, and that a few intelligible definitions would immediately have put an end to the whole controversy. I own that this dispute has been so much canvassed on all hands, and has led philosophers into such a labyrinth of obscure sophistry, that it is no wonder, if a sensible reader indulge his ease so far as to turn a deaf ear to the proposal of such a question, from which he can expect neither instruction or entertainment. But

David Hume, "Of Liberty and Necessity," from *An Inquiry Concerning Human Understanding*, edited by Charles W. Hendel (New York: Macmillan, 1957), pp. 90–104.

the state of the argument here proposed may, perhaps, serve to renew his attention; as it has more novelty, promises at least some decision of the controversy, and will not much disturb his ease by any intricate or obscure reasoning.

I hope, therefore, to make it appear that all men have ever agreed in the doctrine both of necessity and of liberty, according to any reasonable sense, which can be put on these terms; and that the whole controversy has hitherto turned merely upon words. We shall begin with examining the doctrine of necessity.

It is universally allowed that matter, in all its operations, is actuated by a necessary force, and that every natural effect is so precisely determined by the energy of its cause that no other effect, in such particular circumstances, could possibly have resulted from it. The degree and direction of every motion is, by the laws of nature, prescribed with such exactness that a living creature may as soon arise from the shock of two bodies as motion in any other degree or direction than what is actually produced by it. Would we, therefore, form a just and precise idea of *necessity*, we must consider whence that idea arises when we apply it to the question of bodies.

It seems evident that, if all the scenes of nature were continually shifted in such a manner that no two events bore any resemblance to each other, but every object was entirely new, without any similitude to whatever had been seen before, we should never, in that case, have attained the least idea of necessity, or of a connexion among these objects. We might say, upon such a supposition, that one object or event has followed another; not that one was produced by the other. The relation of cause and effect must be utterly unknown to mankind. Inference and reasoning concerning the operations of nature would, from that moment, be at an end; and the memory and senses remain the only canals, by which the knowledge of any real existence could possibly have access to the mind. Our idea, therefore, of necessity and causation arises entirely from the uniformity observable in the operations of nature, where similar objects are constantly conjoined together, and the mind is determined by custom to infer the one from the appearance of the other. These two circumstances form the whole of that necessity, which we ascribe to matter. Beyond the constant *conjunction* of similar objects, and the consequent *inference* from one to the other, we have no notion of any necessity or connexion.

If it appear, therefore, that all mankind have ever allowed, without any doubt or hesitation, that these two circumstances take place in the voluntary actions of men, and in the operations of mind; it must follow that all mankind have ever agreed in the doctrine of necessity, and that they have hitherto disputed, merely for not understanding each other.

As to the first circumstance, the constant and regular conjunction of similar events, we may possibly satisfy ourselves by the following considerations. It is universally acknowledged that there is a great uniformity among the actions of men, in all nations and ages, and that human nature remains still the same, in its principles and operations. The same motives always produce the same actions. The same events follow from the same causes. Ambition, avarice, self-love, vanity, friendship, generosity, public spirit: these passions, mixed in various degrees, and distributed through society, have been, from the beginning of the world, and still are, the source of all the actions and enterprises, which have ever been observed among mankind. Would you know the sentiments, inclinations, and course of life of the Greeks and Romans? Study well the temper and actions of the French and English: You cannot be much mistaken in transferring to the former *most* of the observations which you have made with regard to the latter. Mankind are so much the same, in all times and places, that history informs us of nothing new or strange in this particular. Its chief use is only to discover the constant and universal principles of human nature, by showing men in all varieties of circumstances and situations, and furnishing us with materials from which we may form our observations and become acquainted with the regular springs of human action and behaviour. These records of wars, intrigues, factions, and revolutions, are so many collections of experiments, by which the politician or moral philosopher fixes the principles of his science, in the same manner as the physician or natural philosopher becomes acquainted with the nature of plants, minerals, and other external objects, by the experiments which he forms concerning them. Nor are the earth, water, and other elements, examined by Aristotle and Hippocrates, more like to those which at present lie under our observation than the men described by Polybius and Tacitus are to those who now govern the world.

Should a traveller, returning from a far country, bring us an account of men, wholly different from any with whom we were ever acquainted; men, who were entirely divested of avarice, ambition, or revenge; who knew no pleasure but friendship, generosity, and public spirit; we should immediately, from these circumstances, detect the falsehood, and prove him a liar, with the same certainty as if he had stuffed his narration with stories of centaurs and dragons, miracles and prodigies. And if we would explode any forgery in history, we cannot make use of a more convincing argument, than to prove that the actions ascribed to any person are directly contrary to the course of nature, and that no human motives, in such circumstances, could ever induce him to such a conduct. The veracity of Quintus Curtius is as much to be suspected, when he describes the supernatural courage of Alexander, by which he was hurried on singly to attack multitudes, as when he describes his supernatural force and activity, by which he was able to resist them. So readily and universally do we acknowledge a uniformity in human motives and actions as well as in the operations of body.

Hence likewise the benefit of that experience, acquired by long life and a variety of business and company, in order to instruct us in the principles of human nature, and regulate our future conduct, as well as speculation. By means of this guide, we mount up to the knowledge of men's inclinations and motives, from their actions, expressions, and even gestures; and again descend to the interpretation of their actions from our knowledge of their motives and inclinations. The general observations treasured up by a course of experience, give us the clue of human nature, and teach us to unravel all its intricacies. Pretexts and appearances no longer deceive us. Public declarations pass for the specious colouring of a cause. And though virtue and honour be allowed their proper weight and authority, that perfect disinterestedness, so often pretended to, is never expected in multitudes and parties; seldom in their leaders; and scarcely even in individuals of any rank or station. But were there no uniformity in human actions, and were every experiment which we could form of this kind irregular and anomalous, it were impossible to collect any general observations concerning mankind; and no experience, however accurately digested by reflection, would ever serve to any purpose. Why is the aged husbandman more skillful in his calling than the young beginner but because there is a certain uniformity in the operation of the sun, rain, and earth towards the production of vegetables; and experience teaches the old practitioner the rules by which this operation is governed and directed.

We must not, however, expect that this uniformity of human actions should be carried to such a length as that all men, in the same circumstances, will always act precisely in the same manner, without making any allowance for the diversity of characters, prejudices, and opinions. Such a uniformity in every particular, is found in no part of nature. On the contrary, from observing the variety of conduct in different men, we are enabled to form a greater variety of maxims, which still suppose a degree of uniformity and regularity.

Are the manners of men different in different ages and countries? We learn thence the great force of custom and education, which mould the human mind from its infancy and form it into a fixed and established character. Is the behaviour and conduct of the one sex very unlike that of the other? Is it thence we become acquainted with the different characters which nature has impressed upon the sexes, and which she preserves with constancy and regularity? Are the actions of the same person much diversified in the different periods of his life, from infancy to old age? This affords room for many general observations concerning the gradual change of our sentiments and inclinations, and the different maxims which prevail in the different ages of human creatures. Even the characters, which are peculiar to each individual, have a uniformity in their influence; otherwise our acquaintance with the persons and our observation of their conduct could never teach us their dispositions, or serve to direct our behaviour with regard to them.

I grant it possible to find some actions, which seem to have no regular connexion with any known motives, and are exceptions to all the measures of conduct which have ever been established for the government of men. But if we would willingly know what judgement should be formed of such irregular and extraordinary actions, we may consider the sentiments commonly entertained with regard to those irregular events which appear in the course of nature, and the operations of external objects. All causes are not conjoined to their usual effects with like uniformity. An artificer, who handles only dead matter, may be disappointed of his aim, as well as the politician, who directs the conduct of sensible and intelligent agents.

The vulgar, who take things according to their first appearance, attribute the uncertainty of events to such an uncertainty in the causes as makes the latter often fail of their usual influence; though they meet with no impediment in their operation. But philosophers, observing that, almost in every part of nature, there is contained a vast variety of springs and principles, which are hid, by reason of their minuteness or remoteness, find, that it is at least possible the contrariety of events may not proceed from any contingency in the cause, but from the secret operation of contrary causes. This possibility is converted into certainty by farther observation, when they remark that, upon an exact scrutiny, a contrariety of effects always betrays a contrariety of causes, and proceeds from their mutual opposition. A peasant can give no better reason for the stopping of any clock or watch than to say that it does not commonly go right: But an artist easily perceives that the same force in the spring or pendulum has always the same influence on the wheels; but fails of its usual effect, perhaps by reason of a grain of dust, which puts a stop to the whole movement. From the observation of several parallel instances, philosophers form a maxim that the connexion between all causes and effects is equally necessary, and that its seeming uncertainty in some instances proceeds from the secret opposition of contrary causes.

Thus, for instance, in the human body, when the usual symptoms of health or sickness disappoint our expectation; when medicines operate not with their wonted powers; when irregular events follow from any particular cause; the philosopher and physician are not surprised at the matter, nor are even tempted to deny, in general, the necessity and uniformity of those principles by which the animal economy is conducted. They know that a human body is a mighty complicated machine: That many secret powers lurk in it, which are altogether beyond our comprehension: That to us it must often appear very uncertain in its operations: And that therefore the irregular events, which outwardly discover themselves, can be no proof that the laws of nature are not observed with the greatest regularity in its internal operations and government.

The philosopher, if he be consistent, must apply the same reasoning to the actions and volitions of intelligent agents. The most irregular and unexpected resolutions of men may frequently be accounted for by those who know every particular circumstance of their character and situation. A person of an obliging disposition gives a peevish answer: But he has the toothache, or has not dined. A stupid fellow discovers an uncommon alacrity in his carriage: But he has met with a sudden piece of good fortune. Or even when an action, as sometimes happens, cannot be particularly accounted for, either by the person himself or by others; we know, in general, that the characters of men are, to a certain degree, inconstant and irregular. This is, in a manner, the constant character of human nature; though it be applicable, in a more particular manner, to some persons who have no fixed rule for their conduct, but proceed in a continued course of caprice and inconstancy. The internal principles and motives may operate in a uniform manner, notwithstanding these seeming irregularities; in the same manner as the winds, rain, clouds, and other variations of the weather are supposed to be governed by steady principles; though not easily discoverable by human sagacity and enquiry.

Thus it appears, not only that the conjunction between motives and voluntary actions is as regular and uniform as that between the cause and effect in any part of nature; but also that this regular conjunction has been universally acknowledged among mankind, and has never been the subject of dispute, either in philosophy or common life. Now, as it is from past experience that we draw all inferences concerning the future, and as we conclude that objects will always be conjoined together which we find to have always been conjoined; it may seem superfluous to prove that this experienced uniformity in human actions is a source whence we draw *inferences* concerning them. But in order to throw the argument into a greater variety of lights we shall also insist, though briefly, on this latter topic.

The mutual dependence of men is so great in all societies that scarce any human action is entirely complete in itself, or is performed without some reference to the actions of others, which are requisite to make it answer fully the intention of the agent. The poorest artificer, who labours alone, expects at least the protection of the magistrate, to ensure him the enjoyment of the fruits of his labour. He also expects that, when he carries his goods to market, and offers them at a reasonable price, he shall find purchasers, and shall be able, by the money he acquires, to engage others to supply him with those commodities which are requisite for his subsistence. In proportion as men extend their dealings, and render their intercourse with others more complicated, they always comprehend, in their schemes of life, a greater variety of voluntary actions, which they expect, from the proper motives, to co-operate with their own. In all these conclusions they take their measures from past experience, in the same manner as in their reasonings concerning external objects; and firmly believe that men, as well as all the elements, are to continue, in their operations, the same that they have ever found them. A manufacturer reckons upon the labour of his servants for the execution of any work as much as upon the tools which he employs, and would be equally surprised were his expectations disappointed. In short, this experimental inference and reasoning concerning the actions of others enters so much into human life that no man, while awake, is ever a moment without employing it. Have we not reason, therefore, to affirm that all mankind have always agreed in the doctrine of necessity according to the foregoing definition and explication of it?

Nor have philosophers ever entertained a different opinion from the people in this particular. For, not to mention that almost every action of their life supposes that opinion, there are even few of the speculative parts of learning to which it is not essential. What would become of *history*, had we not a dependence on the veracity of the historian according to the experience which we have had of mankind? How could *politics* be a science, if laws and forms of government had not a uniform influence upon society? Where would be the foundation of *morals*, if particular characters had no certain or determinate power to produce particular sentiments, and if these sentiments had no constant operation on actions? And with what pretense could we employ our *criticism* upon any poet or polite author, if we could not pronounce the conduct and sentiments of his actors either natural or unnatural to such characters, and in such circumstances? It seems almost impossible, therefore, to engage either in science or action of any kind without acknowledging the doctrine of necessity, and this *inference* from motive to voluntary actions, from characters to conduct.

And indeed, when we consider how aptly *natural* and *moral* evidence link together, and form only one chain of argument, we shall make no scruple to allow that they are of the same nature, and derived from the same principles. A prisoner who has neither money nor interest, discovers the impossibility of his escape, as well when he considers the obstinacy of the gaoler, as the walls and bars with which he is surrounded; and, in all attempts for his freedom, chooses rather to work upon the stone and iron of the one, than upon the inflexible nature of the other. The same prisoner, when conducted to the scaffold, foresees his death as certainly from the constancy and fidelity of his guards, as from the operation of the axe or wheel. His mind runs along a certain train of ideas: The refusal of the soldiers to consent to his escape; the action of the executioner; the separation of the head and body; bleeding, convulsive motions, and death. Here is a connected chain of natural causes and voluntary actions; but the mind feels no difference between them in passing from one link to another: Nor is less certain of the future even than if it were connected with the objects present to the memory or senses, by a train of causes, cemented together by what we are pleased to call a *physical* necessity. The same experienced union has the same effect on the mind, whether the united objects be motives, volition, and actions; or figure and motion. We may change the name of things; but their nature and their operation on the understanding never change.

Were a man, whom I know to be honest and opulent, and with whom I live in intimate friendship, to come into my house, where I am surrounded with my servants, I rest assured that he is not to stab me before he leaves it in order to rob me of my silver standish; and I no more suspect this event than the falling of the house itself, which is new, and solidly built and founded—*But he may have been seized with a sudden and unknown frenzy.*—So may a sudden earthquake arise, and shake and tumble my house about my ears. I shall therefore change the suppositions. I shall say that I know with certainty that he is not to put his hand into the fire and hold it there till it be consumed: And this event, I think I can foretell with the same assurance, as that, if he throw himself out at the window and meet with no obstruction, he will not remain a moment suspended in the air. No suspicion of an unknown frenzy can give the least possibility to the former event, which is so contrary to all the known principles of human nature. A man who at noon leaves his purse full of gold on the pavement at Charing-Cross, may as well expect that it will fly away like a feather, as that he will find it untouched an hour after. Above one half of human reasonings contain inferences of a similar nature, attended with more or less degrees of certainty proportioned to our experience of the usual conduct of mankind in such particular situations.

I have frequently considered, what could possibly be the reason why all mankind, though they have ever, without hesitation, acknowledged the doctrine of necessity in their whole practice and reasoning, have yet discovered such a reluctance to acknowledge it in words, and have rather shown a propensity, in all ages, to profess the contrary opinion. The matter, I think, may be accounted for after the following manner. If we examine the operations of body, and the production of effects from their causes, we shall find that all our faculties can never carry us farther in our knowledge of this relation than barely to observe that particular objects are *constantly conjoined* together, and that the mind is carried, by a *customary transition,* from the appearance of one to the belief of the other. But though this conclusion concerning human ignorance be the result of the strictest scrutiny of this subject, men still entertain a strong propensity to believe that they penetrate farther into the powers of nature, and perceive something like a necessary connexion between the cause and the effect. When again they turn their reflections towards the operations of their own minds, and *feel* no such connexion of the motive and the action; they are thence apt to suppose, that there is a difference between the effects which result from material force, and those which arise from thought and intelligence. But being once convinced that we know nothing farther of causation of any kind than merely the *constant conjunction of objects, and the consequent inference of the mind from one to another, and find*ing that these two circumstances are universally allowed to have place in voluntary actions; we may be more easily led to own the same necessity common to all causes. And though this reasoning may contradict the systems of many philosophers, in ascribing necessity to the determinations of the will, we shall find, upon reflection, that they dissent from it in words only, not in their real sentiment. Necessity, according to the sense in which it is here taken, has never yet been rejected, nor can ever, I think, be rejected by any philosopher. It may only, perhaps, be pretended that the mind can perceive, in the operations of matter, some farther connexion between the cause and effect; and connexion that has no place in voluntary actions of intelligent beings. Now whether it be so or not, can only appear upon examination; and it is incumbent on these philosophers to make good their assertion, by defining or describing that necessity, and pointing it out to us in the operations of material causes.

It would seem, indeed, that men begin at the wrong end of this question concerning liberty and necessity, when they enter upon it by examining the faculties of the soul, the influence of the understanding, and the operations of the will. Let them first discuss a more simple question, namely, the operations of body and of brute unintelligent matter; and try whether they can there form any idea of causation and necessity, except that of a constant conjunction of objects, and subsequent inference of the mind from one to another. If these circumstances form, in reality, the whole of that necessity, which we conceive in matter, and if these circumstances be also universally acknowledged to take place in the operations of the mind, the dispute is at an end; at least, must be owned to be thenceforth merely verbal. But as long as we will rashly suppose that we have some farther idea of necessity and causation in the operations of external objects; at the same time, that we can find nothing farther in the voluntary actions of the mind; there is no possibility of bringing the question to any determinate issue, while we proceed upon so erroneous a supposition. The only method of undeceiving us is to mount up higher; to examine the narrow extent of science when applied to material causes; and to convince ourselves that all we know of them is the constant conjunction and inference above mentioned. We may, perhaps, find that it is with difficulty we are induced to fix such narrow limits to human understanding: But we can afterwards find no difficulty when we come to apply this doctrine to the actions of the will. For as it is evident that these have a regular conjunction with motives and circumstances and characters, and as we always draw inferences from one to the other, we must be obliged to acknowledge in words that necessity, which we have already avowed, in every deliberation of our lives, and in every step of our conduct and behaviour.[1]

But to proceed in this reconciling project with regard to the question of liberty and necessity; the most contentious question of metaphysics, the most contentious science; it will not require many words to prove that all mankind have ever agreed in the doctrine of liberty as well as in that of necessity, and that the whole dispute, in this respect also, has been hitherto merely verbal. For what is meant by liberty, when applied to voluntary actions? We cannot surely mean that actions have so little connexion with motives, inclinations, and circumstances, that one does not follow with a certain degree of uniformity from the other, and that one affords no inference by which we can conclude the existence of the other. For these are plain and acknowledged matters of fact. By liberty, then, we can only mean *a power of act-ing or not acting, according to the determinations of the will;* that is, if we choose to remain at rest, we may; if we choose to move, we also may. Now this hypothetical liberty is universally allowed to belong to every one who is not a prisoner and in chains. Here, then, is not subject of dispute.

Whatever definition we may give of liberty, we should be careful to observe two req-uisite circumstances; *first,* that it be consistent with plain matter of fact; *second,* that it be consistent with itself. If we observe these circumstances, and render our defin-ition intelligible, I am persuaded that all mankind will be found of one opinion with regard to it.

It is universally allowed that nothing exists without a cause of its existence, and that chance, when strictly examined, is a mere negative word, and means not any real power which has anywhere a being in nature. But it is pretended that some causes are necessary, some not necessary. Here then is the advantage of definitions. Let any one *define* a cause, without comprehending, as a part of the definition, a *necessary con-nexion* with its effect; and let him show distinctly the origin of the idea, expressed by the definition; and I shall readily give up the whole controversy. But if the foregoing explication of the matter be received, this must be absolutely impracticable. Had not objects a regular conjunction with each other, we should never have entertained any notion of cause and effect; and this regular conjunction produces that inference of the understanding, which is the only connexion, that we can have any comprehen-sion of. Whoever attempts a definition of cause, exclusive of these circumstances, will be obliged either to employ unintelligible terms or such as are synonymous to the term which he endeavours to define.[2] And if the definition above mentioned be admitted; liberty, when opposed to necessity, not to constraint, is the same thing with chance; which is universally allowed to have no existence.

## NOTES

1. The prevalence of the doctrine of liberty may be accounted for, from another cause, viz, a false sensation or seeming experience which we have, or may have, of liberty or indifference, in many of our actions. The necessity of any action, whether of matter or of mind, is not, prop-erly speaking, a quality in the agent, but in any thinking or intelligent being, who may consider the action; and it consists chiefly in the determination of his thoughts to infer the existence of that action from some preceding objects; as liberty, when opposed to necessity, is nothing but the want of that determination, and a certain looseness or indifference, which we feel, in passing, or not passing, from the idea of one object to that of any succeeding one. Now we may observe, that, though, in *reflecting* on human actions, we seldom feel such a looseness, or indif-ference, but are commonly able to infer them with considerable certainty from their motives, and from the dispositions of the agent; yet it frequently happens, that, in *performing* the actions themselves, we are sensible of something like it: And as all resembling objects are readily taken for each other, this has been employed as a demonstrative and even intuitive proof of human liberty. We feel, that our actions are subject to our will, on most occasions; and imagine we feel that the will itself is subject to nothing, because, when by a denial of it we are provoked to try,

we feel that it moves easily every way, and produces an image of itself (or a *Velleïty*, as it is called in the schools) even on that side on which it did not settle. This image, or faint motion, we persuade ourselves, could, at that time, have been completed into the thing itself; because, should that be denied, we find upon a second trial, that, at present, it can. We consider not that the fantastical desire of showing liberty is here the motive of our actions. And it seems certain that, however we may imagine we feel a liberty within ourselves, a spectator can commonly infer our actions from our motives and character; and even where he cannot, he concludes in general, that he might, were he perfectly acquainted with every circumstance of our situation and temper, and the most secret springs of our complexion and disposition. Now this is the very essence of necessity, according to the foregoing doctrine.

2. Thus, if a cause be defined, *that which produces any thing;* it is easy to observe, that *producing* is synonymous to *causing.* In like manner, if a cause be defined, *that by which any thing exists;* this is liable to the same objection. For what is meant by these words, *by which?* Had it been said, that a cause is *that* after which *any thing constantly exists;* we should have understood the terms. For this is, indeed, all we know of the matter. And this constancy forms the very essence of necessity, nor have we any other idea of it.

# C. A. CAMPBELL

# Has the Self "Free Will"?

In this excerpt from his book ***On Selfhood and Godhood*** (1957), Campbell defends a libertarian solution to the problem of free will. He argues that we know by introspection that some of our actions are free. Campbell claims that these actions, therefore, cannot possess causal explanations.

1. ... It is something of a truism that in philosophic enquiry the exact formulation of a problem often takes one a long way on the road to its solution. In the case of the Free Will problem I think there is a rather special need of careful formulation. For there are many sorts of human freedom; and it can easily happen that one wastes a great deal of labour in proving or disproving a freedom which has almost nothing to do with the freedom which is at issue in the traditional problem of Free Will. The abortiveness of so much of the argument for and against Free Will in contemporary philosophical literature seems to me due in the main to insufficient pains being taken over the preliminary definition of the problem. ...

Fortunately we can at least make a beginning with a certain amount of confidence. It is not seriously disputable that the kind of freedom in question is the freedom which is commonly recognised to be in some sense a precondition of moral responsibility. Clearly, it is on account of this integral connection with moral responsibility that such exceptional importance has always been felt to attach to the Free Will problem. But in what precise sense is free will a precondition of moral responsibility, and thus a postulate of the moral life in general? This is an exceedingly troublesome

C. A. Campbell, "Has the Self 'Free Will'?" from *On Selfhood and Godhood* (London: Unwin Hyman Ltd., 1957), pp. 158–165, 167–179. Reproduced with permission of Taylor & Francis Books, Ltd.

question; but until we have satisfied ourselves about the answer to it, we are not in a position to state, let alone decide, the question whether "Free Will" in its traditional, ethical, significance is a reality.

Our first business, then, is to ask, exactly what kind of freedom is it which is required for moral responsibility? And as to method of procedure in this inquiry, there seems to me to be no real choice. I know of only one method that carries with it any hope of success; viz. the critical comparison of those acts for which, on due reflection, we deem it proper to attribute moral praise or blame to the agents, with those acts for which, on due reflection, we deem such judgments to be improper. The ultimate touchstone, as I see it, can only be our moral consciousness as it manifests itself in our more critical and considered moral judgments. . . .

2. The first point to note is that the freedom at issue (as indeed the very name "Free *Will* Problem" indicates) pertains primarily not to overt acts but to inner acts. The nature of things has decreed that, save in the case of one's self, it is only overt acts which one can directly observe. But a very little reflection serves to show that in our moral judgments upon others their overt acts are regarded as significant only in so far as they are the expression of inner acts. We do not consider the acts of a robot to be morally responsible acts; nor do we consider the acts of a man to be so save inso- far as they are distinguishable from those of a robot by reflecting an inner life of choice. Similarly, from the other side, if we are satisfied (as we may on occasion be, at least in the case of ourselves) that a person has definitely elected to follow a course which he believes to be wrong, but has been prevented by external circumstances from translating his inner choice into an overt act, we still regard him as morally blameworthy. Moral freedom, then, pertains to *inner* acts.

The next point seems at first sight equally obvious and controversial; but, as we shall see, it has awkward implications if we are in real earnest with it (as almost nobody is). It is the simple point that the act must be one of which the person judged can be regarded as the *sole* author. It seems plain enough that if there are any *other* deter- minants of the act, external to the self, to that extent the act is not an act which the *self* determines, and to that extent not an act for which the self can be held morally responsible. The self is only part-author of the act, and his moral responsibility can logically extend only to those elements within the act (assuming for the moment that these can be isolated) of which he is the *sole* author.

The awkward implications of this apparent truism will be readily appreciated. For, if we are mindful of the influences exerted by heredity and environment, we may well feel some doubt whether there is any act of will at all of which one can truly say that the self is sole author, sole determinant. No man has a voice in determining the raw material of impulses and capacities that constitute his hereditary endowment, and no man has more than a very partial control of the material and social environment in which he is destined to live his life. Yet it would be manifestly absurd to deny that these two factors do constantly and profoundly affect the nature of a man's choices. That this is so we all of us recognise in our moral judgments when we "make allowances," as we say, for a bad heredity or a vicious environment, and acknowledge in the victim of them a diminished moral responsibility for evil courses. Evidently we do *try*, in our moral judgments, however crudely, to praise or blame a man only in respect of that of which we can regard him as *wholly* the author. And evidently we do recognize that, for a man to be the author of an act in the full sense required for moral responsibility, it is enough merely that he "wills" or "chooses" the act: since even the most unfortunate victim of heredity or environment does, as a rule, "will" what he does. It is significant, however, that the ordinary man, though well enough aware of the influence upon choices of heredity and environment, does not feel obliged thereby to give up his assumption that moral predicates are somehow applicable. Plainly he still believes that there is *something* for which a man is morally responsible, something of which we can fairly say that he is the sole author. *What is this something?* To that question common sense is not ready with an explicit answer—though an answer is, I think, implicit in the line which its moral judgments take. I shall do what I can to give an explicit answer later in this Chapter. Meantime it must suffice to observe that, if we are to be true to the deliverances of our moral consciousness, it is very difficult to deny that *sole* authorship is a necessary condition of the morally responsible act.

Thirdly we come to a point over which much recent controversy has raged. We may approach it by raising the following question. Granted an act of which the agent is sole author, does this "sole authorship" suffice to make the act a morally free act? We may be inclined to think that it does, until we contemplate the possibility that an act of which the agent is sole author might conceivably occur as a necessary expression of the agent's nature; the way in which, e.g., some philosophers have supposed the Divine act of creation to occur. This consideration excites a legitimate doubt, for it is far from easy to see how a person can be regarded as a proper subject for moral praise or blame in respect of an act which he *cannot help* performing—even if it be his own "nature" which necessitates it. Must we not recognize it as a condition of the morally free act that the agent "could have acted otherwise" than he in fact did? It is true, indeed, that we sometimes praise or blame a man for an act about which we are prepared to say, in the light of our knowledge of his established character, that he "could do no other." But I think that a little reflection shows that in such cases we are not praising or blaming the man strictly for what he does *now* (or at any rate we ought not to be), but rather for those past acts of his which have generated the firm habit of mind from which his *present* act follows "necessarily." In other words, our praise and blame, so far as justified, are really retrospective, being directed not at the agent *qua* performing *this* act, but to the agent *qua* performing those past acts which have built up his present character, and in respect to which we presume that he *could* have acted otherwise, that there really *were* open possibilities before him. These cases, therefore, seem to me to constitute no valid exception to what I must take to be the rule, viz. that a man can be morally praised or blamed for an act only if he could have acted otherwise.

Now philosophers today are fairly well agreed that it is a postulate of the morally responsible act that the agent "could have acted otherwise" in *some* sense of that phrase. But sharp differences of opinion have arisen over the way in which the phrase ought to be interpreted. There is a strong disposition to water down its apparent meaning by insisting that it is not (as a postulate of moral responsibility) to be understood as a straightforward categorical proposition, but rather as a disguised hypothetical proposition. All that we really require to be assured of, in order to justify our holding X morally responsible for an act, is, we are told, that X could have acted otherwise *if* he had *chosen* otherwise (Moore, Stevenson); or perhaps that X could have acted otherwise *if* he had had a different character, or *if* he had been placed in different circumstances.

I think it is easy to understand, and even, in a measure, to sympathise with, the motives which induce philosophers to offer these counter-interpretations. It is not just the fact that "X could have acted otherwise," as a bald categorical statement, is incompatible with the universal sway of causal law—though this is, to some philosophers, a serious stone of stumbling. The more widespread objection is that it at least looks as though it were incompatible with that causal continuity of an agent's character with his conduct which is implied when we believe (surely with justice) that we can often tell the sort of thing a man will do from our knowledge of the sort of man he is.

We shall have to make our accounts with that particular difficulty later. At this stage I wish merely to show that neither of the hypothetical propositions suggested— and I think the same could be shown for *any* hypothetical alternative—is an acceptable substitute for the categorical proposition "X could have acted otherwise" as the presupposition of moral responsibility.

Let us look first at the earlier suggestion—"X could have acted otherwise *if* he had chosen otherwise." Now clearly there are a great many acts with regard to which we are entirely satisfied that the agent is thus situated. We are often perfectly sure that—for this is all it amounts to—if X had chosen otherwise, the circumstances presented no external obstacle to the translation of that choice into action. For example, we often have no doubt at all that X, who in point of fact told a lie, could have told the truth *if* he had so chosen. But does our confidence on this score allay all legitimate doubts about whether X is really blameworthy? Does it entail that X is free in the sense required for moral responsibility? Surely not. The obvious question immediately arises: "But *could* X have *chosen* otherwise than he did?" It is doubt about the true answer to *that* question which leads most people to doubt the reality of moral responsibility. Yet on this crucial question the hypothetical proposition which is offered as a sufficient statement of the condition justifying the ascription of moral responsibility gives us no information whatsoever.

Indeed this hypothetical substitute for the categorical "X could have acted otherwise" seems to me to lack all plausibility unless one contrives to forget why it is, after all, that we ever come to feel fundamental doubts about man's moral responsibility. Such doubts are born, surely, when one becomes aware of certain reputable worldviews in religion or philosophy, or of certain reputable scientific beliefs, which in their several ways imply that man's actions are necessitated, and thus could not be otherwise than they in fact are. But clearly a doubt so based is not even touched by the recognition that a man could very often act otherwise *if* he so chose. That proposition is entirely compatible with the necessitarian theories which generate our doubt: indeed it is this very compatibility that has recommended it to some philosophers, who are reluctant to give up either moral responsibility or Determinism. The proposition which we *must* be able to affirm if moral praise or blame of X is to be justified is the categorical proposition that X could have acted otherwise because—not if—he could have chosen otherwise; or, since it is essentially the inner side of the act that matters, the proposition simply that X could have chosen otherwise.

For the second of the alternative formulae suggested we cannot spare more than a few moments. But its inability to meet the demands it is required to meet is almost transparent. "X could have acted otherwise," as a statement of a precondition of X's moral responsibility, really means (we are told) "X could have acted otherwise *if* he were differently constituted, or *if* he had been placed in different circumstances." It seems a sufficient reply to this to point out that the person whose moral responsibility is at issue is X; a specific individual, in a specific set of circumstances. It is totally irrelevant to X's moral responsibility that we should be able to say that some person differently constituted from X or X in a different set of circumstance, could have done something different from what X did.

3. Let me, then, briefly sum up the answer at which we have arrived to our question about the kind of freedom required to justify moral responsibility. It is that a man can be said to exercise free will in a morally significant sense only insofar as his chosen act is one of which he is the sole cause or author, and only if—in the straightforward, categorical sense of the phrase—he "could have chosen otherwise."

I confess that this answer is in some ways a disconcerting one. Disconcerting, because most of us, however objective we are in the actual conduct of our thinking, would *like* to be able to believe that moral responsibility is real: whereas the freedom required for moral responsibility, on the analysis we have given, is certainly far more difficult to establish than the freedom required on the analyses we found ourselves obliged to reject. If, e.g., moral freedom entails only that I could have acted otherwise *if* I had chosen otherwise, there is no real "problem" about it at all. I am "free" in the normal case where there is no external obstacle to prevent my translating the alternative choice into action, and not free in other cases. Still less is there a problem if all that moral freedom entails is that I could have acted otherwise *if* I had been a differently constituted person, or been in different circumstances. Clearly I am *always* free in *this* sense of freedom. But, as I have argued, these so-called "freedoms" fail to give us the pre-conditions of moral responsibility, and hence leave the freedom of the traditional free-will problem, the freedom that people are really concerned about, precisely where it was. . . .

5. That brings me to the second, and more constructive, part of this Chapter. From now on I shall be considering whether it is reasonable to believe that man does in fact possess a free will of the kind specified in the first part of the Chapter. If so, just how and where within the complex fabric of the volitional life are we to locate it?—for although free will must presumably belong (if anywhere) to the volitional side of human experience, it is pretty clear from the way in which we have been forced to define it that it does not pertain simply to volition as such; not even to all volitions that are commonly dignified with the name of "choices." It has been, I think, one of the more serious impediments to profitable discussion of the Free Will problem that Libertarians and Determinists alike have so often failed to appreciate the comparatively narrow area within which the free will that is necessary to "save" morality is required to operate. It goes without saying that this failure has been gravely prejudicial to the case for Libertarianism. I attach a good deal of importance,

therefore, to the problem of locating free will correctly within the volitional orbit. Its solution forestalls and annuls, I believe, some of the more tiresome clichés of Determinist criticism.

We saw earlier that Common Sense's practice of "making allowances" in its moral judgments for the influence of heredity and environment indicates Common Sense's conviction, both that a just moral judgment must discount determinants of choice over which the agent has no control, and also (since it still accepts moral judgments as legitimate) that *something* of moral relevance survives which can be regarded as genuinely self-originated. We are now to try to discover what this "something" is. And I think we may still usefully take Common Sense as our guide. Suppose one asks the ordinary intelligent citizen *why* he deems it proper to make allowances for X, whose heredity and/or environment are unfortunate. He will tend to reply, I think, in some such terms as these: that X has more and stronger temptations to deviate from what is right than Y or Z, who are normally circumstanced, so that he must put forth a *stronger moral effort* if he is to achieve the same level of external conduct. The intended implication seems to be that X is just as morally praiseworthy as Y or Z *if* he exerts an equivalent moral effort, even though he may not thereby achieve an equal success in conforming his will to the "concrete" demands of duty. And this implies, again, Common Sense's belief that *in moral effort* we have something for which a man is responsible *without qualification,* something that is *not* affected by heredity and environment but depends *solely* upon the self itself.

Now in my opinion Common Sense has here, in principle, hit upon the one and only defensible answer. Here, and here alone, so far as I can see, in the act of deciding whether to put forth or withhold the moral effort required to resist temptation and rise to duty, is to be found an act which is free in the sense required for moral responsibility; an act of which the self is sole author, and of which it is true to say that "it could be" (or, after the event, "could have been") "otherwise." Such is the thesis which we shall now try to establish.

6. The species of argument appropriate to the establishment of a thesis of this sort should fall, I think, into two phases. First, there should be a consideration of the evidence of the moral agent's own inner experience. What is the act of moral decision, and what does it imply, from the standpoint of the actual participant? Since there is no way of knowing the act of moral decision—or for that matter any other form of activity—except by actual participation in it, the evidence of the subject, or agent, is on an issue of this kind of primary importance. It can hardly, however, be taken as in itself conclusive. For even if that evidence should be overwhelmingly to the effect that moral decision does have the characteristics required by moral freedom, the question is bound to be raised—and in view of considerations from other quarters pointing in a contrary direction is *rightly* raised—Can we *trust* the evidence in inner experience? That brings us to what will be the second phase of the argument. We shall have to go on to show, if we are to make good our case, that the extraneous considerations so often supposed to be fatal to the belief in moral freedom are in fact innocuous to it.

In the light of what was said [previously] about the self's experience of moral decision as a *creative* activity, we may perhaps be absolved from developing the first phase of the argument at any great length. The appeal is throughout to one's own experience in the actual taking of the moral decision in the situation of moral temptation. "Is it possible," we must ask, "for anyone so circumstanced to *dis*believe that he could be deciding otherwise?" The answer is surely not in doubt. When we decide to exert moral effort to resist a temptation, we feel quite certain that we *could* withhold the effort; just as, if we decide to withhold the effort and yield to our desires, we feel quite certain that we *could* exert it—otherwise we should not blame ourselves afterwards for having succumbed. It may be, indeed, that this conviction is mere self-delusion. But that is not at the moment our concern. It is enough at present to establish that the act of deciding to exert or to withhold moral effort, as we know it from the inside in actual moral living, belongs to the category of acts which "could have been otherwise."

*Mutatis mutandis,* the same reply is forthcoming if we ask, "Is it possible for the moral agent in the taking of his decision to *dis*believe that he is the *sole* author of that decision?" Clearly he cannot disbelieve that it is *he* who takes the decision. That, however, is not in itself sufficient to enable him, on reflection, to regard himself as *solely* responsible for the act. For his "character" as so far formed might conceivably be a factor in determining it, and no one can suppose that the constitution of his "character" is uninfluenced by circumstances of heredity and environment with which *he* has nothing to do. But as we pointed out . . . , the very essence of the moral decision as it is experienced is that it is a decision whether or not to *oppose* our character. I think we are entitled to say, therefore, that the act of moral decision is one in which the self is for itself not merely "author" but "sole author."

7. We may pass on, then, to the second phase of our constructive argument; and this will demand more elaborate treatment. Even if a moral agent *qua* making a moral decision in the situation of "temptation" cannot help believing that he has free will in the sense at issue—a moral freedom between real alternatives, between genuinely open possibilities—are there, nevertheless, objections to a freedom of this kind so cogent that we are bound to distrust the evidence of "inner experience"?

I begin by drawing attention to a simple point whose significance tends, I think, to be underestimated. If the phenomenological analysis we have offered is substantially correct, no one while functioning as a moral agent can help believing that he enjoys free will. Theoretically he may be completely convinced by Determinist arguments, but when actually confronted with a personal situation of conflict between duty and desire he is quite certain that it lies with him here and now whether or not he will rise to duty. It follows that if Determinists could produce convincing theoretical arguments against a free will of this kind, the awkward predicament would ensue that man has to deny as a theoretical being what he had to assert as a practical being. Now I think the Determinist ought to be a good deal more worried about this than he usually is. He seems to imagine that a strong case on general theoretical grounds is enough to prove that the "practical" belief in free will, even if inescapable for us as practical beings, is mere illusion. But in fact it proves nothing of the sort. There is no reason whatever why a belief that we find ourselves obliged to hold *qua* practical beings should be required to give way before a belief which we find ourselves obliged to hold *qua* theoretical beings; or, for that matter, vice versa. All that the theoretical arguments of Determinism can prove, unless they are reinforced by a refutation of the phenomenological analysis that support Libertarianism, is that there is a radical conflict between the theoretical and the practical sides of man's nature, an antinomy at the very heart of the self. And this is a state of affairs with which no one can easily rest satisfied. I think therefore that the Determinist ought to concern himself a great deal more than he does with phenomenological analysis, in order to show, if he can, that the assurance of free will is not really an inexpungable element in man's practical consciousness. There is just as much obligation upon him, convinced though he may be of the soundness of his theoretical arguments, to expose the errors of the Libertarian's phenomenological analysis, as there is upon us, convinced though we may be of the soundness of the Libertarian's phenomenological analysis, to expose the errors of the Determinist's theoretical arguments.

8. However, we must at once begin the discharge of our own obligation. The rest of this Chapter will be devoted to trying to show that the arguments which seem to carry most weight with Determinists are, to say the least of it, very far from compulsive.

Fortunately a good many of the arguments which at an earlier time in the history of philosophy would have been strongly urged against us make almost no appeal to the bulk of philosophers today, and we may here pass them by. That applies to any criticism of "open possibilities" based on a metaphysical theory about the nature of the universe as a whole. Nobody today *has* a metaphysical theory about the nature of the universe as a whole! It applies also, with almost equal force, to criticisms based upon the universality of causal law as a supposed postulate of science. There have always been, in my opinion, sound philosophic reasons for doubting the validity, as distinct from the convenience, of the causal postulate in its universal form, but at the present time, when scientists themselves are deeply divided about the need for postulating causality even within their own special field, we shall do better to concentrate our attention upon criticisms which are more confidently advanced. I propose to ignore also, on different grounds, the type of criticism of free will that is sometimes advanced from the side of religion, based upon religious postulates of Divine Omnipotence and Omniscience. So far as I can see, a postulate of human freedom is every bit as necessary to meet certain religious demands (e.g., to make sense of the "conviction of sin"), as postulates of Divine Omniscience and Omnipotence are to meet certain other religious demands. If so, then it can hardly be argued that religious experience as such tells more strongly against than for the position we are defending; and we may be satisfied, in the present context, to leave the matter there. It will be more profitable to discuss certain arguments which contemporary philosophers do think important, and which recur with a somewhat monotonous regularity in the literature of anti-Libertarianism.

These arguments can, I think, be reduced in principle to no more than two; first, the argument from "predictability"; second, the argument from the alleged meaninglessness of an act supposed to be the self's act and yet not an expression of the self's character. Contemporary criticism of free will seems to me to consist almost exclusively of variations on these two themes. I shall deal with each in turn.

9. On the first we touched in passing at an earlier stage. Surely it is beyond question (the critic urges) that when we know a person intimately we can foretell with a high degree of accuracy how he will respond to at least a large number of practical situations. One feels safe in predicting that one's dog-loving friend will not use his boot to repel the little mongrel that comes yapping at his heels; or again that one's wife will not pass with incurious eyes (or indeed pass at all) the new hat-shop in the city. So to behave would not be (as we say) "in character." But, so the criticism runs, you with your doctrine of "genuinely open possibilities," of a free will by which the self can diverge from its own character, remove all rational basis from such prediction. You require us to make the absurd supposition that the success of countless predictions of the sort in the past has been mere matter of chance. If you *really* believed in your theory, you would not be surprised if tomorrow your friend with the notorious horror of strong drink should suddenly exhibit a passion for whisky and soda, or if your friend whose taste for reading has hitherto been satisfied with the sporting columns of the newspapers should be discovered on a fine Saturday afternoon poring over the works of Hegel. But of course you *would* be surprised. Social life would be sheer chaos if there were not well-grounded social expectations; and social life is not sheer chaos. Your theory is hopelessly wrecked upon obvious facts.

Now whether or not this criticism holds good against some versions of Libertarian theory I need not here discuss. It is sufficient if I can make it clear that against the version advanced in this Chapter according to which free will is localised in a relatively narrow field of operation, the criticism has no relevance whatsoever.

Let us remind ourselves briefly of the setting within which, on our view, free will functions. There is X, the course which we believe we ought to follow, and Y, the course towards which we feel our desire is strongest. The freedom which we ascribe to the agent is the freedom to put forth or refrain from putting forth the moral effort required to resist the pressure of desire and do what he thinks he ought to do.

But then there is surely an immense range of practical situations—covering by far the greater part of life—in which there is no question of a conflict within the self between what he most desires to do and what he thinks he ought to do? Indeed such conflict is a comparatively rare phenomenon for the majority of men. Yet over that whole vast range there is nothing whatever in our version of Libertarianism to prevent our agreeing that character determines conduct. In the absence, real or supposed, of any "moral" issue, what a man chooses will be simply that course which, after such reflection as seems called for, he deems most likely to bring him what he most strongly desires; and that is the same as to say the course to which his present character inclines him.

Over by far the greatest area of human choices, then, our theory offers no more barrier to successful prediction on the basis of character than any other theory. For where there is no clash of strongest desire with duty, the free will we are defending has no business. There is just nothing for it to do.

But what about the situations—rare enough though they may be—in which there *is* this clash and in which free will does therefore operate? Does our theory entail that there at any rate, as the critic seems to suppose, "anything may happen"?

Not by any manner of means. In the first place, and by the very nature of the case, the range of the agent's possible choices is bounded by what he thinks he ought to do on the one hand, and what he most strongly desires on the other. The freedom claimed for him is a freedom of decision to make or withhold the effort required to do what he thinks he ought to do. There is no question of a freedom to act in some "wild" fashion, out of all relation to his characteristic beliefs and desires. This so-called "freedom of caprice," so often charged against the Libertarian, is, to put it bluntly, a sheer figment of the critic's imagination, with no *habitat* in serious Libertarian theory. Even in situations where free will does come into play it is perfectly possible, on a view like ours, given the appropriate knowledge of a man's character, to predict within certain limits how he will respond.

But "probable" prediction in such situations can, I think, go further than this. It is obvious that where desire and duty are at odds, the felt "gap" (as it were) between the two may vary enormously in breadth in different cases. The moderate drinker and the chronic tippler may each want another glass, and each deem it his duty to abstain, but the felt gap between desire and duty in the case of the former is trivial beside the great gulf which is felt to separate them in the case of the latter. Hence it will take a far harder moral effort for the tippler than for the moderate drinker to achieve the same external result of abstention. So much is matter of common agreement. And we are entitled, I think, to take it into account in prediction, on the simple principle that the harder the moral effort required to resist desire the less likely it is to occur. Thus in the example taken, most people would predict that the tippler will very probably succumb to his desires, whereas there is a reasonable likelihood that the moderate drinker will make the comparatively slight effort needed to resist them. So long as the prediction does not pretend to more than a measure of probability, there is nothing in our theory which would disallow it.

I claim, therefore, that the view of free will I have been putting forward is consistent with predictability of conduct on the basis of character over a very wide field indeed. And I make the further claim that the field will cover all the situations of life concerning which there is any empirical evidence that successful prediction is possible.

10. Let us pass on to consider the second main line of criticism. This is, I think, much the more illuminating of the two, if only because it compels the Libertarian to make explicit certain concepts which are indispensable to him, but which, being desperately hard to state clearly, are apt not to be stated at all. The critic's fundamental point might be stated somewhat as follows:

"Free will as you describe it is completely unintelligible. On your own showing no *reason* can be given, because there just *is* no reason, why a man decides to exert rather than to withhold moral effort, or vice versa. But such an act—or more properly, such an 'occurrence'—it is nonsense to speak of as an act of a *self*. If there is nothing in the self's character to which it is, even in principle, in any way traceable, the self has nothing to do with it. Your so-called 'freedom,' therefore, so far from supporting the self's moral responsibility, destroys it as surely as the crudest Determinism could do."

If we are to discuss this criticism usefully, it is important, I think, to begin by getting clear about two different senses of the word "intelligible."

If, in the first place, we mean by an "intelligible" act one whose occurrence is in principle capable of being inferred, since it follows necessarily from something (though we may not know in fact from what), then it is certainly true that the Libertarian's free will is unintelligible. But that is only saying, is it not, that the Libertarian's "free" act is not an act which follows necessarily from something! This can hardly rank as a *criticism* of Libertarianism. It is just a description of it. That there can be nothing unintelligible in *this* sense is precisely what the Determinist has got to *prove*.

Yet it is surprising how often the critic of Libertarianism involves himself in this circular mode of argument. Repeatedly it is urged against the Libertarian, with a great air of triumph, that on his view he can't say *why* I now decide to rise to duty, or now decide to follow my strongest desire in defiance of duty. Of course he can't. If he could he wouldn't *be* a Libertarian. To "account for" a "free" act is a contradiction in terms. A free will is *ex hypothesi* the sort of thing of which the request for an *explanation* is absurd. The assumption that an explanation must be in principle possible for the act of moral decision deserves to rank as a classic example of the ancient fallacy of "begging the question."

But the critic usually has in mind another sense of the word "unintelligible." He is apt to take it for granted that an act which is unintelligible in the *above* sense (as the morally free act of the Libertarian undoubtedly is) is unintelligible in the *further* sense that we can attach no meaning to it. And this is an altogether more serious matter. If it could really be shown that the Libertarian's "free will" were unintelligible in this sense of being meaningless, that, for myself at any rate, would be the end of the affair. Libertarianism would have been conclusively refuted.

But it seems to me manifest that this can *not* be shown. The critic has allowed himself, I submit, to become the victim of a widely accepted but fundamentally vicious assumption. He has assumed that whatever is meaningful must exhibit its meaningfulness to those who view it from the standpoint of external observation. Now if one chooses thus to limit one's self to the role of external observer, it is, I think, perfectly true that one can attach no meaning to an act which is the act of something we call a "self" and yet follows from nothing in that self's character. But then *why should we* so limit ourselves, when what is under consideration is a subjective activity? For the apprehension of subjective acts there is *another* standpoint available, that of *inner experience*, of the practical consciousness in its actual functioning. If our free will should turn out to be something to which we can attach a meaning from *this* standpoint, no more is required. And no more ought to be expected. For I must repeat that only from the inner standpoint of living experience *could* anything of the nature of "activity" be directly grasped. Observation from without is in the nature of the case impotent to apprehend the active *qua* active. We can from without observe sequences of states. If into these we read activity (as we sometimes do), this can only be on the basis of what we discern in ourselves from the inner standpoint. It follows that if anyone insists upon taking his criterion of the meaningful simply from the standpoint of external observation, he is really deciding in advance of the evidence that the notion of activity, and *a fortiori* the notion of a free will, is "meaningless." He looks for the free act through a medium which is in the nature of the case incapable of revealing it, and then, because inevitably he doesn't find it, he declares that it doesn't exist!

But if, as we surely ought in this context, we adopt the inner standpoint, then (I am suggesting) things appear in a totally different light. From the inner standpoint, it seems to me plain, there is no difficulty whatever in attaching meaning to an act which is the self's act and which nevertheless does not follow from the self's character. So much I claim has been established by the phenomenological analysis . . . of the act of moral decision in face of moral temptation. It is thrown into particularly clear relief where the moral decision is to make the moral effort required to rise to duty. For the very function of moral effort, as it appears to the agent engaged in the act, is to enable the self to act against the line of resistance, against the line to which his character as so far formed most strongly inclines him. But if the self is thus conscious here of *combating* his formed character, he surely cannot possibly suppose that the act, although his own act, *issues from* his formed character? I submit, therefore, that the self knows very well indeed—from the inner standpoint—what is meant by an act which is the *self's* act and which nevertheless does not follow from the self's character.

What this implies—and it seems to me to be an implication of cardinal importance for any theory of the self that aims at being more than superficial—is that the nature of the self is for itself something more than just its character as so far formed. The "nature" of the self and what we commonly call the "character" of the self are by no means the same thing, and it is utterly vital that they should not be confused. The "nature" of the self comprehends, but is not without remainder reducible to, its "character"; it must, if we are to be true to the testimony of our experience of it, be taken as including *also* the authentic creative power of fashioning and re-fashioning "character."

The misguided, and as a rule quite uncritical, belittlement, of the evidence offered by inner experience has, I am convinced, been responsible for more bad argument by the opponents of Free Will than has any other single factor. How often, for example, do we find the Determinist critic saying, in effect, "*Either* the act follows necessarily upon precedent states, *or* it is a mere matter of chance and accordingly of no moral significance." The disjunction is invalid, for it does not exhaust the possible alternatives. It seems to the critic to do so only because he *will* limit himself to the standpoint which is proper, and indeed alone possible, in dealing with the physical world, the standpoint of the external observer. If only he would allow himself to assume the standpoint which is not merely proper for, but necessary to, the apprehension of subjective activity, the inner standpoint of the practical consciousness in its actual functioning, he would find himself obliged to recognise the falsity of his disjunction. Reflection upon the act of moral decision as apprehended from the inner standpoint would force him to recognise a *third* possibility, as remote from chance as from necessity, that, namely, of *creative activity*, in which (as I have ventured to express it) nothing determines the act save the agent's doing of it.

11. There we must leave the matter. But as this Chapter has been, I know, somewhat densely packed, it may be helpful if I conclude by reminding you, in bald summary, of the main things I have been trying to say. Let me set them out in so many successive theses.

(1) The freedom which is at issue in the traditional Free Will problem is the freedom which is presupposed in moral responsibility.

(2) Critical reflection upon carefully considered attributions of moral responsibility reveals that the only freedom that will do is a freedom which permits to inner acts of choice, and that these acts must be acts *(a)* of which the self is *sole* author, and *(b)* which the self could have performed otherwise.

(3) From phenomenological analysis of the situation of moral temptation we find that the self as engaged in this situation is inescapably convinced that it possesses a freedom of precisely the specified kind, located in the decision to exert or withhold the moral effort needed to rise to duty where the pressure of its desiring nature is felt to urge it in a contrary direction.

(4) Of the two types of Determinist criticism which seem to have most influence today, that based on the predictability of much human behaviour fails to touch a Libertarianism which confines the area of free will as above indicated. Libertarianism so understood is compatible with all the predictability that the empirical facts warrant. And:

(5) The second main type of criticism, which alleges the "meaninglessness" of an act which is the self's act and which is yet not determined by the self's character, is based on a failure to appreciate that the standpoint of inner experience is not only legitimate but indispensable where what is at issue is the reality and nature of a subjective activity. The creative act of moral decision is inevitably meaningless to the mere external observer, but from the inner standpoint it is as real, and as significant, as anything in human experience.

## PLATO

# What Motivates People to Act Justly?

In this excerpt from *The Republic*, Plato (approx. 427–347 B.C.E.) describes an argument that Glaucon makes to Socrates. Socrates was Plato's teacher. Glaucon argues that people are never motivated by a concern for justice, but are motivated only by a concern for wealth, reputation, and so on. He also offers a theory about why human societies came to have institutions of justice. Glaucon also argues, against Socrates, that the lives that unjust people lead are better than the lives that just people have. The passage begins with Socrates speaking.

[Glaucon] said to me: Socrates, do you wish really to persuade us, or only to seem to have persuaded us, that to be just is always better than to be unjust?

From Plato, *The Republic*, Book 2, 357A-367E, translated by Benjamin Jowett.

I should wish really to persuade you, I replied, if I could.

Then you certainly have not succeeded. Let me ask you now:—How would you arrange goods—are there not some which we welcome for their own sakes, and independently of their consequences, as, for example, harmless pleasures and enjoyments, which delight us at the time, although nothing follows from them?

I agree in thinking that there is such a class, I replied.

Is there not also a second class of goods, such as knowledge, sight, health, which are desirable not only in themselves, but also for their results?

Certainly, I said.

And would you not recognize a third class, such as gymnastic, and the care of the sick, and the physician's art; also the various ways of money-making—these do us good but we regard them as disagreeable; and no one would choose them for their own sakes, but only for the sake of some reward or result which flows from them?

There is, I said, this third class also. But why do you ask?

Because I want to know in which of the three classes you would place justice?

In the highest class, I replied,—among those goods which he who would be happy desires both for their own sake and for the sake of their results.

Then the many are of another mind; they think that justice is to be reckoned in the troublesome class, among goods which are to be pursued for the sake of rewards and of reputation, but in themselves are disagreeable and rather to be avoided.

I know, I said, that this is their manner of thinking, and that this was the thesis which Thrasymachus was maintaining just now, when he censured justice and praised injustice. But I am too stupid to be convinced by him.

I wish, he said, that you would hear me as well as him, and then I shall see whether you and I agree. For Thrasymachus seems to me, like a snake, to have been charmed by your voice sooner than he ought to have been; but to my mind the nature of justice and injustice have not yet been made clear. Setting aside their rewards and results, I want to know what they are in themselves, and how they inwardly work in the soul. If you, please, then, I will revive the argument of Thrasymachus. And first I will speak of the nature and origin of justice according to the common view of them. Secondly, I will show that all men who practise justice do so against their will, of necessity, but not as a good. And thirdly, I will argue that there is reason in this view, for the life of the unjust is after all better far than the life of the just—if what they say is true, Socrates, since I myself am not of their opinion. But still I acknowledge that I am perplexed when I hear the voices of Thrasymachus and myriads of others dinning in my ears; and, on the other hand, I have never yet heard the superiority of justice to injustice maintained by any one in a satisfactory way. I want to hear justice praised in respect of itself; then I shall be satisfied, and you are the person from whom I think that I am most likely to hear this; and therefore I will praise the unjust life to the utmost of my power, and my manner of speaking will indicate the manner in which I desire to hear you too praising justice and censuring injustice. Will you say whether you approve of my proposal?

Indeed I do; nor can I imagine any theme about which a man of sense would oftener wish to converse.

I am delighted, he replied, to hear you say so, and shall begin by speaking, as I proposed, of the nature and origin of justice.

They say that to do injustice is, by nature, good; to suffer injustice, evil; but that the evil is greater than the good. And so when men have both done and suffered injustice and have had experience of both, not being able to avoid the one and obtain the other, they think that they had better agree among themselves to have neither; hence there arise laws and mutual covenants; and that which is ordained by law is termed by them lawful and just. This they affirm to be the origin and nature of justice;—it is a mean or compromise, between the best of all, which is to do injustice and not be punished, and the worst of all, which is to suffer injustice without the power of retaliation; and justice, being at a middle point between the two, is tolerated not as a good, but as the lesser evil, and honoured by reason of the inability of men to do injustice. For no man who is worthy to be called a man would ever submit to such an agreement if he were able to resist; he would be mad if he did. Such is the received account, Socrates, of the nature and origin of justice.

Now that those who practice justice do so involuntarily and because they have not the power to be unjust will best appear if we imagine something of this kind: having given both to the just and the unjust power to do what they will, let us watch and see whither desire will lead them; then we shall discover in the very act the just and unjust man to be proceeding along the same road, following their interest, which all natures deem to be their good, and are only diverted into the path of justice by the force of law. The liberty which we are supposing may be most completely given to them in the form of such a power as is said to have been possessed by Gyges the ancestor of Croesus the Lydian. According to the tradition, Gyges was a shepherd in the service of the king of Lydia; there was a great storm, and an earthquake made an opening in the earth at the place where he was feeding his flock. Amazed at the sight, he descended into the opening, where, among other marvels, he beheld a hollow brazen horse, having doors, at which he stooping and looking in saw a dead body of stature, as appeared to him, more than human, and having nothing on but a gold ring; this he took from the finger of the dead and reascended. Now the shepherds met together, according to custom, that they might send their monthly report about the flocks to the king; into their assembly he came having the ring on his finger, and as he was sitting among them he chanced to turn the collet of the ring inside his hand, when instantly he became invisible to the rest of the company and they began to speak of him as if he were no longer present. He was astonished at this, and again touching the ring he turned the collet outwards and reappeared; he made several trials of the ring, and always with the same result—when he turned the collet inwards he became invisible, when outwards he reappeared. Whereupon he contrived to be chosen one of the messengers who were sent to the court; where as soon as he arrived he seduced the queen, and with her help conspired against the king and slew him, and took the kingdom. Suppose now that there were two such magic rings, and the just put on one of them and the unjust the other; no man can be imagined to be of such an iron nature that he would stand fast in justice. No man would keep his hands off what was not his own when he could safely take what he liked out of the market, or go into houses and lie with any one at his pleasure, or kill or release from prison whom he would, and in all respects be like a God among men. Then the actions of the just would be as the actions of the unjust; they would both come at last to the same point. And this we may truly affirm to be a great proof that a man is just, not willingly or because he thinks that justice is any good to him individually, but of necessity, for wherever any one thinks that he can safely be unjust, there he is unjust. For all men believe in their hearts that injustice is far more profitable to the individual than justice, and he who argues as I have been supposing, will say that they are right. If you could imagine any one obtaining this power of becoming invisible, and never doing any wrong or touching what was another's, he would be thought by the lookers-on to be a most wretched idiot, although they would praise him to one another's faces, and keep up appearances with one another from a fear that they too might suffer injustice. Enough of this.

Now, if we are to form a real judgment of the life of the just and unjust, we must isolate them; there is no other way; and how is the isolation to be effected? I answer: Let the unjust man be entirely unjust, and the just man entirely just; nothing is to be taken away from either of them, and both are to be perfectly furnished for the work of their respective lives. First, let the unjust be like other distinguished masters of craft; like the skilful pilot or physician, who knows intuitively his own powers and keeps within their limits, and who, if he fails at any point, is able to recover himself. So let the unjust make his unjust attempts in the right way, and lie hidden if he means to be great in his injustice (he who is found out is nobody): for the highest reach of injustice is: to be deemed just when you are not. Therefore I say that in the perfectly unjust man we must assume the most perfect injustice; there is to be no deduction, but we must allow him, while doing the most unjust acts, to have acquired the greatest reputation for justice. If he have taken a false step he must be able to recover himself; he must be one who can speak with effect, if any of his deeds come to light, and who can force his way where force is required his courage and strength, and command of money and friends. And at his side let us place the just man in his nobleness and simplicity, wishing, as Aeschylus says, to be and not to seem good. There must be no seeming, for if he seem to be just he will be honoured and rewarded, and then we shall not know whether he is just for the sake of justice or for the sake of honours and rewards; therefore, let him be clothed in justice only, and have no other covering; and he must be imagined in a state of life the opposite of the former. Let him be the best of men, and let him be thought the worst; then he will have been put to the proof; and we shall see whether he will be affected by the fear of infamy and its consequences. And let him continue thus to the hour of death; being just and seeming to be unjust. When both have reached the uttermost extreme, the one of justice and the other of injustice, let judgment be given which of them is the happier of the two.

Heavens! my dear Glaucon, I said, how energetically you polish them up for the decision, first one and then the other, as if they were two statues.

I do my best, he said. And now that we know what they are like there is no difficulty in tracing out the sort of life which awaits either of them. This I will proceed to describe; but as you may think the description a little too coarse, I ask you to suppose, Socrates, that the words which follow are not mine.—Let me put them into the mouths of the eulogists of injustice: They will tell you that the just man who is thought unjust will be scourged, racked, bound—will have his eyes burnt out; and, at last, after suffering every kind of evil, he will be impaled: Then he will understand that he ought to seem only, and not to be, just; the words of Aeschylus may be more truly spoken of the unjust than of the just. For the unjust is pursuing a reality; he does not live with a view to appearances—he wants to be really unjust and not to seem only:—

> His mind has a soil deep and fertile,
> Out of which spring his prudent counsels.

In the first place, he is thought just, and therefore bears rule in the city; he can marry whom he will, and give in marriage to whom he will; also he can trade and deal where he likes, and always to his own advantage, because he has no misgivings about injustice and at every contest, whether in public or private, he gets the better of his antagonists, and gains at their expense, and is rich, and out of his gains he can benefit his friends, and harm his enemies; moreover, he can offer sacrifices, and dedicate gifts to the gods abundantly and magnificently, and can honour the gods or any man whom he wants to honour in a far better style than the just, and therefore he is likely to be dearer than they are to the gods. And thus, Socrates, gods and men are said to unite in making the life of the unjust better than the life of the just.

I was going to say something in answer to Glaucon, when Adeimantus, his brother, interposed: Socrates, he said, you do not suppose that there is nothing more to be urged?

Why, what else is there? I answered.

The strongest point of all has not been even mentioned, he replied.

Well, then, according to the proverb, 'Let brother help brother'—if he fails in any part do you assist him; although I must confess that Glaucon has already said quite enough to lay me in the dust, and take from me the power of helping justice.

Nonsense, he replied. But let me add something more: There is another side to Glaucon's argument about the praise and censure of justice and injustice, which is equally required in order to bring out what I believe to be his meaning. Parents and tutors are always telling their sons and their wards that they are to be just; but why? not for the sake of justice, but for the sake of character and reputation; in the hope of obtaining for him who is reputed just some of those offices, marriages, and the like which Glaucon has enumerated among the advantages accruing to the unjust from the reputation of justice. More, however, is made of appearances by this class of persons than by the others; for they throw in the good opinion of the gods, and will tell you of a shower of benefits which the heavens, as they say, rain upon the pious; and this accords with the testimony of the noble Hesiod and Homer, the first of whom says, that the gods make the oaks of the just—

> To bear acorns at their summit, and bees in the middle;
> And the sheep the bowed down bowed the with the their fleeces.

and many other blessings of a like kind are provided for them. And Homer has a very similar strain; for he speaks of one whose fame is—

> As the fame of some blameless king who, like a god,
> Maintains justice to whom the black earth brings forth
> Wheat and barley, whose trees are bowed with fruit,
> And his sheep never fail to bear, and the sea gives him fish.

Still grander are the gifts of heaven which Musaeus and his son vouchsafe to the just; they take them down into the world below, where they have the saints lying on couches at a feast, everlastingly drunk, crowned with garlands; their idea seems to be that an immortality of drunkenness is the highest meed of virtue. Some extend their rewards yet further; the posterity, as they say, of the faithful and just shall survive to the third and fourth generation. This is the style in which they praise justice. But about the wicked there is another strain; they bury them in a slough in Hades, and make them carry water in a sieve; also while they are yet living they bring them to infamy, and inflict upon them the punishments which Glaucon described as the portion of the just who are reputed to be unjust; nothing else does their invention supply. Such is their manner of praising the one and censuring the other.

Once more, Socrates, I will ask you to consider another way of speaking about justice and injustice, which is not confined to the poets, but is found in prose writers. The universal voice of mankind is always declaring that justice and virtue are honourable, but grievous and toilsome; and that the pleasures of vice and injustice are easy of attainment, and are only censured by law and opinion. They say also that honesty is for the most part less profitable than dishonesty; and they are quite ready to call wicked men happy, and to honor them both in public and private when they are rich or in any other way influential, while they despise and overlook those who may be weak and poor, even though acknowledging them to be better than the others. But most extraordinary of all is their mode of speaking about virtue and the gods: they say that the gods apportion calamity and misery to many good men, and good and happiness to the wicked. And mendicant prophets go to rich men's doors and persuade them that they have a power committed to them by the gods of making an atonement for a man's own or his ancestor's sins by sacrifices or charms, with rejoicings and feasts; and they promise to harm an enemy, whether just or unjust, at a small cost; with magic arts and incantations binding heaven, as they say, to execute their will. And the poets are the authorities to whom they appeal, now smoothing the path of vice with the words of Hesiod;—

> Vice may be had in abundance without trouble; the way is smooth and her dwelling-place is near. But before virtue the gods have set toil

and a tedious and uphill road: then citing Homer as a witness that the gods may be influenced by men; for he also says:

> The gods, too, may he turned from their purpose; and men pray to them and avert their wrath by sacrifices and soothing entreaties, and by libations and the odour of fat, when they have sinned and transgressed.

And they produce a host of books written by Musaeus and Orpheus, who were children of the Moon and the Muses—that is what they say—according to which they perform their ritual, and persuade not only individuals, but whole cities, that expiations and atonements for sin may be made by sacrifices and amusements which fill a vacant hour, and are equally at the service of the living and the dead; the latter sort they call mysteries, and they redeem us from the pains of hell, but if we neglect them no one knows what awaits us.

He proceeded: And now when the young hear all this said about virtue and vice, and the way in which gods and men regard them, how are their minds likely to be affected, my dear Socrates,—those of them, I mean, who are quickwitted, and, like bees on the wing, light on every flower, and from all that they hear are prone to draw conclusions as to what manner of persons they should be and in what way they should walk if they would make the best of life? Probably the youth will say to himself in the words of Pindar—

> Can I by justice or by crooked ways of deceit ascend a loftier tower which may he a fortress to me all my days?

For what men say is that, if I am really just and am not also thought just profit there is none, but the pain and loss on the other hand are unmistakable. But if, though unjust, I acquire the reputation of justice, a heavenly life is promised to me. Since then, as philosophers prove, appearance tyrannizes over truth and is lord of happiness, to appearance I must devote myself. I will describe around me a picture and shadow of virtue to be the vestibule and exterior of my house; behind I will trail the subtle and crafty fox, as Archilochus, greatest of sages, recommends. But I hear some one exclaiming that the concealment of wickedness is often difficult; to which I answer, Nothing great is easy. Nevertheless, the argument indicates this, if we would be happy, to be the path along which we should proceed. With a view to concealment we will establish secret brotherhoods and political clubs. And there are professors of rhetoric who teach the art of persuading courts and assemblies; and so, partly by persuasion and partly by force, I shall make unlawful gains and not be punished. Still I hear a voice saying that the gods cannot be deceived, neither can they be compelled. But what if there are no gods? or, suppose them to have no care of human things—why in either case should we mind about concealment? And even if there are gods, and they do care about us, yet we know of them only from tradition and the genealogies of the poets; and these are the very persons who say that they may be influenced and turned by 'sacrifices and soothing entreaties and by offerings.' Let us be consistent then, and believe both or neither. If the poets speak truly, why then we had better be unjust, and offer of the fruits of injustice; for if we are just, although we may escape the vengeance of heaven, we shall lose the gains of injustice; but, if we are unjust, we shall keep the gains, and by our sinning and praying, and praying and sinning, the gods will be propitiated, and we shall not be punished. 'But there is a world below in which either we or our posterity will suffer for our unjust deeds.' Yes, my friend, will be the reflection, but there are mysteries and atoning deities, and these have great power. That is what mighty cities declare; and the children of the gods, who were their poets and prophets, bear a like testimony.

On what principle, then, shall we any longer choose justice rather than the worst injustice? when, if we only unite the latter with a deceitful regard to appearances, we shall fare to our mind both with gods and men, in life and after death, as the most numerous and the highest authorities tell us. Knowing all this, Socrates, how can a man who has any superiority of mind or person or rank or wealth, be willing to honor justice; or indeed to refrain from laughing when he hears justice praised?

And even if there should be some one who is able to disprove the truth of my words, and who is satisfied that justice is best, still he is not angry with the unjust, but is very ready to forgive them, because he also knows that men are not just of their own free will; unless, peradventure, there be some one whom the divinity within him may have inspired with a hatred of injustice, or who has attained knowledge of the truth—but no other man. He only blames injustice who, owing to cowardice or age or some weakness, has not the power of being unjust. And this is proved by the fact that when he obtains the power, he immediately becomes unjust as far as he can be.

The cause of all this, Socrates, was indicated by us at the beginning of the argument, when my brother and I told you how astonished we were to find that of all the professing panegyrists of justice—beginning with the ancient heroes of whom any memorial has been preserved to us, and ending with the men of our own time—no one has ever blamed injustice or praised justice except with a view to the glories, honours, and benefits which flow from them. No one has ever adequately described either in verse or prose the true essential nature of either of them abiding in the soul, and invisible to any human or divine eye; or shown that of all the things of a man's soul which he has within him, justice is the greatest good, and injustice the greatest evil. Had this been the universal strain, had you sought to persuade us of this from our youth upwards, we should not have been on the watch to keep one another from doing wrong, but every one would have been his own watchman, because afraid, if he did wrong, of harboring in himself the greatest of evils. I dare say that Thrasymachus and others would seriously hold the language which I have been merely repeating, and words even stronger than these about justice and injustice, grossly, as I conceive, perverting their true nature. But I speak in this vehement manner, as I must frankly confess to you, because I want to hear from you the opposite side; and I would ask you to show not only the superiority which justice has over injustice, but what effect they have on the possessor of them which makes the one to be a good and the other an evil to him. And please, as Glaucon requested of you, to exclude reputations; for unless you take away from each of them his true reputation and add on the false, we shall say that you do not praise justice, but the appearance of it; we shall think that you are only exhorting us to keep injustice dark, and that you really agree with Thrasymachus in thinking that justice is another's good and the interest of the stronger, and that injustice is a man's own profit and interest, though injurious to the weaker. Now as you have admitted that justice is one of that highest class of goods which are desired indeed for their results, but in a far greater degree for their own sakes—like sight or hearing or knowledge or health, or any other real and natural and not merely conventional good—I would ask you in your praise of justice to regard one point only: I mean the essential good and evil which justice and injustice work in the possessors of them. Let others praise justice and censure injustice, magnifying the rewards and honours of the one and abusing the other; that is a manner of arguing which, coming from them, I am ready to tolerate, but from you who have spent your whole life in the consideration of this question, unless I hear the contrary from your own lips, I expect something better. And therefore, I say, not only prove to us that justice is better than injustice, but show what they either of them do to the possessor of them, which makes the one to be a good and the other an evil, whether seen or unseen by gods and men.

## Suggestions for Further Reading

### ON THE MIND/BODY PROBLEM
Ned Block (ed.), *Readings in the Philosophy of Psychology,* 2 vols., Cambridge, Massachusetts, MIT
  Press, 1981.
Daniel Dennett, *Brainstorms,* Cambridge, Massachusetts, MIT Press, 1978.
Jerry Fodor, *Psychological Explanation,* New York, Random House, 1968.
George Graham, *Philosophy of Mind—An Introduction,* Oxford University Press, 1993.
John Haugland, *Mind Design,* Cambridge, Massachusetts, MIT Press, 1981.
Jaegwon Kim, *Philosophy of Mind,* Boulder, Colorado, Westview Press, 1997.
David Rosenthal (ed.), *Materialism and the Mind-Body Problem,* Englewood Cliffs, New Jersey,
  Prentice–Hall, 1971.
John Searle, "Minds, Brains, and Programs," in *Behavior and Brain Sciences,* vol. 3, pp. 417–457,
  1980.

### ON FREEDOM OF THE WILL
Daniel Dennett, *Elbow Room,* Cambridge, Massachusetts, MIT Press, 1985.
Gerald Dworkin (ed.), *Determinism, Free Will, and Moral Responsibility,* Englewood Cliffs, New Jer-
  sey, Prentice–Hall, 1970.
John Martin Fischer (ed.), *Moral Responsibility,* Ithaca, New York, Cornell University Press,
  1986.
Robert Nozick, "Free Will," in *Philosophical Explanation,* Cambridge, Massachusetts, Harvard Uni-
  versity Press, 1981.
Timothy O'Connor (ed.), *Agents, Causes, and Events,* Oxford, Oxford University Press, 1995.
Gary Watson (ed.), *Free Will,* New York, Oxford University Press, 1982.

### ON EGOISM AND ALTRUISM
Robert Axelrod, *The Evolution of Cooperation,* New York, Basic Books, 1985.
Joel Feinberg, "Psychological Egoism," in J. Feinberg (ed.), *Reason and Responsibility,* Belmont,
  California, Wadsworth, 1981.
Elliott Sober and David Sloan Wilson, *Unto Others: The Evolution and Psychology of Unselfish
  Behavior.* Cambridge, Massachusetts, Harvard University Press, 1998.

# PART V
# ETHICS

## CHAPTER 28

## *Ethics—Normative and Meta*

The philosophical study of ethics (morality) concerns the nature of good and bad, right and wrong, justice and injustice. In the section of this book on the theory of knowledge, I addressed the question of what a person should *believe*. Ethics focuses on the question of *action*—what actions should a person undertake to perform? Ethics deals with what may be the most fundamental personal question of all—how should you lead your life?

### ETHICS AND RELIGION

People often think that ethical questions are inseparable from religious ones. During childhood, many of us had our moral training and our religious training mixed together. We were taught basic ethical principles (such as the Golden Rule) by being told how God wants us to act. In adulthood, disagreements about some ethical questions (for example, the permissibility of contraception or abortion) sometimes reflect differences over some religious doctrine.

If you think that ethics and religion are tightly bound together, it may well puzzle you how an atheist or an agnostic could have strong moral convictions. Maybe you suspect that such people are being inconsistent. If someone doesn't believe that God exists, how can he or she hold that there is a difference between right and wrong? A character in Fyodor Dostoyevsky's novel *The Brothers Karamazov* expresses this idea when he says, "If God is dead, then everything is permitted."

If you tend to connect God and morality in this way, it may surprise you that a very central tradition in Western philosophy has sought to separate questions of ethics from the issue of what God wants us to do. This tradition goes back to Plato in fourth-century B.C.E. Greece. The philosophers in this tradition usually were not atheists. They believed in God (or in the gods, in Plato's case), but thought that ethical questions should be addressed independently of assumptions about whether there is a God and what God commands. I'll discuss this idea in Chapter 31.

## METAETHICS AND NORMATIVE ETHICS

The study of ethics is usually divided into two large areas. These are *metaethics* and *normative ethics*. The prefix *meta* suggests the idea of "aboutness." For example, meta-mathematics is a part of mathematics in which the objects studied are mathematical axioms and proofs; metalinguistic statements are statements about language. In metaethics, we consider general questions about the nature of morality and about the meaning of moral concepts. In metaethics we don't ask whether murder is wrong rather than right. Rather, we ask whether there really is a difference between right and wrong, and we try to clarify what it means to classify an action as "wrong" or "right." In normative ethics, on the other hand, the usual procedure is to assume that there is a difference between right and wrong and then to ask which actions fall into the one category and which into the other. For example, utilitarians say that whether an action should be performed depends on whether it promotes the greatest happiness for the greatest number of people. An alternative position is that actions should not be performed if they are unjust, where the dictates of justice may not always coincide with what makes people happy. This dispute assumes that there is a correct answer to the question of what principles people should use to guide their actions. The problem in normative ethics is to determine what those principles are.

## TRUTH AND OPINION

Back in Chapters 1 and 2, I drew a distinction between truth and opinion. It is one thing to say that the Rockies are more than 10,000 feet tall. It is something else to say that many people believe the Rockies are more than 10,000 feet tall. The first of these propositions is true independently of anyone's believing it or saying that it is so. The second, obviously, depends for its truth on what people believe. There are objective facts about geology, over and above the subjective opinions that people happen to have about geology.

Does this distinction apply to ethics? There is variation in ethical opinions—people sometimes disagree about whether a given action is right or wrong. But is there, in addition, a fact of the matter as to whether the action really *is* right or wrong? That is, are there objective facts in ethics that exist above and beyond the subjective opinions that people happen to have? This is the primary question I'll consider in metaethics.

After surveying a range of possible answers to this question, I'll move on to normative ethics in Chapter 32. When I do this, I'll simply assume that there is a real difference between right and wrong. Given this assumption, I'll ask what makes some actions have the one property and other actions have the other.

## ALTERNATIVE METAETHICAL POSITIONS

To get started on the metaethical question of whether there are objective facts in ethics, I'm going to provide a road map to the different positions I'll consider. These positions divide up according to how they answer the following two questions:

(1)  Are there any ethical truths?

(2)  If so, what makes the ethical truths true?

## SUBJECTIVISM

What would it mean to answer "no" to the first question? The idea here is that there are various ethical *opinions* that people have about right and wrong. But no statement that says that an action *is* right (or wrong) is, in fact, *true.* Opinions occupy what I've called *the subjective realm.* So the theory that says there is opinion but no truth in ethics is called *ethical subjectivism.*

One way to describe this position is to use a distinction David Hume made famous. It is the distinction between *is* and *ought.* Science aims to discover what *is* the case; ethics tries to describe the way things *ought* to be. A negative answer to question (1) might be understood to mean that all true propositions are *is*-propositions; there are no true *ought*-propositions. I'll consider in the next two chapters several arguments that have been given for saying that "no" is the correct answer to question (1).

## REALISM

Consider next what the options are if you answer "yes" to question (1). That is, suppose that some ethical statements are true. Question (2) then becomes relevant: What makes those statements true? One possibility is that they are true independently of anyone's say-so. Ethical truths are true whether or not anyone thinks they are. This position is called *ethical realism.*

When philosophers talk about ethical realism, the term "realism" does not mean what it means in politics—as when we say that someone is a political realist. We sometimes call people "political realists" when they are "practical"—they don't try too hard to do the right thing, because they think that justice is unattainable anyway. Humphrey Bogart is a realist of this sort at the beginning of the movie *Casablanca,* though he changes at the end. Rather, ethical realism is the view that there are objective ethical facts that exist independently of anyone's say-so. If murder is wrong, this isn't because you, I, or anyone says (or thinks) it is wrong. Hamlet says that nothing is right or wrong, unless thinking makes it so. This bit of poetry rejects ethical realism.

## CONVENTIONALISM

The remaining option in metaethics asserts that there are ethical truths, but maintains that these truths are true because of someone's say-so. I call this point of view *conventionalism.* Conventionalists differ from subjectivists in the way they answer question (1); they differ from realists in the way they answer question (2).

In the United States, people drive on the right side of the road. In England, they drive on the left. There is nothing inherently better about one procedure (suppose). They are equally workable, as long as everybody in a country does the same thing. The key idea about conventions is that they embody *arbitrary decisions*. The reason you should drive on the right in the United States is simply that the people there have agreed that that is the rule to follow. In this case, a fact (you should drive on the right) is brought into being by people's saying that things shall be one way rather than the other.

In Chapter 2, I made a general remark about how we should avoid "wishful thinking." For the vast majority of propositions we could consider, thinking (or saying) that they are true does not, all by itself, make them true. Saying or thinking that the Rocky Mountains are more than ten thousand feet high does not make them so. Descartes (Chapter 13) thought he had found an exception to this pattern; he thought that the proposition "I am thinking" is made true by my thinking it is true. Conventionalism in ethics holds that the same goes for right and wrong. Someone's saying (or believing) that murder is wrong makes murder wrong. Conventionalists, however, disagree among themselves as to whose say-so does the job.

## THREE VARIETIES OF CONVENTIONALISM

The first conventionalist theory I'll consider is called the *Divine Command Theory*. It says that an act is right or wrong because and only because God says that it is. It isn't that murder (or whatever) is inherently bad. Rather, murder has the moral status it does only because God commanded that we behave in a certain way.

The second conventionalist theory is called *ethical relativism*. This view says that what is right or wrong is determined by the society you inhabit. If your society adopts norms that prohibit murder, then it is wrong for you to murder. If some other society adopts different standards, then it may be quite permissible for someone in that society to murder. Ethical truths are relative, not absolute. Murder isn't wrong absolutely; it is wrong relative to the norms of one society but may be right relative to the norms of another. According to ethical relativism, it isn't God's say-so that makes the ethical truths true, but society's.

The third and last conventionalist theory I'll consider asserts that each individual constructs his or her own morality. It isn't just that each of us must decide for ourselves how we should live. Rather the idea is that we make our actions right or wrong by deciding which standards to adopt. This idea is part of one version of the philosophy called *existentialism*. In his book *Existentialism*, the French philosopher Jean-Paul Sartre (1905–1980) describes a young Frenchman during World War II who must decide between joining the Resistance to fight the Nazis or staying home to care for his ailing mother. Sartre says that there is no standard of conduct that determines what the young man ought to do. *He* must choose whether he wants to be one sort of person or another. Once this choice is made, his subsequent action thereby counts as good or bad. For Sartre's existentialism, it is the individual's say-so that makes an action right or wrong.

This menu of options in metaethics is summarized in the following flow chart. At the bottom of the chart are the names of the positions described above them:

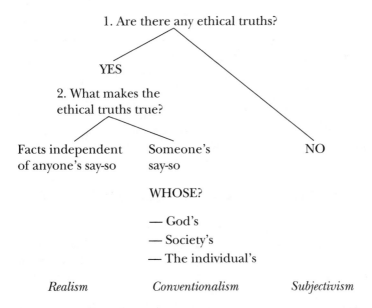

In the next two chapters, I'll consider various arguments that have been made for subjectivism. After that, I'll discuss various conventionalist theories in metaethics, beginning with the Divine Command Theory and Plato's famous criticism of it. The position I'll reach by the end of my discussion of metaethics is that there is no good argument against ethical realism. I don't claim that I can prove that realism is true, but I do think the attempts to refute it by conventionalists and subjectivists have not worked.

## Review Questions

1. What is subjectivism? What does it mean to distinguish objective fact from subjective opinion in science? In ethics?
2. What does it mean to say that ethical truths are "conventional?"
3. What does it mean to say that ethical truths are "relative," as ethical relativism asserts? Relative to what?
4. What is ethical realism? How is it similar to conventionalism? How is it different?

## A Problem for Further Thought

The study of ethics often involves discussion of principles that tell people they should have acted in a way different from the way they did act; sometimes these principles require people to be less selfish and more altruistic. In the previous section of the book, I argued that people have free will and that the thesis of psychological egoism is false. If either of these claims were mistaken, would there still be a point to discussing ethical principles? Defend your answer.

## CHAPTER 29

# *The Is/Ought Gap and the Naturalistic Fallacy*

Based on the previous chapter, you now should have a preliminary grasp of what eth-ical subjectivism is and of how it differs from ethical realism and ethical conven-tionalism. In this chapter and the next, I'll consider several arguments for thinking that subjectivism is true, and I'll suggest that none of them is convincing.

### SUBJECTIVISM: ETHICAL STATEMENTS ARE NEITHER TRUE NOR FALSE

In the previous Chapter, I said that subjectivism is the view that no ethical statement is true. Often the view is given a slightly different formulation: Subjectivism says that ethical statements are *neither true nor false.* I think this representation of the doctrine is less apt to mislead, and so I'll use it from now on. This is a small change, since if a statement is neither true nor false, it isn't true.

Subjectivism says that ethical statements have a particular characteristic. But what is an ethical statement? Examples include any statement of the form "*X* is morally wrong," "*X* is morally permissible," "*X* is unfair," or "*X* is unjust." The *X* may be filled in by a description of an action. So *both* the following statements are ethical statements:

(1)  Murder is always morally wrong.

(2)  Murder is sometimes morally permissible.

Ethical subjectivism claims the first of these statements is not true. According to subjectivism, it isn't true that murder is always wrong. But the reason (1) isn't true is

---

**Emotivism**

Subjectivism says that there are no ethical facts. If subjectivism is true, why do we have ethical sentences in our language? What function do they perform if there are no ethical facts for them to describe? The emotive theory of ethics ("emotivism") attempts to provide an answer.

"Ouch!" I exclaim when I hit my thumb with a hammer. "Whoopee!" I exclaim when a birth-day cake is placed before me. In both cases, I've used language, but not to make an assertion. It would be a mistake to ask whether my utterances were true or false. They were neither.

"Ouch!" and "whoopee!" *express* how I feel. Emotivism claims that ethical sentences allow speakers to express their feelings and attitudes. To say "Murder is wrong" is not to make an assertion that is either true or false; it is to express a certain sort of attitude toward murder.

There is no doubt that ethical language is sometimes used in this expressive way. The ques-tion is whether there is anything more to ethical discourse than this.

When someone says "You are an ignorant pig," the sentence is used to express the speaker's attitudes or feelings. However, that does not show that the sentence is neither true nor false. Besides having an expressive function, the sentence makes an assertion, which is either true or false depending on the characteristics of the person whom the speaker is addressing.

not that it is sometimes morally permissible to murder. Remember, (1) and (2) are *both* ethical statements, and subjectivism claims no ethical statement is true.

At first glance, it might seem that (1) and (2) have the following characteristic: One of them must be true. Ethical subjectivism denies this, because it holds there do not exist any ethical facts about murder. The formulation of ethical subjectivism that I'm using—that ethical statements are *neither true nor false*—should alert you to the fact that subjectivism says that (1) and (2) are *both* untrue.

## DOES THE EXISTENCE OF ETHICAL DISAGREEMENT SHOW THAT SUBJECTIVISM IS TRUE?

What arguments might be presented to support subjectivism? Sometimes it is suggested that there can't be any ethical facts on the grounds that people disagree over what's right and what's wrong. In our own society, there are moral controversies. Some people hold that abortion is sometimes permissible, others that it never is. And even when you find actions about which there is broad consensus in our society, you often can find other times and places at which there was no such consensus. For example, most people in our society would now agree that slavery is wrong; however, if you go back 150 years (or even less), there was no such broad consensus.

Is the fact that ethical opinions vary (in space and time) a reason to accept subjectivism? I don't think so. Science also contains controversies. And what now is accepted often was controversial in the past. To use an example discussed in Chapters ch5 and 6, scientists now accept the idea that life has evolved. This scientific consensus, however, didn't always exist. And even now, there are people—creationists—who deny that evolution is a fact. Even though there is and has been variation in opinion about whether evolution has occurred, all parties in this dispute believe there is a fact of the matter about whether life has evolved. No one denies that there are facts about the history of life on earth. So lack of consensus about what the answer is to a question does not show that there is no objective answer to the question.

It is important to remember that ethical subjectivism is *not* the view that some ethical statements are controversial or are hard to prove or disprove. It says that each and every ethical statement is untrue. This includes "slavery is wrong" and "torturing babies for fun is wrong," just as much as it includes presently controversial claims about the moral status of abortion or capital punishment. If you are prepared to say that even one moral statement is true, you are rejecting subjectivism.

## THE GENETIC FALLACY

Another argument for subjectivism focuses on the explanation of why we hold the ethical beliefs we do. To formulate this argument, consider the fact that most people think it is wrong for parents to totally neglect their children. What might account for why we think this? Two kinds of explanation come to mind. First, society teaches us to think this way. Second, evolution may have led us to think this way; people who totally neglected their children would have been less reproductively successful than people who didn't, and so the less fit trait of total child neglect would gradually have disappeared from the population. (The basics on how a selection process works were outlined in Chapter 6.)

Suppose there is a social or an evolutionary explanation for why people now think it is wrong to totally neglect their children. Does it follow that the ethical statement "it is wrong to totally neglect your children" is untrue? I don't think so. A belief is not shown to be untrue by the mere fact that you can explain why people hold the belief.

Consider arithmetic. How do you explain the fact that most of us think that $2 + 3 = 5$? Society has taught us to think this, and I suppose evolution has somehow contributed to our capacity to have opinions about mathematics. However, this does not show that there is no fact of the matter about whether $2 + 3 = 5$.

Philosophers call the mistake I'm discussing here "the Genetic Fallacy." The word *genetic* means "cause" (as in the genesis of a belief). The Genetic Fallacy has nothing to do with chromosomes. The mistake is to think that a fact about how you come to believe something by itself settles whether the belief is true. In the next chapter, I consider a slightly different and more subtle version of this argument. For now, the point is that you can't prove that subjectivism is true just by pointing out that there is a social or an evolutionary explanation for why we have the ethical beliefs we do.

So much for these two arguments for subjectivism. I now turn to two others. The first focuses on Hume's distinction between is-statements and ought-statements; the second involves G. E. Moore's idea of a "naturalistic fallacy."

## HUME: THE IS/OUGHT GAP

Hume claimed that an ethical statement (describing what *ought* to be the case) can't validly be deduced from a premises that describes only what *is* the case. Consider the following argument:

> Torturing babies for fun causes great suffering.
> _____
> Hence, torturing babies for fun is wrong.

The single premise of this argument describes what is the case, not what ought to be the case. The conclusion concerns what ought to be the case. Hume said you can't deduce an ought-conclusion from exclusively is-premises. The above argument, he claimed, is not deductively valid.

Of course, this argument can be turned into a deductively valid argument by adding another premise. The following argument *is* deductively valid:

> Torturing babies for fun causes great suffering.
> Causing great suffering is wrong.
> _____
> Hence, torturing babies for fun is wrong.

Remember what it means to say that an argument is deductively valid (Chapter 2). In a deductively valid argument, *IF* the premises are true, then the conclusion can't fail to be true. In saying that an argument is valid, I'm not saying that the premises are true (remember the *IF!*).

The last argument displayed does not deduce an ought-conclusion from exclusively is-premises. The second premise in the argument is an ought-statement. So Hume's point might be put like this: If a deductively valid argument has an ethical conclusion, at least one of the premises must be ethical in character as well.

Hume's point is sometimes characterized by saying that you can't infer an ethical conclusion from purely nonethical premises. This is an acceptable rendition of Hume's thesis, if "infer" is taken to mean *validly deduce*. However, if nondeductive inference (Chapter 3) is involved, I don't accept the formulation just given. It seems to me that the fact that torturing babies causes great suffering is an excellent reason for thinking that the action is wrong. *X* can be a reason for *Y* even though *Y* doesn't deductively follow from *X*.

## (S1): AN ARGUMENT FOR SUBJECTIVISM WITH HUME'S THESIS AS A PREMISE

Hume's thesis concerns a fact about deductive implication. Does this thesis lead to subjectivism? Again, I think the answer is *no*. To see why, consider the following argument for subjectivism:

> You can't validly deduce an ethical statement from purely is-premises (Hume's thesis).
> _____
> Hence, ethical statements are neither true nor false.

This argument is not deductively valid. A premise can be added, however, so that the resulting argument is valid:

> You can't deduce an ethical statement from purely is-premises (Hume's thesis).
> (S1)  If ethical statements are not deducible from purely is-premises, then ethical statements are neither true nor false (reductionist premise).
> _____
> Hence, ethical statements are neither true nor false.

(S1) is a deductively valid argument for subjectivism. I find the second premise highly dubious, however. Why not adopt an antireductionist view of the status of ethical statements? That is, why not hold that some ethical statements are true, even though they aren't reducible to (deducible from) purely is-statements?

Here's an analogy. It is pretty clear that astronomy and anthropology describe different sorts of facts. Astronomers are interested in planets, stars, and other heavenly objects. Anthropologists, on the other hand, study similarities and differences among human cultures. What does it mean to say that these are different subjects? One implication is that you can't deduce anthropological statements from purely astronomical ones. Describing the orbits and masses of the planets in the solar system does not allow you to deduce which customs are followed in which human cultures. Would it be plausible to conclude from this that there are no anthropological facts, simply because anthropological statements can't be deduced from astronomical statements? Presumably not. That is, the following argument is not deductively valid:

> You can't deduce anthropological statements from purely astronomical premises.
>
> ──────────────
>
> Hence, anthropological statements are neither true nor false.

The next argument, though deductively valid, has a dubious reductionist second premise:

> You can't deduce anthropological statements from purely astronomical premises.
>
> If a statement isn't deducible from purely astronomical premises, then the statement is neither true nor false (reductionist premise).
>
> ──────────────
>
> Hence, anthropological statements are neither true nor false.

We should reject this argument. A perfectly sensible position is that there are facts in anthropology and facts in astronomy even though neither reduces to (is deducible from) the other. The facts coexist as separate aspects of reality.

## THE NATURALISTIC FALLACY

The idea of a "naturalistic fallacy" is due to the English philosopher G. E. Moore (1873–1958). In his book *Principia Ethica* (1903), Moore criticized the idea that the ethical properties of an action—for example, its rightness or wrongness—might be identical with some "natural" property of that action. An example of such a naturalistic theory is provided by one form of utilitarianism, which I'll call hedonistic utilitarianism. This theory says that for an action to be ethically right is for it to maximize pleasure and minimize pain for those affected by it.

I'm not suggesting this theory is correct. My point is that it is an example of a moral theory that says that an ethical property is identical with some natural property. This theory says that the rightness of an action is one and the same property as the action's maximizing pleasure and minimizing pain. A natural scientist—a psychologist—could inquire whether one action produces more pleasure and less pain than another. According to hedonistic utilitarianism, this scientist would be investigating whether the first action is ethically preferable to the second.

Utilitarianism proposes an "identity thesis," which bears a logical similarity to the Mind/Brain Identity Theory discussed in Chapter 22. An ethical property is said to be identical with a natural property. By natural property, I mean a property that the natural sciences (including psychology) might investigate.

Moore thought that hedonistic utilitarianism and theories like it make a mistake, which he called the Naturalistic Fallacy. Moore thought it is always a mistake to say that an ethical property of an action is the same property as one of its natural properties. Why is it a fallacy to do this? According to Moore, we can see this by considering the meanings of the terms involved. The term "morally right" doesn't mean the same thing as the term "maximizes pleasure and minimizes pain." From this, Moore thought it followed that hedonistic utilitarianism is mistaken. Moore's argument goes like this:

(NFA)

> The expression "x is morally preferable to y" does not mean the same thing as the expression "x produces more pleasure and less pain than y."
> ————————————
> Hence, the property named by the first expression is not identical with the property named by the second.

Moore thought that any ethical theory that equates an ethical property with a natural property could be refuted by this type of argument. Any such theory, he said, commits the Naturalistic Fallacy. Let's call this argument of Moore's the Naturalistic Fallacy Argument (NFA).

I claim that Moore is mistaken. For two terms to refer to the same property, it isn't essential that they mean the same thing—they need not be synonymous. Chemistry tells us that the temperature of a gas is one and the same property as the gas's mean molecular kinetic energy. This claim is not refuted by the fact that "temperature" and "mean kinetic energy" are not synonymous expressions. Consider the following argument:

> The expression "temperature" differs in meaning from the expression "mean kinetic energy."
> ————————————
> Hence, the property named by the first expression is not identical with the property named by the second.

This argument is a fallacy. So is Moore's. That is, I think Moore's argument concerning the Naturalistic Fallacy is itself a fallacy. He commits what I'll call (following John Searle) the Naturalistic Fallacy Fallacy.

Moore failed to establish the thesis that ethical properties are not identical with naturalistic properties. Call this "Moore's thesis." I now want to consider a quite separate question. Suppose, just for the sake of argument, that Moore's thesis is correct. Would subjectivism follow from this?

Moore didn't think so. Moore was no subjectivist. He believed that there are ethical facts and that these ethical facts exist quite apart from the naturalistic facts investigated by science. For Moore, there are two kinds of truths—ethical truths and naturalistic ones. Others have gone in the opposite direction. They have thought that Moore's thesis leads to ethical subjectivism; they have claimed that if ethics fails to reduce to naturalistic facts, then there are no ethical facts at all.

## (S2): AN ARGUMENT FOR SUBJECTIVISM WITH MOORE'S THESIS AS A PREMISE

Moore's thesis does not, all by itself, imply subjectivism. Rather, Moore's thesis, combined with a second idea, leads to subjectivism. Here's the argument we need to consider:

> Ethical properties are not identical with naturalistic properties (Moore's thesis).
>
> (S2) If ethical properties are not identical with naturalistic properties, then ethical statements are neither true nor false (reductionist thesis).
> _____
>
> Hence, ethical statements are neither true nor false.

I'll call this argument (S2).

I've suggested that Moore's argument for the first premise in (S2) doesn't work. What I want you to see now is that the first premise, even if it were true, would not be enough to establish subjectivism. To reach the conclusion that subjectivism is true, (S2) requires the reductionist thesis as well as Moore's thesis. I call the second premise "reductionist" because it says that a property must reduce to (be identical with) a naturalistic (scientific) property if there are to be any ethical facts.

Is the second premise in (S2) plausible? Why not reject it and adopt, instead, an *antireductionist* position, according to which ethical statements are sometimes true, even though ethical properties are not identical with naturalistic properties? We agree that anthropological statements are sometimes true even though anthropological properties aren't identical with astronomical properties. Why not take the same view with respect to the relation of ethics and natural science?

## SUMMARY

Hume correctly noted that you can't deduce an ought-conclusion from purely is-premises. This thesis of Hume's is true. Subjectivism does not follow just from this point, however. Rather, to get subjectivism from Hume's insight, you've got to make a reductionist assumption. I see no compelling reason to be a reductionist about ethical statements. I conclude that (S1) isn't a convincing argument for ethical subjectivism.

Moore correctly claimed that ethical expressions are not synonymous with naturalistic expressions. Moore, however, went on to claim that ethical properties are not identical with naturalistic properties. This thesis of Moore's doesn't follow. Even if Moore were right that ethical properties are irreducibly different from natural properties, subjectivism wouldn't follow from that. So I reject argument (S2).

Although (S1) and (S2) are different arguments for subjectivism, they have something in common. Both assume that if there are ethical truths, these truths must be connected in an especially intimate way with naturalistic truths; ethical statements must somehow "boil down to" the facts described by is-propositions, if ethical statements are to be true. Can this assumption that the two arguments share be defended or refuted?

## Review Questions

1. How do subjectivists view the statement "lying is always wrong"? Do subjectivists reject this statement because they think lying is sometimes morally legitimate?
2. Does the fact that people disagree about ethical issues show subjectivism is true?
3. Suppose there is a social or a biological explanation for why people have the ethical beliefs they do. Does this show that those beliefs are untrue?
4. Hume saw that there is a "gap" between *is* and *ought*. What does this mean? Does Hume's insight show that subjectivism is true?
5. What does Moore mean by the *naturalistic fallacy*? If Moore were right about the naturalistic fallacy, would subjectivism follow?

## Problems for Further Thought

1. In Chapter 19, I explained Frege's distinction between *sense* and *reference*. How can this distinction be used to clarify the mistake Moore makes in his Naturalistic Fallacy Argument (NFA)?
2. In discussing the Genetic Fallacy, I argued that can't prove that a sentence is untrue just by showing that there is a causal explanation for why people believe the sentence. Can you construct an example in which the explanation for why people believe a sentence makes it highly improbable that the sentence is true? If such an example can be constructed, does this show that the so-called genetic fallacy isn't a fallacy at all?

## CHAPTER 30

# *Observation and Explanation in Ethics*

Some people find ethical subjectivism an attractive philosophical position because they think ethics and science are fundamentally different. For them, it seems reasonable to talk about scientific facts. It strikes them, however, that ethics is very different—different enough that it is a mistake to think there are ethical facts. The problem for subjectivism is to make precise the gut feeling that there is a difference here: Can it be stated in such a way that a convincing argument in favor of ethical subjectivism emerges?

## REASONING ABOUT ETHICAL ISSUES

All too often the idea that there is an important difference between science and ethics rests on a misconception of one, the other, or both. One such misconception is the idea that reasoning can play no role in ethics—that ethics is nothing more than the irrational outpouring of feelings about what we think and do.

It isn't to be denied that people often are strongly moved by feelings when they talk about right and wrong. However, people sometimes care passionately about scientific matters and about nonethical matters that arise in everyday life. In addition, it is important to see that reasoning *can* play a role in ethics—that ethical statements can be subjected to rational criticism. An example of how this can occur is provided by Gilbert Harman (in his book *The Nature of Morality,* Oxford University Press, 1977). He asks us to consider the following principle: "If you have a choice between five people alive and one dead, or one alive and five dead, you should always choose the first option over the second." This principle is a generalization. Should we accept it?

One way to tell is to see what it implies about specific examples—about concrete situations that people might sometimes confront. Harman asks us to consider the following example, which is one test case for the principle:

> You are a doctor in a hospital's emergency room when six accident victims are brought in. All six are in danger of dying but one is much worse off than the others. You can just barely save that person if you devote all your resources to him and let the others die. Alternatively you can save the other five if you are willing to ignore the most seriously injured person.

Harman says that in this case, the doctor should save the five and let the sixth person die. This is Harman's moral judgment about the example problem. I agree with Harman about this, and I'll assume that you do too. So in this case, what we are prepared to say about the example is consistent with the dictates of the principle we are considering. Harman concludes that this example is *evidence in favor* of the principle.

Harman next considers a very different situation that a doctor might face:

> You have five patients in the hospital who are dying, each in need of a separate organ. One needs a kidney, another a lung, a third a heart, and so forth. You can save all five if you take a single healthy person and remove his heart, lungs, kidneys, and so forth, to distribute to these five patients. Just such a healthy person is in Room 306. He is in the hospital for routine tests. Having seen his test results, you know that he is perfectly healthy and of the right tissue compatibility. If you do nothing, he will survive without incident; however, the other five patients will die. These five patients can be saved only if the person in Room 306 is cut up and his organs distributed (and you can kill him painlessly). In that case, there would be one dead but five saved.

Harman's judgment about this case, with which I also agree, is that it would be wrong for the doctor to save the five by killing the sixth and harvesting his organs. This example, then, is evidence that the general principle stated before is false.

## TESTING GENERAL PRINCIPLES BY APPLYING THEM TO SPECIFIC EXAMPLES

As Harman's example illustrates, we can reason about the correctness of a general principle by seeing what it implies about concrete cases. We reject the principle because of an ethical judgment we are prepared to make about a concrete case (the second example situation mentioned above). Or, if we disagree with Harman about his judgment on this second case, we might conclude that the general principle is plausible after all. The point is that we can run a *consistency check* on the various ethical opinions we have, making sure that our general principles do not contradict what we believe about specific cases.

This kind of procedure is very important in ethics. Philosophers frequently evaluate a general moral theory by seeing what it implies about specific examples. For this procedure to be possible, we must be prepared to make ethical judgments about the cases considered. This is what Harman did when he used his moral judgment about the second example to argue that the general principle is false.

Let's compare this specimen of ethical reasoning to what scientists do when they want to test a theory. Scientists also test general theories and they do so by seeing what they imply about particular cases. For example, a general theory about electrons might predict that a laboratory instrument in a certain experiment will register "7.6" at a certain time. The scientist then can look at the instrument and see if it says what the theory predicts. If the reading differs from what is predicted, this may count against the theory.

## THOUGHT EXPERIMENTS VERSUS EMPIRICAL EXPERIMENTS

In science, one sees what a theory implies about what can be observed; then one goes ahead and makes the required observations. In the ethical case just discussed, however, no observation was required. We figured out what the general principle implies about the hypothetical case of the doctor contemplating the transplant operations, decided that this implication is unacceptable, and thereby rejected the general principle. The ethics case involved what is sometimes called a *thought experiment*.

Thought experiments differ from empirical experiments in that thought experiments don't involve *actually* making observations. So we now face this question: Does ethics differ from science in that science involves observation, whereas ethics does not? Harman poses the question as follows:

> You can observe someone do something, but can you ever perceive the rightness or wrongness of what he does? If you round a corner and see a group of young hoodlums pour gasoline on a cat and ignite it, you do not need to

*conclude* that what they are doing is wrong; you do not need to figure anything out; you can *see* that it is wrong. But is your reaction due to the actual wrongness of what you see or is it simply a reflection of your moral "sense," a "sense" that you have acquired perhaps as a result of your moral upbringing?

## OBSERVATIONS ARE "THEORY LADEN"

Harman then argues that there are no "pure" observations, that all observation is "theory laden." What does this mean? For you to see *that the children have poured gasoline on a cat and have ignited it,* you have to understand the concepts involved. If you don't know what a child is, or what a cat is, or what gasoline is, then you won't see that this is what is going on.

To make this more precise, let's distinguish two aspects of the process we call *seeing.* We talk about seeing objects ("*S* sees the cat"), and we talk about seeing that this or that proposition is true ("*S* sees that the cat is on fire"). I'll call these *objectual seeing* and *propositional seeing.* Notice that the expression following the verb in objectual seeing names an object (the cat), whereas the expression following the verb in propositional seeing expresses a proposition (that the cat is on fire). The distinction between these two kinds of seeing is somewhat similar to that drawn in Chapter 12 between objectual and propositional knowledge.

Can you see a cat without knowing what a cat is? I would say *yes.* Young children can see a nuclear power plant without knowing what they're looking at. Propositional seeing, however, is different. To see that it is a cat that is on fire, you must understand the concepts that are found in the proposition. So propositional seeing is "theory laden" in this sense: you must have information of various sorts if you are to see that a particular proposition is true.

Now let's go back to the comparison between ethics and science. When you round the corner and see what the children are doing, do you see *that they are doing something wrong?* I agree with Harman that the answer is *yes.* You make use of your background information—in this case, information about right and wrong. In just the same way, when you round the corner, you are able to see *that the children are setting a cat on fire;* you do this by making use of your background information (concerning what a cat looks like, etc.). So Harman concludes (and I agree) that we make ethical observations every day, just as we make observations that concern nonethical matters. We are able to do this by using background information to interpret the visual, auditory, and other sensory signals we receive.

Of course, a person who had no beliefs at all about right and wrong wouldn't be able to see that what the children are doing is wrong. It also is true, however, that the child who has no information about what a nuclear power plant is would be unable to see that there is a nuclear power plant on the hill. The child's incapacity does not show that there are no objective facts about whether the hill has a nuclear power plant on it. I claim that we should say the same thing about the moral ignoramus. This person is unable to see that what the children are doing is wrong, but that does not refute the thesis that what the children are doing is objectively wrong. You don't prove that subjectivism is true just by describing the incapacities of a moral ignoramus.

## OBSERVATION DOES NOT IMPLY OBJECTIVITY

Saying that people make ethical observations does not imply that ethical facts exist. Consider aesthetic judgments—judgments about the beauty of a painting, for example. Suppose you are looking at a painting by Monet and judge that it is a beautiful example of French Impressionism. You wouldn't be able to do this without a certain fund of background information. In addition you needed to use your visual system to make this judgment. So perhaps it is true that you see that the painting has the characteristic just mentioned. We may conclude that observations occur in aesthetics. This, however, is not enough to show that there are "aesthetic facts"—that it is an objective question whether a given painting is beautiful. Someone might concede that people make aesthetic observations and still insist that beauty is in the eye of the beholder.

So far I've criticized two ideas: that ethics does not involve reasoning and that there is no such thing as observation in ethics. Both may seem to mark a difference between ethics and science, but neither really does, or so I have argued. At the same time, I have to admit that the fact that ethics involves both reasoning and observation does not prove there are ethical facts.

## INSOLUBLE DISAGREEMENTS

I'll now consider a third possible difference between science and ethics. It sometimes seems that there isn't much possibility of rational persuasion in ethics. Two people may quite sincerely hold the views they do, and no matter how much they discuss their differences, neither will budge. In science, disagreements are common, but often they can be solved by bringing in new evidence that neither party initially has available. In ethics, it seems that people sometimes stick to their convictions no matter how much new information is imported. If so, there are some *insoluble* disagreements about ethics. Perhaps this marks a difference between ethics and science.

I won't argue that there is no difference here (though we should not forget that people can be pigheaded about nonethical matters as well). I do want to claim, however, that the alleged difference is not enough to establish ethical subjectivism.

Think of a slave owner and an abolitionist in the United States in the 1850s arguing at length over the morality of slavery. The slave owner has shut his eyes to the humanity of slaves and to the suffering they have endured. Imagine that the slave owner was made to take these facts to heart. Maybe some slave owners would have changed their minds if they had had to confront the full implications of slavery. But probably there were some slave owners whose hearts were sufficiently hardened (at least partly out of economic self-interest) that even full information would not have made a difference to them. Let's imagine that the slave owner and the abolitionist are caught in an insoluble disagreement of this kind. Does it follow that there are no ethical facts?

Ethical facts, if they exist, often will be very hard for people to grasp. The reason is that our apprehension of them often will be clouded over by self-interest and self-deception. As difficult as scientific questions about atoms and cells sometimes are, ethics is in this respect even harder. Maybe ethics will be the last frontier of human knowledge; even after we have unlocked the secrets of the atom and of life itself, the problem of discovering the truths of ethics may remain unsolved.

So *IF* ethical facts exist, it wouldn't be surprising that there are ethical disagreements, even insoluble ones. And of course, *IF* subjectivism were true, it likewise wouldn't be surprising that there are ethical disagreements. So both hypotheses—that there are ethical facts and that there are not—can account for the observation that insoluble ethical disputes sometimes occur.

---

### Values in Science

Hume's distinction between is-statements and ought-statements often leads people to think that science is value-free. This seems to follow from the idea that science aims to establish what is the case and takes no stand on any ethical issue.

It is important not to confuse a distinction between different kinds of *statements* with a distinction between different sorts of *activities*. Hume's distinction concerned the former; it does not follow from Hume's distinction that science is an activity that is value-free. In fact, the practice of science is saturated with values. Some of these are more or less internal to the practice of research; others have to do with how science affects the rest of society.

A scientist's decision to pursue one research problem rather than another is a decision about what is of value. Sometimes a problem is worth pursuing because it promises to yield practical benefits. Research in medicine and engineering provides obvious examples. At other times, a scientist will pursue a problem because it is thought to be theoretically important. This too is a judgment of value; in sciences that are more theoretical than practical (more "pure" than "applied"), a problem may be judged important because scientists believe that its solution would advance our understanding of the world.

Judging the value of pursuing a research problem, whether practical or theoretical, becomes especially important when the research would impose significant costs. Research is often expensive, and the expense is often supported by government money. Another cost arises when the research is done on living things who may suffer and die in the course of the investigation. Responsible science requires that these considerations be taken into account.

After the scientist chooses a problem, value issues continue to be important. When scientists judge that the available evidence counts strongly against some theory, they will conclude that they *ought not to believe* the theory. Judgments about plausibility and evidence are *normative*; they concern what we should and should not believe.

Once the scientist has reached some judgment about what the solution is to the problem under investigation, another value issue arises. Should the results be published? If so, in what forum should they be aired? It is sometimes suggested that scientists should keep their results to themselves if publishing would be harmful. Others hold that society is better off in the long run if even the most unpleasant scientific results are made public. Notice that both these opposing positions take a stand on an issue of value: When should a scientist publicize the carefully tested results of inquiry?

## IS SUBJECTIVISM PREFERABLE TO REALISM, ON GROUNDS OF PARSIMONY?

We are considering two competing hypotheses—subjectivism, which denies that there are ethical truths, and realism which asserts that there are ethical truths that are true independently of anyone's say-so. Is there any way to choose between these two hypotheses?

Perhaps subjectivism has the advantage of being more *parsimonious* (an idea discussed in Chapter 22 on the Mind/Brain Identity Theory). If subjectivism can explain everything we observe just as well as the hypothesis that says there are ethical facts, then perhaps we should prefer the former hypothesis.

Harman advances an argument of this sort. He thinks that in spite of the similarities between science and ethics just described, there is nevertheless one big difference. It concerns the problem of explanation. In abductive arguments (Chapter 3), you produce a reason for thinking that something exists by showing that the existence of the thing is needed to explain some observation. Recall that Mendel never saw a gene, but he had a good abductive reason to think that genes exist. Harman argues that we don't need to postulate the existence of ethical facts to explain any observations. Adding to this a principle of parsimony (which tells you that you should assume that something does not exist if it isn't needed to explain anything), Harman concludes that subjectivism is correct.

Harman describes a physicist who is looking at the screen of a cloud chamber (a device for observing particle interactions). He sees a vapor trail on the screen and says, "There goes a proton." How should we explain why the scientist believes that a proton is present? The answer, according to Harman, involves a fact about what is going on inside the cloud chamber—namely, there really is a proton in there. The proton produces the vapor trail; the scientist sees the vapor trail and comes to believe that a proton is present in the chamber. Part of the explanation of why the scientist has the belief is that what he believes is, in fact, true. The causal chain that explains the scientist's belief goes like this:

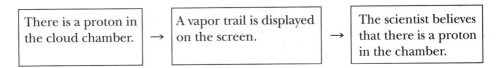

Notice that the causal chain traces something in the subjective realm (a belief) back to something in the objective realm (a proton).

Our commonsense beliefs often have a similar explanation. Suppose you want to explain why Jane believes there is a tiger in the cage. You might do this by citing the fact that her visual system is in good working order, that she knows what a tiger looks like, and that, indeed, there *is* a tiger in the cage that Jane is looking at. We explain a person's perceptual beliefs (apart from their hallucinations) by describing the ways things are outside the mind. In this case, the causal chain looks like this:

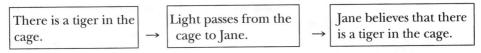

Part of the explanation of why Jane believes the proposition is that the proposition, in fact, is true.

Let's compare Harman's example from science and the similar example about Jane to the moral judgment we made when we saw the hoodlums set fire to the cat. How are we to explain the fact that we hold this ethical belief? Harman says that we don't need to postulate the existence of an ethical fact to explain this. All we need to do is show how our moral beliefs were shaped by our upbringing—by the society in which we live (and perhaps by the genes we possess).

According to Harman, there is a striking difference between ethics and science. Scientific facts *are* needed to explain why people have the scientific beliefs they do, but ethical facts are *not* needed to explain why people have the ethical beliefs they do. Harman concludes that this is why we have a good abductive reason to think that there are protons, genes, and so on, but no good abductive reason to think that there are ethical facts.

Harman concedes that we will cite moral principles when we are asked to explain why it is wrong for the children to have acted as they did. If asked why the children were wrong to have set the cat on fire, we might appeal to some general ethical principle (for example, its being wrong to impose gratuitous suffering). Here we cite a general ethical principle to explain some more specific ethical conclusion. Harman's point, however, is that you don't need to postulate ethical facts to explain why we *believe* the children were wrong in what they did. Ethical facts aren't needed to explain why people have *beliefs* about right and wrong (though scientific facts *are* needed to explain why scientists have some of the scientific beliefs they do).

Harman's picture of the explanatory relationships is as follows:

I'm not going to contest Harman's claim that this diagram is correct. What I do want to argue is that subjectivism does not follow.

## DOES SUBJECTIVISM FOLLOW?

The Principle of Parsimony says that we should not postulate the existence of something, if the something isn't needed to explain *anything*. If postulating the existence of ethical facts served no explanatory purpose whatever, the Principle of Parsimony would conclude that there are no ethical facts. But Harman has not shown that ethical facts aren't needed to explain *anything*. Rather, he has shown something more modest—simply that you don't need to postulate ethical facts to explain why people have the ethical beliefs they do. Ethical facts aren't needed to explain this fact about our *psychology*.

Harman grants that we sometimes make ethical observations. We look at the children and say, "What they are doing is wrong." Harman also grants that the ethical properties of specific actions may be explained by general ethical principles. As noted earlier, a general principle might help explain why what the children did was wrong. Putting these two points together, we may conclude that *general ethical principles can help explain the ethical properties of specific actions.*

The point I want to make here is similar to what I said about Hume's distinction between is-statements and ought-statements in the previous chapter. The argument for subjectivism I called (S1) says that since ought-conclusions aren't deducible from is-statements, there are no ethical facts. I pointed out that this argument requires a reductionist premise. To reach the subjectivist conclusion, you need to assume that if ethical facts exist, they must be deducible from is-statements.

Harman's argument is abductive, not deductive. I grant that ethical facts aren't needed to explain why we have the beliefs we do. Nevertheless, for subjectivism to follow from this, an additional assumption is needed. Harman needs to assume that we should not postulate the existence of ethical facts if they aren't needed to explain why we have the beliefs we do. I find this assumption implausible. Why should the reality of ethical facts stand or fall on their role in psychological explanation?

## AN EXPLANATORY ROLE FOR ETHICAL PRINCIPLES

The previous diagram *does* accord an explanatory role to some ethical facts. If you think that what the children did was wrong, then there is at least one ethical truth that requires explanation. General ethical theories may be evaluated by their ability to explain this and other specific ethical facts about example situations. If one theory does a better job of explaining such ethical facts than another, it is plausible to hold that the former is more likely to be true.

Thus, if you concede that there are at least *some* ethical facts, then postulating *other* ethical facts can be justified on abductive grounds. On the other hand, if you demand that ethical facts be judged by their ability to explain facts in psychology, you'll end up with subjectivism. I conclude that Harman's argument does not justify subjectivism. He has not shown that there are no ethical facts. Nor has he shown that postulating ethical facts isn't needed to explain *anything*. Rather, the more limited conclusion he has established (I grant) is that postulating ethical facts isn't needed to explain certain facts about psychology (that is, about why we believe what we do).

## WHAT IS THE POINT OF ETHICS?

Harman claims that ethical statements should be regarded as true only if they are needed to explain why we have the beliefs we do. However, the point of ethics isn't to explain or describe what we think. Ethics isn't psychology. The point of an ethical statement is to *guide* behavior—to say how we *ought* to think and act, not to describe how we actually think and act. Ethics is in a normative, not a descriptive, line of work. But that does not show that there are no ethical facts.

## Review Questions

1. Why does Harman think that reasoning from general principles to claims about specific cases occurs in both science and ethics? Why does he think that observation is something we do in both science and ethics?

2. Does the occurrence of reasoning and observation in ethics show that there are ethical facts?

3. Suppose there is someone who can't be convinced that slavery is wrong. Does this show that subjectivism is true?

4. What does the Principle of Parsimony have to do with the question of whether there are ethical facts?

5. Harman says that an abductive argument can be found for thinking that protons exist, but none for thinking that ethical facts exist. Why does he think this? Is his argument convincing?

## Problems for Further Thought

1. If parsimony is a good reason to prefer a materialistic theory like the Mind/Brain Identity Theory or for preferring functionalism over dualism, why isn't it also a good reason to favor ethical subjectivism over ethical realism?

2. Consider the following passage from Hume's *Treatise of Human Nature* (1739; III,1,1):

> Morality [does not consist] in any matter of fact, which can be discover'd by the understanding.... Take any action allow'd to be vicious: Wilful murder, for instance. Examine it in all lights, and see if you can find that matter of fact, or real existence, which you call vice. In whichever way you take it, you find only certain passions, motives, volitions, and thoughts. There is no other matter of fact in the case. The vice entirely escapes you, as long as you consider the object. You never can find it, till you turn your reflexion into your own breast, and find a sentiment of disapprobation, which arises in you, toward this action. It lies in yourself, not in the object. So that *when you pronounce any action or character to be vicious, you mean nothing but that from the constitution of your nature you have a feeling or sentiment of blame from the contemplation of it.* Vice or virtue, therefore, may be compar'd to sounds, colours, heat and cold, which according to modern philosophy, are not qualities in objects, but perceptions in the mind: And this discovery in morals, like that other in physics, is to be regarded as a considerable advancement of the speculative sciences; tho', like that too, it has little or no influence on practice. Nothing can be more real, or concern us more, than our own sentiments of pleasure or uneasiness; and if these be favourable to virtue, and unfavourable to vice, no more can be requisite to the regulation of our conduct and behavior.

What analogy is Hume drawing between moral properties and colors? Is Hume right to think they are similar? Does Hume's analogy justify ethical subjectivism?
3. Is it question-begging to claim, as I do in this chapter, that ethical facts are needed to explain other ethical facts?


# CHAPTER 31

## *Conventionalist Theories*

In philosophical writing about ethics, it is not customary to lump together under one heading the three theories I'll discuss in this chapter. Nor is it especially standard to label any of these theories "conventionalist." So let me explain why I'm lumping and labeling in this way.

The Divine Command Theory holds that an action is right or wrong because God says that it is; ethical relativism maintains that an action is made right or wrong in a society by the norms the society adopts; and the existentialism of Jean-Paul Sartre says that individuals freely create the ethical standards that determine whether their lives are good ones or bad ones. Existentialist writers often begin with the idea that there is no God and argue that people therefore must create their own ethical facts. This is obviously very different from the framework of the Divine Command Theory, which sees ethical truth as flowing from God. Both these positions differ from ethical relativism, which views ethics as neither divinely given nor individually chosen, but as socially constructed.

### WHAT MAKES A VIEW CONVENTIONALIST?

In spite of these differences, the three views have two things in common. First, they agree that there are ethical truths. Second, they agree that those truths are made true by someone's say-so. All three theories reject ethical subjectivism on the one hand and ethical realism on the other. The disagreement among them arises when these theories are asked to specify *whose* say-so does the trick—are ethical propositions made true by God's, society's, or each individual's decision?

Why say that these theories are forms of "conventionalism"? Each claims there is nothing inherent in an action (torture, for example) that makes it right or wrong. The action, considered all by itself, could easily be right or wrong. Rather, something outside of the action (extrinsic to it) makes the action right or wrong. It is God, society, or an individual who makes a pronouncement on the action and thereby endows it with one ethical property rather than the other. In Chapter 28, I gave an example of something that I think really is conventional. It is a conventional matter which side of the road people should drive their cars on. The essential ingredients in a convention are *arbitrariness* and *decision*. Let me give another example that illustrates what this means.

## TRIVIAL SEMANTIC CONVENTIONALISM

Consider the fact that we use the word "dog" to refer to dogs. Things didn't have to be this way. Other words would have worked just fine. We could have called dogs by the name "cat" and cats by the name "dog." So how did dogs come to have the one name rather than the other? Dogs have the name they do because of a *decision. We* make it true that, in our language community, dogs are called "dogs." The rules of our language are something we control; they aren't forced on us from the outside. I'll call this kind of conventionalism *trivial semantic conventionalism.* I call it trivial because it describes a fairly boring and unimportant fact. I call it *semantic* because it describes how pieces of language come to refer to things in the world.

A philosophically interesting conventionalist theory must say something beyond what trivial semantic conventionalism says. The ethical views I'll consider here don't make the trivial point that the words "right" and "good" might have been used to mean something different from what they mean in present-day English. If we used the word "right" to mean *morally wrong,* then most of us would treat the sentence "torturing babies for fun is right" as expressing a truth. But this is trivial.

## SUBSTANTIVE VERSUS TRIVIAL CONVENTIONALISM

To see how a substantive form of conventionalism (SC) differs from trivial semantic conventionalism (TSC), we need to distinguish a proposition from the sentence that expresses it (a distinction drawn in Chapter 4). The first of the following claims is true, whereas the second is false:

> (TSC)  If we used language differently, the word "dog" might not name a four-legged animal.

> (SC)    If we used language differently, dogs might not be four-legged animals.

The sentence "dogs are four-legged animals" would not express a truth if we used the word "dog" to refer to fish. But changing the way we talk would not affect the proposition that the sentence expresses; talking differently wouldn't turn dogs into fish!

Conventionalism in ethics isn't a thesis about language. It does not assert that ethical *language* is under the control of someone's say-so; it says that the ethical *facts* are determined by someone's say-so. It says that ethical *propositions* are made true or false by someone's decision. Ethical conventionalism asserts a substantive thesis, not to be confused with trivial semantic conventionalism. Ethical conventionalism holds that ethical propositions are very different from most other propositions. Consider the fact that the Rocky Mountains are more than ten thousand feet high. This proposition isn't made true by someone's believing it or saying it; rather, it is true *independent* of anyone's say-so. Conventionalism in ethics rejects the idea that ethical propositions have the same status as geological propositions like this one.

## PLATO'S CRITIQUE OF THE DIVINE COMMAND THEORY

One of the earliest discussions of the Divine Command Theory is in Plato's dialogue *The Euthyphro.* This is a dialogue between Socrates, who was Plato's teacher, and Euthyphro. They meet in a law court where Euthyphro has just made a charge of murder against his own father. A servant of his father's had killed a slave. Euthyphro's father had the servant chained up and thrown in a ditch while someone went to the priest to ask what should be done. In the meantime, the servant died. Euthyphro is confident that indicting his father is the pious thing to do, though Euthyphro's relatives are angry at him for prosecuting his father for murdering a murderer. Socrates and Euthyphro discuss what piety is. Euthyphro claims to have a clear view of this, but Socrates shows that Euthyphro is very confused.

The Divine Command Theory comes up in this dialogue when Socrates asks: Is an action pious because it is loved by the gods, or is it loved by the gods because it is pious? We might substitute any moral term we wish (like "obligatory," "right," "good," or "just") for piety. And also, if we wish, we may substitute monotheism for the polytheism of the ancient Greeks. With these substitutions, we can reformulate Socrates' question as follows: Is an action morally obligatory because God commands us to do it, or does God command us to do it because the action is morally obligatory? Socrates' question has to do with which item is the cause and which the effect in the following diagram:

The Divine Command Theory says that the arrow goes from left to right. Ethical realism, on the other hand, holds that an action is right or wrong independent of anyone's say-so (even God's). So if you are a realist and think that God exists and makes true pronouncements on ethical matters, you'll think that the arrow goes from right to left. Your view will be that God knows a fact that exists independently of him and correctly describes what that fact is.

Notice that both the options in the preceding diagram assume there is a God. So rejecting the Divine Command Theory isn't the same as embracing atheism. A number of philosophers, beginning with Plato himself, were theists and ethical realists at the same time. Since the problem that Socrates poses assumes that the gods exist (in our reformulation, that there is a God), I'll go along with this assumption. We now want to ask what determines what in the diagram. Which way should the arrow of influence point?

One point that Socrates emphasizes is that the gods sometimes disagree with each other. (In many of the Greek myths, one god approves of an action, while another disapproves.) This allows Socrates to convict the Divine Command Theory of being contradictory. Socrates does this by supposing that the Divine Command Theory says that an action is right (or wrong) if at least one god says that it is. So, if the gods disagree about an action, the theory entails that the action is both right and wrong at the same time. Socrates sees that it is easy to reformulate the theory so that it avoids this problem. Suppose the theory says that an action is right (or wrong) if *all* the gods say it is. The theory then says nothing about those actions on which the gods disagree. Plato thinks this theory is still not satisfactory, but I won't go into his reasons for saying this.

If the theism we assume is monotheistic, what happens to this problem? There is no longer a question of what the theory says when the gods disagree, since the assumption is that there is just one God. However, two further problems have been posed for monotheistic versions of the Divine Command Theory.

## TWO OBJECTIONS TO THE DIVINE COMMAND THEORY

Although monotheists hold that there is just one God, they recognize that there are many *religions*. If different religions disagree about what God commands, how are we to tell what God wants us to do? Even if all religions agree about how God regards some action, there is still the question of whether they correctly report what God commands. Although this point is often offered as an objection to the Divine Command theory, I do not think that it shows that the theory is false. The theory doesn't describe how we can find out which actions are right or wrong; the theory describes only what makes one action right or wrong. This epistemological criticism of the theory is, therefore, off the mark.

The second difficulty is deeper; it is separate from this problem about knowledge. To pinpoint this further problem, let's suppose not just that there is a God, but that we know what God wants us to do. For example, let's suppose that God wants us to follow the Ten Commandments. We now can ask Socrates' question: Does God say that we should not murder (for example) because it is wrong to murder, or is it wrong to murder because God says so?

If the Divine Command Theory were true, then *anything at all* would be right (even torturing babies for fun), if God said that it were. Likewise, *anything at all* would be wrong (even reducing the suffering of sick children), if God said that it were. The idea that God might order us to torture babies for fun probably strikes you as quite horrible. "Surely, God wouldn't order us to do this," you'll say, "since God is good." Let's analyze this reaction more carefully. The point to notice is that this reaction is actually *inconsistent* with the Divine Command Theory. For this reaction to make sense, there would have to be such a thing as goodness, which exists independently of God's say-so. To say that "God would not do X, since X is wrong" is to say that the arrow points from right to left, not from left to right, in the diagram. Remember, the Divine Command Theory says that there is nothing inherent in an action that makes it good or bad; the action has its moral status simply because God chooses to label it good or bad.

I'm not doubting here that God has the power to make us the kinds of creatures we are. Let's assume that God has given us bodies that make us capable of feeling pain. It follows that God is partly responsible for why the following ethical truth is true: Stabbing someone for fun is wrong.

God helps make this ethical proposition true, because God is responsible for the fact that stabbing people causes them pain (if he had made our bodies otherwise, that might not be so). However, the Divine Command Theory says much more than this. It claims that the following ethical proposition is true only because God says it is: Inflicting pain for fun is wrong. I think that this last proposition is true, independent of anyone's say-so, even God's.

This is the most famous of Plato's objections to the Divine Command Theory. If the *only* thing that makes an action right or wrong is God's say-so, then God has no *reason* to decide one way or the other. According to the theory, God makes an *arbitrary* decision about what to say, but his say-so somehow creates an ethical fact. Before the pronouncement, there is no ethical fact; afterward, there is. Frankly, I find it baffling how facts can be brought into being by someone's say-so. If God makes an arbitrary decision when he issues his decree, what binds us to think that what he says is true? To be sure, God can punish us if we disobey his orders. This, however, only makes it *prudent* for us to go along with what he says; it does not show that what he says is true. (Recall the distinction between prudential and evidential reasons discussed in Chapter 10 in connection with Pascal's Wager.) If God's decision to say that *X* is wrong is arbitrary, then the proposition that *X* is wrong seems to be arbitrary as well—there is no reason to think that it is true.

It may be replied that the ways of God are mysterious—God can bring ethical facts into being just by issuing a decree, even though we can't understand how this is possible. To this reply I say that if the matter *is* mysterious, then we should decline to endorse the Divine Command Theory. If we can't understand the process postulated by a theory, that is hardly a reason to accept what the theory says.

## ETHICAL RELATIVISM

I now want to consider ethical relativism. This theory holds that the rightness or wrongness of an action is settled by the say-so of the society to which the actor belongs. In traditional Eskimo culture, it was customary for people to put their aging ailing parents outside to die in winter; according to ethical relativism, an Eskimo who did this would have been doing the right thing. In contemporary American society, this isn't the social norm; so relativism asserts that in our society, it would be wrong for us to act in this way. Ethical relativism says that what it is right or wrong to do depends on (is relative to) the society in which you live.

## ETHICAL RELATIVISM IS NORMATIVE, NOT DESCRIPTIVE

Let's make this theory more precise. First, we need to be clear that ethical relativism is a normative thesis, not a descriptive one. It makes a claim about how people *should* act. There is a quite separate descriptive thesis, which says that customs and norms *in fact* vary from society to society. Having already absorbed Hume's point about the is/ought gap (Chapter 29), you should be able to see that descriptive relativism (an is-proposition) does not deductively imply normative relativism (an ought-proposition).

A comment on the descriptive claim: It is fairly obvious that societies do vary in their customs and values. It is less obvious, however, that they do so with respect to the values that are most fundamental. For example, someone might grant that traditional Eskimos practiced euthanasia ("mercy killing") in contexts that we do not, but still maintain that deep down Eskimo culture and our own have the same fundamental values. Perhaps both societies adopt norms that aim to promote the general welfare, but because of different conditions of life, we and they end up arranging the details of life in different ways. I don't maintain that there are such "fundamental universals." I merely point out that descriptive relativism might be granted for some "superficial" customs but denied for some more "fundamental" ones. Anthropology is the subject that can assess whether this is correct.

## A FURTHER CLARIFICATION OF ETHICAL RELATIVISM

The second point of clarification is that there is an obvious sense in which what we ought to do depends on (is relative to) the situation we are in. I think that in most situations, it is wrong to steal. Suppose, however, that your family is starving and you have no money to buy food for them. Suppose you have the opportunity to steal a loaf of bread from a prosperous baker (this is the situation that Jean Valjean faced in Victor Hugo's novel *Les Miserables*). In this case, I think you would be doing the right thing to steal the loaf. Whether it is right or wrong to steal the bread depends on your circumstances.

People in different societies often live in different circumstances. People in one society may face situations in which it is wrong for them to steal. People in another may face situations in which stealing is the right thing to do. Ethical relativism, however, says more than this. It goes beyond the uncontroversial fact that what you ought to do depends on the situation you are in.

## ETHICAL RELATIVISM IS A VERSION OF CONVENTIONALISM

To see what this extra ingredient is, we must remind ourselves that normative ethical relativism is a conventionalist theory. It doesn't just say that what someone should do varies from society to society. It says that an action is right or wrong *solely because* of society's say-so. An ethical realist can grant that people in one society shouldn't steal whereas those in another should do so; a realist, however, will reject the relativist's explanation of why this is so. For, according to ethical relativism, ethical facts are brought into being simply by a society's adopting various norms of behavior.

So far, I've presented two clarifications of ethical relativism. First, it is a normative theory, not a descriptive one. Second, it is a conventionalist theory. Having said this, let's see whether there is any reason to think that the theory is true.

## IF IMPERIALISM IS WRONG, DOES THAT JUSTIFY ETHICAL RELATIVISM?

Ethical relativism enjoyed a fair amount of popularity in the social sciences (in anthropology, especially) during the twentieth century. As Western social scientists improved their understanding of other cultures, they often came to feel considerable respect for those cultures. The idea took hold that it is wrong for Western nations to impose their own standards on other cultures. From the sixteenth century down to the present, many Western nations created and extended empires by conquest and commercial domination. Often this was said to be justified in the name of bringing Christianity to the conquered peoples; Europeans sometimes talked of a "white man's burden"—of a responsibility to bring Western civilization to the rest of the world.

Maybe you'll find ethical relativism an attractive moral theory if this sort of imperialism strikes you as wrong. If you think that the idea of a "white man's burden" was simply a rationalization for exploitation, what better way to express this than by saying that each society determines its own ethical values? Europe and the United States don't get to decide what's right and wrong for the rest of the world. Rather each society decides this matter for itself. Partly for this reason, ethical relativism became popular among those who defended a kind of *noninterventionism* (this is the idea that one society should not meddle in the affairs of another).

Let's assume that there have been many cases in history in which one society was wrong to impose its will on another. Does this view make ethical relativism plausible? I think not. Are we prepared to say that a society can do anything it pleases to the individuals in it, as long as most of the people in the society believe that this is the right thing to do? It could become "customary" in a society that a certain group of people is oppressed (like the lower castes in India), even systematically murdered (like Jews, Gypsies, and homosexuals in Nazi Germany). Would this be made right if most people in the society thought it was right? I find this highly dubious.

Don't confuse the question of rightness with the question of whether some other country should intervene militarily to put a stop to the objectionable practice. These are separate issues. There might be cases in which foreign intervention would be wrong, even though some practices going on inside the country are wrong. For a practice to be wrong is one thing; what steps should be taken to end the wrong is a separate matter.

In addition, it is important to see that ethical relativism does not prohibit the kind of interventionism that its supporters tend to condemn. Should members of my society engage in colonial conquest? According to ethical relativism, I should answer this question by seeing whether the norms of my society permit people to engage in colonial conquest. Far from condemning interventionism, this consideration will have the consequence of justifying it. If you asked in nineteenth-century Britain whether it was "customary" for individuals to help extend and maintain the British Empire, the answer would have been *yes*. Paradoxically, ethical relativism does not imply that societies ought to respect each other.

Finally, it is worth noticing that the kinds of objections I made against the Divine Command Theory also apply to ethical relativism. A conventionalist view of this kind says that an action is made right in a society simply because it is the norm. This, however, has such bizarre consequences as the following:

> If our society considered it ethically permissible to torture babies for fun, then it would be ethically permissible for us to do this.

Ethical relativism doesn't say that our society *will* ever be like this. It does, however, endorse the above if/then statement. My view is that the above if/then statement is false. If our society were to adopt this norm, then our society would have become morally abhorrent. To say this is to talk like an ethical realist. What is morally right and wrong isn't settled by society's say-so.

Ethical relativism has the consequence that *conformism* is always right. It entails that a person should *always* conform to the norms laid down by his or her society. If you think that the norms in a society can be wrong, you are rejecting ethical relativism. Consider what ethical relativism says about a society that *changes* its norms. Some two hundred years ago, most of the people living in the United States probably believed that slavery was ethically permissible. Later the majority opinion changed. According to relativism, slavery was right until a certain date, but then it suddenly became wrong, *simply because the number of people who endorsed slavery dropped below 50 percent.* Just as in the case of the Divine Command Theory, I find it baffling how ethical truths can flip-flop simply because of someone's say-so. It seems to me that if slavery was wrong after 1865, it was wrong before that date as well.

---

**Two Views of Democracy**

Why is it right for a society to decide certain issues by majority vote? We can reformulate this question by mimicking the question that Plato posed in *The Euthyphro*. Is *X* wrong simply because the majority thinks that it is, or is the rightness and wrongness of *X* not settled by the majority say-so?

Believing that democratic procedures are the best way to decide what a society ought to do does not require one to endorse ethical conventionalism. One can be an ethical realist and still maintain that democracy is often the best practical procedure a society can use for discovering what it should do. According to this position, the opinion of the majority is fallible, but majority rule is *less* fallible than other procedures (dictatorship, for example) that might be adopted.

---

## SARTRE'S EXISTENTIALISM

I now turn to the third conventionalist theory—existentialism. There is a lot more to existentialism than I can discuss here. It is important to realize that existentialist writers differ a great deal among themselves. Here I'm focusing on a single strand in the thinking of some important existentialists; this is the idea (expressed by Sartre and by Søren Kierkegaard, a nineteenth-century Danish philosopher and religious thinker) that individual human beings must freely create their own moral values.

Sartre holds that the scope of human freedom is far wider than most of us suspect. People often believe that only a small range of options is open to them—that the large-scale features of their lives are forced upon them from the outside. Sartre thinks this is an illusion; people stumble without reflection into stereotyped and conventional ways of life without realizing that they in fact are making a choice. Freedom is a frightening burden that we must shoulder without kidding ourselves. Sartre goes so far as to say that we are responsible for every feature of the lives we live. Although I think that this last idea is a piece of rhetorical overstatement, Sartre's general stress on the responsibility of individuals to shape their own lives is important. There is a lot to be said for really reflecting about what you think and do—for regarding options critically and not falling into a pattern out of unreflective habit. However, Sartre says something more than this; this something more is the conventionalist element in his existentialism that I want to identify and criticize.

In Chapter 28, I mentioned that Sartre (in his book *Existentialism*) describes a young Frenchman during World War II who has to decide whether to join the Resistance or stay at home to care for his ailing mother. Let's distinguish two claims that might be made about this young man:

(1) He should think the choice over carefully and not do what he does out of unreflective habit.

(2) There is no moral fact of the matter about what he should do until he makes a decision. If he decides that he wants above all to be a good son, he should stay home; if he decides that he wants above all to be a good Frenchman, he should join the Resistance. But there is no standard that exists independently of his choice that determines what he should want most of all.

Sartre claimed that both (1) *and* (2) are true. He thought that this story about the young Frenchman exhibits a very general pattern. In *every* choice we make, we create moral facts. It is (2) that embodies the conventionalist element in Sartre's existentialism.

Sartre chose this example because he thought it poses a difficult moral problem. But even if the problem were one that we might see as clear-cut, Sartre would view it as calling for an arbitrary decision. Consider a third option that the young man has. He could leave home and volunteer to torture prisoners for the Gestapo. The young man has to decide whether he wants to be a good son, a good Frenchman, or a good Nazi. Sartre's position is that there is no fact of the matter about what the young man should do until he makes a decision about what he wants most. Just like the other conventionalist theories discussed in this chapter, Sartre's existentialism implies the following if/then statement:

If the young man decides that he wants above all to be a good *X*, then it is morally permissible for him to do what it takes to be a good *X*.

I've already noted why I find this claim implausible. Sartre thinks this conventionalist thesis follows from the fact that there is no God If there is no God to lay down the moral law, then each of us must lay down the law for ourselves. An ethical realist would disagree. Why can't moral facts exist independently of anyone's (God's, society's, or the individual's) say-so? Sartre has no very good argument against this realist alternative.

In this and the previous few chapters, I have not provided any strong argument in favor of ethical realism. Rather, I have criticized the subjectivist and conventionalist alternatives to realism. In what follows, I'll assume that there are ethical truths that are true independently of anyone's say-so. The goal will be to consider some theories that try to say what those truths are.

## Review Questions

1. What is the difference between trivial semantic conventionalism and substantive conventionalism?
2. Consider this statement: "We should do what God says we should do." Can an ethical realist and a defender of the Divine Command Theory agree on this? If not, what do they disagree about?
3. Consider this statement: "What may be right for a person in one culture to do may not be right for a person in another culture to do." Can an ethical realist and a defender of ethical relativism agree on this? If not, what do they disagree about?
4. Does ethical relativism entail that people in one culture should respect the standards of conduct obeyed in another culture?
5. Consider this statement: "People must figure out for themselves what they should do." Can an ethical realist and a defender of Sartre's existentialism agree on this? If so, what do they disagree about?
6. There is a Yiddish story about the wise men of Chelm. The town council met to discuss what could be done about the shortage of sour cream. They decided to solve the problem by calling water "sour cream." (The problem of what they would do about the resulting water shortage they put aside for future deliberation.) How does this story illustrate the difference between trivial semantic conventionalism and substantive conventionalism?

## Problems for Further Thought

1. Is there a third coherent option for the theist that rejects both the Divine Command Theory and ethical realism? Defend your answer.
2. Do facts about evolution suggest that there may be fundamental norms that are cultural universals despite the numerous ways in which human cultures differ from each other?

# CHAPTER 32

## *Utilitarianism*

Utilitarianism is an ethical theory whose central idea is "the greatest good for the greatest number." The idea is that ethically correct actions are ones that promote the greatest happiness of the individuals affected by it. We will soon see that this formulation of the theory requires fine-tuning.

Utilitarianism is a philosophical idea that has exercised considerable influence on the world of practical affairs. Jeremy Bentham (1748–1832) and John Stuart Mill (1806–1873) were deeply involved in the political controversies of their age. Both defended utilitarianism in publications that the educated classes in England read with great attention. Utilitarianism wasn't an abstract "ivory tower" theory that only professors found worth discussing. It stirred the interest of great numbers of people who cared about the institutions of their society.

Bentham and Mill thought that many of these institutions needed reform because they failed to promote human welfare. A central political agenda at this time was extending the vote to men who didn't own property. Mill also wrote in favor of women's suffrage, although women didn't receive the vote until much later. The abolition of slavery was another political struggle in which utilitarians participated. In these and other cases, utilitarians argued that institutions had to be changed because they advanced the interests of the few to the detriment of the many. Utilitarians attacked the idea that the rich and powerful had some special "right" to arrange society as they saw fit. On the contrary, the point of utilitarianism is that each individual must be taken into account, because each individual is capable of experiencing happiness.

In this chapter, I'll discuss the general ethical theory, not the specific political issues that at one time were the focus of utilitarian concern. By now (at the end of this book), it should be abundantly clear that the following isn't a valid deduction:

> If utilitarianism is true, then slavery is morally wrong.
> Slavery is morally wrong.
> ———————
> Utilitarianism is true.

I don't doubt the premises, but I'll try to show that there is plenty of room to doubt the conclusion.

### MILL'S DEFENSE OF THE GREATEST HAPPINESS PRINCIPLE

Before describing in more detail what utilitarianism says, I want to discuss how someone might go about evaluating whether the most basic principle in utilitarianism is true. Mill calls this basic idea the Greatest Happiness Principle. It says that the action we ought to perform in a given situation is the one that promotes the greatest happiness.

In his essay "Utilitarianism," Mill attempted to prove that the Greatest Happiness Principle is correct. Mill's argument begins with an analogy between desirability and visibility. He says that just as the only proof that something is visible is that someone sees it, so the only proof that something is desirable is that someone desires it. He then claims that what people ultimately want is their own happiness. Mill concludes from this that the most desirable action is the one that produces the most happiness overall.

Let's reconstruct Mill's argument as follows:

(1) Seeing something proves that it is visible.

———————

(2) Hence, desiring something proves that it is desirable.

(3) The only thing that each person ultimately desires is his or her own happiness.

———————

(4) The only thing that is ultimately desirable for a person is his or her own happiness.

———————

Hence, each person should perform those actions that promote the greatest happiness.

I've drawn three horizontal lines in this argument to indicate that (2) is supposed to follow from (1), (4) is supposed to follow from (2) and (3), and the final conclusion is supposed to follow from (4).

There are several problems with this reasoning. First, (1) doesn't provide much of a reason for accepting (2). Visibility and desirability are different. If something is visible, this means that it is possible to see it. However, if something is desirable, this doesn't mean that it is *possible* to desire it, but that it *should* be desired. Visibility is a descriptive concept, while desirability is a normative one. So although "*x* is visible" does follow from "*x* is seen," "*x* is desirable" does *not* follow from "*x* is desired."

What does the word *ultimately* mean in step (3)? It means that everything else people want they want only as a means to the end of securing their own happiness. If I desire that the starving receive food, Mill is saying that I want this only as a means to securing a certain end—namely, my own happiness. I argued against this thesis in Chapter 27; it simply asserts a form of psychological egoism. Three of the four preference structures discussed there (all except Pure Egoism) involve the thought that people care about the welfare of others in addition to caring about their own well-being. If Psychological Egoism is false (as I think it is), then premise (3) of Mill's argument is false.

Does (4) follow from (3)? No—for the same reason that (2) doesn't follow from (1). Even if a person ultimately desires his or her own happiness, it doesn't follow that the most desirable thing is for the person to have his or her desires satisfied. What people ultimately desire is a *descriptive* question, but what is desirable is a *normative* question. Hume was right that ought-statements do not follow from exclusively is-premises.

Finally, even if (4) were true, the conclusion of the argument would not follow. The fact that your own happiness is the most desirable thing *for you* does not imply that you should try to maximize *everyone's* happiness. The conclusion of this argument sometimes requires you to act unselfishly—to sacrifice your own happiness if doing so brings with it a more than compensating increase in the happiness of others. This does not follow from (4).

## RECIPROCAL ILLUMINATION

Mill had another idea about how utilitarianism could be rationally justified. Instead of trying to deduce the Greatest Happiness Principle from premises that would be plausible even to a nonutilitarian, we can evaluate the principle by seeing how it measures up against the moral judgments we are prepared to make about concrete cases. This was the method I described Harman as using in Chapter 30. A general principle has implications about what it is wrong or right to do in specific situations. If we are prepared to make ethical judgments about these situations, we can use these judgments to evaluate the general theory (recall Harman's example about the transplant operation). If a theory implies that an action is right in a given situation and we believe that the action would clearly be wrong, we might take this as evidence that the theory is false.

So judgments about specific cases can lead us to reject a general theory. The reverse can happen as well. If we think that a theory is very plausible and then find that it implies that a given action is wrong (which, before thinking about it much, we thought was right), we might decide to allow the theory to guide us—to lead us to revise our opinions about the ethical problem posed by the particular case. We see here a two-way influence—a process of *reciprocal illumination*—by which our judgments about specific cases can influence how we regard a theory, and our views about a theory can affect our judgments about specific cases. A utilitarian who does not think that slavery is wrong might come to see that one or the other of these ideas must be abandoned. Which idea should be abandoned depends on which is overall more plausible (the general theory or the judgment about the specific institution), given the other beliefs that he or she has. I now want to use this technique of evaluation to fine-tune utilitarianism and then to suggest that it faces some very serious difficulties.

## WHAT IS HAPPINESS?

I'll begin by focusing on the idea of happiness. What is happiness? I'm not asking for *examples* of activities that make us happy. Rather, I want to know what happiness itself is. Compare: If I ask you what bankruptcy is, I'm not asking you what activities cause bankruptcy. Bankruptcy isn't the same as reckless investment; neither is happiness the same thing as a warm puppy. A partial answer might be that happiness is a feeling. This is only partial, of course, because there are many other feelings besides happiness. If, however, happiness is something in the mind (something purely subjective), we can formulate a problem that utilitarianism must address.

## THE PROBLEM OF THE EXPERIENCE MACHINE

In Chapter 13, I discussed how Descartes grappled with the problem of refuting the hypothesis that he was systematically misled by an evil demon. Contemporary philosophers sometimes give Descartes' problem a modern twist by asking how we know that we aren't brains in vats. According to the brain-in-the-vat hypothesis, your brain now rests in a vat filled with a liquid that keeps it alive. It is hooked up to a giant computer, whose electrical impulses furnish you with a rich stream of experiences. These impulses generate the illusion that you have a body and that you are having sensory contact (sight, smell, hearing, touch, etc.) with the external world. According to the brain-in-the-vat hypothesis, almost everything you believe about your present and past is false. You don't really have a face; you're not really looking at a philosophy book right now and so on.

The point of this bizarre hypothesis is that it poses a philosophical challenge. The challenge is to show how you know that the brain-in-the-vat hypothesis is false. None of us believes this hypothesis about ourselves. Can this conviction be rationally justified, or is it just a groundless prejudice?

As just formulated, the brain-in-the-vat problem falls within the theory of knowledge; it is a part of epistemology. I now will reformulate the problem so as to turn it into an ethical issue, one that tells us something about utilitarianism. The computer described in the brain-in-the-vat problem is an *experience machine*. Suppose that the machine could be set up so it would provide you with whatever experiences would make you the happiest, and that it is up to you to decide whether you wish to be plugged into the machine. If being a great concert violinist would give you pleasure, plugging into the machine will give you a rich, complex sequence of experiences of this sort. If you would be happiest being a political leader loved and admired by millions of people, the experience machine can furnish the feelings that would derive from being loved and admired by millions. Of course, the experience machine does not make you into a concert violinist or a political leader. Rather, the machine gives you the precise set of experiences you would get from having those sorts of lives.

If utilitarianism were true, it would be preferable for people to plug into experience machines rather than lead real lives that provide a lesser degree of happiness. But, contrary to what utilitarianism says about this kind of choice, I for one (and I bet you feel the same way) put considerable value on leading a real life. If you're plugged into the experience machine, virtually all your beliefs are false. You are proud of yourself because you think you are a great violinist and you take pleasure in your skill. If the machine leads you to think that you are a great political leader, you may think you have created world peace and so you feel good about doing so. However, in both cases, your pride and your pleasure rest on an illusion. Most of us value something beyond the feeling of happiness that comes from doing certain things. We also place a value on the reality of the doing. However, to think this way is to say that something matters beyond the subjective feeling of happiness. This goes contrary to the form of utilitarianism we're considering. (The example of the experience machine comes from Robert Nozick's *Anarchy, State, and Utopia,* New York, Basic Books, 1974.)

There are a number of science fiction novels and movies that make this same point. Aldous Huxley's *Brave New World* and Woody Allen's *Sleeper* are examples. These works of fiction describe a future in which people are drugged by their governments into being docile, happy citizens. People are contented, but the novel or movie usually takes the point of view that there is something deeply wrong with a society like this. Usually what's wrong is that people lack *autonomy*. Their own beliefs and desires have been distorted or altogether destroyed; what they do and feel is the result of the drugs they take. If you agree that there is something wrong with a society of this sort, you may have to say that there is something over and above "happiness" (a state of mind) that is ethically important.

## MILL ON "HIGHER" AND "LOWER" PLEASURES

Mill himself grappled with a problem of this kind. He asked why it is better to be "Socrates dissatisfied" rather than a satisfied fool. Socrates was acutely aware of the imperfections of the world around him; it wasn't true that each of his daily experiences filled him with pleasure. But a "satisfied fool," Mill says, might be delighted by every detail of life. If the latter individual is happier, utilitarianism seems to recommend that we become more like the fool and less like Socrates.

Mill denied that utilitarianism has this implication. He thought that Socrates was capable of enjoying "higher" pleasures, whereas the fool, he says, could only experience "lower" pleasures. Higher pleasures derive from exercising higher mental abilities (such as abstract reasoning); lower pleasures come from using mental abilities that are lower (such as sensation). Mill claimed that higher pleasures provide more happiness than lower ones. To see that this is true, Mill recommends that you ask individuals who have experienced both sorts of pleasures which they enjoyed more. Mill was confident that these "competent judges" would say that the higher pleasures bring more happiness than the lower ones.

There are some higher and lower pleasures for which Mill's prediction might be true. For example, someone who does nothing but drink beer and watch television might find that "higher" pleasures are better, once he or she is exposed to them. There are other cases, however, in which Mill's prediction seems mistaken. Imagine someone who has been leading a real life and then is plugged into an experience machine. Once he is unplugged, we could ask him which life made him happier. I think most people would have to admit that their life while plugged in provided more happiness than the real life they led before. This doesn't mean that people *prefer* to live the phony life that results from being plugged into the experience machine; it just means that life in the experience machine provides a greater quantity of happiness.

The same may be true of the people in the science fiction works described earlier. Maybe drugs provide them with more happiness than they would receive if they were autonomous. Again this doesn't mean that they *prefer* being drugged by their governments, but that they receive a greater quantity of happiness in that state. To move closer to real life, consider a drug like heroin. Suppose someone could live a life as a heroin addict without facing dangers like AIDS and being killed by drug dealers. Maybe in that case the drug would be so intensely pleasurable that people who had experienced life with it and life without it would have to concede that life is happier with it. This doesn't mean that we would *prefer* to have such a life. Rather, what it shows is that our preferences are influenced by factors other than the quantity of happiness we receive.

## OBJECTION TO HEDONISTIC UTILITARIANISM

My conclusion is that Mill's argument about higher and lower pleasures does not work. Mill believed that Socrates dissatisfied had a better life than a satisfied fool, but I don't see that Mill has a way of explaining why this is so. So we have here an objection to the first form of utilitarianism I want to distinguish. It is *hedonistic utilitarianism,* which says that the right action is the one that maximizes pleasure and minimizes pain (not just for the agent, but for all individuals who are affected). According to this form of utilitarianism, we should plug into the experience machine; we should become more like the fool and less like Socrates. However, both these ought-statements strike me as false. If they are false, then hedonistic utilitarianism should be rejected.

## PREFERENCE UTILITARIANISM

There is another form of utilitarianism, which is not undermined by these problems. I call it *preference utilitarianism.* The idea of this kind of utilitarianism is not to maximize pleasure, but to maximize the degree to which people get their preferences satisfied. If people generally prefer to lead real lives rather than to plug into experience machines, then a preference utilitarian will have no problem explaining why it would be wrong to plug people into experience machines. And if people prefer to live their lives drug-free, then preference utilitarianism can easily explain why it would be wrong for the government to surreptitiously give people a diet of pleasure-producing drugs. So preference utilitarianism avoids a problem that is fatal to hedonistic utilitarianism. But preference utilitarianism has problems of its own. The first of these becomes clear when we try to apply the view to specific cases.

## THE APPLES AND ORANGES PROBLEM

The problem is that it often is difficult to know how to compare one person's preferences with those of another. This is something that a preference utilitarian must do if those preferences conflict. Consider a state government that has to decide whether a tract of land should be opened to commercial use or reserved for recreational use. There are the profits and jobs that some people will receive on the one hand, and the enjoyment from camping and swimming that other people will receive on the other. How are these two interests to be compared? For preference utilitarians to answer this question, they need to measure how intensely each person prefers one option over the other. Then they need to sum over this totality of individual preferences to decide which action maximizes the satisfaction of preferences collectively. Suppose that the economic losses from not going the commercial route were small, whereas the recreational (and aesthetic) losses from going the commercial route were large. What conclusion would preference utilitarians extract from this? The problem is that it is often obscure what "small" and "large" mean in such cases. Let's call this the *Apples and Oranges Problem:* How can you compare the intensity of one person's gain with the intensity of another person's loss?

Sometimes this kind of question is settled by using money as a mode of comparison. If we want to know how intensely the developers want to develop the land commercially, we can find out how much they are prepared to pay to do so; to ascertain how intensely other people want the land to be preserved for recreational use, we can see how much they are prepared to pay to attain this goal. Then see how much money stacks up on the one side and how much on the other—which option has attracted the higher bid? The problem with this procedure is that how much money people are willing to spend is often influenced by factors other than the intensity of their desires. A rich person may be prepared to pay more for a loaf of bread than a poor one, but that doesn't mean that the rich person wants it more.

Sometimes the Apples and Oranges Problem is addressed by taking a vote among the individuals affected; let a referendum be held, with each person having a single vote. The problem with using voting as a way of solving the this problem (which economists call the problem of interpersonal utility comparison) is that voting does not represent the *intensities* of people's desires. If I mildly prefer the commercial option to the recreational one, I'll vote for the commercial option; if you strongly prefer the recreational use to the commercial one, you will vote for the recreational use. Your vote and mine count equally, but this fails to represent something that is important to the calculation that a preference utilitarian must make.

In practical politics, voting is often a reasonable procedure (whether it *always* is reasonable will be discussed in what follows). However, I'm not talking about choosing a workable (if imperfect) procedure. I'm talking about the problem of making sense of what preference utilitarianism actually says. The problem is that it often is unclear what it means to say that a given action has a higher utility for one person than the opposite action has for another person. Although this is a serious problem for preference utilitarianism, I'm going to assume in what follows that the Apples and Oranges Problem can be solved—that the intensity of people's preferences can be compared. I make this assumption in order to explore some additional criticisms that have been made of preference utilitarianism.

## UTILITARIANISM AND JUSTICE: THE CASE OF THE LONESOME STRANGER

I'll begin with a problem that can be illustrated by an example. A gruesome murder has occurred in a town. The sheriff has discovered that the murderer himself is dead; however, the sheriff knows that no one will believe him if he says this, even if he lays out all the evidence he has. Meanwhile, the townspeople are becoming more and more agitated. The sheriff realizes that if a suspect isn't put on trial very soon, there will be a riot and it is quite probable that many innocent people will be injured and a few killed. As the sheriff is mulling this over in his office, in strolls a lonesome stranger. This fellow tells the sheriff that he has no friends or relations in the world and that he is feeling depressed and has no particular desire to continue living. The sheriff then gets an idea: Why not frame the lonesome stranger? There is capital punishment in this locale, so the sheriff can arrange that the stranger be tried, convicted, and executed. Suppose the sheriff can arrange it so that the framing will always remain a secret. Should the sheriff frame the stranger?

What would a utilitarian say here? For a hedonistic utilitarian, the answer is easy. If you frame the stranger (and keep the facts secret), one person dies, but the peace of mind of the townspeople is restored; if you don't frame him, a bloody riot will ensue and more than one person will die. The way to maximize happiness is for the sheriff to frame the stranger and always keep this secret. For a preference utilitarian, the question is more complicated. If the people in the town have strong preferences that innocent people should not be punished, then the sheriff should not frame the stranger. Suppose, however, the people don't care about this; let's suppose they care only about their own safety and peace of mind. In this case, preference utilitarianism will tell the sheriff that he ought to frame the stranger. The problem here is that utilitarian considerations seem to conflict with considerations of *justice*. It is unjust to punish people for crimes they did not commit. If you think this moral requirement overrides considerations that reflect the utility of punishing the lonesome stranger, then you will interpret this example as an objection to utilitarianism.

## PUNISHMENT

Before considering how a utilitarian might reply to this objection, I want to say a little more about punishment. A utilitarian will answer the question of whether someone should be punished by asking whether the punishment do have good consequences. If punishment does not deter people from similar wrongdoing and does not reform the character of the person punished, then a utilitarian may say that there is no point in punishing people who are guilty of even the most awful crimes. For a utilitarian, the distinction between guilt and innocence does not have to coincide with the distinction between those who should be punished and those who should not be.

A nonutilitarian view of punishment (there is more than one) will see things differently. The principle of an eye for an eye—of retribution for wrongdoing—is not a utilitarian idea. Retributivists want the punishment to fit the crime; they will say that someone should be punished if and only if they deserve to be punished. People who are innoncent of any wrongdoing must never be punished and people who are guilty of some wrongdoing must be punished. For retributivists (people who think that punishment is justified because it is retribution for wrongdoing), it doesn't matter whether punishing improves anything after the crime is committed. For utilitarians, it is precisely the consequences of punishment (not the crime committed) that is relevant to deciding whether someone should be punished.

Utilitarian discussion of punishment usually focuses on the question of why *the guilty* should be punished. But, as the case of the lonesome stranger illustrates, the question can also be posed of why the innocent should *not* be punished. According to utilitarianism there is no absolute requirement that the guilty must be punished and that the innocent must not be. What should be done depends entirely on which course of action will maximize the collective happiness.

## A REPLY: DISTINGUISH RULE AND ACT UTILITARIANISM

I've argued that the lonesome stranger example provides an objection to utilitarianism (whether of the hedonistic or the preference variety). It illustrates how considerations of justice can conflict with utilitarianism. Recall that this assessment of utilitarianism depends on making a moral judgment about the example situation. Without this, there is no way to use specific cases to evaluate the general principle.

There is a standard reply that utilitarians often make to this and similar objections. Their strategy is to distinguish two kinds of utilitarian theory and to claim that one of them is perfectly consistent with the idea that the sheriff should not frame the lonesome stranger. I described utilitarianism as saying that an action should be performed only if it promotes the greatest happiness or the greatest preference satisfaction. However, there is an ambiguity here. Are we evaluating *kinds* of actions, or individual actions, one by one? That is, are we to use utilitarian considerations to decide what general rules to follow, or are we told to apply these considerations each time a specific act is at issue? Here I'm drawing the type/token distinction discussed in Chapter 23 and applying it to the question of how utilitarianism should be formulated.

That is, utilitarianism (regardless of whether it says to maximize happiness or preference satisfaction) can take the form of *rule utilitarianism* or *act utilitarianism*. How does this choice affect the way we understand the lonesome stranger example? According to the rule utilitarian, the sheriff's decision making should have two parts. First, he must decide what general rule to adopt. Second, he must determine how that general rule applies to the concrete case he confronts.

The first problem involves deciding which of the following two alternatives has better consequences:

(R1)  Punish the innocent when it is convenient.

(R2)  Never punish the innocent.

A rule utilitarian will argue that (R2) has better consequences for people's welfare, and so it is (R2) that the sheriff should use. Note that once (R2) is applied to the specific situation the sheriff confronts, he will decide *not* to frame the stranger. Why think that (R2) has better consequences than (R1)? Part of the reason is that rules that are used again and again become generally known. If people generally believe that (R1) is the policy the government follows, this will produce a great deal of unhappiness. An act utilitarian, on the other hand, will not focus on general rules, but will focus instead on the specific choice at hand. The act utilitarian's procedure has one step, not two. In the unique, concrete situation that the sheriff faces, he will maximize utility by framing the lonesome stranger. Which general rule has the best overall consequences is not relevant to the sheriff's deliberation, according to the act utilitarian.

Thus the defender of utilitarianism is suggesting the following: The claim is that the example of the lonesome stranger constitutes an objection to *act* utilitarianism, not to *rule* utilitarianism. The idea is that rule utilitarianism recommends that the sheriff not frame the stranger, and this recommendation coincides with what most people find plausible.

In reply, I want to argue that adopting a rule utilitarian formulation won't save utilitarianism from the difficulty posed by the example of the lonesome stranger. I agree that (R2) has better consequences as a general policy than (R1) does. However, I think that a utilitarian must concede that (R2) is inferior to the following rule:

(R3)  Don't punish the innocent, unless doing so will maximize utility.

I think a utilitarian must agree that (R3) is preferable on utilitarian grounds to (R2). And the sheriff, acting on (R3), will frame the lonesome stranger. I conclude that rule utilitarianism and act utilitarianism are equally subject to the objection posed by the example of the lonesome stranger.

## UTILITARIANISM AND TOLERANCE: THE PROBLEM OF THE FANATICAL MAJORITY

I now turn to a different objection to utilitarianism. An important fact about preference utilitarianism is that it does not allow you to ignore people's preferences on the grounds that you morally disapprove of them. People's preferences, whether we approve of them or not, must be taken into account when we decide what laws our society should adopt or what actions each of us should perform. The problem for utilitarianism is that we sometimes think it is our moral duty to *ignore* people's preferences because we think those preferences are morally objectionable. If it is ever morally legitimate to do this, preference utilitarianism is in trouble.

Consider what happens to nonconformists in a society of fanatics. Here we might be talking about people in a minority religion, who live in a society in which the majority is made of religious fanatics. Or consider a society in which a minority of people are homosexual and the heterosexual majority is very intolerant. Another case concerns political nonconformity—a minority with one set of political beliefs living with a majority that not only disagrees with them, but is extremely hostile toward them. How would a utilitarian view the idea that people should be free to live as they see fit?

A utilitarian will decide this question by calculating how policies of repression or toleration would satisfy people's preferences. If the intolerant majority is fanatical enough, the utilitarian scales may tip in favor of prohibiting nonconformity. If a fanatical majority gets upset enough at the presence of nonconformists, then there will be a utilitarian justification for banning nonconformity. Of course, this sort of policy will not be the one that the nonconformists prefer. However, since they are in the minority, their strong preferences may be outweighed by the strong preferences of the fanatical majority.

Many of us would want to say that people have certain rights—to freely pursue the religion of their choice (or no religion at all), to engage in the sexual practices they prefer (or none at all), to discuss and promulgate their favored political opinions (or to be apolitical)—as long as doing so does not endanger the life and property of others. The fact that these practices might enrage an intolerant majority, many of us would want to say, simply does not count against a person's being entitled to do what he or she wants. To think this way is *not* to think like a utilitarian.

We have here an objection to utilitarianism. I'll call it the *Problem of the Fanatical Majority.* John Stuart Mill considered this issue in his famous essay "On Liberty." Mill was a liberal in the sense of that word used in the nineteenth century. Liberals believed in liberty. An imprecise slogan embodying liberalism is that "people should be free to do what they want, as long as doing so does not hurt others." One reason this is imprecise is that fanatics might claim to be "hurt" (offended, distressed, outraged, etc.) simply by knowing there are people who live their lives differently from the way they do.

Mill was a utilitarian who believed in the kinds of personal liberties I just mentioned. His problem was to reconcile utilitarianism with the idea that people have a right to the kinds of freedoms I've just enumerated. Mill sought to effect this reconciliation by distinguishing *public* and *private* actions. A public action affects individuals in addition to the actor; a private action, on the other hand, does not affect others. Mill argued that people are entitled to live lives of nonconformity, if they wish, since the activities involved here are private, not public.

---

### Liberalism and Conservatism

Mill believed that the right to personal nonconformity flows from utilitarian considerations. He also thought that economic activity is public and therefore might have to be limited for utilitarian reasons. A corporation's activities (even a single person's buying and selling) affects others. A regulated economy (as opposed to an absolutely free market) therefore is preferable, Mill thought, on utilitarian grounds. Mill was a *liberal,* in the nineteenth-century meaning of that term. Liberals believed in liberty—that each person should have the maximum amount of freedom, consistent with not compromising the freedom of others.

The terms "liberal" and "conservative" have different meanings in the United States today. To understand what each involves, let's distinguish two "markets" in which each of us participates: the marketplace of *ideas* and the *economic* marketplace (of goods and services that we buy and sell).

Liberals in the United States now often oppose censorship and think that the government should not promote religion (or promote one religion over any other). They believe that the government should not interfere in the marketplace of ideas. Yet they tend to believe, on utilitarian grounds, that the government should regulate the economy.

So-called "conservatives," on the other hand, tend to take the opposite view. They often favor some sorts of censorship and want the government to promote religion (by encouraging prayer in the public schools, for example). Yet, when it comes to the economic marketplace, they tend to favor more freedom and less regulation.

Although both political positions are influenced by utilitarian considerations, each makes use of nonutilitarian ideas as well. Liberals often talk about "rights" of free speech, which people are said to have even if some forms of free speech make lots of people very unhappy. And conservatives sometimes argue that pornography should be censored on religious grounds or on other grounds that are not utilitarian.

Liberalism and conservatism are not the only political options available. In the United States, both hold that capitalism is a workable form of economic organization, and both have favored military interventions of various kinds (in Korea and Vietnam, for example). Some critics on the left—socialists and communists, for example—doubt the viability of capitalism and have opposed military interventions such as the ones mentioned. Critics on the right—libertarians, for example—reject the government's entitlement to intervene in people's lives without their consent—for example, to collect taxes, to censor pornography, and to regulate the economy.

Mill defended a totally free (*laissez-faire*) marketplace of ideas. He described ideas as being in competition. Everyone benefits from unrestrained competition, Mill said, because competition tends to select the best ideas. Ideas compete in the way organisms do in the process of Darwinian natural selection (Chapter 6).

Defenders of a free economic marketplace have often put forward a similar argument. In *The Wealth of Nations*, the eighteenth-century economist Adam Smith argued that when everyone freely pursues his or her selfish economic interests, everyone benefits. The nation as a whole becomes richer, and so prosperity "trickles down" to even the worst off in the society. Liberals have criticized this trickle down defense of a perfectly free market economy. They claim that an unregulated economy produces catastrophic swings ("boom and bust cycles," like the one that produced the Crash of 1929 and the ensuing Great Depression). An unfettered market, they argue, can make everyone worse off than they would be if the market were regulated. This liberal argument against a perfectly free market is utilitarian in character.

Does this argument secure the kinds of freedoms I have been discussing? Not entirely. In a society in which most people are intolerant fanatics, the most that a nonconforming minority can hope for is the right to be *secret* nonconformists. It is only when such practices are performed in secret that they can count as private in Mill's sense. However, I think most of us believe in liberties that are more extensive than ones that are kept in the closet. Whether it be in the religious, sexual, or political arenas, most of us think there are practices affecting others (because they are not kept secret) that a minority is entitled to engage in, even if this distresses fanatics.

## UTILITARIANISM AND PERSONAL INTEGRITY: THE PROBLEM OF DIRTY HANDS

The next objection to utilitarianism I want to discuss I'll call the *Dirty Hands Objection.* Consider an individual contemplating a choice between an action that is clearly right and one that is clearly wrong. Suppose, however, that the morally wrong action has this characteristic: If the individual does not perform this bad action himself or herself, someone else will. An example of this kind of situation is provided by a case I discussed in connection with Sartre's existentialism in Chapter 31. Imagine someone who is considering whether he should become a torturer for the Nazis. Suppose that if he doesn't do this, someone else will. Examples less horrible than this are common in everyday life. Maybe if you are studying to be an engineer, you'll get a job offer to work on developing a new weapon for the government. Perhaps you will feel that it is wrong to have this weapon developed—that it will provide new ways to harm people without making our country or any other more secure. Of course, your participation in the development of this weapon is not *necessary* for the weapon to get produced. If you don't do the job, someone else will.

What will a utilitarian say about such cases? If you decline the job offer, the bad consequences (the torturing, the development of the weapon) occur nonetheless, but without your participation. If you accept, the same bad consequences occur, this time with your participation. A utilitarian will have to conclude that *it makes no difference,* morally speaking, whether you accept the job offer or decline it. The net consequences are the same. I think that in many cases like this, it *does* make a moral difference what you decide to do. For example, it is wrong to be a torturer for the Nazis. If you become a torturer, you have done something wrong; if you don't become a torturer, you have avoided doing something evil. There is a moral difference here that should guide your conduct. The moral issue of what sort of a person you ought to be is not something that utilitarianism takes into account. According to utilitarianism, what you should do in such cases is to look at the net consequences that would occur under different circumstances; this is different from considering what kind of a person you ought to be.

Sometimes utilitarians reply to this objection in the same way I described them replying to the lonesome stranger example. They propose a distinction between rule and act utilitarianism and claim that rule utilitarianism has the plausible consequence that it *does* make a moral difference whether you become a torturer or not. Utilitarians who make this reply reason as follows. To decide what you ought to do in this specific situation, you first must decide which general rule should be followed by you and others. The two rules you might consider are as follows:

(S1)  If the government offers someone a job as a torturer, the offer should be accepted.

(S2)  If the government offers someone a job as a torturer, the offer should be rejected.

The rule utilitarian then points out that the consequences would be better if everyone adopted (S2) than if everyone adopted (S1). The conclusion about this pair of rules is then applied to the specific choice you confront. You should apply (S2) to decide what to do; hence, you should decline the offer from the Nazis.

I hope you see how this pattern of argument parallels what rule utilitarians have said in reply to the objection based on the lonesome stranger example. My view is that this reply to the problem of dirty hands is no more successful than the previous reply to the lonesome stranger problem. I grant that (S2) has better consequences than (S1).

However, it seems to me that a utilitarian can't explain why (S2) is superior to the following rule:

(S3) If the government offers someone a job as a torturer, the offer should be rejected, unless it makes no difference to the collective utility whether it is accepted or rejected.

A utilitarian can't explain why (S2) is a better rule than (S3). For this reason, the dirty hands problem is, I think, a telling objection to utilitarianism.

## UTILITARIANISM AND PERSONAL LOYALTIES

The last problem I want to consider concerns the role that personal loyalties play in our judgments about morality. Imagine that a boating accident occurs and you have to choose which of two people you are going to save from drowning. One of them is your own daughter. The other is another child. What should you do? If you think it makes a moral difference what you do, how can this be explained? It may be true that the consequences for the collective welfare are the same, whether your child lives and the other child dies, or yours dies and the other lives. If so, utilitarianism can't explain the special obligations we have to our own family.

By now, the rule utilitarian reply to this objection should be something you can anticipate. Compare the general consequences of obeying each of the following general rules:

(T1) People should not make an effort to preserve the lives of their own children.

(T2) People should make an effort to preserve the lives of their own children.

Of course, general adherence to (T2) has better consequences than general adherence to (T1). But that isn't enough to get utilitarianism out of trouble, since it is hard to see how a utilitarian can argue that (T2) is superior to (T3).

(T3) People should make an effort to preserve the lives of their own children, except when no additional utility comes from doing so.

## A PSYCHOLOGICAL OBJECTION TO MY CRITICISMS OF UTILITARIANISM

There is a different sort of reply that utilitarians sometimes make to examples like this one. They say that in a situation of crisis, people don't have time to calculate what they ought to do. They merely act on impulse. What they do in such cases is more a consequence of the habits of character they have developed than of reasoning from general principles.

I grant this psychological point, but it seems to me to be irrelevant. Utilitarianism makes a claim about which actions are right and which are wrong. It doesn't demand that people take the time and energy to reason abstractly about what the Greatest

Happiness Principle implies. Nor does utilitarianism say that people in fact engage in dispassionate calculation in situations of crisis. My criticisms of utilitarianism have to do with what the theory says people *ought* to do; in each of the cases I surveyed, I argued that the theory errs in its moral recommendations.

## SUMMARY

I've raised several objections to utilitarianism. The lonesome stranger objection is supposed to show how utilitarianism can conflict with the value of justice. The problem of the fanatical majority shows how utilitarianism can conflict with the value of liberty. Finally, the problem of dirty hands and the problem of loyalty both show that utilitarianism can fail to detect moral differences between alternative actions that really do differ morally. In each of these cases, utilitarianism was judged by seeing what it implies about a concrete example situation. The arguments all proceeded by advancing a moral judgment about the examples and then showing that this judgment conflicts with the dictates of utilitarianism. I grant that someone who is not prepared to endorse the moral claims I've made about the examples will not find this discussion a conclusive refutation of utilitarianism. However, agreeing with what I've said about one or more of these examples should be enough to make you doubt that utilitarianism is correct.

## Review Questions

1. Mill presents an argument for the Greatest Happiness Principle and also says that the principle can be defended by what I've called "reciprocal illumination." Explain what the argument is and what reciprocal illumination is.
2. What is the difference between hedonistic utilitarianism and preference utilitarianism? How does the example of the experience machine bear on each of these theories?
3. What is the Apples and Oranges Problem?
4. How does the case of the lonesome stranger pose a problem for utilitarianism?
5. How does the Problem of the Fanatical Majority present a difficulty for utilitarianism?
6. How does the Dirty Hands Objection present a difficulty for utilitarianism?
7. How might a utilitarian use the distinction between act utilitarianism and rule utilitarianism to reply to the objections involved in questions 4–6?

## Problems for Further Thought

1. In defending the Greatest Happiness Principle, Mill says that the only proof that something is visible is that someone sees it. Is this a correct claim to make about

dispositional properties (discussed in Chapter 20) like visibility? Is it true that the only proof that something is soluble is that someone dissolves it?

2. In discussing the Apples and Oranges Problem, I argued that the problem would not be solved by having a referendum in which each person casts a single vote. Would it be a solution to give each person 10 votes, and to ask people to cast the number of votes that reflects the intensity of their preferences?

3. When I discussed preference utilitarianism, I interpreted that theory to mean that what should be maximized is the satisfaction of the preferences that people *actually* have. However, there is another form of utilitarianism that is important to consider. Let's say that a person's *revealed preferences* are the preferences he or she would have if provided with full factual information about the situation at hand. A person's actual preferences and his or her revealed preferences may differ if the actual preferences are based on incomplete or incorrect assumptions. Can some of the objections to preference utilitarianism discussed in this chapter be met if we shift our formulation of utilitarianism from actual to revealed preferences?

4. Hedonistic utilitarianism says that the pleasure and pain of *all beings* affected by an act must be taken into account in deciding whether that act should be performed. Preference utilitarianism says that the preferences of *all beings* affected by an act must be taken into account in deciding whether that act should be performed. Some utilitarians (for example, Peter Singer, in *Animal Liberation,* New York, Random House, 1975) have drawn the conclusion that the way human beings treat animals is morally outrageous. They argue that the pleasure and nutrition people obtain from eating meat does not outweigh the suffering and death of the animals that are eaten. Is there any way to avoid this conclusion while still remaining true to utilitarian principles?

5. If utilitarianism requires us to maximize the amount of happiness there is in the world, won't it require us to have as many children as possible? Even if overpopulation lowers the *average* (per person) quality of life, won't this be outweighed by the total number of individuals who obtain some amount of happiness from the lives they lead? How could a utilitarian argue for the desirability of zero population growth?

# CHAPTER 33

## *Kant's Moral Theory*

To understand the basic approach that Immanuel Kant (1724–1804) developed in his moral theory, it is useful to begin with a somewhat commonsensical idea—an idea that Kant rejects. This is the idea that reason can play only an instrumental role in guiding people's actions. Reason does not tell you what your ultimate goals should be; rather, it tells you what you should do, given the goals you have. To say that reason is purely instrumental is to say that it is merely a tool (an instrument) that helps you achieve your goals, your goals having been determined by something other than reason.

This simple idea can be elaborated by viewing actions as the joint products of beliefs and desires. Reason can tell you what to believe, given the evidence at hand. However, reason cannot tell you what to want. Desires must have some other, nonrational, source:

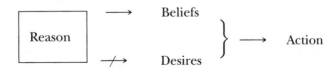

## HUME ON REASON'S ROLE

David Hume articulated this idea about the contribution that reason makes to the actions we perform. In *A Treatise of Human Nature* (1738), he says that "reason is and ought to be the slave of the passions." Hume expresses the same idea in the following passage:

> 'Tis not contrary to reason to prefer the destruction of the whole world to the scratching of my finger. . . .
>
> 'Tis as little contrary to reason to prefer even my own acknowledg'd lesser good to my greater, and have a more ardent affection for the former than the latter.

The main point about Hume's idea is that actions *never derive from reason alone; they must always have a nonrational source.*

## KANT REJECTS THE IDEA THAT REASON IS PURELY INSTRUMENTAL

Kant's theory of morality rejects this Humean doctrine. According to Kant, it is only sometimes true that actions are produced by the agent's beliefs and (nonrationally generated) desires. When we act out of "inclination," this is what happens. However, when we act out of duty—when our actions are guided by moral considerations rather than by our inclinations—matters are entirely different. When we act, there is a goal we have in mind—an end in view—and also a means we use to try to achieve that goal. Hume thought that reason determines the means we choose, but not the end we have in mind. Kant agreed that this is correct when we act out of inclination. But when morality drives our actions, reason determines the end as well as the means. Kant thought that morality derives its authority from reason alone. Reason alone determines whether an action is right or wrong, regardless of the desires that people happen to have. According to Kant, when we act morally, our actions are guided by reason in a way that Hume's theory says is impossible.

## KANT: MORAL RULES ARE CATEGORICAL IMPERATIVES

It is clear, as Hume said, that reason can show us which means to use, given the ends we have. If I want to be healthy, reason may tell me that I should stop smoking. Here reason provides an imperative that is *hypothetical* in form: It says that I should stop smoking *if* I want to protect my health. Hume thought that reason can do no more than this. Kant, however, held that moral rules are *categorical*, not hypothetical, in form. An act that is wrong, is wrong—period. Moral rules say "Don't do X." They do not say "Don't do X if your goal is G." Kant tried to show that these moral rules—these *categorical* imperatives—are derived from reason just as surely as hypothetical imperatives are. Moral rules, which take the form of categorical imperatives, describe what we must do whether we want to or not. They have an authority that is separate from the inclinations we happen to have. So, when we act morally, Kant thought, we are guided by reason, not by inclination. In this case, reason plays more than an instrumental role.

## THE MORAL LAW

Another important ingredient in Kant's moral philosophy is his idea that moral laws and scientific laws have something deep in common. A scientific law is a generalization that says what *must* be true in a specified kind of situation. For example, Newton's universal law of gravitation says that the magnitude of the gravitational force $F_g$ between two objects is proportional to the products of their masses ($m_1$ and $m_2$) and inversely proportional to the square of the distance ($r$) between them:

$$F_g = Gm_1m_2/r^2$$

That is, the law says that if the masses are $m_1$ and $m_2$ and if the distance is $r$, then the gravitational force *must* take the value $Gm_1m_2/r^2$, where $G$ is the gravitational constant.

There is clearly a difference between scientific laws and moral rules (like "Don't cause gratuitous suffering"). Newton's law doesn't say what the planets ought to do; it says what they do, of necessity. If a scientific law is true, then nothing in the universe disobeys it. On the other hand, people sometimes violate moral laws. Moral laws say how people ought to behave; they don't say what people in fact will do. To use vocabulary introduced earlier, moral laws are normative, while scientific laws are descriptive.

In spite of this difference, Kant thought that there is a deeper similarity between them. Scientific laws are *universal*—they involve *all* phenomena of a specified kind. They are not limited to certain places or certain times. Furthermore, a proposition that states a law does not mention any particular person, place, or thing. "All of Napoleon's friends spoke French" may be a true generalization, but it can't be a law, since it mentions a specific individual—Napoleon. I'll mark this feature of scientific laws by saying that they are "impersonal." Moral laws, Kant thought, also must be universal and impersonal. If it is right for me to do something, then it is right for anyone in similar circumstances to do the same thing. It isn't possible that Napoleon should have the right to do something simply because he is Napoleon. Moral laws, like scientific laws, don't mention specific people.

One more element in Kant's moral philosophy must be mentioned before I can describe how Kant thought that reason alone dictates what our moral principles should be. Recall from the previous chapter that utilitarianism asserts that the moral characteristics of an action are settled by the consequences the action would have for people's happiness or preference satisfaction. Utilitarianism is therefore said to be a "consequentialist" ethical theory. Kant's theory is not consequentialist. Kant rejected the idea that the consequences an action would have settle whether the action is morally obligatory. This may come as a surprise to you — what else, besides the consequences the action would have if it were performed, could be relevant to deciding whether the action is right?

## KANT: THE MORAL VALUE OF AN ACT DERIVES FROM ITS MAXIM, NOT FROM ITS CONSEQUENCES

Each action can be described as an action of a certain kind. If you help someone, you may think of this as an act of charity. In this case, you may be acting on the maxim that you should help others. Alternatively, when you provide the help, you perhaps are thinking of this as a way of making the recipient feel indebted to you. Here the maxim of your action might be that you should place others in your debt. To see what moral value your action has, look at the maxim you had in mind that led you to do what you did.

The reason we need to look at the agent's motives, and not at the action's consequences, is not hard to grasp. Kant describes a shopkeeper who never cheats his customers. The reason is that he's afraid that if he cheats them, they will stop patronizing his store. Kant says that the shopkeeper does the right thing, but not for the right reason. He acts *in accordance with* morality, but not *from* morality. To discover the moral value of an action, Kant says we must see *why* the actor performs it; the consequences the action happens to have does not reveal this.

If the shopkeeper acts by applying the maxim "Always be honest," his action has moral value. If, however, his action is a result of the maxim "Don't cheat people if it is likely to harm you financially," his action is merely prudent. Moral value comes from motives, and the motives are given by the maxim that the agent applies in deciding what to do.

## KANT REJECTED CONSEQUENTIALISM

Kant is undoubtedly correct in saying that knowing an individual's motives is important in assessing *some* moral properties of an action. For example, if we wish to evaluate an agent's moral character, knowing the agent's motives is important; the consequences the action has may be an imperfect guide. After all, a good person can unintentionally cause harm to others and a malevolent person can unintentionally provide others with a benefit. However, it is important to see that this point does not imply that an action's consequences are irrelevant to deciding whether to do it. Kant maintains this further thesis: What makes an action right or wrong is not whether the consequences are harmful or beneficial. Kant rejects *consequentialism* in ethics.

## THE UNIVERSALIZABILITY CRITERION

I now can describe Kant's idea that reason determines what it is right and wrong to do. Recall that a moral law (like a scientific law) must be universal. This means that a moral action must embody a maxim that is *universalizable*. To decide whether it would be right to perform a particular action, Kant says you should ask whether you can intend that the maxim of your act should be a universal law. Universalizability is the basis of all categorical imperatives—that is, of all unconditional moral injunctions. Moral acts can be universalized; immoral acts cannot be.

It is important to grasp what Kant's proposed test involves. Kant is *not* saying that you should ask whether it would be a good thing or a bad thing if everyone did the act you are contemplating. The point about immoral actions is not that it would be *bad* if everyone did them; rather, the point is that it is *impossible* for everyone to do them (or, more accurately, Kant thinks it is *impossible* for you to will that everyone do them). As Kant's examples illustrate, Kant is proposing a logical test for whether an action is moral.

## FOUR EXAMPLES

In his book *The Groundwork of the Metaphysics of Morals* (1785), Kant applies the universalizability criterion to four examples. He first describes a man who is tired of life and is contemplating suicide. Kant says that the maxim the man is considering is to end one's life if continuing to live would produce more pain than pleasure. Kant says that it is

> questionable whether this principle of self-love could become a universal law of nature. One immediately sees a contradiction in a system of nature whose law would be to destroy life by the feeling whose special office is to impel the improvement of life. In this case it would not exist as nature; hence that maxim cannot obtain as a law of nature, and thus it wholly contradicts the supreme principle of all duty.

Kant is suggesting that it is impossible for there to exist a world in which all rational living things rationally decide to commit suicide when their lives promise more pain than pleasure. Since there could be no such world, it is wrong for the individual in Kant's example, to commit suicide. The act is wrong because it cannot be universalized.

Kant's second example concerns promise keeping. You need money and are deciding whether to borrow. The question is whether it would be permissible for you to promise to pay back the money even though you have no intention of doing so. Kant argues that morality requires you to keep your promise (and therefore not borrow it under false pretenses):

> For the universality of a law which says that anyone who believes himself to be in need could promise what he pleased with the intention of not fulfilling it would make the promise itself and the end to be accomplished by it impossible; no one would believe what was promised to him but would only laugh at any such assertion as vain pretense.

Kant is saying that promise keeping could not exist as an institution if everyone who made promises did so with the intention of breaking them whenever they felt like doing so. That is, the institution can exist only because people are usually trustworthy. Again, the reason we are obliged to keep our promises is that it is impossible to have a world in which everyone made promises with the intention of breaking them at will. Universalizability is the acid test.

Kant's third example is intended to show that each of us has an obligation to develop our talents. Why should we work hard at "broadening and improving our natural gifts"? Why not, instead, choose a life of "idleness, indulgence, and propagation"? Each person must choose the former, Kant says, "for, as a rational being, he necessarily wills that all his faculties should be developed, inasmuch as they are given to him for all sorts of possible purposes."

Kant's fourth example concerns a man whose life is going well, but who sees that others live lives of great hardship. Is he obliged to help others? Kant grants that the human race could exist in a state in which some do well while others suffer, but he claims that no rational agent could intend (will) that the world be that way:

> Now although it is possible that a universal law of nature according to that maxim could exist, it is nevertheless impossible to will that such a principle should hold everywhere as a law of nature. For a will which resolved this would conflict with itself, since instances can often arise in which he would need the love and sympathy of others, and in which he would have robbed himself, by such a law of nature springing from his own will, of all hope of the aid he desires.

Kant's point is not that the pattern cannot be universal, but that no rational agent could will that it be universal.

## EVALUATION OF KANT'S EXAMPLES

Of these examples, the first is perhaps the weakest. It is not impossible for there to be a world in which all terminally ill people who are the victims of great suffering commit suicide. Moreover, it seems perfectly possible for a rational agent to will that all people spare themselves a pointlessly agonizing death.

The second example is somewhat more plausible. The institution of promise keeping does seem to rely on the fact that people usually believe the promises made to them. If people intended to break their promises whenever they felt like doing so, could the institution persist? Kant says no. However, perhaps circumstances can be contrived in which this conclusion is evaded. For example, couldn't promise making and believing the promises that people make to us persist as social institutions if people intend to try hard to keep their promises while recognizing that they may have to break them if sufficiently weighty considerations of utility present themselves?

Perhaps there is something to be said for Kant's argument about our duty to help others. Each of us needs some sort of help at some time in our lives. Each of us therefore would wish to avoid a situation in which no one would give us the help we need. We therefore can't will that no one should ever provide help. This means it would be wrong for us to lead a life in which we totally refuse to help others. Again the reason it would be wrong is that we cannot will that the pattern be universal.

What is Kant's argument, in his third example concerning the duty each of us has to develop our talents? The thought here seems to be similar to the one Kant deploys in his discussion of the duty to help others. I want others to develop talents that would be beneficial to me; for example, I want physicians to perfect their skills, since one day I'll need them. This means, however, that I can't will that everyone should neglect to develop their talents. It is supposed to follow that I have a duty to develop my own talents.

I emphasized earlier that the universalizability criterion does not ask whether it would be a good thing if everyone performed the action the agent is contemplating. Kant is not asking a consequentialist question. Rather, Kant's question is whether it would be *possible* for everyone to do so, or whether it would be *possible to will* that everyone should do so. If we keep this point clearly in mind, it is doubtful whether Kant can reach the conclusions he wants concerning his last two examples without taking consequences into account. Clearly, it *is* possible that the world be a place in which no one helps others and no one develops his or her talents. This is a sorry state of affairs, not an impossible one. What about Kant's second formulation of his universalizability criterion—could a rational agent *will* that people never help others or develop their talents? That depends on what one means by "rational." If rational means *instrumentally* rational, then there seems to be no impossibility here. As Hume says, I might be perfectly clear in my means/end reasoning (and so be instrumentally rational) and still have the most bizarre desires you can imagine. On the other hand, there is a sense of "rational" according to which a rational agent would not want the world to be a place in which people never help others or develop their talents. A rational agent would not want this *because of the consequences such behaviors would have.* There would be a great deal of suffering, alienation, and despair; life would be bleak. I conclude that it is unclear how Kant can analyze his last two examples as he does without considering the consequences that would follow from making the actions universal.

## A PROBLEM FOR THE UNIVERSALIZABILITY CRITERION

There is a general problem that pertains to all of Kant's examples—indeed, to the whole idea of the universalizability criterion. Recall a simple point from the chapter on functionalism (Chapter 23): *A token exemplifies many types.* This means that a given (token) action can be described as embodying many different properties. Kant seems to assume that there is just one maxim that each action embodies, so we can test the morality of the token act by looking at the universalizability of this maxim. But there are many maxims that might lead to a given action; some of these may universalize whereas others do not.

Let's see how this problem arises in the context of Kant's example about promise keeping. A man has to decide whether to borrow money by promising to repay it, though he has no intention of keeping his promise. What would it mean for everyone to behave like this? One way to describe this action is to say that it flows from the maxim "Make a promise even though you intend to break it." Kant claims universalizing this is impossible because the following proposition is a contradiction: "Everyone makes promises, even though no one intends to keep the promises he makes." However, we can also describe the man's action as flowing from a rather different maxim: "Don't make a promise unless you intend to keep it, except when you are in a life and death situation and your intention to break your promise would not be evident to others." Universalizing *this* maxim does not lead to contradiction, since the following is a perfectly possible way the world might be:

> Everyone makes promises, and people generally expect to keep their promises. Rare exceptions arise when there is an enormous personal advantage to making a promise without the intention to keep it, and the intention to break the promise is not evident to others.

Far from being impossible, the above generalization seems to describe fairly accurately the world we actually inhabit.

You should notice a similarity between the problem that Kant faces and a problem that rule utilitarianism encountered in the previous chapter. "What would happen if everyone did it?" is a question that the rule utilitarian thinks is important in assessing the moral properties of an action. Kant's question is a different one; he asks, "Could everyone do it?" or "Could a rational agent will that everyone does it?" Though the questions differ, similar problems derive from the fact that there are multiple ways of describing any action.

The universalizability criterion may seem plausible if one takes seriously the analogy between moral laws and scientific laws. Both must be universal and impersonal. However, another comparison of these two ideas may diminish the plausibility that anything like Kant's universalizability criterion can be made to work. Scientific laws must be universal, but no one thinks the true explanation of a specific phenomenon can be derived *a priori*. Reason alone can't tell me why the earth moves in an elliptical orbit around the sun, even if I assume that the explanation of this fact must hold true for all similar planetary systems. On the other hand, Kant held that what it is right to do in a specific situation is dictated by the rational requirement of universalizability.

Evidently it is an important fact about morality that if it is right for me to do a particular action, then it is right for anyone similarly situated to perform the same action. This is the idea that moral laws—the general principles that dictate what it is right to do—are universal and impersonal. The problem is that this requirement is not *sufficient* to reveal which moral generalizations are true. If so, the analogy between scientific laws and moral laws has implications different from the ones Kant tried to develop.

## KANT: PEOPLE ARE ENDS IN THEMSELVES

Kant believed that an important consequence of his universalizability test is that we should treat people as ends in themselves, and not as mere means. By this, Kant meant that we should not treat people as means to ends to which they could not rationally consent. Kant believed that slavery is prohibited by this principle. The same may be true for punishing someone for a crime he did not commit, even if doing so would placate a dangerous mob. Kantian theory seems to provide firmer grounds than utilitarianism does for the idea that individuals have rights that can't be overridden by considerations of utility. It isn't the maximization of happiness that matters in Kant's theory. Reason alone is supposed to dictate principles of fairness, impartiality, and justice.

Even though Kant predates the utilitarians, his theory seems designed to correct the defects present in utilitarianism. The idea of rights is a plausible corrective to the idea that every aspect of an individual's life has to pass the test of maximizing the happiness of all. Even so, there are major logical difficulties in Kant's theory. And the absoluteness of some of his pronouncements seems to be wildly at odds with strongly held commonsense moral convictions. Surely it is extremely implausible to think that promises must *always* be kept—that we must *never* tell a lie—no matter what the consequences are. Besides noting the defects in the arguments that Kant gave to justify such injunctions, we also should note that these moral requirements should not receive an unconditional justification in the first place.

If the universalizability criterion fails to provide a procedure for deciding which actions are right, and if Kant's moral judgments about promise keeping, suicide, and other actions are implausible, what is of value in his ethical theory? Many philosophers find Kant's description of *the moral point of view* to be one of his enduring contributions. Desires and preferences can move us to action, and these actions can produce different mixtures of pleasure and pain. This sequence of events, however, occurs among creatures—cows and dogs, perhaps—who by no stretch of the imagination have a morality. What, then, distinguishes action motivated by morality from action driven by inclination, whether benevolent or malevolent?

Kant's answer was that moral action is driven by principles that have a special sort of rational justification. Ordinary language is perhaps a little misleading here, since we can talk about the desire to act morally as if it were on the same footing with the desire for pleasure or profit. But Kant did not think of the determination to do what morality requires as one inclination among many. He saw morality and inclination as existing in entirely different realms. To identify the moral thing to do, one must *set aside* one's inclinations. By fixing our attention on universal and impersonal laws, we can hope to diminish the degree to which self-interest distorts our judgment concerning what we ought to do.

## Review Questions

1. What does it mean to say, as Hume did, that every action has a cause that is "nonrational"? Why did Kant reject this thesis?
2. Kant believed there are important similarities between scientific laws and moral laws. What are these?
3. What does Kant's universalizability criterion assert? Does it say that you shouldn't perform an action if the world would be a worse place if everyone did the same? What does it mean to say that the universalizability criterion is nonconsequentialist?
4. How does Kant try to show that the obligation of promise keeping follows from the universalizability criterion? Is he successful?
5. You are in a boat that is tipping dangerously to one side because all the passengers are on the right. You are considering whether it would be a good idea to move to the left. You ask yourself, "What would happen if everyone did this?" This question has an ambiguity in it. What is it? How is this ambiguity relevant to assessing Kant's universalizability criterion?

## Problems for Further Thought

1. Kant believes that the duty to treat others as ends in themselves, not as means, follows from the universalizability criterion. Try to construct an argument that shows how this might be true. Is Kant correct in thinking these two principles are closely related?
2. Kant thought of the moral law as constraining what one's life should be like, but not as determining each and every detail of it. That is, for Kant, one is free to pursue one's private goals and projects as long as these do not violate any categorical imperatives. These particular projects are morally permissible, not morally obligatory.

   Utilitarianism, by contrast, sees morality as determining each and every aspect of one's life. Each action one performs must be evaluated in terms of the Greatest Happiness Principle. A private project is permissible only if it promotes the greatest good for the greatest number of people. Such acts aren't just permissible; they are obligatory.

   Construct a concrete example in which these features of the two theories lead them to make opposite judgments about whether an act is morally permissible. Which theory strikes you as more plausible in what it says about your example?

3.  Kant's ethics had a powerful influence on the political philosophy of John Rawls. In *A Theory of Justice* (Harvard University Press, 1971), Rawls argues that the correct rules of justice for a society are the ones that all persons would choose if (1) they were self-interested, and (2) they didn't know various details about themselves (like their talents, sex, race, and what projects they will want to pursue). The only facts that people know in this hypothetical situation are general facts about human psychology and human life. Rawl's idea is partially an attempt to capture Kant's idea that personal inclinations must be set to one side if you want to see what your moral obligations are. What principles of conduct do you think people would choose in this hypothetical situation?

# CHAPTER 34

## *Aristotle on the Good Life*

### HOW FAR DO OBLIGATIONS EXTEND?

Some ethical theories hold that each and every aspect of a person's life is to be decided by ethical principles that describe obligations. Utilitarianism, for example, says that it is wrong to do some action if an alternative action could be performed that would better promote people's happiness or preference satisfaction. Other ethical theories hold that considerations of obligation don't answer every question about how people should lead their lives. Kant's ethical theory is often thought to be of this type. According to Kant, you must treat others with justice and accord them dignity and respect. However, this seems to leave open a large number of issues concerning what sort of life you ought to pursue.

The same would be true of an ethical theory that held that all obligations flow from the principle that people have the right to structure their own lives, as long as doing so doesn't infringe on the rights of others. If you accepted an ethics of this sort, many questions concerning how you should live your life would remain to be answered. The reason these questions are left open is that the ethical principle just mentioned is largely *negative* in its implications. It mainly tells you what you should *not* do. In consequence, questions like the following are left unanswered: What sort of work should you take up? Should you get married? Should you have children? What sorts of friendships should you try to nurture? Should you try to develop talents you have other than those that figure in the work you do? Should you participate in the political affairs of your community? Nation? The Earth? What importance should you assign to these various activities? The ethical principle of *do no harm* provides little or no guidance on these matters.

## THE THEORY OF THE RIGHT AND THE THEORY OF THE GOOD

Philosophers sometimes distinguish the *theory of the right* from the *theory of the good*. In doing so, they are indicating that principles of obligation and prohibition fail to address questions like the ones listed in the previous paragraph. The theory of the good attempts to describe what the good life would be like.

According to this distinction, living a good life is not limited to fulfilling your obligations. It is easy to miss this point, since "be good" may sound like the same advice as "do the right thing." One way to see that there is a difference here is to imagine someone who breaks no moral prohibitions, but still fails to lead a good life. An example might be someone who breaks no laws, but shuns all human contact, has a dull and repetitive job, and spends all time outside work reading comic books. This person may do no harm, but it would be implausible to say of him, "he really led a good life."

## ARE THERE GENERAL PRINCIPLES ABOUT THE GOOD LIFE?

It seems plausible that the theory of the right will include principles of some generality. "Do not murder" is a rule that covers you, me, and everyone else. Are there comparable principles to be found in the theory of the good? That is, are there principles that describe what a good life would be like that cover all human beings? Or is the issue of the good life more personal and individual? Even if we all are subject to the same obligations and prohibitions (described in the theory of the right), perhaps there is nothing interesting in common between what would be a good life for you and a good life for me.

In his ethical theory (as developed primarily in *The Nicomachean Ethics*), Aristotle (384–322 B.C.) attempts to describe what a good life would be like. In fact, his goal is to describe what *the* good life for human beings amounts to. As I'll soon explain, he maintains that since we're all members of the same biological species, general principles can be described that specify what a good life would be for any human being. For Aristotle, the good life is to be understood by way of the concept of human nature.

## WHAT IS A GOOD *X*?

A good person lives a good life. But what makes a person good? Aristotle proposes to understand the idea of a *good human being* by first considering what it means to say that something is good. What is a good hammer? Here we aren't talking about ethical issues, of course. A hammer is a tool. A hammer is a good hammer when it is able to perform the tasks that are specific to hammers. Hammers have the function of driving nails into wood. A good hammer optimally performs that function. Consider another example, this one having to do with the roles that human beings play. What is a good father? To answer this question, we have to ask what the function of a father is. Plausibly, a father's function is to help his children grow into loving, responsible, and independent adults. If so, a good father is one who optimally performs that function. Human beings perform other functions. What is a good nurse? Nurses train to help the sick. Evidently, the function of a nurse is to help patients return to full health as much as possible. If this is right, we can tell from the function of a nurse what a good nurse would be.

---

**Good versus Green**

A green apple and a green shirt must have something in common. However, according to Aristotle a good hammer and a good violinist need have nothing in common. What is the difference between greenness and goodness that accounts for this?

To be a green apple is to be green *and* an apple. To be a green shirt is to be green *and* a shirt. Being a green apple is a conjunctive property ("conjunction" means *and*). Being a green apple involves having two properties; the same is true of being a green shirt. This explains why there is something that green apples and green shirts have in common; there is a property—greenness—that they share.

To be a good hammer is not the same as being good *and* a hammer. To be a good violinist is not the same as being good *and* a violinist. Neither is a conjunctive property in which *being good* is one of the conjuncts. This is why good hammers and good violinists need have no property in common.

Consider other adjectives. We use terms like "big," "soft," and "old." Are these more like "green" or more like "good"?

---

These examples—the hammer, the father, the nurse—tell us something about the concept of goodness. The first lesson is that we can decide what it is to be a good *X* by seeing what the function is of *X*s. The concept of goodness is intimately connected with concepts of goal, function, and purpose. The second lesson is that what it takes to be a good *X* depends on the choice of *X*. For example, the character traits required for being a good father may be very different from the ones required for being a good harpist or a good baseball player. Aristotle emphasizes both these points about the concept of goodness.

It is no mystery what a good hammer is, and it isn't that difficult to say what it means to be a good father or a good nurse. Perhaps the same strategy will work when we ask what a good person is. Aristotle thought that once we figure out what the function is of human life, we'll thereby know what a good human being is. This, in turn, will tell us what the good life amounts to.

## HUMAN BEINGS ARE GOAL-DIRECTED SYSTEMS

In Chapter 5, I briefly explained how Aristotle's biology and physics are *teleological* in character. Aristotle thought that living things as well as inanimate objects are goal-directed systems. The goal of a living thing is to grow and reproduce. The goal of a rock is to reach the place where the center of the earth now is. Of course, not all living things grow and reproduce, and not all rocks find their way to the earth's center.

But each has a *natural tendency* to do those things. *Interfering forces* may prevent an object from reaching its natural state.

We human beings are goal-directed systems. What is the end state that we seek? Aristotle's answer is that human beings seek *happiness*. A good life is a life of happiness— a life in which the goal of human life has been achieved.

Before saying how Aristotle understood happiness, it is important to note a difference between human beings and other goal-directed systems. Human beings seek happiness; trees aim to grow and reproduce. The difference between us and other living things comes from *how* we pursue the goals we have. Other living things pursue the goals of growth and reproduction *innately* and *mindlessly*. A tree doesn't have to be taught to send its roots deep into the soil or to send its leaves where they can absorb sunlight. In fact, trees don't need to have beliefs and desires to engage in these activities. Trees do these things *by nature*. In contrast, we human beings are better or worse at seeking happiness according to the upbringing we receive. Some people seek their happiness in wealth or fame or power. Others seek it in love. *How* we seek our happiness is not determined by our nature, but by our upbringing. For Aristotle, a good upbringing is one that helps us develop habits and character traits that are conducive to the good life.

In Chapter 21, on methodological behaviorism, I briefly discussed the nature/nurture controversy. We now understand that dispute in terms of the task of explaining variation in some characteristic (like height or intelligence). Human beings have various heights. How much of that variation is explained by genetic differences, and how much by differences in environment (like nutrition)? Aristotle also drew the nature/nurture distinction, but in a rather different way. First, he didn't have the idea of genes. Second, the fact of variation within a species was much less important to him than it is in present-day biology. For Aristotle, what is biologically significant about human beings is that human beings have something in common; this is what *human nature* is. When Aristotle thought about "nature" (as opposed to nurture), he thought about characteristics that all members of a species *share;* current biology thinks about "nature" (as opposed to nurture) in terms of genetic *differences* among members of the same species. For Aristotle, human beings have a common nature that sets them apart from the rest of the living world. It is part of human nature to seek happiness. How human beings go about doing this varies from person to person. The explanation for this variation, Aristotle held, is environmental. It is differences in nurture—in our upbringing—that explain why human beings live their lives in different ways.

## THE CAPACITY TO REASON

The function of a hammer is something that distinguishes hammers from other tools. A hammer that is able to perform that function well is a good hammer. By the same line of thinking, we can approach the question of what function human beings have by asking what distinguishes human beings from other beings. A human being who is able to perform that function well will count as a good human being.

Human beings are organisms, and so survival, growth, and reproduction are goals that human beings try to achieve. However, in addition, there is a characteristic that distinguishes human beings from other organisms. This is the development of rationality—the capacity for abstract thinking. The basic contours of Aristotle's theory of happiness can now be stated. Human beings, unique among living things, possess the capacity of rationality. The good life for human beings is one in which rational capacities are developed and exercised to a high degree. In doing this, human beings find the best sort of happiness that is possible for them.

Aristotle draws a distinction between theoretical and practical reasoning. Practical reasoning involves the kind of means/ends reasoning so familiar in everyday life. The conclusion you draw in practical reasoning is a decision to do something—to perform some action. For example, you want an article of clothing that will keep you warm in winter. You realize that a cloak will perform this task. So you decide to buy a cloak. Note that this bit of reasoning concludes with the intention to buy a cloak, not with a prediction that you will do so. In contrast, the conclusion you draw in theoretical reasoning is that some proposition is true. Theoretical reasoning is reasoning given over to the disinterested search for knowledge. It is "pure" inquiry, not "applied." In theoretical inquiry, you seek understanding for its own sake. The life of contemplation is devoted to the sort of intellectual activity that occurs in science, philosophy, and the arts. The best life, for Aristotle, is the life of theoretical reason.

## ARISTOTLE: HAPPINESS IS NOT A SUBJECTIVE STATE

When Aristotle asked what happiness is, he wanted to know what sorts of activities make for a happy life. The word "activity" is important here; a happy life is a life of *doing*. The good life is one in which those traits that are specifically human are brought to a high level of cultivation. The happy life is one of flourishing—of doing well. Happiness, for Aristotle, is emphatically not the same as pleasure. The sensation of pleasure is possible for a brain in a vat, but a brain in a vat is not a flourishing human being, even if it has the illusion of leading an ideal life.

Real happiness, then, is not a sensation (compare this with the discussion of happiness in Chapter 32). People can believe themselves to be happy and still not be. Whether you are flourishing is not settled by the mere fact that you think you are.

Although pleasure is not the goal of human life, pleasure naturally accompanies the good life. For Aristotle, the good life involves exercising the faculty of reason. It is natural for people to take pleasure in exercising this ability, just as people take pleasure in the vigorous functioning of a healthy body, as in athletics.

Aristotle thought that human beings have godlike as well as animal characteristics. Our nature as animals decrees we must eat, grow, breathe, and reproduce. In addition, we are social beings by nature, and so the good life includes participation in politics. But the divine spark also is present, and this means that we're directed toward the divine activity of contemplation. When Aristotle says that the good life consists in contemplation (intellectual activity), he is not denying that the activities we share with animals are important to us; nor did he mean that involvement in practical political affairs is unimportant. But the life of contemplation was for him a life that emphasized what was best ( = highest) in us. It is an expression of what we have in common with the gods.

## WHY THE LIFE OF RATIONAL ACTIVITY IS BEST: TWO MORE REASONS

I've already mentioned Aristotle's main reason for thinking that the human goal of happiness is best achieved by the life of rational activity; our capacity to be rational is unique in the living world. However, Aristotle had two other ways of reaching this conclusion.

The first is more specifically tied to his conception of how the human mind works. Aristotle thought that activities that call for fine and multifaceted discriminations make people happier than activities that call for fewer and more one-dimensional discriminations. Chess is superior to checkers, and checkers is superior to tic-tac-toe. Sports that require a variety of skills are better than ones that require fewer, and sports that require fine discriminations are better than sports that require only coarse discriminations.

Aristotle saw this as a basic feature of the human mind. Its highest happiness is to be found in activities of these sorts. Aristotle thought that theoretical reasoning—the kind that artists, scientists, and philosophers pursue—involves mental activities in which the finest and most multifaceted discriminations are drawn.

A further consideration led Aristotle to this conclusion. In choosing a life for ourselves, we must decide which of our capacities we wish to develop. For example, this might involve trying to become a great athlete or a great politician. Aristotle thinks it is highly significant that success in sports or politics depends on a number of factors that are outside the individual's control. Athletes of great talent can suffer injuries. Politicians can be deprived of power if others oppose them. In contrast, the life of rational activity is much less dependent on factors outside the agent's control. Contemplation can last a lifetime. It does not require a youthful body, wealth, power, or the admiration of others. Of course, it isn't wholly independent of external circumstance, but given the perils that can subvert other plans for a life, the life of contemplation makes the most sense, according to Aristotle.

Although Aristotle holds that the good life is devoted to theoretical reasoning, he has a great deal to say about the character traits that good people will display in dealing with other human beings. For example, Aristotle discusses friendship, justice, liberality (generosity), and courage. These virtues, he believes, can be understood within a single theoretical framework, provided by his Doctrine of the Mean.

## THE DOCTRINE OF THE MEAN

The Doctrine of the Mean says that many (if not all) virtues are located on a continuum, their perfection consisting in the fact that they avoid both excess and deficiency. For example, courage is a virtue; Aristotle claims that it is in between foolhardiness and cowardice. Similarly, liberality is a virtue; people who are liberal with their money are neither misers nor spendthrifts.

Aristotle didn't think that the mean had to be an arithmetic average. If 10 units of food is too much and 2 units is too little, the correct amount is somewhere in between; it needn't be 6. Furthermore, Aristotle emphasized that the right amount for one person might not be the right amount for another. The wrestler Milo requires more food than other people do. The mean for him may differ from the mean for others.

Although the Doctrine of the Mean is sometimes represented by the slogan "moderation in all things," this is a rather misleading summary of Aristotle's idea. Aristotle says that spitefulness and envy are bad, as are adultery, theft, and murder. They are wrong in themselves; virtue doesn't consist in doing them a little but not too much.

Once these clarifications are noted, however, it is unclear how much of a theory the Doctrine of the Mean actually provides. To apply it in a given case, we first must decide what the continuum is on which the activity or virtue is located. Generosity is fairly easy; the scale on which it is located is the amount of money you give away. But what is the scale on which justice is located? And if abstaining from murder is a mean, what is the scale on which it is to be represented?

A second problem arises after one has identified the scale on which the activity or character trait is to be represented. Let's grant that being liberal with money is a mean between being a miser and being a spendthrift. The question is why the intermediacy of the trait should be what makes it a virtue. Is being courageous better than being cowardly or foolish *because* courage falls between cowardice and foolhardiness? Aristotle thought that this is so, but it is by no means clear he was correct.

## A SECOND CRITICISM OF ARISTOTLE'S THEORY – DEFINING WHAT A GOOD *X* IS DIFFERS FROM SAYING WHAT IS GOOD FOR *X*S

Let's recall the overall strategy of Aristotle's argument. He begins by asking what the good life is for human beings. This question, he believes, would be answered if we knew what a good human being is. He then proposes to say what a good human being is by inquiring what function human beings have. It is the first step in this reasoning that I want to question. Aristotle assumes that if a good human being is rational, then rationality is good for human beings. The general principle Aristotle uses here is this:

If a good $X$ is $F$, then $F$ is good for $X$s.

To say that someone is a good $X$ is often just to say that they are good at $X$-ing: a good teacher is good at teaching, a good parent is good at parenting, a good butcher is good at butchering, and a good torturer is good at torturing.

As the last example suggests, to say that you are a good $X$ is not to say that it is a good thing for you to be an $X$. You might be a good torturer, even though torturing is bad for you. The same may be true for other, less gruesome, activities at which you excel. This is why I reject the principle just displayed.

---

**"Natural" and "Normal"**

The term *natural* is used in two very different ways. Sometimes it has a normative meaning, as when "natural" and "unnatural" are used as code words for *good* and *bad*. Sometimes it has a purely descriptive meaning, as when "natural" is used to mean *found in nature*.

The same is true of the term *normal*. Usually, when we say that something is "abnormal," we mean that there is something wrong with it. But there is a purely descriptive meaning that the term also has. Sometimes saying that an activity is "normal" just means that often occurs.

It is clear that there are some unusual characteristics that are undesirable. More people have healthy blood than cancerous blood, and so when we say that leukemia is an abnormal condition, we mean both that it is uncommon and that there is something wrong with having leukemia.

In other cases, matters are just the reverse. Most adults in the United States are overweight. Given this, how should you interpret the doctor's comment that your weight is "normal"? If this means that it is common, you might decide that there is something wrong. If the comment means that your weight is healthy, then you may be pleased.

These two examples—of leukemia and weight—illustrate that there is no simple connection between what's common and what's good. Given this, you should be skeptical of any argument that attempts to show that some activity is wrong or bad simply by pointing out that the activity is rare. And the claim that something is "natural" or "normal" also should not be taken as providing an automatic justification.

What bearing do these observations have on Aristotle's attempt to explain what the good life is by developing a theory of human nature?

---

A good human being, Aristotle holds, is someone who is good at characteristically human activities. Aristotle singles out the use of reason as the characteristic activity; he concludes that good human beings devote themselves to lives of contemplation, developing their rational faculties to the utmost.

My criticism suggests that it is not always correct to think about the concept of a good *X* in the functional way that Aristotle proposes. It is plausible to think of a good hammer and a good harpist in the way Aristotle suggests, but the concept of a good human being seems to require a different treatment.

## A THIRD CRITICISM—WHY SINGLE OUT CONTEMPLATION AS THE BEST LIFE?

My last criticism of Aristotle's theory has to do with his exclusive focus on rationality. He notes that human beings share with other animals the tendency to grow and reproduce. He then asks which characteristic is uniquely human, and he comes up with rationality as his answer. But surely there are many behaviors and capacities that are unique to human beings. Collecting money for charity is one of them; engaging in genocide is another. If the good life consists in developing those capacities that are uniquely human, why should contemplation constitute the good life? There are many ways to be uniquely human.

Aristotle provides a second reason for singling out the life of theoretical reason as best. As noted earlier, Aristotle thinks human beings find happiness in drawing fine discriminations and in mastering complex tasks. The life of contemplation provides the greatest opportunity for these activities.

Even if we accept this as a basic fact about the human mind, it is unclear why this shows that the life of contemplation is best. Human beings find happiness in other activities as well. Why think of mastering complexity as *the best* activity? Aristotle's answer seems to be the one just discussed: What's best for human beings is the development of traits that are uniquely human. I've already noted why I find this answer unsatisfactory.

Aristotle gives a third reason for thinking that the life of contemplation is best. This life is least dependent on others. However, here again it is hard to see that this characteristic is unique to the life devoted to theoretical reason. It also is hard to see why this characteristic should make that life the one most worth living.

Aristotle thinks that loving others, including your children, is part of the good life. He goes so far as to say that you can't be happy—lead a good life—if your children suffer or hate you. Notice that in saying this, Aristotle is granting that the good life involves dependency on others. Given this, it is hard to see why the life of contemplation is best *because* it is relatively independent of others.

In summary, Aristotle offers three arguments for thinking that the life of theoretical reason provides the best form of happiness. The first and most important argument appeals to the fact that the capacity to reason is uniquely human. The second claims that human beings find happiness in drawing fine discriminations and in mastering complex tasks. The third sees the contemplative life as supremely good because it is the life in which one is most independent of others. I've suggested that none of these arguments is very persuasive.

In each of them, Aristotle attempts to show why the contemplative life is the best one for human beings without assuming a fully developed theory of value. For example, in the first argument, it is a fact about human biology that justifies his conclusion. In suggesting these arguments, Aristotle is following the analogy with other goal-directed systems. We can say what a good hammer is, or a good father, or a good nurse, without assuming anything about whether it is a good thing or a bad thing to be a hammer, a father, or a nurse. Perhaps the reason that Aristotle's various arguments run into trouble is that there is a *dis*analogy between these cases and the problem of describing what the good life is. The good life must be a life that is worth living. A good life must be a life that would be good to have. You can approach questions about what a good teacher is (or a good general, or a good nurse) with a certain detachment. You can say what this role requires without committing yourself to taking it up for yourself. The problem of the good life, however, admits no such detachment. If you grant that the life of contemplation is the good life for human beings, you commit yourself to the desirability of living such a life.

This may help explain why Aristotle's strategy for solving this important problem was unsuccessful. Another reason may be that Aristotle thought that there is a single form of life that is *the* best one for everyone. His arguments pay scant attention to the differences that distinguish each of us from other human beings. As noted before, the good life for human beings is to be discovered by investigating human nature, and human nature is what all human beings have in common.

Aristotle had the idea that the good life involves actualizing the best capacities we possess. We must find what's best in ourselves and build a whole life on that foundation. Perhaps we should accept this idea, even if we reject Aristotle's suggestion that the good life for every human being consists in actualizing a characteristic that is uniquely human. Perhaps there is no such thing as *the* good life for human beings; rather, there may be many good lives, each uniquely fitted to the unique constellation of traits that each of us possesses.

## Review Questions

1. What is the difference between the theory of the right and the theory of the good?
2. What do a good pizza and a good dancer have in common? What does "good" mean?
3. Why did Aristotle think that the good life for human beings would be a life of contemplation?
4. What is the Doctrine of the Mean? Does it say that we should pursue each activity a little but not too much?
5. What connection did Aristotle see between the concept of *a good human being* and the idea that certain activities would be *good for human beings?* Was he right in connecting these ideas in the way he did?

## Problems for Further Thought

1. Aristotle says that the function of human beings is to reason well. This is what human beings are *for*. In Chapter 26, on the Weather Vane Theory of Freedom, I defined what it means to say that *the function of the heart is to pump blood*. The definition I offered involves the modern idea of natural selection; the theory of natural selection, of course, was unknown to Aristotle. Apply this definition of function to the statement *the function of human beings is to be rational*. Is what Aristotle says plausible if his claim about function is understood in this modern way? Explain your answer.
2. There is an interpretation of what Aristotle thinks the good life is that differs from the one I've offered. Instead of seeing the good life as given over to contemplation, this interpretation has Aristotle saying that a good life is one in which reason suffuses all human activities, both theoretical and practical. This interpretation relies on the fact that human beings are *not* the only things capable of rationality—there are the gods as well. What's unique to human beings is the *mixture* of animal nature and the capacity to reason. Gods can engage in pure contemplation; human beings must lead less monolithic lives.

   According to this interpretation, Aristotle is saying that good human beings judiciously apply reason to the activities they take up. If Aristotle is interpreted in this way, two problems remain for his view. The first is that we need to provide a list of the activities that comprise the good life. The second is that a principle needs to be provided that says how these various activities are to be integrated and balanced against each other. For example, if the good life includes a family, participation in politics, and contemplation, how are the demands each activity places on your time and energy to be judged?

Without answering these questions, the advice to use reason in all your activities seems to be pretty empty. Do the passages from Aristotle's *Nicomachean Ethics* reprinted at the end of this chapter help provide any answers?

# Readings

JEAN-PAUL SARTRE

## Existentialism

In this section of his essay *Existentialism Is a Humanism,* Sartre explains the fundamental ideas in his version of this philosophy. Human beings must realize that there is no God who dictates what is morally required of them. Instead, morality is a free creation that each individual must fashion for himself or herself.

What is meant by the term *existentialism?* Can it be that what really scares [people] in the doctrine I shall try to present here is that it leaves to man a possibility of choice? To answer this question, we must reexamine it on a strictly philosophical plane.

Actually, it is the least scandalous, the most austere of doctrines. It is intended strictly for specialists and philosophers. Yet it can be easily defined. What complicates matters is that there are two kinds of existentialist; first, those who are Christian, among whom I would include Jaspers and Gabriel Marcel, both Catholic; and on the other hand the atheistic existentialists, among whom I class Heidegger, and then the French existentialists and myself. What they have in common is that they think that existence precedes essence, or, if you prefer, that subjectivity must be the starting point.

Just what does that mean? Let us consider some object that is manufactured, for example, a book or a paper-cutter: here is an object which has been made by an artisan whose inspiration came from a concept. He referred to the concept of what a

Jean-Paul Sartre, from *Existentialism Is a Humanism,* translated by Bernard Frechtman (New York: Philosophical Library, 1947), pp. 14–33. Copyright Les Editions Nagel & Briquet Geneva (Switzerland). All rights reserved in all countries.

paper-cutter is and likewise to a known method of production, which is part of the concept, something which is, by and large, a routine. Thus, the paper-cutter is at once an object produced in a certain way and, on the other hand, one having a specific use; and one can not postulate a man who produces a paper-cutter but does not know what it is used for. Therefore, let us say that, for the paper-cutter, essence—that is, the ensemble of both the production routines and the properties which enable it to be both produced and defined—precedes existence. Thus, the presence of the paper-cutter or book in front of me is determined. Therefore, we have here a technical view of the world whereby it can be said that production precedes existence.

When we conceive God as the Creator, He is generally thought of as a superior sort of artisan. Whatever doctrine we may be considering, whether one like that of Descartes or that of Leibniz, we always grant that will more or less follows understanding or, at the very least, accompanies it, and that when God creates He knows exactly what He is creating. Thus, the concept of man in the mind of God is comparable to the concept of paper-cutter in the mind of the manufacturer, and, following certain techniques and a conception, God produces man, just as the artisan, following a definition and a technique, makes a paper-cutter. Thus, the individual man is the realization of a certain concept in the divine intelligence.

In the eighteenth century, the atheism of the *philosophes* discarded the idea of God, but not so much for the notion that essence precedes existence. To a certain extent, this idea is found everywhere; we find it in Diderot, in Voltaire, and even in Kant. Man has a human nature; this human nature, which is the concept of the human, is found in all men, which means that each man is a particular example of a universal concept, man. In Kant, the result of this universality is that the wild-man, the natural man, as well as the bourgeois, are circumscribed by the same definition and have the same basic qualities. Thus, here too the essence of man precedes the historical existence that we find in nature.

Atheistic existentialism, which I represent, is more coherent. It states that if God does not exist, there is at least one being in whom existence precedes essence, a being who exists before he can be defined by any concept, and that this being is man, or, as Heidegger says, human reality. What is meant here by saying that existence precedes essence? It means that, first of all, man exists, turns up, appears on the scene, and, only afterwards, defines himself. If man, as the existentialist conceives him, is indefinable, it is because at first he is nothing. Only afterward will he be something, and he himself will have made what he will be. Thus, there is no human nature, since there is no God to conceive it. Not only is man what he conceives himself to be, but he is also what he wills himself to be after this thrust toward existence.

Man is nothing else but what he makes of himself. Such is the first principle of existentialism. It is also what is called subjectivity, the name we are labeled with when charges are brought against us. But what do we mean by this, if not that man has a greater dignity than a stone or table? For we mean that man first exists, that is, that man first of all is the being who hurls himself toward a future and who is conscious of imagining himself as being in the future. Man is at the start a plan which is aware of itself, rather than a patch of moss, a piece of garbage, or a cauliflower; nothing exists prior to this plan; there is nothing in heaven; man will be what he will have planned to be. Not what he will want to be. Because by the word "will" we generally mean a conscious decision, which is subsequent to what we have already made of ourselves. I may want to belong to a political party, write a book, get married; but all that is only a manifestation of an earlier, more spontaneous choice that is called "will." But if existence really does precede essence, man is responsible for what he is. Thus existentialism's first move is to make every man aware of what he is and to make the full responsibility of his existence rest on him. And when we say that a man is responsible for himself, we do not only mean that he is responsible for his own individuality, but that he is responsible for all men.

The word subjectivism has two meanings, and our opponents play on the two. Subjectivism means, on the one hand, that an individual chooses and makes himself; and, on the other, that it is impossible for man to transcend human subjectivity. The second of these is the essential meaning of existentialism. When we say that man chooses his own self, we mean that every one of us does likewise; but we also mean by that that in making this choice he also chooses all men. In fact, in creating the man that we want to be, there is not a single one of our acts which does not at the same time create an image of man as we think he ought to be. To choose to be this or that is to affirm at the same time the value of what we choose, because we can never choose evil. We always choose the good, and nothing can be good for us without being good for all.

If, on the other hand, existence precedes essence, and if we grant that we exist and fashion our image at one and the same time, the image is valid for everybody and for our whole age. Thus, our responsibility is much greater than we might have supposed, because it involves all mankind. If I am a workingman and choose to join a Christian trade-union rather than be a communist, and if by being a member I want to show that the best thing for man is resignation, that the kingdom of man is not of this world, I am not only involving my own case—I want to be resigned for everyone. As a result, my action has involved all humanity. To take a more individual matter, if I want to marry, to have children; even if this marriage depends solely on my circumstances or passion or wish, I am involving all humanity in monogamy and not merely myself. Therefore, I am responsible for myself and for everyone else. I am creating a certain image of man of my own choosing. In choosing myself, I choose man.

This helps us understand what the actual content is of such rather grandiloquent words as anguish, forlornness, despair. As you will see, it's all quite simple.

First, what is meant by anguish? The existentialists say at once that man is anguish. What that means is this: the man who involves himself and who realizes that he is not only the person he chooses to be, but also a lawmaker who is, at the same time, choosing all mankind as well as himself, can not help escape the feeling of his total and deep responsibility. Of course, there are many people who are not anxious; but we claim that they are hiding their anxiety, that they are fleeing from it. Certainly, many people believe that when they do something, they themselves are the only ones involved, and when someone says to them, "What if everyone acted that way?" they shrug their shoulders and answer, "Everyone doesn't act that way." But really, one should always ask himself, "What would happen if everybody looked at things that way?" There is no escaping this disturbing thought except by a kind of double-dealing. A man who lies and makes excuses for himself by saying "not everybody does that," is someone with an uneasy conscience, because the act of lying implies that a universal value is conferred upon the lie.

Anguish is evident even when it conceals itself. This is the anguish that Kierkegaard called the anguish of Abraham. You know the story: an angel has ordered Abraham to sacrifice his son; if it really were an angel who has come and said, "You are Abraham, you shall sacrifice your son," everything would be all right. But everyone might first wonder, "Is it really an angel, and am I really Abraham? What proof do I have?"

There was a madwoman who had hallucinations; someone used to speak to her on the telephone and give her orders. Her doctor asked her, "Who is it who talks to you?" She answered, "He says it's God." What proof did she really have that it was God? If an angel comes to me, what proof is there that it's an angel? And if I hear voices, what proof is there that they come from heaven and not from hell, or from the subconscious, or a pathological condition? What proves that they are addressed to me? What proof is there that I have been appointed to impose my choice and my conception of man on humanity? I'll never find any proof or sign to convince me of that. If a voice addresses me, it is always for me to decide that this is the angel's voice; if I consider that such an act is a good one, it is I who will choose to say that it is good rather than bad.

Now, I'm not being singled out as an Abraham, and yet at every moment I'm obliged to perform exemplary acts. For every man, everything happens as if all mankind had its eyes fixed on him and were guiding itself by what he does. And every man ought to say to himself, "Am I really the kind of man who has the right to act in such a way that humanity might guide itself by my actions?" And if he does not say that to himself, he is masking his anguish.

There is no question here of the kind of anguish which would lead to quietism, to inaction. It is a matter of a simple sort of anguish that anybody who has had responsibilities is familiar with. For example, when a military officer takes the responsibility for an attack and sends a certain number of men to death, he chooses to do so, and in the main he alone makes the choice. Doubtless, orders come from above, but they are too broad; he interprets them, and on this interpretation depend the lives of ten or fourteen or twenty men. In making a decision he can not help having a certain anguish. All leaders know this anguish. That doesn't keep them from acting; on the contrary, it is the very condition of their action. For it implies that they envisage a number of possibilities, and when they choose one, they realize that it has value only because it is chosen. We shall see that this kind of anguish, which is the kind that existentialism describes, is explained, in addition, by a direct responsibility to the other men whom it involves. It is not a curtain separating us from action, but is part of action itself.

When we speak of forlornness, a term Heidegger was fond of, we mean only that God does not exist and that we have to face all the consequences of this. The existentialist is strongly opposed to a certain kind of secular ethics which would like to abolish God with the least possible expense. About 1880, some French teachers tried to set up a secular ethics which went something like this: God is a useless and costly hypothesis; we are discarding it; but, meanwhile, in order for there to be an ethics, a society, a civilization, it is essential that certain values be taken seriously and that they be considered as having an *a priori* existence. It must be obligatory, *a priori*, to be honest, not to lie, not to beat your wife, to have children, etc., etc. So we're going to try a little device which will make it possible to show that values exist all the same, inscribed in a heaven of ideas, though otherwise God does not exist. In other words—and this,

I believe, is the tendency of everything called reformism in France—nothing will be changed if God does not exist. We shall find ourselves with the same norms of honesty, progress, and humanism, and we shall have made of God an outdated hypothesis which will peacefully die off by itself.

The existentialist, on the contrary, thinks it very distressing that God does not exist, because all possibility of finding values in a heaven of ideas disappears along with Him; there can no longer be an *a priori* Good, since there is no infinite and perfect consciousness to think it. Nowhere is it written that the Good exists, that we must be honest, that we must not lie; because the fact is we are on a plane where there are only men. Dostoevsky said, "If God didn't exist, everything would be possible." That is the very starting point of existentialism. Indeed, everything is permissible if God does not exist, and as a result man is forlorn, because neither within him nor without does he find anything to cling to. He can't start making excuses for himself.

If existence really does precede essence, there is no explaining things away by reference to a fixed and given human nature. In other words, there is no determinism, man is free, man is freedom. On the other hand, if God does not exist, we find no values or commands to turn to which legitimize our conduct. So, in the bright realm of values, we have no excuses behind us, nor justification before us. We are alone, with no excuses.

That is the idea I shall try to convey when I say that man is condemned to be free. Condemned, because he did not create himself, yet, in other respects is free; because, once thrown into the world, he is responsible for everything he does. The existentialist does not believe in the power of passion. He will never agree that a sweeping passion is a ravaging torrent which fatally leads a man to certain acts and is therefore an excuse. He thinks that man is responsible for his passion.

The existentialist does not think that man is going to help himself by finding in the world some omen by which to orient himself. Because he thinks that man will interpret the omen to suit himself. Therefore, he thinks that man, with no support and no aid, is condemned every moment to invent man. Ponge, in a very fine article, said, "Man is the future of man." That's exactly it. But if it is taken to mean that this future is recorded in heaven, that God sees it, then it is false, because it would really no longer be a future. If it is taken to mean that, whatever a man may be, there is a future to be forged, a virgin future before him, then this remark is sound. But then we are forlorn.

To give you an example which will enable you to understand forlornness better, I shall cite the case of one of my students who came to see me under the following circumstances: his father was on bad terms with his mother, and, moreover, was inclined to be a collaborationist; his older brother had been killed in the German offensive in 1940, and this young man, with somewhat immature but generous feelings, wanted to avenge him. His mother lived along with him, very much upset by the half-treason of her husband and the death of her older son; the boy was her only consolation.

The boy was faced with the choice of leaving for England and joining the Free French Forces—that is, leaving his mother behind—or remaining with his mother and helping her to carry on. He was fully aware that the woman lived only for him and that his going off—and perhaps his death—would plunge her into despair. He was also aware that every act that he did for his mother's sake was a sure thing, in the sense that it was helping her to carry on, whereas every effort he made toward going off and fighting was an uncertain move which might run aground and prove completely useless; for example, on his way to England he might, while passing through Spain, be detained indefinitely in a Spanish camp; he might reach England or Algiers and be stuck in an office at a desk job. As a result, he was faced with two very different kinds of action: one, concrete, immediate, but concerning only one individual; the other concerned an incomparably vaster group, a national collectivity, but for that very reason was dubious, and might be interrupted en route. And, at the same time, he was wavering between two kinds of ethics. On the one hand, an ethics of sympathy, of personal devotion; on the other, a broader ethics, but one whose efficacy was more dubious. He had to choose between the two.

Who could help him choose? Christian doctrine? Christian doctrine says, "Be charitable, love your neighbor, take the more rugged path, etc., etc." But which is the more rugged path? Whom should he love as a brother? The fighting man or his mother? Which does the greater good, the vague act of fighting in a group, or the concrete one of helping a particular human being to go on living? Who can decide *a priori*? Nobody. No book of ethics can tell him. The Kantian ethics says, "Never treat any person as a means, but as an end." Very well, if I stay with my mother, I'll treat her as an end and not as a means; but by virtue of this very fact, I'm running the risk of treating the people around me who are fighting, as means; and, conversely, if I go to join those who are fighting, I'll be treating them as an end, and, by doing that, I run the risk of treating my mother as a means.

If values are vague, and if they are always too broad for the concrete and specific case that we are considering, the only thing left for us is to trust our instincts. That's what this young man tried to do; and when I saw him, he said, "In the end, feeling is what counts. I ought to choose whichever pushes me in one direction. If I feel that I love my mother enough to sacrifice everything else for her—my desire for vengeance, for action, for adventure—then I'll stay with her. If, on the contrary, I feel that my love for my mother isn't enough, I'll leave.

But how is the value of a feeling determined? What gives his feeling for his mother value? Precisely the fact that he remained with her. I may say that I like so-and-so well enough to sacrifice a certain amount of money for him, but I may say so only if I've done it. I may say "I love my mother well enough to remain with her" if I have remained with her. The only way to determine the value of this affection is, precisely, to perform an act which confirms and defines it. But, since I require this affection to justify my act, I find myself caught in a vicious circle.

On the other hand, Gide has well said that a mock feeling and a true feeling are almost indistinguishable; to decide that I love my mother and will remain with her, or to remain with her by putting on an act, amount somewhat to the same thing. In other words, the feeling is formed by the acts one performs; so, I can not refer to it in order to act upon it. Which means that I can neither seek within myself the true condition which will impel me to act, nor apply to a system of ethics for concepts which will permit me to act. You will say, "At least, he did go to a teacher for advice." But if you seek advice from a priest, for example, you have chosen this priest; you already knew, more or less, just about what advice he was going to give you. In other words, choosing your adviser is involving yourself. The proof of this is that if you are a Christian, you will say, "Consult a priest." But some priests are collaborating, some are just marking time, some are resisting. Which to choose? If the young man chooses a priest who is resisting or collaborating, he has already decided on the kind of advice he's going to get. Therefore, in coming to see me he knew the answer I was going to give him, and I had only one answer to give: "You're free, choose, that is, invent." No general ethics can show you what is to be done; there are no omens in the world. The Catholics will reply, "But there are." Granted—but, in any case, I myself choose the meaning they have.

## JOHN STUART MILL

# Defense of Utilitarianism

This selection is divided into two main sections. In the first, from his book **Utilitarianism,** Mill (1806–1873) explains some of the basic principles of his theory. He states and defends the Greatest Happiness Principle, and explains why he thinks that higher pleasures are better on utilitarian grounds than lower ones. In the second section, from **On Liberty,** Mill tries to show why extensive personal liberties are protected by the utilitarian philosophy.

## A. FROM *UTILITARIANISM*

### Chapter I: General Remarks

There are few circumstances among those which make up the present condition of human knowledge, more unlike what might have been expected, or more significant of the backward state in which speculation on the most important subjects still lingers, than the little progress which has been made in the decision of the controversy respecting the criterion of right and wrong. From the dawn of philosophy, the question concerning the *summum bonum*, or, what is the same thing, concerning the foundation of morality, has been accounted the main problem in speculative thought, has occupied the most gifted intellects, and divided them into sects and schools, carrying on a vigorous warfare against one another. And after more than two thousand years the same discussions continue, philosophers are still ranged under the same contending banners, and neither thinkers nor mankind at large seem nearer to being unanimous on the subject, than when the young Socrates listened to the old Protagoras, and asserted

From "Utilitarianism," in *The English Utilitarians,* edited by John Plamenatz (Oxford: Basil Blackwell, 1948), pp. 163, 166–167, 169–174, 179–186, 195–204.

(if Plato's dialogue be grounded on a real conversation) the theory of utilitarianism against the popular morality of the so-called sophist.

       •       •       •

On the present occasion, I shall, without further discussion of the other theories, attempt to contribute something towards the understanding and appreciation of the Utilitarian or Happiness theory, and toward such proof as it is susceptible of. It is evident that this cannot be proof in the ordinary and popular meaning of the term. Questions of ultimate ends are not amenable to direct proof. Whatever can be proved to be good, must be so by being shown to be a means to something admitted to be good without proof. The medical art is proved to be good by its conducing health; but how is it possible to prove that health is good? The art of music is good, for the reason, among others, that it produces pleasure; but what proof is it possible to give that pleasure is good? If, then, it is asserted that there is a comprehensive formula, including all things which are in themselves good, and that whatever else is good, is not so as an end, but as a means, the formula may be accepted or rejected, but is not a subject of what is commonly understood by proof. We are not, however, to infer that its acceptance or rejection must depend on blind impulse, or arbitrary choice. There is a larger meaning of the word proof, in which this question is as amenable to it as any other of the disputed questions of philosophy. The subject is within the cognisance of the rational faculty; and neither does that faculty deal with it solely in the way of intuition. Considerations may be presented capable of determining the intellect either to give or withhold its assent to the doctrine; and this is equivalent to proof.

We shall examine presently of what nature are these considerations; in what manner they apply to the case, and what rational grounds, therefore, can be given for accepting or rejecting the utilitarian formula. But it is a preliminary condition or rational acceptance or rejection, that the formula should be correctly understood. I believe that the very imperfect notion ordinarily formed of its meaning, is the chief obstacle which impedes its reception; and that could it be cleared, even from only the grosser misconceptions, the question would be greatly simplified, and a large proportion of its difficulties removed. Before, therefore, I attempt to enter into the philosophical grounds which can be given for assenting to the utilitarian standard, I shall offer some illustrations of the doctrine itself; with the view of showing more clearly what it is, distinguishing it from what it is not, and disposing of such of the practical objections to it as either originate in, or are closely connected with, mistaken interpretations of its meaning. Having thus prepared the ground, I shall afterwards endeavor to throw such light as I can upon the question, considered as one of philosophical theory.

## Chapter II: What Utilitarianism Is

The creed which accepts as the foundation of morals, Utility, or the Greatest Happiness Principle, holds that actions are right in proportion as they tend to promote happiness, wrong as they tend to produce the reverse of happiness. By happiness is intended pleasure, and the absence of pain; by unhappiness, pain, and the privation of pleasure. To give a clear view of the moral standard set up by the theory, much more requires to be said; in particular, what things it includes in the ideas of pain and pleasure; and to what extent this is left an open question. But these supplementary explanations do not affect the theory of life on which this theory of morality is grounded—namely, that pleasure, and freedom from pain, are the only things desirable as ends; and that all desirable things (which are as numerous in the utilitarian as in any other scheme) are desirable either for the pleasure inherent in themselves, or as means to the promotion of pleasure and the prevention of pain.

Now, such a theory of life excites in many minds, and among them in some of the most estimable in feeling and purpose, inveterate dislike. To suppose that life has (as they express it) no higher end than pleasure—no better and nobler object of desire and pursuit—they designate as utterly mean and groveling; as a doctrine worthy only of swine, to whom the followers of Epicurus were, at a very early period, contemptuously likened; and modern holders of the doctrine are occasionally made the subject of equally polite comparisons by its German, French, and English assailants.

When thus attacked, the Epicureans have always answered, that it is not they, but their accusers, who represent human nature in a degrading light; since the accusation supposes human beings to be capable of no pleasures except those of which swine are capable. If this supposition were true, the charge could not be gainsaid, but would then be no longer an imputation; for if the sources of pleasure were precisely the same to human beings and to swine, the rule of life which is good enough for the one would be good enough for the other. The comparison of the Epicurean life to that of beasts is felt as degrading, precisely because a beast's pleasures do not satisfy a human being's conceptions of happiness. Human beings have faculties more elevated than the animal appetites, and when once made conscious of them, do not regard anything as happiness which does not include their gratification. I do not, indeed, consider the Epicureans to have been by any means faultless in drawing out their scheme of consequences from the utilitarian principle. To do this in any sufficient manner, many Stoic, as well as Christian elements require to be included. But there is no known Epicurean theory of life which does not assign to the pleasures of the intellect, of the feelings and imagination, and of the moral sentiments, a much higher value as pleasures than to those of mere sensation. It must be admitted, however, that utilitarian writers in general have placed the superiority of mental over bodily pleasures chiefly in the greater permanency, safety, uncostliness, etc., of the former—that is, in their circumstantial advantages rather than in their intrinsic nature. And on all these points utilitarians have fully proved their case; but they might have taken the other, and, as it may be called, higher ground, with entire consistency. It is quite compatible with the principle of utility to recognise the fact, that some kinds of pleasure are more desirable and more valuable than others. It would be absurd that while, in estimating all other things, quality is considered as well as quantity, the estimation of pleasures should be supposed to depend on quantity alone.

If I am asked what I mean by difference of quality of pleasures, or what makes one pleasure more valuable than another, merely as a pleasure, except its being greater in amount, there is but one possible answer. Of two pleasures, if there be one to which all or almost all who have experience of both give a decided preference, irrespective of any feeling of moral obligation to prefer it, that is the more desirable pleasure. If one of the two is, by those who are competently acquainted with both, placed so far above the other that they prefer it, even though knowing it to be attended with a greater amount of discontent, and would not resign it for any quantity of the other pleasure which their nature is capable of, we are justified in ascribing to the preferred enjoyment a superiority in quality, so far outweighing quantity as to render it, in comparison, of small account.

Now it is an unquestionable fact that those who are equally acquainted with, and equally capable of appreciating and enjoying, both, do give a most marked preference to the manner of existence which employs their higher faculties. Few human creatures would consent to be changed into any of the lower animals, for a promise of the fullest allowance of a beast's pleasures; no intelligent human being would consent to be a fool, no instructed person would be an ignoramus, no person of feeling and conscience would be selfish and base, even though they should be persuaded that the fool, the dunce, or the rascal is better satisfied with his lot than they are with theirs. They would not resign what they possess more than he for the most complete satisfaction of all the desires which they have in common with him. If they ever fancy they would, it is only in cases of unhappiness so extreme, that to escape from it they would exchange their lot for almost any other, however undesirable in their own eyes. A being of higher faculties requires more to make him happy, is capable of more acute suffering, and certainly accessible to it at more points, than one of an inferior type; but in spite of these liabilities, he can never really wish to sink into what he feels to be a lower grade of existence. We may give what explanation we please of this unwillingness; we may attribute it to pride, a name which is given indiscriminately to some of the most and to some of the least estimable feelings of which mankind are capable: we may refer it to the love of liberty and personal independence, an appeal to which was with the Stoics one of the most effective means for the inculcation of it; to the love of power, or to the love of excitement, both of which do really enter into and contribute to it: but its most appropriate appellation is a sense of dignity, which all human beings possess in one form or other, and in some, though by no means in exact, proportion to their higher faculties, and which is so essential a part of the happiness of those in whom it is strong, that nothing which conflicts with it could be, otherwise than momentarily, an object of desire to them. Whoever supposes that this preference takes place at a sacrifice of happiness—that the superior being, in anything like equal circumstances, is not happier than the inferior— confounds the two very different ideas, of happiness, and content. It is indisputable that the being whose capacities of enjoyment are low, has the greatest chance of having them fully satisfied; and a highly endowed being will always feel that any happiness which he can look for, as the world is constituted, is imperfect. But he can learn to bear its imperfections, if they are at all bearable; and they will not make him envy the being who is indeed unconscious of the imperfections, but only because he feels not at all the good which those imperfections qualify. It is better to be a human being dissatisfied than a pig satisfied; better to be Socrates dissatisfied than a fool satisfied. And if the fool, or the pig, are of a different opinion, it is because they only know their own side of the question. The other party to the comparison knows both sides.

It may be objected, that many who are capable of the higher pleasures, occasionally, under the influence of temptation, postpone them to the lower. But this is quite compatible with a full appreciation of the intrinsic superiority of the higher. Men often, from infirmity of character, make their election for the nearer good, though they know it to be the less valuable; and this no less when the choice is between two bodily pleasures, than when it is between bodily and mental. They pursue sensual indulgences to the injury of health, though perfectly aware that health is the greater good. It may be further objected, that many who begin with youthful enthusiasm for everything noble, as they advance in years sink into indolence and selfishness. But I do not believe that those who undergo this very common change, voluntarily choose the lower description of pleasures in preference to the higher. I believe that before they devote themselves exclusively to the one, they have already become incapable of the other. Capacity for the nobler feelings is in most natures a very tender plant, easily killed, not only by hostile influences, but by mere want of sustenance; and in the majority of young persons it speedily dies away if the occupations to which their position in life has devoted them, and the society into which it has thrown them, are not favourable to keeping that higher capacity in exercise. Men lose their higher aspirations as they lose their intellectual tastes, because they have not time or opportunity for indulging them; and they addict themselves to inferior pleasures, not because they deliberately prefer them, but because they are either the only ones to which they have access, or the only ones which they are any longer capable of enjoying. It may be questioned whether any one who has remained equally susceptible to both classes of pleasures, ever knowingly and calmly preferred the lower; though many, in all ages, have broken down in an ineffectual attempt to combine both.

From this verdict of the only competent judges, I apprehend there can be no appeal. On a question which is the best worth having of two pleasures, or which of two modes of existence is the most grateful to the feelings, apart from its moral attributes and from its consequences, the judgment of those who are qualified by knowledge of both, or, if they differ, that of the majority among them, must be admitted as final. And there needs be the less hesitation to accept this judgment respecting the quality of pleasures, since there is no other tribunal to be referred to even on the question of quantity. What means are there of determining which is the acutest of two pains, or the intensest of two pleasurable sensations, except the general suffrage of those who are familiar with both? Neither pains nor pleasures are homogeneous, and pain is always heterogeneous with pleasure. What is there to decide whether a particular pleasure is worth purchasing at the cost of a particular pain, except the feelings and judgment of the experienced? When, therefore, those feelings and judgment declare the pleasures derived from the higher faculties to be preferable *in kind,* apart from the question of intensity, to those of which the animal nature, disjoined from the higher faculties, is susceptible, they are entitled on this subject to the same regard.

I have dwelt on this point, as being a necessary part of a perfectly just conception of Utility or Happiness, considered as the directive rule of human conduct. But it is by no means an indispensable condition to the acceptance of the utilitarian standard; for that standard is not the agent's own greatest happiness, but the greatest amount of happiness altogether; and if it may possibly be doubted whether a noble character is always the happier for its nobleness, there can be no doubt that it makes other people happier, and that the world in general is immensely a gainer by it. Utilitarianism, therefore, could only attain its end by the general cultivation of nobleness of character, even if each individual were only benefited by the nobleness of others, and his own, so far as happiness is concerned, were a sheer deduction from the benefit. But the bare enunciation of such an absurdity as this last, renders refutation superfluous.

According to the Greatest Happiness Principle, as above explained, the ultimate end, with reference to and for the sake of which all other things are desirable (whether we are considering our own good or that of other people), is an existence exempt as far as possible from pain, and as rich as possible in enjoyments, both in point of quantity and quality; the test of quality, and the rule for measuring it against quantity, being the preference felt by those who in their opportunities of experience, to which must be added their habits of self-consciousness and self-observation, are best furnished with the means of comparison. This, being, according to the utilitarian opinion, the end of human action, is necessarily also the standard of morality; which may accordingly be defined, the rules and precepts for human conduct, by the observance of which an existence such as has been described might be, to the greatest extent possible, secured to all mankind; and not to them only, but, so far as the nature of things admit, to the whole sentient creation.

•          •          •

I must again repeat, what the assailants of utilitarianism seldom have the justice to acknowledge, that the happiness which forms the utilitarian standard of what is right in conduct, is not the agent's own happiness, but that of all concerned. As between his own happiness and that of others, utilitarianism requires him to be as strictly impartial as a disinterested and benevolent spectator. In the golden rule of Jesus of Nazareth, we read the complete spirit of the ethics of utility. To do as you would be done by, and to love your neighbour as yourself, constitute the ideal perfection of utilitarian morality. As the means of making the nearest approach to this ideal, utility would enjoin, first, that laws and social arrangements should place the happiness, or (as speaking practically it may be called) the interest, of every individual, as nearly as possible in harmony with the interest of the whole; and secondly, that education and opinion, which have so vast a power over human character, should so use that power as to establish in the mind of every individual an indissoluble association between his own happiness and the good of the whole; especially between his own happiness and the practice of such modes of conduct, negative and positive, as regard for the universal happiness prescribes; so that not only he may be unable to conceive the possibility of happiness to himself, consistently with conduct opposed to the general good, but also that a direct impulse to promote the general good may be in every individual one of the habitual motives of action, and the sentiments connected therewith may fill a large and prominent place in every human being's sentient existence. If the impugners of the utilitarian morality represented it to their own minds in this its true character, I know not what recommendation possessed by any other morality they could possibly affirm to be wanting to it; what more beautiful or more exalted developments of human nature any other ethical system can be supposed to foster, or what springs of action, not accessible to the utilitarian, such systems rely on for giving effect to their mandates.

The objectors to utilitarianism cannot always be charged with representing it in a discreditable light. On the contrary, those among them who entertain anything like a just idea of its disinterested character, sometimes find fault with its standard as being too high for humanity. They say it is exacting too much to require that people shall always act from the inducement of promoting the general interests of society. But this is to mistake the very meaning of a standard of morals, and confound the rule of action with the motive of it. It is the business of ethics to tell us what are our duties, or by what test we may know them; but no system of ethics requires that the sole motive of all we do shall be a feeling of duty; on the contrary, ninety-nine hundredths of all our actions are done from other motives, and rightly so done, if the rule of duty does not condemn them. It is the most unjust to utilitarianism that this particular misapprehension should be made a ground of objection to it, inasmuch as utilitarian moralists have gone beyond almost all others in affirming that the motive has nothing to do with the morality of the action, though much with the worth of the agent. He who saves a fellow creature from drowning does what is morally right, whether his motive be duty, or the hope of being paid for his trouble; he who betrays the friend that trusts him, is guilty of a crime, even if his object be to serve another friend to whom he is under greater obligations. But to speak only of actions done from the motive of duty, and in direct obedience to principle: it is a misapprehension of the utilitarian mode of thought, to conceive it as implying that people should fix their minds upon so wide a generality as the world, or society at large. The great majority of good actions are intended not for the benefit of the world, but for that of individuals, of which the good of the world is made up; and the thoughts of the most virtuous man need not on these occasions travel beyond the particular persons concerned, except so far as is necessary to assure himself that in benefiting them he is not violating the rights, that is, the legitimate and authorized expectations, of any one else. The multiplication of happiness is, according to the utilitarian ethics, the object of virtue: the occasions on which any person (except one in a thousand) has it in his power to do this on an extended scale, in other words to be a public benefactor, are but exceptional; and on these occasions alone is he called on to consider public utility; in every other case, private utility, the interest or happiness of some few persons, is all he has to attend to. Those alone the influence of whose actions extends to society in general, need concern themselves habitually about so large an object. In the case of abstinence indeed— of things which people forbear to do from moral considerations, though the consequences in the particular case might be beneficial—it would be unworthy of an intelligent agent not to be consciously aware that the action is of a class which, if practised generally, would be generally injurious, and that this is the ground of the obligation to abstain from it. The amount of regard for the public interest implied in this recognition, is no greater than is demanded by every system of morals, for they all enjoin to abstain from whatever is manifestly pernicious to society.

The same considerations dispose of another reproach against the doctrine of utility, founded on a still grosser misconception of the purpose of a standard of morality, and of the very meaning of the words right and wrong. It is often affirmed that utilitarianism renders men cold and unsympathising; that it chills their moral feelings towards individuals; that it makes them regard only the dry and hard consideration of the consequences of actions, not taking into their moral estimate the qualities from which those actions emanate. If the assertion means that they do not allow their judgment respecting the rightness or wrongness of an action to be influenced by their opinion of the qualities of the person who does it, this is a complaint not against utilitarianism, but against having any standard of morality at all; for certainly no known ethical standard decides an action to be good or bad because it is done by a good or bad man, still less because done by an amiable, a brave, or a benevolent man, or the contrary. These considerations are relevant, not to the estimation of actions, but of persons; and there is nothing in the utilitarian theory inconsistent with the fact that there are other things which interest us in persons besides the rightness and wrongness of their actions. The Stoics, indeed, with the paradoxical misuse of language which was part of their system, and by which they strove to raise themselves above all concern about anything but virtue, were fond of saying, that he who has that has everything; that he, and only he, is rich, is beautiful, is a king. But no claim of this description is made for the virtuous man by the utilitarian doctrine. Utilitarians are quite aware that there are other desirable possessions and qualities besides virtue, and are perfectly willing to allow to all of them their full worth. They are also aware that a right action does not necessarily indicate a virtuous character, and that actions which are blamable, often proceed from qualities entitled to praise. When this is apparent in any particular case, it modifies their estimation, not certainly of the act, but of the agent. I grant that they are, notwithstanding, of opinion, that in the long run the best proof of a good character is good actions; and resolutely refuse to consider any mental disposition as good, of which the predominant tendency is to produce bad conduct. This makes them unpopular with many people; but it is an unpopularity which they must share with every one who regards the distinction between right and wrong in a serious light; and the reproach is not one which a conscientious utilitarian need be anxious to repel.

If no more be meant by the objection than that many utilitarians look on the morality of actions, as measured by the utilitarian standard, with too exclusive a regard, and do not lay sufficient stress upon the other beauties of character which go towards making a human being lovable or admirable, this may be admitted. Utilitarians who have cultivated their moral feelings, but not their sympathies nor their artistic perceptions, do fall into this mistake; and so do all other moralists under the same conditions. What can be said in excuse for other moralists is equally available for them, namely, that, if there is to be any error, it is better that it should be on that side. As a matter of fact, we may affirm that among utilitarians as among adherents of other systems, there is every imaginable degree of rigidity and of laxity in the application of their standard: some are even puritanically rigorous, while others are as indulgent as can possibly be desired by sinner or by sentimentalist. But on the whole, a doctrine which brings prominently forward the interest that mankind have in the repression and prevention of conduct which violates the moral law, is likely to be inferior to no other in turning the sanctions of opinion against such violations. It is true, the question, What does violate the moral law? is one on which those who recognize different standards of morality are likely now and then to differ. But difference of opinion on moral questions was not first introduced into the world by utilitarianism, while that doctrine does supply, if not always an easy, at all events a tangible and intelligible mode of deciding such differences.

It may not be superfluous to notice a few more of the common misapprehensions of utilitarian ethics, even those which are so obvious and gross that it might appear impossible for any person of candour and intelligence to fall into them; since persons, even of considerable mental endowments, often give themselves so little trouble to understand the bearings of any opinion against which they entertain a prejudice, and men are in general so little conscious of this voluntary ignorance as a defect, that the vulgarest misunderstandings of ethical doctrines are continually met with the deliberate writings of persons of the greatest pretensions both to high principle and to philosophy. We not uncommonly hear the doctrine of utility inveighed against as a *godless* doctrine. If it be necessary to say anything at all against so mere an assumption, we may say that the question depends upon what idea we have formed of the moral character of the Deity. If it be a true belief that God desires, above all things, the happiness of his creatures, and that this was his purpose in their creation, utility is not only not a godless doctrine, but more profoundly religious than any other. If it be meant that utilitarianism does not recognise the revealed will of God as the supreme law of morals, I answer, that a utilitarian who believes in the perfect goodness and wisdom of God, necessarily believes that whatever God has thought fit to reveal on the subject of morals, must fulfil the requirements of utility in a supreme degree. But others besides utilitarians have been of opinion that the Christian revelation was intended, and is fitted, to inform the hearts and minds of mankind with a spirit which should enable them to find for themselves what is right, and incline them to do it when found, rather than to tell them, except in a very general way, what it is; and that we need a doctrine of ethics, carefully followed out, to *interpret* to us the will of God. Whether this opinion is correct or not, it is superfluous here to discuss; since whatever aid religion, either natural or revealed, can afford to ethical investigation, is as open to the utilitarian moralist as to any other. He can use it as the testimony of God to the usefulness or hurtfulness of any given course of action, by as good a right as others can use it for the indication of a transcendental law, having no connexion with usefulness or with happiness.

Again, Utility is often summarily stigmatised as an immoral doctrine by giving it the name of Expediency, and taking advantage of the popular use of that term to contrast it with Principle. But the Expedient, in the sense in which it is opposed to the Right, generally means that which is expedient for the particular interest of the agent himself; as when a minister sacrifices the interests of his country to keep himself in place. When it means anything better than this, it means that which is expedient for some immediate object, some temporary purpose, but which violates a rule whose observance is expedient in a much higher degree. The Expedient, in this sense, instead of being the same thing with the useful, is a branch of the hurtful. Thus, it would often be expedient, for the purpose of getting over some momentary embarrassment, or attaining some object immediately useful to ourselves or others, to tell a lie. But inasmuch as the cultivation in ourselves of a sensitive feeling on the subject of veracity, is one of the most useful, and the enfeeblement of that feeling one of the most hurtful, things to which our conduct can be instrumental; and inasmuch as any, even unintentional, deviation from truth, does that much towards weakening the trustworthiness of human assertion, which is not only the principal support of all present social well-being, but the insufficiency of which does more than any one thing that can be named to keep back civilisation, virtue, everything on which human happiness on the largest scale depends; we feel that the violation, for a present advantage, of a rule of such transcendant expediency, is not expedient, and that he who, for the sake of a convenience to himself or to some other individual, does what depends on him to deprive mankind of the good, and inflict upon them the evil, involved in the greater or less reliance which they can place in each other's word, acts the part of one of their worst enemies. Yet that even this rule, sacred as it is, admits of possible exceptions, is acknowledged by all moralists; the chief of which is when the withholding of some fact (as of information from a malefactor, or of bad news from a person dangerously ill) would save an individual (especially an individual other than oneself) from great and unmerited evil, and when the withholding can only be effected by denial. But in order that the exception may not extend itself beyond the need, and may have the least possible effect in weakening reliance on veracity, it ought to be recognised, and, if possible, its limits defined; and if the principle of utility is good for anything, it must be good for weighing these conflicting utilities against one another, and marking out the region within which one or the other preponderates.

Again, defenders of utility often find themselves called upon to reply to such objections as this—that there is not time, previous to action, for calculating and weighing the effects of any line of conduct on the general happiness. This is exactly as if any one were to say that it is impossible to guide our conduct by Christianity, because there is not time, on every occasion on which anything has to be done, to read through the Old and New Testaments. The answer to the objection is, that there has been ample time, namely, the whole past duration of the human species. During all that time, mankind have been learning by experience the tendencies of actions; on which experience all the prudence, as well as all the morality of life, are dependent. People talk as if the commencement of this course of experience had hitherto been put off, and as if, at the moment when some man feels tempted to meddle with the property or life of another, he had to begin considering for the first time whether murder and theft are injurious to human happiness. Even then I do not think that he would find the question very puzzling; but, at all events, the matter is now done to his hand. It is truly a whimsical supposition that, if mankind were agreed in considering utility to be the test of morality, they would remain without any agreement as to what *is* useful, and would take no measures for having their notions on the subject taught to the young, and enforced by law and opinion. There is no difficulty in proving any ethical standard whatever to work ill, if we suppose universal idiocy to be conjoined with it; but on any hypothesis short of that, mankind must by this time have acquired positive beliefs as to the effects of some actions on their happiness; and the beliefs which have thus come down are the rules of morality for the multitude, and for the philosopher until he has succeeded in finding better. That philosophers might easily do this, even now, on many subjects; that the received code of ethics is by no means of divine right; and that mankind have still much to learn as to the effects of actions on the general happiness, I admit, or rather, earnestly maintain. The corollaries from the principle of utility, like the precepts of every practical art, admit of indefinite improvement, and, in a progressive state of the human mind, their improvement is perpetually going on. But to consider the rules of morality as improvable, is one thing; to pass over the intermediate generalisations entirely, and endeavour to test each individual action directly by the first principle, is another. It is a strange notion that the acknowledgment of a first principle is inconsistent with the admission of secondary ones. To inform a traveller respecting the place of his ultimate destination, is not to forbid the use of landmarks and direction-posts on the way. The proposition that happiness is the end and aim of morality does not mean that no road ought to be laid down to that goal, or that persons going thither should not be advised to take one direction rather than another. Men really ought to leave off talking a kind of non-sense on this subject, which they would neither talk nor listen to on other matters of practical concernment. Nobody argues that the art of navigation is not founded on astronomy, because sailors cannot wait to calculate the Nautical Almanack. Being rational creatures, they go to sea with it ready calculated; and all rational creatures go out upon the sea of life with their minds made up on the common questions of right and wrong, as well as on many of the far more difficult questions of wise and foolish. And this, as long as foresight is a human quality, it is to be presumed they will continue to do. Whatever we adopt as the fundamental principle of morality, we require subordinate principles to apply it by; the impossibility of doing without them, being common to all systems, can afford no argument against any one in particular; but gravely to argue as if no such secondary principles could be had, and as if mankind had remained till now, and always must remain, without drawing any general conclusions from the experience of human life, is as high a pitch, I think, as absurdity has ever reached in philosophical controversy.

The remainder of the stock arguments against utilitarianism mostly consist in laying to its charge the common infirmities of human nature, and the general difficulties which embarrass conscientious persons in shaping their course through life. We are told that a utilitarian will be apt to make his own particular case an exception to moral rules, and, when under temptation, will see a utility in the breach of a rule, greater than he will see in its observance. But is utility the only creed which is able to furnish us with excuses for evil doing, and means of cheating our own conscience? They are afforded in abundance by all doctrines which recognise as a fact in morals the existence of conflicting considerations; which all doctrines do, that have been believed by sane persons. It is not the fault of any creed, but of the complicated nature of human affairs, that rules of conduct cannot be so framed as to require no exceptions, and that hardly any kind of action can safely be laid down as either always obligatory or always condemnable. There is no ethical creed which does not temper the rigidity of its laws, by giving a certain latitude, under the moral responsibility of the agent, for accommodation to peculiarities of circumstances; and under every creed, at the opening thus made, self-deception and dishonest casuistry get in. There exists no moral system under which there do not arise unequivocal cases of conflicting obligations. These are the real difficulties, the knotty points both in the theory of ethics, and in the conscientious guidance of personal conduct. They are overcome practically, with greater or with less success, according to the intellect and virtue of the individual; but it can hardly be pretended that any one will be the less qualified for dealing with them, from possessing an ultimate standard to which conflicting rights and duties can be referred. If utility is the ultimate source of moral obligations, utility may be invoked to decide between them when their demands are incompatible. Though the application of the standard may be difficult, it is better than none at all; while in other systems, the moral laws all claiming independent authority, there is no common umpire entitled to interfere between them; their claims to precedence one over another rest on little better than sophistry, and unless determined, as they generally are, by the unacknowledged influence of considerations of utility, afford a free scope for the action of personal desires and partialities. We must remember that only in these cases of conflict between secondary principles is it requisite that first principles should be appealed to. There is no case of moral obligation in which some secondary principle is not involved; and if only one, there can seldom be any real doubt which one it is, in the mind of any person by whom the principle itself is recognised.

## Chapter IV: Of What Sort of Proof the Principle of Utility Is Susceptible

It has already been remarked that questions of ultimate ends do not admit of proof, in the ordinary acceptation of the term. To be incapable of proof by reasoning is common to all first principles; to the first premises of our knowledge, as well as to those of our conduct. But the former, being matters of fact, may be the subject of a direct appeal to the faculties which judge of fact—namely, our senses, and our internal consciousness. Can an appeal be made to the same faculties on questions of practical ends? Or by what other faculty is cognisance taken of them?

Questions about ends are, in other words, questions about what things are desirable. The utilitarian doctrine is, that happiness is desirable, and the only thing desirable, as an end; all other things being only desirable as means to that end. What ought to be required of this doctrine—what conditions is it requisite that the doctrine should fulfil—to make good its claim to be believed?

The only proof capable of being given that an object is visible, is that people actually see it. The only proof that a sound is audible, is that people hear it: and so of the other sources of our experience. In like manner, I apprehend, the sole evidence it is possible to produce that anything is desirable, is that people actually do desire it. If the end which the utilitarian doctrine proposes to itself were not, in theory and in practice, acknowledged to be an end, nothing could ever convince any person that it was so. No reason can be given why the general happiness is desirable, except that each person, so far as he believes it to be attainable, desires his own happiness. This, however, being a fact, we have not only all the proof which the case admits of, but all which it is possible to require, that happiness is a good: that each person's happiness is a good to that person, and the general happiness, therefore, a good to the aggregate of all persons. Happiness has made out its title as *one* of the ends of conduct, and consequently one of the criteria of morality.

But it has not, by this alone, proved itself to be the sole criterion. To do that, it would seem, by the same rule, necessary to show, not only that people desire happiness, but that they never desire anything else. Now it is palpable that they do desire things which, in common language, are decidedly distinguished from happiness. They desire, for example, virtue, and the absence of vice, no less really than pleasure and the absence of pain. The desire of virtue is not as universal, but is as authentic a fact, as the desire of happiness. And hence the opponents of the utilitarian standard deem that they have a right to infer that there are other ends of human action besides happiness, and that happiness is not the standard of approbation and disapprobation.

But does the utilitarian doctrine deny that people desire virtue, or maintain that virtue is not a thing to be desired? The very reverse. It maintains not only that virtue is to be desired, but that it is to be desired disinterestedly, for itself. Whatever may be the opinion of utilitarian moralists as to the original conditions by which virtue is made virtue; however they may believe (as they do) that actions and dispositions are only virtuous because they promote another end than virtue; yet this being granted, and it having been decided, from considerations of this description, what *is* virtuous, they not only place virtue at the very head of the things which are good as means to the ultimate end, but they also recognise as a psychological fact the possibility of its being, to the individual, a good in itself, without looking to any end beyond it; and, hold, that the mind is not in a right state, not a state conformable to Utility, not in the state most conducive to the general happiness, unless it does love virtue in this manner—as a thing desirable in itself, even although, in the individual instance, it should not produce those other desirable consequences which it tends to produce, and on account of which it is held to be virtue. This opinion is not, in the smallest degree, a departure from the Happiness principle. The ingredients of happiness are very various, and each of them is desirable in itself, and not merely when considered as swelling an aggregate. The principle of utility does not mean that any given pleasure, as music, for instance, or any given exemption from pain, as for example health, is to be looked upon as means to a collective something termed happiness, and to be desired on that account. They are desired and desirable in and for themselves; besides being means, they are a part of the end. Virtue, according to the utilitarian doctrine, is not naturally and originally part of the end, but it is capable of becoming so; and in those who love it disinterestedly it has become so, and is desired and cherished, not as a means to happiness, but as a part of their happiness.

To illustrate this farther, we may remember that virtue is not the only thing, originally a means, and which if it were not a means to anything else, would be and remain indifferent, but which by association with what it is a means to, comes to be desired for itself, and that too with the utmost intensity. What, for example, shall we say of the love of money? There is nothing originally more desirable about money than about any heap of glittering pebbles. Its worth is solely that of the things which it will buy; the desires for other things than itself, which it is a means of gratifying. Yet the love of money is not only one of the strongest moving forces of human life, but money is, in many cases, desired in and for itself; the desire to possess it is often stronger than the desire to use it, and goes on increasing when all the desires which point to ends beyond it, to be compassed by it, are falling off. It may, then, be said truly, that money is desired not for the sake of an end, but as part of the end. From being a means to happiness, it has come to be itself a principal ingredient of the individual's conception of happiness. The same may be said of the majority of the great objects of human life—power, for example, or fame; except that to each of these there is a certain amount of immediate pleasure annexed, which has at least the semblance of being naturally inherent in them; a thing which cannot be said of money. Still, however, the strongest natural attraction, both of power and of fame, is the immense aid they give to the attainment of our other wishes; and it is the strong association thus generated between them and all our objects of desire, which gives to the direct desire of them the intensity it often assumes, so as in some characters to surpass in strength all other desires. In these cases the means have become a part of the end, and a more important part of it than any of the things which they are means to. What was once desired as an instrument for the attainment of happiness, has come to be desired for its own sake. In being desired for its own sake it is, however, desired as *part* of happiness. The person is made, or thinks he would be made, happy by its mere possession; and is made unhappy by failure to obtain it. The desire of it is not a different thing from the desire of happiness, any more than the love of music, of the desire of health. They are included in happiness. They are some of the elements of which the desire of happiness is made up. Happiness is not an abstract idea, but a concrete whole; and these are some of its parts. And the utilitarian standard sanctions and approves their being so. Life would be a poor thing, very ill provided with sources of happiness, if there were not this provision of nature, by which things originally indifferent, but conducive to, or otherwise associated with, the satisfaction of our primitive desires, become in themselves sources of pleasure more valuable than the primitive pleasures, both in permanency, in the space of human existence that they are capable of covering, and even in intensity.

Virtue, according to the utilitarian conception, is a good of this description. There was no original desire of it, or motive to it, save its conduciveness to pleasure, and especially to protection from pain. But through the association thus formed, it may be felt a good in itself, and desired as such with as great intensity as any other good; and with this difference between it and the love of money, of power, or of fame, that all of these may, and often do, render the individual noxious to the other members of society to which he belongs, whereas there is nothing which makes him so much a blessing to them as the cultivation of the disinterested love of virtue. And consequently, the utilitarian standard, while it tolerates and approves those other acquired desires, up to the point beyond which they would be more injurious to the general happiness than promotive of it, enjoins and requires the cultivation of the love of virtue up to the greatest strength possible, as being above all things important to the general happiness.

It results from the preceding considerations, that there is in reality nothing desired except happiness. Whatever is desired otherwise than as a means to some end beyond itself, and ultimately to happiness, is desired as itself a part of happiness, and is not desired for itself until it has become so. Those who desire virtue for its own sake, desire it either because the consciousness of it is a pleasure, or because the consciousness of being without it is a pain, or for both reasons united; as in truth the pleasure and pain seldom exist separately, but almost always together, the same person feeling pleasure in degree of virtue attained, and pain in not having attained more. If one of these give him no pleasure, and the other no pain, he would not love or desire virtue, or would desire it only for the other benefits which it might produce to himself or to persons whom he cared for.

We have now, then, an answer to the question, of what sort of proof the principle of utility is susceptible. If the opinion which I have now stated is psychologically true—if human nature is so constituted as to desire nothing which is not either a part of happiness or a means of happiness, we can have no other proof, and we require no other, that these are the only things desirable. If so, happiness is the sole end of human action, and the promotion of it the test by which to judge of all human conduct; from whence it necessarily follows that it must be the criterion of morality, since a part is included in the whole.

And now to decide whether this is really so; whether mankind do desire nothing for itself but that which is a pleasure to them or of which the absence is a pain; we have evidently arrived at a question of fact and experience, dependent, like all similar questions, upon evidence. It can only be determined by practised self-consciousness and self-observation, assisted by observation of others. I believe that these sources of evidence, impartially consulted, will declare that desiring a thing and finding it pleasant, aversion to it and thinking of it as painful, are phenomena entirely inseparable, or rather two parts of the same phenomenon; in strictness of language, two different modes of naming the same psychological fact: that to think of an object as desirable (unless for the sake of its consequences), and to think of it as pleasant, are one and the same thing; and that to desire anything, except in proportion as the idea of it is pleasant, is a physical and metaphysical impossibility...

## B. FROM *ON LIBERTY*

### Introductory

The subject of this essay is not the so-called "liberty of the will," so unfortunately opposed to the misnamed doctrine of philosophical necessity; but civil, or social liberty; the nature and limits of the power which can be legitimately exercised by society over the individual. A question seldom stated, and hardly ever discussed in general terms, but which profoundly influences the practical controversies of the age by its latent presence, and is likely soon to make itself recognized as the vital question of the future. It is so far from being new that, in a certain sense, it has divided mankind almost from the remotest ages; but in the stage of progress into which the more civilized portions of the species have now entered, it presents itself under new conditions and requires a different and more fundamental treatment.

From *On Liberty,* edited by Currin Shields (New York: Macmillan, 1956), pp. 3–8, 13–16, 19–25, 43–45, 64, 67–68, 77–78, 82–83.

The struggle between liberty and authority is the most conspicuous feature in the portions of history with which we are earliest familiar, particularly in that of Greece, Rome, and England. But in old times this contest was between subjects, or some classes of subjects, and the government. By liberty was meant protection against the tyranny of the political rulers. The rulers were conceived (except in some of the popular governments of Greece) as in a necessarily antagonistic position to the people whom they ruled. They consisted of a governing One, or a governing tribe or caste, who derived their authority from inheritance or conquest, who, at all events, did not hold it at the pleasure of the governed, and whose supremacy men did not venture, perhaps did not desire, to contest, whatever precautions might be taken against its oppressive exercise. Their power was regarded as necessary, but also as highly dangerous; as a weapon which they would attempt to use against their subjects, no less than against external enemies. To prevent the weaker members of the community from being preyed upon by innumerable vultures, it was needful that there should be an animal of prey stronger than the rest, commissioned to keep them down. But as the king of the vultures would be no less bent upon preying on the flock than any of the minor harpies, it was indispensable to be in a perpetual attitude of defense against his beak and claws. The aim, therefore, of patriots was to set limits to the power which the ruler should be suffered to exercise over the community; and this limitation was what they meant by liberty. It was attempted in two ways. First, by obtaining a recognition of certain immunities, called political liberties or rights, which it was to be regarded as a breach of duty in the ruler to infringe, and which if he did infringe, specific resistance or general rebellion was held to be justifiable. A second, and generally a later, expedient was the establishment of constitutional checks by which the consent of the community, or of a body of some sort, supposed to represent its interests, was made a necessary condition to some of the more important acts of the governing power. To the first of these modes of limitation, the ruling power, in most European countries, was compelled, more or less, to submit. It was not so with the second; and, to attain this, or, when already in some degree possessed, to attain it more completely, became everywhere the principal object of the lovers of liberty. And so long as mankind were content to combat one enemy by another, and to be ruled by a master on condition of being guaranteed more or less efficaciously against his tyranny, they did not carry their aspirations beyond this point.

A time, however, came, in the progress of human affairs, when men ceased to think it a necessity of nature that their governors should be an independent power opposed in interest to themselves. It appeared to them much better that the various magistrates of the state should be their tenants or delegates, revocable at their pleasure. In that way alone, it seemed, could they have complete security that the powers of government would never be abused to their disadvantage. By degrees this new demand for elective and temporary rulers became the prominent object of the exertions of the popular party wherever any such party existed, and superseded, to a considerable extent, the previous efforts to limit the power of rulers. As the struggle proceeded for making the ruling power emanate from the periodical choice of the ruled, some persons began to think that too much importance had been attached to the limitation of the power itself. *That* (it might seem) was a resource against rulers whose interests were habitually opposed to those of the people. What was now wanted was that the rulers should be identified with the people, that their interest and will should be the interest and will of the nation. The nation did not need to be protected against its own will. There was no fear of its tyrannizing over itself. Let the rulers be effectually responsible to it, promptly removable by it, and it could afford to trust them with power of which it could itself dictate the use to be made. Their power was but the nation's own power, concentrated and in a form convenient for exercise. This mode of thought, or rather perhaps of feeling, was common among the last generation of European liberalism, in the Continental section of which it still apparently predominates. Those who admit any limit to what a government may do, except in the case of such governments as they think ought not to exist, stand out as brilliant exceptions among the political thinkers of the Continent. A similar tone of sentiment might by this time have been prevalent in our own country if the circumstances which for a time encouraged it had continued unaltered.

But, in political and philosophical theories as well as in persons, success discloses faults and infirmities which failure might have concealed from observation. The notion that the people have no need to limit their power over themselves might seem axiomatic, when popular government was a thing only dreamed about, or read of as having existed at some distant period of the past. Neither was that notion necessarily disturbed by such temporary aberrations as those of the French Revolution, the worst of which were the work of a usurping few, and which, in any case, belonged, not to the permanent working of popular institutions, but to a sudden and convulsive outbreak against monarchical and aristocratic despotism. In time, however, a democratic republic came to occupy a large portion of the earth's surface and made itself felt as one of the most powerful members of the community of nations; and elective and responsible government became subject to the observations and criticisms which wait upon a great existing fact. It was now perceived that such phrases as "self-government," and "the power of the people over themselves," do not express the true state of the case. The "people" who exercise the power are not always the same people with those over whom it is exercised; and the "self-government" spoken of is not the government of each by himself, but of each by all the rest. The will of the people, moreover, practically means the will of the most numerous or the most active *part* of the people—the majority, or those who succeed in making themselves accepted as the majority; the people, consequently, *may* desire to oppress a part of their number, and precautions are as much needed against this as against any other abuse of power. The limitations, therefore, of the power of government over individuals loses none of its importance when the holders of power are regularly accountable to the community, that is, to the strongest party therein. This view of things, recommending itself equally to the intelligence of thinkers and to the inclination of those important classes in European society to whose real or supposed interests democracy is adverse, has had no difficulty in establishing itself; and in political speculations "the tyranny of the majority" is now generally included among the evils against which society requires to be on its guard.

Like other tyrannies, the tyranny of the majority was at first, and is still vulgarly, held in dread, chiefly as operating through the acts of the public authorities. But reflecting persons perceived that when society is itself the tyrant—society collectively over the separate individuals who compose it—its means of tyrannizing are not restricted to the acts which it may do by the hands of its political functionaries. Society can and does execute its own mandates; and if it issues wrong mandates instead of right, or any mandates at all in things with which it ought not to meddle, it practices a social tyranny more formidable than many kinds of political oppression, since, though not usually upheld by such extreme penalties, it leaves fewer means of escape, penetrating much more deeply into the details of life, and enslaving the soul itself. Protection, therefore, against the tyranny of the magistrate is not enough; there needs protection also against the tyranny of the prevailing opinion and feeling, against the tendency of society to impose, by other means than civil penalties, its own ideas and practices as rules of conduct on those who dissent from them; to fetter the development and, if possible, prevent the formation of any individuality not in harmony with its ways, and compel all characters to fashion themselves upon the model of its own. There is a limit to the legitimate interference of collective opinion with individual independence; and to find that limit, and maintain it against encroachment, is as indispensable to a good condition of human affairs as protection against political despotism.

But though this proposition is not likely to be contested in general terms, the practical question where to place the limit—how to make the fitting adjustment between individual independence and social control—is a subject on which nearly everything remains to be done. All that makes existence valuable to anyone depends on the enforcement of restraints upon the actions of other people. Some rules of conduct, therefore, must be imposed—by law in the first place, and by opinion on many things which are not fit subjects for the operation of law. What these rules should be is the principal question in human affairs. . . .

The object of this essay is to assert one very simple principle, as entitled to govern absolutely the dealings of society with the individual in the way of compulsion and control, whether the means used by physical force in the form of legal penalties or the moral coercion of public opinion. That principle is that the sole end for which mankind are warranted, individually or collectively, in interfering with the liberty of action of any of their number is self-protection. That the only purpose for which power can be rightfully exercised over any member of a civilized community, against his will, is to prevent harm to others. His own good, either physical or moral, is not a sufficient warrant. He cannot rightfully be compelled to do or forbear because it will be better for him to do so, because it will make him happier, because, in the opinions of others, to do so would be wise or even right. These are good reasons for remonstrating with him, or reasoning with him, or persuading him, or entreating him, but not for compelling him or visiting him with any evil in case he do otherwise. To justify that, the conduct from which it is desired to deter him must be calculated to produce evil to someone else. The only part of the conduct of anyone for which he is amenable to society is that which concerns others. In the part which merely concerns himself, his independence is, of right, absolute. Over himself, over his own body and mind, the individual is sovereign.

It is, perhaps, hardly necessary to say that this doctrine is meant to apply only to human beings in the maturity of their faculties. We are not speaking of children or of young persons below the age which the law may fix as that of manhood or womanhood. Those who are still in a state to require being taken care of by others must be protected against their own actions as well as against external injury. For the same reason we may leave out of consideration those backward states of society in which the race itself may be considered as in its nonage. The early difficulties in the way of spontaneous progress are so great that there is seldom any choice of means for overcoming them; and a ruler full of the spirit of improvement is warranted in the use of any expedients that will attain an end perhaps otherwise unattainable. Despotism is a legitimate mode of government in dealing with barbarians, provided the end be their improvement and the means justified by actually effecting that end. Liberty, as a principle, has no application to any state of things anterior to the time when mankind have become capable of being improved by free and equal discussion. Until then, there is nothing for them but implicit obedience to an Akbar or a Charlemagne, if they are so fortunate as to find one. But as soon as mankind have attained the capacity of being guided to their own improvement by conviction or persuasion (a period long since reached in all nations with whom we need here concern ourselves), compulsion, either in the direct form or in that of pains and penalties for noncompliance, is no longer admissible as a means to their own good, and justifiable only for the security of others.

It is proper to state that I forgo any advantage which could be derived to my argument from the idea of abstract right as a thing independent of utility. I regard utility as the ultimate appeal on all ethical questions; but it must be utility in the largest sense, grounded on the permanent interests of man as a progressive being. Those interests, I contend, authorize the subjection of individual spontaneity to external control only in respect to those actions of each which concern the interest of other people. If anyone does an act hurtful to others, there is a *prima facie* case for punishing him by law or, where legal penalties are not safely applicable, by general disapprobation. There are also many positive acts for the benefit of others which he may rightfully be compelled to perform, such as to give evidence in a court of justice, to bear his fair share in the common defense or in any other joint work necessary to the interest of the society of which he enjoys the protection, and to perform certain acts of individual beneficence, such as saving a fellow creature's life or interposing to protect the defenseless against ill usage—things which whatever it is obviously a man's duty to do he may rightfully be made responsible to society for not doing. A person may cause evil to others not only by his actions but by his inaction, and in either case he is justly accountable to them for the injury. The latter case, it is true, requires a much more cautious exercise of compulsion than the former. To make anyone answerable for doing evil to others is the rule; to make him answerable for not preventing evil is, comparatively speaking, the exception. Yet there are many cases clean enough and grave enough to justify that exception. In all things which regard the external relations of the individual, he is *de jure* amenable to those whose interests are concerned, and, if need be, to society as their protector. There are often good reasons for not holding him to the responsibility; but these reasons must arise from the special expediencies of the case: either because it is a kind of case in which he is on the whole likely to act better when left to his own discretion than when controlled in any way in which society have it in their power to control him; or because the attempt to exercise control would produce other evils, greater than those which it would prevent. When such reasons as these preclude the enforcement of responsibility, the conscience of the agent himself should step into the vacant judgment seat and protect those interests of others which have no external protection; judging himself all the more rigidly, because the case does not admit of his being made accountable to the judgment of his fellow creatures.

But there is a sphere of action in which society, as distinguished from the individual, has, only an indirect interest: comprehending all that portion of a person's life and conduct which affects only himself or, if it also affects others, only with their free, voluntary, and undeceived consent and participation. When I say only himself, I mean directly and in the first instance; for whatever affects himself may affect others through himself; and the objection which may be grounded on this contingency will receive consideration in the sequel. This, then, is the appropriate region of human liberty. It comprises, first, the inward domain of consciousness, demanding liberty of conscience in the most comprehensive sense, liberty of thought and feeling, absolute freedom of opinion and sentiment on all subjects, practical or speculative, scientific, moral, or theological. The liberty of expressing and publishing opinions may seem to fall under a different principle, since it belongs to that part of the conduct of an individual which concerns other people, but, being almost of as much importance as the liberty of thought itself and resting in great part on the same reasons, is practically inseparable from it. Secondly, the principle requires liberty of tastes and pursuits, of framing the plan of our life to suit our own character, of doing as we like, subject to such consequences as may follow, without impediment from our fellow creatures, so long as what we do does not harm them, even though they should think our conduct foolish, perverse, or wrong. Thirdly, from this liberty of each individual follows the liberty, within the same limits, of combination among individuals; freedom to unite for any purpose not involving harm to others: the persons combining being supposed to be of full age and not forced or deceived.

$$\bullet \qquad \bullet \qquad \bullet$$

## Of the Liberty of Thought and Discussion

The time, it is to be hoped, is gone by when any defense would be necessary of the "liberty of the press" as one of the securities against corrupt or tyrannical government. No argument, we may suppose, can now be needed against permitting a legislature or an executive, not identified in interest with the people, to prescribe opinions to them and determine what doctrines or what arguments they shall be allowed to hear. This aspect of the question, besides, has been so often and so triumphantly enforced by preceding writers that it needs not be specially insisted on in this place. Though the law of England, on the subject of the press, is as servile to this day as it was in the time of the Tudors, there is little danger of its being actually put in force against political discussion except during some temporary panic when fear of insurrection drives ministers and judges from their propriety; and, speaking generally, it is not, in constitutional countries, to be apprehended that the government, whether completely responsible to the people or not, will often attempt to control the expression of opinion, except when in doing so it makes itself the organ of the general intolerance of the public. Let us suppose, therefore, that the government is entirely at one with the people, and never thinks of exerting any power of coercion unless in agreement with what it conceives to be their voice.

But I deny the right of the people to exercise such coercion, either by themselves or by their government. The power itself is illegitimate. The best government has no more title to it than the worst. It is as noxious, or more noxious, when exerted in accordance with public opinion than when in opposition to it. If all mankind minus one were of one opinion, mankind would be no more justified in silencing that one person than he, if he had the power, would be justified in silencing mankind. Were an opinion a personal possession of no value except to the owner, if to be obstructed in the enjoyment of it were simply a private injury, it would make some difference whether the injury was inflicted only on a few persons or on many. But the peculiar evil of silencing the expression of an opinion is that it is robbing the human race, posterity as well as the existing generation—those who dissent from the opinion, still more than those who hold it. If the opinion is right, they are deprived of the opportunity of exchanging error for truth; if wrong, they lose, what is almost as great a benefit, the clearer perception and livelier impression of truth produced by its collision with error.

It is necessary to consider separately these two hypotheses, each of which has a distinct branch of the argument corresponding to it. We can never be sure that the opinion we are endeavoring to stifle is a false opinion; and if we were sure, stifling it would be an evil still.

First, the opinion which it is attempted to suppress by authority may possibly be true. Those who desire to suppress it, of course, deny its truth; but they are not infallible. They have no authority to decide the question for all mankind and exclude every other person from the means of judging. To refuse a hearing to an opinion because they are sure that it is false is to assume that *their* certainty is the same thing as *absolute* certainty. All silencing of discussion is an assumption of infallibility. Its condemnation may be allowed to rest on this common argument, not the worse for being common.

Unfortunately for the good sense of mankind, the fact of their fallibility is far from carrying the weight in their practical judgment which is always allowed to it in theory; for while everyone well knows himself to be fallible, few think it necessary to take any precautions against their own fallibility, or admit the supposition that any opinion of which they feel very certain may be one of the examples of the error to which they acknowledge themselves to be liable. Absolute princes, or others who are accustomed to unlimited deference, usually feel this complete confidence in their own opinions on nearly all subjects. People more happily situated, who sometimes hear their opinions disputed and are not wholly unused to be set right when they are wrong, place the same unbounded reliance only on such of their opinions as are shared by all who surround them, or to whom they habitually defer; for in proportion to a man's want of confidence in his own solitary judgment does he usually repose, with implicit trust, on the infallibility of "the world" in general. And the world, to each individual, means the part of it with which he comes in contact: his party, his sect, his church, his class of society; the man may be called, by comparison, almost liberal and large-minded to whom it means anything so comprehensive as his own country or his own age. Nor is his faith in this collective authority at all shaken by his being aware that other ages, countries, sects, churches, classes, and parties have thought, and even now think, the exact reverse. He devolves upon his own world the responsibility of being in the right against the dissentient worlds of other people; and it never troubles him that mere accident has decided which of these numerous worlds is the object of his reliance, and that the same causes which make him a churchman in London would have made him a Buddhist or a Confucian in Peking. Yet it is as evident in itself, as any amount of argument can make it, that ages are not more infallible than individuals—every age having held many opinions which subsequent ages have deemed not only false but absurd; and it is as certain that many opinions, now general, will be rejected by future ages, as it is that many, once general, are rejected by the present.

The objection likely to be made to this argument would probably take some such form as the following. There is no greater assumption of infallibility in forbidding the propagation of error than in any other thing which is done by public authority on its own judgment and responsibility. Judgment is given to men that they may use it. Because it may be used erroneously, are men to be told that they ought not to use it at all? To prohibit what they think pernicious is not claiming exemption from error, but fulfilling the duty incumbent on them, although fallible, of acting on their conscientious conviction. If we were never to act on our opinions, because those opinions may be wrong, we should leave all our interests uncared for, and all our duties unperformed. An objection which applied to all conduct can be no valid objection to any conduct in particular. It is the duty of governments, and of individuals, to form the truest opinions they can; to form them carefully, and never impose them upon others unless they are quite sure of being right. But when they are sure (such reasoners may say), it is not conscientiousness but cowardice to shrink from acting on their opinions and allow doctrines which they honestly think dangerous to the welfare of mankind, either in this life or in another, to be scattered abroad without restraint, because other people, in less enlightened times, have persecuted opinions now believed to be true. Let us take care, it may be said, not to make the same mistake; but governments and nations have made mistakes in other things which are not denied to be fit subjects for the exercise of authority: they have laid on bad taxes, made unjust wars. Ought we therefore to lay on no taxes and, under whatever provocation, make no wars? Men and governments must act to the best of their ability. There is no such thing as absolute certainty, but there is assurance sufficient for the purposes of human life. We may, and must, assume our opinion to be true for the guidance of our own conduct; and it is assuming no more when we forbid bad men to pervert society by the propagation of opinions which we regard as false and pernicious.

I answer, that it is assuming very much more. There is the greatest difference between presuming an opinion to be true because, with every opportunity for contesting it, it has not been refuted, and assuming its truth for the purpose of not permitting its refutation. Complete liberty of contradicting and disproving our opinion is the very condition which justifies us in assuming its truth for purposes of action; and on no other terms can a being with human faculties have any rational assurance of being right.

When we consider either the history of opinion or the ordinary conduct of human life, to what is it to be ascribed that the one and the other are no worse than they are? Not certainly to the inherent force of the human understanding, for on any matter not self-evident there are ninety-nine persons totally incapable of judging of it for one who is capable; and the capacity of the hundredth person is only comparative, for the majority of the eminent men of every past generation held many opinions now known to be erroneous, and did or approved numerous things which no one will now justify. Why is it, then, that there is on the whole a preponderance among mankind of rational opinions and rational conduct? If there really is this preponderance—which there must be unless human affairs are, and have always been, in an almost desperate state—it is owing to a quality of the human mind, the source of everything respectable in man either as an intellectual or as a moral being, namely, that his errors are corrigible. He is capable of rectifying his mistakes by discussion and experience. Not by experience alone. There must be discussion to show how experience is to be interpreted. Wrong opinions and practices gradually yield to fact and argument; but facts and arguments, to produce any effect on the mind, must be brought before it. Very few facts are able to tell their own story, without comments to bring out their meaning. The whole strength and value, then, of human judgment depending on the one property, that it can be set right when it is wrong, reliance can be placed on it only when the means of setting it right are kept constantly at hand. In the case of any person whose judgment is really deserving of confidence, how has it become so? Because he has kept his mind open to criticism of his opinions and conduct. Because it has been his practice to listen to all that could be said against him; to profit by as much of it as was just, and to expound to himself, and upon occasion to others, the fallacy of what was fallacious. Because he has felt that the only way in which a human being can make some approach to knowing the whole of a subject is by hearing what can be said about it by persons of every variety of opinion, and studying all modes in which it can be looked at by every character of mind. No wise man ever acquired his wisdom in any mode but this; not is it in the nature of human intellect to become wise in any other manner. The steady habit of correcting and completing his own opinion by collating it with those of others, so far from causing doubt and hesitation in carrying it into practice, is the only stable foundation for a just reliance on it; for, being cognizant of all that can, at least obviously, be said against him, and having taken up his position against all gainsayers—knowing that he has sought for objections and difficulties instead of avoiding them, and has shut out no light which can be thrown upon the subject from any quarter—he has a right to think his judgment better than that of any person, or any multitude, who have not gone through a similar process.

•          •          •

Let us now pass to the second division of the argument, and dismissing the supposition that any of the received opinions may be false, let us assume them to be true and examine into the worth of the manner in which they are likely to be held when their truth is not freely and openly canvassed. However unwillingly a person who has a strong opinion may admit the possibility that his opinion may be false, he ought to be moved by the consideration that, however true it may be, if it is not fully, frequently, and fearlessly discussed, it will be held as a dead dogma, not a living truth.

There is a class of persons (happily not quite so numerous as formerly) who think it enough if a person assents undoubtingly to what they think true, though he has no knowledge whatever of the grounds of the opinion and could not make a tenable defense of it against the most superficial objections. Such persons, if they can once get their creed taught from authority, naturally think that no good, and some harm, comes of its being allowed to be questioned. Where their influence prevails, they make it nearly impossible for the received opinion to be rejected wisely and considerately, though it may still be rejected rashly and ignorantly; for to shut out discussion entirely is seldom possible, and when it once gets in, beliefs not grounded on conviction are apt to give way before the slightest semblance of an argument. Waiving, however, this possibility—assuming that the true opinion abides in the mind, but abides as a prejudice, a belief independent of, and proof against, argument—this is not the way in which truth ought to be held by a rational being. This is not knowing the truth. Truth, thus held, is but one superstition the more, accidentally clinging to the words which enunciate a truth.

If the intellect and judgment of mankind ought to be cultivated, a thing which Protestants at least do not deny, on what can these faculties be more appropriately exercised by anyone than on the things which concern him so much that it is considered necessary for him to hold opinions on them? If the cultivation of the understanding consists in one thing more than in another, it is surely in learning the grounds of one's own opinions. Whatever people believe, on subjects on which it is of the first importance to believe rightly, they ought to be able to defend against at least the common objections. But, someone may say, "Let them be *taught* the grounds of their opinions. It does not follow that opinions must be merely parroted because they are never heard controverted. Persons who learn geometry do not simply commit the theorems to memory, but understand and learn likewise the demonstrations; and it would be absurd to say that they remain ignorant of the grounds of geometrical truths because they never hear anyone deny and attempt to disprove them." Undoubtedly; and such teaching suffices on a subject like mathematics, where there is nothing at all to be said on the wrong side of the question. The peculiarity of the evidence of mathematical truths is that all the argument is on one side. There are no objections, and no answers to objections. But on every subject on which difference of opinion is possible, the truth depends on a balance to be struck between two sets of conflicting reasons. Even in natural philosophy, there is always some other explanation possible of the same facts; some geocentric theory instead of heliocentric, some phlogiston instead of oxygen; and it has to be shown why that other theory cannot be the true one; and until this is shown, and until we know how it is shown, we do not understand the grounds of our opinion. But when we turn to subjects infinitely more complicated, to morals, religion, politics, social relations, and the business of life, three-fourths of the arguments for every disputed opinion consist in dispelling the appearances which favor some opinion different from it. The greatest orator, save one, of antiquity, has left it on record that he always studies his adversary's case with as great, if not still greater, intensity than even his own. What Cicero practiced as the means of forensic success requires to be imitated by all who study any subject in order to arrive at the truth. He who knows only his own side of the case knows little of that. His reasons may be good, and no one may have been able to refute them. But if he is equally unable to refute the reasons on the opposite side, if he does not so much as know what they are, he has no ground for preferring either opinion. The rational position for him would be suspension of judgment, and unless he contents himself with that, he is either led by authority or adopts, like the generality of the world, the side to which he feels most inclination. Nor is it enough that he should hear the arguments of adversaries from his own teachers, presented as they state them, and accompanied by what they offer as refutations. That is not the way to do justice to the arguments or bring them into real contact with his own mind. He must be able to hear them from persons who actually believe them, who defend them in earnest and do their very utmost for them. He must know them in their most plausible and persuasive form; he must feel the whole force of the difficulty which the true view of the subject has to encounter and dispose of, else he will never really possess himself of the portion of truth which meets and removes that difficulty. Ninety-nine in a hundred of what are called educated men are in this condition, even of those who can argue fluently for their opinions. Their conclusion may be true, but it might be false for anything they know; they have never thrown themselves into the mental position of those who think differently from them, and considered what such persons may have to say; and, consequently, they do not, in any proper sense of the word, know the doctrine which they themselves profess. . . .

We have now recognized the necessity to the mental well-being of mankind (on which all their other well-being depends) of freedom of opinion, and freedom of the expression of opinion, on four distinct grounds, which we will now briefly recapitulate:

First, if any opinion is compelled to silence, that opinion may, for aught we can certainly know, be true. To deny this is to assume our own infallibility.

Secondly, though the silenced opinion be an error, it may, and very commonly does, contain a portion of truth; and since the general or prevailing opinion on any subject is rarely or never the whole truth, it is only by the collision of adverse opinions that the remainder of the truth has any chance of being supplied.

Thirdly, even if the received opinion be not only true, but the whole truth; unless it is suffered to be, and actually is, vigorously and earnestly contested, it will, by most of those who receive it, be held in the manner of a prejudice, with little comprehension or feeling of its rational grounds. And not only this, but, fourthly, the meaning of the doctrine itself will be in danger of being lost or enfeebled, and deprived of its vital effect on the character and conduct; the dogma becoming a mere formal profession, inefficacious for good, but cumbering the ground and preventing the growth of any real and heartfelt conviction from reason or personal experience.

•          •          •

## Of Individuality, as One of the Elements of Well-Being

Such being the reasons which make it imperative that human beings should be free to form opinions and to express their opinions without reserve; and such the baneful consequences to the intellectual, and through that to the moral nature of man, unless this liberty is either conceded or asserted in spite of prohibition; let us next examine whether the same reasons do not require that men should be free to act upon their opinions—to carry these out in their lives without hindrance, either physical or moral, from their fellow men, so long as it is at their own risk and peril. This last proviso is of course indispensable. No one pretends that actions should be as free as opinions. On the contrary, even opinions lose their immunity when the circumstances in which they are expressed are such as to constitute their expression a positive instigation to some mischievous act. An opinion that corn dealers are starvers of the poor, or that private property is robbery, ought to be unmolested when simply circulated through the press, but may justly incur punishment when delivered orally to an excited mob assembled before the house of a corn dealer, or when handed about among the same mob in the form of a placard. Acts, of whatever kind, which without justifiable cause do harm to others may be, and in the more important cases absolutely require to be, controlled by the unfavorable sentiments, and, when needful, by the active interference of mankind. The liberty of the individual must be thus far limited; he must not make himself a nuisance to other people. But if he refrains from molesting others in what concerns them, and merely acts according to his own inclination and judgment in things which concern himself, the same reasons which show that opinion should be free prove also that he should be allowed, without molestations, to carry his opinions into practice at his own cost. That mankind are not infallible; that their truths, for the most part, are only half-truths; that unity of opinion, unless resulting from the fullest and freest comparison of opposite opinions, is not desirable, and diversity not an evil, but a good, until mankind are much more capable than at present of recognizing all sides of the truth, are principles applicable to men's modes of action not less than to their opinions. As it is useful that while mankind are imperfect there should be different opinions, so it is that there should be different experiments of living; that free scope should be given to varieties of character, short of injury to others; and that the worth of different modes of life should be proved practically, when anyone thinks fit to try them. It is desirable, in short, that in things which do not primarily concern others individuality should assert itself. Where not the person's own character but the traditions or customs of other people are the rule of conduct, there is wanting one of the principal ingredients of human happiness, and quite the chief ingredient of individual and social progress.

&bull;        &bull;        &bull;

Having said that individuality is the same thing with development, and that it is only the cultivation of individuality which produces, or can produce, well-developed human beings, I might here close the argument; for what more or better can be said of any condition of human affairs than that it brings human beings themselves nearer to the best thing they can be? Or what worse can be said of any obstruction to good than that it prevents this? Doubtless, however, these considerations will not suffice to convince those who most need convincing; and it is necessary further to show that these developed human beings are of some use to the undeveloped—to point out to those who do not desire liberty, and would not avail themselves of it, that they may be in some intelligible manner rewarded for allowing other people to make use of it without hindrance.

In the first place, then, I would suggest that they might possibly learn something from them. It will not be denied by anybody that originality is a valuable element in human affairs. There is always need of persons not only to discover new truths and point out when what were once truths are true no longer, but also to commence new practices and set the example of more enlightened conduct and better taste and sense in human life. This cannot well be gainsaid by anybody who does not believe that the world has already attained perfection in all its ways and practices. It is true that this benefit is not capable of being rendered by everybody alike; there are but few persons, in comparison with the whole of mankind, whose experiments, if adopted by others, would be likely to be any improvement on established practice. But these few are the salt of the earth; without them, human life would become a stagnant pool. Not only is it they who introduce good things which did not before exist; it is they who keep the life in those which already exist. If there were nothing new to be done, would human intellect cease to be necessary? Would it be a reason why those who do the old things should forget why they are done, and do them like cattle, not like human beings? There is only too great a tendency in the best beliefs and practices to degenerate into the mechanical; and unless there were a succession of persons whose ever-recurring originality prevents the grounds of those beliefs and practices from becoming merely traditional, such dead matter would not resist the smallest shock from anything really alive, and there would be no reason by civilization should not die out, as in the Byzantine Empire. . . .

I have said that it is important to give the freest scope possible to uncustomary things, in order that it may in time appear which of these are fit to be converted into customs. But independence of action and disregard of custom are not solely deserving of encouragement for the chance they afford that better modes of action, and customs more worthy of general adoption, may be struck out; nor is it only persons of decided mental superiority who have a just claim to carry on their lives in their own way. There is no reason that all human existence should be constructed on some one or some small number of patterns. If a person possesses any tolerable amount of common sense and experience, his own mode of laying out his existence is the best, not because it is the best in itself, but because it is his own mode. Human beings are not like sheep; and even sheep are not undistinguishably alike. A man cannot get a coat or a pair of boots to fit him unless they are either made to his measure or he has a whole warehouseful to choose from; and is it easier to fit him with a life than with a coat, or are human beings more like one another in their whole physical and spiritual conformation than in the shape of their feet? If it were only that people have diversities of taste, that is reason enough for not attempting to shape them all after one model. But different persons also require different conditions for their spiritual development; and can no more exist healthily in the same moral than all the variety of plants can in the same physical, atmosphere and climate. The same things which are helps to one person toward the cultivation of his higher nature are hindrances to another. The same mode of life is a healthy excitement to one, keeping all his faculties of action and enjoyment in their best order, while to another it is a distracting burden which suspends or crushes all internal life. Such are the differences among human beings in their sources of pleasure, the susceptibilities of pain, and the operation on them of different physical and moral agencies that, unless there is a corresponding diversity in their modes of life, they neither obtain their fair share of happiness, nor grow up to the mental, moral, and aesthetic stature of which their nature is capable.

## IMMANUEL KANT

# Ethics Founded on Reason

In this excerpt from his ***Groundwork of the Metaphysics of Morals,*** Kant (1724–1804) tries to show that ethics is founded on reason, not on inclinations. It is acting from duty, not from inclination, that endows an action with moral value. But what is the source of the duties that structure the moral life? These are founded on reason. The universalizability criterion provides a logical test for determining whether an action is morally permissible.

## CHAPTER I
## PASSAGE FROM ORDINARY RATIONAL KNOWLEDGE OR MORALITY TO PHILOSOPHICAL KNOWLEDGE

### [The Good Will]

It is impossible to conceive anything at all in the world, or even out of it, which can be taken as good without qualification, except a **good will.** Intelligence, wit, judgement, and any other *talents* of the mind we may care to name, or courage, resolution, and constancy of purpose, as qualities of *temperament,* are without doubt good and desirable in many respects; but they can also be extremely bad and hurtful when the will is not good which has to make use of these gifts of nature, and which for this reason has the term *"character"* applied to its peculiar quality. It is exactly the same with *gifts of fortune.* Power, wealth, honour, even health and that complete well-being and contentment with one's state which goes by the name of *"happiness"*, produce boldness, and as a consequence often overboldness as well, unless a good will is present by which their influence on the mind—and so too the whole principle of action—may be corrected and adjusted to universal ends; not to mention that a rational and impartial spectator can never feel approval in contemplating the uninterrupted prosperity of a being graced by no touch of a pure and good will, and that consequently a good will seems to constitute the indispensable condition of our very worthiness to be happy.

Some qualities are even helpful to this good will itself and can make its task very much easier. They have none the less no inner unconditioned worth, but rather presuppose a good will which sets a limit to the esteem in which they are rightly held and does not permit us to regard them as absolutely good. Moderation in affections and passions, self-control, and sober reflexion are not only good in many respects; they may even seem to constitute part of the *inner* worth of a person. Yet they are far from being properly described as good without qualification (however unconditionally they have been commended by the ancients). For without the principles of a good

Immanuel Kant, "Ethics Founded on Reason," from *Groundwork of the Metaphysics of Morals,* translated by H. J. Paton (London: Unwin Hyman Ltd., 1956), pp. 61–62, 64–67, 74, 80–92, 95–107. Reprinted by permission of Taylor & Frances Books, Ltd.

will they may become exceedingly bad; and the very coolness of a scoundrel makes him, not merely more dangerous, but also immediately more abominable in our eyes than we should have taken him to be without it.

## [The Good Will and Its Results]

A good will is not good because of what it effects or accomplishes—because of its fitness for attaining some proposed end: it is good through its willing alone—that is, good in itself. Considered in itself it is to be esteemed beyond comparison as far higher than anything it could ever bring about merely in order to favour some inclination or, if you like, the sum total of inclinations. Even if, by some special disfavour of destiny or by the niggardly endowment of step-motherly nature, this will is entirely lacking in power to carry out its intentions; if by its utmost effort it still accomplishes nothing, and only good will is left (not, admittedly, as a mere wish, but as the straining of every means so far as they are in our control); even then it would still shine like a jewel for its own sake as something which has its full value of itself. Its usefulness or fruitlessness can neither add to, nor subtract from, this value. Its usefulness would be merely, as it were, the setting which enables us to handle it better in our ordinary dealings or to attract the attention of those not yet sufficiently expert, but not to commend it to experts or to determine its value.

## [The Good Will and Duty]

We have now to elucidate the concept of a will estimable in itself and good apart from any further end. This concept, which is already present in a naturally sound understanding and requires not so much to be taught as merely to be clarified, always holds the highest place in estimating the total worth of our actions and constitutes the condition of all the rest. We will therefore take up the concept of **duty,** which includes that of a good will, exposed, however, to certain subjective limitations and obstacles. These, so far from hiding a good will or disguising it, rather bring it out by contrast and make it shine forth more brightly.

## [The Motive of Duty]

I will here pass over all actions already recognized as contrary to duty, however useful they may be with a view to this or that end; for about these the question does not even arise whether they could have been done *for the sake of duty* inasmuch as they are directly opposed to it. I will also set aside actions which in fact accord with duty, yet for which men have *no immediate inclination,* but perform them because impelled to do so by some other inclination. For there it is easy to decide whether the action which accords with duty has been done *from duty* or from some purpose of self-interest. This distinction is far more difficult to perceive when the action accords with duty and the subject has in addition an *immediate* inclination to the action. For example, it certainly accords with duty that a grocer should not overcharge his inexperienced customer; and where there is much competition a sensible shopkeeper refrains from so doing and keeps to a fixed and general price for everybody so that a child can buy from him just as well as anyone else. Thus people are served *honestly;* but this is not nearly enough to justify us in believing that the shopkeeper has acted in this way from duty or from principles of fair dealing; his interests required him to do so. We cannot assume him to have in addition an immediate inclination towards his customers, leading him, as it were out of love, to give no man preference over another in the matter of price. Thus the action was done neither from duty nor from immediate inclination, but solely from purposes of self-interest.

On the other hand, to preserve one's life is a duty, and besides this every one has also an immediate inclination to do so. But on account of this the often anxious precautions taken by the greater part of mankind for this purpose have no inner worth, and the maxim of their action is without moral content. They do protect their lives *in conformity with duty,* but not *from the motive of duty.* When, on the contrary, disappointments and hopeless misery have quite taken away the taste for life; when a wretched man, strong in soul and more angered at his fate than faint-hearted or cast down, longs for death and still preserves his life without loving it—not from inclination or fear but from duty; then indeed his maxim has a moral content.

To help others where one can is a duty, and besides this there are many spirits of so sympathetic a temper that, without any further motive of vanity or self-interest, they find an inner pleasure in spreading happiness around them and can take delight in the contentment of others as their own work. Yet I maintain that in such a case an action of this kind, however right and however amiable it may be, has still no genuinely moral worth. It stands on the same footing as other inclinations—for example, the inclination for honour, which if fortunate enough to hit on something beneficial and right and consequently honourable, deserves praise and encouragement, but not esteem; for its maxim lacks moral content, namely, the performance of such actions, not from inclination, but *from duty.* Suppose then that the mind of this friend of man was overclouded by sorrows of his own which extinguished all sympathy with the fate of others, but that he still had power to help those in distress, though no longer stirred by the need of others because sufficiently occupied with his own; and suppose that, when no longer moved by any inclination, he tears himself out of this deadly insensibility and does the action without any inclination for the sake of duty alone; then for the first time his action has its genuine moral worth. Still further: if nature had implanted little sympathy in this or that man's heart; if (being in other respects an honest fellow) he were cold in temperament and indifferent to the sufferings of others—perhaps because, being endowed with the special gift of patience and robust endurance in his own sufferings, he assumed the like in others or even demanded it; if such a man (who would in truth not be the worst product of nature) were not exactly fashioned by her to be a philanthropist, would he not still find in himself a source from which he might draw a worth far higher than any that a good-natured temperament can have? Assuredly he would. It is precisely in this that the worth of character begins to show—a moral worth and beyond all comparison the highest—namely that he does good, not from inclination, but from duty.

To assure one's own happiness is a duty (at least indirectly); for discontent with one's state, in a press of cares and amidst unsatisfied wants, might easily become a great *temptation to the transgression of duty.* But here also, apart from regard to duty, all men have already of themselves the strongest and deepest inclination towards happiness, because precisely in this Idea of happiness there is combined the sum total of inclinations. The prescription for happiness is, however, often so constituted as greatly to interfere with some inclinations, and yet men cannot form under the name of "happiness" any determinate and assured conception of the satisfaction of all inclinations as a sum. Hence it is not to be wondered at that a single inclination which is determinate as to what it promises and as to the time of its satisfaction may outweigh a wavering Idea; and that a man, for example, a sufferer from gout, may choose to enjoy what he fancies and put up with what he can—on the ground that on balance he has here at least not killed the enjoyment of the present moment because of some possibly groundless expectations of the good fortune supposed to attach to soundness of health. But in this case also, when the universal inclination towards happiness has failed to determine his will, when good health, at least for him, has not entered into his calculations as so necessary, what remains over, here as in other cases, is a law—the law of furthering his happiness, not from inclination, but from duty—and in this for the first time his conduct has a real moral worth.

It is doubtless in this sense that we should understand too the passages from Scripture in which we are commanded to love our neighbour and even our enemy. For love out of inclination cannot be commanded; but kindness done from duty—although no inclination impels us, and even although natural and unconquerable disinclination stands in our way—is *practical*, and not *pathological*, love, residing in the will and not in the propensions of feeling, in principles of action and not of melting compassion; and it is this practical love alone which can be an object of command.

# CHAPTER II
## PASSAGE FROM POPULAR MORAL PHILOSOPHY TO A METAPHYSIC OF MORALS

### [Imperatives in General]

Everything in nature works in accordance with laws. Only a rational being has the power to act *in accordance with his idea* of laws—that is, in accordance with principles—and only so has he a *will*. Since *reason* is required in order to derive actions from laws, the will is nothing but practical reason. If reason infallibly determines the will, then in a being of this kind the actions which are recognized to be objectively necessary are also subjectively necessary—that is to say, the will is then a power to choose *only that* which reason independently of inclination recognizes to be practically necessary, that is, to be good. But if reason solely by itself is not sufficient to determine the will; if the will is exposed also to subjective conditions (certain impulsions) which do not always harmonize with the objective ones; if, in a word, the will is not *in itself* completely in accord with reason (as actually happens in the case of men); then actions which are recognized to be objectively necessary are subjectively contingent, and the determining of such a will in accordance with objective laws is *necessitation*. That is to say, the relation of objective laws to a will not good through and through is conceived as one in which the will of a rational being, although it is determined by principles of reason, does not necessarily follow these principles in virtue of its own nature.

The conception of an objective principle so far as this principle is necessitating for a will is called a command (or reason), and the formula of this command is called an **Imperative.**

All imperatives are expressed by an *"ought" (Sollen).* By this they mark the relation of an objective law of reason to a will which is not necessarily determined by this law in virtue of its subjective constitution (the relation of necessitation). They say that something would be good to do or to leave undone; only they say it to a will which does not always do a thing because it has been informed that this is a good thing to do. The practically *good* is that which determines the will by concepts of reason, and therefore not by subjective causes, but objectively—that is, on grounds valid for every rational being as such. It is distinguished from the *pleasant* as that which influences the will, not as a principle of reason valid for every one, but solely through the medium of sensation by purely subjective causes valid only for the senses of this person or that.

A perfectly good will would thus stand quite as much under objective laws (laws of the good), but it could not on this account be conceived as *necessitated* to act in conformity with law, since of itself, in accordance with its subjective constitution, it can be determined only by the concept of the good. Hence for the *divine* will, and in general for a *holy* will, there are no imperatives: *"I ought"* is here out of place, because *"I will"* is already of itself necessarily in harmony with the law. Imperatives are in consequence only formulae for expressing the relation of objective laws of willing to the subjective imperfection of the will of this or that rational being—for example, of the human will.

## [Classification of Imperatives]

All *imperatives* command either *hypothetically* or *categorically.* Hypothetical imperatives declare a possible action to be practically necessary as a means to the attainment of something else that one wills (or that one may will). A categorical imperative would be one which represented an action as objectively necessary in itself apart from its relation to a further end.

Every practical law represents a possible action as good and therefore as necessary for a subject whose actions are determined by reason. Hence all imperatives are formulae for determining an action which is necessary in accordance with the principle of a will in some sense good. If the action would be good solely as a means *to something else, the imperative is hypothetical; if the action is represented as good in itself* and therefore necessary, in virtue of its principle, for a will which of itself accords with reason, then the imperative is *categorical.*

An imperative therefore tells me which of my possible actions would be good; and it formulates a practical rule for a will that does not perform an action straight away because the action is good—whether because the subject does not always know that it is good or because, even if he did know this, he might still act on maxims contrary to the objective principles of practical reason.

A hypothetical imperative thus says only that an action is good for some purpose or other, either *possible* or *actual*. In the first case it is a **problematic** practical principle; in the second case an **assertoric** practical principle. A categorical imperative, which declares an action to be objectively necessary in itself without reference to some purpose—that is, even without any further end—ranks as an **apodeictic** practical principle.

Everything that is possible only through the efforts of some rational being can be conceived as a possible purpose of some will; and consequently there are in fact innumerable principles of action so far as action is thought necessary in order to achieve some possible purpose which can be effected by it. All sciences have a practical part consisting of problems which suppose that some end is possible for us and of imperatives which tell us how it is to be attained. Hence the latter can in general be called imperatives of **skill.** Here there is absolutely no question about the rationality or goodness of the end, but only about what must be done to attain it. A prescription required by a doctor in order to cure his man completely and one required by a poisoner in order to make sure of killing him are of equal value so far as each serves to effect its purpose perfectly. Since in early youth we do not know what ends may present themselves to us in the course of life, parents seek above all to make their children learn things *of many kinds;* they provide carefully for *skill* in the use of means to all sorts of *arbitrary* ends, of none of which can they be certain that it could not in the future become an actual purpose of their ward, while it is always *possible* that he might adopt it. Their care in this matter is so great that they commonly neglect on this account to form and correct the judgement of their children about the worth of things which they might possibly adopt as ends.

There is, however, *one* end that can be presupposed as actual in all rational beings (so far as they are dependent beings to whom imperatives apply); and thus there is one purpose which they not only *can* have, but which we can assume with certainty that they all *do* have by a natural necessity—the purpose, namely, of *happiness.* A hypothetical imperative which affirms the practical necessity of an action as a means to the furtherance of happiness is **assertoric.** We may present it, not simply as necessary to an uncertain, merely possible purpose, but as necessary to a purpose which we can presuppose a priori and with certainty to be present in every man because it belongs to his very being. Now skill in the choice of means to one's own greatest well-being can be called *prudence* in the narrowest sense. Thus an imperative concerned with the choice of means to one's own happiness—that is, a precept of prudence—still remains *hypothetical;* an action is commanded, not absolutely, but only as a means to a further purpose.

Finally, there is an imperative which, without being based on, and conditioned by, any further purpose to be attained by a certain line of conduct, enjoins this conduct immediately. This imperative is **categorical.** It is concerned, not with the matter of the action and its presumed results, but with its form and with the principle from which it follows; and what is essentially good in the action consists in the mental disposition, let the consequences be what they may. This imperative may be called the imperative of **morality.**

Willing in accordance with these three kinds of principle is also sharply distinguished by a *dissimilarity* in the necessitation of the will. To make this dissimilarity obvious we should, I think, name these kinds of principle most appropriately in their order if we said they were either *rules* of skill or *counsels* of prudence or *commands (laws)* of morality. For only *law* carries with it the concept of an *unconditioned,* and yet objective and so universally valid, *necessity;* and commands are laws which must be obeyed— that is, must be followed even against inclination. *Counsel* does indeed involve necessity, but necessity valid only under a subjective and contingent condition— namely, if this or that man counts this or that as belonging to his happiness. As against this, a categorical imperative is limited by no condition and can quite precisely be called a command, as being absolutely, although practically, necessary. We could also call imperatives of the first kind *technical* (concerned with art); of the second kind *pragmatic* (concerned with well-being); of the third kind *moral* (concerned with free conduct as such—that is, with morals).

## [How Are Imperatives Possible?]

The question now arises "How are all these imperatives possible?" This question does not ask how we can conceive the execution of an action commanded by the imperative, but merely how we can conceive the necessitation of the will expressed by the imperative in setting us a task. How an imperative of skill is possible requires no special discussion. Who wills the end, wills (so far as reason has decisive influence on his actions) also the means which are indispensably necessary and in his power. So far as willing is concerned, this proposition is analytic: for in my willing of an object as an effect there is already conceived the causality of myself as an acting cause—that is, the use of means; and from the concept of willing an end the imperatives merely extracts the concept of actions necessary to this end. (Synthetic propositions are required in order to determine the means of a proposed end, but these are concerned, not with the reason for performing the act of will, but with the cause which produces the object.) That in order to divide a line into two equal parts on a sure principle I must from its ends describe two intersecting arcs—this is admittedly taught by mathematics only in synthetic propositions; but when I know that the aforesaid effect can be produced only by such an action, the proposition "If I fully will the effect, I also will the action required for it" is analytic; for it is one and the same thing to conceive something as an effect possible in a certain way through me and to conceive myself as acting in the same way with respect to it.

If it were only as easy to find a determinate concept of happiness, the imperatives of prudence would agree entirely with those of skill and would be equally analytic. For here as there it could alike be said "Who wills the end, wills also (necessarily, if he accords with reason) the sole means which are in his power." Unfortunately, however, the concept of happiness is so indeterminate a concept that although every man wants to attain happiness, he can never say definitely and in unison with himself what it really is that he wants and wills. The reason for this is that all the elements which belong to the concept of happiness are without exception empirical—that is, they must be borrowed from experience; but that none the less there is required for the Idea of happiness an absolute whole, a maximum of well-being in my present, and in every future, state. Now it is impossible for the most intelligent, and at the same time most powerful, but nevertheless finite, being to form here a determinate concept of what he really wills. Is it riches that he wants? How much anxiety, envy, and pestering might he not bring in this way on his own head! Is it knowledge and insight? This might perhaps merely give him an eye so sharp that it would make evils at present hidden from him and yet unavoidable seem all the more frightful, or would add a load of still further needs to the desires which already give him trouble enough. Is it long life? Who will guarantee that it would not be a long misery? Is it at least healthy? How often has infirmity of body kept a man from excesses into which perfect health would have let him fall—and so on. In short, he has no principle by which he is able to decide with complete certainty what will make him truly happy, since for this he would require omniscience. Thus we cannot act on determinate principles in order to be happy, but only on empirical counsels, for example, of diet, frugality, politeness, reserve, and so on—things which experience shows contribute most to well-being on the average. From this it follows that imperatives of prudence, speaking strictly, do not command at all—that is, cannot exhibit actions objectively as practically *necessary;* that they are rather to be taken as recommendations *(consilia),* than as commands *(praecepta),* of reason; that the problem of determining certainly and universally what action will promote the happiness of a rational being is completely insoluble; and consequently that in regard to this there is no imperative possible which in the strictest sense could command us to do what will make us happy, since happiness is an Ideal, not of reason, but of imagination—an Ideal resting merely on empirical grounds, of which it is vain to expect that they should determine an action by which we could attain the totality of a series of consequences which is in fact infinite. Nevertheless, if we assume that the means to happiness could be discovered with certainty, this imperative of prudence would be an analytic practical proposition; for it differs from the imperative of skill only in this—that in the latter the end is merely possible, while in the former the end is given. In spite of this difference, since both command solely the means to something assumed to be willed as an end, the imperative which commands him who wills the end to will the means is in both cases analytic. Thus there is likewise no difficulty in regard to the possibility of an imperative of prudence.

As against this, the question "How is the imperative of *morality* possible?" is the only one in need of a solution; for it is in no way hypothetical, and consequently we cannot base the objective necessity which it affirms on any presupposition, as we can with hypothetical imperatives. Only we must never forget here that it is impossible to settle *by an example,* and so empirically, whether there is any imperative of this kind at all: we must rather suspect that all imperatives which seem to be categorical may none the less be covertly hypothetical. Take, for example, the saying "Thou shalt make no false promises." Let us assume that the necessity for this abstention is no mere advice for the avoidance of some further evil—as it might be said "You ought not to make a lying promise lest, when this comes to light, you destroy your credit." Let us hold, on the contrary, that an action of this kind must be considered as bad in itself, and that the imperative of prohibition is therefore categorical. Even so, we cannot with any certainty show by an example that the will is determined here solely by the law without any further motive, although it may appear to be so; for it is always possible that fear of disgrace, perhaps also hidden dread of other risks, may unconsciously influence the will. Who can prove by experience that a cause is not present?

Experience shows only that it is not perceived. In such a case, however, the so-called moral imperative, which as such appears to be categorical and unconditioned, would in fact be only a pragmatic prescription calling attention to our advantage and merely bidding us take this into account.

We shall thus have to investigate the possibility of a *categorical* imperative entirely a priori, since here we do not enjoy the advantage of having its reality given in experience and so of being obliged merely to explain, and not to establish, its possibility. So much, however, can be seen provisionally—that the categorical imperative alone purports to be a practical **law,** while all the rest may be called *principles* of the will but not laws; for an action necessary merely in order to achieve an arbitrary purpose can be considered as in itself contingent, and we can always escape from the precept if we abandon the purpose; whereas an unconditioned command does not leave it open to the will to do the opposite at its discretion and therefore alone carries with it that necessity which we demand from a law.

In the second place, with this categorical imperative or law of morality the reason for our difficulty (in comprehending its possibility) is a very serious one. We have here a synthetic a priori practical proposition; and since in theoretical knowledge there is so much difficulty in comprehending the possibility of propositions of this kind, it may readily be gathered that in practical knowledge the difficulty will be no less.

## [The Formula of Universal Law]

In this task we wish first to enquire whether perhaps the mere concept of a categorical imperative may not also provide us with the formula containing the only proposition that can be a categorical imperative; for even when we know the purport of such an absolute command, the question of its possibility will still require a special and troublesome effort, which we postpone to the final chapter.

When I conceive a *hypothetical* imperative in general, I do not know beforehand what it will contain—until its condition is given. But if I conceive a *categorical* imperative, I know at once what it contains. For since besides the law this imperative contains only the necessity that our maxim should conform to this law, while the law, as we have seen, contains no condition to limit it, there remains nothing over to which the maxim has to conform except the universality of a law as such; and it is this conformity alone that the imperative properly asserts to be necessary.

There is therefore only a single categorical imperative and it is this: *"Act only on that maxim through which you can at the same time will that it should become a universal law."*

Now if all imperatives of duty can be derived from this one imperative as their principle, then even although we leave it unsettled whether what we call duty may not be an empty concept, we shall still be able to show at least what we understand by it and what the concept means.

## [The Formula of the Law of Nature]

Since the universality of the law governing the production of effects constitutes what is properly called *nature* in its most general sense (nature as regards its form)—that is, the existence of things so far as determined by universal laws—the universal imperative of duty may also run as follows: *"Act as if the maxim of your action were to become through your will a Universal Law of Nature."*

## [Illustrations]

We will now enumerate a few duties, following their customary division into duties towards self and duties towards others and into perfect and imperfect duties.

1. A man feels sick of life as the result of a series of misfortunes that has mounted to the point of despair, but he is still so far in possession of his reason as to ask himself whether taking his own life may not be contrary to his duty to himself. He now applies the test "Can the maxim of my action really become a universal law of nature?" His maxim is "From self-love I make it my principle to shorten my life if its continuance threatens more evil than it promises pleasure." The only further question to ask is whether this principle of self-love can become a universal law of nature. It is then seen at once that a system of nature by whose law the very same feeling whose function *(Bestimmung)* is to stimulate the furtherance of life should actually destroy life would contradict itself and consequently could not subsist as a system of nature. Hence this maxim cannot possibly hold as a universal law of nature and is therefore entirely opposed to the supreme principle of all duty.
2. Another finds himself driven to borrowing money because of need. He well knows that he will not be able to pay it back; but he sees too that he will get no loan unless he gives a firm promise to pay it back within a fixed time. He is inclined to make such a promise; but he has still enough conscience to ask "Is it not unlawful and contrary to duty to get out of difficulties in this way?" Supposing, however, he did resolve to do so, the maxim of his action would run thus: "Whenever I believe myself short of money, I will borrow money and promise to pay it back, though I know that this will never be done." Now this principle of self-love or personal advantage is perhaps quite compatible with my own entire future welfare; only there remains the question "Is it right?" I therefore transform the demand of self-love into a universal law and frame my question thus: "How would things stand if my maxim became a universal law?" I then see straight away that this maxim can never rank as a universal law and be self-consistent, but must necessarily contradict itself. For the universality of a law that every one believing himself to be in need may make any promise he pleases with the intention not to keep it would make promising, and the very purpose of promising, itself impossible, since no one would believe he was being promised anything, but would laugh at utterances of this kind as empty shams.
3. A third finds in himself a talent whose cultivation would make him a useful man for all sorts of purposes. But he sees himself in comfortable circumstances, and he prefers to give himself up to pleasure rather than to bother about increasing and improving his fortunate natural aptitudes. Yet he asks himself further "Does my maxim of neglecting my natural gifts, besides agreeing in itself with my tendency to indulgence, agree also with what is called duty?" He then sees that a system of nature could indeed always subsist under such a universal law,

although (like the South Sea Islanders) every man should let his talents rust and should be bent on devoting his life solely to idleness, indulgence, procreation, and, in a word, to enjoyment. Only he cannot possibly **will** that this should become a universal law of nature or should be implanted in us as such a law by a natural instinct. For as a rational being he necessarily wills that all his powers should be developed, since they serve him, and are given him, for all sorts of possible ends.

4. Yet a *fourth* is himself flourishing, but he sees others who have to struggle with great hardships (and whom he could easily help); and he thinks "What does it matter to me? Let every one be as happy as Heaven wills or as he can make himself; I won't deprive him of anything; I won't even envy him; only I have no wish to contribute anything to his well-being or to his support in distress!" Now admittedly if such an attitude were a universal law of nature, mankind could get on perfectly well—better no doubt than if everybody prates about sympathy and good will, and even takes pains, on occasion, to practise them, but on the other hand cheats where he can, traffics in human rights, or violates them in other ways. But although it is possible that a universal law of nature could subsist in harmony with this maxim, yet it is impossible to **will** that such a principle should hold everywhere as a law of nature. For a will which decided in this way would be at variance with itself, since many a situation might arise in which the man needed love and sympathy from others, and in which, by such a law of nature sprung from his own will, he would rob himself of all hope of the help he wants for himself.

### [The Canon of Moral Judgement]

These are some of the many actual duties—or at least of what we take to be such—whose derivation from the single principle cited above leaps to the eye. We must *be able to will* that a maxim of our action should become a universal law—this is the general canon for all moral judgement of action. Some actions are so constituted that their maxim cannot even be *conceived* as a universal law of nature without contradiction, let alone be *willed* as what *ought* to become one. In the case of others we do not find this inner impossibility, but it is still impossible to *will* that their maxim should be raised to the universality of a law of nature, because such a will would contradict itself. It is easily seen that the first kind of action is opposed to strict or narrow (rigorous) duty, the second only to wider (meritorious) duty; and thus that by these examples all duties—so far as the type of obligation is concerned (not the object of dutiful action)—are fully set out in their dependence on our single principle.

If we now attend to ourselves whenever we transgress a duty, we find that we in fact do not will that our maxim should become a universal law—since this is impossible for us—but rather that its opposite should remain a law universally; we only take the liberty of making an *exception* to it for ourselves (or even just for this once) to the advantage of our inclination. Consequently if we weighed it all up from one and the same point of view—that of reason—we should find a contradiction in our own will, the contradiction that a certain principle should be objectively necessary as a universal law and yet subjectively should not hold universally but should admit of exceptions.

Since, however, we first consider our action from the point of view of a will wholly in accord with reason, and then consider precisely the same action from the point of view of a will affected by inclination, there is here actually no contradiction, but rather an opposition of inclination to the precept of reason *(antagonismus)*, whereby the universality of the principle *(universalitas)* is turned into a mere generality *(generalitas)* so that the practical principle of reason may meet our maxim half-way. This procedure, though in our own impartial judgement it cannot be justified, proves none the less that we can in fact recognize the validity of the categorical imperative and (with all respect for it) merely permit ourselves a few exceptions which are, as we pretend, inconsiderable and apparently forced upon us.

We have thus at least shown much—that if duty is a concept which is to have meaning and real legislative authority for our actions, this can be expressed only in categorical imperatives and by no means in hypothetical ones. At the same time—and this is already a great deal—we have set forth distinctly, and determinately for every type of application, the content of the categorical imperative, which must contain the principle of all duty (if there is to be such a thing at all). But we are still not so far advanced as to prove a priori that there actually is an imperative of this kind—that there is a practical law which by itself commands absolutely and without any further motives, and that the following of this law is duty.

## [The Formula of the End in Itself]

The will is conceived as a power of determining oneself to action *in accordance with the idea of certain laws*. And such a power can be found only in rational beings. Now what serves the will as a subjective ground of its self-determination is an *end;* and this, if it is given by reason alone, must be equally valid for all rational beings. What, on the other hand, contains merely the ground of the possibility of an action whose effect as an end is called a *means*. The subjective ground of a desire is an *impulsion (Triebfeder);* the objective ground of a volition is a *motive (Bewegungsgrund)*. Hence the difference between subjective ends, which are based on impulsions, and objective ends, which depend on motives valid for every rational being. Practical principles are *formal* if they abstract from all subjective ends; they are *material,* on the other hand, if they are based on such ends and consequently on certain impulsions. Ends that a rational being adopts arbitrarily as *effects* of his action (material ends) are in every case only relative; for it is solely their relation to special characteristics in the subject's power of appetition which gives them their value. Hence this value can provide no universal principles, no principles valid and necessary for all rational beings and also for every volition—that is, no practical laws. Consequently all these relative ends can be the ground only of hypothetical imperatives.

Suppose, however, there were something *whose existence* has *in itself* an absolute value, something which as *an end in itself* could be a ground of determinate laws; then in it, and in it alone, would there be the ground of a possible categorical imperative— that is, of a practical law.

Now I say that man, and in general every rational being, *exists as an end in himself, not merely as a means* for arbitrary use by this or that will: he must in all his actions, whether they are directed to himself or to other rational beings, always be viewed *at the same time as an end.* All the objects of inclination have only a conditioned value; for if there were not these inclinations and the needs grounded on them, their object would be valueless. Inclinations themselves, as sources of needs, are so far from having an absolute value to make them desirable for their own sake that it must rather be the universal wish of every rational being to be wholly free from them. Thus the value of all objects that can *be produced* by our action is always conditioned. Beings whose existence depends, not on our will, but on nature, have none the less, if they are non-rational beings, only a relative value as means and are consequently called *things.* Rational beings, on the other hand, are called *persons* because their nature already marks them out as ends in themselves—that is, as something which ought not to be used merely as a means—and consequently imposes to that extent a limit on all arbitrary treatment of them (and is an object of reverence). Persons, therefore, are not merely subjective ends whose existence as an effect of our actions has a value *for us:* they are *objective ends*—that is, things whose existence is in itself an end, and indeed an end such that in its place we can put no other end to which they should serve *simply* as means; for unless this is so, nothing at all of *absolute* value would be found anywhere. But if all value were conditioned—that is, contingent—then no supreme principle could be found for reason at all.

If then there is to be a supreme practical principle and—so far as the human will is concerned—a categorical imperative, it must be such that from the idea of something which is necessarily an end for every one because it is an *end in itself* it forms an *objective* principle of the will and consequently can serve as a practical law. The ground of this principle is: *Rational nature exists as an end in itself.* This is the way in which a man necessarily conceives his own existence; it is therefore so far a *subjective* principle of human actions. But it is also the way in which every other rational being conceives his existence on the same rational ground which is valid also for me; hence it is at the same time an *objective* principle, from which, as a supreme practical ground, it must be possible to derive all laws for the will. The practical imperative will therefore be as follows: *Act in such a way that you always treat humanity, whether in your own person or in the person of any other, never simply as a means, but always at the same time as an end.* We will now consider whether this can be carried out in practice.

### [Illustrations]

Let us keep to our previous examples.

*First,* as regards the concept of necessary duty to oneself, the man who contemplates suicide will ask "Can my action be compatible with the Idea of humanity *as an end in itself*?" If he does away with himself in order to escape from a painful situation, he is making use of a person merely as a *means* to maintain a tolerable state of affairs till the end of his life. But man is not a thing—not something to be used *merely* as a means: he must always in all his actions be regarded as an end in himself. Hence I cannot dispose of man in my person by maiming, spoiling, or killing. (A more precise determination of this principle in order to avoid all misunderstanding—for example, about having limbs amputated to save myself or about exposing my life to danger in order to preserve it, and so on—I must here forgo: this question belongs to morals proper.)

*Secondly,* so far as necessary or strict duty to others is concerned, the man who has a mind to make a false promise to others will see at once that he is intending to make use of another man *merely as a means* to an end he does not share. For the man whom I seek to use for my own purposes by such a promise cannot possibly agree with my way of behaving to him, and so cannot himself share the end of the action. This incompatibility with the principle of duty to others leaps to the eye more obviously when we bring in examples of attempts on the freedom and property of others. For then it is manifest that a violator of the rights of man intends to use the person of others merely as a means without taking into consideration that, as rational beings, they ought always at the same time to be rated as ends—that is, only as beings who must themselves be able to share in the end of the very same action.

*Thirdly,* in regard to contingent (meritorious) duty to oneself, it is not enough that an action should refrain from conflicting with humanity in our own person as an end in itself: it must also *harmonize with this end.* Now there are in humanity capacities for greater perfection which form part of nature's purpose for humanity in our person. To neglect these can admittedly be compatible with the *maintenance* of humanity as an end in itself, but not with the *promotion* of this end.

*Fourthly,* as regards meritorious duties to others, the natural end which all men seek is their own happiness. Now humanity could no doubt subsist if everybody contributed nothing to the happiness of others but at the same time refrained from deliberately impairing their happiness. This is, however, merely to agree negatively and not positively with *humanity as an end in itself* unless every one endeavours also, so far as in him lies, to further the ends of others. For the ends of a subject who is an end in himself must, if this conception is to have its *full* effect in me, be also, as far as possible, *my* ends.

## [The Formula of Autonomy]

This principle of humanity, and in general of every rational agent, *as an end in itself* (a principle which is the supreme limiting condition of every man's freedom of action) is not borrowed from experience; firstly, because it is universal, applying as it does to all rational beings as such, and no experience is adequate to determine universality; secondly, because in it humanity is conceived, not as an end of man (subjectively)—that is, as an object which, as a matter of fact, happens to be made an end—but as an objective end—one which, be our ends what they may, must, as a law, constitute the supreme limiting condition of all subjective ends and so must spring from pure reason. That is to say, the ground for every enactment of practical law lies *objectively in the rule* and in the form of universality which (according to our first principle) makes the rule capable of being a law (and indeed a law of nature); *subjectively,* however, it lies in the *end;* but (according to our second principle) the subject of all ends is to be found in every rational being as an end in himself. From this there now follows our third practical principle for the will—as the supreme condition of the will's conformity with universal practical reason—namely, the Idea *of the will of* every rational being as a will which makes universal law.

By this principle all maxims are repudiated which cannot accord with the will's own enactment of universal law. The will is therefore not merely subject to the law, but is so subject that it must be considered as also *making the law* for itself and precisely on this account as first of all subject to the law (of which it can regard itself as the author).

## [The Exclusion of Interest]

Imperatives as formulated above—namely, the imperative enjoining conformity of actions to universal law on the analogy of a *natural order* and that enjoining the universal *supremacy* of rational beings in themselves *as ends*—did, by the mere fact that they were represented as categorical, exclude from their sovereign authority every admixture of interest as a motive. They were, however, merely *assumed* to be categorical because we were bound to make this assumption if we wished to explain the concept of duty. That they were practical propositions which commanded categorically could not itself be proved, any more than it can be proved in this chapter generally; but one thing could have been done—namely, to show that in willing for the sake of duty renunciation of all interest, as the specific mark distinguishing a categorical from a hypothetical imperative, was expressed in the very imperative itself by means of some determination inherent in it. This is what is done in the present third formulation of the principle—namely, in the Idea of the will of every rational being as *a will which makes universal law.*

Once we conceive a will of this kind, it becomes clear that while a will *which is subject to law* may be bound to this law by some interest, nevertheless a will which is itself a supreme lawgiver cannot possibly as such depend on any interest; for a will which is dependent in this way would itself require yet a further law in order to restrict the interest of self-love to the condition that this interest should itself be valid as a universal law.

Thus the *principle* that every human will is *a will which by all its maxims enacts universal law*—provided only that it were right in other ways—would be *well suited* to be a categorical imperative in this respect: that precisely because of the idea of making universal law it is *based on no interest* and consequently can alone among all possible imperatives be *unconditioned*. Or better still—to convert the proposition—if there is a categorical imperative (that is, a law for the will of every rational being), it can command us only to act always on the maxim of such a will in us as can at the same time look upon itself as making universal law; for only then is the practical principle and the imperative which we obey unconditioned, since it is wholly impossible for it to be based on any interest.

We need not now wonder, when we look back upon all the previous efforts that have been made to discover the principle of morality, why they have one and all been bound to fail. Their authors saw man as tied to laws by his duty, but it never occurred to them that he is subject only to *laws which are made by himself* and yet are *universal*, and that he is bound only to act in accordance with a will which is his own but has for its natural purpose the function of making universal law. For when they thought of man merely as subject to a law (whatever it might be), the law had to carry with it some interest in order to attract or compel, because it did not spring as a law from *his own* will: in order to conform with the law his will had to be necessitated by *something else* to act in a certain way. This absolutely inevitable conclusion meant that all the labour spent in trying to find a supreme principle of duty was lost beyond recall; for what they discovered was never duty, but only the necessity of acting from a certain interest. This interest might be one's own or another's; but on such a view the imperative was bound to be always a conditioned one and could not possibly serve as a moral law. I will therefore call my principle the principle of the **Autonomy** of the will in contrast with all others, which I consequently class under **Heteronomy.**

## [The Formula of the Kingdom of Ends]

The concept of every rational being as one who must regard himself as making universal law by all the maxims of his will, and must seek to judge himself and his actions from this point of view, leads to a closely connected and very fruitful concept—namely, that of a *kingdom of ends.*

I understand by a *"kingdom"* a systematic union of different rational beings under common laws. Now since laws determine ends as regards their universal validity, we shall be able—if we abstract from the personal differences between rational beings, and also from all the content of their private ends—to conceive a whole of all ends in systematic conjunction (a whole both of rational beings as ends in themselves and also of the personal ends which each may set before himself); that is, we shall be able to conceive a kingdom of ends which is possible in accordance with the above principles.

For rational beings all stand under the *law* that each of them should treat himself and all others, *never merely as a means,* but always *at the same time as an end in himself.* But by so doing there arises a systematic union of rational beings under common objective laws—that is, a kingdom. Since these laws are directed precisely to the relation of such beings to one another as ends and means, this kingdom can be called a kingdom of ends (which is admittedly only an Ideal).

A rational being belongs to the kingdom of ends as a *member,* when, although he makes its universal laws, he is also himself subject to these laws. He belongs to it as its *head,* when as the maker of laws he is himself subject to the will of no other.

A rational being must always regard himself as making laws in a kingdom of ends which is possible through freedom of the will—whether it be as member or as head. The position of the latter he can maintain, not in virtue of the maxim of his will alone, but only if he is a completely independent being, without needs and with an unlimited power adequate to his will.

Thus morality consists in the relation of all action to the making of laws whereby alone a kingdom of ends is possible. This making of laws must be found in every rational being himself and must be able to spring from his will. The principle of his will is therefore never to perform an action except on a maxim such as can also be a universal law, and consequently such *that the will can regard itself as at the same time making universal law by means of its maxim.* Where maxims are not already by their very nature in harmony with this objective principle of rational beings as makers of universal law, the necessity of acting on this principle is practical necessitation—that is, *duty.* Duty does not apply to the head in a kingdom of ends, but it does apply to every member and to all members in equal measure.

The practical necessity of acting on this principle—that is, duty—is in no way based on feelings, impulses, and inclinations, but only on the relation of rational beings to one another, a relation in which the will of a rational being must always be regarded as *making universal law*, because otherwise he could not be conceived as *an end in himself*. Reason thus relates every maxim of the will, considered as making universal law, to every other will and also to every action towards oneself: it does so, not because of any further motive or future advantage, but from the Idea of the *dignity* of a rational being who obeys no law other than that which he at the same time enacts himself.

## [The Dignity of Virtue]

In the kingdom of ends everything has either a *price* or a *dignity*. If it has a price, something else can be put in its place as an *equivalent*; if it is exalted above all price and so admits of no equivalent, then it has a dignity.

What is relative to universal human inclinations and needs has a *market price*; what, even without presupposing a need, accords with a certain taste—that is, with satisfaction in the mere purposeless play of our mental powers—has a *fancy price (Affektionspreis)*; but that which constitutes the sole condition under which anything can be an end in itself has not merely a relative value—that is, a price—but has an intrinsic value—that is, *dignity*.

Now morality is the only condition under which a rational being can be an end in himself; for only through this is it possible to be a law-making member in a kingdom of ends. Therefore morality, and humanity so far as it is capable of morality, is the only thing which has dignity. Skill and diligence in work have a market price; wit, lively imagination, and humour have a fancy price; but fidelity to promises and kindness based on principle (not on instinct) have an intrinsic worth. In default of these, nature and art alike contain nothing to put in their place; for their worth consists, not in the effects which result from them, not in the advantage or profit they produce, but in the attitudes of mind—that is, in the maxims of the will—which are ready in this way to manifest themselves in action even if they are not favoured by success. Such actions too need no recommendation from any subjective disposition or taste in order to meet with immediate favour and approval; they need no immediate propensity or feeling for themselves; they exhibit the will which performs them as an object of immediate reverence; nor is anything other than reason required to *impose* them upon the will, not to *coax* them from the will—which last would anyhow be a contradiction in the case of duties. This assessment reveals as dignity the value of such a mental attitude and puts it infinitely above all price, with which it cannot be brought into reckoning or comparison without, as it were, a profanation of its sanctity.

What is it then that entitles a morally good attitude of mind—of virtue—to make claims so high? It is nothing less than the *share* which it affords to a rational being *in the making of universal law*, and which therefore fits him to be a member in a possible kingdom of ends. For this he was already marked out in virtue of his own proper nature as an end in himself and consequently as a maker of laws in the kingdom of ends—as free in respect of all laws of nature, obeying only those laws which he makes himself and in virtue of which his maxims can have their part in the making of universal law (to which he at the same time subjects himself). For nothing can have a value other than that determined for it by the law. But the law-making which determines all value must for this reason have a dignity—that is, an unconditioned and incomparable worth—for the appreciation of which, as necessarily given by a rational being, the word *"reverence"* is the only becoming expression. *Autonomy* is therefore the ground of the dignity of human nature and of every rational nature.

## [REVIEW OF THE FORMULAE]

The aforesaid three ways of representing the principle of morality are at bottom merely so many formulations of precisely the same law, one of them by itself containing a combination of the other two. There is nevertheless a difference between them, which, however, is subjectively rather than objectively practical; that is to say, its purpose is to bring an Idea of reason nearer to intuition (in accordance with a certain analogy) and so nearer to feeling. All maxims have, in short,

1.  a *form*, which consists in their universality; and in this respect the formula of the moral imperative is expressed thus: "Maxims must be chosen as if they had to hold as universal laws of nature";
2.  a *matter*—that is, an end; and in this respect the formula says: "A rational being, as by his very nature an end and consequently an end in himself, must serve for every maxim as a condition limiting all merely relative and arbitrary ends";
3.  a *complete determination* of all maxims by the following formula, namely: "All maxims as proceeding from our own making of law ought to harmonize with a possible kingdom of ends as a kingdom of nature." This progression may be said to take place through the categories of the *unity of* the form of will (its universality); of the *multiplicity* of its matter (its objects—that is, its ends); and of the *totality* or completeness of its systems of ends. It is, however, better if in moral *judgement* we proceed always in accordance with the strictest method and take as our basis the universal formula of the categorical imperative; *"Act on the maxim which can at the same time be made a universal law."* If, however, we wish also to secure acceptance for the moral law, it is very useful to bring one and the same action under the above-mentioned three concepts and so, as far as we can, to bring the universal formula nearer to intuition.

### [Review of the Whole Argument]

We can now end at the point from which we started out at the beginning—namely, the concept of an unconditionally good will. The *will* is *absolutely good* if it cannot be evil—that is, if its maxim, when made into a universal law, can never be at variance with itself. This principle is therefore also its supreme law: "Act always on that maxim whose universality as a law you can at the same time will." This is the one principle on which a will can never be at variance with itself, and such an imperative is categorical. Because the validity of the will as a universal law for possible actions is analogous to the universal interconnexion of existent things in accordance with universal laws—which constitutes the formal aspect of nature as such—we can also express the categorical imperative as follows: *"Act on that maxim which can at the same time have for its object itself as a universal law of nature."* In this way we provide the formula for an absolutely good will.

Rational nature separates itself out from all other things by the fact that it sets itself an end. An end would thus be the matter of every good will. But in the Idea of a will which is absolutely good—good without any qualifying condition (namely, that it should attain this or that end)—there must be complete abstraction from every end that has to be *produced* (as something which would make every will only relatively good). Hence the end must here be conceived, not as an end to be produced, *but as a self-existent* end. It must therefore be conceived only negatively—that is, as an end against which we should never act, and consequently as one which in all our willing we must never rate *merely* as a means, but always at the same time as an end. Now this end can be nothing other than the subject of all possible ends himself, because this subject is also the subject of a will that may be absolutely good; for such a will cannot without contradiction be subordinated to any other object. The principle "So act in relation to every rational being (both to yourself and to others) that he may at the same time count in your maxim as an end in himself" is thus at bottom the same as the principle "Act on a maxim which at the same time contains in itself its own universal validity for every rational being." For to say that in using means to every end I ought to restrict my maxim by the condition that it should also be universally valid as a law for every subject is just the same as to say this—that a subject of ends, namely, a rational being himself, must be made the ground for all maxims of action, never *merely* as a means, but as a supreme condition restricting the use of every means—that is, always also as an end.

Now from this it unquestionably follows that every rational being, as an end in himself, must be able to regard himself as also the maker of universal law in respect to any law whatever to which he may be subjected: for it is precisely the fitness of his maxims to make universal law that marks him out as an end in himself. It follows equally that this dignity (or prerogative) of his above all the mere things of nature carries with it the necessity of always choosing his maxims from the point of view of himself—and also of every other rational being—as a maker of law (and this is why they are called persons). It is in this way that a world of rational beings *(mundus intelligibilis)* is possible as a kingdom of ends—possible, that is, through the making of their own laws by all persons as its members. Accordingly every rational being must so act as if he were through his maxims always a law-making member in the universal kingdom of ends. The formal principle of such maxims is "So act as if your maxims had to serve at the same time as a universal law (for all rational beings)." Thus a kingdom of ends is possible only on the analogy of a kingdom of nature; yet the kingdom of ends is possible only through maxims—that is, self-imposed rules—while nature is possible only through laws concerned with causes whose action is necessitated from without. In spite of this difference, we give to nature as a whole, even although it is regarded as a machine, the name of a "kingdom of nature" so far as—and for the reason that—it stands in a relation to rational beings as its ends. Now a kingdom of ends would actually come into existence through maxims which the categorical imperative prescribes as a rule for all rational beings, *if these maxims were universally followed.* Yet even if a rational being were himself to follow such a maxim strictly, he cannot count on everybody else being faithful to it on this ground, nor can he be confident that the kingdom of nature and its purposive order will work in harmony with him, as a fitting member, towards a kingdom of ends made possible by himself—or, in other words, that it will favour his expectation of happiness. But in spite of this the law "Act on the maxims of a member who makes universal laws for a merely possible kingdom of ends" remains in full force, since its command is categorical. And precisely here we encounter the paradox that without any further end or advantage to be attained the mere dignity of humanity, that is, of rational nature in man—and consequently that reverence for a mere idea—should function as an inflexible precept for the will; and that it is just this freedom from dependence on interested motives which constitutes the sublimity of a maxim and the worthiness of every rational subject to be a law-making member in the kingdom of ends; for otherwise he would have to be regarded as subject only to the law of nature—the law of his own needs. Even if it were thought that both the kingdom of nature and the kingdom of ends were united under one head and that thus the latter kingdom ceased to be a mere Idea and achieved genuine reality, the Idea would indeed gain by this the addition of a strong motive, but never any increase in its intrinsic worth; for, even if this were so, it would still be necessary to conceive the unique and absolute lawgiver himself as judging the worth of rational beings solely by the disinterested behaviour they prescribed to themselves in virtue of this idea alone. The essence of things does not vary with their external relations; and where there is something which, without regard to such relations, constitutes by itself the absolute worth of man, it is by this that man must also be judged by everyone whatsoever—even by the Supreme Being. Thus *morality* lies in the relation of actions to the autonomy of the will—that is, to a possible making of universal law by means of its maxims. An action which is compatible with the autonomy of the will is *permitted;* one which does not harmonize with it is *forbidden.* A will whose maxims necessarily accord with the laws of autonomy is a *holy,* or absolutely good, will. The dependence of a will not absolutely good on the principle of autonomy (that is, moral necessitation) is *obligation.* Obligation can thus have no reference to a holy being. The objective necessary to act from obligation is called *duty.*

From what was said a little time ago we can now easily explain how it comes about that, although in the concept of duty we think of subjection to the law, yet we also at the same time attribute to the person who fulfils all his duties a certain sublimity and *dignity.* For it is not in so far as he is *subject* to the law that he has sublimity, but rather in so far as, in regard to this very same law, he is at the same time its *author* and is subordinated to it only on this ground. We have also shown above how neither fear nor inclination, but solely reverence for the law, is the motive which can give an action moral worth. Our own will, provided it were to act only under the condition of being able to make universal law by means of its maxims—this ideal will which can be ours is the proper object of reverence; and the dignity of man consists precisely in his capacity to make universal law, although only on condition of being himself also subject to the law he makes.

ARISTOTLE

# Morality and Human Nature

In these passages from **The Nicomachean Ethics,** Aristotle (384–322 B.C.E) presents several of his central views on ethics. He argues that we can discover what a good life is for human beings by considering what the function of human beings is. This function is to be found in reasoning well. Aristotle also defends his Doctrine of the Mean, which is intended to explain which character traits (virtues) best promote human flourishing.

## 1. THE HIGHEST GOOD: HAPPINESS

### 1.1 The Highest Good Is Supreme in the Hierarchy of Goods

i 1    *Goods Correspond to Ends*

1094a    Every craft and every investigation, and likewise every action and decision, seems to aim at some good; hence the good has been well described as that at which everything aims.

However, there is an apparent difference among the ends aimed at. For the end is sometimes an activity, sometimes a product beyond the activity; and when there is an end beyond the action, the product is by nature better than the activity.

*The Hierarchy of Goods Corresponds to the Hierarchy of Ends*

Since there are many actions, crafts and sciences, the ends turn out to be many as well; for health is the end of medicine, a boat of boatbuilding, victory of generalship, and wealth of household management.

But whenever any of these sciences are subordinate to some one capacity—as e.g. bridlemaking and every other science producing equipment for horses are subordinate to horsemanship, while this and every action in warfare are in turn subordinate to generalship, and in the same way other sciences are subordinate to further ones—in each of these the end of the ruling science is more choiceworthy than all the ends subordinate to it, since it is the end for which those ends are also pursued. And here it does not matter whether the ends of the actions are the activities themselves, or some product beyond them, as in the sciences we have mentioned.

*The Highest Good*

Suppose, then, that (a) there is some end of the things we pursue in our actions

i 2    which we wish for because of itself, and because of which we wish for the other things; and (b) we do not choose everything because of something else, since (c) if we do, it will go on without limit, making desire empty and futile; then clearly (d) this end will be the good, i.e. the best good.

Reprinted from Aristotle, *Nicomachean Ethics,* translated by T. Irwin (Indianapolis: Hackett Publishing Co., 1985), 1094a1–1096a10, 1097a15–1099b8, 1102a5–1109b27, 1177a11–1179a132. Copyright © 1985 by Terence Irwin. Reprinted by permission of Hackett Publishing Company, Inc.

## 1.2 The Ruling Science Studying the Highest Good Is Political Science

### *The Importance of Finding the Science of the Highest Good*
Then surely knowledge of this good is also of great importance for the conduct of our lives, and if, like archers, we have a target to aim at, we are more likely to hit the right mark. If so, we should try to grasp, in outline at any rate, what the good is, and which science or capacity is concerned with it.

### *The Relevant Science Is Political Science*
It seems to concern the most controlling science, the one that, more than any other, is the ruling science. And political science apparently has this character.

1. For it is the one that prescribes which of the sciences ought to be studied in cities, and which ones each class in the city should learn, and how far.
2. Again, we see that even the most honoured capacities, e.g. generalship, household management and rhetoric, are subordinate to it.
3. Further, it uses the other sciences concerned with action, and moreover legislates what must be done and what avoided.

1094b

Hence its end will include the ends of the other sciences, and so will be the human good.

[This is properly called political science;] for though admittedly the good is the same for a city as for an individual, still the good of the city is apparently a greater and more complete good to acquire and preserve. For while it is satisfactory to acquire and preserve the good even for an individual, it is finer and more divine to acquire and preserve it for a people and for cities. And so, since our investigation aims at these [goods, for an individual and for a city], it is a sort of political science.

## 1.3 The Method of Political Inquiry

### *The Demand for Exactness Must Be Limited by the Nature of Ethics*
i 3   Our discussion will be adequate if its degree of clarity fits the subject-matter; for we should not seek the same degree of exactness in all sorts of arguments alike, any more than in the products of different crafts.

Moreover, what is fine and what is just, the topics of inquiry in political science, differ and vary so much that they seem to rest on convention only, not on nature. Goods, however, also vary in the same sort of way, since they cause harm to many people; for it has happened that some people have been destroyed because of their wealth, others because of their bravery.

### *The Proper Aim of Ethical Theory*
Since these, then, are the sorts of things we argue from and about, it will be satisfactory if we can indicate the truth roughly and in outline; since [that is to say] we argue from and about what holds good usually [but not universally], it will be satisfactory if we can draw conclusions of the same sort.

### *How to Judge an Ethical Theory*

Each of our claims, then, ought to be accepted in the same way [as claiming to hold good usually], since the educated person seeks exactness in each area to the extent that the nature of the subject allows; for apparently it is just as mistaken to demand demonstrations from a rhetorician as to accept [merely] persuasive arguments from a mathematician.

1095a     Further, each person judges well what he knows, and is a good judge about that; hence the good judge in a particular area is the person educated in that area, and the unconditionally good judge is the person educated in every area.

### *Qualifications of the Student of Ethics*

This is why a youth is not a suitable student of political science; for he lacks experience of the actions in life which political science argues from and about.

Moreover, since he tends to be guided by his feelings, his study will be futile and useless; for its end is action, not knowledge. And here it does not matter whether he is young in years or immature in character, since the deficiency does not depend on age, but results from being guided in his life and in each of his pursuits by his feelings; for an immature person, like an incontinent person, gets no benefit from his knowledge.

If, however, we are guided by reason in forming our desires and in acting, then this knowledge will be of great benefit.

These are the preliminary points about the student, about the way our claims are to be accepted, and about what we intend to do.

## 1.4 Common Beliefs About the Highest Good Are Inadequate

### *1.4.1 Most People Identify the Good with Happiness, but Disagree About the Nature of Happiness*

i 4     Let us, then, begin again. Since every sort of knowledge and decision pursues some good, what is that good which we say is the aim of political science? What [in other words] is the highest of all the goods pursued in action?

As far as its name goes, most people virtually agree [about what the good is], since both the many and the cultivated call it happiness, and suppose that living well and doing well are the same as being happy. But they disagree about what happiness is, and the many do not give the same answer as the wise.

For the many think it is something obvious and evident, e.g. pleasure, wealth or honour, some thinking one thing, others another; and indeed the same person keeps changing his mind, since in sickness he thinks it is health, in poverty wealth. And when they are conscious of their own ignorance, they admire anyone who speaks of something grand and beyond them.

[Among the wise,] however, some used to think that besides these many goods there is some other good that is something in itself, and also causes all these goods to be goods.

### 1.4.2 Ethical Method

#### We Must Examine These Common Beliefs; but We Must Not Take for Granted Our First Principles, Since We Are Arguing Towards Them, Not from Them

Presumably, then, it is rather futile to examine all these beliefs, and it is enough to examine those that are most current or seem to have some argument for them.

We must notice, however, the difference between arguments from origins and arguments towards origins. For indeed Plato was right to be puzzled about this, when he used to ask if [the argument] set out from the origins or led towards them—just as on a race course the path may go from the starting-line to the far end, or back again.

#### To Argue Towards First Principles We Must Begin from Common Beliefs That Are Familiar to Us

For while we should certainly begin from origins that are known, things are known in two ways; for some are known to us, some known unconditionally [but not necessarily known to us]. Presumably, then, the origin *we* should begin from is what is known to *us*.

#### To Become Familiar with Common Beliefs We Need a Good Upbringing

This is why we need to have been brought up in fine habits if we are to be adequate students of what is fine and just, and of political questions generally. For the origin we begin from is the belief that something is true, and if this is apparent enough to us, we will not, at this stage, need the reason why it is true in addition; and if we have this good upbringing, we have the origins to begin from, or can easily acquire them. Someone who neither has them nor can acquire them should listen to Hesiod: 'He who understands everything himself is best of all; he is noble also who listens to one who has spoken well; but he who neither understands it himself nor takes to heart what he hears from another is a useless man.'

### 1.4.3 Three Conceptions of the Best Life Reflect Common Beliefs About the Good, but Face Criticism from Other Common Beliefs

But let us begin again from [the common beliefs] from which we digressed. For, it would seem, people quite reasonably reach their conception of the good, i.e. of happiness, from the lives [they lead]; for there are roughly three most favoured lives— the lives of gratification, of political activity, and, third, of study.

#### The Life of Gratification: Pleasure

The many, the most vulgar, would seem to conceive the good and happiness as pleasure, and hence they also like the life of gratification. Here they appear completely slavish, since the life they decide on is a life for grazing animals; and yet they have argument in their defence, since many in positions of power feel the same way as Sardanapallus [and also choose this life].

#### The Life of Action: Honour or Virtue

The cultivated people, those active [in politics], conceive the good as honour, since this is more or less the end [normally pursued] in the political life. This, however,

1095b

i 5

appears to be too superficial to be what we are seeking, since it seems to depend more on those who honour than on the one honoured, whereas we intuitively believe that the good is something of our own and hard to take from us.

Further, it would seem, they pursue honour to convince themselves that they are good; at any rate, they seek to be honoured by intelligent people, among people who know them, and for virtue. It is clear, then, that in the view of active people at least, virtue is superior [to honour].

Perhaps, indeed, one might conceive virtue more than honour to be the end of the political life. However, this also is apparently too incomplete [to be the good]. For it seems, someone might possess virtue but be asleep or inactive throughout his life; or, further, he might suffer the worst evils and misfortunes; and if this is the sort of life he leads, no one would count him happy, except to defend a philosopher's paradox. Enough about this, since it has been adequately discussed in the popular works also.

1096a

### The Life of Study
The third life is the life of study, which we will examine in what follows.

### The Life of Money-Making May Be Safely Ignored
The money-maker's life is in a way forced on him [not chosen for itself]; and clearly wealth is not the good we are seeking, since it is [merely] useful, [choice-worthy only] for some other end. Hence one would be more inclined to support that [any of] the goods mentioned earlier is the end, since they are liked for themselves. But apparently they are not [the end] either; and many arguments have been presented against them. Let us, then, dismiss them.

•          •          •

### (1) The Good Is the End of Action
i 7

But let us return once again to the good we are looking for, and consider just what it could be, since it is apparently one thing in one action or craft, and another thing in another; for it is one thing in medicine, another in generalship, and so on for the rest.

What, then, is the good in each of these cases? Surely it is that for the sake of which the other things are done; and in medicine this is health, in generalship victory, in house-building a house, in another case something else, but in every action and decision it is the end, since it is for the sake of the end that everyone does the other things.

And so, if there is some end of everything that is pursued in action, this will be the good pursued in action; and if there are more ends than one, these will be the goods pursued in action.

Our argument has progressed, then, to the same conclusion [as before, that the highest end is the good]; but we must try to clarify this still more.

### (2) The Good Is Complete
Though apparently there are many ends, we choose some of them, e.g. wealth, flutes and, in general, instruments, because of something else; hence it is clear that not all ends are complete. But the best good is apparently something complete.

Hence, if only one end is complete, this will be what we are looking for; and if more than one are complete, the most complete of these will be what we are looking for.

### *Criteria for Completeness*

An end pursued in itself, we say, is more complete than an end pursued because of something else; and an end that is never choiceworthy because of something else is more complete than ends that are choiceworthy both in themselves and because of this end; and hence an end that is always [choiceworthy, and also] choiceworthy in itself, never because of something else, is unconditionally complete.

### *(3) Happiness Meets the Criteria for Completeness, but Other Goods Do Not*

1097b   Now happiness more than anything else seems unconditionally complete, since we always [choose it, and also] choose it because of itself, never because of something else.

Honour, pleasure, understanding and every virtue we certainly choose because of themselves, since we would choose each of them even if it had no further result, but we also choose them for the sake of happiness, supposing that through them we shall be happy. Happiness, by contrast, no one ever chooses for their sake, or for the sake of anything else at all.

### *(4) The Good Is Self-Sufficient; So Is Happiness*

The same conclusion [that happiness is complete] also appears to follow from self-sufficiency, since the complete good seems to be self-sufficient.

Now what we count as self-sufficient is not what suffices for a solitary person by himself, living an isolated life, but what suffices also for parents, children, wife and in general for friends and fellow-citizens, since a human being is a naturally political [animal]. Here, however, we must impose some limit; for if we extend the good to parents' parents and children's children and to friends of friends, we shall go on without limit; but we must examine this another time.

Anyhow, we regard something as self-sufficient when all by itself it makes a life choiceworthy and lacking nothing; and that is what we think happiness does.

### *(5) What Is Self-Sufficient Is Most Choiceworthy; So Is Happiness*

Moreover, we think happiness is most choiceworthy of all goods, since it is not counted as one good among many. If it were counted as one among many, then, clearly, we think that the addition of the smallest of goods would make it more choiceworthy; for [the smallest good] that is added becomes an extra quantity of goods [so creating a good larger than the original good], and the larger of two goods is always more choiceworthy. [But we do not think any addition can make happiness more choiceworthy; hence it is most choiceworthy.]

Happiness, then, is apparently something complete and self-sufficient, since it is the end of the things pursued in action.

### *1.5.2 A Clearer Account of the Good: The Human Soul's Activity Expressing Virtue*

But presumably the remark that the best good is happiness is apparently something [generally] agreed, and what we miss is a clearer statement of what the best good is.

### *(1) If Something Has a Function, Its Good Depends on Its Function*

Well, perhaps we shall find the best good if we first find that function of a human being. For just as the good, i.e. [doing] well, for a flautist, a sculptor, and every craftsman, and, in general, for whatever has a function and [characteristic] action, seems to depend on its function, and the same seems to be true for a human being, if a human being has some function.

### *(2) What Sorts of Things Have Functions?*

Then do the carpenter and the leatherworker have their functions and actions, while a human being has none, and is by nature idle, without any function? Or, just as eye, hand, foot and, in general, every [bodily] part apparently has its functions, may we likewise ascribe to a human being some function besides all of theirs?

### *(3) The Human Function*

1098a
What, then, could this be? For living is apparently shared with plants, but what we are looking for is the special function of a human being; hence we should set aside the life of nutrition and growth. The life next in order is some sort of life of sense-perception; but this too is apparently shared, with horse, ox and every animal. The remaining possibility, then, is some sort of life of action of the [part of the soul] that has reason.

#### *Clarification of "Has Reason" and "Life"*

Now this [part has two parts, which have reason in different ways], one as obeying the reason [in the other part], the other as itself having reason and thinking. [We intend both.] Moreover, life is also spoken of in two ways [as capacity and as activity], and we must take [a human being's special function to be] life as activity, since this seems to be called life to a fuller extent.

### *(4) The Human Good Is Activity Expressing Virtue*

(a) We have found, then, that the human function is the soul's activity that expresses reason [as itself having reason] or requires reason [as obeying reason]. (b) Now the function of F, e.g. of a harpist, is the same in kind, so we say, as the function of an excellent F, e.g. an excellent harpist. (c) The same is true unconditionally in every case, when we add to the function the superior achievement that expresses the virtue; for a harpist's function, e.g. is to play the harp, and a good harpist's is to do it well. (d) Now we take the human function to be a certain kind of life, and take this life to be the soul's activity and actions that express reason. (e) [Hence by (c) and (d)] the excellent man's function is to do this finely and well. (f) Each function is completed well when its completion expresses the proper virtue. (g) Therefore [by (d), (e) and (f)] the human good turns out to be the soul's activity that expresses virtue.

### *(5) The Good Must Also Be Complete*

And if there are more virtues than one, the good will express the best and most complete virtue. Moreover, it will be in a complete life. For one swallow does not make a spring, nor does one day; nor, similarly, does one day or a short time make us blessed and happy.

## 1.6 Defence of the Account of the Good, from Principles of Ethical Method

### 1.6.1 It Is Reasonable That Our Account Is Only a Sketch

This, then, is a sketch of the good; for, presumably, the outline must come first, to be filled in later. If the sketch is good, then anyone, it seems, can advance and articulate it, and in such cases time is a good discoverer or [at least] a good co-worker. That is also how the crafts have improved, since anyone can add what is lacking [in the outline].

### 1.6.2 The Inexactness of Our Account Suits the Subject-Matter

However, we must also remember our previous remarks, so that we do not look for the same degree of exactness in all areas, but the degree that fits the subject-matter in each area and is proper to the investigation. For the carpenter's and the geometer's inquiries about the right angle are different also; the carpenter's is confined to the right angle's usefulness for his work, whereas the geometer's concerns what, or what sort of thing, the right angle is, since he studies the truth. We must do the same, then, in other areas too, [seeking the proper degree of exactness], so that digressions do not overwhelm our main task.

### 1.6.3 Having Found a First Principle, We Should Not Demand a Further Principle Beyond It

1098b    Nor should we make the same demand for an explanation in all cases. Rather, in some cases it is enough to prove that something is true without explaining why it is true. This is so, e.g. with origins, where the fact that something is true is the first principle, i.e. the origin.

Some origins are studied by means of induction, some by means of perception, some by means of some sort of habituation, and others by other means. In each case we should try to find them out by means suited to their nature, and work hard to define them well. For they have a great influence on what follows; for the origin seems to be more than half the whole, and makes evident the answer to many of our questions.

## 1.7 Defence of the Account of the Good, from Common Beliefs

i 8    However, we should examine the origin not only from the conclusion and premises [of a deductive argument], but also from what is said about it; for all the facts harmonize with a true account, whereas the truth soon clashes with a false one.

### 1.7.1 A Common Classification of Goods

Goods are divided, then, into three types, some called external, some goods of the soul, others goods of the body; and the goods of the soul are said to be goods to the fullest extent and most of all, and the soul's actions and activities are ascribed to the soul. Hence the account [of the good] is sound, to judge by this belief anyhow—and it is an ancient belief agreed on by philosophers.

Our account is also correct in saying that some sort of actions and activities are the end; for then the end turns out to be a good of the soul, not an external good.

### 1.7.2 A Common Conception of Happiness
The belief that the happy person lives well and does well in action also agrees with our account, since we have virtually said that the end is a sort of living well and doing well in action.

### 1.7.3 Commonly Accepted Features of Happiness
Further, all the features that people look for in happiness appear to be true of the end described in our account. For to some people it seems to be virtue; to others intelligence; to others some sort of wisdom; to others again it seems to be these, or one of these, involving pleasure or requiring its addition; and others add in external prosperity as well.

Some of these views are traditional, held by many, while others are held by a few reputable men; and it is reasonable for each group to be not entirely in error, but correct on one point at least, or even on most points.

#### Virtue
First, our account agrees with those who say happiness is virtue [in general] or some [particular] virtue; for activity expressing virtue is proper to virtue. Presumably, though, it matters quite a bit whether we suppose that the best good consists in possessing or in using, i.e. in a state or in an activity [that actualizes the state]. For while someone may be in a state that achieves no good, if, e.g., he is asleep or inactive in some other way, this cannot be true of the activity; for it will necessarily do actions and do well in them. And just as Olympic prizes are not for the finest and strongest, but for contestants, since it is only these who win; so also in life [only] the fine and good people who act correctly win the prize.

1099a

#### Pleasure
Moreover, the life of these [active] people is also pleasant in itself. For being pleased is a condition of the soul, [hence included in the activity of the soul]. Further, each type of person finds pleasure in whatever he is called a lover of, so that a horse, e.g. pleases the horse-lover, a spectacle the lover of spectacles, and similarly what is just pleases the lover of justice, and in general what expresses virtue pleases the lover of virtue. Hence the things that please most people conflict, because they are not pleasant by nature, whereas the things that please lovers of what is fine are things pleasant by nature; and actions expressing virtue are pleasant in this way; and so they both please lovers of what is fine and are pleasant in themselves.

Hence their life does not need pleasure to be added [to virtuous activity] as some sort of ornament; rather, it has its pleasure within itself. For besides the reasons already given, someone who does not enjoy fine actions is not good; for no one would call him just, e.g., if he did not enjoy doing just actions, or generous if he did not enjoy generous actions, and similarly for the other virtues. If this is so, then actions expressing the virtues are pleasant in themselves.

#### Hence Our Account Satisfies Traditional Ideals
Moreover, these actions are good and fine as well as pleasant; indeed, they are good, fine and pleasant more than anything else, since on this question the excellent person has good judgement, and his judgement agrees with our conclusions.

Happiness, then, is best, finest and most pleasant, and these three features are not distinguished in the way suggested by the Delian inscription: 'What is most just is finest; being healthy is most beneficial; but it is most pleasant to win our heart's desire.' For all three features are found in the best activities, and happiness we say is these activities, or [rather] one of them, the best one.

### External Goods

Nonetheless, happiness evidently also needs external goods to be added [to the activity], as we said, since we cannot, or cannot easily, do fine actions if we lack the resources.

1099b     For, first of all, in many actions we use friends, wealth and political power just as we use instruments. Further, deprivation of certain [externals]—e.g. good birth, good children, beauty—mars our blessedness; for we do not altogether have the character of happiness if we look utterly repulsive or are ill-born, solitary or childless, and have it even less, presumably, if our children or friends are totally bad, or were good but have died.

And so, as we have said, happiness would seem to need this sort of prosperity added also; that is why some people identify happiness with good fortune, while others [reacting from one extreme to the other] identify it with virtue.

•       •       •

A further reason why this would seem to be correct is that happiness is an origin; for the origin is what we all aim at in all our other actions; and we take the origin and cause of goods to be something honourable and divine.

## 1.9 Introduction to the Account of Virtue

i 13     *1.9.1 An Account of Happiness Requires an Account of Virtue*

Since happiness is an activity of the soul expressing complete virtue, we must examine virtue; for that will perhaps also be a way to study happiness better.

Moreover, the true politician seems to have spent more effort on virtue than on anything else, since he wants to make the citizens good and law-abiding. We find an example of this in the Spartan and Cretan legislators and in any others with their concerns. Since, then, the examination of virtue is proper for political science, the inquiry clearly suits our original decision [to pursue political science].

### *1.9.2 A Discussion of Virtue Requires a Discussion of the Soul*

It is clear that the virtue we must examine is human virtue, since we are also seeking the human good and human happiness. And by human virtue we mean virtue of the soul, not of the body, since we also say that happiness is an activity of the soul. If this is so, then it is clear that the politician must acquire some knowledge about the soul, just as someone setting out to heal the eyes must acquire knowledge about the whole body as well. This is all the more true to the extent that political science is better and more honourable than medicine—and even among doctors the cultivated ones devote a lot of effort to acquiring knowledge about the body. Hence the politician as well [as the student of nature] must study the soul.

But he must study it for the purpose [of inquiring into virtue], as far as suffices for what he seeks; for a more exact treatment would presumably take more effort than his purpose requires. [We] have discussed the soul sufficiently [for our purposes] in [our] popular works as well [as our less popular], and we should use this discussion.

### 1.9.3 The Rational and Nonrational Parts of the Soul

We have said, e.g., that one [part] of the soul is nonrational, while one has reason. Are these distinguished as parts of a body and everything divisible into parts are? Or are they two only in account, and inseparable by nature, as the convex and the concave are in a surface? It does not matter for present purposes.

### The Nonrational Part: (a) One Part of It Is Unresponsive to Reason

Consider the nonrational [part]. One [part] of it, i.e. the cause of nutrition and
1102b growth, is seemingly plant-like and shared [with other living things]: for we can ascribe this capacity of the soul to everything that is nourished, including embryos, and the same one to complete living things, since this is more reasonable than to ascribe another capacity to them.

Hence the virtue of this capacity is apparently shared, not [specifically] human. For this part and capacity more than others seem to be active in sleep, and here the good and the bad person are least distinct, which is why happy people are said to be no better off than miserable people for half their lives.

And this lack of distinction is not surprising, since sleep is inactivity of the soul in so far as it is called excellent or base, unless to some small extent some movements penetrate [to our awareness], and in this way the decent person comes to have better images [in dreams] than just any random person has. Enough about this, however, and let us leave aside the nutritive part, since by nature it has no share in human virtue.

### (b) Another Part Is Also Nonrational

Another nature in the soul would also seem to be nonrational, though in a way it shares in reason.

[Clearly it is nonrational]. For in the continent and the incontinent person we praise their reason, i.e. the [part] of the soul that has reason, because it exhorts them correctly and towards what is best; but they evidently also have in them some other [part] that is by nature something besides reason, conflicting and struggling with reason.

For just as paralysed parts of a body, when we decide to move them to the right, do the contrary and move off to the left, the same is true of the soul, for incontinent people have impulses in contrary directions. In bodies, admittedly, we see the part go astray, whereas we do not see it in the soul; nonetheless, presumably, we should suppose that the soul also has a [part] besides reason, contrary to and countering reason. The [precise] way it is different does not matter.

### But It Is Responsive to Reason

However, this [part] as well [as the rational part] appears, as we said, to share in reason. At any rate, in the continent person it obeys reason; and in the temperate and the brave person it presumably listens still better to reason, since there it agrees with reason in everything.

### *Hence It Differs Both from the Wholly Unresponsive Part . . .*

The nonrational [part], then, as well [as the whole soul] apparently has two parts. For while the plant-like [part] shares in reason not at all, the [part] with appetites and in general desires shares in reason in a way, in so far as it both listens to reason and obeys it.

It listens in the way in which we are said to 'listen to reason' from father or friends, not in the way in which we ['give the reason'] in mathematics.

The nonrational part also [obeys and] is persuaded in some way by reason, as is shown by chastening, and by every sort of reproof and exhortation.

1103a

### *And from the Wholly Rational Part*

If we ought to say, then, that this [part] also has reason, then the [part] that has reason, as well [as the nonrational part] will have two parts, one that has reason to the full extent by having it within itself, and another [that has it] by listening to reason as to a father.

### *1.9.4 The Division of the Virtues Corresponds to the Parts of the Soul*

The distinction between virtues also reflects this difference. For some virtues are called virtues of thought, other virtues of character; wisdom, comprehension and intelligence are called virtues of thought, generosity and temperance virtues of character.

For when we speak of someone's character we do not say that he is wise or has good comprehension, but that he is gentle or temperate. [Hence these are the virtues of character.] And yet, we also praise the wise person for his state, and the states that are praiseworthy are the ones we call virtues. [Hence wisdom is also a virtue.]

## 2. VIRTUES OF CHARACTER IN GENERAL

### 2.1 How a Virtue of Character Is Acquired

ii 1    Virtue, then, is of two sorts, virtue of thought and virtue of character. Virtue of thought arises and grows mostly from teaching, and hence needs experience and time. Virtue of character [i.e. of *ēthos*] results from habit [*ethos*]; hence its name 'ethical', slightly varied from *'ethos'*.

#### *Virtue Comes About, Not by a Process of Nature, but by Habituation*

Hence it is also clear that none of the virtues of character arises in us naturally.

#### *(1) What Is Natural Cannot Be Changed by Habituation*

For if something is by nature [in one condition], habituation cannot bring it into another condition. A stone, e.g., by nature moves downwards, and habituation could not make it move upwards, not even if you threw it up ten thousand times to habituate it; nor could habituation make fire move downwards, or bring anything that is by nature in one condition into another condition.

Thus the virtues arise in us neither by nature nor against nature. Rather, we are by nature able to acquire them, and reach our complete perfection through habit.

### (2) Natural Capacities Are Not Acquired by Habituation

Further, if something arises in us by nature, we first have the capacity for it, and later display the activity. This is clear in the case of the senses; for we did not acquire them by frequent seeing or hearing, but already had them when we exercised them, and did not get them by exercising them.

Virtues, by contrast, we acquire, just as we acquire crafts, by having previously activated them. For we learn a craft by producing the same product that we must produce when we have learned it, become builders, e.g., by building and harpists by playing the harp; so, also, then, we become just by doing just actions, temperate by doing temperate actions, brave by doing brave actions.

1103b

### (3) Legislators Concentrate on Habituation

What goes on in cities is evidence for this also. For the legislator makes the citizens good by habituating them, and this is the wish of every legislator; if he fails to do it well he misses his goal. [The right] habituation is what makes the difference between a good political system and a bad one.

### (4) Virtue and Vice Are Formed by Good and Bad Actions

Further, just as in the case of a craft, the sources and means that develop each virtue also ruin it. For playing the harp makes both good and bad harpists, and it is analogous in the case of builders and all the rest; for building well makes good builders, building badly, bad ones. If it were not so, no teacher would be needed, but everyone would be born a good or a bad craftsman.

It is the same, then, with the virtues. For actions in dealing with [older] human beings make some people just, some unjust; actions in terrifying situations and the acquired habit of fear or confidence make some brave and others cowardly. The same is true of situations involving appetites and anger; for one or another sort of conduct in these situations makes some people temperate and gentle, others intemperate and irascible.

### Conclusion: The Importance of Habituation

To sum up, then, in a single account: A state [of character] arises from [the repetition of] similar activities. Hence we must display the right activities, since differences in these imply corresponding differences in the states. It is not unimportant, then, to acquire one sort of habit or another, right from our youth; rather, it is very important, indeed all-important.

### 2.1.2 What Is the Right Sort of Habituation?

### This Is an Appropriate Question, for the Aim of Ethical Theory Is Practical

ii 2    Our present inquiry does not aim, as our others do, at study; for the purpose of our examination is not to know what virtue is, but to become good, since otherwise the inquiry would be of no benefit to us. Hence we must examine the right way to act, since, as we have said, the actions also control the character of the states we acquire.

First, then, actions should express correct reason. That is a common [belief], and let us assume it; later we will say what correct reason is and how it is related to the other virtues.

1104a    But let us take it as agreed in advance that every account of the actions we must
do has to be stated in outline, not exactly. As we also said at the start, the type of
accounts we demand should reflect the subject-matter; and questions about actions
and expediency, like questions about health, have no fixed [and invariable answers].

And when our general account is so inexact, the account of particular cases is
all the more inexact. For these fall under no craft or profession, and the agents
themselves must consider in each case what the opportune action is, as doctors
and navigators do.

The account we offer, then, in our present inquiry is of this inexact sort; still, we
must try to offer help.

### *The Right Sort of Habituation Must Avoid Excess and Deficiency*

First, then, we should observe that these sorts of states naturally tend to be ruined
by excess and deficiency. We see this happen with strength and health, which we
mention because we must use what is evident as a witness to what is not. For both
excessive and deficient exercises ruin strength; and likewise, too much or too little
eating or drinking ruins health, while the proportionate amount produces, increases
and preserves it.

The same is true, then, of temperance, bravery and the other virtues. For if, e.g.,
someone avoids and is afraid of everything, standing firm against nothing, he becomes
cowardly, but if he is afraid of nothing at all and goes to face everything, he becomes
rash. Similarly, if he gratifies himself with every pleasure and refrains from none, he
becomes intemperate, but if he avoids them all, as boors do, he becomes some sort
of insensible person. Temperance and bravery, then, are ruined by excess and deficiency but preserved by the mean.

The same actions, then, are the sources and causes both of the emergence and
growth of virtues and of their ruin; but further, the activities of the virtues will be
found in these same actions. For this is also true of more evident cases, e.g. strength,
which arises from eating a lot and from withstanding much hard labour, and it is
the strong person who is most able to do these very things. It is the same with the
virtues. Refraining from pleasures make us become temperate, and when we have
1104b    become temperate we are most able to refrain from pleasures. And it is similar
with bravery; habituation in disdaining what is fearful and in standing firm against
it makes us become brave, and when we have become brave we shall be most able
to stand firm.

### *2.1.3 Pleasure and Pain Are Important in Habituation*

ii 3    But [actions are not enough]; we must take as a sign of someone's state his pleasure or pain in consequence of his action. For if someone who abstains from bodily
pleasures enjoys the abstinence itself, then he is temperate, but if he is grieved by it,
he is intemperate. Again, if he stands firm against terrifying situations and enjoys it,
or at least does not find it painful, then he is brave, and if he finds it painful, he is
cowardly.

[Pleasures and pains are appropriately taken as signs] because virtue of character
is concerned with pleasures and pains.

### Virtue Is Concerned with Pleasure and Pain

1. For it is pleasure that causes us to do base actions, and pain that causes us to abstain from fine ones. Hence we need to have had the appropriate upbringing—right from early youth, as Plato says—to make us find enjoyment or pain in the right things; for this is the correct education.

2. Further, virtues are concerned with actions and feelings; but every feeling and every action implies pleasure or pain; hence, for this reason too, virtue is concerned with pleasures and pains.

3. Corrective treatment [for vicious actions] also indicates [the relevance of pleasure and pain], since it uses pleasures and pains; it uses them because such correction is a form of medical treatment, and medical treatment naturally operates through contraries.

4. Further, as we said earlier, every state of soul is naturally related to and concerned with whatever naturally makes it better or worse; and pleasures and pains make people worse, from pursuing and avoiding the wrong ones, at the wrong time, in the wrong ways, or whatever other distinctions of that sort are needed in an account.

These [bad effects of pleasure and pain] are the reason why people actually define the virtues as ways of being unaffected and undisturbed [by pleasures and pains]. They are wrong, however, because they speak [of being unaffected] unconditionally, not of being unaffected in the right or wrong way, at the right or wrong time, and the added specifications.

We assume, then, that virtue is the sort of state [with the appropriate specifications] that does the best actions concerned with pleasures and pains, and that vice is the contrary. The following points will also make it evident that virtue and vice are concerned with the same things.

5. There are three objects of choice—fine, expedient and pleasant—and three objects of avoidance—their contraries, shameful, harmful and painful. About all these, then, the good person is correct and the bad person is in error, and especially about pleasure. For pleasure is shared with animals, and implied by every object of choice, since what is fine and what is expedient appear pleasant as well.

1105a

6. Further, since pleasure grows up with all of us from infancy on, it is hard to rub out this feeling that is dyed into our lives; and we estimate actions as well [as feelings], some of us more, some less, by pleasure and pain. Hence, our whole inquiry must be about these, since good or bad enjoyment or pain is very important for our actions.

7. Moreover, it is harder to fight pleasure than to fight emotion, [though that is hard enough], as Heracleitus says. Now both craft and virtue are concerned in every case with what is harder, since a good result is even better when it is harder. Hence, for this reason also, the whole inquiry, for virtue and political science alike, must consider pleasures and pains; for if we use these well, we shall be good, and if badly, bad.

In short, virtue is concerned with pleasures and pains; the actions that are its sources also increase it or, if they are done differently, ruin it; and its activity is concerned with the same actions that are its sources.

### 2.1.4 But Our Claims About Habituation Raise a Puzzle: How Can We Become Good Without Being Good Already?

ii 4    However, someone might raise this puzzle: 'What do you mean by saying that to become just we must first do just actions and to become temperate we must first do temperate actions? For if we do what is grammatical or musical, we must already be grammarians or musicians. In the same way, then, if we do what is just or temperate, we must already be just or temperate.'

#### First Reply: Conformity Versus Understanding

But surely this is not so even with the crafts, for it is possible to produce something grammatical by chance or by following someone else's instructions. To be a grammarian, then, we must both produce something grammatical and produce it in a way in which the grammarian produces it, i.e. expressing grammatical knowledge that is in us.

#### Second Reply: Crafts Versus Virtues

Moreover, in any case what is true of crafts is not true of virtues. For the products of a craft determine by their own character whether they have been produced well; and so it suffices that they are in the right state when they have been produced. But for actions expressing virtue to be done temperately or justly [and hence well] it does not suffice that they are themselves in the right state. Rather, the agent must also be in the right state when he does them. First, he must know [that he is doing virtuous actions]; second, he must decide on them, and decide on them for themselves; and, third, he must also do them from a firm and unchanging state.

1105b    As conditions for having a craft these three do not count, except for the knowing itself. As a condition for having a virtue, however, the knowing counts for nothing, or [rather] for only a little, whereas the other two conditions are very important, indeed all-important. And these other two conditions are achieved by the frequent doing of just and temperate actions.

Hence actions are called just or temperate when they are the sort that a just or temperate person would do. But the just and temperate person is not the one who [merely] does these actions, but the one who also does them in the way in which just or temperate people do them.

It is right, then, to say that a person comes to be just from doing just actions and temperate from doing temperate actions; for no one has even a prospect of becoming good from failing to do them.

#### Virtue Requires Habituation, and Therefore Requires Practice, Not Just Theory

The many, however, do not do these actions but take refuge in arguments, thinking that they are doing philosophy, and that this is the way to become excellent people. In this they are like a sick person who listens attentively to the doctor, but acts on none of his instructions. Such a course of treatment will not improve the state of his body; any more than will the many's way of doing philosophy improve the state of their souls.

## 2.2 A Virtue of Character Is a State Intermediate Between Two Extremes, and Involving Decision

### 2.2.1 The Genus

#### Feelings, Capacities, States

ii 5    Next we must examine what virtue is. Since there are three conditions arising in the soul—feelings, capacities, and states—virtue must be one of these.

By feelings I mean appetite, anger, fear, confidence, envy, joy, love, hate, longing, jealousy, pity, in general whatever implies pleasure or pain.

By capacities I mean what we have when we are said to be capable of these feelings—capable of, e.g., being angry or afraid or feeling pity.

By states I mean what we have when we are well or badly off in relation to feelings. If, e.g., our feeling is too intense or slack, we are badly off in relation to anger, but if it is intermediate, we are well off; and the same is true in the other cases.

#### Virtue Is Not a Feeling . . .

First, then, neither virtues nor vices are feelings. (a) For we are called excellent or base in so far as we have virtues or vices, not in so far as we have feelings. (b) We are neither praised nor blamed in so far as we have feelings; for we do not praise the angry or the frightened person, and do not blame the person who is simply angry,

1106a    but only the person who is angry in a particular way. But we are praised or blamed in so far as we have virtues or vices. (c) We are angry and afraid without decision; but the virtues are decisions of some kind, or [rather] require decision. (d) Besides, in so far as we have feelings, we are said to be moved; but in so far as we have virtues or vices, we are said to be in some condition rather than moved.

#### Or a Capacity . . .

For these reasons the virtues are not capacities either; for we are neither called good nor called bad in so far as we are simply capable of feelings. Further, while we have capacities by nature, we do not become good or bad by nature; we have discussed this before.

#### But a State

If, then, the virtues are neither feelings nor capacities, the remaining possibility is that they are states. And so we have said what the genus of virtue is.

### 2.2.2 The Differentia

ii 6    But we must say not only, as we already have, that it is a state, but also what sort of state it is.

#### Virtue and the Human Function

It should be said, then, that every virtue causes its possessors to be in a good state and to perform their functions well; the virtue of eyes, e.g., makes the eyes and their functioning excellent, because it makes us see well; and similarly, the virtue of a horse makes the horse excellent, and thereby good at galloping, at carrying its rider and at standing steady in the face of the enemy. If this is true in every case, then the virtue of a human being will likewise be the state that makes a human being good and makes him perform his function well.

We have already said how this will be true, and it will also be evident from our next remarks, if we consider the sort of nature that virtue has.

### The Numerical Mean and the Mean Relative to Us

In everything continuous and divisible we can take more, less and equal, and each of them either in the object itself or relative to us; and the equal is some intermediate between excess and deficiency.

By the intermediate in the object I mean what is equidistant from each extremity; this is one and the same for everyone. But relative to us the intermediate is what is neither superfluous nor deficient; this is not one, and is not the same for everyone.

If, e.g., ten are many and two are few, we take six as an intermediate in the object, since it exceeds [two] and is exceeded [by ten] by an equal amount, [four]; this is what is inter-

1106b  mediate by numerical proportion. But that is not how we must take the intermediate that is relative to us. For if, e.g., ten pounds [of food] are a lot for someone to eat, and two pounds a little, it does not follow that the trainer will prescribe six, since this might also be either a little or a lot for the person who is to take it—for Milo [the athlete] a little, but for the beginner in gymnastics a lot; and the same is true for running and wrestling. In this way every scientific expert avoids excess and deficiency and seeks and chooses what is intermediate—but intermediate relative to us, not in the object.

### Virtue Seeks the Mean Relative to Us: Argument from Craft to Virtue

This, then, is how each science produces its product well, by focusing on what is intermediate and making the product conform to that. This, indeed, is why people regularly comment on well-made products that nothing could be added or subtracted, since they assume that excess or deficiency ruins a good [result] while the mean preserves it. Good craftsmen also, we say, focus on what is intermediate when they produce their product. And since virtue, like nature, is better and more exact than any craft, it will also aim at what is intermediate.

### Arguments from the Nature of Virtue of Character

By virtue I mean virtue of character; for this [pursues the mean because] it is concerned with feelings and actions, and these admit of excess, deficiency and an intermediate condition. We can be afraid, e.g., or be confident, or have appetites, or get angry, or feel pity, in general have pleasure or pain, both too much and too little, and in both ways not well; but [having these feelings] at the right times, about the right things, towards the right people, for the right end, and in the right way, is the intermediate and best condition, and this is proper to virtue. Similarly, actions also admit of excess, deficiency and the intermediate condition.

Now virtue is concerned with feelings and actions, in which excess and deficiency are in error and incur blame, while the intermediate condition is correct and wins praise, which are both proper features of virtue. Virtue, then, is a mean, in so far as it aims at what is intermediate.

Moreover, there are many ways to be in error, since badness is proper to what is limited; but there is only one way to be correct. That is why error is easy and correctness hard, since it is easy to miss the target and hard to hit it. And so for this reason also excess and deficiency are proper to vice, the mean to virtue; 'for we are noble in only one way, but bad in all sorts of ways.'

### 2.2.3 Definition of Virtue

1107a   Virtue, then, is (a) a state that decides, (b) [consisting] in a mean, (c) the mean relative to us, (d) which is defined by reference to reason, (e) i.e., to the reason by reference to which the intelligent person would define it. It is a mean between two vices, one of excess and one of deficiency.

It is a mean for this reason also: Some vices miss what is right because they are deficient, others because they are excessive, in feelings or in actions, while virtue finds and chooses what is intermediate.

Hence, as far as its substance and the account stating its essence are concerned, virtue is a mean; but as far as the best [condition] and the good [result] are concerned, it is an extremity.

#### The Definition Must Not Be Misapplied to Cases in Which There Is No Mean

But not every action or feeling admits of the mean. For the names of some automatically include baseness, e.g. spite, shamelessness, envy [among feelings], and adultery, theft, murder, among actions. All of these and similar things are called by these names because they themselves, not their excesses or deficiencies, are base.

Hence in doing these things we can never be correct, but must invariably be in error. We cannot do them well or not well—e.g. by committing adultery with the right woman at the right time in the right way; on the contrary, it is true unconditionally that to do any of them is to be in error.

[To think these admit of a mean], therefore, is like thinking that unjust or cowardly or intemperate action also admits of a mean, an excess and a deficiency. For then there would be a mean of excess, a mean of deficiency, an excess of excess and a deficiency of deficiency.

Rather, just as there is no excess or deficiency of temperance or of bravery, since the intermediate is a sort of extreme [in achieving the good], so also there is no mean of these [vicious actions] either, but whatever way anyone does them, he is in error. For in general there is no mean of excess or of deficiency, and no excess or deficiency of a mean.

### 2.3 The Definition of Virtue as a Mean Applies to the Individual Virtues

ii 7   However, we must not only state this general account but also apply it to the particular cases. For among accounts concerning actions, though the general ones are common to more cases, the specific ones are truer, since actions are about particular cases, and our account must accord with these. Let us, then, find these from the chart.

#### 2.3.1 Classification of Virtues of Character

#### Virtues Concerned with Feelings

1107b   (1)  First, in feelings of fear and confidence the mean is bravery. The excessively fearless person is nameless (and in fact many cases are nameless), while the one who is excessively confident is rash; the one who is excessively afraid and deficient in confidence is cowardly.

(2)  In pleasures and pains, though not in all types, and in pains less than in pleasures, the mean is temperance and the excess intemperance. People deficient

in pleasure are not often found, which is why they also lack even a name; let us call them insensible.

### Virtues Concerned with External Goods

(3) In giving and taking money the mean is generosity, the excess wastefulness and the deficiency ungenerosity. Here the vicious people have contrary excesses and defects; for the wasteful person spends to excess and is deficient in taking, whereas the ungenerous person takes to excess and is deficient in spending. At the moment we are speaking in outline and summary, and that suffices; later we shall define these things more exactly.

(4) In questions of money there are also other conditions. Another mean is magnificence; for the magnificent person differs from the generous by being concerned with large matters, while the generous person is concerned with small. The excess is ostentation and vulgarity, and the deficiency niggardliness, and these differ from the vices related to generosity in ways we shall describe later.

(5) In honour and dishonour the mean is magnanimity, the excess something called a sort of vanity, and the deficiency pusillanimity.

(6) And just as we said that generosity differs from magnificence in its concern with small matters, similarly there is a virtue concerned with small honours, differing in the same way from magnanimity, which is concerned with great honours. For honour can be desired either in the right way or more or less than is right. If someone desires it to excess, he is called an honour-lover, and if his desire is deficient he is called indifferent to honour, but if he is intermediate he has no name. The corresponding conditions have no name either, except the condition of the honour-lover, which is called honour-loving.

This is why people at the extremes claim the intermediate area. Indeed, we also sometimes call the intermediate person an honour-lover, and sometimes call him
1108a indifferent to honour; and sometimes we praise the honour-lover, sometimes the person indifferent to honour. We will mention later the reason we do this; for the moment, let us speak of the other cases in the way we have laid down.

### Virtues Concerned with Social Life

(7) Anger also admits of an excess, deficiency and mean. These are all practically nameless; but since we call the intermediate person mild, let us call the mean mindless. Among the extreme people let the excessive person be irascible, and the vice be irascibility, and let the deficient person be a sort of inirascible person, and the deficiency be inirascibility.

There are three other means, somewhat similar to one another, but different. For they are all concerned with association in conversations and actions, but differ in so far as one is concerned with truth-telling in these areas, the other two with sources of pleasure, some of which are found in amusement, and the others in daily life in general. Hence we should also discuss these states, so that we can better observe that in every case the mean is praiseworthy, while the extremes are neither praiseworthy nor correct, but blameworthy. Most of these cases are also nameless, and we must try, as in the other cases also, to make names ourselves, to make things clear and easy to follow.

(8) In truth-telling, then, let us call the intermediate person truthful, and the mean truthfulness; pretence that overstates will be boastfulness, and the person who has it boastful; pretence that understates will be self-deprecation, and the person who has it self-deprecating.

(9) In sources of pleasure in amusements let us call the intermediate person witty, and the condition wit; the excess buffoonery and the person who has it a buffoon; and the deficient person a sort of boor and the state boorishness.

(10) In the other sources of pleasure, those in daily life, let us call the person who is pleasant in the right way friendly, and the mean state friendliness. If someone goes to excess with no [further] aim he will be ingratiating; if he does it for his own advantage, a flatterer. The deficient person, unpleasant in everything, will be a sort of quarrelsome and ill-tempered person.

### Mean States That Are Not Virtues

(11) There are also means in feelings and concerned with feelings: shame, e.g., is not a virtue, but the person prone to shame as well as the virtuous person we have described receives praise. For here also one person is called intermediate, and another—the person excessively prone to shame, who is ashamed about everything—is called excessive; the person who is deficient in shame or never feels shame at all is said to have no sense of disgrace; and the intermediate one is called prone to shame.

1108b

(12) Proper indignation is the mean between envy and spite; these conditions are concerned with pleasure and pain at what happens to our neighbours. For the properly indignant person feels pain when someone does well undeservedly; the envious person exceeds him by feeling pain when anyone does well, while the spiteful person is so deficient in feeling pain that he actually enjoys [other people's misfortunes].

There will also be an opportunity elsewhere to speak of these [means that are not virtues].

### Justice

We must consider justice after these other conditions, and, because it is not spoken of in one way only, we shall distinguish its two types and say how each of them is a mean. Similarly, we must consider the virtues that belong to reason.

### 2.3.2 The Relations Between Means and Extremes

### The Mean Is Opposed to Each Extreme

ii 8    Among these three conditions, then, two are vices—one of excess, one of deficiency—and one—the mean—is virtue. In a way each of them is opposed to each of the others, since each extreme is contrary both to the intermediate condition and to the other extreme, while the intermediate is contrary to the extremes. For as the equal is greater in comparison to the smaller, and smaller in comparison to the greater, so also the intermediate states are excessive in comparison to the deficiencies and deficient in comparison to the excesses—both in feelings and in actions.

For the brave person, e.g., appears rash in comparison to the coward, and cowardly in comparison to the rash person; similarly, the temperate person appears intemperate in comparison to the insensible person, and insensible in comparison with the temperate person, and the generous person appears wasteful in comparison to the ungenerous, and ungenerous in comparison to the wasteful person. That is why each of the extreme people tries to push the intermediate person to the other extreme, so that the coward, e.g., calls the brave person rash, and the rash person calls him a coward, and similarly in the other cases.

### Extremes Are More Opposed to Each Other Than to the Mean

Because these conditions of soul are opposed to each other in these ways, the extremes are more contrary to each other than to the intermediate. For they are further from each other than from the intermediate, just as the large is further from the small, and the small from the large, than either is from the equal.

Moreover, sometimes one extreme, e.g. rashness or wastefulness, appears somewhat like the intermediate state, e.g. bravery or generosity; but the extremes are most unlike one another; and the things that are furthest apart from each other are defined as contraries. Hence also the things that are further apart are more contrary.

### Sometimes One Extreme Is More Opposed Than the Other to the Mean

1109a    In some cases the deficiency, in others the excess, is more opposed to the intermediate condition; e.g. it is cowardice, the deficiency, not rashness, the excess, that is more opposed to bravery; on the other hand, it is intemperance, the excess, not insensibility, the deficiency, that is more opposed to temperance. This happens for two reason.

One reason is derived from the object itself. Since sometimes one extreme is closer and more similar to the intermediate condition, we oppose the contrary extreme, more than this closer one, to the intermediate condition. Since rashness, e.g., seems to be closer and more similar to bravery, and cowardice less similar, we oppose cowardice more than rashness to bravery; for what is further from the intermediate condition seems to be more contrary to it. This, then, is one reason, derived from the object itself.

The other reason is derived from ourselves. For when we ourselves have some natural tendency to one extreme more than the other, this extreme appears more opposed to the intermediate condition; since, e.g., we have more of a natural tendency to pleasure, we drift more easily towards intemperance than towards orderliness. Hence we say that an extreme is more contrary if we naturally develop more in that direction; and this is why intemperance is more contrary to temperance, since it is the excess.

### 2.3.3 Practical Advice on Ways to Achieve the Mean

ii 9    We have said enough, then, to show that virtue of character is a mean and what sort of mean it is; that it is a mean between two vices, one of excess and one of deficiency; and that it is a mean because it aims at the intermediate condition in feelings and actions.

Hence it is hard work to be excellent, since in each case it is hard work to find what is intermediate; e.g. not everyone, but only one who knows, finds the midpoint in a circle. So also getting angry, or giving and spending money, is easy and anyone can do it; but doing it to the right person, in the right amount, at the right time, for the right end, and in the right way is no longer easy, nor can everyone do it. Hence [doing these things] well is rare, praiseworthy and fine.

### Avoid the More Opposed Extreme

Hence if we aim at the intermediate condition we must first of all steer clear of the more contrary extreme, following the advice that Calypso also gives—'Hold the ship outside the spray and surge.' For since one extreme is more in error, the other less, and since it is hard to hit the intermediate extremely accurately, the second-best tack, as they say, is to take the lesser of the evils. We shall succeed best in this by the method we describe.

1109b

### Avoid the Easier Extreme

We must also examine what we ourselves drift into easily. For different people have different natural tendencies towards different goals, and we shall come to know our own tendencies from the pleasure or pain that arises in us. We must drag ourselves off in the contrary direction; for if we pull far away from error, as they do in straightening bent wood, we shall reach the intermediate condition.

### Be Careful with Pleasures

And in everything we must beware above all of pleasure and its sources; for we are already biased in its favour when we come to judge it. Hence we must react to it as the elders reacted to Helen, and on each occasion repeat what they said; for if we do this, and send it off, we shall be less in error.

### These Rules Do Not Give Exact and Detailed Guidance

In summary, then, if we do these things we shall best be able to reach the intermediate condition. But no doubt this is hard, especially in particular cases, since it is not easy to define the way we should be angry, with whom, about what, for how long; for sometimes, indeed, we ourselves praise deficient people and call them mild, and sometimes praise quarrelsome people and call them manly. Still, we are not blamed if we deviate a little in excess or deficiency from doing well, but only if we deviate a long way, since then we are easily noticed.

But how far and how much we must deviate to be blamed is not easy to define in an account; for nothing perceptible is easily defined, and [since] these [circumstances of virtuous and vicious action] are particulars, the judgement about them depends on perception.

All this makes it clear, then, that in every case the intermediate state is praised, but we must sometimes incline towards the excess, sometimes toward the deficiency; for that is the easiest way to succeed in hitting the intermediate condition and [doing] well.

•          •          •

## [BOOK X]

### 13.3 Theoretical Study Is the Supreme Element of Happiness

x 7　　If happiness, then, is activity expressing virtue, it is reasonable for it to express the supreme virtue, which will be the virtue of the best thing.

The best is understanding, or whatever else seems to be the natural ruler and leader, and to understand what is fine and divine, by being itself either divine or the most divine element in us.

Hence complete happiness will be its activity expressing its proper virtue; and we have said that this activity is the activity of study. This seems to agree with what has been said before, and also with the truth.

#### 13.3.1 The Activity of Theoretical Study Is Best

For this activity is supreme, since understanding is the supreme element in us, and the objects of understanding are the supreme objects of knowledge.

#### 13.3.2 It Is Most Continuous

Besides, it is the most continuous activity, since we are more capable of continuous study than of any continuous action.

#### 13.3.3 It Is Pleasantest

We think pleasure must be mixed into happiness; and it is agreed that the activity expressing wisdom is the pleasantest of the activities expressing virtue. At any rate, philosophy seems to have remarkably pure and firm pleasures; and it is reasonable for those who have knowledge to spend their lives more pleasantly than those who seek it.

#### 13.3.4 It Is Most Self-Sufficient

Moreover, the self-sufficiency we spoke of will be found in study above all.

For admittedly the wise person, the just person and the other virtuous people all need the good things necessary for life. Still, when these are adequately supplied, the just person needs other people as partners and recipients of his just actions; and the same is true of the temperate person and the brave person and each of the others.

1177b　But the wise person is able, and more able the wiser he is, to study even by himself; and though he presumably does it better with colleagues, even so he is more self-sufficient than any other [virtuous person].

#### 13.3.5 It Aims at No End Beyond Itself

Besides, study seems to be liked because of itself alone, since it has no result beyond having studied. But from the virtues concerned with action we try to a greater or lesser extent to gain something beyond the action itself.

#### 13.3.6 It Involves Leisure

Happiness seems to be found in leisure, since we accept trouble so that we can be at leisure, and fight wars so that we can be at peace. Now the virtues concerned with action have their activities in politics or war, and actions here seem to require trouble.

This seems completely true for actions in war, since no one chooses to fight a war, and no one continues it, for the sake of fighting a war; for someone would have to be a complete murderer if he made his friends his enemies so that there could be battles and killings.

But the actions of the politician require trouble also. Beyond political activities themselves these actions seek positions of power and honours; or at least they seek happiness for the politician himself and for his fellow-citizens, which is something different from political science itself, and clearly is sought on the assumption that is different.

Hence among actions expressing the virtues those in politics and war are pre-eminently fine and great; but they require trouble, aim at some [further] end, and are choice-worthy for something other than themselves.

But the activity of understanding, it seems, is superior in excellence because it is the activity of study, aims at no end beyond itself and has its own proper pleasure, which increases the activity. Further, self-sufficiency, leisure, unwearied activity (as far as is possible for a human being), and any other features ascribed to the blessed person, are evidently features of this activity.

Hence a human being's complete happiness will be this activity, if it receives a complete span of life, since nothing incomplete is proper to happiness.

### 13.3.7 It Is a God-like Life

Such a life would be superior to the human level. For someone will live it not in so far as he is a human being, but in so far as he has some divine element in him. And the activity of this divine element is as much superior to the activity expressing the rest of virtue as this element is superior to the compound. Hence if understanding is something divine in comparison with a human being, so also will the life that expresses understanding be divine in comparison with human life.

We ought not to follow the proverb-writers, and 'think human, since you are human', or 'think mortal, since you are mortal'. Rather, as far as we can, we ought to be pro-immortal, and go to all lengths to live a life that expresses our supreme element; for however much this element may lack in bulk, by much more it surpasses everything in power and value.

1178a

### 13.3.8 It Realizes the Supreme Element in Human Nature

Moreover, each person seems to be his understanding, if he is his controlling and better element; it would be absurd, then, if he were to choose not his own life, but something else's.

And what we have said previously will also apply now. For what is proper to each thing's nature is supremely best and pleasantest for it; and hence for a human being the life expressing understanding will be supremely best and pleasantest, if understanding above all is the human being. This life, then, will also be happiest.

## 13.4 The Relation of Study to the Other Virtues in Happiness

### 13.4.1 The Other Virtues Are Human, Not Divine

x 8    The life expressing the other kind of virtue [i.e. the kind concerned with action] is [happiest] in a secondary way because the activities expressing this virtue are human.

For we do just and brave actions, and the others expressing the virtues, in relation to other people, by abiding by what fits each person in contracts, services, all types of actions, and also in feelings; and all these appear to be human conditions.

Indeed, some feelings actually seem to arise from the body; and in many ways virtue of character seems to be proper to feelings.

Besides, intelligence is yoked together with virtue of character, and so is this virtue with intelligence. For the origins of intelligence express the virtues of character; and correctness in virtues of character expresses intelligence. And since these virtues are also connected to feelings, they are concerned with the compound. Since the virtues of the compound are human virtues, the life and the happiness expressing these virtues is also human.

The virtue of understanding, however, is separated [from the compound]. Let us say no more about it, since an exact account would be too large a task for our present project.

### 13.4.2 The Other Virtues Require More External Goods Than Study Requires

Moreover, it seems to need external supplies very little, or [at any rate] less than virtue of character needs them. For grant that they both need necessary goods, and to the same extent, since there will be only a very small difference even though the politician labours more about the body and suchlike. Still, there will be a large difference in [what is needed] for the [proper] activities [of each type of virtue].

For the generous person will need money for generous actions; and the just person will need it for paying debts, since wishes are not clear, and people who are not just pretend to wish to do justice. Similarly, the brave person will need enough power, and the temperate person will need freedom [to do intemperate actions], if they are to achieve anything that the virtue requires. For how else will they, or any other virtuous people, make their virtue clear?

Moreover, it is disputed whether it is decision or actions that is more in control of virtue, on the assumption that virtue depends on both. Well, certainly it is clear that 1178b what is complete depends on both; but for actions many external goods are needed, and the greater and finer the actions the more numerous are the external goods needed.

But someone who is studying needs none of these goods, for that activity at least; indeed, for study at least, we might say they are even hindrances.

In so far as he is a human being, however, and [hence] lives together with a number of other human beings, he chooses to do the actions expressing virtue. Hence he will need the sorts of external goods [that are needed for the virtues], for living a human life.

### 13.4.3 Beliefs About the Gods Support the Supremacy of Study

In another way also it appears that complete happiness is some activity of study. For we traditionally suppose that the gods more than anyone are blessed and happy; but what sorts of actions ought we to ascribe to them? Just actions? Surely they will appear ridiculous making contracts, returning deposits and so on. Brave actions? Do they endure what [they find] frightening and endure dangers because it is fine? Generous actions? Whom will they give to? And surely it would be absurd for them to have currency or anything like that. What would their temperate actions be? Surely it is vulgar praise to say that they do not have base appetites. When we go through them all, anything that concerns actions appears trivial and unworthy of the gods.

However, we all traditionally suppose that they are alive and active, since surely they are not asleep like Endymion. Then if someone is alive, and action is excluded, and production even more, what is left but study? Hence the gods' activity that is superior in blessedness will be an activity of study. And so the human activity that is most akin to the gods' will, more than any others, have the character of happiness.

A sign of this is the fact that other animals have no share in happiness, being completely deprived of this activity of study. For the whole life of the gods is blessed, and human life is blessed to the extent that it has something resembling this sort of activity; but none of the other animals is happy, because none of them shares in study at all. Hence happiness extends just as far as study extends, and the more someone studies, the happier he is, not coincidentally but in so far as he studies, since study is valuable in itself. And so [on this argument] happiness will be some kind of study.

### 13.4.4 But a Human Being Also Needs Moderate External Goods

However, the happy person is a human being, and so will need external prosperity also; for his nature is now self-sufficient for study, but he needs a healthy body, and needs to have food and the other services provided.

1179a     Still, even though no one can be blessedly happy without external goods, we must not think that to be happy we will need many large goods. For self-sufficiency and action do not depend on excess, and we can do fine actions even if we do not rule earth and sea; for even from moderate resources we can do the actions expressing virtue. This is evident to see, since many private citizens seem to do decent actions no less than people in power do—even more, in fact. It is enough if moderate resources are provided; for the life of someone whose activity expresses virtue will be happy.

### Traditional Views Held by the Wise Support Us

Solon surely described happy people well, when he said they had been moderately supplied with external goods, had done what he regarded as the finest actions, and had lived their lives temperately. For it is possible to have moderate possessions and still to do the right actions.

And Anaxagoras would seem to have supposed that the happy person was neither rich nor powerful, since he said he would not be surprised if the happy person appeared an absurd sort of person to the many. For the many judge by externals, since these are all they perceive.

Hence the beliefs of the wise would seem to accord with our arguments.

### But Theory Must Be Tested in Practice

These considerations do indeed produce some confidence. The truth, however, in questions about action is judged from what we do and how we live, since these are what control [the answers to such questions]. Hence we ought to examine what has been said by applying it to what we do and how we live; and if it harmonizes with what we do, we should accept it, but if it conflicts we should count it [mere] words.

### 13.4.5 The Person Who Studies Is Most Loved by the Gods

The person whose activity expresses understanding and who takes care of understanding would seem to be in the best condition, and most loved by the gods. For if the gods pay some attention to human beings, as they seem to, it would be reasonable for them to take pleasure in what is best and most akin to them, namely understanding; and reasonable for them to benefit in return those who most of all like and honour understanding, on the assumption that these people attend to what is beloved by the gods, and act correctly and finely.

Clearly, all this is true of the wise person more than anyone else; hence he is most loved by the gods. And it is likely that this same person will be happiest; hence the wise person will be happier than anyone else on this argument too.

---

## Suggestions for Further Reading

Gilbert Harman, *The Nature of Morality*, New York, Oxford University Press, 1977.

Thomas Nagel, *Mortal Questions*, London, Cambridge University Press, 1979.

Derek Parfit, *Reason and Persons*, New York, Oxford University Press, 1984.

John Rawls, *A Theory of Justice*, Cambridge, Massachusetts, Harvard University Press, 1971.

J. J. C. Smart and Bernard Williams, *Utilitarianism: For and Against*. London, Cambridge University Press, 1973.

Peter Unger, *Living High and Letting Die—Our Illusion of Innocence*, New York, Oxford University Press, 1996.

Bernard Williams, *Morality*, New York, Harper Torchbooks, 1972.

# GLOSSARY

**abduction**    A form of nondeductive inference, also known as inference to the best explanation. The Surprise Principle and the Only Game In Town Fallacy are relevant to deciding how strong an abductive inference is.

**altruism**    An ultimate desire (a desire that one wants to come true for its own sake, not because it instrumentally contributes to some other goal) is altruistic if it seeks the well-being of some other person. If there are ultimate altruistic desires, then psychological egoism is false. *See* psychological egoism.

**analogy argument**    A nondeductive inference in which one infers that a target object *T* has some characteristic on the ground that *T* is similar to some other object *A* (the analog), and *A* is known to possess that characteristic. Example: "Other galaxies probably contain life, since they are quite similar to our own galaxy and our own galaxy contains life." The strength of analogy arguments is an issue relevant to the Argument from Design and to the problem of other minds.

**analytic**    An analytic sentence is one whose truth or falsehood is deductively entailed by definitions. Many philosophers have held that mathematical statements are analytic. If a sentence isn't analytic, it is synthetic.

*a posteriori*    A proposition that can be known or justified only by sense experience. An *a posteriori* argument is an argument in which at least one premiss is an *a posteriori* proposition. See *a priori*.

*a priori*    A proposition that can be known or justified independent of sense experience. An *a priori* proposition can be known or justified by reason alone (once you grasp the constituent concepts). Truths of mathematics and definitions are often thought to be a priori. An *a priori* argument is an argument in which all the premises are *a priori* propositions. The Ontological Argument for the existence of God was supposed to be an *a priori* argument. See *a posteriori*.

**Argument from Design**    An *a posteriori* argument that God exists, advanced by Aquinas and Paley, criticized by Hume. The argument claims that some feature of the world (like the simplicity of its laws or the fact that organisms are intricate and well adapted) should be explained by postulating the existence of an intelligent designer, namely God.

**Argument from Evil**    An argument that claims that the existence of evil shows either that there is no God, or that God can't be all-powerful, all-knowing, and all-good.

**axiom**    In mathematics, a starting assumption from which conclusions (theorems) are deduced.

**begging the question**    An argument begs the question when you wouldn't accept the premises unless you already believed the conclusion.

**behaviorism**    *See* logical behaviorism and methodological behaviorism.

**bias**    *See* sample bias.

**Birthday Fallacy**    The error in reasoning that one would make in thinking that "everyone has a birthday" deductively implies that "there is a single day on which everyone was born."

**categorical imperative**    An imperative (a command) that is unconditional (no if's). In contrast, a hypothetical imperative is a command of the form, "If you have goal *G*, then perform action *A*." Kant thought that moral rules (like "don't lie") take the form of categorical imperatives. In contrast, rules of prudence (like "stop smoking if you want to be healthy") are hypothetical.

**causal argument for the existence of God**    An argument that Descartes gives in the *Meditations* for the claim that God exists and is no deceiver: Since (1) I have an idea of a perfect being, and (2) there is at least as much perfection in the cause as there is in the effect, it is said to follow that the cause of that idea must be a perfect being, namely, God himself.

**circularity**    *See* begging the question.

**clarity and distinctness criterion**    Descartes maintained that if a belief is clear and distinct, then it can't fail to be true. The reason clear and distinct ideas must be true is that God exists and is no deceiver.

**compatibilism**    The thesis that free will and determinism are compatible. Soft determinism is a version of compatibilism. Hard determinism and libertarianism are incompatibilist theories.

**compatibility**    Two propositions are compatible if the truth of one wouldn't rule out the truth of the other. Example: (i) this shirt is blue; (ii) this shirt is torn. Propositions (i) and (ii) are compatible. This doesn't mean that either is true.

**conditional**    An if/then statement. The if-clause is called the antecedent; the then-clause is called the consequent.

**consequentialism**    A kind of ethical theory that holds that the ethical properties of an action (its rightness or wrongness, its justness or unjustness, etc.) can be determined by seeing what consequences the action would have if it were performed. Utilitarianism is a consequentialist doctrine. Kant's theory isn't.

**conservation law**    A law in physics that says that some quantity (like matter or mass/energy) can neither increase nor decrease in a closed system.

**contingent**    A being is contingent if it exists in some but not all possible worlds; a proposition is contingent if it's true in some but not all possible worlds. You are an example of a contingent thing; though you exist in the actual world, you could have failed to exist.

**conventionalism**    Trivial semantic conventionalism holds that a true sentence might have been false if we had defined our terms differently. For example, the sentence "dogs have four legs" might have been false if we had used the word "dog" to refer to fish. A philosophically interesting conventionalism must go beyond this unsurprising point. Substantive conventionalism holds that a particular proposition is true only because of someone's say-so. For example, the following is a substantive conventionalist claim (and a false one): Dogs would have lacked four legs if we had used the word "dog" to refer to fish. *See* ethical conventionalism and proposition.

**cosmological argument**   An argument for the existence of God that cites some large-scale feature of the universe as a whole—for example that things are in motion, that events are related by cause and effect, or that contingent beings exist. Aquinas's first three ways are instances of this type of argument.

**counterexample**   A counterexample to a generalization is an object that refutes the generalization. A rotten apple in the barrel is a counterexample to the claim "All the apples in this barrel are unspoiled."

**deductive validity**   An argument is deductively valid because of the logical form it has. A deductively valid argument is one in which the conclusion must be true if the premises are true.

**descriptive/normative distinction**   A descriptive claim says what is the case, without commenting on whether that is good or bad. A normative claim says whether something should be the case, or whether it is good or bad. "Drunk drivers kill thousands of people every year" is a descriptive claim; "drunk driving shouldn't be so lightly punished" is a normative claim.

**design argument**   An argument for the existence of God that begins with the observation that features of the universe show evidence of design. The inference is then drawn that an intelligent designer brought these features into being. The most familiar form of this argument cites the complex adaptive features of organisms. Creationists use the argument from design and reject evolutionary theory.

**determinism**   The thesis that a complete description of the causal facts at one time uniquely determines what must happen next. There is only one possible future, given a complete description of the present. Newtonian physics says that the behavior of physical objects is deterministic. *See* indeterminism.

**Divine Command Theory**   The theory that ethical statements are made true or false by God's decreeing how we should act.

**dualism**   The thesis that the mind and the body are two distinct entities. Dualists claim that a person's mind is made of a nonphysical substance. Dualism rejects materialism.

**Duhem's thesis.**   The thesis that theories in physics typically do not, by themselves, make predictions about observations, but do so when supplemented with auxiliary information. See box 9 ("Neptune and Vulcan") for an example. Pierre Duhem states this in his 1914 book *La Théorie Physique—Son Object, Sa Structure* (translated as *The Aim and Structure of Physical Theory*, Princeton University Press, 1954). The thesis is generally thought to apply to science in general, not just to physics.

**egoism**   *See* psychological egoism.

**emotivism**   A theory about how ethical statements are used. Such statements are never true or false; rather, they merely allow the speaker to express feelings and attitudes. Emotivism accepts ethical subjectivism.

**empirical**   For a proposition to be empirical is for it to be *a posteriori*. See *a posteriori*.

**epistemology**   The branch of philosophy concerned with concepts like knowledge and rational justification.

**equivocation, fallacy of**   An argument commits this fallacy when it uses a term with one meaning for part of the argument and then shifts to another meaning for the rest of the argument. Example: "I put my money in the bank. A bank is a side of a river. Hence, I put my money in the side of a river." Arguments that commit this fallacy should be clarified so that the terms in them are used with a single meaning throughout.

**ethical conventionalism**    The thesis that ethical statements are made true by someone's say-so. The divine command theory, ethical relativism, and Sartre's version of existentialism are conventionalist theories. *See* conventionalism.

**ethical realism**    The thesis that some ethical statements are true, and are true independently of anyone's thinking or saying that they are.

**ethical relativism**    The thesis that an ethical statement is true or false in a society because of the norms adopted in that society. Ethical relativism is a normative, not a descriptive, thesis.

**ethical subjectivism**    The thesis that there are no ethical facts, only ethical opinions. Ethical statements are neither true nor false.

**evil**    *See* Argument from Evil and theodicy.

**existentialism**    A twentieth-century philosophical movement that places great weight on the fact that individuals are free and so must take responsibility for how they live their lives. In Sartre's version of existentialism, each person creates ethical facts for himself or herself by a free decision.

**fallacy**    An error in reasoning.

**falsifiability**    *See* strong falsifiability.

**fatalism**    The theory loosely expressed by the slogan "whatever will be, will be" (*que sera, sera*). According to this theory, what happens to us doesn't depend on what we think or want or try to do. Example: Oedipus, the myth says, was fated to kill his father and marry his mother. Fatalism and determinism are different.

**foundationalism**    The view that all the propositions we know to be true can be divided into two categories. First, there are the foundational propositions, which have some special property (like indubitability) that explains why we know them to be true. Second, there are the superstructural propositions, which we know because they bear some special relationship (like deductive implication) to the foundational propositions. Sometimes foundationalism is understood as a thesis about justified belief, not knowledge.

**functionalism**    The theory in the mind/body problem that says that psychological properties (types) aren't identical with physical properties, because psychological properties are multiply realizable. In addition, functionalism maintains that psychological properties are to be understood in terms of their causal roles.

**genetic fallacy**    The mistake of thinking a statement can't be true simply because there's a causal explanation for why people believe that it's true.

**hard determinism**    The incompatibilist doctrine that holds that human actions are unfree because they are causally determined.

**identity theory**    The thesis that the mind and the brain are identical. Also, that psychological properties are identical with physical properties.

**if and only if**    "*X* is true if and only if *Y* is true" means that the truth of *X* is both necessary and sufficient for the truth of *Y*. "*X* if and only if *Y*" means that *X* and *Y* are either both true or both false.

**incompatibilism**    *See* compatibilism.

**incorrigibility of the mental, thesis of the**   This thesis claims that we can't be mistaken in the beliefs we have about the contents of our own minds. If you believe that you believe *P* or want *Q* to be true, then it must be true that you believe *P* or want *Q* to be true.

**independent**   Two propositions are logically independent of each other if the truth or falsity of one doesn't deductively imply the truth or falsity of the other. Example: It was discovered in the eighteenth and nineteenth centuries that Euclid's parallel postulate is independent of the other axioms and postulates of his system of geometry.

**indeterminism**   The thesis that even a complete description of the present doesn't uniquely determine what will happen next. There's more than one possible future, each with its own probability of coming true, given a complete description of the present.

**induction**   A nondeductive argument in which characteristics of individuals not in a sample are inferred from the characteristics of individuals in the sample. The strength of an inductive inference is influenced by sample size and sample bias.

**is/ought gap**   Hume argued that ethical statements concerning what ought to be the case can't be deduced from statements that describe only what is the case.

**JTB theory**   The theory that knowledge is justified true belief. In other words, the theory advances the following proposal: For any person *S* and any proposition *p*, *S* knows that *p* if and only if (1) *S* believes that *p*; (2) *p* is true; (3) *S* is justified in believing that *p*.

**KK-principle**   This principle says that if *S* knows that *p*, then *S* knows that *S* knows that *p*. The principle is rejected by the reliability theory of knowledge.

**law**   A scientific law is a proposition that is general (it concerns all objects of a certain kind), that doesn't refer to any individual, place, or time, and that has a kind of necessity called nomological necessity. The term is often reserved for a posteriori propositions satisfying these conditions.

**Leibniz's Law**   If *a* and *b* are identical, then they must have all the same properties. Mind/body dualists defend their view by attempting to find some property that the mind has but the body lacks; they thereby appeal to Leibniz's Law.

**libertarianism**   The incompatibilist doctrine that holds that some human actions aren't causally determined, since they are free.

**logical behaviorism**   The thesis that the meanings of mentalistic terms can be given in exclusively behavioral terms.

**logical form**   The logical form of an argument is what makes it deductively valid or deductively invalid. *See* deductive validity.

**materialism**   The thesis that every object is a physical object. The mind/brain identity theory and functionalism are materialistic theories about the mind. Both reject the dualist claim that minds are made of an immaterial substance.

**mentalism**   The view that mental states are inner causes of outward behavior. Beliefs and desires are "inside" the subject; they cause behavior, which is more directly observable by others.

**metaphysics**   The branch of philosophy concerned with specifying the basic kinds of things that exist. Whether electrons exist is a problem for physics, not metaphysics, but whether physical objects exist is a metaphysical question. Other metaphysical questions include, Do numbers exist? Does God exist? What is the nature of the relationship between minds and bodies?

**method of doubt**    The method Descartes used to determine which propositions are foundational. If it's possible to doubt the proposition, then it fails the test. To see if it's possible to doubt a proposition, see if you can construct a story in which the proposition is false even though you believe that it's true.

**methodological behaviorism**    The view that science shouldn't talk about the inner states of organisms when it attempts to explain behavior.

**mind/brain identity theory**    *See* identity theory.

**multiple realizability**    A property (type) is multiply realizable if the tokens that fall under the type need have nothing in common physically. Being a mousetrap is multiply realizable. Functionalism claims that psychological properties are multiply realizable.

**mutually exclusive**    Two characteristics are mutually exclusive when nothing can have both of them. Being a triangle and being a circle are mutually exclusive properties.

**naturalistic fallacy**    G. E. Moore argued that the ethical properties of an action (e.g., its being morally obligatory) aren't identical with any "naturalistic" properties of the action. A naturalistic property is a property that might be studied in a natural science. To deny this, Moore held, is to commit the naturalistic fallacy.

**necessary**    Necessary beings exist in all possible worlds; a necessary proposition is true in all possible worlds. It's customary to distinguish three kinds of necessary propositions: ones that are logically necessary (like "bachelors are bachelors"), ones that are nomologically necessary (like "nothing moves faster than the speed of light"), and ones that are circumstantially necessary (like "this bomb will explode in five minutes").

**necessary condition**    "$X$ is a necessary condition for $Y$" means that if $Y$ is true, then so is $X$. That is, it's necessary for $X$ to be true in order for $Y$ to be true. *See* sufficient condition.

**normative claim**    *See* descriptive/normative distinction.

**objective**    A proposition describes an objective matter if the proposition is true or false independently of what anyone believes or thinks.

**observation**    An observational proposition is one you come to believe via the "direct" testimony of sense experience (sight, hearing, taste, touch, smell). One philosophical question about observation concerns what "direct" means in this definition.

**Ockham's Razor**    *See* Principle of Parsimony.

**Only Game in Town Fallacy**    The error of thinking that you are obliged to believe a proposed explanation of an observation just because it's the only explanation that has been proposed.

**Ontological Argument**    An *a priori* argument for the existence of God, proposed by Saint Anselm. It attempts to show that the definition of the concept of God entails that God exists, necessarily.

**other minds, problem of**    This is the problem of explaining how we know that other individuals have minds and how we know what the contents of those minds are.

**physicalism**    *See* materialism.

**positivism**   The philosophical view that sentences about God, morality, aesthetics, and metaphysics are meaningless and are shown to be so by the testability theory of meaning. *See* testability theory of meaning.

**possible**   *See* necessary and contingent.

**pragmatism**   In this book, the philosophical theory that claims that the usefulness of a belief is what makes it reasonable to believe. Pragmatists also proposed a theory about what truth is.

**Principle of Parsimony**   Otherwise known as Ockham's Razor. This principle says that an explanation that postulates fewer entities or processes is preferable to one that postulates more.

**Principle of Sufficient Reason.**   The thesis that everything that happens in nature has an explanation. This idea is part of Aquinas's and Clarke's different versions of the cosmological argument (Lectures 4 and 7).

**Principle of the Common Cause**   A principle governing abductive inference. It asserts that when two or more objects exhibit an intricate series of similarities, the similarities should be explained by postulating a common cause; this is preferable to a separate cause explanation, according to which each object obtained its characteristics independently. Example: Two students hand in identical essays in a philosophy class. It's more plausible to explain this as the result of plagiarism than to think that each student worked independently. The Common Cause Principle is an application of the Surprise Principle.

**Principle of the Uniformity of Nature (PUN)**   The thesis that the future will resemble the past. Hume believed that all inductive arguments presuppose that this principle is true.

**proposition**   That which is expressed by a true or false declarative sentence. Though the sentence "Lemons are yellow" is part of the English language, the proposition that this sentence expresses is no more a part of English than it is a part of any other human language. A variety of philosophical theories maintain that some declarative sentences don't express propositions (though they may seem to). For example, ethical subjectivism says that ethical statements are neither true nor false. Logical positivism maintains that the statement "God exists" is neither true nor false.

**propositional attitudes**   Consider the following statements: "*S* believes that lemons are yellow"; "*S* wants to drink a cup of coffee"; "*S* doubts that it will rain." In each of these, a subject, *S*, is said to have an attitude—believing, desiring, or doubting—toward a proposition.

**psychological egoism**   The doctrine that people's ultimate desires are always self-directed; whenever a person has a desire about the situation of others, this desire is purely instrumental—you care about others only because you think that this will benefit yourself. Psychological egoism denies that people ever have altruistic ultimate motives.

**random**   A sampling process is random when each object in the population from which the sample is drawn has the same probability of being drawn.

**realism**   *See* ethical realism.

**reductio ad absurdum**   A deductively valid form of argument in which one proves that *P* is true by showing that (1) if *P* were false, *A* would have to be true, and (2) *A* is false.

**redundancy theory of truth**     This theory claims that to say that a statement is true is to do nothing more than assert the statement: "It's true that snow is white" is just a long-winded way of saying that snow is white.

**reference**     *See* sense and reference.

**relativism**     *See* ethical relativism.

**relativity**     The truth or falsity of a proposition *p* is a relative matter, if *p*'s truth or falsehood depends on an arbitrary choice. Example: Sue and Mary are walking side by side. Is Sue to the left of Mary? That depends on (is relative to) a choice of point of view. There are several equally correct such choices. Whether it's true or false that Sue is to the left of Mary depends on that (arbitrary) choice.

**Reliability Theory of Knowledge**     A theory that exploits the analogy between a thermometer's reliably representing the temperature and a subject's knowing a proposition to be true. The theory says that *S* knows that *p* if and only if (1) *S* believes that *p*; (2) *p* is true; and (3) in the circumstances that *S* occupies, *S* wouldn't have believed that *p* unless *p* were true.

**sample bias**     An inductive inference is weakened by its being based on a biased sample. If you want to know what percentage of Americans believe in God, don't conduct your survey by using church membership lists. To do so would probably bias your estimate.

**sample size**     An inductive inference is made stronger by increasing its sample size. In telephone surveys, your conclusion about the population sampled is on firmer ground if you call more people than if you call fewer.

**sense and reference**     Two terms in a language may refer to a single object, even though they have different meanings (senses). An example: "The inventor of bifocals" and "the first U.S. ambassador to France" have different senses, though both refer to the same person, namely, Benjamin Franklin. Frege held that terms with the same sense must have the same reference.

**skepticism**     The thesis that knowledge (or rational justification) is unobtainable. Descartes tried to refute skepticism about knowledge; Hume was a skeptic about the rational justifiability of induction.

**soft determinism**     The compatibilist thesis that human actions are both free and causally determined.

**solipsism**     The thesis that the only thing that exists is my mind and its contents.

**strong falsifiability**     A hypothesis is strongly falsifiable if it deductively implies an observation sentence. "Falsifiable" doesn't mean false.

**subjective**     A proposition is subjective if its truth or falsehood depends on what occurs in the mind of some subject. *See* objective.

**subjectivism**     *See* ethical subjectivism.

**sufficient condition**     "*X* is a sufficient condition for *Y*" means that if *X* is true, so is *Y*. That is, for *Y* to be true, it's sufficient for *X* to be true. *See* necessary condition.

**Surprise Principle**     A principle governing abductive inference. An observation *O* strongly favors one hypothesis $H_1$ over another $H_2$ when the following two conditions are satisfied, but not otherwise: (1) If $H_1$ were true, we would expect *O* to be true; (2) if $H_2$ were true, we would expect *O* to be false.

**synthetic**     *See* analytic.

**teleology**   An object is described in a teleological fashion when it is described in terms of its goals, purposes, or ends.

**testability theory of meaning**   A positivist doctrine which says that a meaningful sentence must either be analytic or empirical. Statements whose truth or falsity cannot be decided either by observation or by reasoning are meaningless. Some positivists proposed to understand what it means to be empirical in terms of strong falsifiability. *See* strong falsifiability.

**theodicy**   The attempt to reconcile the existence of evil in the world with the idea that God exists and is all-powerful, all-knowing, and all-good.

**theorem**   *See* axiom.

**type/token distinction**   A type is a property or characteristic. The individual items that populate the world are termed tokens. A given token falls under many types. So, for example, you are a token of the type human being and a token of the type object on the surface of the earth. The type/token distinction is important to functionalism's critique of the mind/brain identity theory.

**universalizability criterion**   Kant thought that the ethical permissibility of an action could be determined by seeing if it passes the universalizability test: See if it's possible for the action to be universal (performed by everyone) or if it's possible for a rational agent to will (intend) that the action be universal.

**utilitarianism**   The ethical theory that the action you should perform in a given situation is the one that would promote the greatest good for the greatest number of individuals. Hedonistic utilitarianism equates goodness with the feeling of pleasure and the absence of the feeling of pain. Preference utilitarianism says that the good to be maximized is the satisfaction of preferences. Utilitarian theories also are distinguished by whether they are act or rule utilitarian. An act utilitarian says that it's the consequences of the token action under consideration that need to be considered. A rule utilitarian says that it's the long-term effects of the type of action that are relevant to deciding whether to perform a token act of that type.

**validity**   *See* deductive validity.

**verifiability**   *See* testability theory of meaning.

**vitalism**   The theory that living things differ from nonliving things because they possess a special immaterial substance—an *élan vital*—that animates them with life. Vitalism and dualism both reject materialism.

# INDEX